OKLAHOMA'S CHIEF OF PUBLIC INSTRUCTION 1890-2015

The Position, The Politics, and The Public Servants (Superintendents)

A. Kenneth Stern

NEW FORUMS PRESS INC.

Published in the United States of America
by New Forums Press, Inc.1018 S. Lewis St.
Stillwater, OK 74074
www.newforums.com

Copyright © 2022 by New Forums Press, Inc.

All rights reserved. No part of this publication may be reproduced or transmitted in any form or by any means, electronic or mechanical, including photocopy, or any information storage or retrieval system, without permission in writing from the publisher.

Library of Congress Cataloging-in-Publication Data Pending

This book may be ordered in bulk quantities at discount from New Forums Press, Inc., P.O. Box 876, Stillwater, OK 74076 [Federal I.D. No. 73 1123239]. Printed in the United States of America.

Jacket design by Chris Sinderson
Collage: E. D. Cameron (Oklahoma Historical Society); Oliver Hodge (Oklahoma Education Association); Oliver Hodge Memorial Education Building and "show and tell" classroom (Lois Brandt); Sandy Garrett (Department of Education); Pleasant Valley School Living History Class (Pleasant Valley School Foundation); Negro Rural School, Creek County, Oklahoma (Library of Congress no. 2017785202); and graduation ceremony (Harvey Brandt)

ISBN 10: 1-58107-363-1
ISBN 13: 978-1-58107-363-8

Contents

Acknowledgements vii
List of Abbreviations and Uppercase Terms ix
Introduction xi

Part I Territorial Period Administration (1890-1910) 1
   1 Laying the Groundwork in Oklahoma Territory (1890-1907) 3
   2 Benedict: Imposing the Federal Will on Tribal Schooling
      in Indian Territory (1899-1910) 25

Part II The Superintendency and the Contestants (1907-2015) 43
   3 The Executive Office of Superintendent (1890-2015) 45
   4 Campaigns and Elections (1907-2014) 63
   5 The Superintendents (1907-2015) 83
   6 Women's Struggle to Achieve Suffrage and Gain Equality
      in Educational Governance (1890-2014) 95

Part III The Superintendents (Public Servants) (1907-2015) 111
   7 Cameron: Managing the Statewide Expansion of the Common
      School System (1907-1911) 113
   8 Wilson: Surviving Turbulence Before Achieving Tranquility (1911-1923) 129
   9 Youthful Nash: Leading Effectively (1923-1927) 155
   10 Vaughan: Navigating the End of the Roaring Twenties
       and the First Half of the Depression Thirties (1927-1936) 167
   11 Crable: Suffering Persistent Chaos for a Decade (1936-1947) 189
   12 Hodge: Creating Stability (1947-1968) 215
   13 Creech and Tuxhorn: Stepping In to Fill the Vacancy (1968-1971) 243
   14 Fisher: Directing Rapid Department Growth and Expansion
       of Services (1971-1984) 253
   15 Folks: Pursuing An Ambitious Reform Agenda (1984-1988) 267
   16 Hoeltzel: Grappling with Excess in the Department (1988-1991) 279
   17 Quintessential Politician Garrett: Maneuvering Through
       Two Decades (1991-2011) 289
   18 Barresi: Faltering in the Changing of the Guard (2011-2015) 315
   19 Hofmeister: Campaigning on Limited Qualifications (2014
       and the Quasquicentennial Anniversary) 331

Epilogue 339

Figures
   2.1 Map of the Indian and Oklahoma Territories 1892 26
   8.1 Publications of the Department 1911-1912 143
   8.2 Select recommendations of the Commission of Educational Survey 150
   10.1 Minutes of the Meeting of the State Board
        of Education, August 19, 1936 186
   11.1 Elementary School Course of Study Completion Certificate, 1938 195
   12.1 Sixth grade student report card, 1960, Thomas, Oklahoma 229

Tables

1.1 Territorial Superintendents' demographic data I 6
1.2 Territorial Superintendents' demographic data II 21
1.3 Territorial Superintendents' demographic data III 21
3.1 Superintendents' constitutional qualifications 56
3.2 Salaries for Superintendent, Federal Indian Superintendent, and Governor for the biennia of the period of 1890-1910 58
4.1 Number of candidates and parties for the election years 1907-2014 66
4.2 Gender and political party of Superintendency candidates 1907-2014 68
4.3 Female candidates, parties, years, and elections 1926-2014 69
4.4 Candidates' average age by gender at filing for their first election 70
4.5 General election results 1907-2014 73
4.6 Oklahoma voter registrations 1960-2014 74
4.7 Number of candidates and campaign expenditures 1910-2014 78
4.8 Campaign expenditures of Sandy Garrett's tenure 1990-2006 79
5.1 Tenure and political party of Superintendents 1907-2015 86
5.2 Superintendents' demographics 87
5.3 Public school/Department experience (years) 92
6.1 Gender of administrative and supervisory employees in the Department 1899-1969 103
6.2 Department employees by classification and gender 104
6.3 Top-level administrative positions at the Department by gender for select years 1975-76 to 2009-10 105
7.1 Population, enrollment, ADA, and number of teachers 1907 and 1908 119
10.1 Vaughan's legislative efforts 1917 and 1919 169
10.2 Statistical comparison of 1926-1927 and 1935-1936 174
10.3 Election results 1934 180
10.4 Enrollments, faculty, and degrees awarded at the teachers colleges 1936 and 1938 187
11.1 Party registration of the Oklahoma Legislature 1937-1945 192
11.2 Department FTE 1936-1946 198
11.3 Supplemental external donations 1916-1943 198
11.4 Common schools data for the years 1935-36 to 1946-47 199
12.1 Number of Democratic and Republican executive office primary candidates 1946-1966 218
12.2 Teachers, students, and expenditures 1946-1947 to 1967-1968 222
12.3 Integration progress in Oklahoma 1956-1960 236
14.1 School district and Department data 1971-1984 259
15.1 School district and Department data 1984-1988 272
16.1 School district and Department data 1988-1991 285
16.2 Sources and amounts of Department expenditures 1988-1991 285
17.1 Department budget FY 91-FY 96 307
17.2 School district data and Department FTE 1991-2011 307
17.3 Enrollment by race/ethnicity 2012-2013 308
18.1 2010 Primary election results 319
18.2 2010 General election results and total campaign expenditures 320
18.3 2014 Republican primary election and campaign expenditures 322
18.4 Department personnel and budget 2010-11 to 2013-14 327

18.5 School district data 2010-2014 328
19.1 2014 Election results and campaign expenditures 335

Abbreviations in the Notes and Appendices 341

Notes 343

Appendices
A Superintendent Demographics 1907-2015 377
B Alphabetized List of Candidates, Year, Election,
   and Party Affiliation 1907-2014 378
C Number of Candidates for the Superintendency 1907-2014 382
D Candidates' Ages at Filing Time 1907-2014 382
E Superintendency Candidates' Other Political Activities 1907-2014 386
F Superintendency Election Results 1907-2014 390
G Superintendent Vote as a Ratio of the Governor Vote 1907-2014 397
H Oklahoma Voter Registration 1960-2017 398
I Ratio of Superintendent's Salary to Governor's Salary 1890-2015 399
J Candidates' Campaign Expenditures 1910-2014 401
K School Age Population, Enrollment, Number of Teachers, State Population,
   and Number of School Districts for Select Years 1891-2014 404
L Number of Districts and Teachers 1907-2014 406
M ADA, Number of Teachers, Department FTE, Number of Districts,
   and Department Expenditures 1970-2014 407
N Superintendent Participation on Agencies, Boards, Commissions,
   and Committees 1907-2014 409

Index 423

About the Author 443

To Aaron who lived generously and taught me how to appreciate life regardless of the challenges confronted.
1979-2007

Acknowledgements

Many people have been involved in this project over the decades beginning about 1985 with the employees in the newspaper section of the Oklahoma History Center who assisted with the navigation of the somewhat obsolete reader machines. When the facilities and equipment improved remarkably upon relocation to the Oklahoma Historical Society Research Center, the dedicated employees there graciously and expeditiously responded to my requests to fetch documents from the stacks and restricted documents collections. Equally attentive to my requests for files, records, and books were multiple persons at the State Archives in the Oklahoma Department of Libraries who assisted me with accessing documents over the decades. Carol Guilliams, and then more recently, Holly Hasenfratz, represented many who quickly and graciously retrieved archival documents and guided me through their Digital Prairie website. Without these unsung employees I would never have been able to engage in the research necessary to write this book.

Communication with David Baird in the mid to late 1980s provided some of the inspiration for investigating the history of the Superintendency. Because my professional career was not centered in history I was seeking confirmation from him of the value of my pursuing research leading to publishing a book. What I received was enthusiastic support, encouragement that I never forgot and that sustained me when I doubted that I would finish.

For more than a quarter century John Phillips in the Documents Section of Oklahoma State University's Edmon Low Library identified resources, retrieved books and materials, and counseled further investigation to bring additional substance to this project. His readiness to assist has resulted in a more thorough investigation of the topic and is deserving of special recognition for his expertise.

Librarians, curators, and archivists at the Bizzell Library and the Western History Collections at the University of Oklahoma, Edmon Low Library at Oklahoma State University, the Max Chambers Library at the University of Central Oklahoma, and the Library of Congress in Washington, DC, provided access to their historical documents sections. Without this assistance and access many original documents would have been unavailable for review.

Appreciation is extended to John Folks and Gerald Hoeltzel, who participated in interviews to provide first hand accounts of their experience in the Superintendency, and those who graciously shared their perspectives even though they contested unsuccessfully for the position: Scott Tuxhorn, Charles Sandmann, Lloyd Roettger, and John Cox. Providing perspective on the position and the incumbents were Clark Ogilvie, W. H. Langley Jr., Rep. Larry Adair, Kara Gae Neal, Lealon Taylor, Velta Reed Johnston, Sharon Lease, and Ellen McCoy. John Scroggins, administrator in the Bartlesville, Muskogee, Norman, and Ponca City school districts, read the manuscript and offered advice and perspective to improve the text and help shape the narrative. Multiple lengthy interviews with Clarence G. Oliver Jr., who was once invited to complete an unexpired term and whose career stretched across the administrations of Oliver Hodge through Joy Hofmeister, a span of seventy years, provided rich perspective of both the behind-the-scenes maneuverings and the public actions of these Superintendents. I owe much to his sage advice and worthy insight. His contributions extended to reading a draft of the manuscript and offering counsel on the analysis.

Significant to the success of my career and this project were a number of men beginning with my Dad, Amos Stern, who taught me to be curious and to develop love of learning. He wished that I would pursue educational achievement to the best of my ability, an opportunity not afforded to him. At Messiah University Professor Morris Sider nurtured my love of history while teaching me the rudiments of historical research. Gene Shepherd at the University of Oklahoma guided my graduate studies in leadership and introduced me to Oklahoma's educational system through various avenues. He believed in my potential to be a contributor to the advancement of public education in Oklahoma. Joining him in advancing my career was Gene Pingleton who challenged me to broaden my perspective to consider alternative career options including a professorship. At Oklahoma State University Professor Kenneth St. Clair mentored me by his actions and gentle advice through exemplifying the role of a professor to assist doctoral students through completion of their dissertations. I would be remiss without mentioning Bill Pennington who was a friend and a fellow traveler in education. Shortly before he was killed in a car accident we discussed the ways in which he would be involved in the final writing of the book. The book would have been better with his expert assistance. Finally, I was fortunate to have an older brother Ron whose education pursuits stirred a desire in me to follow a similar path to earning a doctorate in school administration. With diligence, perseverance, and sacrifice, I could achieve beyond my dreams.

Deserving of my gratitude is my editor Zhanna Shatrova who with a sharp eye, a keen perspective, and a gentle touch insisted on near perfection as her guiding objective in form and format. This book would not have been possible without her participation. Appreciation is also extended to Doug Dollar at New Forums Press for his patience through the process and his support of the goal to bring the book to fruition. His steady guidance and unassuming persona mix to provide a welcoming environment for publishing a book.

Confirmation of one's career accomplishments can arise from a child's success as an adult. My daughter Janelle's dedication and efforts to improve the quality of life for those with epilepsy, including her brother, were founded on the high quality of her public school experience in Oklahoma. Now in the next generation my two grandsons Jonah and Jesse are flourishing from the quality public education they were offered in their foundational years. Posthumously, gratitude is acknowledged for my son Aaron whose life epitomized the strength of the human spirit to overcome obstacles. My hope is that this culmination of effort in some way adds to the improvement in public education for all current and future generations of students.

My greatest gratitude goes to my wife Lois who sacrificed and supported me so that the project could be finished after these many years. Without her steadfastness and quiet encouragement, the goal would have been much more elusive. The many trips to the Oklahoma History Center and the Oklahoma State Archives and the associated incurrence of costs for which there was no reimbursement could have created tension, but these actions were met with support. She also committed her career and devoted her energies for more than thirty years to teaching in the public schools of Oklahoma. She and I have been a team dedicated to serving the public schools, the students, the teachers, and the administrators.

Uppercase Terms and Abbreviations Used in the Text

For ease of presentation, efficiency, and brevity, without unnecessarily causing confusion, special use of uppercase lettering and several abbreviated terms have been employed. Because of the frequent reference to the State Superintendent of Public Instruction and as a contrast to district and county superintendents, the uppercase is used for Superintendent or Superintendency. District and county superintendent references are with lowercase lettering. The same basis was used for the shortened wording of the State Board of Education, the State Department of Education, and the State Secretary of Education (used primarily in chapters 16 and 17).

State Superintendent of Public Instruction	Superintendent
State Superintendency	Superintendency
State Board of Education	Board
State Department of Education	Department or Agency
State Secretary of Education	Secretary
County or district school superintendent	county or district school superintendent

Used less frequently but nonetheless importantly are the numerous names of the colleges and universities in Oklahoma. Below is a list of those institutions with their current names followed by their abbreviations, the chronology of names from most recent to earliest, and the years of establishment.

Oklahoma State University (OSU) — Oklahoma A&M College (1890)

Langston University (LU) — Oklahoma Colored Agricultural and Normal University (1897)

University of Oklahoma (OU) (1890)

Universities — teachers colleges — normal schools:

> East Central University (ECU) — East Central Oklahoma State University — East Central State College — East Central State Normal School (1909)

> Northeastern State University (NSU) — Northeastern Oklahoma State University — Northeastern State College — Northeastern State Teachers Colleges — Northeastern State Normal School (1909)

> Northwestern Oklahoma State University (NWOSU) — Northwestern State

College—Northwestern Oklahoma State Teachers College—Northwestern Territorial Normal School (1897)

Southeastern Oklahoma State University (SEOSU)—Southeastern State College—Southeastern State Teachers College—Southeastern State Normal School (1909)

Southwestern Oklahoma State University (SWOSU)—Southwestern State College—Southwestern Institute of Technology—Southwestern State College of Diversified Occupations—Southwestern Oklahoma State Teachers College—Southwestern Normal School (1901)

University of Central Oklahoma (UCO)—Central State University—Central State College—Central State Normal School—Territorial Normal School (1891)

Introduction

Educational governance and politics joined together on the one hand seem incongruent, but on the other hand, because public education is a function of the government, it cannot occur in a political vacuum. The juxtaposition of the two, set in an ultra-conservative state with rich natural resources, but limited commitment to educational excellence, made for a fascinating study. Oklahoma created the position of superintendent of public instruction at the beginning of the territorial period to lead its education system. Most likely little thought about the selection of the word "instruction" versus "education" entered into the discussions of the lawmakers in the fall of 1890 as they wrote the laws for Oklahoma Territory. Although instruction is a major component of an education system, it is not the totality of the effort of the state to meet its constitutional mandate. Those territorial legislators borrowed heavily from the language of other states where "instruction" was part of the title. Today's terminology in the other states has been updated and typically uses the more encompassing "education," yet there is no indication that a change of wording has ever been considered or will be in the near future. Oklahoma has a secretary of education who reports to the Governor and represents that office's intentions for the three major branches of public education: common schools, career-technical education, and higher education.

Several questions guided the research, description, and analysis that culminated in the writing of this book. What is the history of the position of the territorial/state superintendent of public instruction and how have the incumbents fulfilled their responsibilities in this primarily ministerial administrative position? What kind of people contested for the position? How did they explore the discretionary opportunities afforded them? How did the elective nature of the position discourage or stifle attempts to exemplify leadership and to entertain bold initiatives? Asking these and more questions set the stage for an attempt to present and elucidate a narrow slice of history for the edification of current and future decision-makers. It is a description and analysis of the more salient facets of the political nature of the position and the actions of the individuals charged with leading the state's education system. As such it might be particularly interesting for those who are considering running for the position, for those who study government to ascertain how it could function more effectively and efficiently, for those who study history to learn what has occurred and the ramifications of those decisions, and for those who lived through the past four-five decades and whose careers intersected with the state superintendent.

To set the stage, it is important to note a thread that has permeated the attitude of the state's citizens for many decades. *"The Oklahoman's main characteristic is to be previous. The trait may have originated in the days of soonerism, but it is getting stronger every year. It is in the very air* (author's emphasis)." Angie Debo, noted Oklahoma historian of the twentieth century, wrote that Oklahomans had a great need to be number one, to get there first, whether it be competition in the county fair or in athletics.[1] Her expansion of a journalist's characterization of Oklahomans in the early days has withstood the decades of time in many regards but not including education. Webster's Dictionary of 1937 defines "previous" in part as premature, untimely, unwarranted by developments;

speaking, judging, prematurely or too quickly. In the 1940s and 1950s some Oklahoma City business and civic leaders wished to improve the state's national image after the Dust Bowl, the outward migration, and *The Grapes of Wrath.* They decided that the University of Oklahoma football team should reach a competitive status that would bring national acclaim to the sooner state. In that regard, they reached their goal, one that is emblematic across the state's history. Oklahomans have always prized their athletics at the high school and collegiate levels, but have seemed unable to muster the financial courage to offer an equally stellar academic program. There are, however, two exceptions: a state-of-the-art career-technical system and the Oklahoma School for Science and Math, both without athletic programs and facilities. Most funding for education originates at the state level while most decision-making is at the district level. Because capacity for building construction is based primarily on local property taxes the value of the combination of commercial, agricultural, and residential properties dictates the amount and quality of instructional and athletic facilities. When academic and athletic interests collide usually the latter receive precedence. As an example, Oklahoma is the only state that allows athletics (practices) within the school day. Athletic prowess receives more accolades than academic accomplishment, a reality that the state superintendent constantly confronts in this rural state with more than 500 local school districts.

Possibly because the state superintendency is an elected position, aspirants and incumbents exhibited an expanded optimism, were "previous" on several occasions. First Superintendent E. D. Cameron in 1910, when 2,800 districts had just been created in Indian Territory to add to a greater number already existing in Oklahoma Territory and not all of the kinks had been resolved in the relations with the federal government, stated, "This report will show that we have established in Oklahoma a public school system equal to the best in the world."[2] A short five years passed when R. H. Wilson optimistically stated: "It is the plan of the State Department of Education to organize all the forces making for a better citizenship in an educational crusade that will cause our state to assume first rank when the returns of the decennial census of 1920 are reported."[3] Eighty years later Sandy Garrett's election slogan envisioned a dramatic improvement, "First by the 21st."[4] In light of 100 years of being ranked near the bottom among the fifty states in acquiring resources and results, such slogans and bravado about being first in the nation or the world ring rather hollow, or maybe they reflect more accurately the political nature of the top education position in Oklahoma's executive government.

A late entrant into the Union as the forty-sixth state, Oklahoma's recorded history is not long, expansive, or complete. Some early records are not extant, for example, the minutes of the meetings of the Territorial Board of Education from 1896-1904 and the State Board of Education from 1907-1911. Histories have been written about the governors since the beginning of the territorial days, but there is a dearth of investigations and assessments about the other executive offices and officers. As one of the most important functions of state government as mandated by the state constitution, and as the single largest item in the state budget, the operation of the public education system has been a critical part of the state's history, yet, while considerable factual data exist, there has been no effort to describe and analyze these records systematically. The state superintendents' biennial and later annual reports are extant and provided a rich trove of facts and insight into the education system's highest officers' descriptions of the current status and what needed the attention of the lawmakers and the citizens. Newspapers, particularly *The Oklahoman* with its conservative slant on the role of public education and how it should be financed, and located in the capital city, offered the author insight into the behavior of government officials. Archival documents in multiple university libraries, the Library of Congress, the Oklahoma Historical Society Research Center, and the Oklahoma State Archives were viewed to gain information and perspective.

In this attempt to add to the understanding of a narrow, but extremely important, segment of Oklahoma's history I have researched and written about the executive office of the superintendent of public instruction and a chronological account of the incumbents who held the position. Part I, chapter One begins with the legislative creation of the office in December 1890 and continues to statehood in November 1907. Both educational and political actions of the seven appointees who also served as *ex officio* territorial auditor during this seventeen-year period are described briefly in the context of the political turmoil that roiled these early days. Chapter Two might seemingly fit strangely within the book because it is about the federal government's oversight of education in Indian Territory. It was included, however, because that territory in 1907 became about half of the new state of Oklahoma, the supervisor was an appointee, and the meshing of the two territories pricked the sensitive political skin of the first elected state superintendent.

The four-chapter Part II is a lengthy investigation into, and description and analysis of, the eligibility criteria for the elective position of the state superintendent of public instruction and the efforts to make it appointive, the demographics of the more than seventy-five individuals who contested for the position, and the results of the twenty-eight election cycles since statehood with emphasis on the existence of single political party domination. Not infrequently throughout the 108 years of statehood Democratic and Republican governors have tried through external and internal studies to instigate a constitutional change to allow them to wield more influence in the state's education arena through the appointment of the state superintendent of public instruction. To date all of those efforts have failed because the citizenry has not been convinced of the need to change. The general populace continues to prefer to elect the superintendent, but it did approve an amendment in 2010 to limit that office and a few others to two terms, the same length as the governor's. Possibly more critical to the issues at hand is the residency rule: to be eligible for the office one must have been a resident of the state for the previous ten years. At least in the education sphere, this limitation hinders the ability of the state to move forward as does the lack of any educational qualification. Future attempts to gain a constitutional change either to make it an appointive position or to reduce the residency qualification can be informed of past futile efforts as I have detailed in chapter Three. My historical review of this aspect of the executive office structure is intended to assist future efforts to achieve success in making the office appointive or to reduce or eliminate the ten-year residency criterion. This effort was to peer into the history of a sometimes obscure but highly significant and important executive position and to describe and analyze the most salient aspects of it.

Because gender has played a major role (women were ineligible for the executive offices until 1942), and women have comprised the majority of the education profession, an entire chapter, Six, is devoted to the struggle by women first to gain suffrage, then eligibility for the executive office, and then credibility in education positions at all levels of leadership and administration. This chapter, while it expands upon the direct role of women in the state superintendency to include ancillary topics and issues, nonetheless is vital to the understanding of the evolution of the changes in male-female relationships and the willingness of white males to not only cede authority and influence to females but to purposefully and intentionally advance their interests. One outstanding example was Governor Henry Bellmon who, in the 1980s with his wife Shirley in a less public role, advocated by word and action for women. College professors and school district superintendents held positions in which they were able to encourage women to consider administrative and professorial positions. In my first attempt to obtain a principalship I "lost" in the competition to a woman with less qualification than I, as I was told afterward by the Director of Elementary Schools. The district was being pressured to hire its first female principal regardless of the talent pool from which to select. One door closed but another one opened and several years later my first doctoral student at Oklahoma State University was Sandy Wisley, a highly regarded principal in this same district who went on to become a superintendent in another district. One of the more satisfactory aspects of my career was to be an observer to, and an active participant in, the advancement of women in all aspects of the education field.

Of the fourteen individuals who served as the state superintendent from 1907 to 2015, only three held the position without gaining it by election. Another three were initially appointed to the position to complete unexpired terms and then ran successfully to continue in office. In Part III, chronologically, each of the chapters Seven through Nineteen, with the exception of Thirteen (two appointees), is devoted to one superintendent's brief biographical information and a description of his/her tenure including the political component of elections (campaign expenditures and methods, contestants, voting results, etc.), education aspects and accomplishments, extraordinary occurrences relating to ancillary responsibilities such as the Commissioners of the Land Office and the Textbook Commission, and actions surrounding desegregation. With the number of superintendents involved it was not possible to delve in depth into all of the political history and ramifications of their educational decisions.

After graduating from the public schools in Pennsylvania I earned a degree in history and subsequently taught in a public school in that state. Career advancement aspirations led me to graduate studies in educational leadership of the public schools in Pennsylvania and then in Oklahoma after which I assumed the principalship of a racially integrated school in Kansas. In my studies and work I was fascinated with the sociological and political context in which schools function. Eventually I obtained teaching and leadership positions in higher education spending a combined thirty-three years at Southwestern Oklahoma State University and then at Oklahoma State University. Early in that tenure I began a study of the Oklahoma State Superintendent of Public Instruction position and the incumbents because of my interest in how that office fit in state government, and how the incumbents navigated elections and fulfilled their duties. This book is a culmination of that effort and suggests that changes are necessary if the citizens are to have a higher quality public school system than what minimally meets the Legislature's constitutional mandate in article 1, section 5: "Provisions shall be made for the establishment and maintenance of a system of public schools, which shall be open to all the children of the State and free from sectarian control." Another critical component of the constitution, especially in a state that historically underfunds its public schools, is article 2, section 5: "No public money or property shall ever be appropriated, applied, donated, or used directly or indirectly, for the use, benefit, or support of any sect, church, denomination, or system of religion…" Historically, little political will ever surfaced over allocating public funds for nonpublic options, but that attitude began to change late in the twentieth century and the state superintendent could not avoid the controversy. Siphoning funds from a limited capacity for religiously oriented schools is detrimental to the efforts of the constitutionally mandated public schools. No elected superintendent was going to stake his or her political future on espousing a strong argument for or against in this controversy, or so we thought.

Part I
Territorial Period Administration
(1890-1910)

Educational governance in Oklahoma Territory and Indian Territory evolved very differently because, in the former the people of the territory had a voice in determining the structure of public education beginning in 1890, while in the latter, after initially granting the tribes authority to create their education systems, the federal government decades later in 1899 superimposed a scheme of supervision. Citizens in Oklahoma Territory welcomed at public expense the creation of schools with local boards. Tribal officials in Indian Territory, used to organizing, governing, and financially supporting their schools, looked askance at the federal government's perceived intrusion into what they believed to be tribal prerogatives achieved through treaties. In both territories, the governance was fraught with politics at the federal and territorial levels with the federal supervisor of tribal schools and the Oklahoma Territory governors appointed by the interior secretary and US presidents, respectively.

From the organization of civil government within Oklahoma Territory in late 1890, public education took root slowly in the original few counties and grew rapidly in the next decade and a half. The territorial Superintendents were appointed by the governors who oftentimes were chosen as political payoffs and without any prior connections to the territory. Intense political infighting in the dominant Republican Party in Oklahoma Territory sometimes embroiled the Superintendents who were replaced frequently. Several of the seven Superintendents, also territorial auditors *ex officio*, who served in the seventeen-year territorial period that ended in November 1907 held excellent credentials for the position. Regardless of the frequent transitions, at statehood the rudiments of a functioning public education system were in place with nearly 3,000 school districts in operation.

In Indian Territory for much of the latter half of the nineteenth century each of the Five Civilized Tribes operated its own education system and schools. As the end of that century neared, the US Congress shifted its perspective on the relationship with the tribes and decided to end tribal governance. A component of that transition involved the appointment of a federal supervisor to oversee tribal compliance and to submit annual reports to the interior secretary as a source of information for federal decision-making. Because the composition of Indian Territory population was changing with the number of white students and children of the freedmen overtaking that of tribal school students, it became imperative to provide some feasible education option for the non-Indian students. Within this context the federal supervisor's assessment of the tribal schools was influenced by his advocating for the establishment of schools for the swelling number of other students.

Part I, chapter 1 describes how the Oklahoma Territory's education system evolved under the leadership of the appointed Superintendents. Brief background biographical information is described for each Superintendent to present the level of educational qualification for the position. With a couple of notable exceptions, E. D. Cameron and A. O. Nichols, the appointees had significant educational experiences that provided a framework upon which to lead the Department and the education system. Woven into the descriptions are the political realities in which they governed, the vicissitudes of governors' actions, and the dynamics of the internecine struggles within the dominant Republican Party. Partisan politics was not absent in Indian Territory of this era, but it was only part of the overall political picture. John Benedict, who served 1899-1910, "survived" these politics in part because his experiences, both educational and others and described in some detail, were more extensive than any of the Oklahoma Territory Superintendents. In chapter 2 qualifications developed through Benedict's early career in education in Illinois and subsequent brief venture in New Mexico Territory are presented as a preliminary to a lengthy description of his assessment of, and supervision over, the tribal schools.

Chapter 1
Laying the Groundwork in Oklahoma Territory
(1890-1907)

To the President of the Council, Territorial Legislature:

> I have the honor to return herewith Council Bill No. 4 with my approval. I will however suggest that at an early day the bill be amended so as to provide for an Auditor, rather than have the Territorial Superintendent perform the duties thereof ex-officio; this may be done without at all increasing the salary proposed to be paid to the Superintendent of Public Instruction, and to him as ex-officio Auditor. The labor it seems to me would be more efficiently performed and the public would receive better service. (*Journal of the First Session of the Legislative Assembly of Oklahoma Territory, Beginning August 17, 1890* [Guthrie, 1890], 697.)

With the stroke of a pen, Oklahoma Territory's first governor, George W. Steele, signed the legislation creating the executive offices within the territory December 3, 1890. Council Bill No. 4, "Entitled [*sic*] an act to create the offices of Territorial Auditor, Territorial Treasurer, Territorial Attorney General and Territorial Superintendent of Public Instruction, and prescribing their several duties, and fixing the salaries thereof," was originally introduced September 2, 1890, the seventh day of the session. When the bill finally arrived on the Governor's desk after being under consideration for ninety-nine days, the only part the Governor found objectionable was the combination of the offices of Superintendent and *ex-officio* auditor. Governor Steele's reservations were prescient because that combination resulted in the incumbent being unable to devote adequate attention to the various duties of the two offices. On several occasions during the seventeen years of Oklahoma Territorial government (1890-1907) attempts to separate the two offices were mounted, unsuccessfully.[1]

The Superintendent position was designed to involve that person in numerous education-related leadership responsibilities, while the *ex-officio* auditor position would require that same person to serve on boards related to financial affairs. Some positions were included in the actions of the first legislative session; others were added within a few years. The Superintendent was a member of the Territorial Board, an *ex officio* member of the Board for Leasing School Land (1894), the *ex officio* President of the Territorial Board of Health (until 1903), and an *ex officio* member of the Board of Education of the Normal School (beginning with Edmond and later adding those at Alva and Weatherford). By 1897 the Normal School board also had the responsibility for the management and care of the "deaf and dumb." The Board of Regents of the Colored Agricultural and Normal University also included the territorial Superintendent.[2]

Additionally, the Superintendent (who would serve as Secretary), the Territorial

Secretary, and Territorial Treasurer would constitute a Board of Commissioners for the Management and Investment of the funds appropriated for the operations of territorial permanent schools, the Territorial Normal School, and the Territorial University. As Territorial Auditor he was a member of the Territorial Board of Equalization, Secretary of the Board of Railroad Assessors, a member of the Banking Board, and a member of a board to audit and allow all accounts for services and other liabilities incurred by the National Guard when called into active service. He also was required to audit all accounts of the Board of Regents of the Agricultural College and Experiment Station.[3] Each of these boards and committees was required to meet on a regular basis.

Supplementary legislation was enacted requiring the Governor to appoint, with the advice and consent of the Territorial Council within ten days of the passage of the act, a Territorial Superintendent who would hold office for a two-year term and until the Governor would appoint a qualified (posted a bond) successor. Succession procedures stipulated that, should a vacancy occur by resignation, death, or otherwise, the Governor was to appoint, as soon as practicable, someone to fill the vacancy who would serve until a successor was appointed and qualified.[4]

J. H. Lawhead, Highly Qualified Former Kansas Superintendent

Governor Steele's first appointee was J. H. Lawhead whose initial career move was from his home in Uniontown, Pennsylvania, to Syracuse, Ohio, where he served for several years as President of Carleton College. Enlisting in the Union army in 1861 he served in the Civil War until 1864 when he was mustered out because of a disability, having reached the rank of first lieutenant and adjutant general. In 1871 he uprooted his family and moved 750 miles west to southeastern Kansas, and was there only a few months before being elected Bourbon County's superintendent of schools, a position he held for more than ten years. That was only the beginning of his career in the political arena, and it was during the heady days of early statehood. In 1876 he was appointed to the Central Committee of the Republican Congressional Convention, Second District, at Fort Scott. By 1880 Lawhead was elected to the Kansas House of Representatives from District 37 in Bourbon County by a vote of 617 to 398. On December 26, 1883, at the State Teachers' Association meeting in Topeka he was elected vice-president of that group. Lawhead's political and educational star was rising, destined to greater heights.[5]

At the Republican State Convention in Topeka in July 1884, Lawhead and several others were nominated for state superintendent, and on the third ballot Lawhead was selected. In November's general election, he received 154,940 votes to his opponent's 110,000 to become the ninth superintendent, all Republicans. Two years later he was reelected and served a second two-year term. As superintendent, he served on the State Board of Education along with the State University Chancellor, the State Agricultural College President, and the Emporia and Leavenworth Normal School presidents. For four years Lawhead, the top education official in Kansas, presided over a system of education that included 8,775 school districts, 8,196 buildings, 11,310 teachers, and a student attendance of 403,351.[6]

Lure, excitement, and opportunities afforded in the 1889 Oklahoma land run proved irresistible for Lawhead so he and his family moved again, this time for 300 miles, made the run, and took a claim in Kingfisher County. Barely had he settled when Governor Steele nominated him as Territorial Superintendent for a two-year period. Eminently qualified from his Kansas experience, the Council confirmed his nomination December 9, six days after creating the position. Lawhead assumed the responsibilities very soon thereafter, addressing the closing session of the Legislature for a few minutes regarding school matters. He sent a request to the Attorney General for an opinion relating to the provision in the recently enacted school laws about elections for county superintendents.[7]

Five weeks after his confirmation he called the first meeting of the Territorial Board January 14, 1891. Comprised of the county superintendents of the six organized counties, the Board elected Lawhead chairman, engaged in much discussion about the powers and duties of the Board, discussed the first regular examination of teachers to be held in two weeks, and considered the process for the adoption of textbooks.[8] Beginning a territorial educational system was a challenge for which he was prepared, and he did not disappoint Steele. Lawhead and the Board formulated rules and policies in a precedent setting manner to guide the evolution of the fledgling structure of the education system. It was certainly fortuitous for Steele to have Lawhead available because of his thorough knowledge of Kansas's system and he was the best person to lead in Oklahoma Territory.

J. H. Lawhead
Courtesy of Kansas State Historical Society, Topeka, Kansas

Over the subsequent three months Lawhead called the Board to meet three times. On February 6 it established the process for textbook adoption, including hearing the publishers' propositions. In the last item of business the Board appointed a committee to confer with the Governor about a system for paying the teachers their compensation. On the 19th, it met to implement the Governor's suggestion for a fixed, uniform wage scale throughout the territory based on level of certification and whether the teacher was a principal or teacher or both. Questions for the April teacher examination were approved by the Board at its April 9th meeting as were the textbooks for the high school curriculum. To promote reading and literacy the Board organized itself also as the Board of Directors of the Oklahoma Reading Circle.[9]

Surprisingly, given these early days of establishing an education system, nine months passed before Lawhead scheduled the Board to meet January 20, 1892, when it developed a curriculum for all of the territory's schools and appointed a three-member committee, including J. H. Parker, Kingfisher County superintendent, to suggest amendments to the school laws. Four months later, when the Board met for the last time under Lawhead's leadership, the members presented potential questions for the teachers' examinations, an activity that challenged their ability to generate enough questions.[10]

Lawhead's term was cut short by his untimely death and after serving only twenty months (see table 1.1). That period was critical in the early development of the educational system even though only a small number of counties and districts were organized. His nearly two decade educational and political experience in Kansas laid the groundwork for his brief tenure in Oklahoma Territory where he became a founding member of its education system. Lawhead served three governors: through the end of Steele's abbreviated term, under an Acting Governor Robert Martin for three months, and almost half of Governor Abraham Seay's term. Governor Steele encountered opposition because he was an outsider (He came from Indiana to be the governor and immediately returned to that state upon his resignation.), and he was not hesitant to name recent arrivals for executive positions. Lawhead lived only briefly in the territory before being named Superintendent, but he was eminently qualified from his prior experience in Kansas and he gave every indication that he was planning to live permanently in his new home.[11]

Table 1.1 Territorial Superintendents' demographic data I

Superintendent	AWA	Party	Tenure	Length
James Hadden Lawhead	56	Republican	Dec. 9, 1890-Aug. 15, 1892	1 y, 8.0 m
Joseph Homer Parker	44	Republican	Aug. 20, 1892-Feb. 20, 1894	1 y, 6.0 m
Evan Dhu Cameron	31	Democratic	Feb. 21, 1894-Nov. 30, 1896	2 y, 10.0 m
Albert Owen Nichols	26	Republican	Dec. 1, 1896-Sept. 30, 1897	10.0 m
Stuart N. Hopkins	44	Republican	Oct. 1, 1897-Apr. 3, 1901	3 y, 6.0 m
Louis Warren Baxter	31	Republican	Apr. 4, 1901-Dec. 31, 1906	5 y, 9.0 m
James Edward Dyche	40	Republican	Jan. 1, 1907-Nov. 16, 1907	10.5 m

Note: AWA signifies age when appointed.

J. H. Parker, Minister and Educator

Finding someone to replace Lawhead fell to Governor Seay, who wasted little time naming a successor. Within a few days he selected J. H. Parker, superintendent of schools in Kingfisher County and a Congregational minister, to complete the unexpired term.

Parker had limited experience in schools; one year as a combined teacher and principal, and less than two years as county superintendent; but he possessed great organizational and entrepreneurial skills and appreciated the value of education. Bi-vocational in work in Oklahoma Territory, he split his time between serving the schools and his denomination, but only after having gained special dispensation from the latter through arguing persuasively that he could do both.[12]

Parker's career began with a short stint as a teacher and principal of an academy in Chester, Vermont, during the 1869-70 school year. At Chicago Theological Seminary he earned a Bachelor of Divinity degree in 1873. In September of that year, at age twenty-five, he was ordained to the Congregational ministry at Vermontville, Michigan, and immediately assumed the duties of pastor of the church there. Between 1875 and 1889 Parker pastored churches in Pontiac, Michigan, Peoria and Chicago, Illinois, Storm Lake, Iowa, and Wichita, Kansas. In Wichita he started a college, Fairmount, the forerunner of Wichita State University. After five church pastorates in fifteen years, he accepted an appointment in the summer of 1889 as superintendent of Congregational work in Oklahoma and moved to the territory where he officiated at the organization of a Congregational Church in Kingfisher on December 22. Over the next two years he pastored that church and organized congregations in El Reno, Downs, Hennessey, Seward, and other towns.[13]

J. H. Parker
Courtesy of Oklahoma Education Association

Early in January 1891 Governor Steele appointed Parker as Kingfisher County's superintendent of schools, where he supervised, until August 1892, all of the schools in the county and served *ex-officio* on the Board. He knew Lawhead and the expectations of the Superintendency well from the collegial environment of the Board's work in building the foundation for the Territory's education system. Because of his pastoral, missionary, and educational activities in the county, he was well known in the capital city and thus quite eligible for a promotion. Governor Seay appointed Parker August 26 to complete the unexpired term of Lawhead and the Council, upon the Governor's recommendation, confirmed him at the beginning of the next biennial legislative session, February 3, 1893, for a full two-year term.[14]

Parker chose to assume the duties but not to call the Board together before the previously scheduled November 2 meeting. He deemed it unnecessary to call a special meeting since he was intimately familiar with the Board's activities and the members' concerns and interests. When it met, the Board followed precedent by electing him chairman in the first item of business. Two additional topics, arrangements for territorial certificate examinations and amendments to the school laws, focused their attention. The Board next met in April 1893 but with a radically changed membership due to the second Territorial Legislature replacing county superintendents, who were increasing in number because of the formation of new counties and causing the Board to become unwieldy, with the presidents of Edmond Normal School and OU *ex officio* and the superintendents of a city school district and of a county as gubernatorial appointments. Because all levels of education, except the Normal school with its own governing board, were under the purview of the Board, it only seemed reasonable to have representation from the various levels. Items of business were the election of Parker as president, a discussion of the course of study for the two-week summer Normal Institute for teachers, the most convenient time to convene the Institute, and correspondence with the American Book Company. The broadened membership and scope of the Board, which previously addressed the concerns of the administrators of the county schools, now expanded to include the perspectives the common schools and higher education in the overall preparation and certification of teachers through the matriculation of secondary students to higher education institutions to earn degrees and/or through participation in summer institutes.[15]

One month later, May 4, when Parker called the Board to his Guthrie office, they decided to adopt the Kansas Course of Study for Institutes with the only modification being to change the cover pages to "Oklahoma." Most likely approval was neither sought nor granted for this "borrowing" of the Kansas plan and no one thought that approval was needed. Why expend precious time and energy when an acceptable alternative already existed? Discussion also involved conductors' and instructors' examinations and certificates. A July 15 meeting determined the times for the examinations of territorial certificate applicants and an October 26 meeting continued the discussion of similar topics.[16]

Politics at the national level affected events in the territorial offices in Oklahoma. Grover Cleveland, a Democrat, was elected president in 1892, and, after Governor Seay's resignation, Cleveland appointed William Renfrow governor. Renfrow, upon assuming the office, wrote Superintendent Parker (with similar letters to the attorney general and the treasurer) June 2, 1893, "You are hereby respectfully requested to deliver to me your resignation as Superintendent of the Territory of Oklahoma to take effect upon the appointment and qualification of your successor."[17]

Much to the delight of the Republican press, Parker refused to resign.

Honorable W.C. Renfrow, Governor:

Your communication of June 2, requesting me to deliver to you my resignation of the offices of territorial superintendent of public instruction and auditor has had careful consideration. After advising with many friends of education throughout the territory, not a few of whom I am pleased to say are of your political faith, I have decided to respectfully decline your request. While I deprecate the spirit that will narrow our educational interests within partisan lines, my main reason for declining to join my confreres in their exit is that in the present disturbed condition of school affairs in our territory, largely consequent upon change of our school law, I can not [sic] lay down the unsought position bestowed upon me by governor and council and generously confirmed by the loyal support of my fellow citizens, irrespective of party without a betrayal of trust.

Respectfully Yours, J. H. Parker, Terr. Supt. and Auditor (*Weekly Oklahoma State Capital*, July 29, 1893.)

That action began a protracted, difficult, and stormy relationship between Parker and the Governor that continued until February 1894. Parker's refusal to resign forced Renfrow and his newly appointed attorney general to accuse him of negligence of duty and malfeasance. He was charged with receiving income of $2,000 for his duties as Superintendent and auditor and $1,500 for his services from the extension society of the Congregational Church. In that triple capacity he was prevented from giving due attention to his official government duties. The charge of malfeasance accused Parker of illegally and wrongfully auditing and allowing certain accounts for mileage and expenses of the Oklahoma Agricultural and Mechanical College's board of regents. When Parker answered all of the charges in early September, the Governor then pursued a different route to have the office vacated by appointing E. D. Cameron as Parker's successor. Cameron had to pursue legal action through a quo warranto on February 21, 1894, to force Parker from office and a writ of mandamus to get his papers and records. Thus ended Parker's term as Superintendent and auditor, but not before it pitted two ministers of the gospel in a lawsuit over a secular position.[18]

Political tensions in the Territory knew no boundaries where much in the government's operation was up for scrutiny and many were maneuvering for power and influence. Parker was in office less than a year before he faced an attempt to oust him. Trumped up charges by the Governor and attempted enforcement by his minion were an affront to Parker's reputation both professionally and religiously. Raw politics was the game and he did not wish to be a player. Not much time passed before his bi-vocational approach was replicated by his successor and, ironically, Renfrow chose to overlook the hypocrisy.

After leaving office Parker continued his ministerial efforts in addition to devoting a lot of energy to the growth of Kingfisher College which he had founded as an academy in 1890. He was President of the Kingfisher Chautauqua Association during its existence, and in his later years he served temporary pastorates at Okarche and Vinita. Parker served the Territorial education system with Board membership for three years *ex officio*, first as a county superintendent and then as Superintendent. In the latter role he led the Board when its membership transitioned from county superintendents to educators of various institutions and entities. His religious reputation and political party affiliation led to his county superintendency and Superintendency appointments, but politics proved to be the main cause for his ouster.[19]

E. D. Cameron, Minister and Democrat

E. D. Cameron began his tenure February 21, 1894, five days before his thirty-second birthday and eight months after he was appointed to complete Parker's unexpired term. Born on his father's plantation in North Carolina ten months after the beginning of the Civil War and seven months before President Lincoln issued the Emancipation Proclamation, he was home-schooled for his first twelve years before enrolling in the Rockingham Academy where he graduated as class valedictorian at age sixteen. He attended Trinity University (now Duke University), and in 1881 he graduated from law school in Greensboro, North Carolina.[20]

After practicing law for a few years Cameron became a licensed minister, picked up roots, and moved to Henrietta, Texas, where, at the 1889 annual meeting of the North Texas Conference of the Methodist Episcopal Church, South, he was "admitted on trial" and assigned to pastor the Archer City Mission. Not long thereafter, he was assigned by the Indian Mission Conference of the Methodist Episcopal Church, South to pastor the Methodist church in Norman. Barely two years passed before he captured the attention of the Governor and was appointed Superintendent and Auditor.[21]

E. D. Cameron

W. P. Campbell Collection, Courtesy of Oklahoma Historical Society, no. 696

A Democrat, but with no teaching or administration experience at any level in any public or private school, Cameron was named to lead the education system. His political affiliation and church pastorates in Oklahoma Territory made him visible among the territory's leadership. A month after assuming the Superintendency he scheduled his first meeting with the Board for March 21, whereupon he was elected president. Over the next twenty-two months he called the Board together nineteen times, dealing most frequently with topics such as teacher examinations and certificates, territorial and county institutes, and textbooks. Not only was he leading the Board, he was trying to inform himself of the many tasks, duties, and responsibilities of the educators at all levels of the system.[22]

Compliance with the statutes required the Superintendent to submit a biennial report to the Governor who then included it in his message to the Legislature. Recommendations for statutory changes were an essential component of the report. Among the twelve recommendations Cameron submitted in his early 1895 report were: enactment of a separate school law (primarily to deal with Black schools); specification of the authority of county superintendents to remove district officers for willful neglect of duty; repeal of the section of the school law that required district bond elections to be held under the general election laws; and prohibition of all school officials from employment as salesmen for companies selling supplies and furniture to schools.[23]

An examination of the reasons supporting some of these recommendations identifies and describes the context in which these suggestions were offered. Mid-1890s saw a flurry of enactments across the South establishing separate schools and access to other facilities as a consequence of the Supreme Court's decision in *Plessy v Ferguson*. Also, Cameron perceived a direct conflict of interest when school officials were moonlighting as salesmen for companies conducting business with the schools. Rapidly expanding school enrollments and erection of school buildings created a need for many desks, books, lumber and other construction materials. In an environment of lax standards regarding conflicts of interests, it is not surprising that school officials might engage in ethically questionable practices to further their own financial advantage. At this early date educators apparently perceived no ethical constraints from gaining personally from public funds, but, as a lawyer and minister, Cameron wanted strict prohibition of the practice.

For thirty-three months Cameron tried to juggle the duties of the Territorial offices as well as the ministerial responsibilities, an effort he finally decided was too strenuous, especially since his bishop transferred him from El Reno, Oklahoma Territory to Muskogee, Indian Territory. Furthermore, he would have to resign because the law forbade him from living in one territory and holding a political position in another. Maybe his conscience pricked him over how he received his appointment in the first place. Regardless, officially, he finished the unexpired term of Parker in early 1895, was nominated by Renfrow for a full two-year term, was confirmed by the Council February 11, 1895, and served until November 30, 1896. However, his public service was not finished as detailed in chapter Six.[24]

By March 1893 the Legislature concurred that the Superintendent needed assistance to fulfill the duties of auditor so D. B. Lawhead was hired to serve in that capacity for one year. In April 1894, A. O. Nichols was hired as clerk to Superintendent/Auditor Cameron. When Cameron resigned, Renfrow appointed the twenty-six-year-old Nichols, who by then had gained the title of Assistant Auditor, to complete the unexpired term. Then, March 9, 1897, the Council confirmed Nichols for a two-year term.[25]

A. O. Nichols, Brief Tenure of An Ill-Fitted Appointee

A. O. Nichols earned degrees from Vanderbilt University and the Missouri School of the Mines before making the Cherokee Outlet run in 1893, settling in Alva. Not long after that he became the Register of Deeds in the county soon-to-be-named Woods. Identified as a promising young, competent, and aspiring professional, he was selected to assist in the territorial auditor's office. Also on the territorial payroll was his wife Belle who worked from January 1896 through early November 1897, quite possibly in the Auditor's Office.[26]

A. O. Nichols
Oklahoma School Herald Collection, 21396.5.12.C,
Courtesy of Oklahoma Historical Society

Young, possessing little political cachet, and minimally prepared to assume the duties of the combined offices, particularly those of the Superintendency, but at the same time sufficiently cognizant of the expectations, he had the confidence and foresight to write in the biennial report to the Governor in December 1896.[27]

> The character of the work of the two offices is entirely different and they seemed to have been combined, in the first instance, solely in the interest of economy. When the territory consisted of but seven counties, as it did at first, this arrangement may have been justified; but under present conditions, I am of the opinion that the two offices should be made separate and distinct…The auditor should be a practical business man; the superintendent, a man learned in the sciences and art of education. The two qualifications are seldom found in the same person. (*Third Biennial Report of the Territorial Superintendent of Public Instruction of Oklahoma, July 1, 1894-June 30, 1896* [Guthrie: State Capital, 1896], 7-8.)

Interpreting his commentary to conclude he considered himself adequately prepared for the auditor responsibilities but not for the Superintendency is not difficult or unreasonable. Thus, it is ironic that Nichols found himself in a quandary within a few short months. While he was prescient regarding the combination of the positions, he was ill prepared for the events of April 1897. Controversy swirled around Nichols over a deal with the American Book Company when he insisted he had no choice but to follow the law that required him, within a sixty-day period, to enter into a five-year contract with a book company to provide textbooks. Because 99 percent of the books being used were published by the American Book Company, he obligated the territory to this company in the contract. Consequences were swift, for soon other companies alleged unfair purchasing practices.[28]

By early July Nichols had had enough and announced his resignation, effective September 30, but his troubles were not over. In late August a second controversy erupted when he refused to issue any more territorial warrants until the US Supreme Court decided whether the one percent limit of the federal Harrison Act of 1889 applied to general debt. Mandamus proceedings were brought against Nichols in September. He left office after ten months, September 30, 1897, and shortly moved to Joplin, Missouri, where he lived most of the remainder of his life with the last twenty-five years at the Elks Club. He engaged in the zinc and lead mining industry in the Joplin area and in coal mining in Arkansas for many years. Nichols and his wife had a daughter in 1897 and twin daughters in December 1899. Complications resulting from the birth of the twins caused his wife's death almost immediately.[29]

Nichols, the first person in the Territorial Auditor's post whose educational preparation was more akin to the business and mining world, was suspect as far as the educators were concerned. And, he succeeded Cameron who was first and foremost a minister and whose predecessor was also viewed primarily as a minister. Educators were itching for one of their own to lead the education system. Within a month after Nichols's confirmation by the Council in March 1897, speculation grew about his replacement. He was ill-fitted for the combined responsibilities and insufficiently savvy to negotiate the political minefields of Territorial government.

S. N. Hopkins, Lifelong Educator

In a front-page article in the *El Reno News* of April 16, 1897, S. N. Hopkins was touted as the next Oklahoma Territory Superintendent through these comments: recognition among the educators of the Territory, personal acquaintance with many territorial teachers, and strong support from persons beyond the education community. The *Guthrie Daily Leader* opined that he was favored by the Territorial Teachers' Association, the faculties of the different universities, and scores of county teachers' organizations. Much interest was expressed in the position with several men applying. Governor C. M. Barnes got the message and named Hopkins to assume the responsibilities October 1. While some were surprised at the selection, "Republicans generally believe a first-rate appointment has been made."[30]

Hopkins, the son of a farmer, lived in Ohio until his family moved to Iowa in 1869. At nineteen he began teaching and soon thereafter entered the Kirksville Normal School in Missouri. Upon graduation in 1877 he moved to Salina, Iowa, to become a principal. Subsequently, he occupied a similar position in Brookville, Iowa, before being elected on the Republican ticket in 1883 to a two-year term as the superintendent of schools in Jefferson County, Iowa. In 1885 and 1887 he was reelected, providing him insight into the machinations of rural politics within the education arena.[31]

Like masses of other people he migrated to Oklahoma in 1890, and soon accepted the El Reno city schools superintendency, a position he held until his appointment as Territorial Superintendent. Sufficient support of the El Reno School Board got him reappointed annually, and his involvement in school affairs across the territory, frequently serving as a speaker at various meetings, increased his visibility among educators. For example, at the Territorial Teachers' Association meeting in December 1895 he spoke on "The Graded Course of Study." He lectured before the Logan County teachers November 25, 1897, and he was elected President of the Territorial Teachers' Association that same year.[32]

S. N. Hopkins
Courtesy of Oklahoma Education Association

Governor Renfrow appointed Hopkins to the Territorial Board in May 1894, and at the next month's meeting in El Reno he was elected Secretary. Thus began his affiliation with that Board, which lasted until 1901, the last three and one-half years in which he served as the Superintendent. As a Board member he was intimately involved with the educational affairs of the territory and the controversy surrounding his predecessor Nichols. Renfrow's successor, Barnes, chose Hopkins, now forty-three, to be Territorial Superintendent to complete Nichols' unexpired term beginning October 1, 1897. Hopkins completed that term and was then nominated and confirmed by the Council in March 1899 for a two-year term, becoming the first of only two territorial Superintendents to complete a full term for which they were nominated and confirmed. Barnes nominated Hopkins to a second term in March 1901, but the discordant Legislature ended the session sans confirming him.[33]

Hopkins's tenure was not free of controversy for, similar to his predecessors, he found himself embroiled in contested legal matters in the spring of 1899. In his Auditor's role, Hopkins refused to produce for an investigating committee of the Council his records relating to vouchers and warrant stubs of the adjutant general's office. A vote in the Council resulted in a warrant for his arrest, and he was arrested by the sergeant-at-arms who had orders to place him in the county jail. Meanwhile, as a result of habeas corpus proceedings, Hopkins was released on his own recognizance. Judge John H. Burford discharged Hopkins from custody and excused him from bringing his vouchers before the investigating committee. A few weeks later Hopkins entered a guilty plea to the charge of contempt for refusing to produce certain vouchers and warrant stubs. Fines and court costs amounted to $15, and the contempt charge for refusing to produce documents for the investigating committee was dismissed.[34]

The *Fourth Biennial Report*, Hopkins' first, offers insight into his description of the territory's schools. Teacher pay amounts and student enrollment and attendance numbers were presented. The *Oklahoma School Herald*, the most informative and widely read monthly magazine, provided the critical assessment of the status: teacher pay was woefully inadequate, barely more than a common laborer, and fewer than half of eligible students attended daily. Because Hopkins and the Board were responsible for the summer normal school institutes, they announced the plans without comment. The *Herald* on the other hand, highly critical of the content and delivery of institutes, described them as essentially a poor use of the participants' time.[35]

Hopkins reported in the *Fifth Biennial Report* that the Board held fifteen meetings from July 1, 1898 to June 30, 1900. Topics of discussion and action taken regarded questions for county teachers' examinations, a course of study for the county normal institutes, and a revision of the course of study for the common schools. He recommended legislation establishing a teachers' association in each county, initiating an Arbor Day observance by the public schools, requiring 15 percent of the lease moneys from the Kickapoo indemnity lands to be apportioned to the public schools in those lands, and making the payment of the last month's salary of all public school teachers contingent upon filing all required reports due the county superintendent and district clerk. Ten years of practice found the flow of paperwork so insufficient that some leverage was needed for compliance. In a general statement, he encouraged the populace to establish closer ties with their schools and to invest in their schools for the advancement of the students and the Territory. In his second report he reiterated his concerns over inadequate teacher pay and poor student attendance but with considerably more passion: "The financial inducements to remain in the profession are not strong…There is a strong argument in these last figures in favor of a compulsory educational law."[36] Other than implying that teacher pay should be increased, he offered no amount that might convince good and highly qualified teachers to remain in the profession. Correspondingly, he omitted any analysis of the consequences of a law requiring student attendance, i.e., compliance, larger class sizes, more teachers, and larger facilities.

When Hopkins agreed to serve another term, and the Governor nominated him, an internecine dispute involving the Council and the Governor caused nominations for several positions, including his, to be scuttled. "The World believes a great injustice was done some of the appointees of Governor Barnes by the late legislature adjourning without confirming them," reported *The Southwest World*, a typical partisan paper of the era. Even *The El Reno Democrat* reminded its readers of the injustice committed by the Legislature's lack of action. Also, not to be minimized were the politics in the presidency at Edmond Normal School where the Board was intimately and consequentially involved. The Republican Legislature domination failed Hopkins in the spring of 1901, but his influence as an *ex officio* member of the Board of Education of the Normal School resulted in his appointment as a professor of arithmetic and advanced algebra at the Edmond school. After eight years there Hopkins was hired to be the principal of Eugene Field School in Oklahoma City, a position he held until 1922.[37]

He was a charter member and elder of the Presbyterian Church of El Reno and a member of the El Reno Lodge, International Order of Foresters. Hopkins served the Territory well and would have had a longer tenure as Superintendent except for the debilitating and simmering contentions within the Republican Party in Oklahoma Territory and between Washington, DC, and Guthrie. His career reflected a cyclical trajectory from a beginning teacher/principal to Superintendent to experienced principal and included the gamut of education positions. In hindsight he discovered the politics of rural southeastern Iowa to be more manageable than the rough and tumble Republican dynamics of Oklahoma Territory.[38]

L. W. Baxter, Longest Serving Territorial Superintendent

When Governor Barnes, who was within a few days of being fired by President William McKinley, was forced to nominate another person, his choice was L.W. Baxter, a professor at Edmond Normal School. Baxter, a native Kansan and son of Canadian born parents, attended the University of Kansas and later earned a degree from Emporia Normal School where, upon graduation, he worked as private secretary to the president and met a gal who became his wife after he moved to Oklahoma Territory.[39]

By 1896 Baxter became school superintendent in Guthrie. That same year Superintendent Cameron, in a bipartisan effort, named Baxter along with Hopkins, both Republicans, to a committee that was required by law to visit the Edmond Normal School and to submit a report to the Superintendent of the school's operation. Expertise and a willingness to serve overrode partisan notions. In the 1897-98 school year Baxter became a professor there teaching history, literature, civics, penmanship, and bookkeeping.[40]

During this time as Guthrie's superintendent and as a professor Baxter was very active in the education arena. For example, he was president of the Territorial Teachers' Association in 1896 and gave the address at its annual meeting. He conducted normal institutes in Blaine and Logan counties in 1897. In October of that year when Hopkins was appointed Territorial Superintendent, Governor Barnes appointed Baxter to replace Hopkins on the Territorial Board. Teaching responsibilities kept him at the Normal School until his appointment as Superintendent and Auditor April 4, 1901, at the youthful age of thirty-one.[41]

The Territorial Legislature in 1890 created the Territorial Board of Education and the Board of Education (Regents) for the Normal School as two separate governance entities (see appendix N) with the Superintendent serving *ex-officio* on both boards. A legislative change in 1893 placed the Edmond Normal president on the Territorial Board *ex-officio* and set the stage for some fascinating decisions. Guthrie, the capital, and Edmond were only fifteen miles apart and that allowed frequent and quick communication. The common school system and the normal schools (now three) were growing rapidly, and it was only natural that the members of the two boards were familiar with the curricula and most of the best administrators and faculty in the schools and at the teacher preparation institutions. Soon after Baxter became Superintendent, his influence on the Board of Regents resulted in the president of the Edmond Normal School (and fellow Territorial Board member) being replaced by one of his (Baxter) faculty colleagues, Frederick Howard Umholtz, and Hopkins, his predecessor, being hired as a mathematics professor. In the highly charged environment of the times, political calculations were ever-present even lacking partisanship.[42]

L. W. Baxter
*Courtesy of Special Collections and University Archives,
Oklahoma State University*

Baxter eventually served longer than any other Territorial Superintendent, nearly six years with the Council officially confirming him for two-year terms on March 11, 1903, and March 10, 1905. The relatively long tenure created stability in the office and facilitated the territory's common school and normal school growth and expansion. Baxter accomplished this in spite of the rapid turnover in the governor's office in his first year. Appointed by Barnes, and serving briefly under Governors William Jenkins and William Grimes, Baxter then enjoyed the relative stability and support of the Thomas Ferguson administration before ending his tenure under Governor Frank Frantz. Baxter was part of five of the nine Oklahoma Territory gubernatorial administrations, a testament to his ability and skills to navigate turbulent political waters.[43]

In his first biennial report, in 1902, he summarized the activities of the Board, commented on the effects of the legislation enacted in 1900, and lauded the efforts of his predecessor for legislative recommendations that had come to fruition. The Board's emphasis in its twenty-five meetings over the two-year period was on the preparation of qualifying examination questions for myriad levels of teacher certification and the revision of courses of study for normal institutes and the common schools. He observed that the separate school law (applying almost exclusively to Black schools) was working very satisfactorily as evidenced by the erection of many school buildings, except in a few counties. Also, the statute of 1900 returning 15 percent of the revenue from the school land leases to the districts in which they were situated, while burdening the Territorial Treasurer, provided relief to the residents and substantially benefited the schools.[44]

Baxter's obligation to recommend legislation to improve the operation of his office and the common schools resulted in a request to authorize county commissioners to levy a tax to be apportioned per capita among the districts of the county, to remove all superintendents from the boards of health, and to require county superintendents (twenty-five in 1902) to forward their annual reports to the Superintendent by October 15 subject to punishment for failure to do so. Impetus for this last recommendation was pragmatic because the Superintendent was required to submit a report to the Governor by December 1 and he did not receive some of the county superintendents' reports until November 25. Baxter suggested to the Governor that pay for the last quarter would be withheld until the report was received.[45]

Legislation relating to the schools was evolving simultaneously with the development and expansion of the schools. The Superintendent was the person most knowledgeable of the Territory's schools who could translate that knowledge into recommendations for statutory changes. In most cases the Legislature cooperated by enacting provisions deemed pertinent by the Superintendent. Baxter's expertise was in the education arena, but that did not exempt him from fulfilling his obligations as *ex officio* Territorial Auditor. Thus, he was required to prepare and submit to the Governor a biennial report of the auditing department. Baxter's second, and last, report emphasized once again the weighty responsibility and monumental task of overseeing two extremely important sections of territorial government. "The work has increased so materially the past few years and is of such magnitude and importance that each office should be recognized as a department of the Territorial Government [sic]. Again the offices are not compatible."[46]

Baxter resigned effective December 31, 1906,[47] and the Board expressed its warm thoughts and complimentary comments:

> Resolved: That the Territorial Board of Education desires to record an expression of its regret at the discontinuance of Honorable L. W. Baxter as member and secretary of the Board after a service of about six years. His energy, conscientious devotion to duty, thoughtful vigilant capacity for grasping details, his integrity and fairness in dealing with men; his knowledge and intelligent sympathy with the work of the school system, have made his services for six years on this Board of exceptional value. In this period of service the school system of Oklahoma has developed

from the crude beginning of the early days of the Territory, to the well established structure of the present date. Every school, almost every teacher, in all of the financial affairs, have felt the touch of Mr. Baxter's well directed energy. No difference what great growth and development the future may bring, the impress and mark of Mr. Baxter's work will never be obliterated. His genial personality, his steadfast fidelity, his remarkable capacity for being and making a friend, have warmly endeared him to the members of this Board. Wherever he may go, in whatever work he may engage, he has the hearty good will and wishes of all the members of this Board *(Territorial Board of Education Meeting Minutes,* January 10, 1907).

The Edmond Sun suggested in mid-December 1906 that one of the reasons for Baxter's resignation was his declining health caused by fulfilling the duties of the combined offices of Superintendent and Auditor. Yet, he was only thirty-six. His career in education and devotion to the growth of the schools and teacher preparation institutions ended just when he could have continued to be very influential. The paper mused that he would engage in business upon regaining his health. Little time passed before Baxter and another fellow organized the American National Bank of Guthrie, which they later sold prior to creating the American National Bank of Tulsa. When his business partner died, he and several others organized the Security National Bank of Tulsa. Another venture involved the oil business in small pools in the Wynona district near Haskell and throughout the Osage district. Banking and the energy industry, certainly a major shift from his early career, occupied him until his death.[48]

J. E. Dyche, Ten-month Transition to Statehood

The seventh and last of the Superintendents, J. E. Dyche, began his brief tenure at the beginning of 1907, having been appointed by Governor Frank Frantz. Dyche finished his early schooling in Hiawatha, Kansas, then spent two years at Garfield University (now Friends University) in Wichita after which he enrolled at the University of Kansas, graduating in 1892. His first employment was as teacher and assistant principal at Wellington, Kansas, and from 1896 to 1900 he was superintendent at Horton, Kansas. He moved to Oklahoma Territory with the opening of the Kiowa and Comanche country in 1901, shifted careers, and with a partner, began and operated Dyche and Fegenbaum Hardware in Lawton. Over the next several years he served as the only Republican on the Comanche County Commission, and he also was appointed assistant postmaster in Lawton. At forty, he was selected by Governor Frantz to be Superintendent and Auditor, essentially to facilitate the transition of the responsibility of the combined Superintendent's and the auditor's offices to the separate offices in the new State of Oklahoma.[49]

During his brief ten and one-half month tenure, the Board met a surprising fourteen times with at least one meeting every month. Dyche brought experience in Kansas school districts to the office and business experience in Lawton to the auditor's office. Much of the emphasis was on the routine, mundane affairs regarding teacher examinations and the issuance of certificates; however, there was an air of expectancy over the joining of the two territories. The Board invited the federal supervisor of the tribal schools in Indian Territory, John Benedict, to meet with them to adopt a course of study for the schools of both territories. At the final meeting of the Board, October 19, 1907, it ordered Dyche to audit all claims against the Board that would be filed between that date and statehood so that there would be no claims passing to the new Board about which they would not be informed.[50]

J. E. Dyche
Courtesy of Oklahoma Historical Society, no. 4447

Dyche's term ended November 16, Statehood Day. During his tenure as a territorial officer he found time to run for the office of state auditor on the Republican ticket, garnering 99,904 votes compared to the Democratic and Socialist candidates who received 132,590 and 10,454 votes, respectively. Soon after Dyche left office he was appointed District Indian agent in the former Indian Territory and was stationed at Chickasha until 1914. He was engaged in several business interests when he became actively involved in politics on a full-time basis as campaign manager for Jake Hamon for national committeeman. In 1921 he was named warden of the federal penitentiary in Atlanta, Georgia. Upon his resignation as warden, he was named the federal prohibition agent for the Oklahoma, Kansas, Missouri, and Arkansas division, with headquarters in Kansas City. A desire to return to Oklahoma and to re-enter politics later led to his resignation. Dyche died at his home in Oklahoma City.[51]

Summary

Commonalities in the profile of the Superintendents (see tables 1.1-1.3) were: white males, members of the Republican Party (except Cameron), married, parents, born in the US (except Parker), prior education administration experiences (Cameron excepted), and no offices gained after statehood (except Cameron). Office tenures ranged from Nichols's ten months to Baxter's five years and nine months. Superintendents' ages ranged from twenty-six to fifty-six at the time of their appointments, with Nichols the youngest and Lawhead the oldest, and the average was thirty-eight and one-half years.

Table 1.2 Territorial Superintendents' demographic data II

Superintendent	Birth date	Place	Death date	Place	Age
J. H. Lawhead	1834	Pennsylvania	Aug. 15, 1892	Kingfisher	58
J. H. Parker	Feb. 20, 1848	Quebec, Canada	July 7, 1915	Oklahoma City	67
E. D. Cameron	Feb. 26, 1862	North Carolina	July 29, 1923	Tahlequah	61
A. O. Nichols	Sept. 17, 1870	Arkansas	July 12, 1954	Joplin, MO	83
S. N. Hopkins	Sept. 27, 1853	Ohio	Nov. 8, 1934	Oklahoma City	81
L. W. Baxter	1870	Kansas	Mar. 6, 1935	Tulsa	65
J. E. Dyche	July 4, 1866	Missouri	Dec. 26, 1926	Oklahoma City	60

All of them graduated from normal school/college or law school, and two of them were ministers, Parker and Cameron. Nichols was the only one to have been employed either in the Auditor's or the Superintendent's office prior to assuming the top position; however, Lawhead served four years as Kansas' state superintendent before moving to Oklahoma Territory. Parker, Hopkins, and Baxter served on the Board prior to becoming the Superintendent, giving them opportunities to gain a working knowledge of the office's responsibilities.

Table 1.3 Territorial Superintendents' demographic data III

Superintendent	Married	Spouse	Child	Normal/college	Denomination
J. H. Lawhead	1858	…	7	Marietta, Ohio	…
J. H. Parker	1874	Carrie Griswold	6	Middlebury, Conn.	Congregational
E. D. Cameron	1890	Clara Williams	6	Trinity/Duke	Methodist S.
A. O. Nichols	1897	Belle Rittenhouse	3	Vanderbilt	…
S. N. Hopkins	1885	Kate Doyle	2	Kirksville, Missouri	Presbyterian
L. W. Baxter	1897	Mary Edith	2	Emporia, Kansas	…
J. E. Dyche	1890	Nora English	6	Univ. of Kansas	…

The combination of the offices of Superintendent and Auditor, and the political milieu of the territorial period, probably affected the success of the men who filled the positions more than any other factors. When Governor Steele signed the legislation December 3, 1890, establishing the combined positions, he wrote of his reservations and said it should be changed as soon as possible. Several Superintendents in their biennial reports to the Governor pled for separation of the offices, but they were not successful; however, the Legislature appropriated salary money for office assistants. By 1893 a clerk was hired for the Auditor's Office and soon thereafter the position was upgraded to Assistant Auditor. Additional assistance was funded in the Superintendent's office in 1895. By 1899 there was a deputy superintendent and, in the Auditor's Office, both a bookkeeper and a stenographer by 1905.[52]

Territorial governors were appointed by the US presidents and consequently reflected the same political affiliations. Governors nominated or appointed Superintendents and *ex-officio* Auditors who aligned with them politically. Partisanship politics and internal conflicts within the Republican Party were the rule and most likely played an important role in Parker's removal from office, Nichols's resignation, and Hopkins's inability to receive Council confirmation.

From 1890 to 1907 the system of education changed dramatically in Oklahoma Territory. It began from nothing and grew into a fledgling organized system of 3,000 regular and separate school districts. County superintendent positions were created to provide assistance and supervision, a Territorial teachers' association was formed, standards and qualifications were established and approved for teacher and instructor certificates, a system for financing schools was developed, Normal schools for preparing educators were created at Edmond, Alva, and Weatherford, and a university was founded for educating the Black citizens, in addition to OU and the Agricultural and Mechanical College (OSU). The Superintendent/Auditor and the Territorial Board of Education of the Normal School were involved in the selection of the administrators and faculty, the curriculum, and the physical facilities for the Normal schools.

Separate schools, few of which enrolled white students, were a settled Supreme Court issue. The mid-1890s *Plessy v. Ferguson* decision formed the legal basis for creating the dual system that would remain in effect for the next six decades and for the prohibition written into the state constitution in 1906 against Black students and white students being taught in the same classroom. Superintendents had to deal with this extra layer of complexity, especially when supervising the funding of the schools, but also with unequal treatment. What was decided at the end of the nineteenth century left a legacy of questionable treatment evident yet today.

The Oklahoma Territorial government interfaced with the national government over the access afforded Native American students with the federal authority's provision of education through tribal schools dating to the middle of the nineteenth century. For the Plains Indians (Kiowa and Cheyenne and Arapaho), federal financial support was directed to both boarding schools and day schools. When Oklahoma Territory was organized and began offering free public schools Indian parents had the additional choice of sending their children to those schools. In 1891 the Cheyenne and Arapaho reservation was divided into counties and Territorial schools were opened. *The Report of the Commissioner of Indian Affairs* in 1896 showed that twenty-five Indian students attended public schools the previous year with the federal government paying tuition of ten dollars per quarter per student to the school districts. In many regards Indian children did not want to attend the public schools because they encountered racist attitudes and the schools were only conditionally receptive of them because they received the tuition funds. Then, circa 1900 tuition payments ceased, engendering more opposition from the Indian parents. A decade later the federal government entered into agreements with local districts to pay a sum equal to the per capita cost of the school only to have that arrangement vacated by the comptroller of the federal treasury because Indian students were entitled to attend the public schools according to Oklahoma law. With no tribal school systems and the vacillations of the payment of tuition by the federal government in the late 1800s and early 1900s the Kiowa, Comanche, Cheyenne, and Arapaho tribes lobbied for better quality public schools and fair access to them.[53] Little in the recorded history reflects overt efforts of the Superintendents to address the challenges faced by the Indian students as they encountered the public schools.

The relationships among the tribes, the federal government, and the Territorial schools involved the Superintendent primarily in the oversight of the funding mechanisms of the Territory and the US government. In this formative period when counties were being formed, county superintendents were being elected, school districts were created including separate schools, and Territorial funding of the schools was evolving Superintendents did not consider the education of the Indians a high priority.

Formation of Oklahoma Territory and its education system were not unique because the federal government dictated how territories would become states. Oklahoma Territory's education system developed concurrently with New Mexico's although the latter did not achieve statehood until early 1912. New Mexico gained territorial status in 1851, legislated a superintendency and a board of education in 1863, failed to fund and implement the statute but created school districts across the territory, and waited until 1891 to form a functioning territorial superintendency and school board. Many of the provisions of Oklahoma and New Mexico were similar except for at least one significant aspect in New Mexico: the Catholic bishop over the Territory held a seat on the Territorial Board of Education.[54]

Oklahoma Territory's experiment in naming a Superintendent through gubernatorial appointment lasted seventeen years, resulting in a mixed success of the individuals who held the position. Politically turbulent times in the Territory created controversies that saw short tenures and rapid turnover both in the governorship and the Superintendency. As constituted, the method of selection of several of the territorial officers was not a success worthy of repetition in statehood. Governors had to be elected, but the extent of their appointment prerogative received considerable consideration at the constitutional convention.

Chapter 2
Benedict: Imposing the Federal Will on Tribal Schooling in Indian Territory
(1899-1910)

In the final quarter of the nineteenth century federal Indian policy shifted from dealing with removals, treaties, reservations, and some wars to breaking up reservations by granting land allotments. Motives were mixed from wanting to make the Indians less dependent upon the government and thus more self-reliant, to enhance their assimilation into white society, and to free up reservation land for white ownership. The Dawes Act, or General Allotment Act of 1887, gave the president the authority to divide the land held in communal ownership. However, this act specifically excluded the Five Civilized Tribes. Subsequent negotiations and laws, including the Curtis Act of 1898, extended the provisions to these tribes based in part on this report to the US Congress in 1894: "The governments (of the tribes) have fallen into the hands of a few able and energetic Indian citizens, nearly all mixed blood, and adopted whites who have so administered their affairs and have enacted such laws that they are enabled to appropriate to their own exclusive use, almost the entire property of the Territory of any kind that can be rendered profitable and available."[1]

The federal government's approach to the Five Civilized Tribes' prerogatives to self-governance of their educational systems shifted from a limited oversight primarily focused on the financial contributions of the federal government to a more extensive involvement in the actual operation of the tribal governance boards and the schools. This new focus was to accomplish greater accountability until all tribal governments were abolished by March 4, 1906, as required by the Act for the Protection of the People of Indian Territory known as the Curtis Act of 1898.[2]

Congress, through the Department of the Interior, determined that the education systems of the Five Civilized Tribes (Cherokee, Chickasaw, Choctaw, Creek, and Seminole) of Indian Territory had deteriorated to the point that outside supervision was immediately necessary. For example, in the Cherokee and Creek boarding schools, wrote Angie Debo, the superintendents owed their appointments to patronage with such practice at its worst in the Black schools. Superintendents were often illiterate or at best ill-prepared as John Benedict portrayed in his first report: "There are at present 26 boarding schools in the Territory, and the superintendents of not more than four of these schools are competent to teach any of the common school branches."[3] Of critical importance here was the practice of these administrators who had unquestioned authority to select, supervise, and manage these teachers.

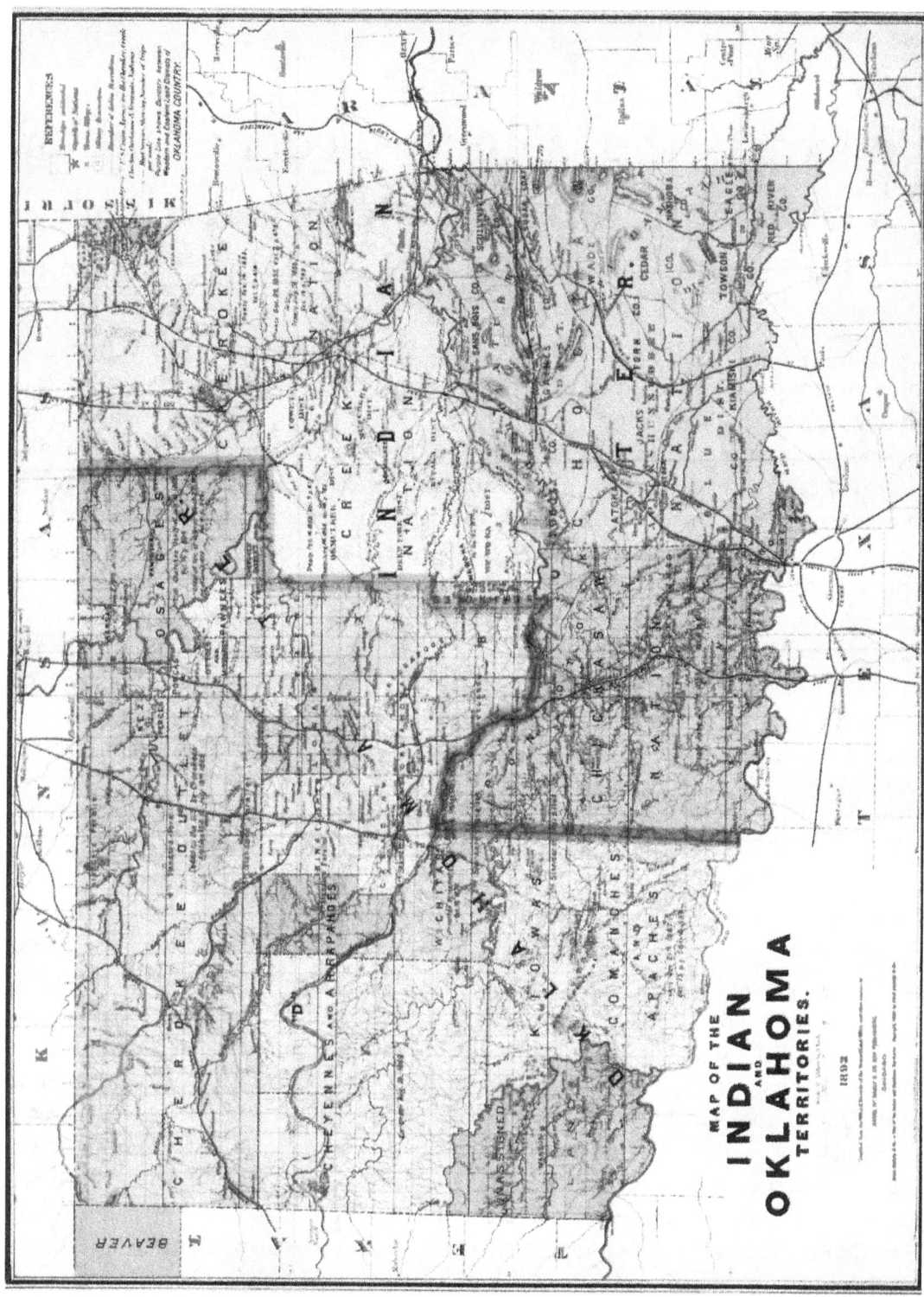

Fig. 2.1 Map of The Indian and Oklahoma territories [S.I., 1892], Rand McNally and Company, https://www.loc.gov/item/98687110/.

Extending beyond the tribal system was this depiction of the perceived crisis: How was it conceivable that thousands of whites who moved to the territory and were substantially responsible for the economic development could be excluded from the benefits and responsibilities of citizenship? To stimulate greater accountability, to assist with the scheduled termination of the tribal governments and schools, and to facilitate the transition from tribal to state education, the secretary of the Interior created the position of superintendent of schools for all of Indian Territory. For this unique position it would take an exceptional person.[4]

Benedict's Experiential Preparation for Indian Territory

Cornelius Bliss, appointed by President McKinley March 6, 1897, to be secretary of the Interior, served for two years and was replaced by Ethan Hitchcock, February 20, 1899. Responsible for Indian Affairs as well as territorial officers' appointments, Interior handled the paperwork and supervised the officials, but the President officially appointed those officers. It was Bliss who initially selected John Benedict to work for the Department of the Interior as the first superintendent of the forest reserves of the New Mexico and Arizona territories. Benedict at the time was serving as Master of Chancery of the Circuit Court in Danville, Illinois. The few months spent in the southwestern territories resulted in a restoration of his health and new appreciation of the geographical ruggedness of that area.[5]

John Dunning Benedict's life and career leading up to his appointment as superintendent of schools for Indian Territory prepared him well for his duties in supervising an education system. From his father, who was a native of New York and who taught school in Clermont, Indiana, and the surrounding area for several years, he learned of the challenges of moving a long distance from family and of teaching school. When he was fifteen he moved with his uncle's family to Rossville, Illinois. By the age of thirty-four he had experience as a rural schoolteacher, city schoolteacher, principal, county superintendent, assistant state superintendent, local school board member, and state school board member in addition to serving the circuit court. His connections to influential people aided him in obtaining employment opportunities.[6]

At Rossville High School, while in the advanced class, the principal suggested to the eighteen-year-old Benedict that he take the teacher's certificate examination just for practice. He passed and earned a first-grade certificate qualifying him to teach in the county and village schools. Such schools in Vermillion County, Illinois, gave John the opportunity for five years to practice and hone his teaching skills before he left to study law in Danville. Out of money after one year, he sat for the city teacher's exam and passed. A year teaching eighth grade followed by a year as principal preceded his election in December 1889 as superintendent of schools in Vermillion County.[7]

Teaching in the rural and city schools in Illinois informed Benedict's subsequent assessment of the deficiency in the Indian nations' schools' curriculum and to see the need for systematic courses. He observed that country school students were not competitive with their age mates when they entered high school. Typical duties of the county superintendents were collecting statistical data, issuing teaching certificates, and reporting to the state officials. Young and ambitious and wanting to improve the educational system, he solicited two other county superintendents who thought similarly and together they outlined a course of study intended to include a minimum of what should be taught at each level each month. Teachers were sent exams monthly to test the students and a final examination was to be given at the end of each year. Events evolved until the Illinois State Teachers' Association petitioned the Legislature to appropriate funds for publishing and distributing a course of study to all the rural schools of the state. Benedict served on the committee to develop this course of study.[8]

Eight years of an industrious and progressive county superintendent career caught the attention of the Illinois state superintendent who offered Benedict the position of his assistant with primary responsibilities to implement the above-mentioned course of study statewide in the rural schools. Soon additional responsibilities increased Benedict's commitments resulting in a nervous breakdown and his moving back to Danville to recuperate. Over the next four years he served as Master in Chancery of the Circuit Court, a member of the Danville Board of Education, and a member of the Illinois State Board of Education. Then came the brief stint in the forests and open country of the great Southwest of the US with his office's headquarters in Santa Fe, New Mexico Territory. It was a political appointment that emphasized his administrative skills over any knowledge of forest reserves or of this large land mass.[9]

Federal Appointment in Indian Territory

After only a few months on the job in Santa Fe and with no advance notice, on February 10, 1899, Benedict was summoned to Washington, DC, by Interior Secretary Bliss to assume responsibilities as superintendent of schools for Indian Territory. Bliss created the position and developed the rationale for his right to control the schools based on this clause of the Curtis Act of 1896: "That no payment of any moneys on any account whatever shall hereafter be paid by the United States to any of the tribal governments or to any officer thereof for any disbursement, but payments of all sums to members of said tribes shall be made under the direction of said Secretary of the Interior by an officer appointed by him."[10] Bliss decided that proper disbursing of the funds of the tribes could occur only after competent teachers and superintendents were employed, and those could be employed only after a representative of his office would supervise and oversee the schools.

For assuming the position Benedict was to be paid $3,500, a princely amount compared to the Oklahoma Territory Governor's salary of $2,500 (determined by the federal government) and the territorial Superintendent's salary of $1,800, including his responsibilities as the auditor. Benedict had no knowledge of the decentralized governance present in Indian Territory, although he might have gained minimal understanding of territorial government having spent the previous few months in the Arizona and New Mexico territories. By the time he arrived in Muskogee, Benedict was given by Bliss's replacement Ethan Hitchcock a set of the rules and regulations to govern the schools of Indian Territory. He, an experienced teacher and administrator, was given, by a non-educator and partisan bureaucrat, a blueprint to follow. He was to assume entire control of the schools, but was not briefed whether or not the tribal officials had relinquished control of their schools to the federal government.[11] A rude awakening was soon to broaden his perspective about the challenge facing him.

Seventeen days after departing the Southwest and a trip to Washington, DC, he arrived in Muskogee, Indian Territory, to represent the federal government in the oversight and supervision of tribal schools that had been functioning independently for decades. Realizing he lacked knowledge of the Indians, their tribal governments and school systems, and the relationship between the government and the Indians, he immediately set about to educate himself and to initiate contact with the tribes, their leaders, and the educational representatives. Whatever his handicaps, he was committed to fulfilling his duties to the extent of his ability: "It was an honor to the Territory that a man of his ability, integrity of purpose, and experiences in the field of public, rural education was appointed to this responsible position."[12] But, the government had an agenda that was not favored by the tribes.

Benedict's first few months on the job were spent traveling to the tribal schools and talking with the officials. Transportation in Indian Territory at the end of the nineteenth century was little more than primitive. Few paved roads existed and few railroads crisscrossed the Territory. Travel primarily was by horse or with horse drawn buggies, consumed much time, and left the traveler weary and tired upon arrival at one's destination. Lodging accommodations were equally primitive and more substandard than desired by one from the more settled areas of Illinois. Thus, timely travel was challenging; regardless, Benedict immediately set out to accomplish his responsibilities with focused purpose.

The prevailing thinking in Washington was that the Indian tribes were having difficulty with self-government and needed external oversight. Of a particular concern was the fact that, in the expenditure of the federal funds, insufficient accounting procedures were in place, resulting in inappropriate spending. Agreements were reached between the government and each of the tribes. Benedict was to persuade the tribes to accept the conditions that the government would impose along the way and to placate the Indian officials while the government stripped them of their control over their own affairs. He was to use his educational preparation and experience to convert the tribal-run schools to schools that would mesh well with the public school system to be established at statehood. The timeline for implementation was not initially in dispute because the Curtis Act of 1898 set a deadline of March 4, 1906, for the completion of the dissolution of the tribal governments.

Benedict had to navigate the administrative hierarchy above him—President, Interior Secretary, and Commissioner of Indian Affairs—and below him—four US supervisors of schools (one each for the Cherokee, Chickasaw, Choctaw, and Creek and Seminole combined nations) and the tribal representatives. An additional layer was added when Indian Territory became part of Oklahoma. Angie Debo, noted historian of tribal affairs, was critical of this administrative overload because it was unnecessary, exceedingly expensive, cumbersome, and funded with the tribal nations' money. Her critique was not without some merit, for Benedict would eventually find himself in an untenable position.[13]

Initial Impressions of Tribal Schools

Benedict's Illinois experience with developing courses of study, administering a county school system, filing of thorough and detailed statistical reports, and working out of the state office for the coordination of the schools statewide provided the framework for his first report to the secretary of the Interior and the commissioner of Indian Affairs.

Defects identified in the tribal schools were: incompetent supervision, irregular student attendance, financial mismanagement, and neglect of the English language. Specifically, incompetent supervision referred to the boarding schools superintendents who held their positions in part by virtue of their membership in the respective tribes.[14]

Benedict suggested that the tribal nations' laws stipulating that superintendents be citizens of their respective nations were stifling any possibilities for progress, a rather inauspicious initial comment. Stressing the attendance problem, he portrayed the Indian parents as not appreciating their children's need for regular attendance to enhance learning. Financial mismanagement resulted from the nations giving the superintendents, in advance, a fourth of the annual funds for their spending discretion and then having insufficient amounts to finish the year. Lastly, it seemed to Benedict that the Indian children would not be able to function in the society if they did not learn the English language well. Superintendent Benedict was describing and assessing primarily the boarding school system; however, there were also 120-day schools operating in the Cherokee nation serving 4,620 children. Debo took umbrage with this description that also included the Choctaws: "Benedict's reports show that he was without tact, and that he failed to appreciate the pride which the Choctaws felt for their most cherished institution."[15]

John Benedict
Courtesy of Oklahoma Historical Society, no. 857

His critique of the defects was followed by an enumeration of some indispensable improvements: competent teachers, better sanitary conditions, and manual training. Two of these three, competent teachers and manual training, were to become major foci of the Superintendent's efforts during his term in office. A third common theme that developed over time surfaced in this initial report—quality of educational opportunities for freedman and whites (particularly outside of the incorporated towns and cities)—is discussed infra. In spite of these general deficiencies, Benedict wrote the commissioner of Indian Affairs in July 1899 and described the exceptional Cherokee schools: "The Cherokees have the finest schools in the Territory. The board examines and appoints all teachers, fixes their salaries and has general supervision over all the schools...They have abolished all winter vacations and are making more progress than is being made by the other Nations."[16]

Benedict's first few months in office resulted in a flurry of correspondence between tribal leaders and Secretary Bliss. The leaders forcefully averred that tribal affairs were the prerogative of the tribes while Bliss claimed his authority rested with the Congress and the federal government. For example, Principal Chief of the Choctaw Nation, Green McCurtain, wrote: "I feel it is my duty to apprise you of the great dissatisfaction which exists among the Choctaw people on account of the transfer of the management of our schools from the Choctaw people to officers appointed by the Interior Department." Continuing, he reviewed the substance of the agreement signed by the tribe and the US Congress, April 23, 1897, extending the government of the Choctaw people to continue for eight years from March 4, 1898. An excerpt from that agreement reads, "This stipulation is made in the belief that the tribal government so modified will prove so satisfactory that there will be no need or desire for further change."[17]

Interior Secretary Hitchcock replied and invoked article 1, section 8, paragraph 3 of the US Constitution, specifically that Congress had the power to regulate commerce with foreign nations, among the states, and with the Indian tribes. Also, appointment of a superintendent of schools and a supervisor for the Choctaw Nation rested upon the imperative accounting for the proper use and expenditure of federal funds, and of general public business.[18]

Sixteen months later, in July 1900, Benedict submitted his second report. Gone were the enumerated criticisms of the tribal school systems lodged in his first report; instead, he chose to accentuate the work of the several supervisors and, by implication, himself: "The federal officials are laboring earnestly and assiduously to protect the interests of the Indian, to fairly adjust their property rights in accordance with the new order of things, and Congress should speedily furnish whatever aid or relief is necessary to complete this enormous task. Owing to these peculiar conditions, the task of improving the educational work of the Territory is an extremely difficult one. Improvement implies change, and the Indians are, by nature, prone to resist change."[19] To add emphasis, Benedict predicted that the Indian would need even more education soon because he would not have the protection of the tribe that he currently enjoyed. Quite possibly the bulk of the Indians' gravamen was to external pressure applied by the federal officials and the apparent violation of the sovereignty status rather than by inherent opposition to change itself.

A Multifaceted Approach to Improving the Tribal Education System

Prior school administration experience in Illinois etched upon Benedict the significance of excellent preparation of teachers through college study and normal schools. Such was the priority of improving the quality of the minimally prepared teachers and their instruction that he addressed the topic in his first report and then, through an annual update, in each of his eight subsequent reports. Steadfastly approaching the problem from several angles, he wrote that whatever normal schools existed in 1899 were poorly organized and poorly operated. Benedict was determined to organize normal schools throughout Indian Territory so that concentrated periods of time could be set aside for teaching the teachers subject matter and teaching strategies. Teacher certification standards had been adopted by 1902 and teachers were required to pass examinations. Three years later all teachers in the Indian nations had to meet the same certification standards. To facilitate increased teacher knowledge and understanding, associations were formed to bring teachers together to discuss common issues. And, as events moved closer to statehood, Benedict joined with the Oklahoma Territory government officials to combine efforts to improve the quality of teaching. He was tireless in pursuing strategies to ensure students were taught by qualified teachers.[20]

In the spring of 1900 Benedict requested financial assistance from Washington to fund the summer normal schools so that teachers would not be required to pay a fee to attend. Funds were not forthcoming, but he, nevertheless, organized and offered summer school sessions in June in the Cherokee, Creek, and Choctaw nations. The twelve-dollar registration fee was the equivalent of one-fourth to one-third of a teacher's monthly pay, not a small amount. To ensure tribal support and cooperation, each nation's federal supervisor was charged with coordinating the meetings.[21]

In spite of the lack of federal financial support in 1900, Benedict wrote a glowing account of the successes of the normal schools in his 1901 report to the Interior Secretary. For example, so favorably impressed was the Cherokee Nation that its Council at the October meeting opted to require its board of education to schedule a four-week normal school at Tahlequah each June.[22] If Benedict believed federal funds were requisite for developing quality normal schools, describing positively those offered without adequate funds seems incongruous.

Benedict's influence and leadership, and federal funds, resulted in an expansion of opportunities for all children and some teachers. By 1901 educational opportunities were afforded not only to Indian and white children; some Black children had their schools and Black teachers. In the Cherokee Nation, a summer normal school operated with eighteen teachers participating. Correspondingly, fifty Black teachers attended the separate normal school held in the Creek Nation.[23]

The fourth year of summer schools witnessed a shift in emphasis from teaching basic subject matter to the study of principles and methods.[24] Benedict determined that teachers were at least minimally competent in the subject matter and needed to learn instructional skills and classroom management. He also decided that expenditure of finite funds and commitment of limited available time would achieve greater results in the classroom through providing teachers techniques for instructing and managing students.

Benedict's desire for improvement in the quality of classroom instruction materialized in his planning of summer institutes and expanded recruiting of teachers. He believed that current teachers needed professional development opportunities and that there was an inadequate supply of qualified Indian teachers in the territory. Word spread of the value of the summer schools, attracting ever-larger numbers of participants. City boards of education, non-tribal, began requiring their teachers to attend, and these participants were joined by others who traveled from adjoining states to improve their instructional skills. It was not long before it became difficult to locate facilities to accommodate the large number of attendees, reaching 1,066 for the area encompassed by the nations by 1906. Commenting on Benedict's favorable description of normal school professional development, Debo agreed that it was no doubt beneficial; however, she averred that Benedict's general assessment of few available qualified Indian teachers provided him the rationale to hire white teachers who did not understand the Indian children or their culture.[25]

Initially, Benedict observed and concluded that the boarding schools' curriculum was inappropriate and insufficient for the practical needs of the students and the tribes. An emphasis on the classical curriculum designed to prepare students for college was not appropriate for the Indian in the post-tribal government days. Teaching female students Latin, instead of sewing, cooking, and other branches of domestic economy, would not prepare them to be housewives. Boarding schools were located on farms, yet the males were not being taught agriculture, a distressing practice to say the least. "A change in direction of intelligent work along these lines of industrial and manual training is badly needed in these schools, yet owing to the natives' dislike for work, this change should be inaugurated gradually."[26]

For someone with no previous connection to, or familiarity with, Indians and their tribes, other than brief exposure for a few months in the Southwest, to arrive at this conclusion reflects the bias Benedict brought to his responsibilities, a bias not unusual among the white citizens of the era. Teach the native children to learn practical skills for subsistence living rather than expand their horizons, stimulate their creativity, and prepare them for continued academic performance. This binary view of assessed needs and capabilities might have reflected financial realities, but that perspective did little to offer the tribal children opportunities similar to their white counterparts.

Benedict set out to encourage change in the curriculum and, by 1901, reported that manual training was introduced in all of the boarding schools over which the government exercised total control as well as in some other schools. Since arriving two short years earlier, he achieved a modicum of success that, for him, was only the beginning. He was cautiously optimistic that the initial efforts would expand and be productive. Apparently his cautiousness had some grounds because by 1904 he reported his regrets that they did not have the funds or facilities for expanding the opportunities. His assessment of the Indian children continued: "It is a well-known fact that the average Indian child learns to write and to draw more readily than the average white child. Whether the outgrowth of inheritance or home environment, the Indian child's fingers are defter and his powers of observation more acutely developed than those of white children."[27] After four years on the job, he appears to be entertaining the possibility that his original assessment of the Indian child's capabilities might have been deficient.

Benedict's actions in Indian Territory did not go unnoticed in Oklahoma Territory education circles as chronicled in the minutes of the Oklahoma Territory Board meeting of May 28, 1904. There he suggested that the two territories agree to a uniform course of study for all of the schools, one that had been developed and adopted by the Illinois

State Board of Education. His suggestion of a uniform course of study was received favorably resulting in the Board establishing a structure for accomplishing this. Each territory would have a committee of two men and these two committees would join together to recommend a course of study.[28]

Eighteen days later the Board considered the Kansas curricular plan, similar to the one in Illinois, and its secretary was ordered to correspond with Benedict concerning the adoption of this course. The Board continued consideration at its September meeting and directed the Secretary to arrange a meeting with Benedict. Oklahoma Territory Board members Superintendent Baxter and Ed Vaught were appointed to act jointly with Benedict and Choctaw Nation Supervisor Calvin Ballard to agree upon any changes necessary in the preferred Illinois curriculum subsequently adopted.[29]

Benedict was supportive of various means of improving the instruction as well as the administration of all schools. One example of the latter was his initiation in 1905 of schoolmasters clubs across the Territory. He was the keynote speaker at the South McAlester meeting of April 28-29 where more than seventy-five superintendents and principals representing tribal, city, and day schools attended. Administrators, with otherwise limited opportunities to meet together, could share the innovative practices occurring in their districts. Different from the summer normal institutes where teachers could meet to learn about teaching techniques and strategies, administrators functioned in a more isolated environment.[30]

Advocating for Schooling for the Whites' and Freedmen's Children

By the late 1890s whites greatly outnumbered Indians in Indian Territory, yet the Indian schools were for tribal children; other children (freedmen's children and white children) were almost totally excluded from educational opportunities, regardless of paying tuition. While the tribes provided for their children, the majority of children living in Indian Territory were not being educated. (In Oklahoma Territory, the opposite was most prevalent where white children were provided schools.) Benedict abhorred these deplorable conditions, but these children were not within the realm of his responsibility for working with the tribes to further the federal government's purposes. He could not resist the temptation to express his grave concern over the appalling conditions; so, he described the conditions and problems in his first report in 1899. While the Choctaw and Chickasaw nations, through the Atoka agreement, were prohibited from sharing their school funds with children of the freedmen, the other tribes were not under similar constraints.[31]

Because some slaves were adopted as citizens of the various Indian nations after the Civil War, their descendants had limited rights that excluded education under tribal government. By 1903 Benedict expanded his urging that provision be made for the education of thousands of Black children in separate schools. Whites, in comparison, had no rights. The estimated 40,000-50,000 white children living in Indian Territory and the children of freedmen had essentially no educational opportunities provided them at government expense. The case for white children was complicated and practices were complex. Some whose parents could afford the tuition were permitted to attend the Indian academies. By 1903, white parents residing in rural districts were permitted to send their children to one of the 400 Indian day schools upon payment of a reasonable tuition. Benedict suggested that these day schools be converted into common schools open to both races. As a March 1906 deadline approached for the dissolution of all tribal governments and the disposal of all tribal property, Benedict grew more and more concerned with the impending doom. Accommodations were not forthcoming from Congress to ameliorate the crisis of March 1906, yet statehood was still more than a year and a half away.[32]

Debo contends that a hidden agenda was driving the efforts of the Interior Secretary when he seized the opportunity afforded by a general clause in the Curtis Act of 1898. By interpreting that it was in his prerogative to establish oversight of the Indian nations' schools, he set up the administrative hierarchy that ostensibly was to improve the tribal schools, but his primary purpose was to organize a way of providing education to the non-Indian (white and Black) who greatly exceeded the number of Indian children being educated by the tribal schools. Dale and Wardell were more straightforward when they wrote that Benedict was "appointed to supervise the building of a public school system."[33]

When the Indian Territory teachers convened their annual meeting in December 1905 in McAlester, they adopted a resolution to Congress requesting appropriate funds for the support of the schools. March 2, 1906, Congress began deliberations on HR 5976 authorizing continuation of the schools for the remainder of the school year. Later, at the end of April, Congress authorized the Secretary of the Interior to continue the schools until such time as the new state was formed and prepared to care for the education of all of the children. By statehood, 990 day schools functioned in Indian Territory, funded by the federal government, tribal funds, surplus court fees, and tuition, and most were available to white children.[34]

Essentially, what Benedict found upon his arrival in 1899 in Indian Territory was a system of tribal schools, led by tribal officials, serving only Indian children, and funded in large part by tribal funds. For the greater number of non-Indian children living in the Territory no organized education system functioned to serve them. Debo contended that Benedict's mandate was to create such a system to prepare Indian Territory to join Oklahoma Territory to form the forty-sixth state. To exacerbate the troubled relations with the tribal governments, five high paid supervisors were put in charge and their salaries were paid with tribal funds.[35] The recalcitrant Indians' resolve to manage their own affairs was not equivalent to the force of federal authorities who controlled the purse strings and had the backing of Congress and the Supreme Court.

Freedmen, Indians and whites lived in Indian Territory in 1899 with the largest number being white, and that group was also the fastest growing subpopulation. Benedict was assigned to deal with the tribes from a superior position with all of the power and force of the federal government and, if compliance was not achieved, he could force them to kowtow to Congress's mandates, for the 1906 deadline was looming. Simultaneously, he had to establish relations with the education officials in neighboring Oklahoma Territory as that part to the west was moving toward statehood. Benedict's assignment was not an easy one: placating the tribes while the government forced them to be submissive, creating a system to provide educational opportunities to all children regardless of race (not a legal duty, but personally a moral imperative), positioning the mishmash of schools in Indian Territory to join Oklahoma Territory at statehood, and functioning as a Republican (and minority) in a Democrat majority area.

Creek Leader Paves Path to the State Constitution

Indian Territory was fortunate to have a native son who advanced the cause of education in the Creek Nation and in the drafting of both the Sequoyah Constitution and the Oklahoma Constitution. Alexander Lawrence Posey, educated at Bacone College, was thrust into key leadership positions in the Creek Nation's governance at an early age. At twenty-one he was elected to the House of Warriors, a representative body of the National Council, and also assigned responsibilities with the Creek national treasury. Simultaneously, he was appointed Superintendent of the Creek Orphan Asylum boarding school which served 100 children age eight to eighteen. After two years, he was appointed the Superintendent of Public Instruction of the Creek Nation to fill the remaining ten months of the unexpired two-year term. In this capacity he oversaw the operation of all of the neighborhood and boarding schools in the Nation including examining and appointing teachers and selecting boarding school superintendents. Placement by the tribal leadership in these positions conveyed their trust in his ability to lead even at such a young age. But his heart was not in it so, at the end of his superintendency, he moved to his farm where he could write poetry.[36]

Posey's lasting influence in Indian Territory's affairs was yet to sprout and grow. Though short in stature, he was first and foremost a scholar, poet, and philosopher, widely read and erudite. His talents were displayed through his service as the Secretary of the Sequoyah Convention and in the writing of much of the Sequoyah Constitution in 1905 in anticipation of Indian Territory becoming a separate state. Of particular importance to education, article 7, section 1, were these words he penned: "…it is a fundamental duty of the State to provide for its citizens the best possible preparation for intelligent and virtuous citizenship; therefore, the General Assembly shall establish and maintain a system of free public education for all persons in the State between the ages of six and twenty-one years, and also shall provide for the maintenance of institutions for the education of the deaf, dumb, and blind of this State."[37] Additionally, he wrote in section 4 that school funds should be distributed regardless of race or color of students, but that separate schools should be provided for Black children. Nearly verbatim provisions were subsequently adopted by the Oklahoma Constitutional Convention in article 13 of the constitution. In education and experience, but not temperament, Posey was most qualified to compete for the Superintendency at statehood but he disliked public life and never again sought public office. Instead he focused his energies on writing poetry until his tragic accidental drowning May 27, 1908.[38]

Transitioning to Statehood

Officially, with statehood, came the dissolution of the Indian schools and the need for a superintendent to supervise the myriad schools within Indian Territory. However, a period of transition to state control was necessary. Federal funding did not cease immediately; in fact, it continued for several years to supplement the state funding of schools in the former territory. Because the Cherokees did not conserve an education fund similar to the other tribes, they were forced to give up their academies to the outstretched arm of the new state that was ready to assume responsibility for their operation. Incorporated town schools and 317 neighborhood units were transferred to the state, giving newly-elected county superintendents in Mayes, Delaware, Adair, Sequoyah, Cherokee, Rogers, Craig, Nowata, and Washington county "…an exceedingly stable base on which to build the rural schools under their jurisdiction."[39]

Two thousand, one hundred and forty-two school districts, formed in Indian Territory with many of those conforming to boundary lines of the previous districts, matched the more than 3,400 formed in Oklahoma Territory from 1890-1907. Rural schoolhouses were constructed by the patrons and thus were located in the more populous areas, allowing for convenience in organizing districts according to topography and population. Many, if not most, of the Indian Territory towns' school systems equaled those of neighboring states and Oklahoma Territory requiring little modification to be integrated into the new state's education system. In some instances, when these districts were formed in Indian Territory, not all were pleased and some pleaded to Benedict to intervene. He informed the four supervisors of the tribal schools the responsibility was now with the state government, not with the federal government, and thus he no longer had authority to act.[40]

In 1907 when the county system was inaugurated, the school term as directed by the federal supervisors had already begun. Sufficient funds were unavailable through local taxation, so the federal government appropriated additional funding of $300,000 to the county schools annually until 1915 for maintaining rural schools in Indian Territory. As is typically the case, the federal government was not interested in appropriating funds without strings attached. Tribal funds, surplus court fees, and appropriations were continued for several years, but the distribution and administration of the Congressional funds were given to Benedict until 1910 and then to several others thereafter.[41]

The methods of operation and funding of the schools in the former Indian Territory became a particularly thorny issue of oversight and control at statehood. State school authorities claimed they had a right to control all of the schools. However, in most of the eastern half of the state, the land had been owned by the Indians and had not been taxed. Interior Secretary James Garfield had no right to turn over the funds that had been appropriated for rural schools to the state authorities, yet he insisted that the superintendent of schools in Indian Territory supervise the disbursement of those funds.[42]

Controversy was brewing as early as December 1907 when, in an interview on the nineteenth, recently elected Superintendent Cameron's frustrations surfaced in comments directed toward Benedict's continued oversight of schools. By early January 1908 the dispute reached a level where Cameron sought the support of Governor Douglas H. Johnston of the Chickasaw Nation to resolve the matter. Obstruction from Benedict blocked the Superintendent from fulfilling his duties, so Cameron solicited the support. House Speaker Alfalfa Bill Murray denounced Benedict's interference, an example of the level to which politics colored the actions of government officials. Governor Haskell and Secretary Garfield settled the controversy through an agreement whereby the state school authorities were to complete the organization of the school districts and conduct the rural schools as long as state funds would carry them, and then the federal government would continue the schools until its special appropriations were exhausted.[43]

The two individuals most directly responsible for the mundane affairs of meshing the federal government's and the state's spheres of influence were Benedict and Cameron, and both had legitimate claims of competence and ability. Cameron, now elected and believing he was accountable to the people, was no novice, but held minimal experience gained ten years previously with the Oklahoma Territory schools. Benedict had superior experience both with earlier public schools in Illinois and recently an aggregate of schools in Indian Territory. On top of that, he commanded a salary twice as much as Cameron's. Benedict had a quarter century experience in the gamut of education positions from classroom teacher to federal government supervisor. Cameron, on the other hand, was a minister of the gospel and briefly served as Territorial Superintendent. To suggest that Benedict had "fallen in line" and that he was subservient to the state's demands would mean that Cameron held the superior position and Benedict was the supplicant, even though he was eight years older and more experienced. After the initial conflict and subsequent resolution, Cameron wrote eloquently of his firm belief in the right of self-government and reported that Benedict acquiesced.

> In the opening of the year we had some trouble with the representatives of the Department of the Interior in regard to certain national schools in the bounds of our State [sic]. I am thankful to say that the matter was adjusted and I have no doubt that the plan agreed upon has worked... I'm glad to say that Hon. John D. Benedict, the representative of the national government, has fallen into line, and I think at the present time, aside from his academies, is aiding district rural schools under the control of our regular teachers employed by our boards, as he agreed to in the beginning of the year. (*Second Biennial Report of the Department of Public Instruction, State of Oklahoma 1908* [Guthrie: State of Oklahoma, 1908], 73)

An agreement between Garfield and Haskell resulted in Benedict's membership on the State Textbook Committee in 1908. Haskell believed that Benedict's knowledge of the Indians would provide insight in the Committee's deliberative process of selecting appropriate textbooks. Five members in addition to the secretary and Haskell, *ex officio*, comprised the Committee that was eliminated in 1911 upon the creation of the new Board. Participation in state textbook oversight was considered prestigious and influential, more than of secondary or tertiary importance. Two years later Benedict's service to the Committee ended when Interior Secretary Richard Ballenger, appointed by President Taft, decided to remove Benedict from his superintendent duties.[44]

That Haskell would appoint Benedict, although of the opposing party, is no surprise considering they both hailed from Muskogee, then a town of 4,000. Benedict was his senior by six years and had already acclimated himself to the territory by the time Haskell arrived. Both were energetic and enterprising, establishing themselves as influencers in the community with Haskell owning a newspaper and Benedict pursuing a banking interest and serving on the school board while focusing on his Indian schools' supervision. Their various business activities and community involvement set the stage for Benedict's appointment to the State Textbook Committee.[45]

Caught in a Political Cauldron

Nineteen hundred seven raised the political stakes when the two territories joined to become Oklahoma and the process began to elect those who would hold the first political positions in state government. The Democratic Party seemed destined to claim the initial prizes, but outstanding men across both territories were encouraged to seek the various offices. Obviously, money was required to run campaigns, so those who held influential positions and were perceived to have money were sought for contributions. Benedict was in this group and was assessed $350 for campaign purposes. He refused for practical reasons: he was unable to spare 10 percent of his salary, he was under no obligation to these politicians for his position, and President Roosevelt had said he was not subject to such assessments. However, more importantly, in all of his school experiences, he refused to consider political affiliation. Instead, he insisted on selecting teachers and superintendents based on educational and moral qualifications.[46]

When he refused to pay the assessed amount and rebuffed the politicians seeking his support, he incurred the wrath of those office seekers. Additionally, a change of presidents (Roosevelt to Taft) and of Interior secretaries (Garfield to Ballinger) brought a different climate to Washington, and complaints of officials in Oklahoma regarding the operation of the Indian Territory schools fell on more receptive ears. As early as June 1909 Ballenger requested from Benedict clarification of three issues: Was he seeking the gubernatorial nomination? Was he a member of the Textbook Commission and was it an honorary position? Finally, was he president of and a stockholder in a banking institution in Muskogee? First, he replied that he was not running for Governor. Second, he informed Ballenger that his predecessor Garfield had agreed with Governor Haskell for his position on the Textbook Commission and that the Commission provided an honorarium and expenses to all members for attendance at its meetings. Third, he stated he once was involved with a bank, but no longer.[47]

Six months later, in early January 1910, charges were leveled against Benedict and three other education officials who were then suspended from their duties. Specifically regarding Benedict, he was derelict in his professional duties by employing incompetent superintendents and teachers and by allowing the Indian Boarding School building to become old and dilapidated. His acceptance of an appointment to the State Textbook Commission and devotion of an excessive amount of time to that effort resulted in an infringement upon his time to fulfill his assigned duties. Likewise, energy and time invested in an external enterprise, organizing the Guaranty Bank of Muskogee and serving as its first president, was detrimental to his work assignment. If the above factors were insufficient, a final charge alleged he led thirteen Chickasaw schoolgirls astray.[48]

Benedict responded to the charges on January 22 with a lengthy written rebuttal of the allegations. Four days later he sent supportive letters from persons knowledgeable of his decade of service and asked for a meeting with Secretary Ballenger in Washington to refute the charges. By now he had been suspended from his duties, but wanted to retire from his position. Following the request, he traveled to meet with the secretary where he was able to defend himself. Ballenger, a few days later, February 19, 1910, sent a telegram to Benedict informing him that his position and those of the supervisors were to be abolished effective February 28 and that his suspension was being removed.[49]

During the suspension Benedict was in a delicate position because he was unsure of the sources of the opposition. Also, a suspension implied a problem that negatively reflected on his performance and brought uncertainty to his status. In his final employment-related correspondence with Ballenger, February 21, he wrote that the decision to abolish his position was satisfactory to him, that he did not wish to continue under the suspension, and that he wished to be paid for the period January 1 to the present.[50]

Difficulty with his employment was not limited to the Interior Department. Benedict was a Republican as was US Third District Representative Charles Creager. Democratic Governor Haskell and Benedict were good friends. Walter Falwell, supervisor of the Creek and Seminole schools, was active in Republican politics: chairman of the first Republican Muskogee County convention, delegate to the first Republican state convention held in Tulsa in 1907, and delegate from the Third District of Oklahoma to the Republican National Convention in Chicago in 1908. Apparently, Congressman Creager wanted Falwell to replace Benedict as Superintendent of Indian Schools.[51] Secretary Ballenger saw no concern over the extent of one of his supervisor's involvement in the political arena, yet the relationship of the Governor and Benedict surfaced in the events leading up to the Secretary's abolition of the position.

Governor Haskell honored his friend when he lauded the work Benedict had accomplished only to be maligned and forced from office.

> It is to reputation acquired by the man or the woman who has devoted his life in a straight forward course and justly earned the favorable commendations of neighbors that is dearest to all of us and I should refuse to speak here tonight in the presence of some recent circumstances, if I did not feel that I would be permitted as a neighbor and friend, to express my condemnation of the political machinations that for the moment have reflected upon one of the most worthy educators of our state...I have never had any business, or even intimate official relations with John D. Benedict, but I for years resided in the same town. I came to know him as a man of high integrity and the best of purposes and intent. ("Address of Welcome," January 12, 1910, Guthrie, Box 1, F 7, RG 8-A-2, Governor Charles Haskell Collection, OSA, ODL, OKC)

Business and Civic Activity in the Final Chapter

Benedict firmly believed in the importance of being an active and participating member of the Muskogee community. He was well educated and had broad experiences living in other parts of the country. Benedict's participation in civic affairs began upon his arrival in Muskogee in 1899 and continued until his death January 26, 1946, in that city. He was a Master Mason, past exalted ruler of the Benevolent Protective Order of Elks, and a past grand chancellor of the Knights of Pythias. Service on the Muskogee Board of Education lasted for ten years, and he was one of eight writers of Muskogee's charter form of government in 1910. A native of Indiana and Illinois, he chose to remain in Oklahoma after his ten years as federal supervisor. His wife of fifty years, nee Alice Miranda Hibbard, died in Muskogee in 1932 at age seventy-three. Three children were born to the Benedicts.[52]

For many years he was active in the real estate and insurance business, but he paused long enough in his endeavors in 1922 to write *Muskogee and Northeastern Oklahoma*, a three-volume history of Muskogee and several northeastern Oklahoma counties. Volume I is more expansive than the title suggests with a descriptive review of the history of the treatment of the Five Civilized Tribes by the US government through the Dawes Commission.[53] This volume offers additional insight into his view of the relationship between the federal government and the tribes in the late nineteenth and early twentieth centuries.

Benedict, a stranger to Indian culture, customs, education, and tribal affairs, reflected the prevailing attitude towards the Indians and tried to bring order and accountability to the tribal operations of their school. The part he played in representing the federal government earned him the wrath and scorn of those who questioned the motives of the government and his commitment to representing those motives. Regardless, he was the one assigned to represent the federal government's interests and, to the best of his ability, performed his duties with the ultimate goal being to provide the most students with an educational opportunity. It was a difficult era for the government-Indian relationships with outcomes reverberating for the next hundred years. Benedict contributed much to the community of Muskogee, proving to be a valuable citizen for nearly a half century.

Part II
The Superintendency and the Contestants
(1907-2015)

The territorial/state Superintendent position has existed continuously since its creation in December of 1890. For the seventeen-year territorial period it was appointive and, since statehood, it has been elective. Why it was appointive and then elective is not a mystery, for its status was determined by what was typical and standard in that era. Oklahoma's first Territorial legislature opted to designate the several executive offices as appointive by the Governor. Federal law required the US president to appoint territorial governors and secretaries of state. By statehood in Oklahoma most states had written into their constitutions provisions for elective superintendents. Part II is a comprehensive examination and analysis of the Superintendency and the demographics of the aspirants for the position.

In chapter Three the position is described through an examination of these aspects: the executive offices and terms, duties and responsibilities, selection, eligibility criteria, compensation, and patronage. Constitutional and statutory revisions over the years have modified some initial provisions that became inconsistent with cultural expectations and the demands of a rapidly changing technological society. A state residency requirement of a minimum of three years initially and then increased to ten years in 1942 constricts unnecessarily the population of qualified candidates. In theory a lengthy residency durational requirement might be more appropriate for the governor, lieutenant governor, attorney general, and secretary of state, but the practical result relative to the Superintendency is that it essentially eliminates candidates external to the state who might bring refreshing and new ideas to the public education system.

Election results, political parties, aspirants' demographics, campaign finances, and campaigning methods are described and given context in chapter Four. Oklahoma's historically weak political party structure, evident in the patterns of election outcomes, and the susceptibility of a few dominant pressure groups combine to present a formidable challenge to substantial change and improvements. That no Superintendent was elected to a higher position in Oklahoma lends credence to the perceived relative insignificance of the Superintendency as a stepping-stone in one's political career.

Chapter Five presents and analyzes the demographic data of the officeholders whether appointed or elected from 1907 to 2015. Considerable homogeneity, as might be expected for the top education management position for which the Constitution stipulated a lengthy state residency, is evident in the backgrounds and careers both of those elected to four-year terms and those appointed to complete unexpired terms. Eight decades had to pass before a woman was elected to the office in 1990.

Women's efforts to achieve suffrage and equality in Oklahoma in general and in educational leadership in particular are chronicled in chapter Six. From the earliest days of Oklahoma Territory women were permitted to vote in local school elections and for county superintendents and to serve on school boards and as county superintendents. After an initial flurry of activity around 1920 women gained suffrage, but not until 1942 did they receive the right to serve in the top executive offices of state government. While their rights expanded, it took decades for societal and cultural change enough that women were given serious consideration for educational leadership at all levels.

Chapter 3
The Executive Office of Superintendent
(1890-2015)

The legal basis for the establishment of Oklahoma Territory, the Organic Act of May 2, 1890 (26 US Statutes at Large, 81-100), excluded any reference to public education other than land grants, giving total prerogative to the territorial Legislature. Similarly, the Enabling Act of June 16, 1906 (34 US Statutes at Large, 267-278) was silent on education because the US Constitution through the Tenth Amendment gave the right to determine public education organization, supervision, and management to the state. The evolution of the legal framework for the office of Superintendent began with the original Oklahoma Territory statutes of 1890 that were then modified and expanded over the seventeen-year territorial period. With statehood in 1907, the Constitution provided for executive offices including the Superintendency (article 6, section 1) and mandated the Legislature to "establish and maintain a system of free public schools wherein all of the children of the State may be educated" (article 13, section 1). Subsequently, the Legislature enacted statutes expanding the Superintendent's duties and responsibilities for managing and supervising the state's public schools.

Unlimited Terms for a Century

Twelve executive offices, including the Superintendent, were enumerated in article 6, section 1, of the Constitution and section 4 established term limits. The Constitutional Convention, or Con Con as it was commonly referenced, delegates believed the citizenry should be able to vote on many positions, but then distrusted them to decide how long a person should be able to serve in these designated offices: governor, secretary of state, state auditor, and state treasurer. All other officers could serve multiple terms if reelected, but these four were prohibited from succeeding themselves until 1966 when the Governor and others were permitted to run for a second term.[1]

Terms for the Superintendent, and several other executive officers, were modified through a constitutional amendment with strong advocacy from Republicans who had grown weary of the perpetual dominance of the Democrats, particularly in the Superintendency, and had calculated that one avenue for change might be term limits. Long tenures, minimal turnover, and relative continuity described the Superintendency for most of the first century of its existence, a state of affairs that the Republicans thought needed to end. Thus, they pushed for State Question No. 747, adopted in November of 2010, and provides: "No person shall be eligible to serve…Superintendent of Public Instruction for a period of time in excess of eight (8) years." Twice in the state's history voters denied the Superintendent a second term, and also once a third term. Seven times the incumbent was rewarded with a second term with three of those reelected twice and one each three, four, and five times. The Democrats had an impressive and sustained record of reelection efforts, but the tide was turning and 2010 was the watershed year with the Republicans sweeping all of the major offices. Ironically, they achieved their goal of term limits, but now they would be subjected to the limitations they thought imperative to compete in the political arena.

One other provision of the Constitution, never modified, was article 6, section 4 stipulating the term of office to be four years beginning with the second Monday of January after the previous November general election. This precise statement setting forth the origination and length of the term, and with no controversial elements, has protected the provision from any attempts to modify it.

Duties and Responsibilities

To be efficient, the territorial Legislature chose to combine the responsibilities of Superintendent and Auditor by assigning the latter an *ex-officio* role of the former. Initially, that move caused no great concern: with only a handful of counties and few school districts, auditing functions were minimal; so the assumption was one person could manage both roles thus saving money which was an important factor in the birth of territorial government. In the early years, performing combined duties caused minimal stress, but soon the Legislature acknowledged the demands on the position and approved an assistant auditor. More personnel were added, but the combined offices functioned satisfactorily in their assigned duties regardless of the concerns expressed by the incumbents. Political chicanery, on the other hand, caused problems for at least two of the Superintendents as auditors, forcing one out by legal maneuver and the other by resignation. Not until statehood were the positions separated and each was afforded an office, staff, and budget.[2]

At the beginning of the territorial period, the Superintendent was supposed to supervise and manage the territory's educational interests, apportion the school fund and the annual school taxes, give his opinion on legal questions involving the schools and keep a record of those opinions, publish the school laws biennially, print forms for district reporting, visit all counties annually (very few in number in the early 1890s), maintain an office at the seat of government where all official documents were to be housed, and deliver to the Governor in December preceding each regular session of the Legislature a report of the demographic data and descriptions of the territory's students and districts along with his recommendations for statutory changes. Superintendent Parker submitted more than fifteen recommendations to the Governor who included them verbatim in his message to the Legislature. Although the Governor used this format, he informed the legislators that he did not agree with all of the ideas, but he declined to identify his preferences.[3]

Of the few provisions stated in Oklahoma's 1907 Constitution regarding expectations of the Superintendent's office, one was general and one was specific. As one of the executive officers, the Superintendent is required by article 6, section 1 to "keep his office and public records, books, and papers at the seat of government and shall perform such duties as may be designated in this Constitution or prescribed by law." More specifically, the Superintendent was to chair a Board of Education vested with the supervision of the public school "whose powers and duties shall be prescribed by law" (article 13, section 5). As originally written and remaining so until 1911, the Board's membership also included the Governor, Secretary of State, and Attorney General. Of note, Oklahoma's Con Con delegates approved the draft of the education committee without any changes beyond the addition of the provision for teaching agriculture. The convention members at large wished to emphasize the importance of agricultural instruction in the schools.[4]

Oklahoma's Superintendents, as executive officers, have always had their duties and responsibilities enumerated by the Legislature. For the most part those assignments have remained consistent, but whatever modifications have been written into the statute, they tend to be additions. As the complexities of the operation of the educational system have grown, so have the Superintendent's obligations. Most of the territorial Superintendent's duties were adopted and retained by the state's first Legislature in 1908: supervise the state's education interests, apportion funds, issue written opinions on the interpretation and construction of the laws, visit each county at least annually, and hold an office and keep official records at the seat of government. By December 1 preceding each regular session of the Legislature the Superintendent was to submit to the Governor a report with statistical data on students, teachers, facilities, etc. of all levels of education; an account of all public school funds including receipts and expenditures; and plans for supervision and improvement of the public schools.[5]

Supervisory responsibilities expanded slightly in 1908 when the Superintendent was authorized to examine the status of instruction in agriculture in the high schools and to disseminate the best curriculum and teaching methods through bulletins and speeches. Agriculture content was to be an integral part of a high school academic program, and the Superintendent was to assist the normal schools to plan and offer training to qualify teachers for employment in the schools. Such efforts were focused on the constitutional requirement for common schools to teach agriculture, horticulture, and the domestic sciences.[6]

By 1931 the Superintendent's duties were modified slightly reflecting the increased complexity of the legal aspects of the operation of the Department and school districts. The Superintendent was to coordinate with the state's Attorney General when developing and interpreting the school law, and he was to inform the district and county superintendents of his decisions. When school employees or district officials were guilty of moral turpitude or of stealing, the Superintendent was to deal with the issues with one potential consequence being the revocation of their teaching or administration certificates.[7]

Tensions within and between the executive and legislative branches are not necessarily inevitable, but are probable. From the beginning the Superintendent administered the Department and was responsible for supervising the few employees, but the Legislature determined the number and title of the positions. Over two to three decades, the Superintendents were granted expanded authority to determine personnel needs. The mid-1930s saw a rapid growth in the personnel numbers as the state and federal governments wrestled with the effects of the Depression and the Dust Bowl. More services and programs required more people, with a concomitant expansion of the Superintendent's responsibilities. Political infighting in the Legislature and between the Superintendent and a contentious Governor resulted in HB 168 in 1941 shifting authority for all of the Department employees but his secretary from the Superintendent to the Board whose members were appointed by the Governor. Governor Leon Phillips got his wish, temporarily, but several years afterwards the Legislature codified the statutes and returned the patronage prerogative to the Superintendent. From the end of the decade of the 1940s to 2011, the Superintendent recommended personnel changes and the Board acted accordingly.[8]

With the exception of the personnel prerogatives in 1949, the Superintendent's employment and duties remained unchanged until minor wording modifications resulted from the 1971 legislative session. More and significant changes were attempted in 1980 because the Board wished to convince the Legislature to augment the Superintendent's compensation by $10,000 with the justification based on the enumeration of five additional duties. The Legislature was convinced and approved the compensation and the altered job description. As one might expect, if this were to be confirmed as permissible, it would be viewed as establishing a precedent for other agencies to pursue. It was not to be as determined by the Attorney General one year later when he referenced the law prohibiting the increasing of salary during the four-year term of office.[9]

Because modifications in the Superintendent duties were minor throughout history with the exception of the disruption in the 1940s relative to patronage, the transfer of authority in 2011 was sudden and profound, greatly expanding the Superintendent's authority and concomitantly diminishing the Board's. The revised wording explicates the Superintendent's duty: "Organize and have control of the administration of the State Department of Education and any other supervisory agencies, divisions, personnel and their appointment and salaries and other operations necessary to carry out the power, duties and functions of the State Superintendent and the State Board of Education."[10] Now, the Superintendent has total discretion to hire, determine salaries, and to terminate employees.

To present a picture of the extent of the Superintendent's responsibilities, data from the beginning of the territorial period to 2014 are displayed in appendixes K and L. Growth in school enrollment and number of teachers is in contrast to the precipitous drop in the number of school districts. Larger numbers of students and teachers placed higher demands on the Department, but fewer districts eased some of the pressures. Still, the "large" number of small elementary (100 with small ADA) and independent districts (ADA <300) together with more than eight large (ADA >15,000) districts presented a challenge for the Department under the Superintendent's leadership to provide curricular, instructional, and financial accounting services.

A large state agency providing assistance to the public schools and collecting data for informing the Legislature, under the watchful eye of that body, requires a cadre of employees and effective leadership from a Superintendent who serves at the pleasure of the electorate. This person must administer an agency that oversees the largest single expenditure of the state budget. The Department's staff numbers from 1970-2015 grew substantially during the 1970s and into the early 1980s, reaching a peak in 1983-84 before beginning a downward trend and reaching the nadir in 2011-12. At the end of these forty-five years, the number of staff increased by only twenty-four. Multiple reasons can explain the rapid rise: passage of the federal law, Education for All Handicapped Children Act, that in the mid 1970s set many standards and provided money to the states; Oklahoma's creation of the regional education service centers requiring personnel to coordinate and offer the services; and HB 1706's redesign of teacher preparation and HB 1017's minimal class sizes and increased teacher pay necessitated personnel changes. Eventually, the service centers were eliminated and the numbers reduced even more with the change to a Republican administration in 2011. Federal and state funding of new initiatives and then shifting priorities caused the breadth and depth of the Department's role, and the Superintendent's supervision to wax and wane (see appendixes L and M).

Critical to the state and mandatory to the Department is oversight of the eligibility and certification of the state's educators. From 1971-72 to 2006-07, the number of teachers nearly doubled from 31,231 to 59,592 before school districts were forced to retrench because of the national economy (see appendix M). Screening applicants for certificates who had criminal backgrounds and following due process for revoking certificates of teachers engaged in illegal conduct were high priorities for the Superintendent and the Board. Keeping 700,000 students safe from sexual predators required constant vigilance. Exacerbating the challenge for the Department to fulfill its duties over the years was a Legislature hesitant to raise taxes and/or bent on reducing state government by refusing to fund the education system adequately. In more recent times the national economy improved slowly, but the legislators held firm on their conservative spending.

By 1915 Oklahoma had 5,800 mostly small, rural, township schools with grades 1-6 or 1-8 scattered across a large geographical area with the Department assigned supervision over them. The process of consolidating and annexing school districts over the next century occurred by fits and spurts eventually leading to the elimination of more than 90 percent of the districts. At the beginning the Legislature provided for an elective intermediate administrative level, the county superintendency, to be responsible for many functions, primarily relating to the thousands of small rural districts. A century later, and decades after its usefulness was mostly exhausted, it was eliminated in 1993. Especially in the formative decades of the state when travel was more complicated and communication was much slower, some functionaries performing at various levels were more competent and cooperative than others. While their elective status allowed them some independence from the Department and the Superintendent, the county superintendents initially performed an important function that gradually lost purpose until the Legislature determined the position had become obsolete. The elimination of this intermediate function and position in conjunction with changing dependent districts to elementary districts that were administered by district superintendents allowed the Superintendent and Department duties to become more efficient.[11]

State Superintendents did not often advocate for greater efficiency through mergers and unification of districts for that would have engendered lots of opposition from the rural communities that viewed their schools with pride, determination, and fierce loyalty. As an elected functionary with no term limits, the Superintendents were hesitant to state more than a general idea that reduction in the number of districts should be pursued. R. H. Wilson was an exception when he called for consolidation to improve upon a fragmented system, formed a subcommittee of Board members to collect data, and published a bulletin to disseminate the information.[12]

School district numbers historically reflected the citizens' preference for accessibility over academic quality, and the state legislature, dominated by rural interests, rejected calls for significant consolidation. The major exception to this influence occurred through HB 85 in 1947 mandating annexations and setting the minimum standards for small rural grades 1-8 schools. From the approximately 5,800 districts in 1915, the number was reduced to 4,450 by 1946, to 2,100 in 1952, and eventually to 517 by 2013. Population losses in rural areas, especially in western Oklahoma, reduced the number of students which, in turn, forced districts to join together as a matter of survival and to offer at least a minimal quality curriculum and educational experience. At the forefront of the technology revolution the Department coordinated efforts for districts to receive instruction by satellite. Oklahoma State University's College of Arts and Sciences played an integral role in designing and developing the curriculum and the delivery was through the University's state of the art studios and technology.[13]

The responsibility and influence of the Superintendent extended beyond the management and supervision of the Department and the oversight of the state's school districts and personnel. First and foremost, however, the Superintendent has always been designated as Chair/President of the Board through the territorial statutes in 1890 and then the constitutional provisions in 1907. Another *ex-officio* role, since 1894, has been that of membership on the Commissioners of the Land Office. This commission was assigned responsibility for the custody of all of the assets attached to the original allotments of land and money by the federal government. A third important role has been oversight of the vocational and technical programs since the second decade of statehood. Until 1968 the Department served this program area and then it became a separate free-standing agency, the State Department of Vocational-Technical Education, with its own director. This new department's board is chaired by the Superintendent *ex-officio*, extending that person's influence over what became known as career education. In 2000 the agency's name was changed to the Department of Career and Technology Education (see Board of Vocational Education, appendix N).

State Superintendents have served on many boards over the years, some as chair and others as a member only. Representative examples are: Board of Pardons from 1908-1913 when it was not unusual for elected officials to serve on ancillary boards, the State Textbook Committee, the Library Commission, and the Dormitory Bond Fund. Oversight of the normal schools/teachers colleges has been provided either by the Board, chaired by the Superintendent, or by a separate free-standing board on which the Superintendent was an *ex officio* member. As the mission of those original normal schools broadened over the decades, the Superintendent's role in those institutions and on the governing board narrowed. By statute Superintendents since 1890 have been designated to chair at least fifteen boards and commissions and to be members of another thirty-five (see appendix N for a partial listing of Agencies, Board, Commissions, and Committees).

Everything the Superintendent attempted or accomplished was done within a political environment fraught with competing interests and under an aura that elevated the significance of actions because children and students were involved. Without doubt, one of the most critical functions of the Superintendent was to work closely with the Legislature as the foremost advocate of education. This key person, or a designee, had to communicate well with the lawmakers to advance the cause of education with the goal of achieving maximum funding. Beyond the written biennial/annual report of the state's schools and testimony before legislative committees, the Superintendent responded to governors' inquiries and coordinated with the Secretary in apposite situations. Performing the enumerated constitutional and statutory duties, leading the Board and the Board of Career and Technology Education, speaking to administrators' and teachers' organizations, visiting schools, managing the Department, et alia, together represented the gamut of the expectations of the office.

Preference for an Elected Superintendent

Throughout state history surveys, committees, and distinguished persons have voiced reservations and concerns of an elective Superintendent position. If not elective, various appointing options are possible with examples of each option existing in other states. In some states the governor appoints while in others, it is the board of education which is either elected or gubernatorial appointed. When, in December 1890, the territorial Legislature created the office of Superintendent and gave Governor George Steele the responsibility for appointing someone to serve a two-year term, it began what eventually became a seventeen-year experiment of filling the office by appointment. The political landscape was dominated by Republicans in both the US presidency, and thus the territorial government, except for the Grover Cleveland term from 1893-1897. Party kinship did not result in harmony with internecine struggles within the territory's Republican Party causing additional stress to the government's operation. Nine men serving as Governor or Acting Governor during the territorial period provided frequent transitions and turnover of personnel and, consequently, uncertainty in continuity of thrusts and programs.[14]

Alfalfa Bill Murray, President of the Con Con and thus a member of every committee, described how the events unfolded in the decision to establish multiple executive positions as elective. During the convention, one of the earliest reports was that of the Executive Branch Committee. Murray, believing that the executive offices of Governor, Auditor, Treasurer, and State Examiner and Inspector needed to be independent of each other because they were responsible for state funds and collusion would be difficult, preferred these and only these to be elective. To provide perspective for their deliberations, other states' arrangements were studied, and it was learned that in some states few offices were elective while in other states few were appointive.[15]

Officers from the Farmers Union and the Labor Union pressured—"lobbying" was forbidden by Murray—the convention members "to elect every-thing [sic]." Murray was opposed but remained silent because the members overwhelmingly wanted the positions to be responsible to the voters. "Officers in the Indian Territory were all appointed, what there was of white man's government, and most of them in Oklahoma Territory and the people were tired of appointive officers."[16] Concerted resistance to a scheme of numerous gubernatorial appointments resulted in a decision described by Murray as a serious mistake that swung the pendulum too far. Within this milieu the Superintendent position transitioned from appointive to elective status, and despite multiple studies and recommendations, remains as such to this day.

Less than fifteen years after statehood and considerable legislative tinkering with various aspects of the state's schools' organization and administration, enough political will was amassed to request an analysis of the entire system. State leaders wished to bring order to some of the more incoherent parts of the system including how the Superintendent was chosen, the relationship between that person and the county superintendents, and the role of the latter. In a 1921 special session, the legislature passed An Act Creating a Commission of Educational Survey and appropriated $20,000 to pay for it. Governor J. B. A. Robertson appointed four members who were joined by Superintendent R. H. Wilson, *ex-officio*. At its first organizational meeting John Vaughan, former legislator and later Superintendent, was hired as the Executive Secretary. The Commission, desiring to seek external expertise and assistance to lend credibility to the report, entered into an agreement with the US Department of the Interior, Bureau of Education to conduct the study. Education experts from seven widely separated states examined the public school system.[17]

The Commission received the report with its analyses and several recommendations including that the elective Superintendency was problematic because it was "subject to the hazards and influences of partisan politics" as was an elective county superintendency "amenable to political vicissitudes." The external experts further opined a preference for a scheme of a Board appointment of the Superintendent, through a national search, of a commissioner of education who held great respect and a resume of appropriate experiences. Constituted as such, Oklahoma's school administration system was "open to criticism as lacking proper organization and coordination."[18] It was an indictment of a selection process that could be improved upon to reduce political influence and increase the probability that better quality individuals could be identified and selected.

A related topic for the Commission was compensation. "The salary paid to the State superintendent of public instruction should be considered as an index of the importance of the responsibilities of the office, and an index of the realization of their importance on the part of the citizens of the State."[19] The report was generally critical of many states' superintendents' low salaries and recommended specifically that the Superintendent's salary be tripled to $7,500. By setting a competitive compensation package, high quality individuals would be encouraged to apply. Eight years passed before the Superintendent's salary was increased and then it was only to $6,000. Not until 1951 did the salary equal or exceed $7,500 (see appendix I).

The Institute for Government Research of the Brookings Institution in 1935 studied the organization and administration of Oklahoma and concluded that the constitutional duty of the Legislature to "provide by law for the establishment and maintenance of an efficient system of checks and balances between the officers of the Executive Department" in practice experienced an "exceedingly doubtful" efficiency. Corrective action necessitated changing the Superintendency to an appointive office. Twenty years later an analysis of Oklahoma's constitution and the motives of its writers were the subject of comment by Thornton, Rushing, and Wood who gave the document high marks, more so than any other state constitution, because it expressed more effectively the objectives of modern enlightened government. However, these authors describe the Constitution writers of a half-century earlier as more proficient at writing a constitution than at administering state government, for the government they designed was equipped with administrative structures, organization, and procedures drawn almost entirely from American political experiences and preconceptions of the early 19th century. "The Framers held strongly to the principle of checks and balances, and were not content to limit its application to relations between the three branches of government…They devised a complex system of checks and balances which operates within the executive branch, and then directed the Legislature to expand on it."[20]

Thornton, Rushing, and Wood continued, "To some extent, in Oklahoma as well as in other states, conflict between the Governor and other elected officials is potential rather than real."[21] A bit puzzling is this foray into the hypothetical "potential" given the intensity and frequency of the conflict that surfaced between the Governor and the Superintendent beginning as early as 1911 and boiling up in the 1930s, 1940s, and again in 2010-2014. On the other hand, conflicts between the chief executive and the top education official may not have been deemed sufficient for specific identification.

For the third time in forty-three years the Superintendency was studied, this time by the Division of Surveys and Field Services at George Peabody College and at the urging of the state's first Republican governor. In 1964 it reported that only twenty-one states elected their Superintendent, down from thirty-four in 1945. Where states had chosen to have their boards of education select the Superintendents, none opted to return to an elective model. From this analysis, the Peabody researchers recommended that the Constitution be amended to direct the Legislature to provide for the Board to select the Superintendent, with guidelines to fix the term of office and to set the salary.[22]

Three years later Republican Governor Bartlett commissioned yet another study to examine state government, the Governor's Management Study Committee. Fifty-six task force members representing business and industry, and financed by 110 corporations, businesses, and schools, spent four months studying ways the state could improve efficiency and save money by reorganizing its operations. Specifically relating to educational governance, the committee recommended that the Superintendent position be appointive, the county superintendent position eliminated, and the number of school districts reduced to 300. None of these three changes was imminent, and the only one ever achieved was the elimination of the county superintendency, but not before the passage of more than twenty-five years. For the third time in five years, in 1969, an assessment of elementary and secondary education in Oklahoma, this time under Title III of the ESEA by SCREL of Little Rock, Arkansas, recommended that the Superintendency be appointive. No explicit rationale was offered for this position; rather, it was stated almost in passing, minimizing the importance of the suggestion. Republican efforts to streamline state government met with great apathy among the dominant Democratic Legislature.[23]

A substantially different approach to improving the efficiency and effectiveness of state government, given no indication that the citizens were imminently going to vote to amend the Constitution to select several executive positions by gubernatorial appointment, was attempted by Governor George Nigh in 1984 through Executive Order 84-1 creating the Commission on Reform of State Government. After studying the executive branch, it recommended the creation of a cabinet organization with all state agencies, board, or commissions being grouped according to the functions and services they provide. This additional layer of administration would create a Secretary of each cabinet office appointed by the Governor, subject to confirmation by the Senate, reporting to the Governor, and serving at the chief executive's pleasure. A further recommendation was that several positions including the Superintendent be appointive.[24]

Two years passed before HB 1944 provided for the Oklahoma Reorganization Council of twenty-five citizens to study the different areas of state government and to recommend how these areas could be implemented into a cabinet system. From the Council's deliberations emerged this consensus: a gubernatorial appointed and Senate-confirmed Secretary, serving at the pleasure of the Governor, should head each cabinet position with sufficient flexibility and authority to influence policies, funds, and personnel. Specifically, the Education Secretary would supervise and assist with coordinating post secondary, career-technical, and common education. The council advised the Superintendency be appointive to enhance cohesion within the executive structure and to be consistent with the other two branches.[25]

The cabinet configuration was implemented by Republican Governor Bellmon and, under it, some of the cabinet secretaries, such as Education, did not control major operating departments. Lacking any operational responsibility, the Education Secretary became little more than a staff advisor to the Governor. The Chancellor for Higher Education and the Director of Career Education were board appointed, with political constituencies of their own, who wished no oversight from a cabinet level Secretary.

Resistance to reorganizing the executive branch was strong: "Government reorganization does represent a drastic change. Not only do such proposals create apprehension among those immediately affected (bureaucrats at all levels), but legislators may be skeptical if not hostile…Clientele groups which often develop special relationships with state offices, likewise want 'their' agencies to remain somewhat removed from the governor's control."[26]

Another analysis was conducted at the direction of another Republican governor, Frank Keating, in 1995 when he obtained the assistance of fifty state employees, the Governor's Performance Team, to find ways to streamline government operation. One recommendation was the creation of "an executive level position appointed by the governor [sic], confirmed by the Senate (based on qualifications) to assume executive and policy management responsibility for a unified educational structure."[27] Implementing this recommendation would cause the elimination of the Superintendent position. Some reformers contended that such changes would save taxpayers a great amount of money, although experience from other states refutes that claim. In effect, reorganization calls for structural changes in the executive branch so as to make departments and agencies more accountable to the Governor. Oklahoma's surveys and studies inevitably included the recommendation that the office of Superintendent be appointive rather than elective.

Changing the Superintendency to an appointive position was not as simple as amending the Constitution although that has thus far been a formidable hurdle. If it were to be by appointment, who would select the person? Former state senator and Chair of the Survey

Commission of 1922, Superintendent Vaughan, in 1932, recommended a constitutional amendment to permit the Board to select the Superintendent. Under his plan, governors could influence the Superintendent selection process through their Board appointees; however, governors then, and until the 1960s, could not serve more than one term and thus would have been exiting office before being able to get "their person" into office. Governors would relish the opportunity to appoint their preferred persons to the position who would then serve at the Governors' pleasure.[28]

Surveys, reports, recommendations, and opinions about how the Superintendent should be selected dot Oklahoma's history since statehood. External professional input has been sought and paid for with tens of thousands of taxpayer and private dollars, but to no avail. While an additional layer of bureaucracy was created by the cabinet system, no corresponding lessening of current structures beneath this system ensued. Change comes slowly in Oklahoma government, but not always free of humor. For, in 2003, two Republican politicians, frustrated at their party never being able to defeat the incumbent Democratic Superintendent, argued that states where the Superintendent was appointed had higher test scores and "superior academic results;" thus, Oklahoma should have an appointed chief school officer. Seven years later a Republican was elected to the office, stifling the clamoring for the position to be appointive. By 2013, in the thirty-eight states where the Superintendent, also known as the Chief State School Officer, was appointed, the Governor appointed that person in fifteen and the Board in twenty-three. By election, the other twelve states, including Oklahoma, chose the top education official.[29]

Elected secondary executive officials can be independent and even oppositional in their dealings with the Governor regardless of party affiliations. All instances of substantial conflict between the Governor and the Superintendent involved individuals of the same political party, not surprising given the dominance of the Democratic Party in Oklahoma's history. Only 13 percent of the time since 1907 were the Governor and Superintendent from opposing parties, and always the former was Republican and the latter Democratic. One can only conjecture what the potential for disagreements might have been if the two offices would have been represented by persons of opposing political parties for a larger percentage of the time.

Qualifications for the Superintendency

Absent of any constitutional or statutory qualifications or restraints for the Superintendency in 1890 and throughout the territorial period, the governors weighed the political mood and sentiments to identify the persons they selected to be the Superintendent. That most of the Superintendents had formal preparation and experience in education conveyed the import that such a background was a prerequisite to eligibility for the highest government position overseeing the public education system. A most critical criterion, before statehood with all appointees and since 1907 for persons selected to complete unexpired terms, was their political party. In all thirteen instances in Oklahoma Territory and during statehood, those appointed were affiliated with the political party of the Governor.

The basic distrust of political officials, manifested in mood of the Con Con delegates and across the twin territories at the writing of the Constitution, took form in the populist spirit to create numerous executive positions with the same few qualifications to be filled by popular vote: male, minimum age of 30, minimum of three years of residency, and US citizenship. Excluding the gender criterion, these requirements were similar to other state constitutions and the US Constitution. United States citizenship, the only unchanged qualification since statehood and gained through naturalization or birth, was deemed critical to prove one's commitment to the virtues and patriotism of the country, though the length of time as a citizen was not stated. The brief Oklahoma residency criterion conveyed the expectation that executive officials would have some attachment to, and understanding of, the state's government and its citizens, but also recognized that the state was young and had many residents who emigrated from other states. Article 6, section 3 of the Oklahoma Constitution set forth these requirements only, obviously excluding any expectation of the Superintendent having any expertise in understanding schools and managing the Department. The electorate could be trusted to select the best of the "qualified" people who would aspire to the position.

United States citizenship, length of state residency, and minimum age specification generated no controversy over the decades, but the exclusion of females proved to be a different issue. Women were not only viewed as unqualified and thus excluded from eligibility, but also were not deemed worthy of suffrage. As time would tell, their eligibility for statewide office would not materialize until decades after they won the right to vote. Multiple times the citizens voted to change the Constitution to include no reference to gender, eventually succeeding in the general election of 1942. (For a more detailed

Table 3.1 Superintendents' constitutional qualifications

Superintendent	Birth state	AA	AE	YinOBBE
E. D. Cameron	North Carolina	n/a	45	16
R. H. Wilson	Kentucky	n/a	37	7
M. A. Nash	Texas	n/a	32	20
John Vaughan	Tennessee	42	45	24
A. L. Crable	Texas	46	48	16
Oliver Hodge	Missouri	n/a	45	35
D. D. Creech	Oklahoma	51	n/a	n/a
Scott Tuxhorn	Oklahoma	41	42	n/a
Leslie Fisher	Oklahoma	n/a	48	48
John Folks	Oklahoma	36	38	12
Gerald Hoeltzel	Oklahoma	54	55	n/a
Sandy Garrett	Oklahoma	n/a	47	47
Janet Barresi	Oklahoma	n/a	58	58
Joy Hofmeister	Missouri	n/a	50	28

Notes: AA is the age at appointment, AE is the age at election, and YinOBBE is the years of residency in Oklahoma before being elected. The first five Superintendents qualified under original constitutional criteria for eligibility for office (male, US citizen, and minimum age of thirty and three years of state residency). The remaining nine met the amended qualifications of 1942 (US citizen, minimum age of thirty-one, and ten years of state residency). Six of the fourteen were initially appointed to the office.

description of this struggle see chapter 6). In that same amendment, the age requirement was raised by one year to 31 and the state residency from three years to ten.[30]

No Superintendent elected or appointed failed to exceed the minimum constitutional standards. Prior to 1942, M. A. Nash was closest to the minimum age of thirty and R. H. Wilson, with seven years in the state, exceeded the three-year standard. After 1942, John Folks was closest to the cutoff with twelve years in Oklahoma following his two-year hiatus in Texas. When governors appointed men to complete unexpired terms, they judged their appointees to subsequently aspire to the position. Only the persons eligible to be elected were appointed, and all appointed, except D. D. Creech, subsequently stood for election.

To reflect the growing importance of the Superintendency, the Legislature opted in 1965 to augment the constitutional requirements with certificate standards that were based on an earned master's degree in school administration. All Superintendents to date were actively involved in education prior to being elected to the position, but formalizing the professional nature of the position would add status and eliminate less qualified individuals. The lawmakers determined that the professional qualifications for Superintendent should equal those for school district administration: "a master's degree in school administration from a college recognized by the State Board of Education and meet the requirements to qualify for an administrator's certificate." No test of the constitutionality of the additional statutory stipulations occurred until 1981 when the Attorney General complied with a request and subsequently ruled: "The legislature may not impose upon the office of Superintendent of Public Instruction eligibility requirements which are additional to or different from those prescribed by the Oklahoma Constitution, article 6, section 3."[31] Although the opinion became effective immediately, almost ten years passed before the Legislature in 1990 deleted the exact wording of the 1965 statute. None of the three Superintendents since 1990 would have been eligible if these statutory stipulations would have continued in operation.

Regardless of elected or appointed, and in spite of no stipulations addressing specific educational preparation or experience in the public schools, Oklahoma's Superintendents, prior to 2011, were career educators. Five governors appointed a total of six persons (Bartlett appointed two) to complete unexpired terms, and five of these had had prior small school superintendent experience. The exception was John Folks who was an employee in the Department when named by Governor Nigh to complete Les Fisher's term in 1984. From 1907 to 1984 three elected Superintendents held the top post in small rural districts, two at the county level, and one, E. D. Cameron, had no superintendent experience at all. Since 1986 none of the four elected Superintendents have had top-level administrative positions in the public schools with the two most recent having only minimal school teaching experience.

Monetary Compensation

To gain insight into the monetary compensation mechanism, one should analyze the constitutional and statutory processes to determine pay, compare two or more positions' remuneration, and describe increases (and decreases) over time. During the territorial period both the Federal Indian Supervisor and the Governor were hired and paid by the US government while the Oklahoma Territory Superintendent was selected by the Governor and paid with territorial funds, the amount of pay determined by the Legislature. Federal salary money ceased with the transition to statehood when all funds for compensation for the Governor and the Superintendent were raised through Oklahoma's taxation system. The Oklahoma Constitution then became the guidebook for determining the compensation scheme and the Legislature determined the amount of executive officers' pay.

Federal statute set Oklahoma Territory officials' (Governor and judges) compensation biennially and the territorial Legislature would in turn set the salaries of the other officials. When the Supervisor of Indian Schools position was created in 1899 as a function of the office of the US Secretary of the Interior, the salary was determined biennially also. The first Oklahoma Territory Legislature in 1890 set the Superintendent's compensation, as shown in table 3.2, at $1,800, and two years later increased it to $2,000, a level sustained only until 1897 when, because of insufficient funds, it reverted to the earlier amount and remained there until statehood. This reduction in pay because of insufficient tax revenues was a harbinger of things to come during statehood. Comparatively, the Governor, paid through federal taxes, fared better by having the initial amount maintained until 1903 when he received a 15 percent increase that continued until statehood. During the territorial period, the Superintendent's salary ranged from 60 percent to 77 percent of the Governor's salary. Superintendent of Indian Schools, Benedict, earned more than or equal to the Governor until 1907 when the Governor's pay increased by 50 percent. Statehood brought a 39 percent increase in the Superintendent's pay, still 17 percent below that of the Superintendent of Indian schools.[32]

Table 3.2 Biennia Salaries for Superintendent, Federal Indian Superintendent, and Governor for the period of 1891-1910

Year	Superintendent Amount	Change	Indian Superintendent Amount	Change	Governor Amount	Change
1891-93	1,800	n/a	n/a	n/a	2,600	n/a
1893-95	2,000	+11	n/a	n/a	2,600	0
1895-97	2,000	0	n/a	n/a	2,600	0
1897-99	1,800	-9	n/a	n/a	2,600	0
1899-01	1,800	0	3,000	n/a	2,600	0
1901-03	1,800	0	3,000	0	2,600	0
1903-05	1,800	0	3,000	0	3,000	+15
1905-07	1,800	0	3,000	0	3,000	0
1907-10	2,500	+39	3,000	0	4,500	+50

Note: Territorial period 1891-November 16, 1907; statehood 1907-1910. Indian superintendent began in 1899. The change is the percentage difference from the prior year.

Determination of the Amount of the Compensation

Since the Legislature at statehood was mandated by the Constitution to determine executive officers' salaries within the parameters of the Constitution, essentially, compensation for these officers' four-year terms were to be set with no allowance for increases during the term, but the amount could be decreased subject to lack of sufficient funds. The method for determining the amount of compensation varied with internal discussions prevailing for some periods of time and input from citizens' committees on other occasions. For decades, salaries for the Governor and several other officials, including the Superintendent, were independent of each other, but then the Legislature decided on a scheme to tie together executive and judicial officers' salaries. In 1995 and, for the next twenty-four years, the Superintendent's pay was to equal that of a district judge's. Four years later the Governor's compensation amount was tied to that of the Chief Justice of the Oklahoma Supreme Court. Citizens appointed by the Governor to the Board of Judicial Compensation determined the pay scale. This scheme continued in effect until 2015 when the Legislature overrode the Governor's veto and decoupled the salaries of the executive and judicial officers. The Governor's opposition stemmed from the belief that a board representing the various sectors of the population could more justly and capably determine a fair compensation than could the politically charged Legislature.[33]

Twice, exceptions to the prohibition of no increases during the Superintendent's term were attempted, a successful one in 1968 and one ruled unconstitutional in 1980. The former instance was when Governor Bartlett wanted to name the superintendent of the Pryor schools to succeed Oliver Hodge who died suddenly. D. D. Creech refused consideration until his current salary was exceeded. Successful lobbying of the Legislature accomplished his wish, and no one questioned the apparent unconstitutionality of the action. In the second instance, the Board, pleased with the performance of the Superintendent and desiring to compensate him accordingly, thought it possible to circumvent the constitutional restriction of increasing the salary during an officer's term if it were to expand the duties significantly. Seemingly, precedent was set twelve years earlier when no one contested the Legislature's action to increase the salary with no additional duties involved. The Board devised a new position description with increased duties and responsibilities and requested the Legislature to increase his compensation. A sympathetic Legislature granted the wish, but a year later, the Attorney General squelched that move, declaring the Legislature's action unconstitutional, and the Board had to reduce the pay to the original amount for the term of the office.[34]

Compensation Ratio of Superintendent to Governor

At statehood the Legislature raised the Governor's pay by 50 percent over the amount of the last four years of territorial governance, an increase certainly justifiable considering that his responsibility doubled regarding geographical size and population. Demographics were similar for the Superintendent plus the number of school districts more than doubled by 1912. However, the Superintendent's salary grew only 39 percent. From 1907 to 1930, the Superintendent's pay relative to the Governor's was 55 percent, a ratio that would prove to be the lowest in the 125 years from 1890-2015 (see appendix I).

Availability of money was the most important factor determining the amount of executive officer compensation with the ratio between the Governor's and Superintendent's salaries shifting periodically from the relative assessments of the significance of the positions. Shortly before the collapse of the stock market in 1929, the Legislature increased the Governor's pay by 167 percent and the Superintendent's by 240 percent to become effective in 1931. This action raised the ratio between the Superintendent's salary ($6,000) and the Governor's ($7,500) to .80, a substantial improvement. Unfortunately, the beginning of the Depression reduced the amount of tax revenue flowing into the state's coffers, causing executive officers' compensation to decrease. The deepening of the Depression and the effects of the passage of the balanced budget amendment in 1942 forced the Legislature to reduce the pay until 1951 (see appendix I).[35]

More revenue was available by the beginning of the 1950s to increase the compensation, this time for the Superintendent and Governor 250 percent and 230 percent, respectively, resulting in a slight increase in the ratio for the former. No similar percentages of increases have been achieved since. In 1982 when the energy sector was booming, both offices were awarded large increases, the Superintendent from $35,000 to $55,000 and the Governor from $48,000 to $70,000. Those amounts did not change for the next four terms or until 1999 when both salaries were tied to the judicial offices. A significant boost to the compensation occurred then with the two offices' salaries being raised to $88,511 and $101,140, respectively. Particularly beneficial to the Superintendent was this decision because now the Superintendent's salary approximated 87 percent of the Governor's, the highest ratio since 1890. In the term 2011-2014 pay for the Superintendent was $102,529 and for the Governor $117,571 for a ratio of .872, very similar to 1999-2010. An analysis of the compensation for the five terms of Sandy Garrett, for example, shows that the ratio of her pay relative to the Governor's grew from .79 to .87. And, in her twenty-year tenure, her pay increased 89 percent (see appendix I).[36]

Superintendent compensation relative to the Governor has ranged from a low of 55 percent from 1907-1930 to a high of 87.5 percent in 1999-2002. Only during two terms in the 1960s was the ratio as low as 60 percent, but then it began trending upward to the current level in excess of 87 percent. When the executive officers' salaries were tied to those of the judicial officers', the Superintendent benefitted considerably. However, the legislators decided after a twenty-five year experiment that they did not wish to abrogate their prerogative, so they discontinued the tie between the executive and judicial officers' pay (see appendix I). Time will tell whether this separation was advantageous.

Superintendent Compensation Relative to Department Employees and District Superintendents

As elected officials, the Superintendents were subject to the whims of the Legislature for the determination of their salaries. In the early decades the Legislature also determined the salaries of the Department's employees. Typically, these administrators and supervisors earned slightly less than the Superintendents. Over time the authority for determining these salaries shifted to the Superintendent and the Board. During the long shadow of the Depression, the Superintendent's salary remained unchanged and low. More money coming into the state's coffers, and into the Department, in the late 1940s allowed the Board to increase these employees' salaries. In 1949-50, the Assistant Superintendent's salary was $6,000 (25 percent more than the Superintendent's) and all of these were paid anywhere from 16 to 50 percent more than the Superintendent: Director of Secondary Education, Director of Rural and Elementary Education, Director of Annexation and Consolidation, Director of Finance (highest at $7,200), Assistant Director of Finance and Supervisor of School Bus Purchase and Rental, Director of Transportation and Safety Education, and Head Examiner.[37]

Compensation for the Superintendent has always been determined relative to the amount paid to the Governor and other executive officers rather than to school district superintendents, the pool of candidates until 1984. Superintendents' (and governors') salaries historically compared unfavorably to those of many of the district superintendents. In 1909-10 the Oklahoma City School District with 200 teachers paid its superintendent $100 more than Superintendent Cameron's salary of $2,500. Ten years later thirty-three district superintendents were paid more than R. H. Wilson whose salary had not been increased from his predecessor's. Teacher numbers in those districts ranged from 9-500 with seventeen districts hiring fewer than fifty. Tulsa's superintendent earned the most at 2.6 times the Superintendent's compensation. By 2015 large numbers of districts were paying their superintendents considerably more than the Superintendent earned.[38]

Patronage at the Forefront

"To the victor belong the spoils" is descriptive of the degree of discretion that voters in a democracy typically give elected officials to select the persons to work in their administrations, but short terms and tenures exacerbate the turnover as does the amount of controversy surrounding the official. Given Oklahoma's political history, how did this attitude and practice play out for a century? The Legislature condoned and even encouraged such a system, and Oklahomans were familiar with, and accepting of, the practice. Oklahoma's Superintendents benefitted from this environment with the lone exception of 1941 to 1949 when the Legislature transferred the discretion of whom to hire to the Board. The prerogative was returned to the Superintendent in early 1947 by the Board when he gained approval to hire his preferred people and then in 1949 by the Legislature. All employees were considered "at will" and subject to the vicissitudes of patronage, limited only by the Board.[39]

Governor Howard Edmondson entered office in 1959 and pushed the Legislature to craft a merit system bill to end the historic pervasive cronyism in Oklahoma government at all levels. Across the country in the 1950s, efforts to achieve the same results were bearing fruit, and Edmondson wanted to avail himself of that environment. Only after much horse-trading and promises of construction projects did the Legislature acquiesce to write a bill that the Governor signed. Oklahoma in 1959 had "merit-based civil service" and a significant blow to patronage politics.[40]

Not long after assuming the Superintendency in 1971, Les Fisher and the Board requested the Senate draft a bill removing all thirty-four Department supervisory personnel from the merit system and its protections stating that he planned to fire no one and that everyone involved supported the request. This is no surprise considering that eight years under two Republican governors had just ended, the entire Board was comprised of gubernatorial appointees, and the Superintendent would desire the freedom to hire his preferred people. Nor was the consent of the employees incongruous when considering that they, no doubt, wished not to jeopardize their status by opposing the Superintendent's idea. To soften the bold request, Fisher stated he had no intent to terminate anyone. In fact, Department staff numbers expanded considerably during his fourteen-year tenure, and his reputation was positive among the employees.[41]

Typical for elected officials, such as Superintendents, is the practice of replacing some or many of those agency administrators who were hired by their predecessors. When Sandy Garrett became Superintendent in 1991, she immediately eliminated many positions and terminated employees, aided by the loosening of the constraints in the merit system of twenty years earlier. But, the Department reorganization, terminations, and new employees required the approval of the Board.

Entirely different events unfolded rapidly in January 2011 when a maverick Republican Superintendent and a holdover Board appointed by a Democratic governor, in their first meeting, quickly became contentious causing the meeting to degenerate into a paroxysm that gave the Republican controlled Legislature the fuel it needed to transfer authority from the Board to the Superintendent. Almost a complete reversal of the Superintendent's misfortune in the 1940s befell Janet Barresi when she was handed the authority to hire and fire employees. Additionally, that legislative action provided for each new Governor to appoint Board members upon the assumption of the office rather than as previously where Board members served six years staggered terms. This return to complete patronage gave the Superintendent total flexibility in staffing the Department, the very situation the Legislature tried to correct in 1959.[42]

Summary

For more than a century the citizens of Oklahoma have entrusted the management of their public education system to a position with no constitutional or statutory requirements unique to the responsibilities assigned to that position. Most of those who competed for the Superintendency were engaged in public education and all of those who held the position until 2011, whether elected or appointed, were career public educators. Changing political dynamics in the twenty-first century allowed a career dentist and then a private entrepreneur to gain the confidence of the voters over the experienced educators. Attempts to modify the selection process and the eligibility requirements have met only a modicum of success (excepting the granting of women the right to hold the office). Business concepts (e.g., accountability, competition, and customers) have become ingrained in the philosophy of schooling resulting in a lessening influence of the educators and an increasing acceptance of other perspectives. Emphasis has shifted from preparing students to become successful adults in a complex world to preparing students to achieve well on tests. Concomitant to that is the effort to grade schools and school districts with the hope that competition will spur greater growth in student achievement. Thus, in the state's elective process the contestants need to endorse school choice and competition. Finally, very little attention across the decades has been directed toward the sufficiency of the financial compensation paid to the Superintendent. Historically, the position's salary has been less than that of many local district superintendents, a status that has been exacerbated in recent years as greater numbers of local officials' salaries have surpassed the Superintendent's remuneration.

Chapter 4
Campaigns and Elections
(1907-2014)

Minimal eligibility qualifications for Oklahoma's elective executive offices, including the Superintendency, allowed for a wide-open field for those courageous enough to mount a campaign, who were capable of raising funds or, in rare cases, had sufficient personal assets to engage in publicity sufficient to inform and persuade voters. From the first day of statehood Oklahomans have voted for their top educator despite multiple efforts to cause the selection to be by appointment. The citizens have not been convinced to change by the learned opinions of educators and the business and professional communities nor the injections of political pragmatism of several governors wishing to consolidate their power and influence.

In this chapter the elections and candidates are described and analyzed in the context of the politics of the position. Political dynamics depended on many factors, some unique and others constant, in each election cycle. Some years saw several contestants; there were periods of no challengers, with the incumbent undistracted from his duties through the campaign months with no need to contend for his office. Two election cycles, 1926 and 1934, witnessed women brave enough to compete for an office of which they were not guaranteed even if they would have garnered the most votes. Three Republican appointees held the office, but were never subsequently elected. Only two tried. Another Superintendent, initially appointed and then elected, did not seek reelection. No Superintendents were able to use their positions to springboard them to a higher elected position. From horse feed to millions of dollars, campaigns have received nonmonetary and financial support. General election outcomes, without exception and regardless of the amount of money spent, reflected voter party registration—when the Democratic Party held 50 percent or more of the registered voters, the Democratic candidate won and, when that party's numbers slipped below half, even slightly, the Republican won.

Ebb and Flow of Candidates' Interest Through Twenty-eight Election Cycles

Election day, September 17, 1907, two months before Oklahoma was admitted to the Union, set the stage for the political process of the election of Oklahoma's governing officials for the abbreviated first term of office. Once the Constitution was written providing for an elected Superintendent, and adopted by the voters, it set the expectations for those aspiring to be the state's top education official. Oklahoma's statutes set the framework for elections, criteria for determining election outcomes, and party recognition. Competition for that office, as for all of the executive offices, reflected the degree of controversy; the power, influence, and success of the incumbent; the strength of the opposition parties; and the overall excitement or malaise in the state. The number of candidates vying for an office and the historical time period determined whether or not a runoff election was necessary or permitted.

Those elected would serve slightly more than three years only, but many of their actions would be precedential. A compressed timeframe for "campaigning" forced events to occur rapidly, but the chosen executive officers and legislators would gain valuable knowledge to assist in planning for the process of subsequent elections. Criticism of the primary voting scheme enacted in 1908, specifically regarding statewide offices, focused on how a candidate's obscurity and order of name placement on the ballot could affect the outcome. The candidate garnering the most votes won even though that person might have received less than a fourth or a third of the votes. Until 1929 winners were determined by plurality and thus there was no need for runoff elections, and thereafter by majority outcomes.[1]

Voters were confronted with rather extensive ballots every four years when they chose their executive officials. Additionally, as one of the minority of states allowing straight party voting, electors, by checking one box, could efficiently choose their party's preferred slate of candidates. Another factor influencing the outcomes was the dominance of one party's voter registration for decades, and more recently the opposing party. With this mix of political ingredients, it is easy to understand that the greatest determinant of the elections' outcomes was voter registration. Even with the ease of straight party voting, party registration was the most influential factor in predicting the outcome prior to the 2010 election (see table 4.6).

Particularly for statewide elections, only parties nationally recognized were permissible: Democratic, Republican, Socialist, Prohibitionist, and Progressive. The three minor parties faded with time and were eventually replaced in 1960 by the American and Libertarian parties, but Independents were never considered a party. In the inaugural election, and throughout the state's history, the two major parties fielded candidates who dominated the process. Also, as was typical in the early days, a third party presented voters with an alternative to the platforms of the Democrats and Republicans. Almost no variation resulted among the twelve executive offices in 1907 with the Democratic candidates garnering 53.5-55.2 percent, Republicans 40.7-42.5 percent, and the Socialists 3.9-4.3 percent, respectively. All were considered plurality winners, including E. D. Cameron, but all were also majority winners, a status not consistent through the teens and 1920s. No limit was ever established for the maximum number of candidates, and the minimum number for an election was one.[2]

In the executive officers' election of 1907 both major parties had only one candidate for each office in its primary representing each of the two territories, a reasonable limit placed on the parties to simplify the process within a shortened timeframe in this initial experiment of campaigning. With the general election scheduled for September, a compressed calendar conveyed urgency in proceeding efficiently. The Republicans, with their party's convention set for early August, knew who the Democratic candidates were, and, no doubt, were optimistic but considered them to be formidable candidates.

The Superintendency election, unsurprisingly, generated considerable excitement as the process evolved in uncharted waters. By late March, Cameron announced his campaign platform followed by Robert L. Knie, superintendent of Washita County, publicizing his in *The Oklahoman* in the first week of June. With their candidates' declarations, the Democrats were eager for their party's first primary election Saturday, June 8. Final tallies were undetermined until almost two weeks later, when with two counties yet to report, Cameron led Knie by over 15,000 votes out of approximately 150,000 counted. In this first "statewide" Democratic primary, the Indian Territory candidate defeated the one from Oklahoma Territory and, two weeks later at the statewide convention, candidate Cameron was nominated by acclamation.[3]

It was a common practice in other states for political parties to hold conventions to generate excitement among the members, to adopt platforms, to nominate their candidates for the several offices, and to discuss strategies for campaigning. Oklahoma's Democratic and Republican parties adopted similar practices in the inaugural year of 1907. Party platforms were adopted in Oklahoma City by the Democrats, June 18, and, in Tulsa, by the Republicans six weeks later, August 2. Contrasted to the Democrats, the Republicans chose not to have a primary, but to select their candidate by a vote at their convention. When conventioneers chose Calvin Ballard, narrowly, of South McAlester over G. D. Moss from Kingfisher, they were not setting a precedent for the party. Rather, that was the most efficacious procedure for the 1907 Republican Party in the lead-up to statehood.[4]

With the unique restriction of only one candidate from each of the two territories for each party's primary in 1907 being replaced by an allowance for unlimited candidates, the second election cycle was truly competitive with multiple candidates of four parties in the fifteen statewide executive offices. For the Superintendency, six candidates ran in the same three parties as three years earlier, giving voters choices both in the hotly contested Democratic primary and an evenly matched Republican primary. The 1910 elections reflected growing interest in the political process as the parties and candidates jostled for power and influence.[5]

Two election cycles that drew much interest and multiple candidates in both the governorship and the Superintendency were 1934 and 1946. Nineteen thirty-four, deep into the Depression and also thick into the controversy brewing in the Commissioners of the Land Office whose membership included both the Governor and the Superintendent, saw a total of eighteen candidates for the former position and ten for the latter. A dozen years later interest was high again in both positions with twelve campaigning for governor and seven for Superintendent. In Oklahoma in the 1930s and 1940s many citizens engaged in efforts to gain political office knowing that success would result in employment and a guaranteed salary. But of particular interest was the 1946 election cycle when the incumbent Superintendent, disputatious and recalcitrant, proved to be too confrontational with the Governor and the Legislature resulting in multiple aspirants who hoped to unseat him.[6]

Political interest in the Superintendency waxed and waned over the decades, in some elections reflecting the overall mood of the state and, in others, recognizing the reality of a popular incumbent running for reelection. From 1910 to 1946 four or more candidates entered every election cycle except in 1930. Conversely, all election cycles from 1950 to 2006 drew three or fewer candidates with six general elections having no challengers to the incumbents and five others with just one challenger either in the primary or the general election. Sandy Garrett's retirement after five terms opened the door in 2010 for a highly competitive election, and Janet Barresi's contentious term attracted six other aspirants to the contest in 2014. This election cycle proved to be an aberration when, different from the fewer candidates for other executive offices, multiple candidates emerged, possibly signaling that events within the Department had reached an unacceptable level. Challengers forced incumbents to explain and defend their actions, to solicit the voters' support, and, in general, to justify to the public why they should be given another term. Oliver Hodge and Les Fisher were given an easy ride when they sought reelection while Garrett drew at least one challenger in every election cycle of her lengthy term (see table 4.1 and appendices C and F).[7]

Table 4.1 Number of candidates and parties for the election years 1907-2014

Candidates	Parties	Election years
1	1	1950, 1954, 1962, 1966, 1974, 1978
2	2	1958, 1982, 1986, 2002, 2006
3	2	1930, 1970, 1990, 1994, 1998
4	2, 3	1918, 1942
5	3, 4, 2, 3, 3	1907, 1914, 1926, 1938, 2010
6	4	1910
7	2, 2, 2	1922, 1946, 2014
8	…	…
9	…	…
10	3	1934

Source: ok.gov/elections/Elections_info/Election_Results/Election_Results_1907-1992.html; *Oklahoma Elections: Statehood to Present*, vol. 1 (OKC: SEB, 1994) for the results of the elections of 1907-1994; Election results from 1998-2014, www.ok.gov/elections (see also appendix C).

Note: To explain, four candidates represented two parties in 1918 and three parties in 1942. In no election years were there eight or nine candidates.

Not only did the Constitution specify the elective process for the executive offices, it also provided for a method for filling a position vacated by a resignation or death of the incumbent during the term. Those appointed temporarily would complete the remainder of the unexpired term with no formal obligation to then compete for the office. However, governors sought the opinion and intent of potential appointees to campaign for the office as the incumbent in the next election. In all six times the Superintendency was vacated before the term expired, when the governors were Democrats (1927, 1936, and 1984), their appointees, also Democrats, subsequently won election to the position. Conversely, when the governors were Republicans (1968, 1969, and 1988), two of their Republican appointees lost in the next election. When Oliver Hodge died in 1968, Governor Bartlett chose D. D. Creech, who served twenty-one months before unexpectedly resigning, and then he named Scott Tuxhorn to complete the term. Unexpired terms ranged from three months less than four years (John Vaughan, 1927-1931) to slightly more than one year (Scott Tuxhorn, January 1, 1970-January 11, 1971). Creech's sudden departure and

Tuxhorn's appointment by Bartlett forced Tuxhorn into the untenable position of immediately needing to fulfill the duties of the office and campaigning for the 1970 election.[8]

Candidates' Political Party Affiliations

Dominance of the Democratic Party's membership and occupation of most of the executive offices in Oklahoma before 2010 did not occur because of a lack of effort by the Republicans. As an example, of the seventy-six individuals who ran for the office of Superintendent from 1907 to 2014, thirty-six were Democrats, thirty-three were Republicans, three were Socialists, and one each Progressive, Prohibition, Progressive/Prohibition, and Independent. Most candidates lost every time they ran, others won every reelection campaign (R. H. Wilson, M. A. Nash, John Vaughan, Oliver Hodge, Les Fisher, and Sandy Garrett), a third group both won and then eventually lost (E. D. Cameron, A. L. Crable, and Janet Barresi), and John Folks ran only once and won. No incumbent ever lost to a challenger from the opposing party. Democratic dominance for decades, reflective of its large political roots of the conservative southern Democrats, left the Republicans with enough frustration to begin exploring ways of working the system to triumph over the inequitable conditions. What happened in the Superintendency was but a microcosm of the political milieu of the state. Waiting what seemed like forever eventually paid dividends in the 2010 election when the Republicans swept the statewide offices and the Legislature. In these first 108 years of statehood eleven individuals were elected to the Superintendency, the first nine were Democrats and the two most recent, Republicans. Only once, in 1914, did a third party candidate, a Socialist, capture more than 20 percent of the votes, resulting in the incumbent's reelection with less than a 45 percent margin. No doubt the state has suffered by a century of one-party dominance, and the immediate future does not bode well for achieving some equilibrium (see appendix B).[9]

Because of the opportunity afforded by the 2009 retirement announcement by the long-tenured, Democrat, the elevated hopes of the Republicans to capture the Superintendency and the other seven executive offices, and the total success of the shift in the 2010 election (Republicans captured those eight offices for the first time since statehood.), the magnitude of the transition was immense. Five candidates filed for the office: two Democrats, two Republicans, and one Independent. Four years later and after a difficult and tumultuous term, the incumbent drew six other candidates, two Republicans and four Democrats, to compete with her for the office in 2014. So contentious was Barresi that many of her staunchest initial supporters directed their support to her Republican challenger.[10]

Candidates' Other Political Activities

The candidates' other political activities beyond interest in the Superintendency indicate the extent of the desire of these individuals for involvement in politics and government service. The interest level can be inferred by examining how often they were candidates and for what offices. Several candidates (John P. Evans, 1910 House; Tuxhorn, 1962 House, and Susan Paddack, 2004 and 2008 Senate) were elected to offices before they filed for the Superintendency while others ran successfully in years thereafter (Robert Knie, 1917 and 1919 Senate and Earl Garrison, 2004-2012 Senate). Others, in the early decades sought varied offices, but were not rewarded by the voters. Since 1942, and with the exceptions of Fisher (governor in 1986) and Bill Crozier (multiple positions from 1972-2010), no Superintendent candidate sought an office other than state senate (see appendix E).

While the Superintendent oversees an extremely important state agency, that position has never been viewed as a significant stepping-stone to a higher position. Nineteen candidates for the Superintendency attempted forty times to be elected to other positions, for example: US representative, clerk of the Oklahoma Supreme Court, corporation commissioner, president of the state board of agriculture, Oklahoma house and senate, and governor. No Superintendent candidate had ever won another statewide office (see appendices B and E). Two Superintendents who subsequently ran for Governor, Wilson and Fisher, failed in their attempts, but the former competed vigorously and nearly achieved his goal. Attempting the most often was John C. Burns in the 1930s and 1940s who lacked perspicacity as a political operative. Nine times he filed for office, sometimes as a Republican and other times as a Democrat. Voters must have been wary of his motives and actions, and never elected him.

Candidates' Demographic Profiles

Since statehood women have dominated teaching positions at all levels and, for much of that time, elementary administrative positions also. Men, conversely, filled most secondary principalships and almost exclusively district superintendencies. By the turn of the twenty-first century, demographic shifts were underway at important levels. Unchanged was the ratio of male to female teachers: 1:2. However, more women were becoming secondary principals without the prerequisite of coaching and then using that administrative experience to burnish their credentials for the district superintendency. Concurrently, more women were moving into administrative roles at the Department. These trends would seem auspicious for those women who might aspire to the Superintendency; now they would have access to the stepping-stones for advancement to the state's highest post (see chapter 6).

Three Democratic and six Republican women (see table 4.2) sought the office in a struggle to achieve political success in a male dominated culture, an obstacle they could not overcome before 1990. Fifty-six years after Jenella Jones's campaign another woman ventured into the predominantly male world. Sandy Garrett's win in 1990 was

Table 4.2 Gender and political party of Superintendency candidates 1907-2014

Political party	Gender	
	Male	Female
Democratic	33	3
Republican	27	6
Minor parties	7	0
Total	67	9

Note: The minor parties were Socialist, Progressive, Prohibition, and Independent although Oklahoma does not recognize Independent as a party.

a harbinger of things to come, for the first female to run and capture the top education position was succeeded by a female. For twenty years, she dominated the education political scene by defeating all challengers although the 1994 election was the closest in history. Only 9,259 votes separated the two candidates in the general election out of 978,115 votes cast. Four years later, and in the only instance in state history, the two major party candidates were identical to the previous election. Linda Murphy's second go-round resulted in a defeat more in line with the historical trend—Democrat 60 percent, Republican 40 percent.[11]

These nine female aspirants competed in twenty-three primary (11), runoff (1), and general (11) elections, as shown in table 4.3, and won eight of the primary and seven of the general elections. Garrett competed in almost a third of the total elections (7) and won every contest. In 1994, 1998, and 2010 both candidates in the general elections were women. Collectively, they represented fewer than one in eight contenders for the office, three when the Constitution prohibited women from being eligible and six from 1990-2014. Only in the 1926 and 2014 Republican primaries and the 1994, 1998, and 2014 general elections did two women compete against each other. At least one female was involved in all elections (primary, runoff, and general) after 1990. With the exception of primary elections in 1926 and 1934, and the general election in 1926, no females were involved in any election prior to 1990. Of the seven general elections since 1990, three saw women exclusively competing for the office. For the Republican women, minority party status also prohibited any success before 2010.

Table 4.3 Female candidates, parties, years, and elections 1926-2014

Candidate	Party	Year	Election
Anna Willis	Republican	1926	*Primary* and General
Mary A. Munson	Republican	1926	Primary
Jenella Jones	Republican	1934	Primary
Sandy Garrett	Democratic	1990	*Primary* and *General*
		1994	*Primary* and *General*
		1998	*General*
		2002	*General*
		2006	*General*
Linda Murphy	Republican	1994	General
		1998	*Primary* and General
Susan Paddack	Democratic	2010	*Primary* and General
Janet Barresi	Republican	2010	*Primary* and *General*
		2014	Primary
Freda Deskin	Democratic	2014	*Primary* and Runoff
Joy Hofmeister	Republican	2014	*Primary* and *General*

Note: Races won are italicized.

With her retirement at the end of her term in January 2011, the first Superintendent in history to end her public service in such manner, Garrett opened the door for other women (and men) to pursue the office. State senator Susan Paddack and dentist Barresi competed for the 2010 general election with the latter winning. Barresi, Joy Hofmeister, and Freda Deskin, were involved in the 2014 primaries with Deskin forcing a runoff in the Democratic primary. Hofmeister, the Republican, received more than half of the primary votes and then the same was true in the general election (see appendix F). Women seized the opportunity, and, in so doing, proved their mettle with Garrett paving the way for women to follow. Eighty-three years of male dominance was then followed by an uninterrupted twenty-four years of females directing the Department and fulfilling the constitutional and statutory mandates of the office.

Male dominance in the Superintendency unsurprisingly reflected the overall trend in how women's qualifications for higher office were defined. While, for example, the state's general population gender ratio was approximately 50-50, females comprised 2/3 of the educators, and until recently, less than one-half of the school administrators. History was repeated in 2010 when both major party candidates for the general election were females, the same as in 1994 and 1998. Also, it was the first election since 1942 when a third "party" candidate ran as an Independent. His participation proved to be inconsequential; females were now energized to engage actively in the process for the long haul, a commitment that continued in the 2014 elections.

In general, women tend to be slightly older than men when attaining their first leadership positions, and this proved to be the case with the Superintendency, but the small number of females, urges caution in drawing any conclusions. Table 4.4 displays the age at filing time of the candidates by gender. Sixty-seven men ran for the office. Three other men with an average age of 48 were appointees, one of whom, Creech, resigned before his term ended. The mean age for all candidates was 45.1 years with the average for females at 50.4, five years higher than for males. Ages for the female winners and losers were higher for the former and lower by 1.3 years for the latter. Somewhat surprisingly, elected females averaged 9.5 years older than their male counterparts, a gender comparison with commonality to the workforce at large, but displaying a wider gap. This gap for the Superintendency was, no doubt, larger than for other leadership positions,

Table 4.4 Candidates' average age by gender at filing for their first election*

Category	Number	Ave. age
Unsuccessful female candidates	6	50.0
Elected female candidates	3	51.3
Total female candidates	9	50.4
Unsuccessful male candidates	56**	44.8
Elected male candidates	8	41.8
Total male candidates	64	44.4
Total unsuccessful candidates	62	45.3
Total elected superintendents	11	44.4
Total candidates' ages	73	45.1

Note: Although multiple candidates filed in multiple election cycles only their ages at first filing are used (see appendix D).

* D. D. Creech was appointed, served twenty months, and resigned, becoming the only person who served and never ran for the office. Thus, he is not included in this table.

** Of the fifty-nine unsuccessful male candidates, ages of three are unknown and those candidates are not included in the table.

but was reflective of the tendency for women to be older when entering historically male dominated arenas. Female Superintendents were older than unsuccessful female candidates, but male Superintendents were three years younger than unsuccessful male candidates. Historically, primarily younger males sought advancement to administrative positions and were selected by predominately male school boards for those positions. Women, particularly young women, were not encouraged to consider secondary school or district superintendent positions. The cultural changes of recent decades, and the recognition that the eligibility criteria are favorable to long-term residents regardless of their gender or experience, have resulted in a more receptive environment for women.

Voting Patterns

Straight ticket, or straight party, voting option, "down ballot" effect, frequent turnover of governors because of a one-term limit until the 1970s, no restrictions on Superintendency terms and longevity in office, two world wars, the Dust Bowl and the Great Depression migrations to the west coast, "boom and bust" in the energy arena, numbers of candidates for the Superintendency, and political dominance of the Democratic Party for a century are the factors that influenced the voting patterns and results in the general elections. Doubling the number of terms in the 1960s allowed to the Governor has resulted in more stability in that office with four of six governors since 1979 having served two terms. Governors and Superintendents, regardless of party affiliations, have served with relative harmony—a key to success for both positions and for political advantage.

Straight ticket voting has been practiced in Oklahoma, although the practice is declining across the country, making the state one of fewer than ten that continue to offer this option. Voters' knowledge and understanding of candidates and their platforms do not need to be extensive, their desire to exercise this significant duty in a democracy may be superficial, party loyalty is almost sacred, and efficiency in performing this responsibility may be paramount. Regardless of their motives, voters find this alternative an attractive one and consequential to consistency in the votes for all of the offices. Straight ticket voting obviously results in ratio of 1.00 between those voting for Governor and Superintendent.

Conversely, for those foregoing the straight ticket option, the "down ballot" effect, or drop off in voting, is intensified when the ballot includes multiple offices. Voters may not be equally interested in all positions listed, so they choose only the ones attractive to them. Others may refuse to vote for candidates for which they have little or no knowledge. Ballots with state questions included often reflect this effect when the voters choose not to mark their preference or they tire of the number of options and quit. Legislative action designates the election (special, primary, or general) for a state question and governors have been known to schedule the election based on their calculation of political advantage.

Because the Governor is the top state executive and the Superintendent administers a large share of the state's budget, these two factors might seem to tie the two positions together in the public's eyes as the voters mark their ballots. However, gubernatorial candidates typically have more name recognition and the voters are more knowledgeable of their platforms than is the case for the lesser offices and candidates further down the ballot. Ballot fatigue occurs when voters pay less attention toward offices and candidates listed nearer the bottom of a long ballot and seems to be a non-factor with the executive offices listed at or near the top. Might it be possible that controversy of some kind involving the Superintendent would affect the voting rate for the Superintendency? It appears as though any controversies were resolved in the primaries with the acceptable winner proceeding to the general elections. In 1930 and 1934, when the ratio was the lowest (.863 and .843), and the severest conflict during this term was the Land Commission scandal pitting the Governor against the Superintendent, one in six who voted for Governor failed to vote for Superintendent. Controversial Democratic primary elections in 1910 and 1946 were not followed by a higher ratio of voters choosing both the Governor and Superintendent in the general election. When electors in the two decades of 1994-2014 voted for Governor and Superintendent at a higher ratio than any other time in history (.983 to .993), citizens' party affiliations were shifting with the tide in the southern states. Neither the controversial times nor the number of entrants into the races seemed to affect the ratio of those voting for both positions on the same ballot, but the increased Republican efforts to gain and keep the Superintendency may be as important factor as any. As the competition for the Superintendency took on a greater sense of urgency and hope, more voters checked boxes on the ballot for both positions (see appendix G).

Striking of the twenty-two general elections (see table 4.5) where both parties fielded Superintendency candidates was the variation in the number of voters from one election to another. Twenty to 25 percent increases or decreases from one election to the next were not uncommon. Elections during the two world wars, 1918 and 1942, showed dramatic drops in votes from the elections before and after, but that would be expected with large numbers of men and women participating in the war effort. In 2002 and 2010 more than one million persons voted, but after each of these elections, the number dropped by 10.1 percent and 20 percent, respectively. Retaining incumbents typically does not generate enthusiasm equal to when first choosing them. Only 882 votes separated the total numbers for the 1986, 1990, and 1998 Superintendent elections for an average of 864,041 while the 1994 election results show the high of 978,115 for these four election cycles. The higher voter interest in 1994 reflected the interest generated in the governorship race and the heated controversy over the pros and cons of Outcomes Based Education, and caused the closest race in history when incumbent Garrett defeated her challenger Murphy by only 9,259 votes. When these two persons competed against each other four years later, the passions of OBE cooled and the result differential returned to the typical pattern.

The share of the vote for the winning candidate in the Superintendent's race, Democrat from 1907 to 2006 and Republican from 2010 to 2014, ranged from a low of 44.7 percent in 1914 when the third-party candidate received 23.9 percent to a high of 74.7 percent in 1958, Hodge's only reelection to draw an opponent. Multiple third-party candidates in 1910 and 1914 siphoned off a combined 10 and 24 percent of the vote, respectively, resulting in 1914 being the only year since statehood when the winning candidate received fewer than half of the votes. From 1918 to 2006 no third party candidate(s) received a total of more than .7 percent of the votes (see appendix F).

General election results since statehood as shown in table 4.5 help explain the dominance of the Democrats in the Superintendency probably better than any other statistic or demographic. Historically a conservative state, it resembled those states south of the Mason-Dixon line. Democrats held the superior numbers since Civil War days in those states organized before 1900, and they voted against civil rights and for states' rights. Religious influences were pervasive, even if the society was divided between Black and white, and Oklahoma reflected the culture and conditions of those states.

As late as 1960, 82 percent of Oklahoma voters were registered Democrats and less than one-half percent Independents (table 4.6). Two decades later that high number was reduced only to slightly less than 76 percent, but the trend was toward fewer Democrats,

Table 4.5 General election results 1907-2014

Supt.	Year	Democratic		Republican		Other		Total
		No.	Per.	No.	Per.	No.	Per.	
Cameron	1907	139,962	54.8	99,912	41.1	9,678	3.9	242,552
Wilson	1910	118,628	50.3	93,549	39.6	23,642	10.1	235,819
Wilson	1914	107,686	44.7	75,705	31.4	57,242	23.9	240,633
Wilson	1918	101,775	56.3	78,818	43.6	n/a	n/a	180,593
Nash	1922	289,447	63.5	165,892	36.4	n/a	n/a	455,309
Nash	1926	203,005	57.7	148,558	42.2	n/a	n/a	351,563
Vaughan	1930	285,719	64.7	155,365	35.2	n/a	n/a	441,084
Vaughan	1934	353,345	66.7	174,312	32.9	1,515	0.2	529,172
Crable	1938	305,349	68.9	135,032	30.4	2,633	0.5	443,104
Crable	1942	184,539	54.9	149,671	44.4	2,419	0.7	336,629
Hodge	1946	263,751	58.6	186,185	41.3	n/a	n/a	449,936
Hodge	1950	n/a	n/a	n/a	n/a	n/a	n/a	n/a
Hodge	1954	n/a	n/a	n/a	n/a	n/a	n/a	n/a
Hodge	1958	350,472	74.7	118,373	25.2	n/a	n/a	468,845
Hodge	1962	n/a	n/a	n/a	n/a	n/a	n/a	n/a
Hodge	1966	n/a	n/a	n/a	n/a	n/a	n/a	n/a
Fisher	1970	384,397	62.1	234,357	37.9	n/a	n/a	618,754
Fisher	1974	n/a	n/a	n/a	n/a	n/a	n/a	n/a
Fisher	1978	n/a	n/a	n/a	n/a	n/a	n/a	n/a
Fisher	1982	511,176	64.2	284,443	35.7	n/a	n/a	795,619
Folks	1986	527,477	61.1	336,643	38.9	n/a	n/a	864,120
Garrett	1990	618,008	71.5	246,435	28.5	n/a	n/a	864,443
Garrett	1994	493,687	50.5	484,428	49.5	n/a	n/a	978,115
Garrett*	1998	520,270	60.2	343,291	39.8	n/a	n/a	863,616
Garrett	2002	609,851	59.7	411,814	40.3	n/a	n/a	1,021,615
Garrett	2006	576,304	62.6	343,900	37.4	n/a	n/a	920,204
Barresi	2010	387,007	37.7	573,716	55.9	65,243	6.4	1,025,966
Hofmeister	2014	361,878	44.2	457,053	55.8	n/a	n/a	818,931

Sources: *Oklahoma Elections: Statehood to Present*, vol.1 (OKC: SEB,1994); www.ok.gov/elections.

Note: Percent totals may not equal 100 as a result of rounding each column's percentage to tenths.

* Only instance when the incumbent and the challenger were the same persons as in the previous election.

more Republicans, and minimal change in the number identifying with either party and labeled Independents. A monumental shift occurred in voter registration and voter action in the two decades leading up to 2000 with a precipitous drop in the ratio of Democrats to Republicans, 56.7 percent to 35 percent. Ten years later the Democrats' piece of the pie chart slipped under half and, by the 2014 election, only 44.8 percent identified themselves as such. Both the Republican and Independent registrations were rising so that by this election they had 43.2 percent and 12 percent, respectively. In all elections prior to 2010, the Democratic candidate won and, in each of the two elections since then, the Republican won. For the Republican to be the winner, some Independents and Democrats had to support the Republican. Whether the shift in voter attitudes has been equally seismic over the long term will play out in the upcoming decades.[12]

Table 4.6 Oklahoma voter registrations 1960-2014

Year	Democratic No.	Per.	Republican No.	Per.	Independent No.	Per.	Total
1960	863,529	82.0	179,645	17.6	3,585	0.4	1,019,759
1970	922,158	76.7	267,284	22.2	6,622	0.6	1,201,666
1980	874,895	75.8	263,008	22.8	15,830	1.4	1,153,733
1990	1,239,275	64.9	624,801	32.7	46,567	2.4	1,910,643
2000	1,189,332	56.7	734,382	35.0	174,649	8.3	2,098,750
2010	999,855	49.0	813,158	39.9	225,607	11.1	2,038,620
2014	885,609	44.8	854,329	43.2	238,870	12.0	1,978,810

Source: State Election Board, www.oklahoma.gov/elections/voter-registration/voter-registration-statistics.

Note: There is only a four-year interval between the bottom two lines.

From Horse Feed to Multi-million Dollar Campaigns

From early days of feeding oats and hay to horses and later to fueling cars and buying television advertisements, funds were necessary. In several instances, aspirants spent either no funds or less than one dollar while others could list the bill for oats and hay for the horse. Obviously, the emphasis was focused on the expenditures and not the sources and amounts of contributions. These figures contrast, for example, with Barresi's report of spending in excess of two million dollars of her own assets in the 2010 and 2014 campaigns combined, far more than her opponents to win one election and lose another. Oklahoma's procedure for campaign reporting of expenditures since statehood and receipts for the past half-century reflects an evolving structure that accounted for increasing complexity in the way those funds are donated and then spent.[13]

By the 1950s, few citizens filed for the Superintendency resulting in no runoff elections and no need to file reports for those intermediate elections until 2010. In campaign finance in general, heightened public interest in expenditures, resulting in legislative action in 1968 to add general election data to the reports, expanded in the next five decades to expect a greater degree of transparency in reporting. Campaign finance laws were on the books for the early years, but numerous loopholes allowed for inconsistent reporting. Impetus for more accurate information was provided by the Watergate scandal in 1974. Oklahoma was one of many states to add campaign finance reforms and ethics rules immediately. For example, individual contributors of $200 or more were listed and a maximum of $5,000 per family was set. Generally, wariness of the contributions to the Superintendency candidates was less than that of other positions such as legislators who were reluctant to open the window of review. The citizens pressed forward and it resulted in legislative enactment of the Oklahoma Ethics Commission with authority to administer greater oversight of campaign finances. Political chicanery and legislator recalcitrance, along with the urging of Governor Bellmon, provided the fuel for an initiative petition in 1990 that led to State Question 627 to enshrine the Oklahoma Ethics Commission in the constitution. But, for each step forward in campaign finance reporting, pushback followed, evident today in the Legislature's refusal to fund the Ethics Commission sufficiently to conduct its investigations and comply with the law.[14]

Throughout the Superintendency campaigning history the amount of money expended by the incumbent, relative to that of the challenger, minimally affected the vote. It was important, however, that those competing raised and spent some money as indicative of their interest in the position, their commitment to assuming the role with an air of confidence and assurance, and their ability to raise money. Until 2010, a Democrat's odds of winning were more than even, and, since then, a Republican has enjoyed a decided advantage. Party affiliation trumped financial contributions as the most salient factor in general elections. Over time, focus on expenditures waned as sources and amounts of contributions attracted greater purview. Monitoring the sources of donations was necessary to determine the donor's purpose, especially when the trend toward greater privatization of education options (e.g., private schools, parochial schools, and virtual schools) opened the door for crass commercialization and opportunism. Analyses of sources of contributions became feasible when such information was required.

Historically, candidates for the Superintendency, particularly incumbents, sought campaign contributions from the education establishment: teachers, administrators, and Department personnel. Large amounts were not needed and educators, for the most part, did not possess expansive assets to donate nor were they inclined to do so for political purposes. Business owners were becoming dissatisfied in the late 1980s with what they perceived as ineffective public schools receiving funds with no plans for significant changes (e.g., public funding for both public and private school options) by the legislative and executive branches of government. Many in the business sector were incensed when a Republican governor, Bellmon, pushed through a bill to infuse a large amount of money into the schools in large part to compensate for several years of insufficient tax revenue. Sandy Garrett, early in her tenure, intentionally and gradually moved to enlarge her support base, realistically sensing a shift in how the Department was viewed in the larger functioning of government and an appreciation of the increasing cost of campaigning. While she enjoyed visibility in the Department, connections to the larger citizenry via her brief stint as Secretary of Education showed her the importance of a broad base. Succeeding her was Janet Barresi whose ties to the business community, especially in Oklahoma City, and to private, for-profit education companies and like-minded educators across the country, and her undisguised disdain for the state's education establishment created a political environment with many voters who were attracted to her campaign platform. Her tumultuous tenure placed her second campaign in great jeopardy for she had alienated much of the corporate, moneyed interest and left her to self-fund the cost of her reelection effort.[15]

Campaign expenditure reports from all candidates for primary elections only were required by statute beginning in 1910. Exact format of the expenditures was not prescribed, thus the reports varied in the presentation of the data. In that election with five candidates, two Democrats and three Republicans, each of the two Democrats reported spending more money than the total of the three Republicans. Passions were running high where the Democratic incumbent E. D. Cameron from the capital city of Guthrie drew challenger R. H. Wilson, Grady County superintendent, and the consensus was that the primary winner would most likely be successful in the general election. Cameron spent $1,428.79 for printing, a stenographer, traveling and lodging, postage, advertising in eighteen newspapers, and a $125 donation to the Democratic Committee. Ironically, his campaign gave money, 11.1 percent of his expenses, to the state Democratic Party in an election where he lost by 14 percentage points. Wilson's largest costs, railroad fares, postage, printing, and advertisements in seventy-three newspapers, totaled $1,454.34. Republican candidate G. D. Moss reported his neatly-presented and categorized expenditures of $225.81 on Cheyenne Public Schools stationery: railroad fares, hotel bills, printing, postage, and horse feed for $1.25. A second Republican, John Evans, listed losses suffered from stolen letters containing cash to pay for newspaper ads. Other expenditures for his campaign included $6.00 for lemonade, cigars, pie, and peanuts at a Flint Ridge fundraiser and $1.00 "cash for negroes [sic] dinner on election day."[16] (see appendix J)

Improvements in the filing process were evident by the 1914 primary, for now there was a prescribed form requiring the candidate to swear to the accuracy of an attached itemized list of expenditures and to have his signature witnessed "before someone authorized to administrator oath [sic]." Incumbent Wilson listed, along with postage and stationery, cigars for $3.00. Although the same form and process continued in 1918, and Wilson complied with both, challenger J. N. Hamilton submitted a statement on Ponca City Public Schools official stationery, "No money expended." The form that year urged the candidate to prepare the application, including the candidate's name, on the typewriter because many wrote illegibly. Both candidates in the 1922 Democratic primary submitted their reports on stationery with affidavits attached. J. P. Battenberg, President of Northwestern State Teachers College, used the college's official stationery for the cover letter and itemized list, and M. A. Nash, Secretary of the Oklahoma Education Association, had personal stationery printed that listed background information, degrees earned, and employment history. Only seventy-five dollars separated the total amounts spent, Nash more, but Battenberg's travel expense was 2.3 times greater because of the distance from remote Alva to other parts of the state. The Democratic incumbent in 1926 drew no opponent in the primary, yet spent $196.25, primarily for newspaper advertising and traveling. Four Republicans vied for their primary with the range of expenditures among them, $.59 to <$25. Winner Anna Willis, Lincoln County superintendent, reported the lone expenditure of $.95 for postage. Candidates for the Superintendency were prompt and compliant with the reporting requirements such as itemization of expenditures and affixation of affidavits, and they attempted to follow the spirit of the law in the absence of guidance on categorization or format. For those few who failed to report, no adverse consequence ensued.[17]

Reporting requirements were modified minimally during the 1930s and 1940s with expenditure categories growing from eight to ten. In these two decades candidates relied primarily on newspaper advertising and printed materials, but the mid 1940s saw the beginning of expenditures for radio time and radio recording. A. L. Crable's 1946 runoff report showed a cost for radio that represented 10 percent of his expenses. This new medium for publicizing a candidate's campaign platform would gain prominence for a few years until it was superseded by a more effective medium, the television. Another expense, unrelated to advertising, yet critical to the functioning of a campaign and comprising but a small percentage of the total costs, was first reported by John Vaughan in the Democratic primary runoff of 1934, the cost for the use of telephones. Over the decades Superintendency candidates quickly adopted whatever new inventions became available to their campaign efforts and strategies.[18]

Total campaign and winning candidate expenditures, as shown in table 4.7, for the period 1910 to 1946 display some variations in trends. As expected, in those years when more than five candidates entered the races (1922, 1934, and 1946), total expenditures were greater than years with fewer candidates with the exception of 1914. Fiercely contested primaries in 1934 and 1946 resulted in runoff elections, thus the amounts spent were nearly double the other highest years except 1914. The only primary with one lone Democratic candidate, 1926, reflects the minimal expenditures of the four Republican contestants. Consistently throughout these decades Republican contenders spent far less money than the Democrats. With the exceptions of 1926 (little competition) and 1946 (great competition), the winning candidates spent between 1,095 and 1,495 dollars not considering inflation. However, a calculation of the inflation over those decades shows the 1934 election to be the only one to exceed the expenditure amounts of the 1910 and 1914 elections. The 1910 winner's expenditures were three-fourths that of the 1946 winner's, but, in inflated dollars, the latter amount of $934 was only 65 percent of the former. In real value, winning candidates in the early years spent considerably more than in the later years.[19]

Because of the absence of contested primaries, no expenditure reports were submitted after 1946 until the 1970 election cycle when a law, enacted in the 1960s, required candidates, in one final report, to identify donors who gave ≥ $500 and the amounts of their donations, and to indicate total contributions in the primary, the general election, or both. Concern over who was trying to influence the politicians through contributions was manifested in this attempt to inform the public of the sources of the money for all elections. Categorization of expenditures was continued, but now with greater differentiation and increased awareness of the electronic media as reflected in these groupings: personal services, printing, radio and television, billboards, general advertising, and miscellaneous expenses. The 1970 election cycle drew candidates Charles Holleyman, Leslie Fisher, and Scott Tuxhorn and they spent 46, 37, and 35 percent of their total funds, respectively, on radio and television advertising. Printing and newspapers were

Table 4.7 Number of candidates and campaign expenditures 1910-2014

Election	No. of cand.*	Total spent	Equiv. 1913 dollars**	Winner spent	Equiv. 1913 dollars
1910	5	3,613	3,613	1,454	1,454
1914	5	4,044	3,963	1,461	1,432
1918	4	2,962	1,922	1,482	962
1922	7	3,287	1,917	1,244	726
1926†	5	233	130	197	110
1930	3	2,296	1,355	1,095	646
1934	9	5,795††	4,238	1,215††	889
1938	4	2,206	1,533	1,478	1,027
1942	3	2,638	1,576	1,495	893
1946	7	6,541††	3,237	1,917	949
			Equiv. 1970 dollars		Equiv. 1970 dollars
1970‡	3	87,159	87,159	52,140	52,140
1982‡‡	2	n/d	n/d	n/d	n/d
1986	2	n/d	n/d	80,000	28,321
1990	3	330,260	95,735	247,626	71,781
1994	3	275,305	70,125	202,883	51,678
1998	3	453,008	104,925	421,835	97,704
2002	2	545,628	114,518	458,741	96,282
2006	2	376,217	69,882	375,617	69,771
2010	4	2,092,445	362,800	1,222,233	211,918
2014	7	3,157,306	500,928	818,932	129,929

Sources: Oklahoma State Archives; State Election Board; bls.gov/data/inflation_calculator.htm.

Note: Election cycles from 1910-1969 required candidates to file expenses only for the primary and any runoff elections. From 1970-2014 candidates were required to file expenditure reports for all elections in a cycle.

* For the years 1910-1946 the number shown is the number of candidates in the primary elections only. The numbers for the years 1970-2014 are for all elections, however, the 2010 election is the only one that includes a third party candidate in the general election.

** For example, the $6,541 spent in 1946 was equivalent to $3,237 in 1913, or $376 less than spent in 1910. January 1, 1913 was chosen as the reference point because the US Bureau of Labor Statistics began its calculation of inflation from that date. July of the election year was selected as the comparison date from 1913 to 2014. To determine equivalent 1970 dollars January 1 of that year was chosen to be the comparison date.

† No Democratic primary, but the candidate reported expenditures.

†† Election cycle included a runoff.

‡ No primary elections occurred during the previous twenty-four years and only one general election in 1956. No elections occurred in 1974 and 1978 because the Superintendent ran unopposed.

‡‡ Neither the Oklahoma State Archives nor the State Election Board could locate campaign expenditure reports for the 1982 and 1986 elections. It is assumed the records are not extant. The winner, John Folks, estimated his expenditures to be the amount shown.

giving way to electronic forms of communication resulting in much broader coverage, but at an increased cost. Regarding identification of donors and amounts of donations, Holleyman, who lost in the primary, listed six donors including himself giving $4,319 of a total of $15,309. Fisher identified only three donors for a total of $2,115 out of more than $52,000 raised, meaning almost all of his donations were small amounts and indicating broad support from many people. Tuxhorn essentially self-funded his campaign by contributing two-thirds of the total spent. Compliance with the reporting law was not complicated and gave the citizens important information about donors and how the funds were spent (see appendix J).[20]

Campaign costs escalated quickly from the 1970 to the 1990 elections with Garrett's expenditure alone in 1990 almost triple the aggregate of the three candidates in the 1970 election. For her five election campaigns she raised $1,706,706, almost six times that of her opponents collectively as shown in table 4.8. No pattern is reflected in her expenditures, but the close outcome in 1994 spurred her to seek greater contributions in 1998 and 2002. After sixteen years, her reputation discouraged any significant competitor, allowing her to decrease the amount spent from 2002 by 18 percent.

Donations and expenditures exploded in the 2010 and 2014 elections when Barresi had "deep pockets" and a willingness to invest whatever was needed to win. However, her strongest opponent in each of those elections spent over $850,000 in 2010 and only $30,000 less than that amount four years later. Election season 2014 offered more of the same as both Republicans and Democrats were determined to replace the incumbent, more so the Republicans because they now had the political leverage in voter support.

Table 4.8 Campaign expenditures of Sandy Garrett's tenure 1990-2006

Election	Candidate	Amount	Election	Candidate	Amount
1990	Sandy Garrett (D)	247,626	2002	Sandy Garrett (D)	458,747
	David Fisher (D)	67,816		Lloyd Roettger (R)	86,881
	Gerald Hoeltzel (R)	14,818		Subtotal	545,628
	Subtotal	330,260			
1994	Sandy Garrett (D)	202,883	2006	Sandy Garrett (D)	375,617
	Earl Garrison (D)	8,930		Bill Crozier (R)	600
	Linda Murphy (R)	63,492		Subtotal	376,217
	Subtotal	275,305			
1998	Sandy Garrett (D)	421,835	1990-2006		
	Tod Williams (R)	1,041		Sandy Garrett	1,706,708
	Linda Murphy (R)	30,133		Opponents	273,711
	Subtotal	453,009		Total	1,980,419

Sources: 1990 data, Oklahoma State Archives, ODL, OKC; 1994-2006 data, Oklahoma State Ethics Commission.

Note: D—Democrat, R—Republican.

Hofmeister, a political novice, raised about half the amount of Barresi and almost twice as much as the Democratic opponent in the general election to ride to victory. All candidates raised a combined total of 3.175 million dollars with Barresi personally donating almost half of that amount.[21]

One egregious method of raising campaign funds over the decades operated within the Department solely, involved employees only, and surfaced in at least two long-tenured administrations. Essentially, administrative level, non-civil service personnel were "informed" of their expected participation in the reelection effort by a deputy superintendent so as to keep the Superintendent above such unscrupulous and despicable deeds and "unaware" of the fund-raising scheme. With some variation in process, the administrations of both Hodge and Garrett participated in this behavior, all the while the Superintendent protesting any knowledge of what was transpiring.

Confirmation of the extent of this support was realized with the enactment of the Ethics Commission rule mandating specificity of donors' names and amounts of contributions. Even before this more recent mandate, rumors surfaced periodically over the seemingly illegal and surreptitiously conducted fund-raising schemes. Hodge initially denied knowledge of any such activity occurring under his watch under pressure from *The Oklahoman*, and then took the noble approach of assuming responsibility. This incident occurred in late spring of 1950, in the fourth year of his first term when he ultimately drew no opponent. There was no hiding the scheme when *The Oklahoman* broke the news and several employees were fingered for participation in the process. Amounts to be donated ranged from a high of two weeks' pay, later reduced to one week's pay, to five dollars. Hodge reported that fifty-seven of 116 employees donated to the cause, all voluntarily, because he was doing such good work and they wanted to see him continue in that role. Just four years earlier he had persuaded the Board to give him patronage "unofficially" because the Legislature had withdrawn it from his predecessor in 1942 over the conflict over the balanced budget. Only was that prerogative returned to him officially in 1949. Most of the employees in the Department were beholden to him for their employment and devotees to his continued tenure. Hodge took umbrage with the newspaper's questioning of a practice "requested" by the employees and sought approbation in the public square by acknowledging the scheme and clarifying his position: "I have no apology to make on behalf of myself and any employees in this matter. We have done only that which the majority of the personnel of the department wanted done in regard to the campaign."[22]

Garrett, on the other hand, never had her Department fund raising scheme exposed by the press; none-the-less, it operated, albeit at a more restricted level. Specifically, administrative meetings over which she presided would have "breaks" when she vacated the room and a deputy would preside. In her absence, plans were laid for the level of involvement of those present from hosting a fund-raising party to contributing a predetermined amount. After this brief interlude, Garrett would return and the "official" meeting would resume. Following such a meeting, those present would return to their respective departments, call the employees within their units together, and explain "what they needed to do." Employees at the Department understood the importance of their donating when they were considered for a promotion: "We definitely know we work in a political environment and you have to be a supporter to get ahead in the Department."[23]

Department employees, at least from the Hodge era and following, were expected to contribute to the reelection of their bosses either through monetary or time donations. Level of responsibility within the organization determined somewhat the amount of the donation with those higher in the hierarchy contributing more generously than lower level employees. Though the Superintendent was not directly involved in the solicitation, the responsible person informed the Superintendent of the amounts and contributors. The State Ethics Commission, when informed of multiple allegations of campaign violations in the 2002 election, mailed warnings to school districts and the Department to cease such actions. When Garrett's chief of staff, Lealon Taylor, was "accused of calling school administrators during work hours for contributions," she responded: "Absolutely no campaign activities are conducted at the state Department of Education."[27] At no time did she acknowledge publicly any unscrupulous behavior or activity.

Candidates running for the Superintendency were engaged in campaign strategies and methods similar to contemporary politicians. Face-to-face contact through speeches, fund-raising dinners, addresses at conventions, and other settings were practiced throughout history. In this capacity, incumbents enjoyed an advantage at no cost to their campaigns. Those Superintendents offering statewide summer conferences for school district administrators promoted their "educational agendas" and tried to create loyalty, all the while benefitting from the taxpayers' dollars.

The print media dominated the publicity efforts before the advent and widespread use of radio and then television. In the earliest days, candidates and campaigns bought advertisements in the newspapers, sometimes using a photo and always a brief caption or a one-to-two column statement of accomplishments and intentions. Friends of the candidates purchased advertisements in the larger town and city newspapers touting the qualifications and strengths of their candidates and highlighting reasons why the opponent was unacceptable. Reputable publications read by educators reported on the activities of the incumbent and would frequently have articles written by the Superintendents who served in influential leadership positions in educators' organizations, giving them visibility among that segment of the voters and opportunities to test the viability of their ideas and programs. Old fashion correspondence was not overlooked as an important means of communication. Wilson, in 1921-22, was completing his third term, and simultaneously running for the governorship by writing and receiving letters requesting and announcing support for his campaign. He was careful to send his letters on non-Department stationery, but originators of letters to him were not. Mack Phillips, Superintendent of McCurtain County schools, wrote of his support under his office's letterhead.[24]

Early day travel by railroad, after a generation or so, evolved into the more flexible automobile transportation as roads and highways became paved and this mode of movement became financially affordable. Over the decades, meeting the voters face-to-face in large and small groups was a priority, and continued so into the twenty-first century. Most candidates logged tens of thousands of miles crisscrossing the state and visited all or many of the seventy-seven counties to inform the citizens of their ideas about how to improve the state's education system.

Crable, probably more than any other Superintendent, was active in the Democratic Party through membership in various groups and participating in annual meetings of the party. Both Crable and his wife were identified as members in the 1945 publication of The Women's Democratic Council of Oklahoma. Earlier, Crable wrote a brief statement, "Keep Roosevelt," in the 1940 Speakers' Manual, issued by the Democratic State Central Committee. Campaign advertisements appeared in publications of several Democratic Party groups.[25]

Television, and more recently internet, advertising became preferred vehicles for widespread communication of the positive aspects of one's candidacy and the undesirable parts of the opponent's platform. To engage this format required large amounts of money and was available only to those who generated sizeable campaign chests. Also, every candidate wished to avoid controversy and to be portrayed positively in the news cycle, thus receiving free advertisement. Advent of the internet and its capability as a relatively inexpensive form of communication became another opportunity for politicians to connect to their constituents. Various social media became vehicles for candidates to raise their profiles and attain name recognition. But, with each new avenue for communication came additional costs and the necessity for aspirants to prioritize their spending. Campaign coordinators and polling experts boosted the cost of running for office. Raising money, always important, became more critical than ever before.

Nothing enhances a political campaign and allows for much publicity more than lots of money from donors willing to exert their influence or from candidates with ample assets. Merging in the 2010 campaign were the Republicans' aspiration finally to win and the Democrats' hope to maintain their historical edge. Coincidentally, Barresi, who was not reluctant to spend from her substantial assets that exceeded any Superintendent candidate ever, was committed to winning regardless of how much of her personal wealth was tapped to achieve the goal. After committing a large sum to win the office initially, she was similarly prepared to repeat the financial commitment of four years previously. In the three months leading up to the unsuccessful 2014 primary, she donated almost $910,000 of her own money, and the campaign spent in excess of $1,000,000 for media placement and production.[26]

Candidates for the Superintendency, including incumbents, had minimal name recognition statewide, always needing to compete with those running for governor, other executive offices, and legislative positions. Incumbents, knowing their records in office would be scrutinized by the media, calculated the political consequence of their decisions. With the internet and more overall intensive analyses of candidates' histories, political campaigns will be particularly attuned to countering negative efforts to discount competitors' allegations. Term limits imposed through the 2010 law should free those Superintendents in their second terms from a tendency to skew their thinking in light of competing for another term. Until the position is no longer elective it will embody the positive and negative aspects of political campaigns.

Chapter 5
The Superintendents
(1907-2015)

Richard Fox and Jennifer Lawless posit that "democracy cannot function as intended if competent, politically interested citizens do not exhibit…interest in running for office and a willingness to present a battle of ideas to voters," while Matt Barreto and Matthew Streb emphasize that "Competitive elections draw larger voter turnouts, encourage greater citizen political engagement, and heighten elected officials' responsiveness to their constituents."[1] The history of the Oklahoma Superintendency when examined by these descriptors of a healthy democracy reflects an executive office that in some decades was healthier than in others. Incumbents drew strong challengers, most frequently in the primary elections, until the mid-forties, the early 1990s, and in 2014. The Superintendency in Oklahoma is unique in the rate of the office holders who obtained their offices through gubernatorial appointment and then seeking the position at the next election cycle, and in the frequency of elections where the incumbent ran unopposed. Six of the fourteen Superintendents were thrust into the job initially by appointment and most can be assumed had not been considering the position. Once in office all of these individuals but one then reconsidered their career goals and decided to compete for the office. Governors were desirous of their appointees achieving success both to finish the terms, seek reelection, and be rewarded with a full term. Appointees had a trial period to test their fitness to the position, but those elected received the affirmation of the voters.

"You Never Know What You Can Do Until You Try…"

Author C. S. Lewis captured to some degree a person's thinking when mulling over the decision to contest for a political office. He did add, however, "very few try unless they have to."[2] Candidates vying for the Superintendency via election were able to ponder their career goals and aspirations, but mid-term resignations from the office, and one death, allowed little time for the governors to find viable replacements and for those accepting to refocus their career plans. Many factors influence a person's decision to seek elective office: (e.g. self-selection, viability, voter acceptance, legal and credential qualification, personality and charisma, personal financial capacity, fund-raising skills, motivation, and political party affiliation). All are important but not all carry equal weight, forcing candidates to consider their strengths and weaknesses. Appointees were faced with varying lengths of time remaining in the terms and thus had to calculate the political headwinds facing them—Democrats always won and Republicans always lost. With minor exception, the Superintendents were career educators who did not begin their life's work aspiring to be the top education officials. Circumstances along the way afforded them the opportunity and they availed themselves of it. Some were more competent and productive while others stumbled and paid the political consequences. Politics prior to their first day on the job affected their performances and their ability to deal with political reality determining their fate.

All but one of the Superintendents competed in the elective process and, by doing so, viewed themselves as possessing sufficient experience, capable of winning, and competently fulfilling the duties of the office. Before completing the filing form and paying the application fee, six had had the advantage of serving a "trial" period and eight contemplated the implications without having intimate position insight. Various angles were approached and personal desires and ambitions were weighed. Beyond the constitutional criteria, what was their familiarity with the duties and responsibilities of the position, reputational strengths, career experiences, and political affiliations? Those who completed unexpired terms could point to their accomplishments as evidence of their ability to perform the duties. Each of the chapters in Part III, except thirteen which describes two appointees and nineteen which introduces Joy Hofmeister only through her inauguration, delves into the life and Superintendency of a person who occupied the office for more than two years.

Because the Superintendency is that arm of the government charged with the administration of the common school system, the overseer of that function is expected to have some knowledge of the schools and ability to manage a large agency. In the early days of the Department a handful of persons carried out the duties working through the county superintendents and, after several decades of district consolidations and eventual elimination of the county superintendency, that number expanded to reach a handful of hundreds of employees. Cameron, whose status as a territorial Superintendent was similar to the appointed Superintendents since statehood, asserted that he was familiar with the position, believed his reputation was broadly known across the new state, and was not averse to the political nature of the position. He would have some leverage to set precedence within the broad spectrum of education. Wilson was known in education circles to be a creative and beneficially aggressive county superintendent, and he hoped to lead the state in the formative decade. Nash advanced through several education positions including the OEA and the Department, but had no aspirations for a long tenure in the Superintendency and used it as a stepping-stone to higher education administration. Vaughan brought a breadth of experiences, having served as an elected state senator and higher education official and was succeeded by Crable with Department and higher education experience, but whose tenure was laden with controversy. Hodge navigated multiple election cycles while serving as Tulsa County superintendent for a decade. Fisher led multiple districts, rural and suburban, and opted to dip his toe into the political water when there was a weak incumbent. He was succeeded by Folks whose short tenure followed nearly a decade of service within the Department. Garrett, with several years of Departmental work on her resumé, filed while serving as the Secretary, appreciating the fact that she had a weak opponent. After another two decades, absent an incumbent, and a culmination of a seismic shift in statewide party devotion, Barresi, with limited experience, mounted a successful campaign with little doubt regarding her motive to shake up the education establishment. Finally, Hofmeister, with the thinnest credentials, seized the moment in fall 2014 to capitalize on Barresi's failed leadership and to carry the Republican banner and agenda forward. All three of the Republican appointees presented credentials in experience and education equal to or greater than their Democratic counterparts, but they could not overcome their party affiliation. In the late 1960s and again in 1990 Republican candidates faced insurmountable obstacles as the minority party with a limited share of the registered voters.

Events shaped the Superintendents who, in turn, affected the direction of the Department. Cameron, slightly, Crable, Hoeltzel, and Barresi, more so, struggled to achieve some equilibrium. Wilson and Fisher led quite well during significant statutory changes, federal and state. Hodge and Garrett served with Republican governors (five and eight years, respectively), adapted well in general and enjoyed long tenures, eventually leaving office with their reputations intact. Nash and Folks left office before lasting changes could materialize and, for the latter, after mounting frustration. Creech and Tuxhorn were the brief and relatively insignificant hyphen between twenty-one and fourteen year tenures; and Hofmeister was just beginning.

Democratic dominance for a century left the Republicans with enough frustration to begin exploring ways of working the system to triumph over what they deemed to be inequitable conditions. Waiting what seemed like forever eventually paid dividends in the 2010 election when the Republicans not only swept the statewide offices and the Legislature, but collected enough support to change the Constitution to restrict the Superintendent to two terms. Oklahoma joined the southern states' moves to the right of the political spectrum to give Republicans the opportunity to govern, in part, by acting quickly to lower taxes and constrict government. The Republican Party in general desired government-funded options for nonpublic school students, requiring all candidates to espouse this particular plank in their platform. A compliant Legislature in Oklahoma opened the door for such funding even though a majority of the citizens opposed using public money for private purposes. Regardless, the minority party's newly-acquired dominance was setting the agenda and the candidates hoping to get elected needed to hew to the party line.

Time in Office

Superintendents' time in office, a critical determinant to assess their potential for fulfillment of significant objectives and strategies, can be characterized by tenures of about ten years or more and less than five years. Appointees to finish unexpired terms are typically constricted to finishing the plans of their predecessors and one-term Superintendents frequently depart prior to pursuing their initiatives to fruition. On the other hand, Superintendents with long tenures are afforded multiple opportunities to try new projects and schemes if they are willing to risk the political challenges to do so. Six elected Superintendents served a combined period of eighty-seven years as opposed to seven elected or appointed with accumulated time of twenty years. Of the ten (Hofmeister excluded) elected Superintendents, three served for short tenures and two for two decades each. The Superintendency, which emphasizes administration and management, is not an office where incumbents are necessarily rewarded for being leaders who are willing to take aggressive stands on cutting edge theories and cultural issues. Hodge, as a long-tenured Superintendent, steered a middle ground regarding the desegregation thrust, Garrett with a similar length of tenure almost was defeated in 1994 over the Outcomes Based Education controversy, and Crable eventually paid the price for his opposition to the balanced budget amendment and participation in an alleged illegal textbook publishing scheme. Likewise, Barresi was not reelected in part over her attempts to force private options to compete with the public schools.

Table 5.1 Tenure and political party of Superintendents 1907-2015

Superintendent	Party	Tenure	Length
E. D. Cameron	Democratic	Nov. 16, 1907-Jan. 9, 1911	3y, 2m
R. H. Wilson	Democratic	Jan. 9, 1911-Jan. 8, 1923	12y
M. A. Nash	Democratic	Jan. 8, 1923-April 9, 1927	4y, 3m
John Vaughan	Democratic	April 9, 1927-Aug. 19, 1936	9y, 4m
A. L. Crable	Democratic	Aug. 19, 1936-Jan. 13, 1947	10y, 5m
Oliver Hodge	Democratic	Jan. 13, 1947-Jan. 14, 1968	21 y
D. D. Creech*	Republican	April 16, 1968-Dec. 31, 1969	1y, 8.5m
Scott Tuxhorn*	Republican	Jan. 1, 1970-Jan. 11, 1971	1y, .5m
Leslie Fisher	Democratic	Jan. 11, 1971-June 30, 1984	13y, 5.5m
John Folks	Democratic	July 1, 1984-June 30, 1988	4y
Gerald Hoeltzel*	Republican	July 19, 1988-Jan. 8, 1991	2.5y
Sandy Garrett	Democratic	Jan. 8, 1991-Jan. 11, 2011	20y
Janet Barresi	Republican	Jan. 11, 2011-Jan. 13, 2015	4y
Joy Hofmeister	Republican	Jan. 13, 2015-	n/a

Notes: E. H. McDonald, Deputy State Superintendent, was appointed by Governor Bartlett to serve as the interim Superintendent from January 14-April 16, 1968. Governor Bellmon waited nineteen days, from July 1 to 19, 1988, while he searched for someone to complete the unexpired term.

* Appointed but not elected.

Demographics

Elected officials' demographics in a representative democracy would logically reflect those of the dominant power group of citizens, and the Superintendency in Oklahoma is no exception. Through the twentieth century, most Oklahoma politicians and Superintendency candidates were white, male, and well educated members of society. To elucidate and expand upon a description of those who served in this important education position, an array of demographics—gender, race or ethnicity, birth state, age, marital status, number of children, and religious affiliation—was analyzed to determine the degree of homogeneity within the Superintendent group and the similarity of that group to the population at large. How much alike were the demographics of those elected and the citizens at-large and were important segments of the population unrepresented or underrepresented because they were powerless and "invisible?"[3]

Gender

Historically women were not deemed qualified for government executive offices in the United States, and particularly in Oklahoma with a constitutional prohibition at statehood that was not removed until 1942. It would be another almost fifty years before a female opted to run for the office and, not surprisingly, it was for the Superintendency. Women dominated the teaching profession, but not the administration of the schools. Regardless, the voters were receptive to having a female head of the agency. Gender ratios were not static across the decades with 115 males to 100 females in 1906, dropping to 110 to 100 in 1920, and eventually reaching a 50.5 to 49.5 percentage split in 2010.[4] More female voters meant more potential support for female candidates. Sandy Garrett had the advantage through a brief tenure as the Secretary, a position to which she was appointed by a respected and popular Republican governor. When she faced a relatively weak opponent in 1990 Democratic primary and a yet weaker Republican opponent in the general election, Garrett won and provided the transition from all male elected or appointed Superintendents to all female thereafter. The public's acceptability of women in leadership positions, in general and in Oklahoma in particular, encouraged women to enter politics and to compete for top positions. After the door opened in 1990, women representing the two major parties contested the Superintendency in four of the next six general elections. (A more detailed examination and analysis of women's struggles for suffrage and equality in the education arena is presented in chapter 6.)

Birthplace/Durational Residency Requirement

Birthplace is not necessarily germane to assessing qualifications of the Superintendent, but one's place of residence prior to becoming Superintendent may affect one's perspective of the education system. Birth states of the first six Superintendents as shown in table 5.2 were not atypical of residents in the first half-century of statehood. These Superintendents came as young adults or were brought as children by their parents and

Table 5.2 Superintendents' demographics

Superintendent	Birthdate	Birth state	Children*	Denomination	AS†
E. D. Cameron	Feb. 26, 1862	N. Carolina	1d, 5s	Meth/Bapt	44
R. H. Wilson	July 25, 1873	Kentucky	1d, 1s	Baptist	37
M. A. Nash	July 20, 1890	Texas	1d, 3s	Baptist	32
John Vaughan	Oct. 29, 1885	Tennessee	1d	Baptist	41
A. L. Crable	Nov. 27, 1889	Texas	1d, 2s	Baptist	47
Oliver Hodge	Sept. 24, 1901	Missouri	-0-	Christian	45
D. D. Creech‡	July 1, 1917	Oklahoma	1d, 2s	Methodist	50
Scott Tuxhorn‡	Mar. 4, 1928	Oklahoma	1d, 2s	Christian	41
Leslie Fisher	Jan. 17, 1992	Oklahoma	2d, 1s	Baptist	48
John Folks	Mar. 17, 1948	Oklahoma	2s	Ch. of Christ	36
Gerald Hoeltzel‡	Dec. 17, 1934	Oklahoma	1d, 2s	Lutheran	53
Sandy Garrett	Feb. 8, 1943	Oklahoma	1s	Methodist	47
Janet Barresi	Mar. 6, 1952	Oklahoma	2s	Catholic	59
Joy Hofmeister	Sept. 7, 1964	Missouri	2d, 2s	Baptist	50

*Children: d—daughter, s—son.
†Age when sworn in.
‡Appointed, but never elected.

easily qualified for the executive office by residing within the state beyond the minimum of three years (until 1942). Joy Hofmeister, the only Superintendent since then born beyond the state's borders, was brought to Oklahoma as a young child. No Superintendent's birth or any part of life was lived north of the Mason-Dixon line or west of Texas. Oklahoma's historically unfavorable educational reputation was not conducive to attracting highly qualified individuals with a record of leadership excellence, and a ten-year durational residency requirement, longer than every other state except Missouri, effectively discouraged "outsiders" from vying for the Superintendency.[5]

Race/Ethnicity

Oklahoma's racial composition since statehood has been a mix of Caucasian, Native American, African American and, to a lesser extent until recently, Latino. With all of the Superintendents elected prior to 1970 born outside of Oklahoma, there was less likelihood any would have Indian blood than if they were native to eastern Oklahoma. Native born Oklahomans Fisher, Folks, and Barresi claimed no Indian blood, nor did Missourian Hofmeister. Garrett's 1/64th Cherokee blood quantum barely stands out in an otherwise all Caucasian Superintendency. With only one Superintendent possessing Native American heritage and tribal membership, the office has been strictly skewed Caucasian. Oklahoma's current racial demography shows significant percentages of Native American, African American, and Latino citizens (11.1 percent in 2010 and growing rapidly), but they remain unrepresented or underrepresented. Eligibility requirements, inadequate political capital, and insufficient financial capacity have challenged minorities' aspirations and desires, and will continue to do so as long as the position is elective. Additionally, attitudes toward minority acceptability discouraged any individuals who might have had aspirations for the position. Legalized segregation was in effect until the 1950's, but its demise did not translate to immediate "qualification." Only recently have more Native Americans begun to pursue high-ranking executive office positions.[6]

Age

Age as a factor when one seeks or is appointed to office is important for reasons beyond meeting the constitutional minimum. More years to compile a varied resumé can better qualify a person for a position, but at some point age then can become a negative factor. Candidates can view their career status with what their ultimate goals might be and how long they might want to serve should they be elected and reelected. Gender and age for the elected Superintendents were intertwined when males assumed office at more than nine years younger than females. Caution is urged, however, in assigning too much significance to this statistic and to the fact that appointed Superintendents who were not subsequently elected were almost seven years older than their counterparts. Significant though is the fact that the males could and did pursue work opportunities beyond their time in the Superintendency with the exceptions of Hodge who died and Fisher who retired, both in their mid sixties. Two of the three who assumed the Superintendency while in their thirties served brief tenures before going on to distinguished careers in other positions.

Marital Status

Marriage compatibility was stronger among this group of educational leaders than the general population in Oklahoma with its relatively high divorce rate. To their advantage, none of the Superintendents had to expend energy explaining personal issues to the media or to being subjected to inquiries into aspects of their lives preferably hidden from public view. All of the Superintendents were married at least several years before assuming the office, and continued so throughout their their terms, except Garrett who was divorced almost two decades prior to her election in 1990 and Barresi whose husband died suddenly the year before her election (see appendix A).[7]

Parenthood

Because the Superintendent administers the department responsible for oversight of the education of the state's school children, that person's understanding of the dynamics of learning and parent-child interaction should naturally be enhanced by being a parent. A parent should better comprehend the challenges and rewards of rearing a child who has to navigate school. Concomitantly, the age of one's children may affect career decisions. Superintendents in their thirties and forties juggled their parental and work responsibilities with the latter infringing on parental responsibilities being a persuasive factor in Folks's decision to resign mid year in 1988. Those with emancipated children were able to devote more of their time to their duties. Except for Hodge, who served the longest tenure, all Superintendents had children with the number ranging from one to six and the average, 2.6.[8]

Religious Affiliation

Superintendents' religious affiliations reflected that of the state's general population. Religious diversity in the state was minimal with conservative Christians (mostly Protestant) dominant and few citizens representing themselves as non-Christian, resulting in an overall conservative bent to religion and many social issues. Catholics comprised 8 percent of the population, equivalent to the denominational affiliation of one of the Superintendents. Oklahomans desired a Superintendent who reflected their traditional values and was an advocate particularly of their rural constituent interests. Superintendents allowed Christian religious practices within the schools that had been forbidden for decades by the US Supreme Court, taking the position that it was a local board issue rather than one on which the Superintendent should take an advocacy stance. Similarly, Tuxhorn, for example, argued that sex education curriculum and materials should be locally determined rather than at the Department or Board level. Somewhat related, Superintendent Hodge pushed for local decision-making on the desegregation issue.[9]

Attaining Office by Appointment

Six Superintendents were initially appointed to complete unexpired terms, but none in the last twenty-five years, the longest time since statehood. Appointee status in an elective system generally connotes a relatively quick decision and consent. Forethought into what considerations would be necessary for subsequently running for the office would not be careful and deliberate. Only Folks had several months to weigh his decision to accept Governor George Nigh's offer of appointment. Ironically, his combined appointed and elected tenure's brevity matched that of Barresi's for being the shortest of elected Superintendents except for Cameron's abbreviated term at the beginning of statehood. The three Democrat appointees subsequently ran for the office and were elected, Vaughan, Crable, and Folks, and, of the three Republicans, two, Tuxhorn and Hoeltzel ran and were defeated. Only Tuxhorn did not have at least two years of an unexpired term to decide to run and to mount a campaign. Creech, the sole appointee not to complete an unexpired term, did not please Governor Bartlett who had spent political capital to persuade the Legislature to increase the Superintendent's salary to a level attractive to Creech.

Summary

The analysis portrays a collective individual representative of the dominant power and cultural structures until 1991 (white, Christian, married, and with 2.6 children), and since then (white or Native American, married/divorced, and 2.3 children). White, Anglo Saxon, Protestant, and married-with-children are the predominant descriptors with none reflecting the historic African American population or the more recent growth of the Latino population. As might be expected, the dominant cultural structure would provide the environment from which viable candidates would emerge and be elected. When a female was elected in 1990, she was in the forefront of a shift in society's thinking about the role of women. As a Native American in Oklahoma, Garrett represented a long history of that group's exclusion from decision-making in the highest offices until her appointment as Secretary. Without that visibility, would she have been able to overcome the historical advantages afforded her white, male opponent with both rural school superintendency and Department experience? While religious persuasion is one's choice, Oklahoma has always been predominantly Protestant. Barresi's Catholicism deviated from that, but not far since she represented Christianity. Gender ratios, disparate at first, evolved over the decades to a near even split by 2010. African-American percentage of the total population remained rather stable for over a century, but produced no Superintendents. Native American population statistics are somewhat difficult to trace to detect a trend, but most likely the data are consistent across the century. The Hispanic/Latino segment of the population is likewise difficult to analyze historically, but the percentage is increasing.[10]

Political Experience

Political experience can be viewed as another factor for the efficacy of the Superintendent as a person should benefit from gaining an elected position prior to running for the Superintendency. Wilson, Vaughan and Hodge, known for their tenure in the position, could credit part of their electoral success to skills and expertise they gained in politics before the Superintendency. Their competitiveness in local elections prepared them for the processes and realities of statewide elections. Vaughan's legislative endeavors not only gained him the reputation of educational expert; they eased his relationship with the legislators while he was Superintendent. Of course, those who won election to the Superintendency and then opted to seek reelection held campaigning experience. However, we can also find the cases when political capital did not translate into election to the

Superintendency: e.g., for Tuxhorn, his winning the 1962 House election from Alfalfa County was informative, but did not translate into election to the Superintendency in 1970 nor did winning an election as a Superintendent spell success for reelection for Cameron, Crable (1946), and Barresi. Not only political experience but also political affiliation were the important factors for successful running for a position. Rural and Republican in 1962 and 1970, and rural and Democratic in 2010, were the demographics not beneficial to a statewide race.

Actual and Expected Pre-Superintendency Career Experience

An absence in the Constitution of any eligibility criteria of knowledge, experience, or expertise for the executive offices, particularly for the Superintendency, was not interpreted by the public, especially those in education, to be impertinent. Generally, it was accepted and expected that educators would compete for the position. After the territorial period when three appointed Superintendents did not bring that background to the position, the consensus was that, to be given serious consideration, a contender needed to have experience in an education setting, i.e., teaching or administration or both. Prior to his brief tenure in the Oklahoma Territory Superintendency Cameron lacked any such experience, but his service then carried him over to the successful election in 1907. After Cameron and until Hofmeister, all twelve Superintendents had several years of teaching experience, half were district and two were county school superintendents, and three had Department experience following their years of teaching. After Fisher, for a period of thirty-one years with the exception of Hoeltzel, no Superintendent had previously been a district or county superintendent (table 5.3).

The location and size of school districts where Superintendents gained their teaching and administrative experiences represented the recipients of the major thrusts of the Department. Wilson through Tuxhorn served in one or more of the 5,000 smaller, mostly rural school districts while Fisher and subsequent superintendents lived in and experienced metropolitan schools. Fisher and Garrett, however, worked in small rural districts before moving to the Oklahoma City area, and thus understood the challenges and needs of non-urban settings. Consolidation of 90 percent of the districts over the decades and the elimination of the county superintendency reduced considerably the dependency of small schools on the Department and the number of rural superintendents and their political influence. Wide variations in size and complexity of districts continued, but influence at the Department level shifted considerably to the urban areas.

From Garrett's tenure onward what grew in significance was a candidate's willingness to accept and to advocate for options other than a traditional school governed by a traditional district board. As Secretary of Education Garrett expressed interest in school boards designing options and loosening student transfer rules. Barresi was instrumental in starting a charter school in Oklahoma City, and built on that success and the support of wealthy and influential citizens in the metropolitan area to achieve the Superintendency. Hofmeister's fifteen months as a Board member earned her enough cachet to parlay it into a primary win in 2014 against a weakened and embattled incumbent. Hofmeister's

Table 5.3 Public school/Department experience (years)

Superintendent	Teacher	B/CO Ad*	Dist. Supt.	CS**	SDE†
E. D. Cameron	0	0	0	0	2.75
R. H. Wilson		8††	0	3	0
M. A. Nash		11†††		0	1
John Vaughan		12†††		0	0
A. L. Crable	10	3	1	0	4
Oliver Hodge		7††	0	10	0
D. D. Creech		25†††		0	0
Scott Tuxhorn	3	4	7	0	0
Les Fisher		8††	16	0	0
John Folks	5	0	0	0	9
Gerald Hoeltzel		10††	25	0	0
Sandy Garrett	12	2‡	0	0	6
Janet Baresi	5‡‡	0	0	0	0
Joy Hofmeister	1	0	0	0	0

*Building/central office administrator: assistant principal, principal, coordinator, or assistant superintendent.
**County superintendent.
†State Department of Education.
††Indicates service as a teacher, teacher/principal, and/or principal.
†††Indicates service as a teacher, teacher/principal, principal, principal/superintendent, and/or superintendent.
‡Administrator of gifted programs.
‡‡Speech pathologist.

extremely limited experience in public education was overlooked as long as she was a Republican who promised less disharmony in the Department and would not be oppositional to multiple options including funding private schools with public money. She also had a fifteen-month period as a Board member to gain insight into the Department's structure and operation.

Expectation of any public school experience, or especially in administration, was waning by the beginning of the twenty-first century and was further eroded in 2014 when the successful candidate's resumé was almost totally devoid of such a background. From secondary student to college graduate Hofmeister was a participant in, and observer of, private schooling. Her one-year stint teaching in a public school gave her an introduction to the challenges faced when the doors are opened to all students. Later, ownership and operation of a for-profit tutoring company, and active involvement in committees and volunteering in the suburban district where her children attended school comprised her knowledge and comprehension of how the schools and teachers were constructing a learning environment.[11]

Life After the Superintendency

While the Superintendency is a key executive office in Oklahoma's state government, responsible for a large slice of the budget pie, it is not perceived to be a stepping-stone to a higher political office or, in the past half-century, to regional college presidencies where the salaries are far more generous. Only four (Nash, Vaughan, Creech, and Folks) of the thirteen Superintendents (not including Hofmeister) moved on to significant positions within Oklahoma and all of them resigned during their terms to accept these positions.

What Superintendents pursued when they left the Superintendency—by resignation, retirement, or electoral defeat—was varied and depended upon their age, aspirations, and political connections. At least two, Wilson and Fisher, desired to continue in the political spotlight, aspiring to the governorship, but were denied the opportunity by the electorate. Wilson was almost fifty and still had valuable years ahead of him, and Fisher, at sixty-four, opted for retirement. Both discovered that their tenures as Superintendents were insufficient to get them elected to the governorship. Nash, Vaughan, and Creech parlayed their experiences and political connections into college presidencies (Oklahoma College for Women, Northeastern State Teachers College, and Northeastern Oklahoma Junior College, respectively) and, for Nash, eventually into the chancellorship of the state's higher education system. Vaughan died suddenly while president at Northeastern after serving a decade and a half and Creech eventually retired from the NEO presidency.

No residual benefits from their experiences at the highest level of the common school system were achieved either by Hodge who died in office and by Garrett and Barresi who retired or by Tuxhorn and Crable who transitioned into non education-related, federal government positions out of state. Garrett, however, was recognized for her expertise and was granted confirmation for her experience through serving as an "advisor" to her successors. Cameron continued his ministries with the Baptist denomination and attempted, with minimal success, to influence politics at the highest levels of the state. Enemies gained during his Superintendency and the contentious 1910 election foreclosed any future political opportunities for him. Crable's plight was similar in 1946. Hoeltzel served briefly in a small school superintendency followed by a consultancy with a private company providing assistance to school districts, both unrelated to his Superintendency experience.

Folks, at age forty and the second youngest to leave office, benefitted from his Superintendency tenure, not so much from knowledge of the statewide system, but his experience as an administrator. He moved to the superintendency of the Mid-Del School District, a position he would not have achieved otherwise because he lacked any public school administrative service. From there he became dean of the small school of education at Southwestern Oklahoma State University. Both that position and two district superintendencies that ensued in Texas were part of his resumé, but the Superintendency affected minimally his overall qualifications after leaving Oklahoma.

Chapter 6
Women's Struggle to Achieve Suffrage and Gain Equality in Educational Governance
(1890-2014)

Because women have always been viewed as the primary caretakers of the family and in the home, they have been given the responsibility for nurturing the education of the children at home and in the school. Particularly was this true from the children's birth through elementary school. Mothering included teaching values at home as well as academics in school where most primary teachers have been women. This valuable and stereotypical role had strong roots and has had an endearing and enduring legacy. Many women, however, have yearned for a more expansive role in the administration and governance of education at all levels: local school districts, county offices, local and county school boards, territorial/state offices, and college presidencies. Women's participation in governance and leadership in the education arena through suffrage or holding office (by election or appointment) was neither substantial nor consistent with some limited exceptions for the 125 years from the beginning of Oklahoma Territory in 1890 to 2015. This book about the Superintendency, the paths taken by the Superintendents prior to their taking the oath of office, and their activities while holding the office shows in part how men were advantaged in myriad ways while women had to meet unique expectations. The proving ground, slanted favorably toward the men for many decades, eventually nearly leveled and allowed women access to all positions in education.

Women faced the dual challenge of legal hurdles to suffrage and executive office holding and cultural and societal norms determining their role in society. However difficult the pursuit of universal suffrage was, it was easier to accomplish than to gain the constitutional right to be elected to any of the state's several executive offices. Even after that right was achieved forty-eight years elapsed prior to a female weighing the pros and cons before throwing her hat into the ring in an arena of state government dominated in the lower ranks by women and in the leadership positions by men. This chapter focuses on some of the struggles of women to gain their rights through legal channels and then through cultural acceptance and acknowledgement of their administrative and leadership abilities. Men were intentional in excluding women in the instances of writing the Constitution, determining the qualifications for executive office, and prohibiting their vote, but also in allowing women to serve as county superintendents, on county and local district school boards and the Board. Over the decades women pushed for their right to be equal, sometimes advancing and other times losing momentum. While the effort was largely theirs, at several key moments women benefitted from the initiatives and efforts of men who firmly believed in their counterparts' right to be equal participants. Most notable was Republican Governor Henry Bellmon who appointed Sandy Garrett Secretary of Education in 1988, setting the stage for her election to the Superintendency two years later. On a smaller scale several school district superintendents in the late 1970s and a Superintendent in the 1980s signaled their support through advocating for, and promoting to administrative roles, aspiring and competent women. This chapter describes and tells part of the century-and-a-quarter effort of women to achieve parity in educational leadership aspects related to the Superintendency.

Limited Suffrage before Full Voting Rights

In the initial session of the Oklahoma Territory Legislature in the fall of 1890 the lawmakers were not prepared to grant women full suffrage, but they also were not willing to deny totally their right to participate in the democratic process. The legislators were being guided by other states' laws and finally decided to grant women a limited right to vote in county and local school district elections, a right that was extended to Indian Territory at statehood and has remained unchanged ever since. The initial provision was clear: "In all elections for school purposes of any kind, whatsoever, all persons possessing the qualifications of electors residing in such district, shall be entitled to vote without distinction of sex."[1] This law reflected recognition of the significant role women played in the development and education of children, but it did not address the question of the right of women to serve on the boards. Superintendent Cameron six months into his term in 1908, and dissatisfied with his fellow Board member Attorney General Charles West's insufficient opinion, clarified the status: "My position is that women are allowed to vote in school elections and under the same rule they should be privileged to sit on school boards."[2] Suffrage in 1890 encouraged female support for school attendance in the early days of the creation of a territorial education system when student attendance was irregular. Allowing women to serve on local boards at statehood expanded the expertise and commitment of those boards especially as thousands of districts were established in Indian Territory.

Seventeen years later the all-male constitutional convention saw no need to extend universal suffrage to women; but the issue arose in 1910 through an initiative petition that allowed all eligible male voters statewide to choose "to authorize women to vote under the same circumstances and conditions as men may now do under the laws of this State [sic]."[3] The sentiment of these male voters in 1910 had not moved from three years earlier, but shifting national currents affected the state in less than a decade. Suffrage was extended to women in all elections through a constitution change in November 1918 when Oklahoman joined twelve other states on the forefront to granting equal suffrage to men and women.[4] The positive action by these states preceded the federal government's successful attempt by two years to amend the US Constitution extending universal suffrage throughout the United States. Women gained parity in voting, but many years would pass before they could enjoy the fruits of equal consideration for employment.

Legal Qualifications for the Superintendency

The all-male constitutional convention writers' firm belief in the supremacy of male leadership in the highest elective executive offices found expression in the eligibility requirements and the process by which the Constitution could be modified. Among the qualifications in 1907 for the state's executive offices as specified in article 6, section 3, was the prohibition of females. Thirty-five years passed before the gender restriction was successfully excised from the founding document. Attention to the rights of women, especially suffrage, in the late teens and early 1920s provided some impetus to encourage citizens to address this glaring sexist language. What began as an attempt to cause a simple modification through amending the Constitution stretched into a two-decade-long campaign. Initially, legislative oversight and the ineptitude of some government officials led to the nullification of a state question by the court, and subsequently another constitutional provision, article 24, section 1, relative to the threshold standard for passage of a state question (see chapter 3 and table 3.1 for additional explication), proved to be a major stumbling block.[5]

In the spirit of the times, when general acceptance of the rights of women in governmental matters was waxing, two women were elected to the Oklahoma Legislature for the first time in 1920 and three years later the voters approved an amendment striking the prohibition of women's eligibility for the executive offices from the constitution. Subsequent invalidation of the results by Governor Martin Trapp postponed further consideration of the issue until former Senator Mrs. Lamar Looney requested a writ of mandamus in 1930 to force the Secretary of State Graves Leeper to submit the amendment to a vote of the people. In the meantime, and in a state of limbo, Anna Willis, superintendent of Lincoln County, and Mary Munson, a Woods County teacher, joined two men in the 1926 Republican primary which Willis won with a plurality of less than 35 percent. Lacking a decisive victory in the primary, Democratic domination of the state's politics, and skepticism of some about a woman being elevated to the highest education office doomed her efforts in the general election.[6]

Women were especially hopeful in 1930 that the two-to-one margin of the vote in 1923 would be replicated and the constitutional barrier to achieving equality would be eliminated. They achieved their goal of a similar ratio, but the supporting vote tally did not reach the threshold of a majority of the overall voters. Astoundingly, an insurmountable constitutional standard prohibited the will of two of every three voters on the amendment. Nevertheless, with no uncertainty about the exclusion of women, in 1934 forty-five-year-old Jenella Jones, superintendent of Woodward County since 1925, entered the Republican primary along with two males. In this three-person race, Jones placed a disappointing second with 22 percent of the votes. Even though the constitution was amended in 1942 to allow women to be qualified, no woman would compete for the office for another forty-eight years.[7]

Three brave women during the 1920s and early 1930s presented themselves as serious candidates for the Superintendency knowing they faced daunting odds of succeeding. Optimism had to offset what they knew would be powerful forces working against them. In both 1926 and 1934 they challenged incumbent males who were riding tides of success and the support of the Democratic Party. Like those males, the women hailed from rural counties, but in contrast they lacked any experience in the capital city, connections to decision makers and other influential people, and relationships to educators beyond their respective counties. Not necessarily a major factor was the belief of a segment of the population in the Biblical principle that women should not be in charge of men. In the conservative rural environment religion was pervasive in the lives of many individuals including those who served on the school boards.[8]

Women's Opportunities in the County and District Superintendencies

Following the structure of government organized by other states in their births in the 1800s and the Organic Act of May 1890, Oklahoma's territorial Legislature in the fall of that year established counties in Oklahoma Territory as an intermediate level of organization and management. Within that unit the elective position of county superintendent was designed to assist in carrying out various educational functions and responsibilities. School district formation soon grew exponentially. County superintendents during an era of thousands of small rural school districts served a vital function in the collection of data, coordinating and supervising the teacher certification process, and submitting reports to the Superintendent. Communication also flowed from the Department to the local districts through the county superintendents. It was this array of administration levels from which most of the candidates for the Superintendency came before 1990. These local district and county superintendents touted their experience in these positions as important credentials on their resumés. Only two county superintendents were able to use their positions successfully as stepping-stones to achieve the office, R. H. Wilson and Oliver Hodge. While the position of county superintendent held a relatively important status in the first half of the twentieth century, consolidations and mergers of districts lessened the county level responsibilities and significance. Administration of a local district (1-12), even if it were relatively small, for the most part was considered more crucial than a county superintendency for M. A. Nash, John Vaughan, A. L. Crable, D. D. Creech, Scott Tuxhorn, Les Fisher, and Gerald Hoeltzel. E. D. Cameron and John Folks were the only two male Superintendents who lacked administrative experience at the county or district level.

Oklahoma's territorial Legislature and then the state Legislature recognized the crucial role women played in the education system. Most of the teachers were women as were many of the county superintendents, but that did not signify that women held equal status in the overall operation of the government's services and agencies. Women were given some legitimacy for their contributions and were permitted limited use of their abilities. In some districts, however, their behavior was circumscribed through being forbidden to being married. No legal gender restrictions existed for the county superintendency or for the local district superintendency, allowing women to seek those positions. For example, in 1899, five of the twenty-three (22 percent) county superintendents were women increasing to one out of every three twenty years later and to 38 percent by 1929-30. In the acknowledgement of professional and highly important occupations, the county superintendency was not considered a prestigious position and thus women were "fully qualified." From its apogee of strategic importance in early statehood the county position declined over the decades as more and more dependent districts (grades 1-8) merged with nearby independent districts (grades1-12). By 1990, long after its value had dwindled almost totally and shortly before the position was eliminated, in only one-fourth of the thirty-two counties still electing a superintendent was that person a female.[9] For the two female county superintendents who sought the Superintendency, their positions proved not to be a sufficient asset to win election. It was during the heightened activism of women in the 1920s-1930s, that county superintendents Anna Willis and Jenella Jones opted to test the political waters but were thwarted in their endeavors to climb the ladder of advancement to the Superintendency through a combination of party affiliation and gender. Especially for these reasons, important avenues to the Superintendency essentially were blocked for women.

The "training ground" of school district administrative positions was closed to women with rare exception from the 1920s to the 1980s when females held elementary school principal and county superintendent positions, but typically not district superintendencies. Women were not viewed acceptably by local district boards of education for the high school principalships that were oftentimes the stepping-stones to the district superintendencies; thus, few women were ever hired to fill those positions. By the twenty-first century women were beginning to be viewed as capable candidates for district superintendencies and in the 2009-2010 school year females held the top position in 25 percent of the state's twenty largest school districts, primarily in the urban areas. Rural independent districts were slower to hire women and had not yet achieved that ratio.[10] Forbidden access to this typical line of accession played an extremely critical role in hindering women's promotion and advancement to administrative positions beyond the school district level. Folks and Sandy Garrett were transitional Superintendents in that they proved it was not a prerequisite to have held prior county, building, or district level responsibilities, and Garrett broke the gender barrier decisively to prove that women could win and succeed in the Superintendency. Her successors built on this changing perspective of what qualified a person for the position.

Female Representation on the State Board of Education

Female representation on the most influential board governing education has been woefully minimal throughout the territorial period and statehood. Statutes in the early years determined eligibility based on position. For example, from 1891 to 1893 all of the few county superintendents comprised the Board, while from 1893 to 1907 heads of designated education institutions made up the Board. All Board members during the territorial period were men. The Constitution in 1907 set the Board's membership as several executive officers *ex officio* including the Superintendent until such time as the Legislature provided otherwise, a move accomplished in early 1911. During this brief hiatus androcentric perspectives were heightened because of the legal exclusion of the participation of women, but these perspectives dominated for 100 years in the arena of governance of education institutions. Typically, a male governor appointed males to the Board that was chaired by a male Superintendent. Few, if any, females were appointed to supervise the overall direction of the education of public school students across the state. Not until 1922 and amidst the spasm of national fervor of women's suffrage was the first woman Ethel Cardiff appointed to the Board. Four years later Bertha Truitt became a member; and for two years these women's terms overlapped, a situation that did not occur again until 1998 with the exception of the period from February 1935 to July 1936. Only during the 1930-1934 timeframe did the Board not have at least one female Board member for the years 1922-1938. Not coincidental were these Board appointments considering that they were in the decades when women gained suffrage and competed for the Superintendency.[11]

It may have been coincidental that two notable actions restricting the political involvement of college administrators and faculty were taken by the Board, first in July 1935 and then in June 1936, a period when two women were among the six members. The 1934 election was particularly controversial when Governor Murray and his supporters fought hard to unseat Vaughan. Former Department employees were involved with one of them filing against Vaughan. Financial contributions were solicited from many state employees including college faculty. Board member Grace Davis seconded a motion to adopt a resolution that read in part "This Board…looks with disfavor on their active or financial participation in partisan and personal politics…this Board hereby requests a semi-annual written statement from each faculty member…under its control that shall read 'I have not been solicited…to make a contribution to a partisan or personal political campaign…I have made no contribution…'"[12] Adoption of the resolution was aided by the votes of Davis and Jane Clark.

In the latter half of 1935 and the first half of 1936 political actions of the Governor and others factored into the resignations of two college presidents and the selections of their successors along with a vacancy resulting from the death of a third president. In the midst of the turmoil, some Board members resigned and new ones were appointed. In 1936 the Council of Presidents of the Teachers Colleges determined that the resolution and requirement of written statements of the Board the previous year were insufficient to inform the faculty and to curb their political behavior. Some faculty were uncertain of the latitude afforded to them while the political involvement of others was deemed excessive and detrimental to the effective functioning of the colleges. The Council pled for further clarification and assistance from the Board, and the Board cooperated. Jane Clark offered a motion that was immediately seconded by Grace Davis to prohibit any candidate for a public office from using the colleges' facilities. A corollary action prohibited faculty members from participating in any organized political activities. The two women, unsympathetic to the politics as usual, led the way and were joined by two of the four male members present to adopt the resolution.[13] These resolutions in the mid-1930s, no doubt viewed as progress, eventually gave way to greater freedoms of faculty political engagement.

The initial accomplishments of the 1920s and 1930s fizzled and the practice of naming women to the Board went dormant. Female advice to the Superintendent disappeared in 1938 and was not regained until the civil rights era of the mid-1960s. Interestingly, only two Superintendents, A. L. Crable and Oliver Hodge, served during these years when androcentric perspectives dominated and the voices of the female majorities of instructional staff and student enrollment in the schools were for the most part not permitted to proffer their arguments and appeals. Exacerbating this dilemma was the almost total exclusion of females from school district superintendencies and the limited opportunities for female principals to influence the decision-making at that level. The appointment of Ruth Musselman to the Board in 1966 began a trend of at least one female Board member that continued until the present day with the exception of fours year from 1977 to 1981. From 1890 to 1990 only eleven women had served on the Board with seven of them completing their six-year terms and the remainder fewer than three years. Collectively, women served approximately fifty-four years out of a possible 600 years, a 9 percent share. Not until 1993 when Garrett was Superintendent did females gain a majority of the Board membership, an atypical division that was not maintained into the twenty-first century when the composition returned to a two-to-one ratio in favor of males. Even that ratio was not sustained by 2012 when only one of six members was female. Governor Mary Fallin eventually named Joy Hofmeister to replace Phil Lakin who had resigned. Hofmeister, after slightly more than one year, resigned to run for the Superintendency and thus became the only Board member to subsequently become Superintendent.[14] Membership on the Board is crucial to the operation of the common school system, but women's voices have been stifled for much of Oklahoma's history.

Winning a College Presidency

As the six normal schools and then teachers colleges evolved their presidencies were considered plum positions, and politics was never far from the selection of the presidents. With the primary mission of these institutions to prepare teachers, local school district superintendents were the aspirants for the top position and almost without exception all of these superintendents were men. Throughout most of Oklahoma's history, governance of the institutions was assigned to a board either chaired by the Superintendent or on which he or she sat as a member. The Board, chaired by the Superintendent, oversaw these institutions from 1911 through 1949 except for the years from 1939-1943. When not under the Board, these institutions' board membership included the Superintendent *ex officio* who could be elected president of the board by the members (see appendix N). The most critical responsibility of these gubernatorial-appointed boards was to hire the presidents and, thus the process for choosing these presidents was not free of political influence either overt or covert or gender preference. Overt politics surfaced late in 1934 in the naming of the first female president to any of these teachers colleges when Governor-elect E. W. Marland persuaded Governor Murray to appoint Kate Galt Zaneis to the Board. A few months later, and now Governor, Marland effected more changes on the Board's membership. The reconstituted Board, chaired by Superintendent Vaughan, named Zaneis to the presidency of Southeastern State Teachers College. Marland "negotiated" these actions so that Zaneis, the coordinator of his Carter County election campaign, could be rewarded for her efforts.[15] Whether Vaughan was fully supportive of this move mattered little. His duty was to see that the Governor's wishes were fulfilled, and under his leadership the Board hired Zaneis. This purely political employment of Zaneis did not bode well and she was forced to resign slightly more than two years later. Her hiring was an aberration in the arc of history for the first one hundred years in Oklahoma.

More than a half-century passed before a board on which the Superintendent served hired another woman to be president of one of the original six teachers colleges. In June 1990 Joe Anna Hibler, a former teacher and college professor, was chosen by the Board of Regents of Oklahoma Colleges (now Regional University System of Oklahoma) to be president of Southwestern Oklahoma State University.[16] The Superintendent was involved in the employment of both Zaneis and Hibler, but his influence was minimal in both instances. For Vaughan, he was doing the Governor's bidding and for appointed Superintendent Gerald Hoeltzel, he was *ex officio* member of the Board of Regents, purely a coincidental circumstance. Not a coincidence or an anomaly was the time period between the naming of Zaneis and Hibler, for it paralleled much of the time when women were virtually unseen and unheard in the governance of education. Between Hibler's retirement in 2001 and 2015, only one female was hired by the Board of Regents of the RUSO to be president of one of the universities under its purview, Janet Cunningham at Northwestern Oklahoma State University in 2007.

Department Secretary to the Superintendency

Creation of positions in the Department and the selection of staff lay almost entirely with the Legislature in the earliest decades; however, these prerogatives slowly shifted to the Superintendent subject to the vicissitudes of the lawmakers to fund the positions. Except for the decade of the 1940s when, in a pique, patronage was assigned to the Board, Superintendents over time assumed greater authority to govern the Department. Superintendents determined who was hired and their assignments subject to approval of the Board which was chaired by the Superintendent. A consistent pattern developed early where the Department staff were men in the professional administrative and supervisory positions and women in the supportive clerk, stenographer, and secretarial positions. But no women were hired at any level in the Department until R. H. Wilson was Superintendent; and by 1914 he had hired four females, three stenographers and one secretary. As shown in table 6.1, only males were employed in the professional levels until the 1920s when Victoria Lyles, Wagoner County superintendent, was hired as a rural school supervisor.[17] In the decades of the 1920s and 1930s when enthusiasm for women's advancement was waxing generally little of it translated into professional jobs in the Department. Examining the common education arena only, positions through the 1960s were created rapidly and then filled by men more than 80 percent of the time. Assignment of the females was to the lower-level supervisory positions such as curriculum and instruction with the males gaining the more prestigious administrative positions (e.g., deputy superintendent and assistant superintendent for finance).

Vocational education within the Department evolved similarly to common education, but the nature of the curricular topic divided males and females. Exclusively, men were drawn to agriculture and trades and industry and women to home economics and secretarial courses. The first fulltime professional woman in the Department, Mabel Potter, was hired in 1917 to supervise home economics.[18] "Naturally," men were viewed as more administratively suited and thus were considered for the administrative positions within the Department, a practice that continued until vocational education was separated from the Department in the late 1960s.

Table 6.1 Gender of administrative and supervisory employees in the Department 1899-1969*

Yr	Common education†					Vocational education					Total				
	Male		Female		Tot.	Male		Female		Tot.	Male		Female		Tot.
	N	%	N	%	N	N	%	N	%	N	N	%	N	%	N
99	0	0	0	0	0	...	...	...	...	...	0	0	0	0	0
09	3	100	0	0	3	...	...	...	...	...	3	100	0	0	3
19	6	100	0	0	6	...	...	1	100	1	6	85.7	1	14.3	7
29	9	90.0	1	10.0	10	5	83.3	1	16.7	6	14	87.5	2	12.5	16
39	17	94.1	1	5.9	18	8	50.0	8	50.0	16	25	73.5	9	26.5	34
49	24	92.3	2	7.7	26	35	83.3	7	16.7	42	59	86.8	9	13.2	68
59	52	89.7	6	10.3	58	16‡	69.6	7	30.4	23	68	84.0	13	16.0	81
69	83	81.4	19	18.6	102	43	81.1	10	18.9	53	126	81.3	29	18.7	155

Sources: Data for each of the years are from the *Educational Directory* published by the Department.

Note: Vocational programs were begun soon after the passage of the federal Smith-Hughes Act in 1917 but positions were not yet created and listed in the *1919-20 Educational Directory*. The first fulltime position was a supervisor of home economics. By 1969 the *Educational Directory* listed the Vocational Department directory as a separate section reflecting its independency from the Department. Excluded were any number of persons hired in the Vocational Rehabilitation Department.

*Included within this group were administrators, supervisors, assistant supervisors, field supervisors, directors, and assistant directors. Excluded were the Superintendents.

†Common education was chosen to designate K-12 education except the vocational education programs within those schools.

‡The large reduction from 1949 to 1959 was from the discontinuance of the Veterans Agricultural Training Program.

Superintendent Fisher's tenure from 1971 to 1984 offers a case study into the evolution in the thinking, if not the practice, of women's advancement into the top echelons of administration in the Department. His predecessors left him with an agency guided exclusively by males in the upper administrative level of deputy state superintendent and three assistant superintendents in charge of finance, state and federal programs, and instruction. When he resigned thirteen years later, this rank of administration had grown by two positions. In 1972-73 and 1981-82 he added an associate deputy superintendent, and in 1982-83 two more. But that last year he eliminated an assistant superintendent position. Among these positions and during his tenure, only one female, his friend June Gruber, served as assistant superintendent in charge of instruction for the years 1972-73 to 1974-75. Even she recognized the significance of her position when she was initially hired, "Willingness is a big factor. Women kind of shy away from this type of responsibility."[19] She did not expand on the reason(s) why women were hesitant to pursue such positions, but cultural expectations and no evidence of employment conspired against women to seriously consider competing for the positions. Her comment may have also reflected her relationship with Fisher who hired her in the mid-1960s to be the elementary coordinator in Moore School District. During her time in that position and until her employment in the Department she was the only female administrator in that district. As a comparison, Norman School District by 1969 had four female principals among its fourteen building administrators.[20] Upon Gruber's departure from the Department,

Fisher selected a male to replace her and delayed for several years the appointment of another female to a high executive position in the Department.

Great stability and continuity in upper-level management allowed Fisher to inspire confidence in those around him and vice versa. It also precluded him from seriously confronting his own sexism, a topic he addressed in 1981. "In the past I have turned down capable people because they were women, and hired less-capable [sic] people because they were men. I'll not do that again. I'll just simply employ the best people I can find."[21] His thinking on the role of females in high positions evolved, but his actions proved otherwise. Neither did he replace men with women nor did he create opportunities to advance women, a wrong that his successor set about immediately to correct.

Fisher's employment and promotion of females in the Department was not particularly different from other organizations in the 1970s. Few women held positions of influence and power in most organizations and professions, but what differentiated the education sector was that it was dominated by female teachers and administered by men. Almost without exception, male rural district superintendents were hired for executive offices in the Department while females holding lower-level district administrative posts were hired for entry-level management positions in the Agency. Rarely, if ever, was a female hired at a junior level promoted to the executive level.

Enlightening is a report prepared for the Board drawn from data submitted to the US Office of Civil Rights of a comparison of Department employees by classification and gender in January 1971 and July 1982. At first glance the data displayed in table 6.2 seem to indicate great progress. No females in the top two categories in 1971 to thirty-two in 1982 indicated that the Department was moving in the direction of greater gender parity. During this same period, thirty-two of the fifty-five new positions in these categories were filled with women, unarguably rapid progress. But what is not explicitly shown is

Table 6.2 Department employees by classification and gender

Class.*	January 1, 1971					July 15, 1982				
	M	%	F	%	T	M	%	F	%	T
Off/Ad.	30	100.0	0	0	30	47	71.2	19	28.8	66
Asst. Ad.	5	100.0	0	0	5	11	45.8	13	54.2	24
Profess.	64	71.1	26	28.9	90	100	35.8	179	64.2	279
Subtotal	99		26		125	158		211		369
Paraprof.	2	14.3	12	85.7	14	4	12.9	27	87.1	31
Cler/Sup.	5	5.0	93	95.0	98	7	4.5	150	95.5	157
Subtotal	7		105		112	11		177		188
Total	106		131		237	169		388		557

Source: Board of Education Meeting Minutes, July 29, 1982, 92.

*Classifications: Official/Administrator, Assistant Administrator, Professional, Paraprofessional, and Clerical/Support personnel.

a description of the gender split in the handful of the highest, most prestigious positions, those in the Department's publicized executive administration levels. Those positions were held by men from 1971 to 1982 and interrupted only by the brief two-year period of assistant superintendent of curriculum Gruber.[22]

Additional light can be shown on Fisher's Department during this eleven-year period by aggregate analyses of the top three categories. Ninety-nine males were employed in 1971 and that number grew substantially to 158 in 1982, a 59 percent increase. Female employee numbers jumped dramatically, from twenty-six to 211 or an 812 percent increase, but most of these were in the lowest of the three categories, the professional level. The overall growth of 295 percent, from 125 to 369, in professional and administrative positions in eleven years presents the opportunities that were afforded to Fisher's Department to hire and advance women.

Table 6.3 shows how the strong gender discrepancy in the Department finally dissipated by the 2007-08 school year, but it does not display the relative significance attached to the four levels and the topic areas. No female served as chief of staff, deputy state superintendent or associate superintendent, excepting Judy Leach as associate superintendent in charge of instruction during Folks's tenure, and no female was responsible for financial, legal, or federal/fiscal programs at any time prior to Garrett's tenure. Rather, they held an assistant superintendency responsible for instruction, personnel/professional services, school improvement, or special education. Garrett leapfrogged all of these administrative levels when she was elected Superintendent in 1990 and then gradually altered the gender pattern existing in the Department for a century.

Table 6.3 Top-level administrative positions at the Department by gender for select years 1975-76 to 2009-10*

School year	Gender M	F	T	Supt.
1975-1976	5	0	5	Fisher
1986-1987	7	1	8	Folks
1992-1993†	3	1	4	Garrett
2007-2008	4	5	9	Garrett
2009-2010	2	5	7	Garrett

Source: Oklahoma Educational Directory for each of the school years.
Note: In some of the years not displayed Sharon Lease served as chief of staff to Garrett.
*Top-level positions were chief of staff, deputy superintendent, associate superintendent, and assistant superintendent.
†Reorganization of the hierarchy through renaming positions and shifting duties.

A "Village" to Raise a Superintendent

"It takes a village to raise a child" is claimed by some to be an African proverb to explain who in the community must be involved in raising a child. Regardless of the origin, it is applicable to most successful individuals who were assisted and mentored by many persons and in a variety of ways. Historically males helped males to advance in their careers. For far too long women (and people of color) were denied opportunities for advancement, particularly in education administration. Slowly, the tide began shifting in the late 1970s and early 1980s. Because males controlled the avenues to women's ascension of the administration ladder, men would need to be the facilitators. Then, as women began to gain some influential positions, they mentored other women who were seeking higher-level positions. The "village's" membership was growing, the number of possible mentors expanding, and women were gaining in their effort to achieve parity with men. In the two main divisions of common education, K-12 and vocational-technical education, Les Fisher and Francis Tuttle, respectively, began some initiatives to improve the preparation of the next generation of leaders. Fisher's oral commitment to the advancement of women in education leadership, somewhat tentative and ambivalent, extended beyond employment decisions within the Department and did gain some minimal substance and direction when in mid-1979 he hired Cecil Yarbrough as a special assistant in administration to create a leadership development program. Tuttle created the Administrators Development Program to address the imminent shortage of leaders caused by anticipated retirements and the expansion of the campuses and programs of the vo-tech system. The first cadre of twenty-four participants, split evenly between men and women, was formed in 1984 and became a model for the cadres over the next several years.[23]

About the same time, and only somewhat aware of these initiatives, Clarence Oliver, superintendent of the Broken Arrow school district, initiated discussions with Tom Payzant, superintendent of the Oklahoma City school district, and Bob Mooneyham, executive director of the Oklahoma Association of School Administrators to design workshops, conferences, administrator internships, and an academy to prepare future principals and superintendents. Oliver's seminal thoughts and efforts were to create a multifaceted approach that would attract quality females especially if they could see that they would be in a non-threatening environment. An example of his concern over what reception women would receive from the state's predominately male administrators was exhibited four or five years earlier when he invited several women teachers who were aspiring to become principals to travel with him to attend OASA meetings. Upon arrival he was greeted by the insulting epithet "Here come Clarence's Angels." Oliver's commitment to advancing women became concrete by hiring Kara Gae (Wilson) Neal in 1977 to be an assistant principal at Broken Arrow High School. Within this context Oliver and several other administrators established the Oklahoma Commission for Future Educational Leadership circa 1980 or 1981. Not long thereafter Yarbrough joined the coordinators and was able to provide some funds from the Oklahoma Curriculum Improvement Commission to offer seminars and conferences to teach aspirants to leadership positions, especially women, the knowledge and skills to be successful leaders. Fisher, mindful of what was percolating, in January 1981, led the Board to issue a resolution "expressing support and commitment to increasing the number of women in educational administration in the public schools."[24] These men through their initiatives recognized the immense reserve of talent available, the gross inequality of exclusion, and their capacity to cause improvements. All that was left was the will to become involved.

Oliver and several other astute district superintendents in the Oklahoma City and Tulsa metropolitan areas in the 1980s knew that opening the door to women was just the beginning of the support needed. Women would seek advancement within the administrative hierarchy leading ultimately to the superintendency of school districts and would need superintendents to provide them the opportunities to do so. On their own initiative these superintendents initially began hiring women in the areas of personnel, curriculum, and instruction, but almost never in the areas of finance, facilities, and transportation. It was an evolutionary process but the gender bias still existed. Slowly, a slight few superintendents then began to create opportunities for these women to develop knowledge and skills in all areas.[25] Now, a cadre of women was being prepared for district superintendencies which made them ultimately eligible for all of the positions at the Department. But, would they be hired? As with school districts the Department eventually filled the upper echelon of administrative ranks with women.

The largest organization of educators throughout the territorial period and statehood was the OEA and its predecessors. Because women dominated the teaching corps they also comprised the majority of the OEA membership. Men, on the other hand, were the presidents for the first forty-five years except in 1917, and the Superintendent was among this group for seven of the years with Nash being the last one in 1929. Men dominated the committees and the leadership at all levels within the organization. Probably not coincidental were the election of Susan Fordyce as president for 1917 in the midst of a heightened interest nationally in the suffrage movement and the creation of the State Council of Administrative and Executive Women in Education. This Oklahoma version of the state councils being established across the US held its foundational meeting November 29, 1917. At that meeting the Council was advised by Grace Strachan-Forsythe, an activist school administrator from New York, and it elected Mary Davis, superintendent of the Claremore school district, president. At least for the year 1917 women in the OEA exerted their influence and showed they could be a significant force, but sixteen years would pass before another woman would be elected president.[26]

Sixty years later a group of women once again organized to create a forum where those who aspired to leadership positions in educational organizations could join together. Velta (Reed) Johnston, hired in 1984 as superintendent of the Western Oklahoma Area Vo-Tech District and the first female to lead such a district, believed strongly that women should be given opportunities equal to men in the superintendency. Johnston was a member of the original cohort in the Administrator Development Program and became a superintendent at the end of that year. Her participation in this formal program led her to begin thinking about starting an organization for women by women. Discussions with, and commitments from, several other women led to the formation of Oklahoma Women in Education Administration to support women's advancement, in part, by affirming them and assisting their efforts in networking.[27]

Key men, and later women, in influential leadership positions as well as in professorships engaged in preparing administrators were welcomed into the group to advance the women's efforts. Bellmon's election in 1986 placed him in a propitious position to advance women, and he exercised that prerogative with great consequence when he named Sandy Garrett as Secretary of Education in 1988. She then had a platform to encourage women through word and action and she had the Governor's blessing and support. Garrett along with Ramona Paul and Sharon Lease in the Department by now were nurturing participants in OWEA as were superintendents Lucy Smith at McAles-

*Governor and Mrs. Shirley Bellmon hosting women superintendents in 1988
Standing, Mrs. Bellmon and Governor Bellmon; seated at the end of the table,
Secretary Garrett (L) and Pat Sholar (R)[28]
(Courtesy of the Governor's photographer)*

ter, Edna Manning at Shawnee and soon to become President of the Oklahoma School for Science and Mathematics, and (Wilson) Neal in Tulsa County. All of these administrators except Garrett had reached the pinnacle of their education careers by earning PhDs and thus by example were modeling the type of behavior and accomplishment of highly successful women. The leadership of OWEA invited men to participate, to be supportive, and to advocate for their advancement. Superintendents Fisher and Folks were solicitous in providing Departmental support in the formative days and Garrett as Secretary and then as Superintendent was instrumental in providing Departmental assistance as well. Garrett had achieved the pinnacle of educational governance, proof that women had achieved remarkable progress in the span of a decade. Never forgetting how the "village" supported her, she spent her time as Superintendent advocating for, and mentoring, other women in their careers.[29]

Taking the Helm and Never Looking Back

The women's toehold on top leadership positions, as exemplified by Garrett's appointment as Secretary and then election to the Superintendency, grew significantly as the end of the twentieth century approached. Achievement of these two positions within two and one-half years proved to be a watershed event in the arc of women's effort to gain parity within the education arena. In four of her five election/reelections Garrett vanquished males on her way to victory. Her two successors, both women, defeated men in the primary as well as the general election. Simultaneously women were slowly gaining school district superintendencies across the state in both urban and rural areas. By 2001 women were leading six of the state's career technology districts/centers and Ann Benson was director of the Oklahoma Department of Career and Technology Education, an appointive position. A short four years later women led three of the eleven interlocal cooperatives providing services to school districts. Similar gains were yet to be realized among the twelve two-year colleges where all of the presidents were male and among the thirteen four-year college and university presidents only two were female.[30]

Women have made significant progress in leadership positions at most levels, but to achieve parity, the struggle will continue. Garrett opened the door and led the common education system for twenty years by navigating through Democratic and Republican administrations. Her immediate successor benefited from being part of a dominant Republican Party governance, yet she failed to lead sufficiently and was denied a second term. Barresi then handed the mantle of the Superintendency to Joy Hofmeister in the first instance of a female challenger ousting a female incumbent.

Part III
The Superintendents (Public Servants)
(1907-2015)

In Part III, a chapter is devoted to a description and analysis of each Superintendent's background (excepting Thirteen with D. D. Creech and Scott Tuxhorn who were both appointees), political involvement by election cycle, Departmental management, annual reporting, suggestions for legislative action, and post tenure activities. Oklahoma's almost total dominance by the Democratic Party for the first hundred years and the Republican Party since then was reflected in the party affiliation of those who were elected as Superintendent. The first nine elected were Democrats and the more recent two Republicans. The elective nature of the office and absence of term limits encouraged the Superintendents to gauge their decision making in light of their relative political standing, but did not discourage some of them from defying the Governor as evidenced by R. H. Wilson, John Vaughan, and A. L. Crable. Strengths and foibles of each Superintendent are described, some of their accomplishments and failures highlighted, and their legacies analyzed. All of them were politicians eventually by dint of the position, some more comfortable in the role than others, but all were political nevertheless. Politics cost several of them their positions (e.g., E. D. Cameron and Crable), but, for one, Janet Barresi, it was not so much her ideas though controversial, but her personality and inflexibility that led to her downfall. Regardless of political leanings, all were conservative, Christian, married (one divorced and one widowed), and willing to participate in the messy process of electoral partisanship. Winners were triumphant while losers were relegated to the arena of rejection, especially those three incumbents who lost to rivals within their own party, but also those neophytes who never did taste victory. To the winners go the spoils and to the unsuccessful, oblivion and sometimes bitterness (e.g., Lloyd Roettger and Barresi).

With no term restrictions and oftentimes uninformed voters, once elected Superintendents could continue in office. Six enjoyed tenures of nine years or greater for a combined eighty-seven years or 82 percent of the time, four served the equivalent of one term and two months or less (two resigned and two were defeated) for a total of fifteen years. Three appointees, not subsequently elected, served a combined six years. Joy Hofmeister's inclusion only pertains to the 2014 election.

Large, urban, and suburban school districts are able to amass resources by virtue of their size and economies, an advantage not typically available to small, rural districts that rely on the Department's services and assistance. Issuing teaching certificates, monitoring districts' hiring of certified teachers, and processing state aid per the legislatively established funding formula are responsibilities applicable to all districts. How the Superintendent manages the Department's operations through the administrative levels, and the description portrayed to the public and the Legislature, determine public perception. Generally, there is a disconnect between the significance of the Department, measured by the percentage of the state budget appropriated to the Department and the many school districts, and the understanding of the general public.

Several issues were time specific while others were woven throughout the Superintendency history. Critical in the earliest administrations was the creation of the Board in 1911 and the controversy over the members' decisions regarding higher education institutions and faculty. Over time the breadth of the Board's responsibility was narrowed as governing boards were created for those institutions. On the other hand, as vocational education expanded so did the Board's supervision of it until the late 1960s. As a contrast, the Superintendent has been a member of the Commissioners of the Land Office since 1890 with little controversy except in the first half of the 1930s. Textbook oversight involved the Superintendent for decades with a major upheaval in the 1940s. Desegregation occurred not as a priority within the state, but from US Supreme Court mandates beginning in the mid-1950s. "Accountability" became part of the lexicon with stirrings in the 1970s and developing into a crescendo in the 1990s. In the twenty-first century public money for nonpublic options has been demanded and allocated.

Male domination for the first eighty-three years was followed by female domination for the next twenty-five. Caucasians, with the exception of Garrett, were the face of the office throughout the history. Offspring of politicians they were not, again with the exception of Garrett, nor were they representative of a wealthier class with one possible exception, Barresi. They were commoners with a dedication to managing the state school system to the best of their abilities within the expectations of the general public. They were public servants dedicated to fulfilling the legislative mandates of the office in a political and cultural environment mired in a habit of satisfaction with mediocrity while trumpeting a desire for excellence.

Chapter	**Superintendent**	**Time in Office**
Seven	E. D. Cameron	November 16, 1907-January 9, 1911
Eight	R. H. Wilson	January 9, 1911-January 8, 1923
Nine	M. A. Nash	January 8, 1923-April 9, 1927
Ten	John Vaughan	April 9, 1927-August 19, 1936
Eleven	A. L. Crable	August 19, 1936-January 13, 1947
Twelve	Oliver Hodge	January 13, 1947-January 14, 1968
Thirteen	E. H. MacDonald (acting)	January 14, 1968-April 15, 1968
Thirteen	D. D. Creech (appointed)	April 16, 1968-December 31, 1969
Thirteen	Scott Tuxhorn (appointed)	January 1, 1970-January 11, 1971
Fourteen	Les Fisher	January 11, 1971-June 30, 1984
Fifteen	John Folks	July 1, 1984-June 30, 1988
Sixteen	Gerald Hoeltzel (appointed)	July 19, 1988-January 8, 1991
Seventeen	Sandy Garrett	January 8, 1991-January 11, 2011
Eighteen	Janet Barresi	January 11, 2011-January 13, 2015
Nineteen	Joy Hofmeister	January 13, 2015-

Chapter 7

Cameron: Managing the Statewide Expansion of the Common School System

(1907-1911)

A nearly two-decade-long evolution of Oklahoma Territory's common school governance—Board, Superintendent, Department, county superintendents and district administrators—provided the blueprint for the structure to be expanded at statehood across what was Indian Territory. Among these various levels of administration, the sole modification was the composition of the Board, from gubernatorial-appointed members to constitutional *ex officio* members: Governor, Attorney General, Secretary of State, and Superintendent as secretary. During the constitutional convention sentiment arose to minimize the politicization of the appointment authorization of the Governor and a way to do that was to create oversight by executive officers. The appointed educators on the Territorial Board were able to offer valuable advice to Oklahoma Territory Superintendents, especially those who lacked an understanding of common school governance. This new Board of executive officials had priorities elsewhere and anticipated the Legislature would very soon create a Board of educators, or so was the hope and expectations of the executives and the state's educators. Even the legislators anticipated a professional Board by appropriating funds of $3.00 per day for meetings plus the per diem cost for members to attend meetings.[1] Pointedly benefitting the Superintendent was a narrowing of responsibilities through the elimination of the Auditor's duties and a guarantee of a designated term exclusive of the whims of the Governor.

No perceived need arose to change substantially the Superintendent's office with the exception of an additional staff member or two to serve the doubled constituency. Problems encountered in the years of governing the schools in Oklahoma Territory were exacerbated with the addition of Indian Territory which previously had no coordinated territorial oversight excepting federal supervision of the tribal schools. Oklahoma Territory Superintendents wrestled with several endemic problems and requested legislative assistance to solve them with mixed results. For example, collection and compilation of data, necessary for preparing an accurate annual report, was oftentimes not forthcoming from county and local district school officials. Approval was sought for financial sanctions for those entities failing compliance with the law. Federal supervisor Benedict still maintained oversight of the federal funds, a festering problem with the new Superintendent who wanted no interference from the federal supervisor, but was restrained because of the extent of the continued funding from Washington to the former Indian Territory schools.

The Superintendent functioned at the apex of the administrative hierarchy responsible for common schools by reporting to the Governor and the Legislature, coordinating textbook selection and distribution, structuring qualifications and professional development for teacher certification and employment, and data gathering and reporting. Expeditiously, many counties were formed and held elections for several positions including superintendent. Thousands of districts were created in a five-year period. In this first term of statehood government the Superintendent had to grapple with bringing order to somewhat chaotic conditions in the former Indian Territory as well as attempt to improve conditions in Oklahoma Territory.[2] Significantly, and implicit in the responsibilities, the Superintendent would be an advocate for public education within the political realities of reelection.

Taking Advantage of a Privileged Legacy

When the major upheavals convulsed the South in the mid and late 1800s, those with wealth and status were better able to withstand the adverse effects of the war. E. D. Cameron inherited an enviable legacy of family reputation and financial advantage for his father was a lawyer, an editor, an owner of a large plantation with many slaves, a colonel in the Confederate Army, and was well respected in the community. He was active in politics as represented by his thirty-year editorship of the *North Carolina Argus*, that state's organ of the old Whig Party. E. D.'s mother, also well educated, was highly influential on his life and became his mainstay after his father died when E. D. was only four. The younger Cameron basked in his privileged childhood and youth, excelling in oration and debating. He acquired a top-quality education and launched a career that could reward him financially. At a young age he won local elections for seven years for city attorney in his hometown of Rockingham, North Carolina, while also maintaining a private practice in a nearby town. Opportunities looked limitless for a highly successful career arising from all of the advantages afforded him through the acquisition of wealth and status by his father and the close nurturing of his abilities by his mother. Cameron's formative years and early career were spent in the cauldron of the Civil War's aftermath and early Reconstruction days, a period of significant influence on his attitudes towards politics and Blacks. But a seed planted in childhood grew to fruition, eventuating in a shift to a sacrificial call to become a minister, choosing the Methodist Episcopal Church, South. Soon, as a dashing, young, well-educated bachelor, he pulled up substantial roots to follow a ministerial commitment 1,200 miles west for a brief, but significant, stay in North Texas where he pastored small churches, met his wife, and their first son was born. They transitioned to Norman, Oklahoma, in November 1891, when he was hired to pastor the First Methodist Episcopal Church there.[3]

Cameron quickly established himself in Norman and became involved in church and political affairs across both Oklahoma Territory and Indian Territory by 1894. Sufficient were his efforts of engagement in both arenas that he gained a favorable reputation that resulted in his gubernatorial appointment to the Superintendency even though he lacked any credible experience in teaching or educational governance. On the other hand, such expectations were not high priorities for the governors, and the Board was comprised of educators who could advise the Superintendents. He anticipated that the appointment was not destined to be long term and that he could continue his ministerial duties with the Methodist denomination (see chapter one for Cameron's accomplishments during his Territorial tenure).

Cameron's return fulltime to his chosen profession in December 1896 both as a church pastor in multiple locations and in denominational leadership and his continued involvement in education affairs through speaking engagements and participation in teacher organizations increased his visibility across the twin territories. When he vacated the office of Oklahoma Territory Superintendent, his assignment was in Muskogee, Indian Territory. Earlier he had been accepted by transfer into the denomination in Oklahoma at the Forty-Seventh Conference held in Ardmore, November 1892. One year later, Reverend Cameron was elected a traveling preacher, a pattern of assignments over the next eight years that caused him to move his expanding family frequently. For almost a decade, he served Methodist churches in Norman, Oklahoma City, El Reno, Muskogee, Chickasha, and Pauls Valley on a fulltime basis with the exception of his term as Oklahoma Territory Superintendent. However, by 1901 and while living in Chickasha, he switched allegiances by withdrawing from the MECS and joining the Baptists, assuming his first assignment in McAlester. Religious affiliation and denominational leadership positions provided Cameron high name recognition across Indian Territory and Oklahoma Territory. For several years, his pastoral duties allowed him time to lead as President of the Indian Territory Baptist Convention. He served also as a state representative on the Southern Baptist Convention Mission Board. Over several years he was active in leadership roles at the Territorial Baptist conventions, and in 1907 in recognition of his Superintendency leadership, he was selected as one of three conventioneers to meet as a group to draft articles of incorporation for a university. Subsequently, he was elected as a trustee for the new Oklahoma Baptist University. Obviously, his influence stretched beyond the confines of the local churches in his circuit, and he was comfortable with the traveling necessitated by his denominational responsibilities.[4] An expansive and growing network associated with his religious activities would eventually serve him well in the first statewide election.

His commitment to vocational activities did not preclude him from pursuing involvement in the Territories' educational affairs and politics. The oratorical skills developed in his youth, honed through his pastoral duties, and the logical reasoning developed and refined through his preparation to be, and practice as, a lawyer burnished his speaking and organizational abilities. Examples are: in May 1897, he was chosen to deliver the commencement sermon, "Man Shall Not Live by Bread Alone," at Edmond Normal School; he was a member of every education convention held in either territory leading up to statehood; he was intimately involved in the establishment of OBU and served on its inaugural board of governance. By the beginning of 1907 Cameron had established impressive credentials from which to legitimate his campaign for the Superintendency at statehood. Although he was well known and connected politically, educationally, and religiously with the dominant power structures across both territories, his influence was less among the Black and Native American populations. However, during his Oklahoma Territory Superintendency he was a proponent for quality for the Black separate schools and appreciated the clarification of the separate school law passed by the 1897 Legislature, even though the law was enacted after his term had ended.[5]

Competing in the Inaugural Election

Because Cameron's numerous pastoral assignments across both territories, leadership in two denominations, and service in the offices of Superintendent and *ex officio* auditor in the sixteen-year territorial period made him a recognized figure throughout the land, that he was a Democrat was only slightly advantageous. Oklahoma Territory was predominately Republican and with the larger population of 733,062, Indian Territory was Democratic and counted 681,115 persons. By late spring 1907, the excitement of the upcoming constitutional convention, the Democratic primaries and convention, and subsequent statehood captured his attention and resulted in his becoming a candidate for Superintendent. At the time he was pastoring a Baptist Church in Sulphur.[6]

As an elected official, he would serve at the pleasure of the people rather than of the Governor as was previously his case. However, he would need to work closely with the Governor as a member of the Board if he wished to advance the cause of public education and project harmony within the highest level of state educational governance. Projecting a successful leadership image would be important to win reelection should he decide to do so in 1910. But for the moment, should he win election, no longer would he need to serve as auditor and, if he wished, subject to his denominational approval, he could continue his ministerial responsibilities.

E. D. Cameron
James T. Brady, The State of Oklahoma, Its Men and Institutions
(Oklahoma City: The Oklahoman, 1908), 19.

Different formats were followed by the two major parties with the Democrats opting for a primary to sift the potential candidates to one while the Republicans chose by election at their August convention. Cameron bested Robert L. Knie in the June 8 primary and Calvin Ballard was preferred over G. D. Moss in the Republican convention to become the party standard bearers heading into the general election. Knie, in 1906, became the first county superintendent to be elected president of the Oklahoma Teachers Association and presided over its demise as the two territorial teachers' organizations merged into one. Some, possibly city superintendents, rumored that he was poorly qualified even though he had a college degree and many years of experience. Knie led the convention in Shawnee in which both territorial associations met jointly. Moss had been active in the educational arena for several years and Ballard was the federal supervisor of the Choctaw Nation schools for the previous eight years. Ballard's initial appointment was in 1899 as the supervisor of the Creek Nation schools. His and John Benedict's appointments stirred resentment among the Creek Council members who believed these positions were a waste of money. Ballard's performance for that year pleased Benedict who then transferred him to the same position with the Choctaws. "Ballard readily won the confidence of the Choctaw people by recognizing their potentialities and calling on them for help as he sought to help them…Because of this attitude and procedure, he was acclaimed throughout the Nation and given credit in Federal circles for the splendid response of the Choctaws after the first initial [sic] difficulties had been settled."[7] Ballard was well known in Indian Territory because of his leadership skills and would have been a capable Superintendent. His chances of winning election to the office would have been greater had he been a Democrat. Knie and Moss were from Oklahoma Territory and Cameron and Ballard from Indian Territory.

Both Democratic candidates campaigned for the office in the popular format of newspaper ads and benefitted from highly complementary articles by supportive editors. Knie purchased an ad in *The Oklahoma Farm Journal* in which he emphasized his major points. First, uniformity of textbooks was critical along with their cost being reasonable. "I shall do my utmost to secure the best books in educational value and quality of material and workmanship for the least possible cost."[8] Second, school consolidation was a necessity because rural children deserved to be provided quality educational opportunities afforded to students in larger schools. Continuing, Knie believed the quality must be sufficient to allow students to matriculate from one level to the next through the university. A similar ad was placed in *The Oklahoman* June 5. Compliments for his efforts to consolidate schools came from the *Oklahoma School Herald* as early as April 1906. Cameron was boosted by a lengthy article in *The Sulphur Democrat* in which he delineated twelve "I favor" statements beginning with separate schools for the Black race equal to those for the white race. *The Oklahoman* published a brief political ad, "Professor E. D. Cameron," submitted by S. M. Barrett. Campaigns sponsored newspaper ads as did individual supporters, but the preferred option was a paper's support through a favorable editorial or article.[9]

Although Cameron was not the incumbent per se, he chose to run on his record of a decade earlier describing in some detail his involvement in organizing the common schools and the normal schools. Specific emphasis was focused on his segregation efforts. Cameron, a slave owner's son, wrote, "I made the first speech delivered in Oklahoma in favor of separate schools for the Negroes. It will be conceded that I took the leading part in keeping Negroes out of our Territorial schools and in separate district and city schools until the democratic legislature passed a separate school law in 1897."[10] He was proud of his influence to discourage a group of Black students from demanding admission to the Edmond Normal School, told them he believed they should have quality separate schools, and said he would recommend to the Legislature that appropriation be made for a territorial school of first-class character combining the features of an industrial school, a normal school, and a university. When he reported to the Legislature January 8, 1895, he fulfilled his promise regarding the segregation effort.[11] What was happening in Oklahoma Territory in the mid 1890's was a microcosm of national events that witnessed the US Supreme Court's *Plessy v Ferguson* decision. Jim Crow laws were alive and well, and boosted by the Court's decision. Cameron's intent on providing "quality" segregated schools both pre- and post-*Plessy* was formed in the cauldron of deep-seated racial experiences of his childhood and early career.

Candidate Cameron parlayed these platform planks, for example, extending the present educational system in Oklahoma Territory to Indian Territory, organizing districts in Indian Territory and erecting buildings, creating a uniform system of textbooks and selling the books at cost to the students, establishing a county high school in each county, articulating a system of free public schools beginning with the district school and ending with higher education, and building two normal schools in Indian Territory, into victory. His opponents, both a Democrat and two Republicans, were not novices with little understanding of educational governance. But none of them had the credentials unique to Cameron, former Superintendent with visibility across both territories. Voters chose the candidate with the most experience. When only a month remained until the election, others who might have been interested, Republicans John Benedict and J. E. Dyche, the incumbent Territorial Superintendent, opted not to run. The former was already earning a $3,000 salary—the Superintendent would earn $2,500—and the latter chose to compete for state auditor. Election day, September 17, Cameron garnered 132,962 votes to Ballard's 99,912 and Socialist Party candidate Joseph Hanna's 9,678.[12] Cameron was to embark on a challenging journey that would set precedent for subsequent administrations.

Setting the Precedents

Six weeks into his term, Cameron was required to submit a report to the Governor. With Baxter's resignation effective December 31, 1906, and Dyche finishing the unexpired term at statehood, Cameron was the third person to hold the office within the previous twelve months, and he did not fail to mention this rapid turnover in the first of his annual reports to the Governor. Brevity of his time should not have precluded his ability to file a report, for the data were already collected and his previous stint informed him of the process.[13] Cameron was at least tangentially aware, if not fully cognizant, of the minimally functional educational conditions pre-existing in Indian Territory: few organized school districts, funding for the tribal schools from the tribes and the federal government, few white and Black children afforded access to an education, and what was available was on a tuition basis. Worsened conditions in the hiatus between his terms as the white population was growing rapidly would have been known to him since he was a resident of Indian Territory for some of those years. His report in December of

1907 was written with the statistical data from Oklahoma Territory and in light of his first-hand knowledge and observations of Indian Territory school offerings.

Statistical data for 1907 and 1908 are by necessity incomplete, but they provide a snapshot of the status of the collection system in the newly joined territories. Data were being collected for fifteen years already in Oklahoma Territory, but such was not the

Table 7.1 Population, enrollment, ADA, and number of teachers 1907 and 1908

	Dec. 31, 1907 O. T.*	Dec. 31, 1907 I. T.*	Dec. 31, 1907 O. T. + I. T.**	Dec. 31, 1908 O. T. + I. T.**
Population				
All ages	733,062	681,115	1,414,177	n/d
Ages 6-21				
White male	118,325	n/d	n/d	235,710
White female	111,089	n/d	n/d	222,771
Black male	5,226	n/d	n/d	19,354
Black female	5,532	n/d	n/d	19,376
Total	240,176	230,000	470,176	497,211
Enrollment				
White male	103,199	n/d	n/d	139,209
White female	79,373	n/d	n/d	137,063
Black male	2,542	n/d	n/d	10,337
Black female	2,289	n/d	n/d	10,466
Total	187,403	32,431	219,834	297,075
ADA				
Male	50,921	n/d	n/d	87,879
Female	52,240	n/d	n/d	87,794
Total	103,161	n/d	103,161	175,673
Teachers				
White male	1,340	n/d	n/d	8,091
White female	2,857	n/d	n/d	
Black male	60	n/d	n/d	645
Black female	129	n/d	n/d	
Total	4,386	2,000	6,386	8,736

Sources: Department of Commerce and Labor, Bureau of the Census, "Population of Oklahoma and Indian Territory 1907" (Washington: GPO, 1907), www.2.census.gov/prod2/decennial/documents/1970pop_OK-IndianTerritory.pdf; Second BRDPIO (Guthrie: SDE, 1908), 132-33.

Note: For 1907, aggregate data are for twenty-six counties in Oklahoma Territory and estimates for sixty-eight cities in Indian Territory. By 1908 the data are for the seventy-five counties in Oklahoma.

*O. T. denotes the former Oklahoma Territory and I. T. denotes the former Indian Territory.

** O. T. + I. T. denotes the former two territories now combined to form the state of Oklahoma.

case in Indian Territory, at least, not to the extent of the former. The 1908 figures in table 7.1 reflect additional time for improvement in the systematic collection and compilation of the data, but obtaining accurate figures was challenging since, in the former Indian Territory, formation of districts and construction of school buildings continued apace.[14]

Collection and categorization of the data reflect what was considered the eligible school age (Oklahoma Constitution, article 13, section 4 set attendance for ages 8-16 for at least three months of the year for all children of sound mind and body). The division of two races had its roots in article 13, section 3: "The term 'colored children,' as used in this section, shall be construed to mean children of African descent. The term 'white children' shall include all other children." *Plessy v Ferguson* in 1896 declared that a child was Black if he or she was any part Black, and Cameron was operating under this legal basis for generating and displaying the figures of children and students. For him personally, such a distinction was also entirely appropriate. Oklahoma's Legislature would not enact a comprehensive separate school law providing guidance for the Superintendent for another six years, but when it did, it left no doubt about the intention to keep the races separate.

Much changed in one year: the number of students, teachers, districts, and county superintendents reporting to the Superintendent increased twofold or more. While there were many problems and considerable chaos, such a dramatic increase no doubt helped the generally optimistic Cameron to write in his second report, "Our resources are abundant, and we can run in Oklahoma, as we now have underway the finest district school system in the world." And he added, "We believe today we have the best system of county institutes known in any State of the Union, in spite of any defect that may exist in the present law, and we hope that we may continue to hold this honored place."[15] Who was to question such audacious claims with no factual data to buttress them and what good would it do?

At statehood the federal government's involvement in, and financial support of, the public schools continued and would do so for almost a decade. The slow transition in governance irked Cameron, for, in his 1908 report, he wrote that only elected officials should control and supervise the schools. "In the opening of the year we had some trouble with the representatives of the Department of the Interior in regard to certain national schools in the bounds of the state…For us to surrender any of the rights of local self-government would be far more disastrous to us than any benefits could possibly be that we would derive from temporary financial aid, no matter how large the amount donated by the national government." Additionally, "If…the gentlemen representing the national schools do not try to interfere in any way with our county and district organizations and recognize the absolute authority of the State [sic], we welcome their assistance."[16] Cameron was determined to wrestle all control away from the federal superintendent and the tribal supervisors; meanwhile, the state was favorably disposed to accepting the desperately needed federal funds. Transitions were made more difficult with the federal representatives being Republicans and the state's leadership Democrats.

Cameron, particularly aggravated by the thorn in his side Benedict, who was unwilling to cede authority as quickly as Cameron preferred, aggressively pursued Benedict and the four supervisors of the national system (tribal nations' schools), essentially saying, if you want to support the schools financially, that assistance will be accepted sans strings attached. Cameron's comments reflected the times. "Federal interference" was a popular term during the Con Con with vestiges following to the present day. However, as the newly organized schools in the former Indian Territory needed the federal money, Governor Haskell did not regard Cameron's report and earlier (Dec. 19, 1908) interview comments necessarily germane to the interest of local self-government. Thus, the schools continued to receive federal appropriations and federal supervision.[17]

Pleasant Valley School District #15, Payne County, operated 1899-1941, reconstructed in 1987, Pleasant Valley School Foundation, Stillwater, Oklahoma

The first of Cameron's annual/biennial reports included recommendations deemed imperative to the continuing evolution of a respectable statewide school system: a gubernatorial appointed textbook commission authorized to enter into multi-year contracts with book publishing companies, normal schools created in the former Indian Territory to equate to the three already existing in the former Oklahoma Territory, a new separate school law, a school for the deaf and mute, schools for blind children and destitute orphans, and several secondary agricultural schools. Those wishes granted by the Legislature were a revised separate school law; a textbook commission; funding for, but no permanent location for, a school for the blind at Fort Gibson and an orphans' home at Pryor; and agricultural schools at Tishomingo and Lawton.[18]

Legislative enumeration of the Superintendent's primary duties, effective May 20, 1908, required him to assess the extent, kinds, and costs of the state's instructional programs (preferably at the secondary level) and then to advise school boards and communities those that were most satisfactory and desired. Second, he was to determine where to recruit highly qualified teachers (out of state?) and to recommend to the normal schools plans for the preparation of teachers. And third, he was to recruit teachers for the various subjects to be taught and to generate public support to the importance of those subjects. While the Legislature enunciated these expectations, reality posed great challenges: county superintendents' independence in decision making, no normal schools in the former Indian Territory, Oklahoma Territory normal schools' ability to recruit quality faculty, Cameron's small office staff, no professional Board to provide guidance to the Superintendent, and operating in a highly-charged political environment. No favor was extended to Cameron when the Legislature created the Board of Pardons, named him *ex officio* president, and set meetings of this board to be the second Monday of each month.[19] The practice of dual assignments was carried over from the territorial period as the Legislature desired to gain maximum benefit from a limited number of government officials.

By the end his first full year in office, Cameron described the status of the schools to the Governor who subsumed the Superintendent's report in his own report to the Legislature. Cameron's statistics reflect substantial increases in enrollment and ADA from 1907 to 1908 (see table 6.1). Obviously, much improvement was desired with an ADA of 175,673 or 35 percent of 497,211 eligible, and the enrollment of 297,075 was but 60 percent of those eligible. But, constrained by an ineffective compulsory attendance law, the standard of a minimal school year of not less than three months between the first days of October and June, and parental purchase of the textbooks, the education system was faced with a severe challenge to increase student participation and time spent in the classroom.[20]

While Territorial Superintendent, he enjoyed the wise counsel of the Board members (president of the Edmond Normal School, president of OU, a city superintendent, and a county superintendent), but now his Board consisted of three other executive officers and himself. Minutes of any meetings are not extant and only a few letters of correspondence give evidence of this Board's functioning. In laudatory comments of the Board Cameron assessed the significance of that body: "Perhaps the most important work of the State board of education [sic] is the proper administration of the law in regard to State certificates." Cameron, as the chief administrator, was responsible for supervising this function and duly reported that, under his direction, questions were prepared for city and county examinations leading to the issuance of 6,471 first through third level certificates and 1,208 temporary certificates.[21]

However, he was complimentary of the critical assistance he received from the Governor, Secretary of State, and Attorney General. What was desperately needed was a Board of educators to lay the foundation of the state's education system, according to Cameron, who realized his own inadequacy in this endeavor. To his chagrin, such preferred assistance and oversight were not forthcoming during his term leaving the Superintendent open to criticism of political maneuvering that eventually led to his defeat in the 1910 Democratic primary. Cameron's recommendations in December 1908 were some of the previous year that failed legislative enactment, modifications of recent enactments, and new ones including the state providing free textbooks to all children, additional Department supervisors of the agricultural and domestic science courses in the high schools, and encouragement for the establishment of accredited high schools in every county. Specifying agricultural and domestic science course supervision was to fulfill article 13, section 7 of the Oklahoma Constitution, the only specific provision referring to subject areas.[22] By now Oklahoma's Legislature was comfortable with expressing expectations and failing to appropriate sufficient funds to implement quality education programs, a practice that continued to plague the state in the decades and century to come.

Mid-term Assessment Amid Political Realities

Essentially lacking Board guidance, and with limited precedence, Cameron was trying to supervise a decentralized system of thousands of school districts, elected county superintendents operating without school boards (only commissioners), and the start-up of eleemosynary institutions and normal schools. He did access a key conduit for communicating with the educators, their association and its annual convention late in the calendar year. But the limitations of that avenue surfaced in the 1909 meeting, "A political row developed when the leadership, prompted by Cameron, refused to endorse Governor Haskell, a move purportedly to keep politics out of the session."[23] Internal politics in the teachers' organization forced the Superintendent into an undesired conundrum since the Governor was a Board member.

Active participation with the association resulted in his selection as its president for 1909. Cameron's position and status helped with this election, and he used his influence in leading the OTA. Under his presidency the membership grew as did the attendance when 3,500 attended the annual meeting in Oklahoma City December 29-31, 1909, an increase of more than 50 percent over the previous year. Rapid growth in the annual meeting of 1909 resulted from convening the meeting in Oklahoma City instead of Shawnee and by an expansion of the number of teachers across the eastern half of the state. What was to have been a significant achievement for Cameron quickly degenerated into a bitter divide that culminated in the following summer's Democratic primary.[24]

When Cameron showed up with supporters, normal school presidents and faculty, who planned to introduce a resolution praising his administration's success, the Resolutions Committee upstaged them with their own resolution to "enhance Cameron's political fortunes." Those opposed to Cameron outnumbered those in favor and, in no time, the antis coalesced around R. H. Wilson. Wilson's supporters would work for ten months to ensure his election and then wait for the spoils to be divvied up. In 1953 Francis Oakes assessed the 1910 campaign: "There has probably never been a more alert and determined opposition to any man who has run for a second term of office in the State of Oklahoma."[25] As president and conference moderator, Cameron supported J. B. Taylor, superintendent of the Oklahoma City school district, to replace himself. Anti-Cameron forces, uniting with the primary aim of replacing him as Superintendent, condemned him for using the OTA for political purposes. Two camps were agitating for the Governor's seat with the election still almost a year away. Cameron had already earned the enmity of Bill Murray and, ironically, both would be unsuccessful in the 1910 election. Taylor, for his part, was fired only a week after assuming the duties for his political support of Cameron. For years, the 1909 convention was described as the "most political."[26]

Cameron, on several occasions, urged establishment of normal schools in the former Indian Territory equal to those currently operating in the former Oklahoma Territory. Simultaneously, W. C. Rogers, Principal Chief of the Cherokee Nation, was pushing Governor Haskell and the Legislature to take advantage of the Federal Act of April 26, 1906, disposing of the public buildings belonging to the Five Civilized Tribes. More specifically, he suggested that the female college and seminary in Tahlequah be bought as a site for a normal school. Various sources of pressure were applied to force the Legislature to act. Timing was exquisite, for the Legislature was receptive to Cameron's urgings to establish normal schools. Southeastern Normal in Durant and Northeastern Normal in Tahlequah were established through HB 25 and HB 236, respectively, March 6, 1909. Less than three weeks later, SB 83 created an unnamed normal school (later named East Central) at Ada. Parity with the west side of the state was now achieved, and Cameron would play an integral part in staffing these new institutions.[27]

The territorial statute creating the Board of Education of the Normal Schools in 1890 was carried forward verbatim of its origin into statehood. A five-member board, three gubernatorial appointees and *ex officio* members Superintendent and state treasurer, held considerable power and influence over the selection and retention of administrators and faculty. Institutional presidents were replaced as well as faculty with barely a moment's notice, setting the stage for animosity to develop against the board members. Politics was no stranger to the actions of the board with Republicans dominating during territorial days and then Democrats thereafter.

Cameron became embroiled in the machinations of the normal school board in 1909 when the eastern side normal schools were established. His earlier stint in the mid-1890s involved only the Normal at Edmond, but even then, politics was ever present since he represented the only Democratic Superintendent of Oklahoma Territory. Opening and staffing three additional normal schools offered Cameron, as president of the governing board, opportunities to extend his influence in the rapidly expanding state education arena. Concomitant with prerogative was the potential for pitfalls, and Cameron had maneuvered both, winning the initial battles, but in 1910 losing the war for reelection.[28]

Notable recommendations in 1909 for legislative action were: a compulsory attendance law, free textbooks for all students (again), three normal schools (again) on the eastern side of the state (achieved), penalties for school officials failing to submit reports to the county superintendents and Superintendent, and school instruction on the humane treatment of animals and birds. Compulsory attendance and parents having to buy the textbooks were tightly connected. When parents were unable to pay for the books, they simply did not send their children to school knowing that the educators could do little to force attendance. When many local school officials, barely better educated than their students, were delinquent in adhering to reporting mandates, Cameron wished for some leverage to enforce compliance. Lastly, the request for instruction on the humane treatment of animals fit nicely with the constitutional mandate for teaching agriculture and the domestic sciences and with the American Humane Society's emphasis on preventing cruelty to animals, especially workhorses who were too old to work.[29]

Mounting Political Opposition in the Final Year

Cameron's priorities for the first eight months of 1910 were split between fulfilling his bi-vocational duties of ministry and managing the duties of his office and campaigning for reelection. Familiarity with all of these responsibilities eased his completion of the activities, but his decision to seek another term focused his political energies. Campaigning for reelection began in earnest in early summer, just three years from the first election. He now had his record both to defend and on which to build his platform. Opposing groups laid out allegations and accusations of political chicanery in dealing with Normal School faculty and the OTA. Undaunted, he traveled to Chickasha, the hometown of his primary rival, R. H. Wilson, to speak. There he defended his record and catered to the locals by reminding them of his efforts to have the Girls' Industrial School located there. Additionally, he expressed approval of the practice of the Superintendent accepting campaign contributions, and he explained his version of the travel expenses to attend the National Education Association meeting in Denver.[30]

Shortly after the Chickasha speech, he was castigated in the *Alva Pioneer* for his part in removing a faculty member at Northwestern Normal School: "This is a notice to every faculty member in the state. Either get in line for Cameron, or a meeting will be called, at which no one but he and his henchmen are present, and the offender retired to private life."[31] The attacks were not over for, a few days later, a circular was sent out alleging graft, corruption, and intimidation of teachers. Presumably originating in his opponent's office, this four-page pamphlet detailed alleged travel reimbursement irregularities and lodging at expensive inns while on official business, and hinted at political persuasion techniques designed to secure campaign financial contributions. Cameron responded to the charges and ascribed responsibility to his opponent. Specifically alleged were non-renewals of some of the Normal School teachers' contracts purely for political reasons. Political opponents accused Cameron of exacting revenge against the Normal School faculty who opposed him in his reelection campaign.[32]

Early state newspapers were highly partisan in their political support, commentary, and endorsement. The *Chickasha Daily Express* was no exception both in its articles and highly prized locations for political endorsements and it was published in the hometown of Grady County superintendent Wilson. A July 20 political advertisement asked several questions of Cameron including: "Did you not use the influence of your high office to elect yourself president of the State Teachers' association at Shawnee? Are you not making your office documents, for instance the pamphlet on Consolidation of Schools, campaign literature paid for by the state? Didn't you give a plum to a county superintendent in the southeastern part of Oklahoma, if he would stump eight counties for you, and isn't he doing it?"[33] Those allegations were not surprising, considering that elections are always political, and Cameron did have a record to defend.

Campaigning for reelection and fulfilling the duties of the office were not the only things on Cameron's mind in July 1910. Previously, the Governor had moved his office from Guthrie to Oklahoma City resulting in a lawsuit to determine the legality of the move. A judge approved that move but prohibited any other executive offices from moving. An ensuing Oklahoma Supreme Court decision rejected the prohibition and allowed other offices to follow the action of the Governor. Reported by the *Oklahoma City Times* of July 25 was Cameron's stated intent also to move his office and documents immediately. Soon he accomplished that move, but that did not deter him from effectuating his other duties. By the end of his term, he was a member of the governing board for several state institutions, commissions, and agencies: normal schools, Colored Agricultural and Normal University, School for the Blind, Industrial Institute and College for Girls, Agricultural and Industrial Commission, Board of Pardons, Board, and School Land Commission. In his office, assistant superintendent, clerk, and stenographer positions in 1907 were augmented by an agricultural assistant and a diploma clerk. Correspondingly, office expenses grew from $1,500 annually to $2,880 by the 1911 fiscal year.[34]

Wilson defeated Cameron in the August 7, 1910, Democratic primary by a 57 to 43 percent margin. Now that Cameron's political and employment status was determined, he applied his energies fulltime to finishing his term. He completed and submitted to the Governor his annual report that, importantly, included a recommendation for a form of tenure for teachers. Ironically, he, only a short time earlier, was accused of voting to summarily dismiss normal school faculty. Teachers in the state's education institutions, he argued, should be provided some protection once they served a successful probationary term.[35]

By the fall, Cameron was compiling the data and considering his third and final report to the Governor and Legislature. As he reviewed the progress and challenges of the fledging statewide common school system and his term as Superintendent, he considered both what the state, the schools, and his office needed. For the state to move forward, the school year needed to be lengthened and the compulsory attendance law strengthened. He believed school districts should be permitted to establish kindergarten classes in recognition of the value of early educational intervention. The Superintendent's advocacy of offering kindergarten is surprising when the state was struggling to organize a coherent system of grades 1-12. Conversely, attendance was minimal and sporadic partly because of the demands of farm labor, the curriculum varied in breadth and depth and lacked coordination and standardization, and teacher competence barely rose above the level of the students in the hundreds of secondary schools scattered across a large geographic area, a dire situation requiring much attention and improvement. Cameron's address of that compelling need was to recommend approval for the employment of a high school inspector, a request that was granted March 22, 1911, through SB 139 that included the salary and specific duties. His recommendation that the Superintendent's salary be doubled to $5,000, no doubt a fully justifiable notion, was a magnanimous gesture towards his successor and bitter rival.[36]

Cameron's assessment of the state system as a justification for his requests to the Governor and Legislature went beyond the financial needs. On the positive side, creation of the 2,200 school districts in the former Indian Territory was more systematic and orderly than that of the 3,441 districts in Oklahoma Territory: "It is the opinion of this department that experience has shown that the average school districts [*sic*] in that part of the state formerly known as Oklahoma Territory are too small for the best school work…We have laid off much larger districts in the new counties in that portion of the state formerly known as Indian Territory."[37] Oklahoma Territory's experience over seventeen years should have provided some guidance for district creation in Indian Territory given that less than half of the state's land mass counted more than 60 percent of the school districts. Now that the state had in excess of 5,600 districts, it was time to rectify this inefficiency through consolidation.

Conclusion

Cameron proved to be a key player in the transition from two territories to one state, the melding of a fairly organized, but somewhat inchoate system in Oklahoma Territory with a mishmash of federal, Indian, religious, and other schools in Indian Territory. Never far from his focus was the desire to implement fully the constitutional mandate of a dual system of schools. Recommendations annually addressed the issues surrounding the organization and administration of separate schools, the majority of which were Black. Given the political climate of the state, concern for equality of the Black schools was less than for white schools, a circumstance that was not going to improve substantially for many decades. What he was attempting was but a microcosm of the larger government. Politics was intense with many plums to be plucked with but one example being the siting of normal schools and other institutions on the eastern side. He did not have the assistance of a fully functioning Board of educators to guide his thinking and actions and to share some of the responsibility. He exercised considerable prerogative regarding personnel in the various schools and institutions, and thus opened himself up to allegations of political maneuvering leading up to the 1910 election season. Ever the optimist, Cameron wrote in 1910, "This report will show we have established in Oklahoma a public school system equal to the best in the world."[38] Yet, he offered no comparative data to support his assertion, and his term ended in January 1911.

E. D. Cameron was very much a product of his era and privileged upbringing during the post-Civil War South, including a penchant for political involvement. The son of a politically active father and member of a wealthy family in North Carolina he migrated to Oklahoma after an abbreviated stay in north Texas. Cameron devoted thirty-two years of his life to the causes of religion and education in the twin territories and then the state. Though a strict segregationist, he directed his energies to providing quality educational opportunities for all students. Politics energized him to serve in Oklahoma's early history, both in Oklahoma Territory and at the beginning of statehood, resulting in several dissimilitudes: the only Democrat to serve as a territorial superintendent, the only Superintendent who served both during the territorial period and statehood, the first elected Superintendent, the only Superintendent to serve without the assistance and guidance of a functional governing board, the only Superintendent to have an institution named after him, the first incumbent to seek reelection unsuccessfully, and one of only three elected Superintendents to fail in their reelection bids. Near the end of his life he tested his political strength in the 1922 Lieutenant Governor's race, finishing last in a group of nine candidates. He was passionately patriotic, strongly devoted to his Christian ministries, particularly partisan in his politics, unabashedly supportive of education, and, perhaps understandingly from his southern upbringing, highly convinced of the appropriateness and necessity of segregation. He was honored while as Superintendent in 1908 when the Legislature created the Cameron State School of Agriculture in Lawton known today as Cameron University. It is one of only three public colleges in Oklahoma named after an Oklahoman.[39]

Chapter 8
Wilson: Surviving Turbulence Before Achieving Tranquility
(1911-1923)

As the first decade of the twentieth century ended and the second began, Oklahoma's political environment was turbulent and fierce, especially in trying to bring some organization and procedure to the provision of public educational opportunities to the citizens. Rapid creation of school districts in Indian Territory accompanied those previously established in Oklahoma Territory, resulting in more than 5,700 districts. Governance of this sprawling and unwieldy education system was assigned to thousands of administrators, hundreds of district superintendents, seventy-five county superintendents, and the Superintendent. Barely a rudimentary education was offered to the rural students who comprised a large majority of the total enrollment. Elected in 1910 R. H. Wilson was accountable to the people and could be somewhat independent of the Governor's desires, but he needed tremendous support from that office and the Legislature to cause significant improvement in the state's effort to educate its citizens.

Incumbent Superintendent Cameron in 1910 knew from his earlier tenure as territorial Superintendent in the mid 1890s the advantages of being assisted by an active Board of educators more knowledgeable than he was. The advice and direction that came from educators in those early days was critical to the founding and establishment of the territory's school system. He also comprehended well the limited expertise offered by the current *ex officio* Board members Governor C. N. Haskell, Attorney General Charles West, and Secretary of State William Cross.[1] During the first three years of statehood, professional education knowledge was absent and any assistance offered was couched in a political context. Service on the Board was intermittent and not the first priority or interest of the executive officers. The resulting vacuum allowed Cameron considerable flexibility and prerogative to act as he saw best, but left him on his own in bearing responsibility for his decisions. In this initial abbreviated term he seized the opportunity to build a substantial political power base with an eye toward seeking the nomination to remain in office. Regardless of the advantages and disadvantages accruing to Cameron from the temporary composition of the Board, creation of a Board of educators to govern the state's schools was a high priority of the Superintendent and the educators across the state.

The Legislature's doubling of the number of normal schools (established three in Indian Territory to equate to the number in Oklahoma Territory) during the first term of statehood was necessary to prepare enough teachers for the rapid growth in the number of students and schools. Cameron's *ex officio* role on the Board of Regents for the Normal Schools, and his election by those members as president of the board in 1908, allowed him considerable influence in staffing those institutions and overseeing the curriculum.[2] At least in this segment of his duties, he shared the responsibility, but ultimately this "protection" was insufficient to shield him from allegations of political favoritism and patronage towards administrators and faculty who were Democrats.

It was inevitable in a sparsely populated, rather large geographical state with an undeveloped transportation system that rural areas would require many small schools to serve the populace. Oklahoma Territory was familiar with the reality of the need for many of these schools, thus, when Indian Territory became part of the state, it developed a similar pattern. Early in statehood it was obvious that rural school districts possessed fewer resources than the larger city districts, and state supervision proved more requisite for the former than the latter. It was in this context of a rural state with thousands of tiny schools and districts, a small Department to administer the system, and the anticipation of the *ex officio* Board of executive officers being replaced by a Board of educators to provide the overall guidance that Wilson decided to contend for the Superintendency. Over time he and his successors would excite an extensive power base that would be greater in rural schools than in the growing cities. Moreover, Superintendents in the early decades would come with rural and small town backgrounds and experience.

From Kentucky to the Grady County Superintendency

Robert H. Wilson, the oldest of eight children, was born August 25, 1873, near Scottsville, a small town in Kentucky, ten miles north of the Tennessee border, and attended the country schools near his home whenever the opportunities were present. School terms were short in the early decades following the end of the Civil War and most of life's lessons were learned from the rigors of farming. The lure of the West became so powerful that the Wilson family pulled up roots, when Wilson was eighteen, and moved to Whitewright, Texas, only fifteen miles south of the Red River near Sherman. Over the next several years R. H., a common form of address in the early twentieth century, completed his preparatory courses and most of his college studies at the recently incorporated Grayson College. However, overwhelming financial demands forced him to discontinue his studies, but the consequence was not detrimental to his plans. Soon he was offered a position in a country school in his community where teaching occupied him during the winter months and farming the remainder of the year. He fell in love with Sarah Grace Womack, the two were married in September 1899, and seventeen months later a son Robert Lee was born. Eight years later, Mary Grace completed the family.[3]

Wilson at the age of thirty moved his family to Chickasha, Indian Territory, in December 1903 and soon began teaching and serving as a school principal in that city. Rapidly changing events offered sufficient opportunities for this young man to assume significant duties so that when the school board voted for non-renewal of the superintendent's contract, it tendered an offer to Wilson who declined it. It was a time of rapid change and excitement. The organization of state, county, and local governments beginning in November 1907 set the stage for county supervision of rural schools. Wilson ran for, and was elected to the new position of Grady County superintendent of schools. Although not initially disposed to pursue the office, he was persuaded otherwise.[4]

Grady County, as with most counties in Indian Territory, had not organized its schools similar to those in Oklahoma Territory counties. Immediacy of work was preeminent and Wilson accepted the challenge. Through his leadership and direction, beginning immediately after his election, he traveled to the state capitol in Guthrie to plead his case for a county high school in Grady County. Subsequently, he organized seventy-one school districts and oversaw the erection of approximately that number of buildings. Concomitant responsibilities were the hiring of the best-qualified teachers available, not an insignificant task, and the provision of activities for the professional growth and improvement of those teachers. Relatively speaking, little assistance, supervision, and oversight emanated from the Superintendent's office and the essentially non-functioning Board leaving teacher testing, qualifications, and certification to the prerogative and responsibility of the county superintendent.[5]

Wilson was concerned about the wise use of the limited financial resources available to support education. His upbringing accomplished through modest means provided an underpinning for his thoughts and decisions in the public arena. In his presidential address to the Oklahoma School Officers Association (OSOA) in January of 1909 he referred to the poor conditions of the rural schools in his native Kentucky when he was a young boy and he did not wish to see those limitations replicated. Purchasing supplies and providing facilities most efficiently were critical considerations to using limited funds wisely when he met with the school officers in Grady County in May 1908 to consider how to establish and operate the schools. Those present created a permanent organization and committees were appointed to study specific topics. Agreement was reached for the county superintendent to coordinate the purchase and delivery of desks, books, supplies, and coal to the several schools.[6]

R. H. Wilson

Fred. Barde Coll., 19383.M.W., courtesy of the Oklahoma Historical Society, no. 4298

His energy, ideas, and leadership in organizing schools soon captured the attention of people beyond Grady County. Election to the presidency of the OSOA in 1908 was followed by election to the chair of the executive committee of the Oklahoma State Teachers Association (OSTA) in 1909. At home he was elected to the Chickasha City school board and served two and a half years. Wilson's professional star was rising, his reputation was flowering, and he did not shy away from presenting his efforts and successes publicly. The *Oklahoma School Herald*, a publication officially endorsed by the Superintendent's Office, carried news from the various counties in its monthly issues. In December 1908 it reported that Wilson organized a Teachers' Institute and Reading Circle Course and served as its president, he divided Grady County into eight institute districts, and he held the first of what was to become monthly county meetings. So complimentary was the *Herald* that it described Wilson as "one of the most progressive and untiring school men in the great State of Oklahoma."[7]

A glimpse of Wilson's educational stance helps understand his perspective. In his speech to the OSOA, referenced above, he emphasized the two primary reasons for the necessity of such an organization: to advocate for and succeed in getting the legislation necessary for the educational system and to develop a collegial relationship and spirit among the public school administrators and teachers. In other words, engage in political activity for the benefit of the schools and develop professionalism. Wilson reviewed the historical development of the association in his address. There was the perceived need to effect good laws, and establishing an organization would facilitate that process. Certainly not a harbinger of things to come in the near future in his relationship with Superintendent Cameron, Wilson spoke these words, "With these objects in view our great and good state superintendent together with a few of the county superintendents who are interested in the building of the schools of the state met in a caucus and decided to call the first meeting of the State School Officers Association, which was held last year. We met and we counciled and for some reason I know not why, I was chosen your first president."[8]

Popular among the meeting's participants, he urged for the hiring of qualified teachers, for school boards to consult county superintendents before hiring teachers, and for increasing county superintendents' pay. His $100/month compensation, set by the state, was the same as for town and village principals in Grady County and they did not incur expenses for keeping a horse, railroad fare, etc. City superintendents received up to $2,500 annually. Wilson was part of an inadequately financed rural education system where the school year was short and qualified educators were sparse. In this environment a proficient and skillful leader with aspirations of advancement captured the attention of many including his peers.[9]

Wilson understood how important it was for every child to acquire a quality education and he knew that those educators responsible for providing the opportunity needed to know how to do it. Many of the county superintendents were inexperienced and had minimal schooling, so they needed knowledge, skills, and encouragement. No one was better prepared than Wilson for he could speak from a wealth of experience and accomplishment and project an image of one who overcame great odds to reach the penultimate level of administration. His school days, from his boyhood in rural Kentucky to his college years in Texas, gave him firsthand experience in the challenges facing poor students in rural areas. Initial teaching assignments in a rural school in Texas and in the Chickasha schools followed by his efforts to establish quality rural schools in Grady County expanded his understanding of the long term negative consequences of the inattention to the deficient and haphazard operation of poorly financed schools. Professionally, he was driven to attain the highest level from which he could positively influence the development of rural schools to be on par with the city schools.

Wilson As a Politician

When the initial, abbreviated term of the state's elected officials neared its end, and primary election campaigns warmed up in late spring and summer 1910, Cameron officially announced his candidacy for the Superintendency as a Democrat as did Wilson. Before it was over, allegations of wrongdoing, political shenanigans, corrupt actions, textbook issues, and other eruptions served as a precursor for the election cycles of the next 100 years. At this early stage politics became deeply embedded in the state's top education position with politicization of the position finding root, growing into an amorphous form that defied satiation.

Whatever harmonious relationship existed between Wilson and Cameron in early 1909, it dissipated later that year going into mid 1910 when both men filed on the Democratic ticket. Wilson, the up and coming, bright and verbally expressive, county superintendent, with the experience of running for his position three years earlier, competing against Cameron, the almost fifty-year old incumbent who was blending his professional with his ministerial duties, and with all of the accoutrements of his office, offered the voters a clear choice. What ensued was a nasty political campaign involving accusations and allegations of political favors engaged in by the Superintendent. Operating essentially without a functioning Board, Cameron had no one to share the blame for the decisions and actions of his office. He wrote in 1908, "Most of the work of the State board of education has been done this year by the State Superintendent, under the advice and direction of the board."[10] His staff of only a handful—courtesy of legislative failure to fund properly—was inadequate for the responsibilities surrounding the administration of a state educational system. Both candidates agreed on the absolute need for a governing Board comprised of educators to replace the current *ex officio* Board. Each platform contained this important plank, unaware obviously of what would transpire within the next two years. Cameron believed expansion of the Superintendent's office was imperative if he were to fulfill his duties more effectively.[11]

Wilson's brief tenure in leadership positions in statewide educational associations gave him a platform to elucidate his philosophy and offer concrete examples of legislation and financial needs for improving the education system statewide. In an era when official speechmaking and active solicitation for office were not developed as appropriate campaigning techniques, achieving name recognition was difficult. County superintendents and teachers were respected in their communities and thus able to help inform the citizenry. Additionally, newspapers, the most feasible communication medium, were highly partisan and pleased to print advertisements, some paid with the candidate's campaign funds and others by local supporters.

Educators across the state at all levels were divided into the Wilson camp or the Cameron camp, in part driven by those who benefitted from Cameron's patronage largesse. It was the incumbent Baptist minister/bureaucrat versus the organizer of a localized county system of schools and leader in the school officers' association. Campaign slogans were bandied about attacking Cameron, for example, alleging he favored ministers for school positions: "Down with preacher domination of our schools! Put the Preachers [sic] back into the churches and the school men into the schools." Cameron knew religious officials, even crediting his 1907 victory in part to the support of the laity and clergy of the Baptist denomination, so his preferences for education positions made him a target of such campaign fodder. He wilted under the withering attacks and Wilson won the Democratic primary with 57 percent of the almost 110,000 votes cast. Accountability for campaign expenditures was accomplished through legislative action but only for primary elections. Wilson's campaign spent $1,454.34 with a considerable amount for newspaper advertising compared to Cameron's costs of $1,428.74.[12]

The Republican primary had three contestants: J. E. Dyche, former Oklahoma Territory Superintendent and auditor, and unsuccessful candidate for state auditor in1907, garnered 32 percent of the votes; John P. Evans, head of the Agricultural Department at Northwestern State Normal for the previous year, and a member of the first state Legislature from Alfalfa County, received 37 percent; and G. D. Moss, professor at Central Normal School and former superintendent of the Cheyenne Public Schools and of Kingfisher County, got 31 percent after spending $225.81 on the campaign. Apparently with no ethical reservations, Moss submitted his expense record on the Cheyenne Public Schools stationery. Evans, with a slim plurality, won the primary after spending $421.53, nearly double what Moss spent but only a third of what each of the Democrats spent. Notable expenditures by Evans were for cigars, pies, donations to Black churches, and livery hire.[13]

The stage was set for the general election of November 1910 and the development of a trend that was to continue for 100 years. Namely, the Democrat would win and any significant excitement would be generated in a Democratic primary. Wilson's share was 50.3 percent, barely a majority, and Evans's 39.6 percent. Evans counted on support earned during his days as superintendent of the Pond Creek Schools and the Kiowa County schools, and as principal of Woods County High School, all in the former Oklahoma Territory. Lacking Wilson's statewide exposure and the support of the dominant political party, Evans was defeated. Finishing a distant third was the Socialist Party candidate, S. S. Smith, with 10 percent of the vote—not surprising with the recent growth of populism in Oklahoma. Rural tenement farmers forced to pay a fourth to a half of their income for rent felt disenfranchised and responded favorably to the Socialist appeal that also included suffrage for Black men. Dislike and disdain for the elite-controlled Democratic Party provided strong motivation for this third party.[14]

Four years later incumbent Wilson drew an opponent in the Democratic primary while only one person filed on the Republican ticket. Clinton M. Allen, head teacher at Marshall High School in Logan County, spent $793.32, but apparently was not very visible in his campaigning efforts. Wilson campaigned actively only seven days, but spent $1,460.92 including $3 for cigars, and won with almost 64 percent of the vote. Only one Republican, C. G. Vannest, superintendent of Noble County Schools, filed and at the state convention was nominated following a spirited contest among several persons, winning on the third ballot. Total primary and general election expenses amounted to $2,011.80.[15]

Wilson, confident of victory, campaigned only one day in the fall of 1914, relying on his record of the previous four years and his name recognition as incumbent. Vannest, on the other hand, stumped for the position and said, if elected, he would work for: free textbooks and fewer textbooks, a civil service system for teachers, equal pay for teachers who did the same work and had the same qualifications regardless of gender, and absolute separation of politics from the schools. Particularly critical of the Superintendent's efforts to curb the prerogatives of the local school districts, Vannest called the new laws requested by Wilson undemocratic and un-American.[16]

When election day arrived, four political parties supported candidates for the Superintendency: Wilson received almost 45 percent; Republican Vannest, 31 percent; Socialist J. O. Welday, 22 percent; and Progressive Cyrus H. Parrick, 2 percent. Parrick, superintendent of the Cushing Public Schools, stated in a political advertisement that his duties as superintendent at Cushing prohibited him from making a personal campaign, leaving the matter to the good judgment of the voters. Welday, state editor of the Socialist paper *The Appeal to Reason* and an instructor at an Oklahoma City high school, rode the wave of populist support generated for all of the executive positions to capture more than one-fifth of the votes. A couple of months following the election, Welday enunciated the Socialist position as a corrective measure to the exploitation of the tenement farmers and poor people.[17] Wilson's reelection was achieved even though he won less than a majority of the votes, as was the case for all of the executive positions that year. The Superintendent never hesitated from emphasizing his lifelong commitment to improving the education opportunities of rural students.

Four years later when the country was in the midst of World War I, the head of the education establishment drew two challengers in the primary election. Wilson built part of his platform for reelection on his leadership in the involvement of the schools in patriotic activities in their communities. He accentuated the virtues of the public schools and how they contributed to the prosperity of society. So successful was he that he entertained the thought of vying for the Governorship, but then opted to focus his energy on his own reelection. As in 1914, he was able to vanquish his opponents, this time Oklahoma A&M Professor of Agriculture for Schools, George Wilson, and A&M Associate Professor of Education, Charles Briles. Briles, the inaugural president at East Central Normal at Ada, survived the Board's purge of 1911 after serving as superintendent of Muskogee Public Schools from 1905 to 1909. During 1916, while professor at A&M, he was president of the OSTA, succeeding Wilson. Presidency of the teachers' association gave a person great statewide visibility in the education community, and Briles, the eighth Superintendent or candidate for the position since 1892, was no exception. During his one-year tenure he set the stage for an expanded legislative agenda and reorganization of the association with input and advice from his predecessor. Within a year following the election Briles was hired by the State Board of Vocational Education, chaired by Wilson, to be the state director of vocational education, proving that political foes need not be permanent antagonists. George Wilson also had been involved in education, holding various positions since 1891.[18]

Absent the benefits of the incumbency, to avoid the appearance of conflicts of interests and to focus their efforts, both Briles and George Wilson requested leaves from their faculty positions in January and campaigned actively until near the end of July. Meanwhile, as Superintendents typically did, R. H. blended his campaigning with his work activities. Just days before the primary, Briles withdrew from the race saying that his and George Wilson's positions ostensibly were parallel. However, Briles' name remained on the ballot and he captured almost 11.5 percent of the votes. Challenger George Wilson, after spending $1,480.10, garnered 36 percent and incumbent Wilson, spending a similar amount, won with 52.6 percent. Superintendent Wilson accused Briles, whom he knew very well and considered a respected educator, and George Wilson of colluding to confuse the voters over the name. In that November 1918 general election Republican J. N. Hamilton, Superintendent of the Ponca City School District, received 43.6 percent of the vote to Wilson's 56.4 percent. Hamilton's scruples allowed him to report on school district stationary that he spent no money on his campaign. Only a few days later the Great War ended, much to the relief of all Americans. Time would tell that this was Wilson's last reelection effort because he was contemplating running for Governor. Following the election, and when the OSTA (renamed OEA) convened its annual meeting in late November, incumbent Wilson received the approbation of the most powerful voice of the education establishment, confirmation that he won their support within the overall voting public.[19]

Leading the Education Establishment

When Wilson assumed the office January 9, 1911, Oklahoma's educational system was still in its infancy. Twenty years passed since the territorial legislature had established the Superintendent and county superintendent positions. The Territorial Board of educators that met frequently was replaced by an *ex officio* Board with no extant record of its meetings. During Cameron's term, there was little buffer between the Superintendent and the political forces at play as the two territories began their compromised marriage. Indian Territory was to receive the kind of benefits with which Oklahoma Territory was already familiar: county systems, school districts, normal schools, and curricula were to be formed. Cameron had considerable leverage to influence these developments and, by taking advantage of a vacuum in oversight and supervision, he operated with little impunity. But this legacy of minimal oversight proved to tax his successor's political acumen in a volatile environment. Wilson began his term following a bitter election season and residual hostilities that engulfed the first year of his term and that of the newly appointed Board.

The rapid expansion by 1912 both of the number of school districts in Indian Territory resulting in a total of nearly 5,800 statewide and of various kinds of colleges, agricultural schools, and eleemosynary institutions created governance challenges. Ten thousand twenty teachers were employed to teach the 556,852 children of school age. Far fewer numbers of these children actually attended the schools and the school year was only five months duration in many of these districts. To supervise and lead the educational community there were three professionals: the Superintendent, the assistant state superintendent, and an agricultural assistant, and three clerical employees: a clerk, stenographer, and a diploma clerk, all housed in the Mercantile Building in Oklahoma City. The citizens of Oklahoma City agreed to provide the money to house the various state offices at no expense until the Capitol was erected. Twenty-five state institutions (OU, two university preparatory schools, A&M College, six state normal schools, School of Mines, Oklahoma College for Women, Colored Agricultural and Normal University, six district agricultural schools, and six eleemosynary institutions) along with forty to fifty private and denominational colleges and academies provided education in addition to the common schools. Rudimentary education was offered in most of these institutions because of the common school system's minimal funding sources and difficulty of attracting qualified teachers. Legislative priorities leaned more toward creating institutions than to carefully and deliberately designing adequate funding and governance mechanisms for them. Governing the state institutions was a mix of independent and uncoordinated boards with the singular commonality of the Superintendent who served on a number of them. Legislative provision for common education's governance in early 1911 satisfied the educators' demand, but an additional burden on the Board was the oversight of numerous other institutions resulting in the Board's first year being the most tumultuous year prior to 2011.[20]

Twenty years of experience in staffing schools with even minimally qualified teachers in Oklahoma Territory showed the daunting challenge confronting the state officials in creating schools in the former Indian Territory. No more than 20 percent of all of the teachers had any college, university, or normal school training, and no more than 5 percent of the rural schoolteachers had any such training. Of those teaching in the rural schools, less than 50 percent had achieved more than the first year of high school and some had not completed the eighth grade. Teacher certification was no better. The Board issued state certificates valid anywhere in the state and counties issued certificates recognized beyond their county lines. In other words, an applicant who failed to qualify in one county could go to a neighboring county with a lower standard, qualify, and then return home with a "valid certificate." And, finally, the race issue involved local politics when, for example, in a district where there were more legal white voters than legal Black voters, but more Black children than white children and the white people paid more taxes than the Blacks, the law mandated that there be a Black board, striking the whites as an unacceptable arrangement. The separate but equal standard, etched into the Constitution, posed problems administratively for the officials responsible for its implementation.[21]

Creation of the State Board of Education

Wilson's support for a governing board of educators to coordinate governance and supervision of the entities that provided services to children at the pre-collegiate level was not unique. For several years the OSTA and the *Oklahoma School Herald*, mouthpiece for all educational matters, pressed for such a board. Newly elected and inaugurated Governor Cruce supported a total reorganization of the governance structure. His message to the Legislature January 10, 1911, reflecting his priorities, began with his recommendations for education. After raising the need for a statewide tax levy to generate funds so that every district could operate at least five months of the year, the Governor specified the form of coordination requisite for education. Part of his critique of the current status, and the concomitant demand for a change, was expressed in his belief that the situation was deplorable and resulted in duplication and wasteful extravagance. "The only hope that I can see for a correction of these conditions, lies in the creation of a Board of Education, and vesting it with adequate powers to deal with all matters educational."[22] Thus the Governor stated his position, somewhat to the disappointment of Wilson who desired a more limited Board, both in responsibility and experience.

Governor Cruce signing SB 132 creating the State Board of Education, March 7, 1911 Standing L to R: S. M. Barrett, W. P. Steward, Robert Dunlop, R. H. Wilson, J. Roy Williams, R. P. Wynne, courtesy of Oklahoma Historical Society, no. 8587

Various bills were submitted in the Legislature, including one to allow a salary for the Board members, and Wilson actively pursued his efforts to influence the legislation. He and two future Board members, Robert Dunlop and Scott Glenn, drafted a version creating a Board that would not supplant any existing boards other than the current constitutionally established Board. In the horse-trading, Wilson told Cruce he did not want to disappoint Dunlop and Glenn because they would lose membership on current boards if those boards were eliminated. Cruce attempted to assuage Wilson's especial concern that Dunlop's and Glenn's effort on the current Board of Regents for the Normal Schools would be for naught if that board were eliminated. Cruce stated that he would name Glenn, but he would need to inquire about Dunlop's eligibility, now that he was the elected state treasurer. Several attorneys were consulted including the attorney general who concluded there were no constitutional or statutory prohibitions. The Governor persuaded Wilson to agree to a compromise lest the Legislature pass no bill. March 6, 1911, the Legislature enacted SB 132, creating a seven-member Board responsible for textbooks and all of education except the A&M College and the agricultural schools. As a "super" Board, its president was the Superintendent who was to work with six other members with at least two of them to be "practical school men" with at least two-years experience in education in Oklahoma and have at least four years total.[23]

Enthusiasm ran high with matching expectation that the educational governance would now be free of politics. "At one strike the present state administration of Oklahoma removed political influences from the schools."[24] Governor Cruce weighed the selection of his appointees for almost a month. Chosen from nearly 200 applicants representing both major political parties, they were announced Saturday, April 8 without the legislatively-mandated Senate approval: Robert Dunlop, State Treasurer and former member of the Board of Regents of the Normal Schools, and Dr. A. C. Scott, Dean of the Graduate School at Epworth University (private) to two year terms; W. E. Rowsey, Muskogee banker, former member of the Board of Regents of OU and W. A. Brandenburg, Superintendent of the Oklahoma City School District to four year terms; and Scott Glenn, Superintendent of the Shawnee Public Schools and member of the former Board of Regents for Normal Schools, and O. F. Hayes, Chandler banker and former Lincoln County superintendent, to six year terms. The Governor met with the Board the same day as the announcement of their membership to convey to them the significance of the Board and their duties. They were not to serve narrow partisan political interests; rather, their obligation was to represent the interests of the state and the children in a non-partisan, cooperative manner.[25]

Writing to the Governor four months after SB 132 established the Board, Wilson, who believed strongly that the Governor reneged on their agreement, reminded the Governor of his disagreement with the bill. Wilson wrote that it was his intention and the authors of the bill to have the Board comprised of educators only. Initially, the bill was to restrict the Board's oversight to the common schools, but later revisions included responsibility for higher education, institutions for students with disabilities, and textbooks. Continuing, Wilson wrote: "We had many conferences in regard to this bill. Finally, at your urgent request and upon your promise that no member of this board should ever be appointed without my endorsement and that I should have your support in carrying out the policies of this Board, I consented and went to my friends in the Senate, at your request, and asked their support, which they gave, and the bill became law."[26]

On the one hand, the Superintendent now served on fewer governing boards and had legislative permission to appoint a secretary to the Board. Conversely, he presided over a Board with expansive authority. Wilson wasted no time in naming a secretary and in calling the Board into session only five days after the appointments were announced. His preference was for the following Monday, but some members could not meet until Wednesday, the twelfth. That day was devoted to organizational activities. Following a mandate of the Governor to investigate the mission and curriculum of the various state institutions, the Board decided that the heads of all of the state's institutions should be notified to appear before the Board, incredibly starting the next day. These leaders were to present an oral appraisal of the status of their institutions and then to follow up with a written report that included a list of the faculty who were designated to be retained or to be released the next year. First up was to be OU. Following the oral reports, the members decided to divide themselves into subcommittees to travel to the various institutions for a visual assessment. Based on this input only and without any due process, the Board decided April 28 through a committee of three to draft a letter to inform institutional heads and faculty of the status of their contracts. Approximately half of the presidents and some of the faculty were terminated.[27]

As might be anticipated, the Governor began to receive letters concerning rumors of these adverse decisions concerning President Grant Evans and some faculty at OU. And, only a few days passed before these individuals received confirmation of their dismissals. President Evans penned letters to Governor Cruce on several occasions expressing his thoughts, frustrations, and opinions. On June 30, he wrote, "Supt. Wilson himself seems to stand for what is most trivial and petty in political interference with University affairs." Again, a few days later, he wrote, "I am enclosing you a copy of a letter with a circular used during the campaign with reference to Supt. Wilson. Making all allowances for any possible personal bitterness, it would seem that there is enough suspicion of Wilson to make it advisable that the State Board of Education should control rather than be controlled by him."[28]

Pressure mounted as President Evans, and various faculty filed charges with the Governor against Wilson, Dunlop, Glenn, and Hayes. Later came a request to the Governor to call a special session of the Legislature to confirm the Governor's appointees to the Board. Former Oklahoma Territory Superintendent J. E. Dyche wrote the Governor to express support for the Board's actions to clean up the educational affairs and to caution him against removing any members. Affidavits, offers to testify, telegrams, letters of character references, and other forms of evidence were sent to the Governor. Finally, the Governor announced that he would conduct a hearing into the charges specifically focusing on Dunlop, Hayes, and Glenn. Wilson would be asked to testify, but would not be directly investigated because he was an elected official.[29]

Cruce's investigation ran two and one-half months, from August 17 to October 28, as he heard testimony from former Oklahoma Territory Superintendent S. N. Hopkins and Board members including Wilson regarding these charges: failure to perform their public duties, permitted politics to affect their deliberations, dismissed teachers without cause and due process, some members were biased in favor of the American Book Company, and unqualified persons were appointed for their positions. Cruce decided then what actions he would pursue, but delayed announcing them because he did not want to continue to roil the political wars. He would wait nine months! Obviously, Cruce had a difficult challenge that was ironically and primarily of his own making. He appointed a Board absent the advice and consent of the Senate. Within five months he personally was conducting a hearing to investigate charges against the members. Institutional heads and faculty lost their jobs without due process. And, he waited many months, and until the Board sitting in the capacity as the State Textbook Commission precipitated his decision, to announce it: "I, Lee Cruce, do hereby remove from position as a member of the State Board of Education, Robert Dunlop (current elected State Treasurer), Scott Glenn, and Frank Hayes."[30] All three members refused to resign.

In July 1912 Cruce met with the Board and ordered it to take no action on textbook adoption and to not enter into any contracts with textbook companies. Wilson wrote to

Cruce and reminded him of his promises on a number of occasions and in various venues not to interfere with the Board's assumption of its duties. He chose to include Cruce's reason for delaying the adoption, that it was bad politics and would injure the Democratic Party. In the final paragraph of that letter, Wilson wrote, "My first duty is to the State, and so long as I am State Superintendent of the State of Oklahoma and Chairman of the State Board of Education, I am going to conduct my Department as a separate and distinct branch of State Government."[31] In other words, Wilson was not going to be cowed by the Governor. Assuming the Governor exceeded his authority, the Board entered into several contracts. Throughout this time the Board continued to meet and to fulfill its legally constituted functions. Minutes of the October 31, 1912, meeting show the Board's assertion through a resolution stating that those three who refused to resign were instead still duly appointed and active members. Those "replacement" members were to be sent a copy of the resolution.

Next, in this continuing saga, when the Governor announced the names of three new Board members to replace the accused members and submitted their names to the Senate for consent, not only did that body not confirm the new names, they refused to confirm the names of any of the originally appointed members. In essence, no Board existed! Relief was on its way when Governor Cruce submitted names of four new members (a quorum) who were confirmed by the Senate in January 1913 with two more confirmed in subsequent months.[32]

Foundational Years: First Term

When Wilson entered office in January 1911 the education system was still under the governance of the *ex officio* Board that included the Governor who was also new to his position. As the Legislature prepared to meet for it biennial session, Wilson moved into his office and quickly assessed the needs of the Department and the common school system. Foremost on his list, besides the restructuring of the Board, was the addition of the position of state inspector of schools to meet the enlarging demands of his office. He immediately began lobbying for a Board comprised of educators and for the state inspector to augment the current staff in the Department. New Governor, several new legislators, and new Superintendent, with their own agendas and varied political skills, settled down to work on legislation. Wilson had to muster whatever political maneuvering strategies he could to achieve his goals. His request to the Legislature for a state inspector was granted in March. That body authorized him to appoint a person at an annual salary of $1,800 who was to visit and inspect the schools and serve as a liaison between the Superintendent's office and the local and county school officials. The Legislature approved the position, determined the salary, and specified the duties and Wilson was to select the person and supervise him. Most likely the Superintendent informed the legislators what the position description should be. By the end of the legislative session Wilson had almost achieved his top two priorities. The inspector position was created and the new Board was comprised of several educators, but not all.

Wilson believed a fragmented rural education system could be improved through consolidation of districts, but he needed data to bolster his argument. With his state inspector heading a committee of Board members Scott, Dunlop, and Rowsey, information was expeditiously compiled and published in a bulletin by September 7, 1911. Producing documents such as the consolidation bulletin required additional secretarial support as did assistance to the schools through the expansion of services and the collection of data. Quick growth in such activity forced Wilson in 1913 to seek legislative approval to hire a second stenographer. The request was granted for the position at $1,000 annually and increased the Department's staff from five to six and total salary appropriation to $9,500.[33] In these early days of statehood the Legislature not only funded the Department, but also decreed the positions therein and the salaries.

The Superintendent's rural school consolidation's high priority did not extend to the normal schools and other institutions. Conversely, Governor Cruce urged the legislature in early 1913 to abolish at least three of the six normal schools, both of the university preparatory schools, and five of the six district agricultural schools. There may have been excellent reasons for such consolidation, but the Legislature then and in the past one hundred years has achieved little progress in streamlining the system with notable exception being the creation of the coordinating board for higher education in 1941. As president of the Board whose purview included normal schools, Wilson was in no position to recommend such drastic action. However, he reiterated in his biennial report of 1913 his position on the composition and oversight of the Board: it should be reduced to four members who would be appointed from a list of twelve names submitted by the Superintendent. Also, another board should be created to govern the five eleemosynary institutions and a separate textbook commission of seven members chosen from a list of twenty-one submitted by the Superintendent. Wilson assumed Cruce was unable to identify or unwilling to nominate qualified individuals to key education boards, and he was offering his expert advice. None of these recommendations materialized that year nor anytime in the near future.[34]

In the Grady County superintendency Wilson was acutely aware of the paramount importance of communications between his office and the multiple schools in his county. The principals or head teachers in these schools lacked information about their responsibilities for reporting and for following the curriculum. He also knew from his experience in the association of county superintendents that many of them were ill-prepared for their duties. Thus, it was with urgency that as Superintendent sufficient curriculum materials, reporting forms and procedures, rules for certifying teachers and administrators, recently enacted school related laws, and other documents be developed, printed, and disseminated to the schools and counties across the state. He had to compensate for his predecessor who, with no county or district level experience, did not fully comprehend the dire need that existed. Wilson in his first year in office set about to correct the situation as reflected in the number and kind of documents listed in figure 8.1.

Wilson's concern for the quality of the teachers, especially in the rural schools, was manifested in multiple ways. Because the state and county officials were responsible for certification, the rigor of the examinations and the processes for issuing certificates varied. As long as the state permitted county certification, no permanent fix was feasible. Seven of twenty-nine recommendations for legislative enactment in 1913 dealt with examinations, certificate registration, county institutes, and minimum standards. By the end of 1914, Wilson reported the issuance of 10,018 county certificates, during the biennium of 1913-1914, as well as 2,118 state certificates of these kinds: primary, grammar, high school, special, normal, university, institute instructor, institute conductor, kindergarten, and temporary. Four fifths of the certificates issued were at the county level and beyond the scrutiny and regulation of the Board.[35]

When his initial thrust to encourage legislative action on rural school consolidation failed to gain traction, Wilson opted for a different approach in his second biennial report. There he urged the Legislature to adopt the county unit plan of administration. Instead of the current configuration of an elected county superintendent and local districts with their own boards, there should be a county superintendent appointed by an elected county education board, thus eliminating the local boards. (A few years later an independent survey commission offered the same suggestion.) Alas, it did not transpire during Wilson's tenure and, in fact, never did happen.[36]

Much to Wilson's dismay, the 1913 Legislature chose not to fund the school inspector's position it funded for the prior two years, causing its discontinuance and revealing the whims of the solons. Later, but not until December 1916 the General Education Board (national charitable foundation) decided to subsidize the position through the Department. Demand and need grew quickly to the extent a second inspector was necessary, vindicating Wilson and uncovering the problematic resistance of the Legislature. Wilson successfully persuaded the Legislature of this imperative, resulting in the Legislature in 1919 funding a second inspector position effective July 1 to complement the one funded by the GEB.[37] Salary appropriation was crucial, but, over the decades, the Legislature was often prone to creating positions and mandates, and then neglecting to fund them.

Wilson, as a former county superintendent, was cognizant of how the vicissitudes of the taxing potential among rural school districts caused a disparity in the lengths of the school years. Wealthier districts could afford to offer classes for more weeks and

Figure 8.1 Publications of the Department 1911-1912

School Laws Passed by the Third Legislature
Rules and Regulations of the State Board of Education Governing State Certificates
Outline of Requirements for the Common Schools
Holiday Programs for 1911 and 1912
Rural School Consolidation Bulletin
Oklahoma Schools
Rules and Regulations Governing Common School Examinations
Annual Statistical Statement
Course of Study for the Summer Institutes and Common Schools
Days We Celebrate (for 1912 and 1913)
High School Manual
School Laws of Oklahoma 1912
Improvement of Conditions in the Rural Schools
Oklahoma Educational Directory (two issues)
Fourth Biennial Report of the State Superintendent of Public Instruction together with the First Report of the State Board of Education 1912

Source: *Fourth Biennial Report of the State Superintendent of Public Instruction and the First Report of the State Board of Education, 1912* (Guthrie: State of OK, 1912), 9.

months than could the poorer districts. As long as the major source of financing schools was heavily dependent upon local taxation, wide variations resulted. Districts with sufficient resources and citizen commitment benefitted while those with less ability to generate revenue were disadvantaged. Funding for "separate schools," most enrolled Black students, was increased by the Legislature in 1917 but the State Supreme Court construed the statute unconstitutional because it exceeded the one mill limit. Wilson wrote in 1920 that, "It remains a solemn fact that the schools for negroes are not as good in many districts as they are for whites."[38] The Superintendent had access to the legislators biennially, placing him in a position to advocate for a solution to the grossly inequitable educational opportunity that saw some districts operate for only three months and others for nine. Wilson was distressed by the extreme variation and pled for the Legislature to address the problem. He informed the lawmakers of the status and sought to work with them to reach a reasonable solution.[39] Insufficient fortitude of the legislators, borne in large part from taxpayer resistance, mitigated attempts to achieve fairness in taxation and educational quality, a critical challenge in the state's early history and a harbinger of later battles over inequitable school financing.

Among the Superintendent's duties was the printing of the school laws biennially and their distribution to school officials and others across the state. The territorial laws, borrowed from other states and modified for Oklahoma's purposes, then amended by the laws passed in the first four years after statehood, were disjointed and thus unnecessarily complicated to understand, collate, and print for dissemination. In January 1913 Wilson recommended to the Legislature a codification of those school laws, and he was rewarded when the Legislature granted his request in May and the Governor signed the bill in early June.[40]

Wilson's leadership was recognized by the education community when he was elected president of the OSTA for 1915 at its November 5-7 meeting in Oklahoma City. Reelection to the Superintendency four days earlier, but with less than half of the vote, reflected the influence of the Socialist Party which was strong in rural Oklahoma, a constituency very critical to Wilson. However, his popularity across the education spectrum was uncontested, and now he assumed leadership of the largest and most powerful group of educators. Internecine rivalries surfaced between rural and urban interests and between Oklahoma City and Tulsa. In this year he emerged as "Mr. Education" in Oklahoma in spite of the OSTA's internal politics. Mostly positive voter confidence and the support of the Association convinced Wilson to engage aggressively in efforts to push for several programs he deemed important for the improvement of the schools, particularly the rural schools.[41]

He wrote a letter two weeks after his highly successful August 4, 1914, primary to the county superintendents, a crucial group politically for accomplishing his progressive goals, in which he described several necessities: a Model School should be established as an exemplar by every county superintendent, the school's patrons should be invited to join a patrons' club, a free community library should be created and stocked with books of interest to all levels of readers, and male students should be assigned maintenance to the exterior of school buildings and females the interior. Wilson aspired for the county superintendent to visit the school monthly and meet with the patrons' club. Spring county teacher association meetings at the county seat could include side trips to the school for the attendees to experience first-hand what a school could and should be.[42]

The Model School concept was sweeping the nation and fit quite nicely Wilson's notion of the school as the center of the community, not only with the educational focus, but also the social center. A high adult illiteracy rate concerned him, and one avenue to address the problem was through a community-centered school. What better resources would be available than the teachers and what better platform did he have to spread the "gospel" than the presidency of the OSTA. He persuaded the executive committee to invite the founder of "moonlight schools" to speak to that year's annual convention. "Moonlight schools" operated in school facilities with the teachers volunteering to teach the adults of the community how to read. As early as 1912 Wilson offered his thoughts of how to make better use of school facilities, another argument for a new perception of "school." A six-month average school year in rural communities left buildings idle much of the time. He harkened back to an earlier time when children had their "exhibitions," the young people their "literaries" and "spellin' bees," the farmers their "alliance," and the church folks went to "meetin." What could be done to tie the community together? He suggested that county superintendents and local school officials should schedule lyceums, presentations by ministers, lawyers, and businessmen, and musical programs. Wilson wanted the educational leaders to be highly visible and influential in the rural communities.[43] Prior county superintendent experience informed his insight into the challenges as well as the opportunities in rural areas.

Leading by Advocacy and Navigating the Great War Years

Wilson used the presidency and visibility of the OSTA in 1915 to promote the cause of education. For example, he initiated a campaign of district and county rallies for better schools, of two weeks' duration, culminating in a statewide rally held at the annual conference of teachers in November in Oklahoma City. The Superintendent's office prepared *A Brief Statement of the Growth of the Schools of Oklahoma for the Past Four Years* for distribution shortly before announcing the campaign. Wilson attributed a 30 percent increase in the average number of days in the school year from 1915 to 1916 to the content of the bulletin and its dissemination. Never losing focus, he recommended again, in 1916, a change in the law to create a county board of education. Such restructuring would, along with financial assistance, facilitate the development of high schools for rural students who had no access. Unimpressed, the Legislature failed to comply with Wilson's request, again.[44]

Because frequent teacher and superintendent turnover hindered the success of schools, Wilson recommended to the Legislature in 1913, and that body enacted, a law permitting districts to offer superintendents multi-year contracts not to exceed three years. Then, in 1916, Wilson requested the same consideration for teachers, limited only by the individual teacher's length of certificate. Going a step farther, he urged the Legislature to specify the conditions under which a teacher could be terminated: conduct unbecoming a teacher, incompetency, failure to comply with the terms of the contract, and failure to follow directives of the superintendent. The Superintendent's modus operandi was to be assertive in representing particularly the rural schools' interests, but also generally the interests of all aspects of education. He wanted the Legislature every biennial session to expend some energy reviewing and reacting to ideas for improving the schools.[45]

Permeating all of Wilson's reports and his activities was an overriding concern for the quality of education and life in the rural areas where resources—money and qualified personnel—were minimal compared to their urban counterparts. Exacerbating the problem he thought was the conservatism of the rural people making it difficult for their districts to make rapid progress. Wilson focused upon the improvement of rural schools in his biennial reports. "Not only in Oklahoma but throughout the nation, the rural school problem is entitled to first consideration because at least sixty percent of our boys and girls attend these schools...The law relating to city schools, because of its general character, is administered better than that relating to rural schools."[46] State oversight of the large number of rural districts rested on the competency of the county superintendents and their willingness to cooperate with the Department. Wilson found this configuration to be inadequate especially regarding the question of which claims of newly consolidated districts for state aid were legitimate. As a strong advocate for consolidation, he believed that if they were provided professional assistance from the Department and financial inducements from the Legislature, more districts might consolidate. With limited staff to meet the demand for assistance, necessitating an additional person to serve as a rural school supervisor, Wilson wanted to hire a person and pay the compensation and expenses from the funds appropriated for the consolidation and development of schools.[47]

When no legislative approval came and Wilson sought assistance from the GEB, which, beginning December 1, 1916, provided a fund for use in paying the salary and traveling expenses of a rural school supervisor, he exhibited his willingness to go beyond the usual political process to accomplish one of his highest priorities. Not until the 1920 FY did the Legislature appropriate the salary and expenses. The rural school supervisor position was not then legislatively created, and the compensation was separate and above the appropriation for the union and consolidated school fund. Wilson was especially pleased to receive the GEB Fund's continued financial support even when the Legislature agreed to fund the position.[48]

Wilson's biennial request for legislative action for a tax to guarantee a minimum six-month school term for all schools, a separate textbook commission, free textbooks and supplies for all students, and separate governing boards for institutions serving individuals with disabilities continued unabated. A new twist arose in 1916 when he asked for a board for the Colored Agricultural and Normal University (Langston) comprised of the Superintendent and two Black members appointed by the Governor: an educator and a successful businessman or in some reputable profession. State Board president Wilson, who grew up in a segregated Kentucky town of 400 ten miles north of the Tennessee border and who named his son Robert Lee, wrote that that Board always gave greater priority to the white institutions of higher learning than to those for the Blacks and less fortunate.[49]

Oklahoma's struggling effort to form a coherent "system" of education to meet the needs of both city and rural students received a much-needed financial boost from the federal government in 1917 with the passage of the Smith-Hughes Act. In most states' schools academics were prioritized over any other curricular areas, but the federal government deemed during the war that, for many students and for the needs of the country, the curriculum was insufficiently robust. While some viewed the national effort as an intrusion on the prerogative of the state to dictate the curriculum, most willingly accepted the money and initiated the program. Oklahoma schools were already offering courses in agriculture and horticulture per the dictate of article 13, section 7 of the Constitution, but the Smith-Hughes Act broadened the spectrum of vocational programs through financing. The Legislature established the five-member State Board of Vocational Education with the Superintendent as its chair to implement and provide oversight of the program. Wilson endorsed this thrust enthusiastically and consistent with his persistent commitment to improving especially the rural schools.[50] Receipt of federal money to augment the insufficient funds provided by the Legislature would help the state to educate its citizenry more fully.

Wilson as Superintendent operated at the pinnacle of an educational establishment in which the more prestigious leadership positions such as independent school district superintendencies were led by men. By the middle of the second decade of the twentieth century nationally few important positions were occupied by women, but deference toward Oklahoma women in leadership was gaining traction alongside the national and state movement toward women's suffrage. Suffrage was one thing, but the hiring of women for leadership positions was another. Wilson's influence and control were considerable at the Department and the Board where in 1918 four of his nine employees were female, but they were a record clerk and three stenographers. The new Vocational Education Board, as of 1917 and chaired by Wilson, hired a female secretary and two female part time temporary supervisors of home economics who, within a few months, were joined by a fulltime supervisor, the first fulltime, non-secretarial position in the state level hierarchy.[51] Even so, no male most naturally would have qualified for this supervisory position, so Wilson's choice was limited to a female.

The Third and Final Term

Oklahoma's seventh legislature provided much for which Wilson was thankful. For years he lobbied for restructuring the sphere of governance of the Board to narrow its jurisdiction and supervision, and 1919 was a watershed year. Textbook oversight was assigned to a state textbook commission formed with both the Superintendent and the Governor *ex-officio* as secretary and chair, respectively, and five other members named by the Governor with at least four of them public school teachers or superintendents. This composition seems redundant, if the Legislature wished to grant the Governor control given that he named five of the members.[52]

Aggregate institutional oversight was shifted from the Board to a board governing some of the eleemosynary institutions collectively and a separate board for each of these institutions: Miami School of Mines; Colored Agricultural and Normal University; University Preparatory School of Tonkawa, School of Mines and Metallurgy; OU; and the Oklahoma College for Women. These eleemosynary institutions (separate training schools for white boys, white girls, Black boys, and Black girls; western and eastern state homes for white children; and the Deaf, Blind, and Orphans Home for Black Children) were grouped under a new board. Consequently, the Board was left with the much more manageable supervision of the six normal schools, the separate state schools for the white deaf children and white blind children, and the common school system. Through the summer and fall of 1919 the Board, now able to focus on the needs of fewer institutions, studied the feasibility of authorizing the six normal schools to offer the bachelor's degree. In its final meeting of 1919 the Board with Wilson's endorsement sanctioned these institutions to expand their curricula and to offer the degree.[53] The Legislature's intent to focus the Board's responsibilities was a recognition of the growth and needs of the Department, the common school system, and the normal schools, but the way the Legislature formed the other governing boards set the stage for a proliferation of governing entities that reflected the influence of populism permeating Oklahoma circa 1920. With no over-arching board to coordinate the competing interests and needs of the other institutions, each institution had considerable leeway to determine its destiny subject only to the oversight of its board whose members were gubernatorial appointees.

Other notable accomplishments that year were the creation of the Department of High School Inspection within the Superintendent's office, the provision for teachers' annuities and benefits, and a state appropriation to benefit schools with insufficient capacity to generate revenues. Teachers would have to wait on the funding for the retirement benefits because the Legislature failed to appropriate funds to vitalize the provision. Through SB 182, authored by future Superintendent John Vaughan, a sum of $100,000 was appropriated to the Board for improving rural schools with the stipulation that no district could receive more than $500 in any year.[54] Wilson was ecstatic with the additional position in the Department, the various boards' construction, and the appropriation for rural schools. From his perspective it was a fruitful legislative session.

When Governor J. B. A. Robertson assumed office in 1919, he was distraught with the persistent inadequate funding of the education system, lack of a functional teacher pension plan, and poor rural schools, as evidenced in his request to the Legislature. His message also emphasized the urgency for more time in school: "Personally I shall not rest content until a full nine months' term is secured for all the primary schools."[55] To him, that esteemed body failed to meet its obligatory duty to improve the schools. Although it did pass legislation to add a unit for high school inspection in the Department, create a teacher pension system, and appropriate money for rural schools, it neither funded the pension plan nor established a stable rural financing plan. Two years later his efforts received more favorable attention when two of his recommendations became laws: a mandated teacher contribution to the retirement plan and a supplement for districts that could not raise sufficient funds through their millage levies. His dream of a nine-month school year for all students was not realized during his term, and the Legislature continued addressing its mandate of providing schools to all students through a piecemeal approach rather than designing a coordinated and comprehensive plan.[56]

The establishment of the High School Inspection Department was not the beginning of the agency's efforts to address the issue of quality and access to a secondary school education. As early as 1915, under Wilson's leadership, A. C. Parsons worked as a high school inspector. These two invited high school educators to attend the High School Conference of May 1916 where resolutions were passed to raise the minimum standards for teacher certification and course units in all high schools. Later in December that year Parsons met with higher education representatives to seek similar input. By 1919, forty-nine Oklahoma high schools were accredited by the North Central Association with the groundwork laid by the Oklahoma City High School in 1910 followed by Enid, McAlester, Muskogee, and Tulsa high schools in 1911. Accreditation of the larger town and city high schools was crucial into this second decade of statehood, but it was the small rural high schools with fewer resources where Wilson was more focused.[57] His own intermittent high school education provided him a background and a strong incentive to create equitable opportunities for rural students.

Enthusiasm was generated for a more permanent fix to school funding through a constitutional amendment, The Better Schools Amendment of 1920, placed on the general election ballot for November 2. Proposed was a 6-10 mill statewide levy, but it was rejected 188,574 to 169,639. Leading and directing the effort of the OEA to secure passage of the Act was their recently hired executive secretary, M. A. Nash. In spite of Wilson's indefatigable exertion and attempts at persuasion during his twelve years in office to get some type of permanent funding for the "weak districts" in the rural areas, it was to no avail. Undaunted and inspired by the vote on the levy, and through his influence and leadership with the OEA, he persuaded that organization to adopt, as part of its legislative program in mid-December 1920, a resolution to support a school survey of Oklahoma. Timing of this sequence of events prohibited him from mentioning in his annual report his support for the survey. However, the passion he felt for the need for quality schools for all (emphasis on rural schools rather than the separate, primarily Black schools) was reflected in these words: "If all men were created equal and if they are to have equal rights in a democracy, as guaranteed by the fundamental laws of our government, they are not only entitled to, but it is necessary that they have equal opportunities to secure an education to fit them for citizenship in this government. Equal educational opportunity does not exist today."[58] His aspiration was focused on opportunities for the large number of rural students and it was assumed that if the state were to comply with its constitutional mandate of equality to those students, Black students in separate schools and Indian students in the white schools would automatically benefit equally.

Legislative action culminated with Governor Robertson's signature on SB 19 May 16, 1921, creating the Commission of Educational Survey to conduct a comprehensive study to determine the efficiency of all public schools and educational institutions receiving public funds. This five-member commission with Wilson as chair, *ex officio*, and tasked with reporting to the Governor by September 1, 1922, chose the US Bureau of Education to conduct the survey. The cooperation of the Bureau of Indian Affairs was enlisted to include "a study of the special problems of education for Indians in Oklahoma."[59] Here, in Wilson's final year in office and the fifteenth year since statehood, a major study was underway to evaluate the progress and status of the state's education system in general and that of the Indians specifically. Although due at the beginning of September, the report was not presented to the Commission until December 14 and shortly thereafter to the Governor.[60]

Significant recommendations affecting the Superintendent's office and the Board would give more power and authority to the state agency (figure 8.2), specifically that that agency should have increased control over the requirements and standards by which counties received state funds, and the Board should be required to set the professional standards and develop an appropriate salary schedule for all educators. Much decentralization should be lessened, resulting in greater efficiency. Also, to accommodate this shift in responsibility and supervision, the Department's staff should be doubled and the budget increased fourfold. The Governor should be given expanded prerogative to influence the education system through a constitutional change of the Superintendent position from elective to appointive.[61]

Figure 8.2 Select recommendations of the Commission of Educational Survey

1. The position of Superintendent should be appointive rather than elective.
2. More authority for setting standards for appropriation, teacher certification, teacher pay, and teacher employment should be given to the Department.
3. The Board should have authority to approve budgets of subsidiary educational boards.
4. The Board should have authority to prescribe all details of school budget procedure.
5. Legislated organization and governance changes should be toward greater centralization.
6. The counsel and suggestions of the state's educational leaders should be valued and given serious consideration by the legislature.
7. From 1920 to 1925 the number of Department employees should be increased from fourteen to thirty and the budget from $26,600 to $102,000.
8. Institutions were identified for closure.
9. Teacher training programs in high schools should be discontinued.
10. An elective county board of education should govern all dependent districts and appoint the superintendent.

Source: *Public Education in Oklahoma, A Report of a Survey of Public Education in the State of Oklahoma* (Washington, DC: Department of the Interior, Bureau of Education, December 11, 1922), 359-404.

Allowing the commission report to speak for itself, Wilson refrained from offering any formal recommendations in his *Ninth Biennial Report* submitted in January 1923 because he believed it inappropriate to do so as he was leaving office and because his successor might not concur. Also, he desired not to detract from the significant assessment of this external review.[62] With these findings, analysis, and recommendations as with multiple other studies both by external and internal groups over the decades, the Legislature essentially did little. Timing may have been a factor as a new administration was inaugurated within a month of the report's release. Much controversy over the ensuing ten months leading to the Governor's impeachment and the inauguration of his successor relegated the report to a low priority level from which it never recovered.

During Wilson's twelve-year tenure, 1911 to 1923, rapid growth occurred in Department personnel and services as well as in the schools. The Department staff increased from six to thirteen. School enrollment grew almost 50 percent from 415,116 to 607,205, but 80,000 of these in 1922 attended schools open for fewer than 140 days; ADA increased from 236,548 to 409,774, teachers from 10,020 to 17,988, and total expenditures from $8,600,450 to $28,368,689. School districts dropped from 5,820 to 5,190 as many tiny one-room schools with few students and minimal finances merged with neighboring districts.[63] The state's common school system was evolving through fits and starts caused by the Legislature's inconsistent and incoherent attention to the needs of the students and the educators.

Wilson's influence was felt on numerous boards, agencies, and commissions. By the time he left office he chaired, or had chaired, the Board, the Board of Regents for the Miami School of Mines, and the Board of Regents for the Colored Agricultural and Normal University, and served as secretary of the Text Book Commission. He was a member of the Board of Regents for the Oklahoma College for Women, the Board of Regents for the School of Mines and Metallurgy, the Oklahoma Library Commission, the Board of Trustees of the Oklahoma State Teachers Retirement and Disability Fund, the State Board of Vocational Education, and the Commissioners of the Land Office.[64] The most important of these were the Textbook Commission, with overall authority for the selection and procurement of the textbooks, the Board, and the Commissioners of the Land Office, with control over all aspects of the mineral rights on, and leasing and sale of, land set aside by the federal Morrill Act.

His term was winding down and his successor was preparing to take office. Most likely had he chosen to run for reelection he would have won because he had strong support from the education establishment including the ever-growing, influential OEA, and he was a well-known figure across Oklahoma. His leadership guided the state's school system through many growing pains. Shifts in emphases were not unusual as evidenced by a stopgap major centralization of board authority in 1911 and then decentralization in 1919. Serious deficiencies in funding and in coordination of teacher certification persisted into late 1922. Those most concerned with education waited to see what the Survey would highlight and recommend, hoping that the Legislature would be proactive and effect the necessary changes.

Wilson provided stability and continuity in the Superintendency at a crucial time in the state's early history. His tenure proved to be the longest in the sixty-nine years from the beginning of the territorial period to near the end of Oliver Hodge's third term in early 1959. During his tenure it became obvious that Oklahoma's Legislature and the general populace, despite the claims of giving high priority to the education system, unfortunately were not able or willing to organize and fund it at the level requisite to creating a high-quality education experience for the students. Proliferation of school districts emphasized access over quality. Political chicanery was not unheard of; rather, it was alive and well. The OEA, dominated by school administrators, especially superintendents, both provided input to the Superintendent and Department and aroused political support for legislative action and the Superintendent's reelection campaigns. Upheavals and pressures from The Great War forced government officials at all levels to adjust to and accommodate the reverberations that roiled the country. That war added strain to an insufficiently funded common school system. Male teachers went off to fight causing a shortage of qualified teachers, and the general public was not sympathetic to imposing additional taxation on itself. Teachers were underpaid and had no pension system: the support was lacking to improve these conditions until 1921 when the Legislature appropriated funds for a minimal retirement plan.

Governor Cruce's attempt to manipulate the Board he appointed in 1911 caused angst for Wilson who was not reticent about standing firm for the Board's independence. With dogged determination Wilson presented the Governor and Legislature with proposals designed to improve the education system, especially the rural schools. Governance and supervision of the state's school districts, county schools, higher education institutions, and schools for those with disabilities, shifted from a centralized form in 1911 to a more manageable array of multiple boards in 1919. The result was a Board more able to focus on the common schools' needs and supportive services but it also led to a fragmentation of the governance of higher education institutions. With the generous assistance of school district superintendent and state senator John Vaughan in the 1917 and 1919 legislative sessions, Wilson achieved success in focusing attention to the precise needs of the schools.

Wilson tirelessly strove to improve common education knowing the importance of every child, regardless of race, receiving quality instruction and learning opportunities. He rejected the notion that rural students could not attend schools equivalent to larger, town and city schools because of a lack of funds and resources. Black students, enrolled primarily in the "separate schools," had a "separate but equal" right to the same education opportunities as white and Native American students. He advocated for district consolidation as an avenue for using limited resources more effectively. Yet, he met opposition from these same citizens who worried how such a combination might affect them adversely. Ironically, he had to convince them that consolidation was in their best interests, a contest still being fought and indicative of the dynamics involved.

Competing for the Governorship and Beyond

Success in three elections for the Superintendency led Wilson to believe that he could compete well in a bid for the Governorship in 1922. Most probably he could have won reelection to his current post, but he decided to test his political cachet for the more influential position. The state's political environment was chaotic with manifestations of Ku Klux Klan involvement. Stanley Frost of *The Outlook* described Oklahoma from an outsider's perspective: "There has not been time for the growth of civic solidarity or much State pride. Her schools are within six of the bottom of the list and her general literacy—and consequently the possibility of education through the press in political morality—is low. Add great discrepancies between the poverty of the farmers and the wealth of the oil boomers… dissatisfaction as a result of recent hard times…and you have the rough outline of conditions with which decency and progress must contend."[65] Of the five Democrats who entered the primary race, Wilson, with the open and dubious endorsement of the Ku Klux Klan (dooming his efforts) and the support of the education community and other public employees, garnered 31 percent of the vote and finished second.[66]

Wilson's political ambitions were not quite satiated as evidence of his effort to win the fifth district for a seat in the US Congress and his service and loyalty to E. W. Marland over several decades. In the congressional race in 1932 he finished third with a mere 14 percent of the vote. Previously, in 1912 and early in his first term as Superintendent and *ex officio* member of the Commissioners of the Land Office, he voted for a lease that helped to make Marland an oil magnate. Decades later he thought his relationship to the now Governor Marland would secure him an appointment to a government position, but he never received one. When Wilson died October 4, 1937, *The Oklahoma City Times* wrote that he was contemplating running for Superintendent once more, in 1938.[67]

Chapter 9
Youthful Nash: Leading Effectively
(1923-1927)

Fifteen years after statehood, and thirty-two years since the initiation of the territorial period, found the education system continuing to evolve with meager financial support from the state coffers. The Department operated with a skeletal staff while desiring to expand its influence for operational efficiency. Resources were limited in the rural schools forcing them to be dependent on the state office to accomplish the constitutional directive to provide an education to all those children within specific age limits. Complicating matters was the interpretation of *Plessy v Ferguson* allowing dual school systems competing with each other for limited resources, thus posing challenges for those especially committed to "equal" while separate. By now it was becoming obvious to some that the separate Black schools were not able to attract and retain the best teachers and to provide equal facilities. The Democratic Party's dominance in the quadrennial elections for the state executive offices gave the party little incentive to initiate bold actions to address the myriad problems facing an underfunded and uncoordinated school system. Even in a rare instance when the Legislature attempted to appropriate additional funds, the citizens responded with forceful opposition.

Wilson's ambition for a higher office, when he could have won reelection most easily, opened the door for someone new to assume the duties of the Superintendency. Economic and social conditions in the state fostered some competition among several political parties that drew support from a diverse group of vested interests. With no incumbent the timing was right for a knowledgeable and youthful person with political aspirations and a desire to be intimately involved in the advancement of education to seek the office. Mel Achilles (M. A.) Nash persuaded the voters that he was the most qualified to assume the mantle of leadership.

Experienced Beyond His Years

M. A. Nash was born in Tryon, a now long forgotten mill town in the pine forest of Hardin County, Texas, July 20, 1890, one year before his family decided to return to their native Georgia. At age twelve his family moved again, and this time it was to Arcadia, Oklahoma. He graduated in 1908 from the high school program at Central Normal School, where he was one of 934 students enrolled in the secondary or college program. Over the next eleven years he taught in three rural schools, served as high school principal at Granite and Madill, and was superintendent at Madill, Noble, and Idabel school districts. Not content to stay in any place very long, he moved frequently, about every two years. But his penchant for moving did not discourage his pursuit of Mae Clark whom he married August 5, 1916. And, all of this was accomplished before obtaining his bachelor's degree at OU in 1919.[1] Few people could have matched the breadth of his experiences as Nash did by his twenty-ninth birthday.

Superintendent Wilson, cognizant of Nash's accomplishments and rural experiences, and confident in his ability to fulfill the duties as the first chief inspector in the new Department of High School Inspection, selected him in 1919 to develop the basis on which that agency would serve the needs of high schools. Specifically, Nash was "to define official standards of excellence in all matters relating to the administration, course of study, instruction in the high schools of the State [sic] and to accredit those schools in which the specific standards are maintained."[2]

M. A. Nash
Courtesy of the Oklahoma Education Association

Consistent with his previous work history, he was again changing positions after a very short tenure. Nash did not stay long in this new position. In 1920 the executive committee of the OEA tabbed him to become executive director. It was a quick decision by both parties because, for the OEA, its previous director died suddenly and the Association needed someone immediately to lead its efforts to facilitate a coordinated attempt to achieve passage of the School Amendment Act of 1920. Nash's move to the Department and the fulfillment of his duties with the OEA for two and one-half years provided him with an avenue for attaining statewide exposure, experience, and publicity. Some observers at the OEA believed Nash's tenure there propelled him into public office. A highly professional performer, although not known especially as an innovator or crusader, he won the attention and support of influential people. No doubt being a Baptist, the largest religious denomination in the state, also worked in his favor.[3]

Politics In Action

Wilson's aspirations for the governorship flowered in early spring 1922, resulting in no wish for a fourth term as Superintendent. Nash seized the opportunity to expand his influence and filed in late April for the office. Others sought the position in the August 1 primary, but lacked the name recognition and breadth of his experience. J. P. Battenberg joined Nash on the Democratic ticket while five filled the Republican slate: G. D. Moss, former Board member and current teacher at Central State Teachers College (recently repurposed from Normal School); Horace F. Dowell, superintendent of Macomb Consolidated District; Otis McCord, former superintendent of Hooker School District living in Stillwater; Ralph H. Record, former superintendent of Waukomis Public Schools from Norman; and C. N. Peak, superintendent of Guthrie Schools. Moss spent only $12, Dowell, $206.75, McCord, $102.95, Record, $367.50; and Peak, $115.10 campaigning for the office. Each of the five received from 18 to 25 percent of the vote with Moss receiving the most and being declared the winner in this plurality system. Twelve years earlier, he had finished third in a three-way race for the Republican primary, but that did not dissuade him from another attempt.[4]

Battenberg, president at Northwestern State Teachers College, former superintendent of Atoka Public Schools, and viewed by Nash as his strongest opponent in either party, ran a spirited campaign in which he spent $1,168.58, as reported on that institution's stationery. Free textbooks, a simplified course of study, and federal and state aid for rural schools were planks in his platform in addition to "Take the schools out of politics and politics out of the schools." Supporting him was a combination of socialists and union leaders under the banner of the farmer-labor league. Much to his chagrin, Battenberg was alleged to have participated in a scheme in which his campaign received a $200 (equivalent to $2,871 in 2015) contribution in exchange for the secretary of the Board issuing two certificates to unqualified individuals. Wilson's Board secretary issued the certificates with the assurance that the recipients would soon be qualified for them. Battenberg and Wilson both denied any involvement or having any knowledge of the affair. In Wilson's tenure the Department issued certificates without his signature, a situation Battenberg vowed would not exist if he were elected Superintendent. To add to his commitment to running a proper office, he stated that he would appoint a Board secretary who was a qualified woman of experience, unquestioned integrity, and honesty.[5]

Nash spent $1,243.90 on printing, stenographic work, travel, and newspaper advertising to defeat Battenberg by a margin of 64 to 36 percent. Pamphlets distributed four days before the election said that Nash was one of several candidates for various offices who were endorsed by the Ku Klux Klan.[6] In the 1922 election, because the Klan overtly supported candidates for various offices, an allegation of that group's support was not preposterous. For some candidates Klan backing occurred regardless of a candidates' overt acceptance or tacit approval. Nash grew up in the segregated South, Georgia and Oklahoma, and lived and worked in southern and southeastern Oklahoma so he understood the racial and political dynamics at play.

A little over three months' time for campaigning gave the two contestants, Nash and Moss, an opportunity to inform the voters of their respective platforms. The former, better known across the state than the latter, when interviewed by a reporter from *The Oklahoman* in September, described the public's changing perception of a teacher and the most effective way to finance particularly rural schools. To Nash, the teacher was becoming more professional, more similar to a doctor, lawyer, or merchant. Primary financial support for school districts was shifting from the local district to the state, driven in large part by the intent to provide equitably for all students. The Legislature was in the throes of facilitating that transition through enabling a constitutional amendment, and Nash, still employed by the OEA, was a vocal advocate for the passage of the amendment. In the November 7 general election Nash, at age thirty-two, became the youngest person elected at the state level that year and, time would prove, the youngest ever elected to the Superintendency. He had reached the pinnacle of education for the common schools, but his influence in education circles at all levels was only in its infancy.[7]

A few short years later, incumbent Nash, having established himself in the position, was the lone entrant on the Democratic ticket for Superintendent in 1926. Voter apathy was identified along with possible perceived significance of the position in an informal poll of only twenty-eight people conducted by *The Oklahoman*. Fewer than half, twelve, knew he was Superintendent, eight knew he was up for reelection, and only five were informed of his duties. Possibly, equivalent percentages of the today's general population would offer similar responses reflecting an endemic problem in the lack of public awareness of secondary elective positions. Nash was a highly competent individual who impressed those with whom he knew and worked, so it was no wonder that he drew no opponent in his own party.[8]

That year's election offered a new twist in the election for the Superintendency when two women filed for the office as Republicans regardless of the uncertainty of their potential qualification. Anna Willis, superintendent of Lincoln County, and Mary Munson, a Woods County teacher, joined the Seminole County superintendent and a Norman teacher in contesting the Republican primary. Willis won that primary with a plurality of 34.6 percent, propelling her to the general election. Any Republican faced a formidable battle against a Democrat, but no candidate, and especially a woman, who invested as little money ($.95) to campaign as Willis did should have expected to win. Nash anticipated little threat from a Republican, spending only $197. A pattern was settling into place where, over the decades, Superintendency election outcomes were constant regardless of any factors except party affiliation—simply, Democrats won and Republicans lost.[9]

Often timing is crucial, and the November 1926 general election was a prime example of this. The Oklahoma College for Women's president George Austin died suddenly October 24, only nine days before the election, leaving the College's board unexpectedly searching for a replacement. As Superintendent for four years, Nash's *ex officio* chairmanship of the OCW Board equipped him with intimate knowledge of the College's progress and challenges, its growth and operation under financial constraints that faced all of education in the mid 1920s in Oklahoma. Thus, he knew firsthand that the president's compensation was considerably greater than his own (He had employees in his own office who were paid the same as he was.) and that it was an appointive position answerable only to a board. Should he apply and be selected, he could devote his total energy to his responsibilities and would no longer need to conduct a statewide campaign to keep his office.[10]

In the two months between the election and inauguration, Nash considered leaving the job for the presidency of the OCW at Chickasha. The opportunity posed a conundrum for two reasons: he had just been elected to another four-year term that he had, in good faith, intended to complete. All the advantages of the incumbency had accrued to him resulting in no contenders for the position on the Democratic primary ticket while all of the other state level executive offices drew multiple candidates. The voters expressed confidence in him and selected him for another four years. On the other hand, the presidency offered him a higher salary, no need to run for office, an entrée into higher education administration, and greater prestige. He wished not to appear to be dismissive of the public's trust in him, yet he would be handing his gubernatorial appointed successor almost a full four-year term.[11]

As chairman of the OCW board, he was responsible for coordinating the process for selecting a new president, giving him a decided advantage in the selection process. With no Board of Regents' prohibition against its own members' eligibility for the presidency, Nash applied. He was still the *ex officio* chair of the College's board and would be until his resignation from the Superintendency and removal from the Board. Following his hiring by the OCW board, he resigned from his elected position, effective April 9. The five-month hiatus between Austin's death and Nash's resignation provided an opportunity for a critique of a complicated political issue with ethical considerations, but nothing substantial ensued and Nash's replacement was involved in a similar imbroglio nine years later.

Leading the Department

Nash wasted no time before firing the first salvo to the Legislature only two weeks into his first term. Adequately financing all aspects of the schools including the textbooks for the students was an evolving process and a continuing challenge. One-third of a century after the founding of Oklahoma Territory and a decade and a half after statehood no fair school financing scheme was in place. The 25-30 thousand dollar Survey of 1922 (see previous chapter) proposed solutions to the problem, chief among them was for the state to create an equitable funding mechanism. Nash challenged the legislators to provide sufficient funds, in part, through the dedication of a third of the gross production tax to the permanent school fund that could benefit schools in perpetuity. From that reservoir the state could assume a large share of the responsibility for the funding of schools, thus removing the vicissitudes of local funding.[12]

All aspects of providing textbooks for the schools proved to be controversial in these early years and beyond as will be described here and in later chapters. Initial issues had surfaced more than a decade before, primarily regarding the selection and influence of vendors. Now, in the first half of the 1920s, the significant concern was the insufficiency of funds for textbooks. Different from his predecessor who surprisingly mentioned nothing about textbooks in his final biennial report, Nash resolutely encouraged the legislators to appropriate enough money to purchase textbooks for all of the students. Soon after Nash assumed the office and certainly to his delight, the Legislature on March 24, 1923, enacted HB 197 to provide free textbooks to grades 1-8 students. Six hundred thousand dollars were appropriated for 1924-25 with another $350,000 for 1925-26. Responsibility for the purchase and distribution of these books lay with the Superintendent, while the selection decisions were the prerogative of the State Textbook Commission where he served as secretary, *ex officio*. Ownership of the books was held by the state. In good faith the books were ordered, but it was discovered that the two-year appropriation of $950,000 was only about 55 percent of the amount needed. When textbook publishers were notified of the shortage of funds, they volunteered to consign the additional 45 percent and trust the Legislature to appropriate sufficient money to liquidate the balance. [13]

Nash provided the Governor in 1924 with a brief description and qualified assessment of the textbook law. Although the textbooks were funded in March 1923 they were unavailable for distribution until September 1924. He reported that a system where all students statewide in a given grade, for example, received the same textbooks worked generally, but occasionally caused some problems because urban schools' needs did not match the books selected. The free textbook law was expected to be advantageous, he said, but insufficient time had elapsed to be able to evaluate its worth, and the state was fortunate to have good textbooks. Certainly, while his comments were positive, they did not reflect the passion and excitement one might expect from the top education official after years of clamoring for such an arrangement by his predecessors and professional organizations such as the OEA.[14] However, it was the state's constitutional duty to provide a free education for the children and the Legislature was now including textbooks within that parameter.

Through SB 87 the Legislature in 1925 appropriated an additional $650,000 to pay for the books. But the Legislature was not finished with the issue of textbooks because, through SB 54, it repealed the free textbook law of 1923 and made the state-furnished textbooks property of the local school districts. Referendum petitions earned a stay of enforcement of the law and forced an election by the people at the November 1926 general election. In the interim, an attorney general's opinion kept the free textbook law in force. When the people spoke, they voted against the state question, thus repealing the free textbook law.[15]

Roiling the waters of the textbook issues in the first half of 1925 and causing headaches for Nash were groups within Oklahoma opposed to the state's provision of "free" textbooks and events occurring nationally, especially in Tennessee. The Oklahoma Farmers Union vociferously opposed the textbook law and mounted a campaign to obtain the necessary signatures for a referendum on it. In April the Union mailed letters to all of the county superintendents urging them to disregard Nash's memo to these administrators specifying the procedure for returning unused textbooks. An additional grievance surfaced when the Union learned that overturning the law would repeal the prohibition to the teaching of evolution in the curriculum. Contemporaneously capturing national attention was the Scopes Trial in June in Tennessee. This event spurred the major Protestant denominations in Oklahoma to enter the fray, siding with the Farmers Union.[16] During these turbulent times Nash as Superintendent and *ex officio* chair of the Textbook Commission was committed to following the law and implementing the decisions of the Commission, not an easy task.

Nash's biennial report of December of 1926 failed to mention the necessity of the Legislature to address the critical nature of free textbooks.[17] Granted, the people voted one month earlier to sustain the Legislature's actions denying free textbooks, but it would seem that the Superintendent would have taken a stand against shifting the burden to parents to pay for their children's textbooks. Granted also, Nash's reelection occurred the same day as the state question was decided, so politics may have played a role leading up to the election, most pointedly the sharp feelings of the public about all things related to textbooks. There were a few weeks between the election and when the Superintendent submitted his report to the Governor, giving Nash an opportunity to press the need for textbook relief. By the time the Legislature met in early 1927 Nash's priorities had shifted to his effort to secure the OCW presidency.

When the Educational Survey Commission in 1922 recommended a specific amount of money per pupil depending on grade level to be apportioned to each school unit based on the number of students, and the Superintendent for several years recommended free textbooks be provided, the Legislature took the bold step to provide funds for textbooks. However, what was a progressive step in 1923 was negated by that same body in 1925 and confirmed by the people in 1926. Obviously, the elected officials and the citizens were not ready yet for textbook costs to be borne by the state.

Another issue that attracted Nash's attention was quality education for the Blacks within the limitations of the separate but equal standard and the state's separate schools (primarily Black with a few white schools) law. In his 1924 biennial report, he suggested it was imperative that Black schools received better supervision and better support, and two years later he described the constitutional and statutory basis for the separate schools and reported on the current conditions: number of schools, students, and buildings. Unsatisfactory conditions caused by insufficient funding were prevalent in spite of these private funds received from several sources external to the state: from 1920 to 1926 the Julius Rosenwald Fund aided in constructing more than 100 school buildings and teacherages ($74,000 toward the total cost of $400,000); in the period 1924-1926 the John F. Slater fund contributed $4,600 for training schools for Blacks, the Anna T. Jeanes fund gave $5,753, and the General Education Fund in New York City provided $19,334 for rural school supervision including in the separate schools. Nash reported that even with these supplemental funds, some counties with large Black populations had no accredited high school. Such description fails to convince one that the state was meeting the separate but equal standard. He wrote about the problems of inadequate funding, yet chose not to highlight their severity through a separate recommendation for legislative action.[18] For a Legislature that struggled to provide adequate funding for white schools, guaranteeing that separate schools were equal even to this low standard was not a high priority. Private funds helped but were not intended to supplant state funds, only to provide stopgap assistance.

Nash's recommendations in 1924 addressed general funding, teacher certificate supervision, compulsory attendance, school governance at the county level, and illiteracy. Sufficient funding to guarantee equal educational opportunities would be possible only through a constitutional amendment that would allow a statewide levy, a necessity, according to Nash, to generate funds that could be distributed across the state on a per pupil basis. Not insignificant was the status of the Indian Trust Periods, lengths of time tribal owned land would continue untaxed by the state and costing the state an estimated $428,000 annually in lost revenue. Lending support to his contention was the above-referenced Oklahoma Educational Survey of two years earlier. Rural school organization was unwieldy and inefficient, demanding services from a Department lacking the resources to provide the assistance needed. Thousands of tiny districts operated, many without high schools, and functioned as independent fiefdoms. Seventy-seven county superintendents examined teacher certificate applicants and issued certificates to teach, creating an impossibility to achieve consistency across counties. Nash asserted that certificates should be issued only by the state even though it would increase state control at the expense of the local officials.[19]

Living History Class, Pleasant Valley School, 2005, courtesy of Pleasant Valley School Foundation, Stillwater, Oklahoma

School attendance rates were at such a low level that a stronger compulsory attendance law was imperative. Of the 723,883 students enrolled, only 441,037 were in average daily attendance, ranking Oklahoma's attendance rate the last among the forty-eight states. Nash believed parents who kept their children from school to assist with farm or other work were irresponsible, and assigned transiency, the apathetic attitude of Indian children especially, and the apathy of parents and guardians as additional causes. He averred a higher attendance rate in the long run would eliminate the need for literacy programs.[20] Nash was convinced that an improved quality in the schools and instruction would solve myriad problems, and that a compulsory attendance policy with some enforcement authority would complement the improved curriculum and instruction. Frequent attention to the issues of the separate schools tended to overlook the unique needs of the Native American students, but the Educational Survey did not. Under a section "Difficulties to be Overcome," the Survey highlighted these points: many fourteen and fifteen year old Indian students were found in first and second grades, Indian students did not always "receive proper consideration from white pupils and teachers," and Indian children attend "so irregularly that they receive little benefit."[21] Nash's perspective of Indian children's apathy, reflective of many educators' attitudes, was representative enough to be detected through the external surveyors' data collection.

Reporting to the Governor in December 1924, Nash referenced the 1920 census data to highlight Oklahoma's standing relative to the other states: thirty-seven had a higher per capita government cost, amount per capita spent for education was less than twenty-three states, and only fourteen had a greater per capita wealth. He concluded explicitly that Oklahoma had sufficient financial capacity for greater education expenditures and implicitly it needed the will to do so. Strengthening his advocacy was the recent study of Oklahoma's education system highlighting the necessity for significant changes to obtain a more effective and efficient delivery of services and instruction.[22]

State inaction to increase and improve its mandate to provide a free public education was one of several criticisms. Lack of parental support in their children's education contributed to the problems. County superintendent supervision over teacher testing and the issuance of teaching certificates exacerbated the problems. Lack of sufficient funding hindered the Department from functioning at a high degree. Existing multitudinous problems at several levels necessitated a coordinated plan to achieve the desired success. School financing, compulsory attendance, and teacher certification were addressed by Nash and his predecessor to no avail. The passage of several years, a vote of the people on a constitutional issue, an educational survey, and exhortations by several Superintendents were not successful. The Legislature initiated annual emergency equalization appropriations in 1923 but had not developed a permanent solution. Additionally, the county unit both for organizational and financing purposes needed to replace the current organizational hodgepodge.[23]

One way to advance the conversation advocating a major change in the method of school financing was to collect and analyze data showing the gross inequities in the financial support of the schools among the several counties of the state. Nash directed E. E. Brown, chief high school inspector, to glean data from multiple reports over three to four years submitted annually by school districts and county superintendents. The analysis showed poor counties with higher tax rates were unable to match per capita collections from rich counties with lower rates resulting in great inequities in teacher-student ratios and resources. Along with the need for financial reform was an increase in the amount of authority of the county superintendents so they could exercise greater oversight of the schools under their jurisdiction. Nash finally resigned himself to the fact that the county school governance plan was not going to be realized: "A pure countywide system of absolute finance and administration is highly desirable, but very difficult to accomplish." One of the many reasons was "the reluctance of many local boards to give up self-governance in a democracy."[24]

One of Nash's priorities unrelated to organization and administration was an initiative begun by his predecessor and labeled The Model School. The concept was advancing through a movement occurring in many states, and was embraced in Oklahoma under Wilson's direction. Participation in this movement meant Oklahoma's education system was in one way attempting to achieve parity with the more established state systems across the country. Through Nash's encouragement and leadership the number of these schools grew to 1,269 in 1924-25 and by another 696 a year later.[25] These grade 1-8 schools successfully met specific standards that had been determined to be advantageous, somewhat analogous to regionally accredited high schools. In some ways, they were the forerunners of the school accreditation for elementary schools.

Nash administered the state's educational system during a time when the Legislature provided significant solutions to few problems. External experts opined as did the Superintendent, yet chronic problems persisted through insufficient legislative resolve and grassroots support. Lacking any coalescence to finding solutions, no permanent financing scheme was achieved and the Legislature lurched from funding crisis to funding crisis. Inadequate financial compensation plagued the office of Superintendent and the other employees and may have influenced Nash's decision to depart for OCW. In the 1925-26 school year the three high school inspectors were paid the same amount as Nash, $2,500, and 110 school district superintendents were compensated at least that amount with some making as much as $13,000.[26]

During Nash's tenure the Department grew to fourteen employees, three were high school inspectors, including A. L. Crable who would become Superintendent a little more than ten years later, and three were rural school supervisors. Of the five women in the Department in 1926 three occupied secretarial positions, one was a rural supervisor, and the other an agricultural assistant. Organizationally, the Department had these service bureaus: school law and administration, reports and statistics, rural and elementary supervision, high school inspection and accreditation, budget and bookkeeping, free textbooks, and certification of teachers. Nash appreciated the Legislature's support to expand the number of employees and firmly believed the Department needed to focus its energies and resources on the improvement of the rural schools. More employees meant more hiring opportunities for the Superintendent who chose from those serving in the rural schools.[27]

The Department's ability to perform its duties depended upon the capability of the elected county superintendents to provide oversight of the thousands of rural, dependent school districts and the superintendents of the hundreds of districts with grades 1-12. It was not unusual for a county to have dozens of one-to-five room schools, each with its governing board of three members, and several grades 1-12 districts governed by five-member boards. This decentralized and somewhat unwieldy structure, while emphasizing local control and prerogative, made it imperative that Nash's employees interact frequently and substantially with large numbers of county and local school district officials.[28] The elective nature of the county superintendency caused the position to be set in a political dynamic that may or may not have been conducive to the effective functioning of the office and the schools within the county.

A Distinguished Career Extended

When Nash was hired by the OCW Board of two men and two women, and left the Superintendency in early 1927, at the youthful age of thirty-seven to lead that institution, its enrollment was growing slowly and positioned in the middle of the cohort of the teachers' colleges. In fiscal year 1928-29, it received general funding equivalent, per enrollment, to the six teachers' colleges plus a $200,000 appropriation for erection of a building. The timing was critical when he assumed the presidency, and he led the college for sixteen years, gaining status among Oklahoma leaders as an effective voice for OCW.[29]

The first four decades of statehood saw higher education frequently intertwined with intrigue and political machinations. Governors, the Board in 1911 especially, Superintendents, and legislators were not hesitant to express their concerns both publicly and privately leaving presidents and professors subject to the whims of politicians. Nash was tabbed in the late 1930s to coordinate the effort to bring cohesion to the higher education system so as to insulate it from meddling and reprisals of politicians. He chaired the group that produced a blueprint for higher education leading to a constitutional amendment establishing an overarching board of regents and a chancellor to lead that segment of education. Recognition of his abilities in this process and the range of his career experiences led to his being named the first chancellor July 10, 1943, a position he held until he retired June 30, 1961. Nash died in Edmond May 10, 1981, at age ninety.[30]

Summary

Nash proved to be an able and effective leader during periods of substantial growth of the institutions and agencies in which he worked. He was not highly political in the sense that he aggressively sought political office frequently. Politically astute, he was chosen to lead the OEA, by the public for two terms as Superintendent, to serve as president of OCW, and then finally to lead and coordinate the state's higher education system. He was a consummate educator, committed to improving educational opportunities for students of all ages including, to the extent possible, the Black students under the constraints of the separate but equal standard. Little, however, is found in the record of his advocacy for the improvement of the educators' attitudes toward the Native American students. He believed educators should act professionally and effectively and be willing to improve themselves. Soon after leaving the OEA and assuming the Superintendency he urged all teachers to be members of the OEA and the National Education Association. He thought teachers should subscribe to one journal related to their teaching expertise and rural teachers should read one farm journal regularly.[31]

His recommendations for legislative changes in the school laws reflected his professional commitment to improving instruction in the common schools. His proficient administration of the Department earned him a backhanded compliment by *The Oklahoman*: "In leaving the office of state superintendent of education to become president of the Oklahoma College for Women, M. A. Nash leaves behind him a record that has never been marred by any charge of maladministration." Chiming in more affirmatively was *The Frederick Leader*: "He has conducted its affairs so as to keep them absolutely above criticism, and at the same time has steadily urged the schools of the state to a higher plane of endeavor and accomplishment."[32]

Nash, arguably so, stands tallest among the Superintendents in state history for his service and contributions to the several levels of education. Although his tenure as Superintendent was short, four years and three months but ranked fourth of the eleven elected to the position, he served well in that capacity and forcefully represented the needs of the common school system to the Legislature. Politically, it was a chaotic time with the Ku Klux Klan's influence at its apogee and a governor who was impeached during Nash's first year in office. The most influential national event was the Scope's Trial with its controversial ripple effect on the content of the state's textbooks that further compounded the state's waffling on the method of financing those books.

His Superintendency tenure was sandwiched between two others whose terms were each more than twice as long as his. However unsettled the times were, great upheaval was looming in the not-so-distant future. Nash had the good fortune to serve the Superintendency in the decade between the Great War and the Depression, and the ability to stay above the skirmishes between the governors and the Legislature. Confident and assured in his outlook and actions, he moved frequently early in his career and then enjoyed long periods at OCW and the chancellor's office.

Chapter 10
Vaughan: Navigating the End of the Roaring Twenties and the First Half of the Depression Thirties
(1927-1936)

Oklahoma in the late 1920s was growing in population and in school enrollments, but continuing to struggle with funding the educational system adequately. Plagued by an excessive number of inefficient, small, rural school districts, the state was saddled with inequalities in facilities, minimally qualified teachers, weak instruction, resources, and programs. Resources from external organizations such as the Jeanes Fund and the General Education Board augmented the meager funding for separate schools that, in reality, were for the Blacks. Supervision of schools in general, and the rural schools in particular continued to be a function of government critical to the progress of the state.

By the time Nash officially resigned and left the office, Governor Henry Johnston had had several weeks to ponder whom he would appoint to replace the Superintendent. Johnston, who himself had just been elected, considered former Superintendent Wilson but chose John Vaughan, a staunch Democrat with an impressive education and political career resumé for the position. John Samuel Vaughan was born in Knoxville, Tennessee, November 29, 1885. While in his youth his family migrated southwest to Thompsonville, a town in south Texas with no post office, two churches and few businesses, where he graduated from high school. Soon thereafter he moved several hundred miles north to southern Oklahoma where his education and political careers took root. Public school experience was gained during his superintendency at Kingston from 1908-1915 and then at Wapanucka beginning in 1917. Typical rural school districts, they had seven and thirteen teachers, respectively, small enough to allow Vaughan flexibility to pursue other interests.[1]

From Solon to Superintendent

State senator C. C. Shaw of Johnston County decided not to run for reelection in the summer of 1916, opening the door for Vaughan to seek to represent Johnston and Marshall counties. The *Kingston Messenger* was courteous in reminding the citizens of Johnston County that since Marshall County had supported Shaw of Johnston County in 1912, the county now could return the favor in helping to elect Vaughan of Marshall County. Vaughan used the legislative arena judiciously to quickly become an influential advocate in the Senate for the cause of education.[2]

As the representative of the twenty-sixth district in the Senate in 1917 Vaughan introduced at least twelve bills relating to education, as shown in table 10.1, and chaired the Education Committee. Most notable provisions becoming law required independent school district boards to file annual statistical and financial reports to the Superintendent or risk losing their school fund apportionment, allowed city school boards to raise additional levies, and stipulated arrangements and appropriations for the formation of the union graded school districts through consolidations. Bills failing to become law addressed school building construction, local district governance, and teacher contracts. Senate Bill 443 would have narrowed the number of public institutions for which the Board provided oversight, a move that many educators endorsed. Although not Vaughan's bill, a similar bill, HB 213, created the State Board of Vocational Education to oversee the federal government's investment and involvement in Oklahoma's public education system. For his first senate term, he achieved some success in key areas, but not what he had hoped for overall.[3]

Two years later chairing the Education Committee again, Vaughan introduced bills similar in number to the previous Legislature. The wishes of Superintendent Wilson were granted through the passage of Vaughan's SB 29 creating the textbook commission. Senate Bill 91, unsuccessful initially, would have tied the county superintendents' salaries to the number of students in the counties exclusive of those enrolled in first class city school districts. Eventually signed was a palatable act that tied the salary to the county clerk's. Vaughan did not get his exact request, but the result was the same—an equal standard for all. Other successful bills addressed student transfers, provided the first state aid through supplemented appropriations to rural schools, set standards for physical facilities, and provided for filling vacancies in the treasurer's office in city school districts.[4] His legislative initiatives tinkered at the edges of the critical issues of school funding and consolidation of small, primary schools, but as a representative from a rural area, he did not broach them from a straightforward approach. Higher taxes for schools and overall consolidation and reorganization were anathema to his constituents.

Senator Vaughan's legislative achievement for the common schools had, however, its limitations for he was unsuccessful in getting a new position in the Superintendent's office—rural state supervisor. Also, he could not convince his fellow senators through SB 145 to attempt administrative efficiency in rural areas through eliminating boards in small non-high school districts and replacing them with a county board of education. His influence during two legislative sessions in the Senate chamber, however, extended beyond the interests of the common schools. A most significant bill he initiated and was eventually enacted into law permitted the six normal schools to transition to four-year colleges.[5] Over his career he would serve in leadership positions in three of those institutions. Vaughan gained valuable insight into the legislative processes and the behind-the-scenes maneuvering that would prove beneficial to him in his future roles as Superintendent and higher education administrator. At a young thirty-one he became comfortable walking the halls of the State Capitol and mingling with the state's politicians and executives.

Southeastern State Teachers College (SESTC) in Durant hired Vaughan in 1919 as dean and registrar during a time of growth and the transition to a four-year college. By 1921 his combination of education and senatorial experience convinced the Educational Survey Commission to choose him to be its executive secretary with Superintendent Wilson to be the chair. Vaughan was a logical choice, and both were well known to each other. Vaughan assumed his duties with the permission of SESTC president Henry Bennett near the end of November 1921 and finished them thirteen months later when the report was submitted in mid-December 1922. Meanwhile, he continued to serve as registrar at Southeastern.[6]

Vaughan's education career trajectory by 1923 was exceptional given the delay in earning his formal post secondary degrees. By the time he earned a bachelor's degree at age thirty-eight he had been a teacher, principal, superintendent, and administrator at a teachers college. Several years prior to and including 1923 Vaughan was pursuing his bachelor's degree at the OU where four years later he earned his master's degree, the culmination of his pursuit of a formal education. Vaughan returned to SESTC in 1925, holding only a bachelor's degree, to serve as acting president while Bennett took sabbatical leave to earn his doctorate at Columbia University.[7] Experience and maturity earned

Table 10.1 Vaughan's legislative efforts 1917 and 1919

1917		
Bill	Outcome	Subject
SB 37	Failed in the Senate	Constructing school buildings from public funds
SB 48	Enacted into law	Board required to make annual reports to the Supt.
SB 141	Died in the Senate	Dividing state into Normal School districts
SB 149	Enacted into law	Local school levies
SB 150	Enacted into law	Consolidation of districts into union graded districts
SB 187	Failed in the Senate	Governance of common schools
SB 248	Failed in the Senate	Governance of common schools
SB 327	Passed in the Senate	Teacher contract unlawful in >1 district at a time
SB 328	Failed in the Senate	Admission of students to Normal Schools
SB 329	Failed in the Senate	Contracts between teachers and school boards
SB 381	Enacted into law	Degree granting authority to colleges and universities
SB 443	Failed, HB 213 passed	Created State Board of Vocational Education
1919		
SB 29	Enacted into law	Created the State Textbook Commission
SB 33	Enacted into law	Inter-district student transfers
SB 91	Enacted into law	Standard for county superintendent salaries
SB 129	Passed the Senate	Teaching thrift and physical training of students
SB 130	Died in the Senate	Teachers' training courses
SB 145	Postponed	Create county school district with a board of education
SB 156	Died in the Senate	Appointment by the Supt. of a rural school supervisor
SB 182	Enacted into law	Improving rural schools by supplementary appropriation
SB 193	Enacted into law	Standards for physical facilities
SB 322	Enacted into law	Filling vacancies in the treasurer's office in the cities' boards of education
SB 338	Died in the Senate	Membership and duties of the Board of Vocational Ed.

Source: Session Laws of Oklahoma 1917 and 1919

him sufficient cachet to be selected for positions beyond the typical levels preferred by those doing the selecting.

Vaughan, among the leading educators of that era, was active with the OEA, serving as executive board member and legislative chairman in 1922. The Association functioned as a united voice for educators of all levels to advocate for public education with top education professionals holding its leadership positions. Failed efforts to get the Better Schools Amendment Act passed in 1923 renewed the educators' resolve to try again. Vaughan actively lobbied the legislators to gain support for the education bill, and the OEA lobbied the public. By legislative referendum State Question 145, to achieve a per pupil statewide appropriation, was presented to the voters in the 1926 general election. To the dismay of the OEA and educators, the question failed by a margin of two-to-one. Educators were undaunted by legislative inaction, for the ESC report stated that Oklahoma was underachieving in its efforts to provide schooling. The state ranked twelfth in ability to pay and forty-second in expenditures based on ability, leading to the conclusion that the state could and should do better.[8] Vaughan led the OEA's legislative efforts, firmly convinced that rural children deserved a better quality education and that the state had the ability, if not the will, to do better.

John Vaughan

Photograph no. 9706.2 by Harry Watton, Oklahoma City, courtesy Oklahoma Historical Society

Needing a revised strategy, the OEA executive board, on the last day of the year, appointed Vaughan to chair a three-member steering committee to attempt to obtain legislation to address the dire financial needs of many rural school districts, both for the immediate and long-term futures. Vaughan and the OEA were rewarded for their efforts on January 29 through an emergency appropriation of 1.5 million dollars for fiscal years 1927 and 1928. Less than two months later, HB 241 created the Common School Equalization Fund to be funded from one-fourth of the gross production tax. Vaughan, as legislative lobbyist receiving the accolades of his fellow educators, must have been especially gratified when he received the Superintendency soon thereafter.[9]

The sole Superintendent in Oklahoma's history to have served as a state senator assumed the position April 9, 1927, when Governor Johnston appointed him. No doubt attractive to Vaughan was almost a full term to accomplish his goals and prepare for a campaign to win election to the position. Election to a senate seat a decade earlier gave him insight into developing a strategy for the 1930 statewide campaign. Accepting the appointment gave him the opportunity to broaden his experience and to see firsthand how his legislative efforts of nearly a decade earlier were affecting the schools. Also, his *ex officio* roles as Board chairman allowed him to be influential in the governance and leadership of the teachers colleges and as Superintendent to be a forceful member of the School Land Commission.

Administering the Department into the Depression

Four years after the Educational Survey Commission report, the Legislature implemented few of its recommendations. Although the ESC was the brainchild of the Governor with the purpose to survey the citizens and generate recommendations based on external expertise the Legislature did very little, though it provided most of the funding. Teacher certificates continued to be issued at the county and state levels, school consolidation was proceeding at a snail's pace, and no comprehensive teacher pension system was established. Textbook selection was perpetually controversial as was the issue of the most efficacious form of county governance of the dependent school districts. Whatever the unfortunate status was, worse conditions were just slightly beyond the horizon.

A mere two days after Vaughn moved into the office, he performed one of his *ex-officio* duties by chairing his first meeting of the board of the Oklahoma College for Women. At the top of the agenda was the hiring of the president—his predecessor. It would be another eleven days before he would chair his first Board of Education meeting at which a resolution was passed expressing appreciation for the service Nash performed while Superintendent. That Board's membership included two women, Ethel Cardiff, who had been a member since 1922 and was the first woman ever to serve on the Board, and Bertha Truitt, whose first meeting was the prior month.[10]

One of Vaughan's earliest emphases involved improvement of a program begun by Wilson and continued under Nash, The Model School. The tool used to evaluate schools that opted to participate was the Model School Report Card. The scheme, implemented in 1923, primarily assessed the physical features of schools, but also included a thrust for adult literacy. By 1928 Model Schools and Superior Model Schools numbered 2,021, and increased to 2,289 by 1936. County superintendents were responsible for visiting the elementary schools within their respective counties to complete the Report Card and arrive at a score for each school. Annually the tool was revised based on the comments and critiques of the teachers and county superintendents.[11]

Under Vaughan's leadership a corollary to the Model School assessment was developed, the Instructional Report Card. If schools were to be evaluated for their physical features by the county superintendent, that person should also complete an assessment of the quality of instruction. It became a prerequisite for a school to be a Model School if it desired to be state accredited. Several years leading up to the summer of 1927 teachers, several county superintendents, and supervisors discussed a need for an instrument to evaluate instruction. In 1927 the Department's Rural School Division in cooperation with teacher preparation units in the teachers colleges developed accreditation standards for instruction in the elementary schools. Vaughan's career experience was at the secondary school teaching level and at the district superintendency. He realized his deficiency of knowledge of the elementary level and fortuitously availed himself of the assistance of a summer 1927 graduate class of eighty-three students at OU that adopted the project of creating the Instructional Score Card to determine a quantitative analysis of instruction. In the first year of implementation 357 schools met the necessary standard to earn state accreditation. Additional revisions in this rating system designed to stimulate improved teaching methods were accomplished during his tenure, and by 1936 state accreditation was earned by 1,948 elementary schools. Many of the smallest schools, those with fewer than five teachers, did not earn the necessary minimum standard and thus were not accredited under this scheme.[12]

Vaughan assumed the duties of the Superintendency in the middle of the 1927 legislative session, too late to influence any legislation that year, and then had more than one and one-half years to develop recommendations to the 1929 session. Measures to assess facilities and instruction to determine Model School designation and state accreditation, respectively, were in place allowing Vaughan to analyze the effectiveness of the common school system and the role of the Department. As with his predecessors he was frustrated with the Legislature's lack of addressing critical areas. Because the problems persisted, he felt compelled to reiterate several issues and areas where legislative action was sorely needed: assign sole responsibility for teacher certification to the Board, strengthen the compulsory attendance law (attendance rate was only 62 percent), enact a teacher retirement law, increase certification standards for elementary grade teachers, and allow the textbook commission greater prerogative to select books for rural and city schools.[13] Altogether these recommendations were a mix of recent and recurring ones for the past decade and beyond.

As the fourth Superintendent and the first appointed to complete an unexpired term, Vaughan served with two governors prior to being elected to his first term. Johnston, who appointed him, was impeached within two years and replaced by Lieutenant Governor, William Holloway. Holloway's acceptance of the Governor's mantle proved to be a highly positive action for the cause of public education for he pursued an aggressive agenda. Vaughan's work in the common schools, higher education administration, and the Legislature forged a breadth and depth of experience that gave him the perspicacity to work with the governors regardless of their difficulties and brevity of terms. He knew the power brokers in the Legislature and was recognized by his peers in the education community for his skill and expertise. The regular session of the 1929 Legislature, chaotic with little accomplished for education and followed shortly by the turnover in the governorship, did not portend positive actions. However, Holloway's directive to

Vaughan to submit measures that could be pushed through the ensuing extraordinary session of the Legislature without the need of lengthy debate and deliberation was an opportune moment.[14]

His engagement with the OEA continued unabated with extensive involvement over many years, but he was the first Superintendent never to serve as its president. (Nash was elected to the presidency in 1929.) Vaughan and the OEA found each other mutually beneficial over the years as he lobbied the Legislature for the interests of the OEA and the public schools while the Association delivered its support during the election campaigns, a symbiotic relationship that would continue for decades. Vaughan in 1929 "continued to serve as the strongest link between the Association and the lawmakers." And, the Association supported Vaughan in 1930 in his first endeavor to be elected. Between the time of the Governor's request to Vaughn and the Legislature's consideration, Vaughan hosted the OEA board, including President Nash, in his office to develop a list of priorities that included a change in the membership of the textbook commission, governance of vocational education, and consolidation of the teacher certification issuance program. A short time later the same group met with the Governor in the Capitol Blue Room and reviewed their list with him.[15]

The joint efforts of Vaughan and the OEA board were rewarded within a few weeks when the Governor signed a good portion of their requests into law. Composition of the textbook commission changed with the elimination of the Governor as an *ex officio* member and the inclusion of at least one female member. Supervision of the Department of Vocational Education was transferred from the State Board of Vocational Education to the Board and the Superintendent was designated as director of Vocational Education. A "Coordinating Board" was established to serve as a central coordinating agent for the higher education institutions and the Superintendent was named as an *ex officio* member.[16]

Credentialing of teachers by multiple agencies resulting in a hodge-podge of certification standards persistently frustrated the Superintendents. Frequent requests over more than a decade came to fruition when all teacher certification was consolidated under the Board through SB 33, effective October 31 of that year, 1929, bringing consistency and certainty to the process of evaluating credentials for teaching applicants. All county and city examining boards were abolished and all authority for examination and certification of teachers was vested in the Board which subsequently established its procedures and set the guidelines for testing certificate applicants and issuing certificates.[17] The efforts of many educators, Vaughan, and his predecessors, came to fruition, and now there could be an organized and systematic approach to certification. Even though state authority expanded at the expense of local control, the decision was critical for achieving some degree of consistency.

The education system in Oklahoma in the "Roaring Twenties" survived the impeachment of two governors and the rise and fall of the Ku Klux Klan influence. Common schools and higher education were increasing their enrollments while no major structural changes occurred in the governance of education at any level. One Superintendent chose not to seek reelection, allowing another to succeed him. The latter resigned from office and authority passed to a new one through gubernatorial appointment. Oversight at the top level proceeded smoothly during this transition. As the third decade of the twentieth century was winding down, Vaughan was at the helm. The educational system was evolving, but at a glacial pace with persistent embedded problems from insufficient revenue. Intransigent as these problems were, the events of late 1929 would only exacerbate them. The "Crash of Wall Street" would reverberate in Oklahoma, the Great Depression would strain the available resources, and the vicissitudes of the weather would likewise be unkind.

Table 10.2 presents the status of the common schools at the bookends of Vaughan's tenure and gives perspective to his 1930 biennial report where he furnished this assessment: of the 4,933 school districts, 4,581 were classified as rural and 2,600 of these rural districts were one-teacher schools, resulting in an inefficient state system of education. All school districts needed to be funded adequately to offer a minimum nine-month standard curriculum. Free textbooks should be provided to all students, and students should be required to attend more than 2/3 of the school days.[18] Large numbers of small, ineffective school districts continued to mitigate efforts to improve the quality of the students' educational experience. These were formidable and seemingly intractable problems resulting in part from a legislature and populace not amenable to funding education properly.

Table 10.2 Statistical comparison of 1926-1927 and 1935-1936

Topic	1926-1927	1935-1936	% Change
Number of districts	5,078	4,760	-6.3
Average daily attendance	432,086	497,974	+11.5
Student per capita	$68.37	$56.38	-17.5
Number of teachers	18,813	19,858	+5.6
Average teacher salary	$1,021.81	981.57	-3.9
State aid	$500,000	$8,180,000	+1636
State total net evaluation	$1,729,432,830	$1,221,659,918	-29.4
General fund expenditures	$29,540,764	$28,077,298	-5.0

Source: Thirty-First Biennial Report of the State Department of Education (OKC: SBE, 1966), 271-74.

The Depression was well entrenched and the Dust Bowl was a reality. Little money was available to the Legislature without an increase in the taxes and, thus, it was not feasible to increase funding for education. From the late 1920s and early 1930s the Legislature was engaged in deficit spending, the size of the debt was growing, and relief was nowhere in sight. Oklahoma had come to rely on the generosity of the General Education Board, a private philanthropic organization in New York City. Nash requested the GEB to donate $33,000 to operate a Division of Schoolhouse Planning from July 1926 to July 1931. The Legislature enacted a law requiring the state to assume the responsibility, but the Governor vetoed it. Vaughan requested more two-year support from the GEB and the request was granted. Two years later Vaughan again requested extension from the GEB to continue the office through June 1935 under the stipulation that there would be no more requests. Additional financial assistance was sought and received for funding the Division of Research and Service. Beginning July 1, 1929, it compiled educational statistics and engaged in educational research.[19] Through these actions Vaughan recognized the need for specific services to improve the Department's oversight of education in spite of the Legislature's failure to provide funding even for basic instructional services.

Among Vaughan's recommendations to the Legislature in 1934 for statutory changes were: permit counties to hire supervisors to assist county superintendents' efforts to improve instruction; establish and fund two rural elementary school supervisors; guarantee a minimum high school program for every student of high school age regardless of residency; allow only two kinds of districts—independent and dependent; provide equal educational opportunities for Blacks; provide a director of adult education in the Vocational Division; increase state financial support to equalize funding through a minimum program; enlarge the unit of school district administration; offer fair salaries, tenure, and a retirement plan to teachers; and provide free textbooks. To emphasize the dire situation in the Black high schools, Vaughan informed the Board a year later, in December 1935, of the status of accreditation in those schools. Only nine of 834 white high schools were denied renewed accreditation while seventeen of sixty Black high schools failed to be accepted.[20] His comprehensive list in late 1934 would have been daunting in a year when the state's revenues were overflowing and the citizens were pushing for a progression agenda; in the mid-1930s when many were struggling to survive, it was audacious.

What is readily evident in Vaughan's request in 1934 is the extent to which the Legislature engaged in the Department's organization and operation. Such involvement was not unique in the mid-1930s, rather, it was descriptive of the modus operandi since statehood. Superintendents were not entrusted with submitting a total budget based on the needs for personnel and operating costs. The Legislature specified all new positions and appropriated the funds to support them.

Vaughan's brief honeymoon with Governor Holloway ended when "Alfalfa Bill" Murray and Vaughan were inaugurated in January 1931. It was not long until they were at odds with each other with neither willing to give ground. Each publicly attacked the other acrimoniously over various topics and issues. Never hesitant to enter into controversy, Murray presented to the Legislature in November 1931 a comprehensive overhaul of the tax structure to support education at all levels. Vaughan responded with his negative assessment of the Governor's proposals in *The Oklahoman*: "The passage of the proposed educational measures will wreck the educational system of Oklahoma from the primary grades through the university…it will place the schools in the whirlpool of politics, further handicap the 1,500 weak school districts, make impossible not only further progress in our schools, but will place Oklahoma educationally in the ranks of the most backward states in the union."[21] Three weeks later he reiterated his earlier comments: "Educational institutions everywhere will be crippled by the ad valorem measure which will limit the amount that will be raised for support of the schools."[22]

Murray in the fall of 1932 tried again to accomplish changes in the tax laws by appealing to schoolteachers and higher education officials for their support through a letter warning them: "I trust that the teachers under you will not be again deceived by John Vaughan."[23] Not surprisingly, Vaughan was critical in his assessment of the plan. The state's worsening economic status was pinching school districts with decreasing land values, resulting in less ad valorem tax revenue. Vaughan found data to show that "Oklahoma is one of only six states in the union whose productive output annually exceeds $1,000,000,000, and yet it ranks thirty-seventh in education." Another comparison he noted was that the state ranked fifth in road construction and thirty-seventh in education.[24]

Oklahoma's Chief of Public Instruction / 175

In February 1934, with school financing in a precarious predicament, Vaughan went to Washington, DC to seek early allotment of federal funds to aid weak schools. It was estimated that Oklahoma schools would need one million dollars or more just to complete the current school year. In good faith with President Roosevelt's New Deal for the nation, Vaughan called for a new deal for education in Oklahoma. His plan included: sufficient and dependable school financing, more effective school administration, more tenure for effective teachers, removing untrained and inefficient teachers, and sufficient compensation to attract more people to teaching as a career. House Bill 312, in the spring of 1935, changed school funding by replacing the earmarking of gross production, income, and sales taxes with an appropriation of $8,200,000 with $5,400,000 being designated for primary aid and the remainder for secondary aid.[25] The effect on the state's budget was the same, deficit spending continued as the national and state economies worsened.

Vaughan's influence extended beyond that of the administration of the Department and the supervision of the common schools. Beginning in 1911 the Board was given oversight of the six normal schools. Over the next twenty-eight years the Board guided their transition from infancy to mature four-year colleges. Governors, not hesitant to meddle in the Board's operation, flexed their political muscle frequently through their appointments to the Board to influence the employment of presidents and faculty members. Turnover in the colleges and the Board was not uncommon with governors serving only single terms. For example, at least fourteen persons served on the six-member Board during the biennium of July 1, 1934 to June 30, 1936. One of those, Kate Gault Zaneis, was appointed to the Board by Governor Murray in early January 1935 as a favor to Governor-elect Marland. A few short months later, May 11, she was named by the Board, effective the 20th, to the presidency of Southeastern Teachers College where she remained until May 1937. At least three teachers colleges had presidents resign or die in 1935 presenting the Board with the obligation to find and hire replacements. The Board chose to hire its own members to fill two of the vacancies. Joining Zaneis fifteen months later in resigning to assume the presidency of an institution governed by the Board was Vaughan in August 1936. At the meeting on the 19th, for four of the seven Board members, it was their first meeting as members.[26]

Controversy swirled around the Board in the mid-1930s specifically regarding several of the teachers colleges' presidencies. Governors not only appointed Board members, but they publicly announced their intentions and desires. Marland, in particular and as Governor-elect, wanted Kate Zaneis appointed to STC because she was an educator and he wanted to reward her for her efforts as his campaign director for the southern part of the state. Also, in 1935, it was rumored that Superintendent Vaughan was itching for a presidency, the consequence of which would be that the Governor could name his choice for Superintendent.[27]

Perpetual Controversy: Textbooks

The Textbook Commission law as amended in 1919 placed almost total control in the hands of the Governor, not only because he chaired the seven-member group, but that he also appointed five members who were to be teachers and administrators. Excluded from his prerogative was the elected Superintendent who served *ex officio* as the secretary. Senate Bill 29 in 1919 was submitted by John Vaughan as senator who, within eight years, would become the Superintendent. Textbooks were selected for a five-year period and were paid for by the local districts. Thus, the Commission needed to meet only every five years. Ten years later, 1929, membership on the Commission was changed to eliminate the Governor who still retained control through the appointment of six persons, one or more of whom were to be women. The Superintendent, again serving *ex officio*, was to call the first meeting when the chair and secretary were to be elected by the group. By virtue of his position, expertise, responsibility, and access to the Governor, the Superintendent influenced the Commission and reported its actions to the Governor. Governor Holloway appreciated the communications and fostered a harmonious relationship with the educators and especially Superintendent Vaughan. He supported the educational community by being receptive to its efforts to improve the schools. To reciprocate, Vaughan kept Holloway informed of the successes and the needs; for example, in July 1929 he reported that the cost of textbooks decreased dramatically. Less than six weeks later Vaughan, responding to allegations that rebound textbooks were being sold to school districts, denied that any such activity surfaced in an investigation.[28]

All aspects of textbooks: the Commission, selection, and purchase were ripe for disagreements with Governor Murray who was not hesitant to lecture Vaughan on constitutional issues: "John Vaughan and others of his machine are telling that the Free Text Book [*sic*] bill is unconstitutional—as if he knew anything about the constitution—in that the bill does not make the state superintendent chairman of the board of education."[29] A bill, with an inadvertent oversight, was passed in the Legislature and signed by the Governor making the Board also the Textbook Commission with the Superintendent serving as chair of the former and secretary of the latter. That wording was clear, but another provision stated, "… wherever herein the word 'text book board' or 'board of education' or 'board' is used, they shall mean the same, and shall exercise all the power provided for in this law." *The Oklahoman* opined that this kerfuffle arose because the Governor was trying to provide an alibi for his oversight when signing the bill.[30] Eighteen months later the issue resurfaced when the Governor attempted to name Vaughan to fill a vacancy on the Commission. Vaughan, confused, said that he would seek legal advice: "I was under the impression the law automatically made me a member and ex officio secretary of the commission."[31] What his political adversary, the Governor, was trying to accomplish was puzzling to him, again.

In May 1933 Murray drew the wrath of Vaughan, and textbook publishing companies, by threatening to have textbooks written by Oklahoma teachers (and himself) and printed by the state penitentiary. The Governor was unhappy because the textbook companies refused to lower their bids even though the cost of paper and labor had dropped. Vaughan interpreted the Governor's intervention as meddling in his and the Commission's business. Nothing in the statutes addressed how the Commission was to conduct the review of bids. Bids were opened in a secret meeting in June 1933 and Vaughan was to report the results when tabulated. Such veiled conduct of an appointed group was deemed unnecessary and led to further skepticism of the Commission headed by the Superintendent.[32]

No sooner had the Commission adopted new textbooks than the State Attorney General ruled that about 40 percent of the adoptions were illegal because the books were chosen before the statutory date allowed. A dispute arose between the Governor and the Commission over what books could be selected and when with Vaughan stating, "Governor Murray said he signed the textbook law and knew what he was doing."[33] Another point of contention, textbook prices, as one might conjecture, ensued with Murray fulminating: "The state will pay no more than the contract price fixed for textbooks and John S. Vaughan, state superintendent of public instruction, can 'smoke that in his pipe.'"[34] At issue were the interpretation of the state code and the behavior of the textbook publishers. Not unrelated was whether the school districts would choose to purchase new books. Hundreds of thousands of dollars would be saved if the "old" books were to be continued.

Neither the animosity nor the controversy disappeared, when a year later the Governor involved himself in textbook decisions through cancelling adoptions. "His executive order is about as legal as a lot of others he has issued," said Vaughan, "It is certainly not valid."[35] The incoming Marland administration, including the reelected Vaughan, brought some relief to the schools. Time and legal action were required to clean up the textbook mess left by Murray.[36] For Vaughan, he would now be dealing with the fourth governor in eight years.

Competing for the Office in 1930 and 1934

Vaughan was no novice politician and campaigner for office. Granted, his prior experience in 1916 and 1918 was only in Senate District 26, and now, in 1930, he had to run a statewide race. The incumbent's advantage was gained from appointment rather than from election, but his tenure was only three months shy of a full four-year term. So, this was the first referendum on his service that to date was relatively free of controversy. He assumed office near the end of the 1927 legislative session, so the only Legislature he dealt with closely was in the 1929 regular and extraordinary sessions.

Charles Evans, a sixty-year old educator, former president of Central State Teachers College, and publisher in Oklahoma City, filed against him in the Democratic primary and proved to be no serious threat even though he outspent Vaughan $1,200 to $1,094.51. Evans campaigned on saving taxpayers thousands of dollars by reducing the number of textbooks required in the schools. He wanted to reduce by 2/3 the fees teachers paid to enroll in college coursework. Lower taxes and more character education were part of his political platform, and he would help Oklahoma's schools earn a high ranking among the states. Vaughan garnered 60 percent of the vote and was ready to do battle with the Republican candidate, Edson Price, superintendent in Enid and well known in educational circles because of his connections with the OEA. In what was by now a significant trend—Democrat wins regardless of money spent—Vaughan defeated Price by a little more than a two-to-one margin, 285,719 to 155,365. This election was to be appreciated by Vaughan because his next election proved to be more competitive.[37]

Almost all of the executive offices, including the Superintendency, in 1934 drew interest from multiple candidates from both the Democratic and Republican parties. Eighteen candidates vied for the governorship while half that number as shown in Table 10.3

sought the Superintendency. Mired in the throes of the Great Depression and the Dust Bowl outward migration, and four years of animosity between Vaughan and Governor Murray over textbooks, the land commission, and school funding offered challengers much grist to grind. Murray was ineligible to run for reelection, but that did not hinder him from scheming to oust Vaughan and have him replaced by a relative.[38]

Vaughan's credentials and experience far exceeded those of all of the contenders, but the dynamics of the race forced him into a runoff with the Governor's nephew. Muddying the water was the attempt by Clay Kerr to gain the office because, as Assistant Superintendent since 1924, he believed educators would support him over his boss. Given the political nature of the office and the Department where employees were expected to be loyal, for Kerr to resign and then to file against his ex-boss, it must have seemed surreal to Vaughan that Kerr would compete against him. Vaughan was surprised by Kerr's decision to run an active campaign and bid for the teacher vote. The Governor's supporters were hoping Kerr would split the vote for Vaughan and allow Governor Murray's nephew John Murray to win.[39]

While the Governor was ineligible for reelection, he supported his kin as a surrogate to defeat Vaughan. The Governor was still seething over losing control of the School Land Commission to Vaughan and his ilk. If Kerr's votes or the combined votes for Jack Cannon, Tivis Nelson, and Roy Welton had gone to Vaughan, the latter would have won the primary outright. Regardless, a runoff between the incumbent and the younger Murray was forced.[40]

With the defeat of the peripheral candidates accomplished, Vaughan and John Murray prepared for the primary runoff a short three weeks later. Additional emphasis was focused on the Superintendent race resulting from the withdrawal of the runners up for governor, state auditor, and insurance commissioner prior to the runoff election. The Governor marshaled his forces both for the primary and the runoff, but much of the luster dissipated with the outcome of the primary, an indication of the inevitability of the runoff election. An *Oklahoman* editorial, gleeful of the vanquishing of the Murray forces, extolled the virtues of the Vaughan administration and the success of the Superintendent on the Land Commission and the State Textbook Committee.[41]

Meanwhile, the Republicans were trying to achieve viability with three names on the primary ticket: John Burns, Jenella Jones, and Thomas Biggs. Again, as in 1926 when Anna Willis ran, Jenella Jones must have counted on some judicial support should she have won the primary and general elections. No resolution in changing the Constitution was yet achieved that would have permitted her to serve in this executive position. The candidates individually and collectively raised and spent less than one hundred dollars to mount the challenge, and the results reflected little chance of victory. Burns won the primary, only to be defeated by Vaughan in a landslide in the November general election.[42]

Vaughan was safely ensconced in the Superintendency after his crushing defeat of the Murray forces, but his somewhat depleted quiver no doubt caused him to pause and consider opportunities beyond the Superintendency. Very public bruising fights with the Governor, now ended, was not something he relished. He was not prone to shy away from such contentious circumstances, but it was a relief to be rid of Murray and his shenanigans. And, the next election was four years away.

Table 10.3 Election results 1934

Primary						
Candidates	Age	Home	Occupation	Amount*	Votes	%
Democrats						
Jack Cannon	36	Seminole	Superintendent	854	53,970	13.8
Clay Kerr	44	Okla. City	Assistant state supt.	1,332	63,012	16.1
John Murray	43	Stillwater	Associate professor	1,110	91,337	23.4
Tivis Nelson	Legal†	Okla. City	Educator	212	12,449	3.1
John Vaughan	48	Okla. City	State Superintendent	1,016	140,401	35.9
Roy Welton	37	Poteau	Educator	747	29,269	7.4
Republicans						
Thomas Biggs	41	Shawnee	Educator	-0-	8,568	15.9
John C. Burns	40	Newcastle	Teacher	75	33,226	61.9
Jenella Jones	36	Woodward	County superintendent	-0-	11,877	22.1
Democratic primary runoff						
John Murray	43	Stillwater	Associate professor	255	140,914	37.3
John Vaughan	48	Okla. City	State Superintendent	199	236,493	62.6
General election						
John Vaughan	48	Okla. City	State Superintendent	n/d	353,345	66.8
John C. Burns	40	Newcastle	Teacher	n/d	174,312	32.9
M. A. Nelson‡	37	Enid	University professor	n/d	1,515	0.2

Source: *Oklahoma Elections: Statehood to Present*, vol. 1 (OKC: SEB, 1992); Election Board Candidate Filings and Campaign Expenses, Primary and Runoff Elections of 1934, RG 24-4-1, Box 23-16, ARD, ODL, OKC.

*In dollars. Reporting of expenditures was required only for the primary and runoff elections.

†Tivis Nelson reported his age as legal rather than as a number.

‡The Election Board identified M. A. Nelson as a Progressive Party candidate, but *The Oklahoman* had three articles that listed him as the Prohibition Party candidate.

Challenging the Governor's Power over the Commissioners of the Land Office

By constitutional provision (article 6, section 6), the School Land Commission, was to provide oversight and control of the use, lease, and sale of public lands and the monies derived therefrom; and its membership was to be the governor as chair *ex officio*, secretary of state, Superintendent, president of the state board of agriculture, and state auditor. Thus, Vaughan became a member upon his appointment as Superintendent, and over the next three years two governors served briefly as chair. The 1930 election saw Murray chosen Governor; Vaughan, Superintendent; Harry Cordell, President of the State Board of Agriculture; R. A. Sneed, Secretary of State; and Frank Carter, State Auditor. Vaughan had just completed almost four years on the Commission and Sneed had served from 1923 to 1927 while Secretary of State.[43]

One of Chairman Murray's earliest moves was to appoint Judge A. L. Beckett as the secretary January 19, 1931, and then to order an audit of the commission. Controversy swirled around alleged corruption and fraud within the agency. Murray was determined to get to the bottom of the matter, but his authority to name the secretary was questioned immediately by several members. Also controversial were several letters Murray wrote to Beckett suggesting individuals deemed qualified for positions in the School Land Department. A majority of the members were not supportive of Murray, and the Governor was quick to point that out in a letter to Meigs Murray of Colbert, Oklahoma, who was unrelated to the Governor and who inquired about the extension of a land loan: "Out of the Commission of five members there are three that were not my friends when they were elected and those three control the patronage."[44]

Beckett, by request of the Governor, submitted a report to the Governor and the Legislature detailing what he thought an audit should cover. The Board of Affairs entered into a contract May 23, 1931, with the accounting firm of Willson and Garnett to audit the School Land Department from November 16, 1907, to the end of 1930. Taking longer than expected because of the chaotic condition of the records, the auditing firm initially filed a preliminary report February 12, 1932, and completed its work in March 1933. Meanwhile, the Governor, the remaining commission members, and the Secretary continued to feud.[45]

Longevity in office with resulting stability in the Commission was lacking because of the turnover in governors and Commission secretaries. From 1926 to 1933 four men held the Governor's office and another four served as Commission secretary. Turbulence struck the economy with the collapse of Wall Street followed by the early years of the Great Depression and the Dust Bowl. All of these factors impinged upon the ability of the Commission to guide the Land Department. Exacerbating the situation was the inability of land lessees to meet their financial obligations. The enticement of easy money proved greater than some could resist, but a few even flaunted their success. Assistant secretary from 1923 to 1929, Sam Pollard bragged about embezzling $48,000 (equivalent to $669,033 in 2014) from May 1927 to June 1929, but was shielded from prosecution by the statute of limitations. Pollard's thievery occurred at the beginning of Vaughan's tenure on the Commission.[46]

With the audit completed, Secretary Beckett tendered his resignation upon the expectation that HB 187 providing for significant changes in the Land Department would fail and thus make the successful functioning of that department impossible. The Commission proceeded to name his successor, J. L. Carpenter, and people for three other positions in the Department. Murray was incensed for at least two reasons. First, he disliked most of the members because they were upset with Beckett's persistent efforts to "unearth irregularities, frauds, and thefts" and they attempted to force him from office. Second, Murray successfully got the Legislature in an extraordinary session to pass the law July 18, 1933, so that he, Governor, could name the secretary. But the Legislature failed to pass the emergency clause delaying the law's implementation until mid October, allowing the commission to pre-empt him. Murray's tactic was, as Commander-in-Chief of the Militia, to order the Brigadier General to place a guard at the door of the School Land Department to prohibit the commissioners' new appointees from assuming their duties. A military zone was declared in and around that office![47]

The Senate's response to the audit report was the establishment of a special investigative committee with subpoena authority. Over the next several months the investigation was completed and a report was given to the Senate. It uncovered considerable corruption including many tens of thousands of dollars squandered as a result of political interference in the Commission's operation from 1907 to 1930. The committee proposed a constitutional amendment to replace the current five-member *ex-officio* Commissioners of the Land Office with a three-member, all-appointed-by-the-governor commission. Additionally, the secretary should be a gubernatorial appointee. Only this latter recommendation, easily accomplished through legislative action, was implemented.[48] While the populace had significant vested interest in a land department that functioned legally and efficiently, insufficient political will within the Legislature translated into no subsequent action. That legislators personally benefited from the department's transgressions may explain the Legislature's disinclination to act.

Relations between the Governor and the other commission members in 1933 further soured as summer turned to fall. Strong emotions bubbled over at the October 17th meeting when the Governor, who had not been present at any meeting over the previous several months, attended and asserted his authority. "Gentlemen, under the law, I assume the Chairmanship of this meeting." Vaughan, chair of the previous several meetings, spoke next, "The matter of the Chairman of the Board is a matter of little consequence so far as I am concerned." Furthermore, he stated that the needs of the Land Department were above the issue of who was chair.[49]

Murray, as chair, continued the meeting and said it was his intention to name the secretary of the Department. J. L. Carpenter, the Commission's appointee since May 29, spoke up to say the position was not vacant. Next, Vaughan introduced a resolution referencing the constitutional authority of the Commission to name a secretary and saying that it superseded the Legislature's enactment of the previous summer giving the Governor that authority. Murray, as chair, refused to entertain the motion moved by Vaughan and seconded by Cordell. State auditor Carter then called for a vote and Cordell seconded it. Murray ordered the clerk to refuse to call the roll, but all excluding Murray voted "aye."[50] Heated discussion continued and comments ensued with Murray expressing his displeasure with the Board's activities over the previous four to five months. Vaughan, patient no more, addressed the Governor:

> I am not concerned about your political threats, Governor, that is a matter of little concern to me. We have sat around this table for two and one-half months not knowing what was going on. We have a Secretary now that seems to be competent and capable, and the office is always open, and there has been no political connivance since he has been here. We have transacted business. We have collected thousands in loans that otherwise cluttered the records of the department and we have collected a great amount of money three and four times as much money as ever was collected under the former Secretary and we are willing for the people of this State to know the excellent record that our Secretary has made while he has been in charge of this department.[51]
>
> A few comments later, Governor Murray said, "If you gentlemen insist in violation of the law, I haven't any more to say." With this, he departed and Vaughan was elected vice-chairman 3-0 with Vaughan abstaining so the voting and the meeting could continue in orderly fashion.[52]

Later, Murray's initial appointee to be secretary, Glenn Young, wrote to Murray to express regret that he was declining the appointment. Young believed he could not be effective working with the Commission. Insistent on naming a secretary, Murray then appointed John H. Casteel, and the two of them attended the regular meeting of the Commission October 31, 1933. In this meeting they were essentially ignored. The irascible Governor and author of the Constitution considered it a personal affront to be lectured on what that document said. Months passed before Murray would attend another Commission meeting claiming the other members had taken charge and selected Vaughan as chairman.[53]

Murray craved the authority to name the Commission secretary and when he persuaded the Legislature to give him that prerogative, he believed he was going to be able to do so. However, when he tried to force the issue in late October 1933, his action backfired. State Auditor Frank Carter was placed in an impossible predicament for he was also a member of the Commission and responsible for seeing that state employees were paid. He was faced with determining whom to pay. In *Carpenter v. Carter* (29 P. 2d 83) the Oklahoma Supreme Court ruled that, while the recent law granted the Governor the authority to name the secretary, he could not do so until there was a vacancy.

The Commissioners of the Land Office controversy consumed a good portion of Murray's term, and served as a good example of the restraints on the Governor's authority when many executive offices were elective. Simultaneously, the problems in the Land Department exposed weakness in a system where there was considerable turnover of elected officials and relative instability in the secretariat. None of the elected officials individually had the primary responsibility for oversight of the Land Department, yet the Superintendent had the greatest vested interest. Furthermore, from 1907 to 1932 fewer individuals, four, served as Superintendent than the other four offices (aggregately thirty-one); thus, institutional memory should have been less interrupted. Vaughan's statement that their appointed secretary recouped more money than did his predecessor Beckett was self-serving for it was under previous governors and Superintendents that the bulk of the embezzlement occurred.

The events of 1931 to 1933 were only a precursor of things to come in the spring of 1935 when the House of Representatives appointed a special investigating committee to delve into the Land Commission's operation. All of the Commission members testified on multiple occasions. Of particular interest to the investigating committee were the number of loans to, and lease transactions through, banks in Durant and surrounding areas. Vaughan found himself in the middle of this fray specifically because of his former residency in Bryan County as senator and as an administrator at SESTC. The committee interrogated Vaughan to learn of his dealings with these banks.[54]

A key witness in the investigations, Haskell Paul, a lawyer and the law and executive clerk of the Land Commission, accused the commissioners of costing the Department (and the school children) approximately $721,950 (equivalent to $10,050,757 in 2014) because of their illegal actions. The Legislature in 1933 through Senate Bill 12 stipulated procedures for the Land Commission to follow (e.g., state employees' wages were to be garnished by 25 percent until their delinquent interest and principal for land and leases were paid) and strengthened various aspects of the original law, but unfortunately decades of questionable practice resulted in large amounts of money unavailable for distribution to school districts. Private citizens and many persons on the public payroll including legislators and other politicians had been enjoying a free ride at the expense of the state's students.[55]

Paul was fired by the Commission even before the investigation was completed. Vaughan stated to the investigating House members that Paul was fired for insubordination. "Well, Mr. Paul was an employee of the department and anytime any employee who works under me openly fights me personally I am going to remove him. In other words, I will be willing to move him."[56] Vaughan was only one of five commissioners, but his testimony seems to suggest that he alone had the authority to fire Paul. Paul testified about the commissioners' fiduciary failure: "My contention is they couldn't make enough money or live long enough to pay back what they have cost the school children of the State through these loans."[57] Paul had studied the documents and knew enough about the procedures that he was able to prove that numerous approvals and actions by the Commission were illegal. Eventually and essentially, he was vindicated through the investigating committee's report and recommendations.

The commissioners, particularly Vaughan, defended their actions by explaining their attitude toward their duties as commissioners. Vaughan indicated that he paid little attention to the overall affairs of the Land Department and deferred to the Department's executive clerk for the operation of the unit. Professionals were hired within the unit to fulfill the duties, and the Superintendent had neither the interest nor the expertise to micromanage the unit. While testifying, Vaughan asserted that the Commissioners should be fulltime people who were not subjected to peculiarities of the election process and defined terms of office.[58]

The Special School Land Investigation Committee concluded that the Land Department was understaffed; the Commissioners: "know practically nothing about the School Land Department, and they have little or no curiosity to learn…The evidence discloses on the part of the School Land Commissioners, incompetence, inefficiency, careless handling, and neglect, and, we believe, willful failure to discharge the duties of their offices as School Land Commissioners, and that such incompetence, neglect, and inefficiency, has resulted in loss of millions to the School [sic] children of this State."[59]

The Committee recommended passage of a constitutional amendment providing for an independent commission to supervise this department. This House version was similar to the earlier Senate report. Additionally, the Legislature should do whatever possible legally to recover lost funds. In spite of the recommendation to change the *ex officio* nature of the Commission membership through a constitutional amendment, today's commissioners are the same as in 1907 with the exception that the Lieutenant Governor replaced the Secretary of State.[60]

No doubt the mutual dislike between the Governor and the Superintendent lessened the possibility for these two strong egos to work cooperatively for the benefit of the state's students. Neither performed the constitutional responsibility expected of him to the detriment of the public schools. They, along with the other Commission members, neglected their duties and allowed millions of dollars to be embezzled. Corruption was pervasive with little effective oversight. In January 1935, when E. W. Marland replaced

Murray in the Governor's chair, Vaughan's involvement with the Land Commission entered a calmer and more peaceful status. Gone were the histrionics of the previous four years allowing the commissioners to focus on the duties of their *ex officio* offices and to maintain a heightened oversight of the Land Department's activities.

Vaughan's experience with the Land Office involved a personal battle with the Governor as well as politics and machinations. During his tenure, two investigations, one each by the Senate and House of Representatives, scrutinized the activities and procedures of the Commission and the Land Department. In the latter House investigation, the conclusion was that the Commission members were too distanced from the Land Department causing that agency to be inefficient and corrupt. Benefits accruing from the turmoil and investigations included closer oversight and less corruption than previously was the case. Eighty years later Commissioners in 2016 oversaw assets of 750,000 surface acres (less than in 1935 and from an original 3 million acres), 1.1 million mineral acres, and a net value of more than $2.5 billion, and the Department was managed by more than sixty employees. After more than 125 years, this asset continues to benefit students at all levels.[61]

Influencing Your Employment Decision

John Vaughan followed the precedent established by his predecessor Nash when, presiding at the August 19, 1936, Board meeting, he called the meeting to order at 10:00 a.m., announced a recess, and then resigned. At 11:45 a.m., with newly-appointed A. L. Crable presiding, the Board reconvened and the Superintendent entered a motion to hire Vaughan to be the president of Northeastern State Teachers College, effective immediately (see figure 10.1).[62] The Northeastern president had died suddenly months earlier and the Board had been unable to find a suitable replacement. When Vaughan informed Governor Marland of his intention to resign to become the president of NESTC, the Governor had little time to name a successor to complete the twenty-eight months of the unexpired term. Vaughan, as president of the Board, would have been privy to the college application process and the Board's consideration of suitability of the applicants for the presidency.

When Vaughan assumed the helm at Northeastern, the College's enrollment was near to the average for the six teachers colleges, but next to last in the number of faculty, resulting in the highest student-faculty ratio as shown in table 10.4. Two years later NESTC's enrollment exceeded the average by 9.5 percent and continued to have the highest ratio of students to faculty, but the 37 percent decrease in that ratio from 30.70 to 19.26 was the second highest percentage change. Aggregately, the six colleges' enrollments dipped by 22 percent, a large decrease in just two years, with NESTC's dropping the least at 13 percent. In spite of the decline in the number of students in all of the colleges, the average number of faculty grew by six. NESTC's status relative to the other five colleges improved rather significantly early in Vaughan's tenure as president of the college, but NESTC had just experienced the traumatic sudden death of the president and the service of an interim president in the previous year.

> MINUTES OF THE MEETING OF THE STATE BOARD OF EDUCATION
>
> August 19, 1936
>
> The State Board of Education met in the State Capitol at 10:00 A.M. August 19, 1936, with the following present:
>
> > Mr. E.L. Rodman
> > Mr. Harry D. Simmons
> > Mr. J.R. Holmes
> > Mr. Stephen A. George
> > Mr. J.L. Newland
> > > Members
> >
> > Mr. John Vaughan
> > > President
>
> The following member was absent:
>
> > Mrs. Grace Norris Davis
>
> The Board recessed.
>
> The Board reconvened at 11:45 A.M. with the following members present:
>
> > Mr. Harry D. Simmons
> > Mr. E.L. Rodman
> > Mr. J.R. Holmes
> > Mr. Stephen A. George
> > Mr. J.L. Newland
> > > Members
> >
> > Mr. A.L. Crable
> > > President
>
> The following member was absent:
>
> > Mrs. Grace Norris Davis
>
> ### Northeastern State Teachers College
>
> Upon motion by Mr. Newland, seconded by Mr. Holmes, Mr. John Vaughan was elected President of Northeastern State Teachers College, effective August 19, 1936.
>
> Mr. Vaughan made the following recommendations which were approved upon motion by Mr. Newland, seconded by Mr. Simmons.

Figure 10.1. Minutes of the August 19, 1936, Board of Education meeting

Table 10.4 Enrollments, faculty, and degrees awarded at the teachers colleges 1936 and 1938

College	1936				1938			
	Enroll	Faculty	Ratio	Degrees	Enroll	Faculty	Ratio	Degrees
Central	1,642	60	27.36	279	1,249	67	18.64	417
ECSTC	1,732	68	25.47	198	1,283	70	18.33	200
NESTC	1,351	44	30.70	155	1,175	61	19.26	228
NWSTC	1,038	42	24.71	90	762	50	15.24	103
SEOSC	1,355	60	22.58	158	999	54	18.50	192
SWOSC	1,159	50	23.18	174	971	59	16.46	246
Average	1,378	54	25.54	176	1,073	60	17.84	231

Sources: Sixteenth Biennial Report of the State Superintendent of Public Instruction of the State of Oklahoma and the Thirteenth Biennial Report of the State Board of Education (OKC: SBE 1936), 217-36; *Seventeenth Biennial Report of the State Superintendent of Public Instruction of the State of Oklahoma and the Fourteenth Biennial Report of the State Board of Education* (OKC: SBE, 1938), 237-44.

Vaughan served with distinction as president of NESTC from August 19, 1936, to January 21, 1951, when he died suddenly and unexpectedly. He was an active participant in the Boy Scouts for thirty-seven years, both locally and on the Executive Committee of the National Council. A lifelong member of the Baptist Church, he taught Sunday School and served as a deacon. He was a loyal supporter of Oklahoma Baptist University, serving on its board of trustees. Vaughan was a dedicated educator who gave selflessly so that students at all levels could have the opportunity to gain an education so critical to achieving maximum success in life. Eunice, his wife of thirty-seven years, a daughter, and a brother survived him.[63]

The Oklahoman editorialized Vaughan: "There is no way to measure the good a man may do in a lifetime devoted to serving his fellowman…He devoted himself to his daily tasks in a quiet and nearly plodding way, and for that reason he rarely appeared in the public eye." It is a bit surprising that this paper described him in this manner, given the very public nature of his career from educator to senator to higher education administrator to Supcrintcndent, and finally to college president. In his battles with the pugnacious Governor Murray, he did not seem conciliatory; rather, he was not hesitant to take a combative approach. The only major stain on his otherwise stellar career was his complicity, even if primarily by omission, in the Land Department scandal.[64]

Chapter 11
Crable: Suffering Persistent Chaos for a Decade
(1936-1947)

For the second time in less than a decade the Superintendent resigned his position to assume a college presidency, Nash in 1927 and Vaughan in 1936. In both instances the Superintendent was hired to be a president by a board he chaired and from which he resigned immediately prior to his appointment. The chairman of the board for the Oklahoma College for Women was the Superintendent *ex officio* while the Board of Education, chaired also by the Superintendent *ex officio*, determined who was hired at NESTC. In neither instance was it illegal nor apparently unethical to lead a board, resign, and then be hired by that board to be president of a college under its jurisdiction. These men supervised what in essence became their own hiring process. By vacating the Superintendency, these presidents led higher education institutions governed by boards chaired by novice Superintendents. Vaughan, in 1927, was politically savvy, having been a state senator and college administrator while Crable in 1936 lacked political experience but had served as the director of correspondence at Oklahoma A&M College for seven years.

Governor Marland had to act expeditiously to name someone to complete Vaughan's term. Crable's acceptance of the Governor's request transpired quickly, in part because of his familiarity with the Department from his former employment there. President Henry Bennett at A&M, in conversation with Marland, facilitated Crable's resignation to assume the Superintendency. Almost overnight Crable moved his family to Oklahoma City to begin leading the Department. At his swearing-in ceremony, he said he had "some definite ideas…serving the schoolchildren of the state" and promised nothing radical but to cooperate with the Governor and continue the policies of Vaughan.[1] He was about to embark upon a venture on which he would find himself in perilous political fights and the center of controversy over corruption in office, all the while trying to guide the Department through significant upheavals caused by political maneuverings, the lingering Depression, the Dust Bowl and outward migration, and World War II.

Wolfe City to the Superintendency via Marietta, the Department, and A&M

Alvin Lawrence Crable (A. L.), born November 27, 1889, in Wolfe City, a small town in northeast Texas, graduated from nearby Lone Oak High School and began his career teaching mathematics at Sherman. The Texas school districts of Sadler and Collinsville, respectively, hired him as their superintendent. Three years before he moved to Oklahoma in 1920, and at age 28, he earned his bachelor's degree at Austin College, a tiny Presbyterian college in Sherman. With all of the requisite components for his preparation, degree, and teaching and administrative experiences achieved in rural Texas, he opted to cross the state line to Oklahoma to continue his career, initially as a high school principal. His first employment was in Marietta from 1921-1923 before moving the following year to Durant High School, schools forty miles apart and with fewer than ten teachers each. When the superintendency opened at Marietta in 1924, he applied and was hired. To date he had taught in three districts and had been superintendent in two others, all small districts in close proximity to the Texas-Oklahoma border. Crable's superintendency at Marietta, as with all his previous employments, was short, in this instance one year.[2]

During his years in Bryan and Love counties Crable met the administrators at Southeastern State Teachers College, including John Vaughan, registrar, and Henry G. Bennett, president, becoming friends of the latter. These professional relationships and cordial friendships proved highly beneficial to Crable in the following decades. In 1928 Bennett became president of Oklahoma A&M, and soon hired Crable as director of correspondence. Eight years later he recommended Crable for the Superintendency.[3]

Superintendent Nash hired Crable in 1925 to serve as a high school inspector in the Department at a legislatively established salary of $2,400 (only $100 less than Nash's salary), and he continued in that position until August 1929. As an inspector, Crable traversed the state assessing high schools' compliance with, and assisting them to meet, state standards. Rural high schools in the 1920s had limited financial and personnel resources, high quality teachers were in short supply, and whatever assistance the De-

A. L. Crable
2021.201.B0245.0146, The Oklahoman, Oklahoma Publishing Company Photography Collection, Oklahoma Historical Society

partment could provide increased the opportunities for the students to receive at least a modicum of educational experience. Oklahoma's nearly 70,000 square miles stretched the inspectors to the limit; nevertheless, that was the model selected. In the four years Crable assisted boards, principals, and teachers and served as a liaison between them and the Department, he found time to earn a master's degree from OU.[4]

Bennett, in 1929, needed someone to direct A&M's correspondence program aimed at an agrarian society. If anyone understood rural folks' educational needs, it was Crable, who also knew personally many of the small schools' teachers and administrators. He was experienced and mature, educated and adroit at navigating the pre-college education world. For the next seven years he served as the director of correspondence during which he expanded a study center plan that focused on the needs of teachers in remote locations. "Extension courses" came into vogue for these teachers and others seeking to upgrade their skills. Carefully watching this development was Bennett, at a top rung of the education ladder, extending his influence over myriad political developments.[5]

Crable, named August 15, began his term four days later at the reconvened Board meeting when he assumed the Superintendency and the *ex officio* Board presidency following Vaughan's resignation. As chair, his first act after summoning the Board to order was to entertain a motion to hire Vaughan at NEOSC and to call for a vote on the motion. After the meeting concluded, Crable, now *ex officio* secretary of the Land Commission, announced a date for a meeting of that group. Events transpired quickly but benefitting him and welcoming him to his office were the familiar faces of ten of the fifteen Department and Board employees from 1928 who now were joined by fourteen others.[6]

Political Appointment and Three Elections

The summer appointment in 1936 allowed Crable time to navigate the politics of the office and to fulfill the duties for more than two years before the next election cycle. He accepted the position with Bennett's blessing and an eye toward the future, knowing that he would have some time to settle into the position before running a statewide campaign. Crable was not naïve about the politics of the position for he gained insight while employed by the Department during the 1926 reelection campaign of Nash. He, as with all Department employees across the decades, was expected to be an ardent promoter of Nash by soliciting support for him as he traveled across the state.

Crable's first test of statewide exposure as an "incumbent" in 1938 encouraged him to marshal resources attendant to the position. All publications of the Department carried Crable's name as Superintendent. Employees were expected to be supportive by working on his behalf, discretely of course, for no one clearly defined the fine line between work functions and political allegiance. Department personnel owed their loyalty and positions to Crable, even those hired by his predecessor. Department employees' interactions with public school persons allowed frequent opportunities for kind words for the incumbent and no watchdog organizations existed to question the propriety of patronage and employee political involvement while conducting official business. Any external purview by the watchful eyes of the written media was in its infancy.

Before a year passed in Crable's tenure, and a year before the 1938 election cycle, *The Oklahoman* speculated who might challenge Crable and Joe Scott, president of the

State Board of Agriculture. Both would be facing their first election and both belonged to a power group that wielded much influence in education and political circles and was led by Bennett. However, a cloud of suspicion was hanging over a decision by Crable and the Board for the firing of Kate Zaneis, president at SESTC, especially for the covert action and discharge without cause. Influential persons were upset over Zaneis's persistence in achieving equity in pay between the male and female faculty members. The newspaper believed that Crable would receive the most criticism for that action.[7] Given the timing and the content, it appears the newspaper had a dearth of news to report and was searching for something to stimulate some controversy. *The Oklahoman*'s proclivity for speculation continued in February of 1938 when it reported that Leslie Chambers, assistant superintendent in the Oklahoma City School District and state senator from Blaine and Kingfisher counties, was considering running for Superintendent. Only thirty-one years old, he had experience as superintendent at Watonga. Eventually, however, he chose not to run, possibly because of the Oklahoma City district's recent unfavorable publicity from an employee's embezzlement case.[8]

R. M. McCool and J. C. White threw their hats into the political ring along with Crable, and the 1938 Democratic primary race was on. McCool, the Democratic state chairman from 1931 to 1934, and, for seventeen years, president of Murray State School for Agriculture, was thought initially to run for president of the Board of Agriculture. White, least known, a mere thirty-three years of age, and a high school teacher in Stilwell, was a nonfactor. Crable avoided a runoff election by outspending McCool $1,478 to $725 and by capturing 52.4 percent of the votes. His campaign expenditures were typical and were for printing envelopes and stationery, postage, and print advertising.[9]

That year's general election pitted Crable against Geen Gilmour, Republican, and Merrill A. Nelson, Prohibition. Nelson was a nonfactor, Gilmour received support from 30.4 percent of the voters, and Crable, with 68.9 percent, achieved the highest winning percentage since statehood. Gilmour had taught in Bartlesville, Yale, and Kingfisher, and served as Kingfisher Junior High School principal, but with limited statewide recognition and as a Republican, it was a futile effort.[10] Crable's overwhelming widespread support framed his thinking about the extent to which he could act independently from, and eventually in opposition to, the Governor. While he received a significant majority, the result was not consistent, as shown in table 11.1, with the counts in the Senate and House where there were zero and three Republicans, respectively. Voters tended toward

Table 11.1 Party registration of the Oklahoma Legislature 1937-1945

		Senate		House		Total	
Election	Session	Dem	Rep	Dem	Rep	Dem	Rep
1936	1937	44	0	114	3	158	3
1938	1939	43	1	102	13	145	14
1940	1941	42	2	114	7	156	9
1942	1943	40	4	94	24	134	28
1944	1945	38	6	96	22	134	28

Source: OA 2015-2016 (OKC: ODL, 2015), 792-95, 827-29.

more discrimination between the two parties in elections for the executive offices than for the Legislature, a pattern consistent throughout Crable's tenure.

More importantly, the election ushered Leon Phillips and lots of bluster into the Governor's office. Three years earlier as speaker, he did not oppose a bill appropriating one million dollars in emergency funding to school districts, but he doggedly pushed his agenda to curtail expenditures while Governor Marland was trying to get teachers paid.[11] Crable, appreciating Marland's commitment and not Phillips' frugality, wanted additional money to improve schools, provide textbooks, and increase teachers' salaries. Phillips's known fiscal restraint and capture of the Governor's office were not a good omen, for the result was an unbridgeable chasm. The obvious difference of opinion was but one of several that caused a difficult relationship to evolve into public vituperations. Both held elected positions and thus were answerable to the people, but the term-limited governor need not ascertain the public's opinions to weigh future political aspirations.

By 1942 Crable had weathered two major storms, but they created a raised level of vulnerability that eventually would contribute to his downfall. The textbook scandal of 1938 and the bitter fight with Phillips over the balanced budget amendment of 1941 had some opponents hoping that another Democrat would challenge Crable. Friends of the Governor sought a candidate to oppose Crable, and Earl Fisher, a relatively unknown educator with teaching experience, administrative experience as high school principal at Waynoka from 1927 to 1935, and Woods County Superintendent from 1935 to 1939, was a willing albeit late entrant. Crable had put his career on the line by opposing the Governor's balanced budget amendment, but the state's educators did not forget what he had risked for them. Fisher campaigned on the need to restore harmony and to improve Oklahoma's thirty-seventh place educationally. When the primary ended, Crable had spent $1,495 and received 55 percent of the vote, numbers nearly the same as the 1938 primary. Fisher spent about 24 per cent less in a losing cause.[12]

To educators interested in reelecting Crable, this election must have seemed highly important and hotly contested. Yet, *The Oklahoman* lamented the lack of interest in the campaign because of the firmly entrenched practice of Democratic primary winners typically being victorious in the general elections. The Democratic primary results showed that, while 289,149 Democrats voted for the Superintendent, this was 105,000 fewer than voted for the Governor. However, of the secondary positions, more people voted for the Superintendent than for almost all of the other positions. Crable captured 55 percent of the vote to beat Republican M. R. Floyd, former OEA secretary, Vinita superintendent, and president of Northeastern Oklahoma Junior College. Ralph Butterfield, Prohibition Party candidate, represented the hopes of very few voters and tallied less than one percent.[13] Crable was victorious in this election cycle, but it would prove to be his last.

In 1946 the most pivotal election in the state's first 100 years occurred with the six candidates in the Democratic primary equaling the number in 1934. In both years, the top vote getters in the primaries won the runoff elections; however, in 1934, the incumbent was the winner where, twelve years later, the challenger won for only the second time since statehood. Also, the 1946 election was the first when a county superintendent from a non-rural county ran for the office and won, eventually becoming the longest tenured Superintendent.[14]

Three district superintendents—Russell Grow, PhD, University of Nebraska and from Barnsdall, H. G. Creekmore of Hitchcock, and Andrew Jackson Brock of Shawnee—and teacher David Crockett from Ardmore, Tulsa County superintendent Oliver Hodge, and Crable competed in the Democratic primary with the vote ranging from 5.4 percent for Brock to 33.5 percent for Hodge. Crable was a close second at 28 percent. The combined percentage of the votes for Crable and Hodge (61.5) correlated closely to the combined 59.4 percent of the total primary expenditures. These two most serious and competitive candidates were able to raise more money: Hodge spent $1,079 and Crable, 32 percent more, $1,424. Lesser knowns Creekmore and Brock failed to file expenditure reports as the law required while Crockett and Grow reported expenses of $912 and $803, respectively (see appendixes F and J).[15]

This election was anticipated to be a challenge for Crable because of the accumulated disagreements and fights with governors and legislators, and a revelatory textbook controversy. An avowed champion of education, schools, and teachers, Crable got crosswise with key individuals and decision makers. His opposition to the balanced budget amendment won him many friends among the education constituency, but engendered political enemies. Winning reelection was an uphill battle complicated by the number of primary candidates and the popularity of the Tulsa County superintendent.

Attacks on Crable and the state textbook system were featured. Crable, in defense, accused Dixie Gilmer, Tulsa County district attorney who was one of nine Democrats running for governor and who led the legal fight over the textbook charges, of "raising dead issues concerning textbook charges that have been thoroughly heard and dismissed." Crable claimed he had "successfully denied his charges in all the courts and the legislatures." Acknowledging the Tulsa opposition, he stated, "In simple words the Tulsa oligarchy would like to have much state aid and low taxes for their area, little state aid and high taxes for the areas which have weak school districts." In an advertisement Crable wrote, "My Record of Achievement [sic] for the past 9 years as your public servant is an open book. I have endeavored to serve faithfully, efficiently and honestly."[16] Hodge sought the support of the public to clean up the school "mess" in one advertisement and acquired the support of more than 100 rural district and county superintendents in another newspaper advertisement the day before the primary runoff.[17]

By forcing Crable into a runoff, in part because of Crable's earlier smear of the Tulsa community, Hodge was able to swing the advantage to himself. He garnered 69 percent of the vote although Crable had the endorsement of Grow, Creekmore, and Brock, and he outspent Hodge $1,486 to $838. "The decisive defeat handed Crable presages the end of a stormy tenure in the office of the state superintendent," predicted *The Oklahoman*, leaving no doubt about the underlying cause for the outcome. Gilmer, for his part, finished a close second in the gubernatorial primary and lost by six percentage points to Roy Turner in the runoff. The textbook scandal provided beneficial sensational grist for Gilmer in his campaigning and an embarrassing millstone for Crable's reelection efforts. In the subsequent general election, the outcome again reflected the dominance of the Democratic Party with Hodge defeating Republican Martin Nelson 59 percent to 41 percent.[18]

Crable's political battles were with legislators and a governor who were of the same party as he but who opposed him nonetheless. Strong stances on several issues obviously trumped party affiliation, especially his high-profile opposition to Speaker, then Governor, Phillips, with residual effects dogging him in subsequent elections. Timing was not in his favor either, but he did have the support of his long-time friend Henry Bennett. Unfortunately, Bennett also got caught up in the textbook controversy as described below, costing him political currency and lessening his influence in Crable's reelection.

Vociferous Advocate for the Department and the Education System

Four months after Crable assumed office in August 1936 he submitted the biennial report, largely under the aegis of his predecessor, to Governor Marland. Crable, familiar with the process from having provided information previously as a Department employee, expressed optimism in the progress achieved but quickly tempered that perception through an assessment of the chronic problems faced by the Department and the state's schools: "In many hundreds of school districts in Oklahoma the program of studies is still narrow and restricted, the salaries and tenure of teachers inadequate and uncertain, and the quality of instruction of a questionable character."[19] Half of the state's students

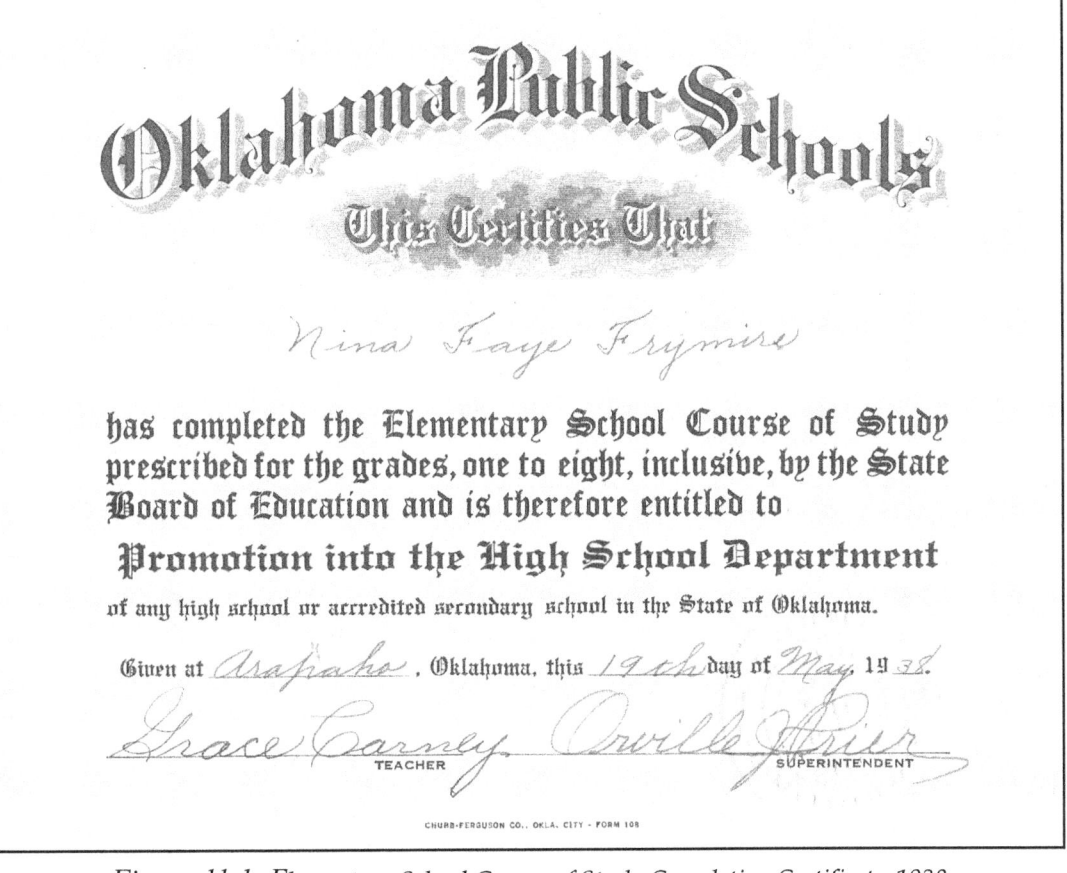

Figure 11.1. Elementary School Course of Study Completion Certificate, 1938, Union Ridge School District #29, Custer County, courtesy of Nina Faye (Frymire) Brandt Family Private Collection

attended dependent (not offering high school grades) school districts where teachers were inexperienced and poorly educated. County superintendents in many instances were not prepared to provide quality supervision for these schools.

Criteria to be a county superintendent were minimal beyond successfully competing in an election to serve, and county structure oftentimes was unwieldy. In 1938 the seventy-seven counties had a total of 4,282 dependent districts (e.g., Jackson had fourteen and Lincoln 110), most with one or two teachers and with countywide enrollments ranging from 574 in Cimarron County to 9,887 in Seminole County. Within this structure of dependent districts were 331 all-Black separate districts in fifty-one counties. Administrative duties hindered even the superintendents with some skills in instructional supervision from assisting the teachers to become better instructors. Crable urged corrective measures and emphasized his point by including reports from the four county superintendents who had hired supervisors. Tulsa County's report of the fifteen dependent districts, four of which were Black, was submitted by Oliver Hodge, who had been in office only one year. He continued the position established by his predecessor but hired a new person to perform the duties.[20]

Crable's earlier stint in the Department and his experience at A&M apprised him of the status of education at multiple levels throughout the state. While his first biennial report reflected data collected by the Department and his predecessor, and his analysis of those data, he further opined about related topics without corresponding facts to bolster his arguments. For example, in the previous sixteen years, fifteen junior colleges had sprung up across the state reaching a total enrollment of 1,067. He conceded some were established in areas that could support them, but others were operating with insufficient enrollment and low paid instructors, potentially draining resources from the common schools. Legislative inquiry and oversight were imperative to clarify the legal status of, need for, and sustainability of such institutions.[21]

Crable's harshest assessment was focused on the separate schools comprised almost exclusively of Black students. Buildings were unsuitable for school purposes and some students were studying in unsanitary and unsightly shacks that were unfit for housing any human beings and should be condemned. More transportation funds to offer students access to better facilities were imperative. Separate schools were far from being equal measured against any reasonable standard, but the Superintendent had little flexibility in ameliorating the conditions of the separate schools. And, the white establishment was little interested in improving the conditions. Only the external Jeanes Fund directed its resources toward these schools and that was in the form of funds to augment the salaries.[22]

James Staten, Board secretary and Department administrator during the interregnum of Crable's exile (described below), prepared the biennial report for the Governor in 1942 and included a description of the status of Black schools considerably more upbeat than Crable and his predecessors' biennial reports. While Crable chose to compare the Black schools with the white schools within Oklahoma, Staten compared the state's Black schools generally with those of the southern states: "Oklahoma is probably doing more towards educating its negro population than any other southern state."[23] Use of the specific example of the teacher salary schedule being the same for equally qualified Black and white teachers, and thus higher than Black teachers' salaries in southern states, played to the obstructionists in the Legislature who harbored racial views, but wanted to appear magnanimous. Pay equality was important but insufficient to assess overall quality of access to resources.

Crable persisted throughout his tenure to highlight the inadequate buildings provided for the Black students. Primarily a responsibility of the county superintendents, and with minimal leverage available to his position to cause change, there was little he could do to improve the situation. Legislative relief was not forthcoming much to the consternation of the Superintendent. "Separate, but equal" was a subjective standard for the decision makers with few moral concerns for the substandard physical learning environments. Crable pled for legislative action to modify the finance laws to remedy not only this four-decade-long glaring problem, but also several other inequities. Nothing less than a vote of the people would accomplish the desired goal. That option became reality through a legislative initiative in 1945 that materialized into a positive vote of the people in 1946 to amend the finance provisions. Crable, hoping the changes in the law would make it possible to provide adequate buildings in the separate, predominantly Black school districts, was a participant in the gathering momentum of the lead-up to the US Supreme Court decisions of the late 1940s into the mid-1950s chiseling at the separate but equal standard. It would still be decades, however, before school facilities improved for many of the rural, predominantly, Black districts.[24]

When Crable entered office the Department comprised three units (general administration and personnel housed in the State Capitol and vocational education: agriculture, home economics, and trades and industrial education located in Stillwater) and thirty-five employees with two-thirds of them in Oklahoma City. Two years later the employee count was sixty-eight with office locations unchanged from 1936. Now, the organizational chart showed eleven divisions under the overarching title of general administration. Crable's first two years in office reflected an 80 percent gain in the number of employees, most of whom were additions rather than replacements. Of those employed in 1936, thirty-three held their offices two years later. Thus, Crable, unlike some Superintendents, kept experienced personnel. In his first two years in office though, he was able to hire forty new people with eighteen of those in vocational education.[25]

A rapid increase (more than 700 percent) in the number of vocational education and vocational rehabilitation employees over the decade of his supervision was necessitated by the federal government's expansion of funding for programs in schools and for persons with disabilities in the workplace, and the requisite need for supervision of these programs. But that does not explain the total picture, for the growth in Department employees was more than 100 percent (see table 11.2). Crable's plea in the annual report was for the state to match the federal funds allocated to Oklahoma.[26]

The *Eighteenth Biennial Report*, crafted by Crable and submitted to his nemesis Governor Phillips, focused most specifically on the lack of a fair, equitable, and easy-to-administer, statewide tax scheme to support the constitutional requirement (article 13, section 1) of "a system of free public schools wherein all the children of the state may be educated." Regarding financing, Crable wrote: "The present plan of local and state financing of schools does not have those elements of permanency, stability, objectivity, and flexibility necessary for planning educational programs covering a period of

Table 11.2 Department FTE 1936-1946

Year (report)	Department (general*)	Voc. Ed. and Voc. Rehab**	Total
1936 (16th)	25	14	39
1938 (17th)	36	32	68
1940 (18th)	33	30	63
1942 (19th)	38	60	98
1944 (20th)	47	76	123
1946†	52	100	152

Source: Biennial Reports of the State Superintendent of Public Instruction, pages iv-v, except for 1946 when the list was compiled from the *OED*, 1946, 4-8.

Note: Vocational Rehabilitation was expanded through federal legislation and funding by 1938 and the office was in the State Capitol. Federal funding for vocational education and vocational rehabilitation was based on two federal laws with separate state offices to administer the respective programs.

*Included all of the divisions except Vocational Education and Vocational Rehabilitation

**Included both the Vocational Education Division and the Vocational Rehabilitation Division

†Since the 1946 report did not include a listing of the staff, the number was compiled from the *OED*, 1946, 4-8.

several years and for adapting the financial program to varied local situations."[27] Placing this report in context, Crable and Phillips were headed to a showdown that would be resolved only by a constitutional amendment in 1941. Phillips was determined to reduce expenditures and balance the budget while Crable was adamant about proper funding of schools.[28]

Crable highlighted the external support provided by several national philanthropic foundations focused on improving the education of Black students. These supplemental funds flowed through the Department under the direction of several Superintendents and were used to pay for the state agent for rural schools, teachers, seminars, buildings, equipment, scholarships, books, and libraries.[29] Table 11.3 shows the amount of money donated to Oklahoma's efforts to provide students an educational opportunity without which many students would have been deprived even of minimal schooling.

Table 11.3 Supplemental external donations 1916-1943

Entity	Years	Amount
General Education Board	1916-1943	$725,000
John F. Slater Fund	Pre-1920	$2,575
John F. Slater Fund	1920-1937	$29,893
Anna T. Jeanes Fund	1919-1937	$34,149
Southern Education Foundation, Inc.	1937-1942	$14,009
Julius Rosenwald Fund	1920-1942	$177,921
Total	1916-1943	$983,606

Source: *Nineteenth Biennial Report of the State Department of Education of Oklahoma*, 1942 (Guthrie: Co-operative, 1942), 14-16.

Note: The John F. Slater Fund and the Anna T. Jeanes Fund combined in 1937 to form the Southern Education Foundation, Inc.

For many Black students, systemic racism created significant obstacles that would have been greater without the ameliorative efforts of philanthropy. The vestiges of slavery and *Plessy v Ferguson* produced an anemic response to the deprivations experienced by Black students.

In the context of the dispute between Crable and Phillips over the balanced budget amendment passed in March 1941, a telling statistic is the per capita expenditure. Crable's persistent rectitude and analysis, somewhat myopic at the time, led him to pronounce that the initial burden of a balanced budget would fall disproportionately on the Department and the common schools. Yet, as seen in table 11.4, in every school year from 1935-36 to 1946-47 the per pupil amount increased with the exception of a minor dip in 1939-40. What was most causational in this per capita increase was the 24 percent loss of ADA between the school years of 1938-39 and 1944-45 and the accompanying 8.3 percent increase in general fund expenditures in that six-year period. In the five years after the balanced budget amendment until 1946-47, per capita spending increased from $76.95 to $113.84, a 47 percent rise. Crable's alarm sounding and subsequent proven error in prognostication gained him much notoriety that critically damaged his political career but resulted in no apparent harm to the funding of the schools. What is not reflected in table 11.4 is how the money was divided, showing only the increase in per student amount.

Table 11.4 Common schools data for the years 1935-36 to 1946-47

Year	ADA	Number of teachers	Average salary	Per capita	General fund expenditure	State aid
1935-36	497,974	19,858	981.57	56.38	28,077,299	8,180,000
1936-37	498,753	20,459	975.61	58.21	29,034,401	8,454,000
1937-38	492,907	20,874	1,060.57	65.76	32,414,918	12,233,733
1938-39	502,561	20,938	1,083.16	66.28	33,307,502	12,737,945
1939-40	485,290	20,980	1,040.32	64.93	31,507,591	11,436,321
1940-41	463,763	20,276	1,068.50	67.59	31,343,562	11,359,758
1941-42	439,238	19,391	1,139.60	72.89	32,015,748	8,208,443
1942-43	413,205	18,084	1,284.05	76.95	31,798,188	7,555,055
1943-44	386,061	17,272	1,417.50	89.84	34,684,381	8,717,239
1944-45	383,028	16,931	1,505.74	94.21	36,083,921	9,542,543
1945-46	391,337	17,863	1,814.75	113.06	44,244,242	15,524,922
1946-47	405,667	18,312	1,837.09	113.84	46,181,682	17,086,149

Source: *Thirty-First Biennial Report of the State Department of Education of Oklahoma* (OKC: SBE, 1966), 272.

Note: Salary, per capita, general fund expenditure, and state aid are shown in dollars.

Underscoring Personnel Issues: A Retirement System and a Teacher Shortage

State Question 242 was proposed in November 1938 to amend the Constitution to permit the Legislature to provide financial security through retirement allowances and death or disability benefits to employees of the common schools and public colleges. Crable, two years in office and running for his first regular term, surprisingly did not adopt an aggressive position on the retirement issue. Had he done so, he would have benefitted personally and he would have gained the appreciation of the teachers across the state. Of the six amendments on the ballot, four were defeated resoundingly while the other two (teacher retirement system and taxation of oleomargarine) less so. Coverage of the retirement amendment leading up to the election showed that the Parent-Teacher Association, the Oklahoma City Classroom Teachers Association, the Oklahoma City Trades and Labor Council, and the Oklahoma Association for Teacher Retirement supported the measure.[30]

A second attempt to give the Legislature flexibility occurred in the July 1942 primary. By then, the teacher shortage was becoming critical with no relief in sight. The Superintendent was in "exile," he was locked in a tight race, and it was only sixteen months after his crushing defeat by Phillips. Crable was not particularly vocal again in his support for the amendment. *The Oklahoman* predicted the amendment would pass because it was the only amendment being voted on, there was no active opposition, and there would be no silent vote issue. Joseph Brandt, president of OU, chaired a retirement commission that proposed the content of the amendment and pushed for its adoption. More than 63 percent of the voters supported the amendment, removing the state from the dubious distinction of being one of only two without such a provision. Enabling legislation on April 3, 1943, created the teachers' retirement system to be administered by a nine-member Board of Trustees that included the Superintendent *ex officio*.[31]

World War II and insufficient salaries created an acute shortage of teachers in 1942. Board executive secretary, Staten, substituting for Crable, reported that schools were experiencing extreme difficulty in retaining and finding teachers because they were entering the military, working in war-related industries, and moving to higher paying private employment. Four hundred twenty-two high schools reported that, of 7,035 teaching positions, 1,792, or 25 percent, were vacated by departing teachers. Males entered one of the three categories, females were concentrated in the defense industry, and collectively the subject area of the curriculum with the heaviest losses was mathematics.[32]

Schools responded to the shortage by relaxing their standard prohibiting married teachers from employment and by hiring substitutes. At the Department level, Crable organized a meeting of superintendents and representatives from teacher preparation institutions to generate ideas and recommendations for solving the problem. Pragmatically, this group recommended relaxing requirements for teaching eligibility and endorsed the proposition that "educated women in domestic life be persuaded to come into classrooms." Women with any college degrees could be considered eligible for teaching. Former Superintendent and now president at Northeastern State College, John Vaughan proposed allowing county superintendents to examine high school graduates to determine qualifications for temporary teaching certificates.[33] Educators joined efforts to weigh options to solve the shortage, but the Legislature, meeting in the odd numbered years only, assumed no obligation or prerogative to ameliorate the emergency.

Crable forwarded these recommendations to the Board where they were adopted in their entirety. Essentially, they were for a reduction in the number of college hours and in the length of issuance for the various levels of the certificates.[34] The teacher shortage solution was not to raise salaries, but to lower eligibility standards, a solution that proved viable enough to be implemented in subsequent decades. Educators were forced to compromise their core belief in the necessity of well-prepared teachers to meet a financial exigency while the Legislature felt no compulsion to robustly fulfill their constitutional mandate of providing a system of free public schools. After all, only eighteen months earlier the citizens voted for a balanced budget and there was no hue and cry for a tax increase to solve a teacher shortage.

Ameliorating the crisis somewhat was the trend beginning in 1939 of a significant reduction in the ADA of students in the state's schools. Table 11.4 shows that the ADA in that year was 502,561 and, by 1944, had dropped to 383,028, a decline of 119,533. For the same six-year period, an equivalent precipitous drop was seen in the number of teachers, 19.1 percent. Fewer students meant fewer teachers were needed, but experienced teachers departing for other work being replaced by lesser-prepared teachers lowered the overall quality. Reductions in ADA, teaching positions, and experienced teachers in conjunction with an insufficient supply of qualified applicants presented challenges to Crable that were somewhat offset by the increase in the per capita expenditure from $64.93 to $94.21, a 45 percent growth, and an equivalent improvement in the average teacher salary. State aid, low in 1935-36, more than doubled a decade later, but not before dipping to its nadir in 1942-43.

Providing Leadership in the Construction of School Facilities

In the late 1930s and early 1940s, the Works Progress Administration provided funds to the states and permitted discretionary spending of those funds. Maximizing that flexibility, Oklahoma chose to erect school buildings with a larger percentage of its monies than any other state. When the WPA projects ended, so did most of the school construction in Oklahoma. Crable, with the exception of 1941-1943, oversaw the Department's division of schoolhouse planning which assisted school districts to design and construct their facilities. This building boom in the early 40s was affected by the Legislature when it changed the pupil-teacher ratio in the finance bill, resulting in only half as many two-teacher buildings constructed in 1941-42 as in the prior year. In larger school districts, the decrease in construction was caused by the curtailment of the WPA program.[35] Uncertainty marked the status of construction and heightened the necessity of careful supervision of the efforts.

Crable was Superintendent during a period of considerable school building construction, much of it funded by the federal government. Only a few months after he left office, the annexation and consolidation act of 1947, HB 85, resulted in the closure of many of the buildings erected under the WPA program. On numerous occasions during his tenure, Crable pressed the Legislature to pass a consolidation law, and his biennial reports consistently emphasized the need to close ineffective schools. Had the Legislature been attuned to his concerns and heeded his urgent and frequent requests, a pre-WPA district consolidation plan would have allowed a better investment of the federal money.[36]

Working with Marland and Feuding with Phillips

When Crable was appointed to the Superintendency, his familiarity with the position and the Department's operation, the rural schools, and their administrators, gained from prior employment at the Department and his responsibilities in the extension office at Oklahoma A&M, bode well for him and informed his assumptions of what the agency's major thrusts should be. Rural schools had been the focus of previous Superintendents, thus the Department should continue its current emphases, perform well, and then expand operations that were meeting the needs of the state's schools. One of the most important growth areas in Crable's early tenure, necessitated in part by district consolidation that increased in speed over the next decade, was student transportation and its oversight, but it was not the only one. City schools could marshal resources to provide students with educational opportunities, but rural schools struggled in the face of daunting odds and desperately needed the assistance of the Department, especially in instructional supervision. County superintendent offices lacked the resources to aid dozens of small schools, often physically isolated, to hire and develop high quality teachers.

Events were set in motion before and when Crable was appointed that would later affect his position. Leon Phillips was running for reelection, unsuccessfully as it turned out, to speaker of the House of Representatives. Governor Marland, who had just lost his US Senate bid, requested the resignations of two Board members because they were "not qualified." Only eighteen months earlier they were no doubt qualified because one was a Rhodes scholar and the other was previously president of the Marland Oil Company of Mexico. What now made their qualification questionable was their refusal to help the Governor win the senate seat. A third member submitted her resignation voluntarily, stating that it was fairly obvious why she did so. Replacing these three were the superintendents of the Muskogee, Wewoka, and Antlers school districts. *The Oklahoman* editorialized over the change in membership of the Board especially with regard to its responsibilities for coordination and oversight of the state's teachers colleges. Typically, it said, changes in faculty and the presidencies followed such shakeups. Now with Crable presiding, the Board hired Vaughan to be president of NESTC even though a majority of the Board's seven members had less than three weeks' experience as members.[37]

Governor Marland's announced intention in December 1936 to achieve a balanced budget in the upcoming legislative session and to erase the state's debt by the end of his term was a harbinger of the political fights to come. In the Governor's favor was a positive trend in tax collections from 1933-34 to 1935-36 when both the income and gross production tax revenues doubled and the sales tax increased one-fourth. House Speaker Phillips adamantly opposed any tax increase. During the 1930s, the Legislature had developed a pattern of deficit spending that allowed the schools' state aid to increase from $1,398,416 in 1931-32 to $8,454,000 in 1936-37 and then to jump to $12,233,945 the next year. The Legislature's recalcitrance in refusing to decrease spending and the Governor's announced intent to achieve a balanced budget provided the impetus for the grumblings to develop into a crescendo over the next several years.[38]

Phillips was first elected in 1932 to represent Okfuskee County, reelected in 1934 with no opposition, and reelected in 1936. In his second term, in 1935, and after only one year of experience, for the Legislature met biennially, he served as speaker of the House. It was with this political background that he was elected Governor in 1938. Planks in his platform were to reduce the number of state employees, cap salaries, and place all departments on strict budgets with the Department seemingly a likely target. It was ironic that when Phillips was House speaker, the Legislature gave a special appropriation to the Department to pay the costs of a director of transportation and a secretary. Two years later another special appropriation provided for the establishment of the division of transportation and the hiring of an assistant director.[39] Phillips's term as House speaker preceded Crable's appointment to the Superintendency, thus the animus between the two developed when Phillips was a representative only and then governor.

When Phillips became Governor in 1939, he now had the important platform to pursue his staunch anti-tax sympathies through his opposition to additional funding for school districts. His objectives were twofold: balance the budget and achieve a constitutional amendment requiring balanced budgets. Crable, disinclined to concede anything to the Governor, pushed for additional money to improve schools, provide textbooks, and increase teachers' salaries.

Phillips waited until the fall after the legislative session in 1939 to launch his attack on the Superintendent. He was seething over his inability for several years to obtain financial data from the Department under Vaughan and then Crable so he issued this threat: "When I was first a member of the legislature [sic] I tried to get information which would show actual school needs. When I was speaker of the house [sic] I tried to get this information. Now even with the power of the office of governor [sic] I have not been able to get proper information. But, I am going to get it."[40]

His wrath was focused on Crable, although Vaughan was in office until August 1936. *The Oklahoman* described Phillips as giving up hope of getting cooperation from Crable, but it believed the Governor would pursue another path because he was convinced the taxpayers would support more money for education if there were actually a need for it.[41] Since 1890 the Legislature, with the Governor's consent, determined the positions and salaries in the Department, and the Governor was not about to cede this prerogative. Vaughan stood his ground with Governor Murray on the Land Commission fight, and Crable decided to expand the independence of the Department to lessen external meddling. Crable was soon to discover at the beginning of 1941 that he miscalculated the willingness of the Legislature to do the Governor's bidding and the sentiment of the people toward a balanced budget.

Two political schemes were percolating in spring 1941: conversation and publicity about several amendments, particularly the balanced budget one, and legislation to modify Department governance and supervision. Governor Phillips was wholeheartedly committed to ending what he deemed to be a pattern of decades of undisciplined legislative spending, and getting legislative support to coerce the Department to submit information and data. The Governor at the onset of 1939 had little time to put together his legislative agenda prior to the beginning of the session. Halfway through his term, and with his earlier experience as House speaker, Phillips was better prepared for the 1941 legislative session. Crable's four and one-half years as Superintendent informed him well what to expect from Phillips. Each had priorities with the Governor claiming to represent the people-at-large while Crable highlighted the needs of the students and promoted the interests of the education establishment. Crable believed his vision was the nobler one since it accentuated the expectations of a rich learning environment for the children. Phillips's proposals included three constitutional amendments: first and foremost, a mandate for a balanced budget; next, the coordination of higher education institutions under one governing board; and last, a pension system for educators. Beyond the amendments, the Governor wanted legislation to improve the textbook selection process and to reconfigure the Department. As noted earlier, Crable vociferously opposed the balanced budget proposal, and he gave a cool reception to the notion of modifying the Department's structure.[42]

In mid-January 1941, the state budget director announced a slash of $7,690,348 from the budget requests of the various institutions and agencies. In its reporting of this announcement *The Oklahoman* emphasized that the arch political foe of the Governor would see a reduction in the Department's appropriations, however, all entities would be affected. For the Department, the appropriation requests for 1941-42 and 1942-43 were $90,330 and 87,030, respectively, while the budget director's announced recommendations were $52,740 and $52,440. Seventy thousand, four hundred nine dollars were spent in 1939-40 and $73,730 were appropriated for the current year.[43]

"Renewal of warfare between Governor Phillips and A. L. Crable...was brewing over control of school funds used in transportation of pupils."[44] The personal feud was intensifying with the Governor accusing Crable of wasteful spending in student transportation and for hiring political hacks as employees in the Department. Within a few days, Crable denied the Governor's charges of waste in transportation, and he seemed to have the Legislature's support. Two years earlier the Legislature had viewed the state supervision of the transportation of students critical and had authorized the continued employment of a director, an assistant, and a secretary in the transportation division. Now specified, these persons were responsible for collecting and compiling data, formulating policies and practices, calculating funds to be allocated to school districts, inspecting equipment, and refereeing controversial problems referred to the Department. Crable believed this law to be one of the most important pieces of legislation in 1939. Power, influence, and egos formed the crux of the matter in the disputes among the executive officers and the Legislature. Partisanship was not an important factor as the decade of the 1930s ended because the Governor, the Superintendent, forty-three of forty-four senators, and 102 of 115 representatives were Democrats.[45]

A Festering Problem, an Explosion, and the Beginning of a Restoration

In Crable's first four years this government agency grew by more than 50 percent. A constricting financial picture of the early 1930s was improving with the return of the energy industry and the infusion of federal funds. While the growth in the number of employees seemed excessive, a need existed for supervision of various expanding programs. At the same time, it subjected the Department to allegations of waste and patronage with the hiring of persons deemed by some to be unqualified.[46] Simultaneous to Crable's early administration was Representative Phillips's laying the political groundwork for a run at the governorship where he could continue more vigorously his crusade for less government spending.

As the legislative process continued in early 1941, department chiefs across all agencies were to testify to the needs of their units. Crable wished to present a decade-long analysis of the trends in the state's common school funding and the enrollment and teacher salaries followed by a report on the Department's employees and expenditures. Major upheavals were occurring in Oklahoma resulting from the collapse of the economy and the outward migration from the Dust Bowl. From a cost of $31,995,433 for 492,864 students in 1930 the amount decreased to $31,507,591 for 463,763 students a decade later, declines of 1.5 percent and 6 percent, respectively. While student enrollment decreased, the number of teachers grew 1.5 percent from 19,978 to 20,276 but their salaries dropped 4.5 percent from $1,120 to $1,069. Crable also outlined, to no avail, a justification for reinstatement of high school inspectors and rural school inspectors. In 1939 the Department hired one chief and three assistant high school inspectors along with one rural school and two assistant supervisors for a total of seven inspector/supervisors. What the Legislature gave him were one chief school inspector and six school examiners for a total of seven but with a different emphasis than he preferred. Crable's assignment of employees in 1939 cost $18,800 for salaries while the Legislature's cost in 1941 was a mere 10 percent less. The legislators were convinced that changes were needed regardless of his assessment, that their perceptions superseded his, and together formed a harbinger of significant re-alignment in the administration and operation of the division. They were not about to cede that authority to the Superintendent.[47]

Department employee numbers and costs grew as the Legislature added services and programs and the federal government implemented initiatives to counteract the devastation from the effects of the Great Depression. Initiation of the transportation program helped to swell the employment numbers also. Any government agency that grew more than 50 percent in four years could expect to be scrutinized. The first hint of a proposed restructuring of the Department appeared in a bill introduced by Rep. Charles Ozmun, a Democrat from Lawton. Fourteen positions were identified for elimination in the Department at an annual savings of $30,000. Supervision of most of the remaining positions would be transferred from the Superintendent to the Board, leaving only three out of the current twenty-four to be supervised by Crable. Ozmun claimed no persecution or personal animosity, but said he would fight hard to trim the positions and offered no reason for the shift in oversight.[48]

Crable was in a fight to protect both the Department and his own political career but that did not stop his vociferous refutations to the Legislature's arguments and the Governor's accusations and schemes. He was upset with Ozmun and his bill and the Governor's aim to balance the budget, vowing to oppose the latter's efforts with "the vim of a 'biting shoat'" and knowing he had the backing of the leadership of the OEA. Phillips, not one to back down, after a meeting with the Schoolmasters Club of Stephens County, reported that some of the teachers told him "the political branch of the education department is more like a hog than just a biting shoat."[49] Name-calling and mudslinging were deployed to maximize opponents' idiocies. In a manner more appropriate to his office Crable contended the Governor's desire to balance the budget might be reasonable if all of the state's revenues were placed in the general fund and then the reductions would occur all across the government agencies. However, 70 percent of the fund was already earmarked so the attempt to balance the budget involved only the remaining 30 percent. It was out of this smaller portion that all of education, higher and common, was funded and, consequently, education would be affected most severely, argued Crable.[50]

Phillips and his administration were relentless in pressuring the Legislature to pass the Ozmun bill to strip Crable of most of his authority and patronage. The Governor's dissatisfaction with the stonewalling of his requests by Department employees reached a crescendo with the demand for more transparency from Crable and the Department. Phillips was also angry with a lack of support and cooperation from some legislators. Crable, in return, accused the Governor of being "power drunk" and "grabbing patronage." Glen Johnson, floor manager of the House and representing the Governor's home county, was "fired" by the Governor for his recalcitrance in not supporting passage of HBs 167 and 168 to strip Crable of his patronage.[51]

Occurring simultaneously in the early months of 1941 was the effort by the Governor to get a trio of constitutional amendments passed. Crable supported the pension amendment and vociferously opposed the amendments for the balanced budget which he believed would result in less money for education, and the higher education coordinating board because it would reduce the influence and prerogative of the Board over the teachers colleges. By the third week of February, the March 11 date for a popular vote on the three amendments was set and the Legislature was nearing a vote on the bills reorganizing the Department and the Board. Phillips and Crable were locked in a battle that played out in the public and was eagerly reported in the newspapers.[52] Phillips appealed to the general public and the teachers while Crable concentrated his efforts on educators at all levels.

No more than ten days later, the Governor sent letters to 20,000 teachers promising them an increase of $10 per month in pay if they supported the budget amendment. Not to be outdone, Crable had 15,000 eight-page pamphlets printed and sent to the members of all of the school boards, and was prepared to send upwards of 35,000 more to the administrators and teachers, that listed eight arguments against the balanced budget and the higher education coordinating board amendments. Among those arguments were: education would bear the brunt of the budget balancing, the burden of financing the schools would shift more to the local districts and thereby increase ad valorem taxes, the governor would be given power to gain control over constitutional agencies of the government, and a state board of regents could "cripple or destroy any or all of our state colleges and universities."[53] The rhetoric was becoming more strident and the stakes were getting higher as the two sides drew on whatever resources were available to them to attract the support of the public. In the midst of this cacophony of voices *The Oklahoman* added some perspective when it editorialized that, "Democracy's ability to survive in spite of the vagaries of some of its disciples is proof of its eternal quality."[54]

Phillips took to the airwaves on the evening of March 3 to explain the amendments' contents and his rationale for supporting them, especially the balanced budget one. Passage of the amendments would rein in the Legislature's penchant for deficit spending if it were forced to adopt balanced budgets, higher education would be less accessible to political whims, and the Department would be operated more efficiently if it were given less money. The Governor's focus on the Department was based on his dislike for what he described as an extravagant and wasteful student transportation plan and a misuse of funds for oversight of instruction: "We must write a progressive education program that will get some relief to the classroom teachers, themselves, rather than continue to squander money by the thousands in duplicating supervision."[55] Phillips's commentary superficially had legitimate justification but the unofficial context for his attack on the Department was his animosity toward Crable.

As the March 11 special election date neared, others spoke out, mostly in support of the amendments. Henry Bennett, ordinarily Crable's staunchest advocate, and W. B. Bizzell, retiring president at OU, announced support of all of the measures but Roscoe Dunjee, editor of *The Black Dispatch*, focused opposition on the balanced budget one. Crable's motive was admirable, but his opposition was doomed to failure. Voters favored the budget balancing and higher education coordinating board amendments by two-to-one margins and the third amendment, old age assistance, which received little pre-election attention, by three-to-one.[56] History would prove this to be a momentous day in Oklahoma, for all three amendments have had far-reaching effects.

It was a crushing defeat for Crable who staked a lot of political capital on its defeat, and a crowning victory for Phillips who sought passage for the state's financial advantage, but also for pressuring Crable to cooperate. Phillips was granted an additional wish a month later when the Legislature handed him a bill stripping Crable of his power and patronage in the Department. The Legislature could not eliminate the constitutional office, but it could severely restrict the Superintendent's authority. "The machinery was greased Tuesday to whip the Ozmun bill through the state senate to complete the political thrashing given A. L. Crable." Also, "It will end the stormy two-year fight between Crable and Governor Phillips with the chief executive the complete victor in the legislative struggles," reported *The Oklahoman*.[57]

For the Governor the votes on the three amendments were a mandate for his administration, so he turned his attention toward passage of the Department reorganization bill. Intense feelings for and against Crable were evident in the Legislature. Some admired him for the stand he had taken, but more were anxious to punish him. House Bill 168 replaced the Board's six appointed members with an eight-member Board and transferred the thirty-five employees officed in Oklahoma City from the Superintendent's oversight to the Board's; those employees located at A&M in Stillwater were under the supervision of the director of vocational programs. Four of the Board's six previous members were reappointed by the Governor along with four new members to form the reconstituted Board. The Superintendent remained *ex-officio* member and president, but all of the authority to manage the Department was now in the hands of the Board except supervision of the Superintendent's secretary. James Staten, director of finance in the Department, became the new assistant state superintendent and executive secretary to the Board with supervisory duties over the Department and at a salary of $3,600. Salaries of the Board's employees were set legislatively as were the details of the reorganization including specific administrative units within the Department.[58] In essence, the Legislature imposed its will to micromanage this government agency, even to a greater extent than was historically the case. Not having the option to eliminate the Superintendency or the incumbent, it found a way to minimize his influence.

Subdivisions within the Department were named in legislation as were the positions within these units: two auditors added, the high school and rural school inspection system with seven employees abolished, stenographers reduced from ten to six, and the assistant state superintendent position eliminated. Crable's opposition to this move to strip him of his power was "to keep the governor from destroying the department and to see that sufficient funds are provided for the schools."[59] Crable was so focused on dueling with the Governor that he momentarily suspended his better judgment and alienated many legislators resulting in the House voting to advance the bill stripping him of his power. Further insult was heaped on Crable April 16 as the new Board immediately fired or kept Department employees based on their political support for the Governor. Replacements were paid less than those fired for the same positions and responsibilities. Crable, Board chair, learned about one of the firings indirectly through a letter from the one discharged.[60] Obviously, the relationships among the Superintendent, the Board, and the Department were strained at best and not conducive to the efficient operation of a government agency.

When Crable worked in the Department from 1924 to 1929 as a high school inspector, the head of that division by statute was the Superintendent, first Nash and then Vaughan. One of his colleagues and mentor was E. A. Duke, a rural school supervisor since 1918, whose first Department employment at age thirty-four was in 1913 as the assistant superintendent and one of only two professional employees beside the Superintendent. Duke held high school principalships in Mangum and Ponca City before becoming Kay County superintendent, served as a rural school supervisor until 1942, and continued with his responsibility as a state agent for Black schools until the end of Crable's term in January 1947. Thus, Crable and Duke had known each other professionally for more than two decades, and the latter's expansive institutional history and stalwart stature were an invaluable influence on the Department and the four Superintendents with whom he worked. When the legislature abruptly altered the Department's organizational chart, these two men's vested interests were adversely affected. Both with experience in inspection and supervision were resistant to external pressure. Duke survived the initial purge but then chose to retire five years later at age sixty-eight. Politics were a key ingredient, but the state's changing school structure, affected by increased transportation of students, needed a Department responsive to the needs.[61]

Crable's role obviously was complicated by the actions of the Governor and the overwhelming majority of the Legislature, yet he was expected to fulfill his responsibilities regardless of how they were modified. He was still chair of the Board and expected to function in that role. From his first Board meeting in August 1936 until April 5, 1941, he missed only two out of fifty-two meeting days or sessions. Of the forty-six meeting days that occurred over the next two years when the Board members were Phillips's appointees, Crable was absent fifteen of those days. Meeting minutes for 1941 and 1942 show that he was present in 1941 for eighteen meeting days and absent for five, while in 1942 he was present for only eleven of nineteen meeting days. Although he was officially chair, the Board's executive secretary was in charge. In April 1943 when the Board was again reconfigured and with Governor Robert Kerr's appointees, the Superintendent's attendance rate improved to that of his first five years. Also significant, the Board met more frequently during the period of Phillips's administration than previously or subsequently. Not to be forgotten was that the nation had entered World War II in December 1941.[62]

Governor Kerr was less than a month into his term in early February 1943 when he persuaded the Legislature through SB 35 to reorganize the Board by reducing the number of members to six. All of the incumbent members lost their positions except Hugh Carroll when the Board was reconfigured, giving Kerr the opportunity to name the new members and to usher in a less contentious period.[63] Sixty-eight years later and in the midst of another kerfuffle the Legislature moved to require Board members to resign when a new governor was elected, giving that person the opportunity to name an entirely new Board.

The relationship between the Board members and chairman Crable improved dramatically from 1943 to the end of his term in January 1947 as evidenced by the Board's "Resolution to Mr. Crable" at his last meeting with the Board. Improvements to education occurring under his leadership were: annual state aid fund increased from 8.2 million to 15.6 million dollars, appropriations to vocational education tripled, teacher certification standards enhanced, improvement of instruction emphasized, Black students' educational opportunities increased through the establishment of additional tuition aid, and more efficient criteria for secondary schools' evaluation and accreditation developed.[64]

At stake in Phillips's administration was the competing power and authority of the Governor and the Superintendent. Both were elected and answerable to the public; however, the Governor did not need to concern himself with reelection while the Superintendent did. Imbedded in the power struggle was the Legislature's redefinition of the Superintendent's role and the Department's (employees and administrators) reconfiguration. From the beginning of the territorial period the Legislature identified titles and salaries while allowing the Superintendents (and Boards) to hire their choices. When the overwhelming majority Democratic House stripped patronage from Crable, a member of their party, and transferred authority exclusively to the Board, the vote was 70 to 27 with 22 absent or excused. In 1949 patronage was officially returned to the Superintendent by a House vote similar to the earlier one along with the prerogative to determine positions and salaries. Of particular historical note, voting with the majority in both years was Representative W. H. Langley of Adair whose daughter Sandy Garrett became Superintendent five decades later in 1991.[65]

Endless Textbook Controversy and an Impeachment Vote

Crable's tenure was dogged by textbook controversies, eventually leading to his indictment and an impeachment attempt. Issues in the late 1930s and early 1940s focused on whether the parents or the state would purchase textbooks, selection processes, authorship, costs, adoption frequency, revisions, publishing companies, vendors, and, of course, political intrigues. Six gubernatorial appointees and the Superintendent, *ex-officio* as secretary, formed the Textbook Commission and, as such, pledged an oath of no interest in, and to receive no benefit from, any contract.[66]

Textbook controversy seemed endemic in the early decades of the state's history, but it was not surprising considering the lure of easy money and an ethical climate amenable to political machinations and graft. Whether at the macro level of the state or at the micro level of the county and local school superintendencies, textbook funds proved irresistible to those bent on circumventing the law. Unscrupulous they were at the expense of the school students and their parents. Periodically, the Legislature from territorial days forward tackled the gamut of selection and acquisition of textbooks, but no consistent approach resulted. It was not a good omen, especially considering the various squabbles embedded in political overtones in which Crable became mired.

In Crable's initial involvement with textbooks, the Attorney General declared in July 1937 the State Welfare Board was legally able to allocate funds for textbooks for children of needy parents and drought-stricken farmers. Crable announced that it would not be difficult to gather data to determine the number of eligible children and families. After his office conducted a survey, he approved the Welfare Board's selection and purchase of $400,000 worth of books.[67] Nothing controversial here, at least he was off to a good start and had the Attorney General's support.

Near the end of 1940 Crable was faced with a conundrum when nine textbook companies filed a federal injunction against him for refusing to comply with the law because he was advising school administrators not to purchase books published by these nine and, instead, to purchase books printed by other companies. At issue was the length of the adoption period, one to five years depending on the book. Simultaneously, he was restrained by a Pontotoc County lawsuit in which the judge ruled parts of the textbook law unconstitutional. The textbook companies believed they were being harmed by Crable's actions, and Crable believed he was constrained by the lawsuit from acting. It was a chaotic situation rooted in the controversy over textbooks having arisen from the Murray administration six years earlier. Fortunately, the Legislature was in session and was able to solve the issue through a resolution to extend the adoption period to five years for all books.[68]

The fall 1942 political season attracted less voter attention than previous years because the United States at war commandeered resources and focused peoples' attention on the events of the day. Speculation by *The Oklahoman* over who would back the respective parties' choices and what the emphases would be focused to some extent on Crable and the festering textbook problems. The conservative Republican attack would be to expose the textbook graft even if those alleged guilty could not be prosecuted. Disappointing, no doubt, for the newspaper was the election's outcome. Crable remained in office.[69]

At 4:50 P.M. of the last day of 1942 Governor Phillips filed suit in federal district court against nineteen publishing companies and fourteen other defendants for harming citizens through fixed textbook adoptions in the years 1933-1937. Only twelve days until the end of his administration, he charged Crable; Henry Bennett; the president of the State Board of Agriculture, Joe Scott; former Superintendent Vaughan; former speaker of the House, T. J. Daniel; president of East Central State College, A. Linscheid; former governor, W. J. Holloway; and others in an eighty-eight-page description of the accusations. Phillips alleged that Bennett and several A&M faculty initially wrote textbooks and then, with few minor modifications, issued new editions so that the revised editions would cost more and earn the authors more money. Another charge was that the American Book Company paid a 10 percent kickback on the more than one million dollars it received from the state for textbook sales. This money was funneled through the William H. Murray Education Foundation created in 1934 by Bennett, Vaughan, Crable, Daniels, Holloway, and others. Purportedly, no one other than the "conspirators" knew the real purpose of the Foundation. Phillips, through the lawsuit, arrived at the amount of the loss to the state by alleging damages of $1,789,183 ($24,859,269 in 2014) but under the "restraint of trade" statutes, three-fold damages, or $5,367,550 ($74,577,820 in 2014), were demanded.[70]

Four days later Crable denounced the allegations of the lawsuit, denied any involvement whatsoever in any conspiracy to rig the costs of textbooks, and advised anyone who had questions to study the record since all of the Textbook Commission's actions were recorded. The plot thickened in early February when Representative Charles Whitford offered a resolution in the House that Crable be impeached for his indiscretions. Offended supporters vouched for his veracity and Guy Massey, Representative from McCurtain County, described him as "my good friend and a good Christian gentleman."[71]

A joint legislative committee, from within which was selected a Board of Managers, was formed to investigate the charges. Federal district attorney Charles Dierker, the first witness, had conducted a grand jury investigation about a year earlier into tax evasion charges resulting from graft in textbook purchasing. J. T. Daniel, the former speaker, was given a two-year sentence in federal prison for failure to pay taxes on the $44,465 in 1937 ($725,064 in 2014) and $53,717 in 1938 ($900,957 in 2014) received from the Jasper Sipes Book Depository. Dierker testified to the Board of Managers that only Daniel and one other person, Howard Drake, a political advisor to Governor Marland, received any money. Drake also was sent to federal prison for two years for his tax evasion. Recovery of the money paid to Daniel and Drake was impossible because of the state statute of limitations. Continued operation of the joint investigating committee was authorized in early April when Governor Kerr signed a bill extending the inquiry. Former Governor Phillips had testified before the committee only days earlier and admitted that the previous December when he was still governor but had less than a month remaining on his term, he accepted $5,000 (nearly five times a teacher's salary then and equivalent to $69,471 in 2014) from E. H. Moore, one of Oklahoma's US senators![72]

A second level of investigation got underway in November 1943 when a Tulsa County grand jury looked into textbook purchases. Crable was viewed as the key witness, and all members of the Textbook Commission in 1937 were called. An additional witness, James Staten, was called because of his role as chief executive officer of the Department during this time when Crable was stripped of most of his authority. Given the politicization of the process in 1943, and now with the former Governor on the periphery, it came as little surprise that the grand jury handed down indictments. Two hundred and thirty-seven witnesses testified and then the jury reported that a conspiracy existed for six years costing the state $1,300,000 ($21,649,333 in 2014), and some defendants received large sums of money from the publishing companies in return for those companies selling their books for excessive prices. Crable was named along with Bennett; Ed Morrison, president of Panhandle A&M; former federal prisoners Daniel and Drake; Willis Smith, president of the Jasper Sipes Book Depository; and others. American Book Company, Follett Publishing Company, Laidlaw Brothers, and other publishers were also named.[73]

Crable and Daniel were arrested after they declined to appear voluntarily to the Tulsa County grand jury for the indictments. Crable showed up at the Ada District Courthouse and claimed he was being unlawfully detained since the Tulsa grand jury had no authority over textbook adoptions; only Oklahoma County had jurisdiction in this matter. Bennett had already raised that issue in the Criminal Court of Appeals (renamed the Court of Criminal Appeals in 1959). Dixie Gilmer, Tulsa County District Attorney, was loath to allow Crable to defy the grand jury and to injure his own political aspirations. The grand jury's findings were submitted to the District Court where the judge sustained a motion to quash the indictment. Gilmer was disappointed and frustrated, but not vanquished. He pursued an opportunity to further his political interests by seeking perjury charges against Crable through a request to the Oklahoma County district attorney's office. Gilmer also testified before the House investigating committee in April 1944 that Crable gave inconsistent statements to that committee and the Tulsa grand jury. "I wouldn't feel like I was a decent citizen if I wasn't willing to sign such a complaint against Crable," Gilmer stated.[74]

Through the investigation by the House that included the years of Crable's administration beginning in 1936, the representatives collected information resulting in a stinging criticism of Crable and a resolution with six articles of impeachment. Five of those articles failed by a consistent range of about 45 to 68, but article two's margin was very narrow 55 to 59. Crable was charged in article two with involvement with the Welfare Board's purchases of textbooks in 1937, some of which expired within two months after the deal closed. All twenty-one Republicans along with the Democratic leadership voted for all six of the articles. Speaker Johnson Hill followed through on his earlier promise to resign if the House failed to impeach, causing bitterness among his friends in that legislative body who believed Governor Kerr had sabotaged the proceedings. Regardless, Crable thought it highly unlikely that the Senate would have supported impeachment even if the House would have.[75]

Crable survived legislative investigations and impeachment votes, a Tulsa County grand jury, and the animus and vitriol of Governor Phillips who had no reluctance to cast aspersions on his performance or intentions. The Governor tried to tie Crable and Bennett, both of whom were his enemies, to nefarious actions and deeds. Both escaped any criminal charges through events that kept them from ever being found guilty. Bennett had sufficient political cachet to avoid any potential criminal outcome prior to the expiration of the statute of limitations. Lost in all of the acrimony and political maneuverings was a determination of who was guilty, but there was no disputing the corruption within the textbook selection and purchasing processes. No persons were ever held accountable, and the state's students were the losers.

Governor Kerr preferred a high level of functioning within the Textbook Commission, so he assembled a distinguished group of members. He requested George Cross, President of OU, to chair the Commission who, when he received the call from the Governor, thought Kerr must be kidding. Assured of no such intent, Cross was appalled at the request for two reasons. It was beneath his dignity as a university president to chair a textbook committee; furthermore, he was somewhat familiar with the recent sordid history of the Commission and did not wish to sully his name with any such affiliation. Rumors were afloat about past attempts from as high as the Governor's office to influence the Commission's decisions on which books to adopt. At Cross's request Kerr listed the names of men he was considering also inviting to serve. Cross was relieved at the quality of those men and agreed to serve.[76]

Crable, *ex-officio* secretary, was held with contempt by Cross and some of the other members who wanted to hear nothing about how the Textbook Commission functioned in the past. In the Commission's first meeting and when the group was discussing procedural questions, Crable proffered, "In the past, the members of the commission have always---" whereupon Otis McClintock, president of the First National Bank of Tulsa, interrupted with "God Damn it, Crable, that's what we're trying to avoid—doing what past commissions have done! I don't want to hear anything more about the past!"[77] It was to be understood that textbooks would be adopted for their merit, not out of economic or political consideration.

Not all of Kerr's motive in wanting Cross and other distinguished Oklahomans to serve on the commission was utilitarian, for he was planning to run for the US Senate in a few years and wanted his record to reflect that he cleaned up the textbook process.[78] Regardless, the state's image suffered through yet another example of corruption, a seemingly endemic characteristic of this young state dominated by one political party and "fueled" by the booms and busts of the energy industry. Textbook selection processes offered opportunities for easy money, and some decision makers succumbed to the temptation to enrich themselves at the expense of taxpayers and students. Conviction of some of the perpetrators was hindered by a short statute of limitations and a fraught political environment.

How ironic it must have seemed to Crable that on the day his successor was elected,

Negro rural school, Creek County, Oklahoma, Library of Congress photograph collection No. 2017785182

Oklahoma's Chief of Public Instruction / 213

the citizens voted by a 61 percent to 39 percent margin to amend the constitution to establish a free textbook system that involved a committee of active educators identifying textbooks from which local district committees could select books for their schools. Enabling legislation was enacted in 1948, effective July 1, specifying the composition of the State Textbook Committee: eight gubernatorial appointees and the Superintendent, *ex officio*, to serve as secretary and vote only when there was a tie vote. These measures did not end all controversy, but they were an attempt to provide some clarity. Future issues would involve protests from companies excluded from the approved adoptions and parents who were dissatisfied with some of the textbooks' contents.[79]

Looking for Work

Crable became the second Superintendent in thirty-six years to lose his position in the Democratic primary and his loss, like the earlier one, was to a sitting county superintendent. He was fifty-eight and out of work, but still friends with Henry Bennett. Crable served with three governors who were term-limited, and it was under Phillips that he had the most conflict. He survived a grand jury investigation and indictment, an attempted impeachment, and unpopular espousal of opposition to the balanced budget amendment to serve for ten years. Controversy, however, did not subside when his term ended January 13, 1947.

Crable's post-Superintendency whereabouts were of such a sufficient interest to *The Oklahoman* that a search was made of the payrolls in the budget department of the Capitol where it was discovered that he was working at Oklahoma A&M in the veterans' guidance division. Inquiry was made through the chairman of the A&M Board of Regents who expressed surprise that Crable was employed by the College. Later when the regents discussed the matter, they were told there was nothing they could do since Crable was employed by the Veterans Administration. However, the regional VA manager said Crable could not be transferred since he did not work for the Administration.[80]

Such was the controversy swirling around Crable even after he left the Superintendency. *The Oklahoman* could not resist the urge to keep the controversy over Crable's alleged involvement in the textbook investigations in the news. Though Crable was not found guilty of any crime, the paper hounded him relentlessly until he announced his intention to resign at the end of February 1948 and after he worked for the VA for seven months. Crable then moved to the General Services Administration in Washington, DC from 1948 to 1956, before he returned to Oklahoma City to become vice president of Bankers Service Life Insurance Co. where he worked until 1970. One of the founders of the National Diabetic Foundation, he served as its vice president until his retirement in 1972.[81]

Death came to Crable August 10, 1976, in Oklahoma City. His alma mater, Austin College, had conferred an honorary doctorate on him in 1937 and two years later he was elected president of the board of trustees of Oklahoma Baptist University. Also, in the fall of 1939 he spoke out against attempts to repeal the prohibition law, "The repeal of the liquor law is not consistent with the objectives we have in our educational program."[82] Supporting prohibition was consistent with the public's expectation of the Superintendent and the Baptists' qualification of the University's governing board chairman.

Chapter 12
Hodge: Creating Stability
(1947-1968)

In early 1947 Oklahoma's transition from wartime sacrifice to peacetime exuberance continued. The election outcome held out hope for change within the Superintendency and Department as Crable exited and Oliver Hodge entered. Increased post-war industrial output of domestic goods gave consumers more of the necessities to enjoy life. People were beginning to feel good about the state's financial condition to the extent that they were willing to invest in infrastructure that had been delayed because of the focus on the war rations and shortages.

A governor who wished to improve the state's transportation and education systems was elected. He was planning first, to construct a toll road between Oklahoma City and Tulsa that would not be a drain on the budget and second, to consolidate rural schools. Rural highways, too long neglected and unsafe, needed to be improved to allow more efficient transportation of agricultural products as well as students to school. Additionally, he wanted teacher compensation to be a function of experience and training. Prepared to work in tandem to propel the state's school system forward was a new Superintendent who had his ideas about how to accomplish that.

Within this context Governor Roy Turner's and Hodge's terms began with the former assessing his future knowing that he had four years to accomplish his goals. Success depended upon his ability to work with, and persuade, the Legislature to support his platform. Hodge, on the other hand, knew that if he were successful, he could seek re-election as often as he desired and could attract a majority of voters to his cause. Thus, any action on his part would need to be imperatively weighed by an educational value as well as by the political.

Oliver Hodge was born in Exeter, a small town in southwest Missouri, September 24, 1901, and spent most of his youth in Collinsville, Oklahoma. In the forty-five students of his freshman class of 1917, he was one of sixteen males, but not one of the three male class officers, and he was one of two freshmen on the eight-member varsity basketball team. From relative obscurity during his early high school years he distinguished himself such that upon graduation in 1921 he was employed as a teacher and coach. For seven years he taught and coached football and basketball at Collinsville High School where he also was principal in 1925-27. During these years, Collinsville's district enrollment of approximately 1,300 students was taught by a faculty of twenty-five.[1]

Hodge was awarded a bachelors degree at the University of Tulsa in 1928 followed by a master's degree at the University of Oklahoma. A three-year stint of teaching and basketball coaching at the University of Tulsa preceded a similar period of study and graduate assistantship at OU where he earned his doctorate in 1937. Not all was work, for Hodge participated in the OU golf doubles championship in 1933.² His career trajectory was upward because he was ambitious and excelling at almost everything he attempted. His resumé was growing in those areas that would provide him the most substantial credentials for his subsequent political career. He had teaching, coaching, and administrative experience, expansive educational preparation, and an aspiration for advancement.

Following the passage of the constitutional amendment in March 1941 creating the higher education system and a governing board, the Governor appointed the board members who then designed the administrative officer position and considered persons for the job. Among those persons rumored to be under review was Hodge. The board chose M. A. Nash, but that Hodge was even considered was a testament to his professional standing in the state's educational and political community.³

Always Ready for the Next Election

At the youthful age of thirty-three Hodge challenged Democrat incumbent L. H. Cates in the 1934 primary for the Tulsa County superintendency. Cates was first elected three years earlier and now faced his most serious challenger. A third person, Lola Covington, joined in the primary, but it was Hodge who forced a runoff election by getting 7,170 out of 22,647 votes cast. Even though the *Tulsa Tribune* editorialized in his favor, expressing the need for the office to be filled by an educator and organizer, he lost 10,993 to 9,008, the only instance of election failure in his long and distinguished political career.⁴

Oliver Hodge
Courtesy of Oklahoma Education Association

Undaunted and optimistic of winning, he entered the Democratic primary against Cates two years later, squeaking by with 52 percent of the vote. That year's general election outcome, two to one margin in his favor, set the political neophyte on a public career that would last more than thirty years. So popular and formidable was he that he drew no opponents in the primary or general elections of 1938, 1940, and 1942. Only in 1944 was he challenged by Republican Leslie Guy Ferguson whom he bested 39,329 to 32,213. With this political experience and the vicissitudes of Crable's tenure, Hodge was encouraged to run against him in the 1946 statewide race for Superintendent.[5]

Hodge and Crable knew each other very well through professional and political relationships beginning in late 1936 when Hodge was elected in Tulsa County. Five months earlier Crable had been appointed to the Superintendency and, over the ten-year period of their concurrent tenures, they would have met numerous times. Hodge oversaw fifteen dependent school districts (only nine with four or more teachers) each with its own three-member governing board and, among the nine, an average of 248 students and seven teachers. Tulsa County's number of dependent school districts, teachers, and students was not an anomaly, being similar to other counties. Annual reports were submitted to Crable accounting for the number of students, expenditures, textbooks, teacher and principal certificates, and buildings. Hodge was responsible for approving the hiring of teachers and verifying their position-appropriate credentials. County superintendents, especially from the more populous counties, had frequent interactions with the Superintendent.[6]

Not only was Hodge aware of Crable's fights with Governor Phillips, the impeachment controversy, and the Tulsa County grand jury indictments, he was also cognizant of the textbook issues and the operation of the Textbook Commission. Of all of the Superintendents, he was the most intimately familiar with the Commissioners of the Land Office, one of the most important commissions on which the Superintendent served *ex officio*, having focused his doctoral dissertation research on it.[7] And by 1946, he was only two years younger than Crable was when appointed to the Superintendency. Hodge pondered the political environment in 1946 and knew that the incumbent was vulnerable, that he had engendered the enmity of some in the Legislature, and thus opened the door for someone knowledgeable of the position to mount a challenge.

Many of the details of the 1946 election cycle are described in the prior chapter, but some additional description is edifying. For both Crable and Hodge, this election proved to be the most formidable of their political careers. Again, as in 1910, an incumbent was defeated in the primary or runoff election. With Crable dispatched, Hodge focused his energy on besting his Republican opponent, Martin Nelson, the relatively unknown superintendent of schools at Shidler from 1927 to 1946 who was also the head of the tiny Shidler Junior College during the 1940s. The 59 percent outcome for the Democrat seemed an almost foregone conclusion, as reflected in the parties' registrations statewide.[8]

Crable's political assets included oversight of the education system for a decade, the support of a bloc whose most visible representative was Henry Bennett, and *ex officio* service on the School Land Commission while it was free of any allegations or accusations of corruption. In general, he was well known across the state, especially among the teachers. But antagonists included former Governor Phillips, members of the House of Representatives, and voters of Tulsa County who he accused of wanting their cake and eating it too when it came to taxation and allocation of state dollars to schools. Also, he had alienated some of the county superintendents with his suggestions over the years for improving the education and instruction in the dependent districts.

Hodge, quite the contrary, sought the support of the county superintendents by emphasizing his kindred spirit and understanding their challenges. One of few people who earned a doctorate, he appreciated the admiration of those who showed deference to highly educated people. An active OEA member, he chaired the resolutions committee in 1941, not necessarily the most influential position in that organization's administrative structure. A county superintendent who had previously been a principal, but not a district superintendent, his experience in the second most populous county gave him the unique perspective of the rural and urban settings. He was prepared with the political foundation to lead the Department into the second half of the twentieth century.

Elevated interest in several of the executive offices in the 1946 election, particularly from the Democrats, continued a pattern present in both parties since 1916, and would eventually extend to 1966 as shown in table 12.1, especially for Governor and Lieutenant Governor. Through the 1946 election, the Superintendent position drew multiple candidates, but then the pattern shifted dramatically. Six filed in the Democrat primary that year, equaling the 1934 election, but not occurring since that year (see appendix F).

Table 12.1 Number of Democratic and Republican executive office primary candidates 1946-1966

	1946		1950		1954		1958		1962		1966		Average	
Position	D	R	D	R	D	R	D	R	D	R	D	R	D	R
Governor	9	3	4	5	16	5	11	4	12	2	13	3	10.8	3.66
Lt. Governor	8	2	14	4	10	2	11	2	15	2	4	2	10.3	2.33
Secretary of State	11	1	9	1	24	1	5	1	4	1	6	1	9.8	1.00
Auditor	2	1	5	1	2	0	3	1	8	0	3	1	3.8	0.67
Attorney General	2	2	3	1	2	1	3	3	8	1	5	1	3.8	1.50
Treasurer	6	1	2	1	3	0	6	1	4	1	5	1	4.3	0.83
Superintendent	6	1	1	0	1	0	1	1	1	0	1	0	1.8	0.33

Source: *Oklahoma Elections: Statehood to Present*, vol. 1 (OKC: SEB, 1994), C-321-C-476.

Note: A number greater than one indicates a primary election occurred. A one indicates there was a candidate in the general election. A zero in either the primary or the general election denotes no candidate.

Interest in the top positions was greater than in the secondary positions from 1946 to 1966, but unique to all of the positions was the Superintendency, possibly because of the perceived invincibility of the incumbent. Hodge enjoyed supremacy in the position with no viable opposition to threaten his legitimacy. Had he not died, with no term limit, and with forceful political acumen, his tenure might have continued uninterrupted for more terms. Hodge drew no Democrat opponents during his tenure, and, only in 1958, was he opposed by a Republican, Clyde Smallwood, an assistant professor of philosophy at Philips University who garnered a mere 25 percent of the votes. That margin of victory for Hodge remains the greatest in the history of the Superintendency.[9]

Hodge was keenly aware of the Superintendent's limited authority to select and oversee the Department's personnel, an awkward and unworkable evolution of the Crable era. Even before assuming the office, Hodge maneuvered to get that patronage returned to him. For the immediate future, he submitted recommendations to the Board for personnel in the Department to be effective January 13, his first day in office. Fortunately for him, Board members were receptive to the proposed changes. Determination of the extent of Hodge's prerogatives was a function subject to the political whims of the legislators, some sympathetic to Hodge's request to be able to exercise flexibility in the Department's operation while others skeptical of the necessity for extensive latitude.[10]

Hodge and the Board compromised to develop a relationship that granted him more authority in all aspects of personnel decision-making; but Hodge wished the Legislature to formally grant him more latitude. Two years later, in 1949 in a legislative rewrite of the school code, the Board membership was reduced from the nine mandated in 1941 to seven, its enumerated duties grew from twelve to twenty-six, and the Superintendent formally regained the patronage privileges of the earlier times. Any who had qualms about the adverse effects of such a system had those concerns confirmed in 1950 when *The Oklahoman* revealed that a move was under way for a "shakedown" of the Department's employees. Alleged was that a Department administrator was collecting money from employees to help defray Hodge's reelection campaign expenses. E. H. McDonald, an assistant division head, was identified as the collector, and the expected amount of contribution was 25 percent of one month's salary. Assistant superintendent Truman Bennett was one of five employees on the strategy committee that planned the collection campaign.[11]

Planning within the Department for Hodge's reelection began the preceding autumn in a meeting of all unit heads. The committee was organized and plans included a "fund raising" scheme that originally called for one half of one month's salary. When no primary opponents materialized, less money was needed, so each person's contribution was reduced. Bennett stated that no one was compelled to contribute and that Hodge had repeatedly said no pressure was to be applied. Hodge's disingenuous description was that some Department employees asked him how they could help in a reelection campaign, they were grateful that they could assist him in such an effort. He also said that, months earlier in an impromptu administrators' meeting, he was asked how they could help. In a subsequent luncheon meeting, Hodge said he emphasized that no pressure should be applied for contributions. "I have always insisted that the raising of funds for any purpose among our employees be on this basis." Having stated his criterion for the fund raising, he continued to explain his rationale for approval of such a scheme, "I have no apology to make on behalf of myself or any of our employees in this matter."[12] For Hodge, if employees wanted to contribute one quarter of one month's salary, they were happy to do so, and it was totally acceptable to be complicit in the exercise. Effects of the practice were to be ameliorated by meetings scheduled at lunch and voluntary contributions.

The Oklahoman speculated that collected funds were not destined for the support of the reelection of the Superintendent who drew no opponent, but rather for the support of legislators who would be sympathetic to the interests of the Department. No evidence seems to support this allegation nor does it seem reasonable to suspect that rank and file employees would contribute voluntarily, knowing that if they supported one who lost, retribution might ensue. The cozy relationship between education and politics was reaffirmed in late 1953 when Hodge surveyed educators across the state to determine their assessment of his chances for reelection in 1954. Of the seven hundred letters received from superintendents and principals, only one was negative. No mention was made of how many letters were sent initially. Hodge concluded that he had about 100 percent favorability and thus, he should run. It is impossible to know how many disapproved, for anyone who would express opposition potentially could face political consequences. No comment by *The Oklahoman* addressed the ethical aspects of querying constituents using state paid stationery, postage, and clerical assistance, although it is difficult to know for certain that this was the case.[13]

In January 1955 news broke that a potential rival to Hodge, Eddie Higgins, was paid $1,500 to help defray campaign expenses and to withdraw his filing application for the office of Superintendent. Higgins two years earlier had been fired from the Department for alleged political maneuvering. Several people testified before a House committee about events surrounding the alleged payoff money and the delivery of the withdrawal letter to the election board by the Department's assistant superintendent. Investigating committee members sought to establish a connection to Hodge who reported, "I didn't authorize anyone to make a payment, not did I make one." Higgins expressed his frustration and disgust with Hodge by describing him as a "75 percent superintendent" who spent twelve weeks each year at his cabin in Canada. Hodge retorted that he spent only one month annually at his Canadian retreat. Higgins escaped punishment even though he refused to name the contact man. Nothing is reported about whether Hodge knew anything about the scheme. An Oklahoma County grand jury eventually indicted Higgins for accepting a bribe, but the payoff was courtesy of Ben Brickell, former legislator and current owner of a beer company.[14]

Communicating his political aspirations to education constituents and friends was important to Hodge, and was viewed as an effective means of generating support. Early in 1958 he announced his plan to run for reelection through a letter to teachers and other friends. Three months earlier he had been feted by more than 1,000 friends, educators, and politicians including Governor Raymond Gary. Optimism was running high as evident in *The Oklahoman*'s assessment, "The voters of the state believe strongly in the program his office and the school people have been attempting to operate and that he will have almost unanimous support of the school people of the state."[15]

Hodge flexed his political muscle in 1962 by announcing publicly his endorsement of former Governor Gary who was now seeking a second term after a one-term hiatus. After the Democratic primary he sent letters to 3,500 principals and superintendents informing them of his reasons for supporting Gary. Drawing no opponent himself freed him to engage in the political arena for what he thought was good for education. Not only did Gary not win the Democratic runoff election, losing by 449 votes out of the 463,539 cast, but also his opponent lost the general election to Henry Bellmon. Stationery, postage, and clerical support paid with taxpayer money for political purposes seemed to be totally acceptable with Hodge commenting that he thought the administrators appreciated his action because they wanted to know who he was supporting and why. Nine years earlier it had been alleged that morale in the Department was adversely affected by the Superintendent's public support of a specific individual for the Governorship.[16]

Hodge's final election cycle, in 1966, was uneventful when Oklahoma City resident A. D. Castle filed for the office, but subsequently withdrew, allowing Hodge to continue in office without contending for it. It was an impressive run of more than twenty years of active involvement in the statewide political arena.[17]

Supervising a Growing Common School System

Prior to 1968 the Board was required to submit a biennial report to the Governor, and annually thereafter, providing a narrative and data description of the education system's status and recommendations for its improvement. Typically, division heads wrote segments of the report and the Superintendent compiled the report, adding comments and perspectives and developing the rationale for the desired improvements or funding. Hodge, as his predecessors, enumerated multiple recommendations in his reports emphasizing the necessity for further consolidations, providing adequate funding for textbooks, "weak" districts, and teacher compensation, and curricular modifications.

Rather significant demographic changes occurred during his twenty-one-year tenure as shown in table 12.2: the number of teachers increased by 53 percent, student attendance grew by 38 percent, and the number of school districts decreased by 79 percent. District consolidation and annexation progressed rapidly in the first ten years, with 1,786 closing after the 1946-47 year, but slowed during the last twelve years.[18]

Much of the consolidation resulted from dependent districts shutting their doors because they were unable to meet the attendance requirements established in the consolidation law of 1946. Just prior to the enactment of this legislation, approximately 36 percent of the state's students attended schools supervised by county superintendents.[19] Consequently, the extent of the role of the county superintendent diminished immensely during Hodge's tenure through the reduced number of school districts and school sites. Less correspondence between the Department, dependent school districts, and county superintendents allowed for more efficiency in operation. Larger dependent district enrollments required fulltime principals who could assist the county superintendent, especially in collecting information and compiling reports. With county superintendents having far fewer schools to visit and supervise, greater efficacy achieved through an economy of scale aided the various administrative levels in fulfilling their responsibilities, allowing Hodge's Department to re-align roles.

A 40 percent increase in ADA over the twenty years reflected the growth in the state's population and an improving attendance rate. Hodge was concerned with student attendance as early at 1952 when he recommended enforcement of the compulsory attendance law for the elementary schools and curricular improvements to lower the dropout rate at the secondary level. The Superintendent decried the irrelevance of segments of the high school curricular offerings, believing revisions would entice more students to opt to pursue their diplomas instead of dropping out when they reached age sixteen and were no longer required to attend school.[20]

The 59 percent expansion in total expenditure of funds (local, state, and federal) in the mid-1960s as shown in table 12.2 allowed per pupil expenditure growth of 46 percent, from $332 in 1963-64 to $483 in 1967-68. While the total amount from all funds averaged almost 15 percent, the state aid portion of that sum grew at a rate of only approximately 11 percent as increased federal aid supplemented (and sometimes supplanted) the state's efforts. For example, in the last three years of data displayed in table 12.2, state aid changed minimally while total expenditures continued to grow. Federal aid in 1965-66 amounted to slightly more than $22,000,000 and the following year to $23,263,000. Substantial yearly influxes of money allowed districts to decrease class sizes, employ more teachers (18 percent over the four years), and add programs. Student attendance growth of 5 percent during this four-year period was not equal to the additional monetary commitment, giving the schools a chance to catch up from prior lean years. At the Department, few additional employees, only 6 percent, were necessary to administer the various federal-funded programs. Typically, morale is higher when the amount of funds allocated to education grows, and school administrators, always desirous of more appropriations, seem to find curricular and instructional areas where student learning can be enhanced.[21]

Table 12.2 Teachers, students, and expenditures 1946-1947 to 1967-1968

School year	Number of teachers	Number of districts	ADA	Per capita	Expenditures	State aid
1946-47	18,312	4,450	405,667	113.84	46,181,682	17,086,149
1947-48	18,097	2,664	399,966	143.43	57,368,768	18,764,958
1948-49	18,447	2,338	395,631	158.37	62,656,628	18,092,215
1949-50	18,885	2,332	401,931	186.04	74,774,461	25,611,082
1950-51	19,244	2,177	409,191	192.66	78,834,478	24,782,979
1951-52	19,477	2,100	404,767	215.99	87,424,082	28,224,464
1952-53	19,411	1,989	411,430	219.42	90,274,234	27,132,130
1953-54	19,695	1,888	425,425	228.99	97,416,867	30,568,973
1954-55	20,075	1,802	447,394	224.37	100,382,127	30,443,402
1955-56	20,512	1,738	453,173	239.73	108,639,187	30,328,425
1956-57	20,683	1,643	460,146	251.94	115,930,959	29,646,372
1957-58	20,698	1,468	460,385	270.09	124,347,106	31,531,572
1958-59	20,858	1,372	476,489	287.32	136,902,684	38,416,359
1959-60	21,530	1,322	485,559	298.31	151,508,111	42,547,117
1960-61	21,983	1,274	495,123	306.00	158,937,206	43,468,203
1961-62	22,466	1,232	503,671	315.56	168,509,664	45,408,599
1962-63	23,026	1,180	518,872	324.76	176,699,792	49,288,292
1963-64	23,687	1,160	532,781	331.66	182,744,540	50,792,242
1964-65	24,377	1,118	541,367	337.56	230,333,636	48,522,031
1965-66	25,380	1,049	545,611	422.16	258,956,700	65,540,880
1966-67	27,062	998	554,860	466.71	270,225,914	65,786,638
1967-68	27,979	940	559,350	483.11	289,997,448	65,648,086

Sources: Annual Report of the Oklahoma SDE, 1981-82, 89-90.

Note: Number of districts gleaned from the Superintendents' biennial/annual reports. ADA is the average daily attendance.

Education Leader and Department Administrator

Hodge entered the Superintendency at an opportune time: many disenchanted with Crable's performance were looking to a more harmonious relationship among the Superintendent, the Legislature, and the Governor; expanding state coffers provided more money for government services including education; WWII had ended two years earlier and the country was returning to civilian status; returning veterans could re-enter the teaching ranks; and the Legislature was exhibiting a willingness to tackle some of the persistent educational problems diverting attention from a unified focus to improve the schools. Significant educational issues confronted the state and the Legislature in the latter half of the 1940s: too many school districts, too much inefficiency, a shortage of teachers, low teacher compensation, textbook controversy, and too many college freshmen students woefully ill-prepared for college-level coursework. Leadership at the Department was sorely needed, and a strong, competent leader with political acumen could step in to guide the Department forward by navigating the legislative waters.

Flexibility to Practice Patronage

Hodge desired the latitude and prerogative to hire the people he wanted to work in the Department's administration. Names of several persons solicited for the work were run by the Board in late December 1946 so that by inauguration day they could be hired and prepared to assume their duties. Cooperative Board members granted Hodge his appointees with one exception. Resignations opened the positions including the Agent for Negro Education who was a Department employee since 1913.[22]

While he opined over the patronage issue and vouchsafed the positive virtues of such prerogative, he denied any interest in exercising similar authority over the distribution of funds to school districts. That responsibility, he said, should rest with the Board. Hodge demurred believing that no single person should be responsible for disbursing that much money. To add credence to his perspective, the previous Legislature generously appropriated $15.6 million (63 percent increase from the 1944-45 school year) for common school aid. His post-election declination to divide the money solely did not address how he thought the state aid should be divided among the hundreds of school districts. Six months earlier on the campaign trail, he said aid should not be divided on a per capita basis; rather, the aid should provide adequate financial assistance to the weaker school districts. Those districts lacked sufficient resources to provide a quality education and often were small, rural, isolated districts. Financial aid, he thought, should be directed toward those most in need, not to those with substantial resources of their own.[23]

Benefitting Hodge, Governor Turner, in May of 1947 appointed three members to the Board. A fourth member, appointed by Governor Kerr but with input from Turner, remained on the Board giving the latter control of the Board early in his term. Relative harmony among the members assisted Hodge at the outset of his tenure to remake the Department to fit his conception of how it should be organized. However, the Legislature still controlled to a great extent what positions there were.[24]

A Mostly Fortuitous Confluence in His First Term

Six months into this first term, the Oklahoma Supreme Court in an eight-to-one decision handed the state officials a victory when it upheld the re-districting or consolidation law (HB 85, O.S.L. 1947) enacted in the recent legislative session that eliminated all districts with fewer than thirteen students. Of the estimated 1,786 districts eliminated (see table 12.2), 1,105 enrolled no students. Another 438 districts were annexed by the county superintendents under the provisions of SB 5 of the 1943 Legislature. More were eliminated though not reported by the county superintendents. Obviously, this was a much-needed efficiency move, but consequently was significant mostly on paper. Eliminating districts was a positive move in several aspects, but all was not rosy for there was a teacher shortage, ameliorated only in minimal part through discontinuance of the small districts.[25]

Simultaneous to the consolidation focus, and in an effort to achieve a better education system, a complete reorganization was suggested by the Oklahoma Public Expenditures Council. It described the administrative structure of Oklahoma's schools antiquated and wasteful. "Reorganization of the school system into larger fiscal and administrative units should be affected before any statewide building program is launched."[26] The Council proffered citizens within each county should be involved in deciding how the schools were organized and administered. Hodge's experience at the county level and now at the state level gave him little confidence that such an approach would be successful. During his decade in Tulsa County, increasing efficiency through combining districts was not a critical issue nor was it politically advantageous for him to advocate further consolidation.[27]

Federal involvement in education, controversial even through contemporary times, expanded in 1946 when the National School Lunch Program was given permanence. Congress acted in June to provide funds and guidelines for program implementation in the nation's public schools. The federal government for three decades had been funding several vocational programs in the high schools so the lunch one was just another avenue for assisting the public schools. Facilitation of the lunch program necessitated the creation of the School Lunch Division within the Department. Not everyone was enthusiastic then nor ten years later about accepting federal funds lest the state lose control over what many thought was a state responsibility. Regardless, more federal money would flow in the coming years, but with similar resistance: "There had been considerable prejudice against the state's receiving money from the federal government."[28] Hodge was prepared to accept money from multiple sources to provide services to the students.

Oklahoma's sordid history of textbook corruption, begun during territorial days, with major scandals about every twenty years that cost the state's students millions of dollars (see previous chapter) was finally addressed early in Hodge's first term. A textbook committee was created with the Superintendent *ex officio* secretary, its duties defined, and the Board directed to provide space for the committee's functions. Appropriations for the 1948-49 and 1949-50 biennia were $500,000 and $1,833,148, respectively. Specific guidance allowed the Board and the Department to administer the textbook program more effectively. For example, the Board was to promulgate rules and regulations for the issuance and preservation of textbooks. It was to develop accounting procedures requiring all county and district superintendents to submit timely reports on forms designed by the Board with "an exact amount of the cost of books distributed to each school district, together with the proper proportion of transportation and accounting charges."[29]

Students with mental or physical disabilities in four districts—Tulsa, Ponca City, Shawnee, and Oklahoma City—began to receive state financial assistance for an education in 1945. Two years later the program was expanded by increasing the funds and number of districts participating, and by authorizing creation of the Division of Special Education in the Department under the direction of the assistant superintendent. Thus began Oklahoma's commitment to the common schools to educate students with disabilities, a commitment not matched by the federal government for another thirty years.[30]

Hodge was Superintendent in 1947 when the first educators began retiring under the provisions of the 1943 law creating the teacher retirement system. E*x officio* and one of nine trustees of the retirement board, he helped oversee a program that required an appropriation greater than three million dollars in the 1949-51 biennium. Teachers retiring in these early years generally received benefits greater than the amount they contributed to the pension system, a phenomenon not unlike the early years of the federal Social Security program, but not until 1955 were teachers permitted to participate in both the state and federal retirement plans.[31]

Concurrent with common school expansion was that of vocational education which by 1947-48 had forty-nine employees within four sections: agricultural education, distributive education, home economics education, and trade and industrial education. Legislation in 1941 created the State Board of Vocational Education to be one in the same as the Board with the Superintendent *ex officio* as the chair. Responsible for leading the division with its headquarters in Stillwater was the director, J. B. Perky. He guided the vocational programs and expanded the political connections that set the stage for its development into a separate department in the mid-60s, one that quickly gained a robust political support of its own. This separation, now six years in operation, narrowed the Superintendent's foci and allowed him to concentrate on the common schools' academic programs, but it fostered the growth and rapid expansion of a segment of education that would compete highly successfully for the taxpayers' dollars.[32]

The last major event during Hodge's first term was the Legislature's decision to rewrite and codify the school code to achieve clarity and coherence of the laws affecting the common education system. Concurrent with the code revision effort was one to update the school finance and consolidation laws. Any one of these thrusts would be a challenge in a single legislative session, but to suggest all three simultaneously would confuse and confound the process that began with a meeting in September 1948 in Okmulgee chaired by Representative E. T. Dunlap from Latimer County. Initial proposals included specifying the Board's duties, changing the selection of county superintendents from elective to appointee by a group of citizens, and including only students six to eighteen years old in the census rather than six to twenty-one, the current practice. A new code eventually was written, but not until after much wrangling and debate. Consolidation was effected by the state school financing scheme, 675 districts eliminated in the next five years, but that scheme allowed the Superintendent some authority over the distribution of money to school districts. This delegation of authority proved to be the most controversial with many thinking Hodge was angling for too much power.[33]

As a secondary teacher and then county level administrator of 1-8 grade schools, Hodge gained foundational experience to develop a firm grasp on the status and conditions of schools statewide as he neared the end of his first term. He was fully aware of the disparities in the quality of instruction and resources between the elementary and secondary schools, and his suggestions for improvement reflect those concerns. His second biennial report proffered the most recommendations of his tenure. First, at the elementary level: add kindergarten programs; employ elementary teachers, supervisory personnel, and principals as qualified as those at the secondary level; standardize first grade entrance age; carefully plan school day; align teaching methods with the students' needs; and assign equitable teaching loads. Recommendations for secondary schools were: offer curriculum evaluation to meet diverse needs of students; develop in-service programs for teachers; schedule pupil-teacher planning time; encourage cooperation among parents, teachers, and students; create richly-resourced libraries managed by well-qualified librarians; and determine why students drop out and then develop measures to reduce the dropout rate.[34] Many of his recommendations required additional funds and thus legislative support, but his suggestion to determine why students dropped out was one that he, the Board, and the Department could have addressed without legislative approval. After collecting data, the Department would have had a stronger rationale for developing preventive measures. To emphasize this point, five years later Hodge surveyed principals over their math curricula and began collecting desegregation data from district superintendents.

Hodge couched his suggestions in the overall climate of the schools and communities, believing that joint cooperation and planning among parents, communities, and schools was necessary to achieve maximum learning environments. For him, several basics for the schools were immutable: meet students' needs, have active community participation, be responsible for instilling democratic ideals and behavior, employ competent teachers, and hire professional and capable leaders.[35] Most beneficial for his ability to succeed during this first term were the cooperation of the Legislature and the infusion of federal funds. Together they primed the pump to improve educational opportunities for many children.

Obviously, state revenues were more plentiful at the end of the decade of the 1940s, for the Legislature that had not increased the Governor's and Superintendent's salaries for fourteen and ten years, respectively, gave hefty raises in 1951. The Governor's salary was raised from $6,500 to $15,000 and the Superintendent's from $4,800 to $12,000. A dire situation had developed in the latter 40s as the Department and the Board, to be competitive, paid administrators salaries higher than the Superintendent's. By the end of the decade eight were paid in excess of the Superintendent with the highest paid 50 percent more. Low pay for the Superintendent was nothing unique then and continued to be throughout history (see appendix I).[36]

Humor sometimes intrudes upon the seriousness and complexities of one's responsibilities, especially if an event can be used for political purposes. Six months before the general election in 1950 Hodge, while driving "a big 1950 model car," had been arrested near Guthrie by a highway patrol officer after which he stated: "I may have been exceeding the speed limit a little bit, but I am not guilty of reckless driving." No charge was filed, according to a Logan County official, "There may have been mitigating circumstances."[37] Traffic rule compliance seemed to be measured by varying standards depending upon the political status of the offender, not uncommon in Oklahoma.

End of a Four-Year Honeymoon

With relative quiet and no overt criminal allegations in his first term, and, thus, no competition in 1950 for the Superintendency, Hodge could continue to focus his attention on the operation of the Department. Politics, however, was never far from the scene, for example, when in 1951 Hodge and the Department were subjected by the Senate to a potential investigation of fraud, graft, and corruption. Before progressing far, it was blocked, but not before Hodge attacked the charges vociferously, defending the Department's reputation.[38]

Two years later the Board fired the Department's head examiner for six years, the above referenced Eddie Higgins, a friend of both Governor Johnston Murray and Speaker James Nance, and replaced him with a friend of the President Pro Tempore of the Senate, Raymond Gary. Higgins, on leave from his Department position to serve as Chief Clerk of the House during the legislative session, remarked that political machinations of the past year were now coming to fruition. Hodge did not vote at the meeting and refrained from commenting to a reporter other than to say there was no discussion at the meeting surrounding the vote. Competing affinities for gubernatorial candidates were playing out in the Board's decisions and Department personnel.[39]

The House committee investigating the Higgins affair in the 1954 election also looked into the involvement of two Department employees relative to bus and textbook sales. Ira Bugg, prior to his 1949 employment as the assistant director of rural and elementary education, was Pottawatomie County superintendent. In that role, he also represented the Denoyer-Gebbert Co. as a book salesman to the independent districts in that county. He did admit to receiving some checks from the company after starting employment at the Department, but claimed those were for sales prior to his departure from the county superintendency. Claiming that book sales while on the county payroll were not illegal, he did admit that it was unethical. Bugg continued employment in the Department until 1965, serving as supervisor of homebound teaching for the final ten years.[40]

Roy Emans, the budget examiner, assistant director of finance, and then director of finance for the Department for the previous eighteen years, testified to the House committee that he touted the Excel Coach Sales Company which built school buses in its Durant plant. He had written to the company president who then circulated widely the letter to school districts. Emans, exhibiting a little naivete and maybe some state pride, offered justification for sending the letter, "I thought that a home industry deserved some recognition." No harm, he directed the finance unit until 1963.[41]

An *Oklahoman* editorial framed the problems within the Department succinctly, and proceeded then to indict the Legislature and the entire political system. First, the investigating committee statement, that it's "of the firm opinion that state employees in their outside business enterprises should not be in the business with those who are doing business with the state and the department in which they are employed," could be a good policy for the state. "Some of the representatives and senators who refuse to investigate the county commissioners are listed as salesmen by the companies selling supplies to the counties."[42] Hodge was responsible for the ethos within the agency, but saw little need to restrict employees' behavior. Politics pervaded much of the decision making not only in the Department, but also at the county and district levels as well as all other government functions. The Department was but a microcosm of the state's governmental functions where ethical considerations seemed secondary to what was politically feasible.

Reacting to an Alleged Curriculum Failure

A curriculum quality controversy erupted in late 1955 when the OU president alleged that incoming freshmen were ill-prepared for the rigors of college causing the professors to teach at a level below which they were hired. Too many students needed remedial instruction to learn what they should already know. Hodge took umbrage with this allegation in a speech to Oklahoma teachers at their annual fall convention, "apparently an effort is being made to indict all of us engaged in public school work." Then, *The Oklahoman* seized the opportunity to criticize Hodge for an attempt to deny the reality rather than to search for solutions to the alleged problem. Reminiscent of the charge is a description of the comments of Territorial Governor T. B. Ferguson in a 1903 letter to D. T. Flynn, delegate to Congress from Oklahoma Territory: "The governor was also disturbed by the large number of high school students being taught in preparatory classes at the colleges. He demanded an end to this practice, emphasizing that it was not right to pay instructors professional salaries for teaching high school level courses."[43]

The final chapter of this event developed immediately when Hodge wrote to 745 high school principals to ask what was being taught and what the students were learning, particularly in math. *The Oklahoman* persisted in its commentary by wondering why he did not already know this, if the Department collected such data, and, if not, why. Incredulous, the paper stated the Department knew what every teacher was paid and all of the approved transfers, but yet totally lacked a system to track curricular content and student performance. Was it not the mission of the Department to collect data to provide a baseline for determination of the success of the schools?[44]

Failure to Adequately Fund the Pension System

When the Legislature in 1955 passed SB 72 allowing educators to participate in Social Security and the teacher retirement system, Governor Gary, believing the state could ill afford both systems, even though Social Security was partially federally funded, predicted that the retirement system would cause financial ruin; nevertheless, he signed the bill into law. Hodge recommended in 1956 the solvency of the teacher retirement system be accomplished through dedicated revenues: "an amount sufficient to guarantee legal commitments to retired teachers would go a long way to make for a better and more efficient system of public education in Oklahoma."[45] The solvency of the retirement system was not addressed adequately in 1955 and for most of the history since then, another example of the Legislature's refusal to consistently fulfill its commitment to the educators.

Integrating External Funds

Growth of programs in the Department in Hodge's third term, 1955-59, reflected greater external influence and sources of funds including increased federal assistance with the concomitant strictures and the expanding needs of a public education system perpetually underfunded and serving high percentages of economically disadvantaged children. Indian education was funded from the federal government since statehood, but, in 1956, the Department assumed supervision. Title V-A of the National Defense Education Act in 1958 funded guidance and counseling services in the schools. The Division of Television Instruction, created in 1956 and funded the first year by the Frontiers of Science Foundation of Oklahoma, expanded services to schools. These augmentations to the curriculum convinced Hodge in 1955 to combine the divisions of Elementary Education and Secondary Education into the Division of Instruction. Three years later Hodge requested $40,000 from the Legislature to assist the efforts of the Curriculum

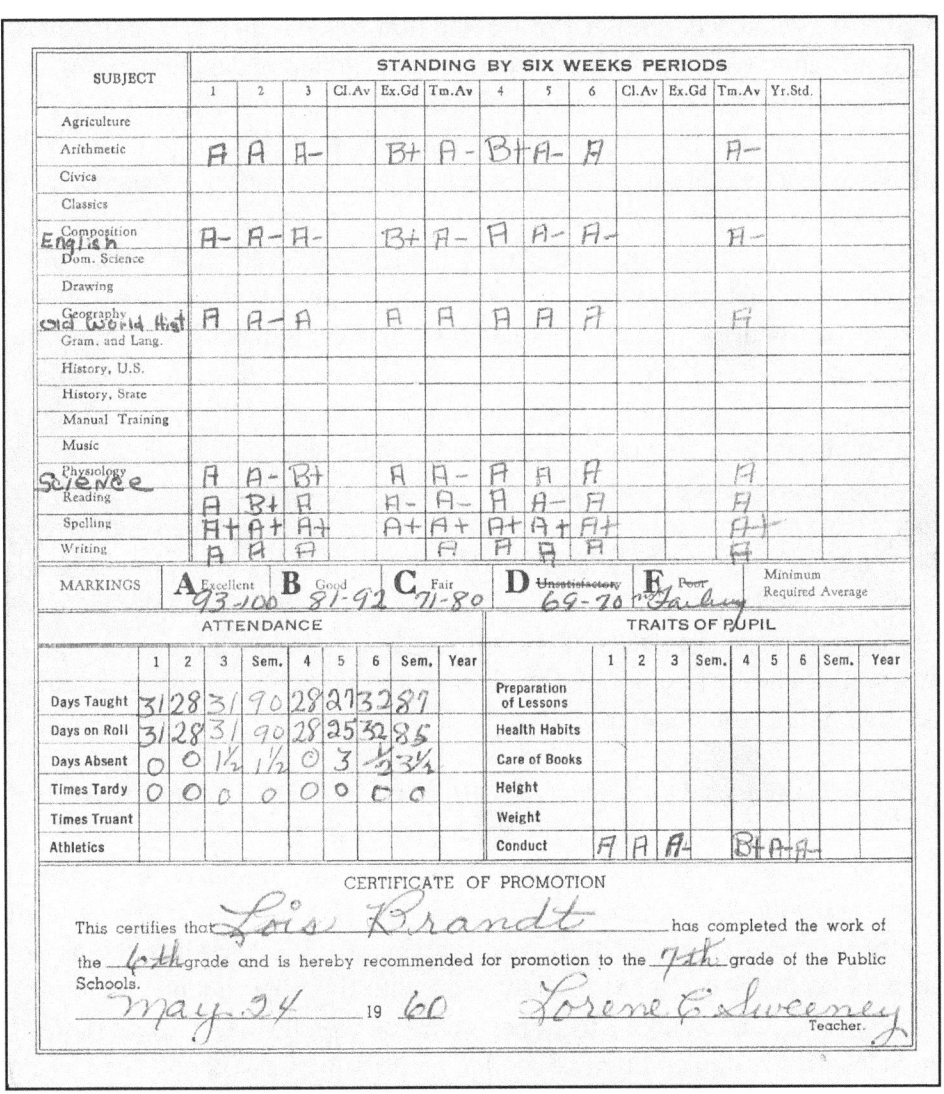

Figure 12.1 Sixth Grade Report Card, 1960, Thomas, Oklahoma

Commission to provide leadership in the schools. Support from an expanding OEA was appreciated, especially when it developed its legislative agenda, an indication of the continuing symbiotic relationship between the state's highest education leader and the largest association representing educators.[46]

Fighting to Protect State Funds from Being Supplanted by Federal Money

The greatest infusion of money accompanied the various federal laws of the 1960s designed to help the economically disadvantaged of the student populace (e.g., Elementary and Secondary Education Act of 1965, Head Start). Title VI of the Civil Rights Act of 1964 challenged those schools that were resisting desegregating by forbidding their receipt of any federal funds. Ten years after the first *Brown* decision, the federal government became impatient with the school boards and offered financial assistance pending full compliance with the court's standard. Hodge welcomed the federal funds even with strings attached, but what distressed him was the threat or actual instance of the state Legislature siphoning funds dedicated to schools for other purposes. Whether it was by sleight of hand or overt action, the Legislature was complicit in taking what legitimately belonged to the students. Hodge specifically addressed this in 1966 when he emphasized that federal funds were to supplement state funds, not to supplant them.[47]

The 1960s, for Hodge, was a time for pleading for adequate school funding as he observed that the Legislature was content with mediocre/average schools. Addressing a complaint evident throughout the state's history, he deemed it important that teacher salaries keep pace with the regional average, important enough that his recommendations to the Legislature in 1962, 1964, and 1966 included such urging. In these same years, he requested adequate funding for textbooks and increases in per pupil expenditure. Financial emphasis aside, the curriculum needed improving and, from his perspective, the Legislature needed to provide the capability for accomplishing this. Hodge's biennial reports lacked specificity in what curricular improvements should entail except that in 1958, 1960, and 1962 he wrote that the OEA's recommendations should be adopted. For the 1962 to 1968 reports the wording was the same. "We must continue to improve our curriculum to meet the needs of the boys and girls who will be living in a rapidly changing world. The curriculum of a generation or two ago is no longer adequate. We are working on this problem constantly."[48]

Milestones to the Creation of the Vocational-Technical Education Department

Evolving parallel to the Department's growth was the emphasis on the Division of Vocational Education. Governance of the division had been assigned to the State Board for Vocational Education for decades, a board with dual identity since its membership was the same as the State Board of Education with the Superintendent chairing both boards *ex officio*. Under Hodge's leadership the Vocational Board hired Francis Tuttle, superintendent of Muskogee Public Schools, in 1964 to be the coordinator of the area schools unit, and area schools began forming. In May 1966 voters approved State Question 434 (51 to 49 percent) permitting multiple school districts to form single vocational districts that were funded by a tax assessment on all of the participating districts. Rapid events and growth continued apace, and in 1967, Tuttle replaced long-tenured J. B. Perky as state director of Vocational and Technical Education. A year later the federal government repurposed vocational education giving Oklahoma an incentive to redesign the governing board and to create a separate and independent department with Tuttle as the director.[49] Hodge was an integral part of these developments until his death six months prior to the fruition of his efforts.

Knowing When to Avoid Playing—Athletics Sanctioning

Lest athletics be overlooked, it is informative to describe briefly the origin of the Oklahoma Secondary Schools Activities Association and Hodge's opining on it. The forerunner of the OSSAA, the Oklahoma High School Athletic Association, began in 1911 and served to coordinate athletics only. In late summer 1962 the Oklahoma Coaches Association and the North Central Association of Colleges and Secondary Schools were at odds over the number of permissible mid-week athletic events. Simultaneously, preliminary plans for the formation of an inclusive activities association solidified into the creation of such an association through a compromise with the NCACSS. The OSSAA would sanction all secondary school athletic and most extracurricular activities and remove the coaches association from having to regulate practices. Hodge, the former athlete and basketball coach, wholly supported the effort to form a self-governing organization to regulate school activities rather than have the Board assume responsibility.[50]

Teachers Demand Collective Bargaining

By the time of Hodge's death, national trending in the relationships among teachers, administrators, and school boards began to have residual effects on Oklahoma's education system. Historically, teachers and administrators belonged to the same professional organizations with subdivisions catering to the different levels of responsibility. Typically, administrators dominated the leadership of these organizations, but the teachers began to attempt to wrest control from the administrators by the mid-1960s into the early 1970s. First the superintendents and then the principals left to form their professional associations as teacher empowerment gained traction. Teachers across the country were pressuring their legislators to grant them collective bargaining rights similar to those held by employees in private industry. In this milieu Governor Bellmon appreciated Hodge for mediating the relationship between him and the teachers. Beyond that, the Governor considered Hodge a friend and professional who advocated for the students without political hindrances.[51]

Cultivating Positional Qualification and Respect

During Hodge's tenure the Department evolved from essentially a compliance-checking, regulatory and record keeping agency to a service-oriented one of supervising federal programs and providing many kinds of curriculum guidance and assistance. Instead of almost exclusively state efforts, it became a joint operation with the federal government, causing the Department employment numbers to double and then double again. Appreciation of the growing challenges of the Superintendency, and Hodge's administrative leadership, quickened the perspective of the legislators who believed a greater status would add esteem to the position and raise the standards for aspirants to the position. Desired efficacy of the state's schools, and the Department being led by someone who qualified for an administrator's certificate, focused their thinking. Since statehood, requirements for the several executive offices changed minimally (state residency from three to ten years and elimination of gender requirement). The Legislature was urged by the Board to add two prerequisites: a master's degree in school administration (admission and coursework specified by the college/university) and an administrator's certificate (requirements set by the Department and Board). Never before had this issue surfaced, and it was non-controversial when it passed in 1965. Only a mere sixteen years passed, however, before the state's attorney general, when asked through an inquiry by a non-educator who pondered seeking the office, ruled the additional standards unconstitutional.[52]

Hodge's lengthy tenure intersected that of six governors, four Democrats and two Republicans. He gained the respect singularly of Gary for his leadership of the Board in the desegregation efforts and of Bellmon for his mediation of the relationship between the teachers and the Governor. Although Republican governors won elections in 1962 and 1966, not only did Hodge win reelection, but he also drew no opposition. He was able to maneuver through the political minefields without earning the wrath of legislators and governors. He was the face of the education establishment and represented the interests of the students. Considerable effort of the last fourteen years of his tenure was leading the Board and the Department to improve the educational opportunities of African American students. Equal opportunity was demanded by the Supreme Court and the federal government with no minimal state effort permissible.

From "Separate But Equal" to "Integration 'With All Deliberate Speed'"

By far the greatest education issue confronting government officials at the executive, legislative, and judicial levels in the twentieth century was the US Supreme Court's landmark decision in *Brown v Board of Education of Topeka* (347 U.S. 483). This 1954 decision, overturning *Plessy v Ferguson* (163 U.S. 537) from fifty-eight years earlier and declaring that racial segregation violated the equal protection clause of the Fourteenth Amendment, roiled public education. To add specificity to its decision, the court a year later mandated that integration proceed "with all deliberate speed."[53]

Separate and Mostly Unequal

Plessy v Ferguson, a seven-to-one decision in 1896, set the stage for Oklahoma to enshrine racial segregation in its original constitution of 1907, the only state to do so, and then to somewhat auspiciously set the standard: "Separate schools for white and colored children with like accommodation shall be provided by the legislature and impartially maintained. The term 'colored children,' as used in this section, shall be construed to mean children of African descent. The term 'white children' shall include all other children." (article 13, section 3). This Constitutional inclusion became the basis for a statute in 1913 stipulating parameters and prohibitions for racial segregation of students. For example, section 6 prohibited a teacher at any level of education from teaching a mixed-race classroom (referring to Black and white students with no mention of Native American, Asian, or other minorities) and prescribed the penalty for any violation as a misdemeanor with a fine of $10-$50 per day. Children with any African blood were deemed Black and restricted to attending Black schools.[54] Schools were to be segregated, fairly easy to do given the criteria, but also impartially maintained, a standard that allowed for variance in its interpretation and resulted often times in deplorable conditions for Black students.

Racial segregation for the first fifty years of statehood proved to be complicated, complex, expensive, and time consuming. Separate dual systems were created, financed, administered, and staffed, but they were rarely equal. Oklahoma, with a fairly large geographic and predominantly rural area and a history of insufficient funding, could not afford dual systems, although it was legally required to have them. Elected county superintendents administered separate schools and often times lacked the resources to meet the letter of the law if not the intent. The state relied for many years on outside resources, money and personnel, to give instruction to the "separate schools" that existed in about 75 percent of the counties. Without the external assistance these schools would have experienced direr conditions for racial prejudices were not minimal.[55]

Multiple factors were causing consternation among Oklahoma officials and legislators. Denied admission to the OU law school six years earlier, in 1948, Ada Lois Sipuel Fisher successfully sued the University (332 U.S. 631), claiming that the state constitutional provision prohibited the mixing of the races in the classroom. Although admitted, she was segregated in the classroom and the dining area, indicating the court's decision was accepted reluctantly by the University officials. Education officials, the Governor, and legislators were under great pressure from segregationists to maintain the status quo and integrationists to respond to court mandates and restrictions. Over the years several Supreme Court decisions were necessary inducements to effect sufficient change in Oklahoma.

It was in this milieu that Hodge, eight years in office, Attorney General Mac Q. Williamson, almost twenty years in office, and governors Johnston Murray, briefly, and Raymond Gary, for a full term, were expected to forge a response to the Supreme Court's decisions. They, along with the Legislature, were required to move forward aggressively, but, at the same time, not totally disrupt the state's education system or cause violence. How they accomplished this in the near and long terms would have significant consequences.

Brown v Board of Education of Topeka (I and II)

Within a day or so of the 1954 decision *The Oklahoman* opined that the state would comply with the law, the legislators had an ineluctable duty to significantly overhaul the segregation laws, and the citizens would remain law abiding: "The law…is going to be obeyed in Oklahoma…It will be observed faithfully by those who occupy positions of authority. And it will be well for the state if the people as individuals show full respect for the court's decision."[56] Hodge's immediate reaction to the decision was to do nothing except to write the county and district superintendents advising them to continue their current operations because no one knew exactly what to do. Three months later the Oklahoma Cooperative Program in Educational Administration presented him a proposal to help school districts and the state move to a desegregation plan. Providing additional support to the Superintendent's approach was Attorney General Williamson who stated he would file a brief with the court explaining the difficulty the state would have in compliance because of its constitutional and 1913 statutory mandates.[57]

Newly elected in January 1955, Governor Gary was a strong and immediate supporter of the court's decision. His attitude toward segregation began in his youth and matured as a county superintendent when he observed the white school boards and white superintendents who administered the funds for the Black schools siphon those funds off for their own schools. Now, as Governor, he was poised to do something about that, so he pushed for the passage of the Better Schools Amendment, a proposal "diplomatically silent on its long-term effect, the financial emasculation of the state's segregated school system." This amendment to alter the way schools were financed and to comply with the Supreme Court's decision was approved decisively by the voters April 5, 1955, only three months past Gary's inauguration and almost two months before the court imposed the standard that desegregation proceed with all deliberate speed. What the Legislature and citizens did not do was remove the Constitution's language mandating separate schools.[58]

The Oklahoman, not acknowledging Governor Gary's intent, but predicting the Legislature's moves, editorialized: "Proposed in Oklahoma is legislation aimed frankly at gerrymandering public school attendance in such a way as to defeat the spirit of the court's ruling while preserving a façade of compliance." If, as Attorney General Williamson requested, no deadline for implementation be imposed, would not negligence or malingering occur? The Gary administration assumed a middle ground position by urging financial overhaul to push districts to desegregate and then wait for action, hoping to avoid violence.[59]

Hodge's biennial reports to the Governor from 1948 to 1954 were silent on any racial issues with the exception of 1948 when he wrote that the out-of-state tuition fund for Blacks should be increased because Oklahoma students did not wish to attend OU. Oklahoma had had an out-of-state tuition assistance fund since 1935 and the Legislature added to the fund several times, but the initial legislation also included aspects deterring students from availing themselves of the assistance. These restrictions were relaxed in 1941-42, yet several years later attendance at OU was still not appealing to them. Hodge requested additional appropriations to the fund so that more of the students' college related and travel expenses could be paid.[60]

Essentially, the 1954-55 school year was one of waiting and seeing, with much speculation regarding what the immediate future held. What would the Supreme Court mandate education administrators and government officials to do? The answer came in mid 1955 through *Brown v Board of Education* II with the admonition that governments would act with "all deliberate speed." This mantra set the standard but with wide-ranging opinions of the definition. Included in *The Oklahoman's* assessment of the current status and immediate challenges were: school districts must make their own decisions, the Board's policy must apply equally to every district, some districts are ready to integrate, but they do not want to be the first, and some districts are overcrowded currently and would be placed in a bind if forced to integrate immediately. Hodge unequivocally believed and stated that desegregation was to be achieved by the local districts with minimal involvement of the Board and the Department.[61]

Monitoring the Desegregation Process: the First Five Years

Under Hodge's leadership as chair of the Board, the Board adopted its desegregation policies at the June 1955 meeting: parents, regardless of color could choose the school for their children to attend; Black schools previously receiving aid when having too few students would no longer be permitted to do so; and districts could apply for continuation of separate schools as long as they stated reasons and be acting in good faith. Parental option eliminated the county superintendent's prerogative to transfer any student to any district in the county.[62]

The Board continued its mostly permissive stance at the next month's meeting. At issue was whether districts not integrating would be required to submit their plans for achieving desegregation as a condition for receiving state aid: "any plan submitted by local boards—or none at all—would be acceptable." With that less than ringing endorsement, boards could proceed. "The board of education must solve its own problems on de-segregation…must be proceeding, in good faith, towards an objective of disregard of color or race in offering, sponsoring or financing educational opportunities."[63]

Specific circumstances were anticipated and predicted by Hodge when he stated that the Black high schools in Oklahoma City, Tulsa, and Muskogee would no doubt be continued as segregated schools. He also believed that many Black elementary schools would continue to be segregated in communities where the Black high schools would be closed. Hodge advised everyone to continue the status quo until further guidance was forthcoming, and that was the case early in the fall of 1955. Integration began in Oklahoma under the court's standard of speed of progress when the Department designed a brief questionnaire of five items and sent it to all district and county superintendents requesting the latter to report only on the non-high schools. What was not done then or any time later was to set a deadline for total good faith compliance with the court's admonishment of "all deliberate speed."[64]

Prior to the mid-January 1956 Board meeting, Hodge and Department administrators formulated a proposal for how the Board should clarify its policy of the previous June for allocating funds to mix-raced districts through alteration of the formula for distribution of state aid. Disagreement arose among the Board members about the necessity of adding to the earlier policy, and a vote to continue the present policy was turned down five to two. A second motion, offered to modify the previous policy by adding specificity to financial aid for teachers and transportation, passed five to two with all members voting consistently with the previous vote. Though not required or expected to participate unless the vote was tied, Hodge wanted to be on record siding with the majority on both of these decisions. Unanimity among the Board members was unachievable, emblematic of the environment of the early desegregation efforts.[65]

Following Board adoption of the Department's plan for implementing disincentives to school districts continuing segregation, Hodge notified all districts. A purposeful intent of the decision was that, rather than ceding all authority to local districts, the Board, under Department direction, would retain some influence, specifically financial. It was anticipated that more than one million dollars per year would be saved through reduced appropriations to teacher and transportation aid to districts planning non-compliance. As time would tell, some districts' recalcitrance to comply resulted in reduced funds. Aid reduction as the sole disincentive would not suffice to change some peoples' attitudes about how their schools should be modified. Operating with less money was preferable to desegregating their schools, a stance adopted by a large number of school districts in the state's southeastern corner.[66]

March 22, 1956, Hodge wrote to superintendents of all districts where Black high schools were operating asking them of their plans for integration for the next school year. Ten failed to respond and were sent a follow up request April 10. Thirty-two superintendents reported some kind of integration plan while an equal number reported no such plan. Almost without exception, responding districts with integration schemes indicated they planned to integrate the white high school by closing the Black high school or by ending the payment of transportation of Black students to the Black high school.

Table 12.3 Integration progress in Oklahoma 1956-1960

Category	Year				
	1956*	1957	1958	1959	1960
Districts with Black students eligible for school	312	359	353	342	334
Integrated schools (Black and white students)					
Number of high schools	178	181	190	182	187
Enrollment	n/d	2,508	3,321	3,578	3,441
Number of junior high schools	90	89	100	100	102
Enrollment	n/a	1,087	1,703	1,798	1,505
Elementary schools	172	161	168	183	196
Enrollment	n/d	3,038	3,327	4,870	4,860
Schools closed since beginning of integration	112	138	163	179	186
High schools	n/d	56	61	63	67
Junior high schools	n/d	4	8	15	16
Elementary schools	n/d	78	94	101	103
Black teachers lost positions since integration	304	298	344	360	379
Schools with Black attendance only					
High schools†	44	39	35	33	29
Junior high schools	15	14	7	13	15
Elementary schools	192	130	135	131	124

* Enrollment and level of school data were not collected in 1956.

† Before the Supreme Court decision of 1954 there were 96 Black high schools. Hodge to Paul H. Douglas, 12 May 1959, Superintendent's Collection, 18-3-3, Box 2, FF 2-31, OSA, ODL, OKC.

Many districts with multiple elementary schools continued operating separate white and Black schools, complying with the desegregation demand that districts be integrated.[67]

Hodge surveyed district and county superintendents again in the fall of 1956 to assess integration efforts and compliance. This more comprehensive survey became a baseline for data collected and analyzed for the next four years. While the data in table 12.3 do not necessarily provide consistency, they do show several trends over the five years. Three important ones are: the increase (by approximately 37 percent) in the number of students enrolled in integrated high schools, the cumulative number of Black teachers losing their positions (379), and the decrease in the number of high schools and elementary schools, 34 and 35 percent, respectively, with Black students only.[68]

Hodge's assessment of the progress is apparent in correspondence with John Rogers in December 1958: "I think we have made remarkable progress, with a minimum of conflicts. We have Negro children eligible to attend school in sixty-two of our seventy-seven counties. Some integration has actually taken place in sixty of the sixty-two counties."[69] Surveyed were the seventy-seven county superintendents, who had authority over the dependent schools only, and the district superintendents in Oklahoma City, Tulsa, and Muskogee; yet, every county had at least one high school and a district superintendent. All independent districts and superintendents were excluded from the survey. Also, threatening the validity of the survey was the Department's discontinuance two years earlier of collecting data by race because, with constitutional and statutory changes, it determined it was no longer expedient to track students by this demographic. Hodge commented regarding the integration effort, "I have also felt that the least we could say about this program the better off we would be."[70] To discontinue collecting important student racial data because it was expedient seems almost incredulous and suggests that the Department wished not to have the data so that it did not then need to deal with it. By continuing to amass the numbers the Department could have monitored local districts to determine accuracy of compliance with the law and court decisions.

Five months later Hodge received a request from Illinois Senator Paul Douglas for a written summary of Oklahoma's integration progress in lieu of Hodge's testifying before judiciary committees of the US House and Senate. Hodge wrote: three high schools were in all-Black communities in the three largest cities and eight in rural areas; out of 1,600 Black teachers before the Supreme Court's decision, 344 lost their jobs; and another estimated twelve to fifteen were teaching in all white classrooms. Hodge next corresponded with Oklahoma's Senator Robert Kerr April 1, 1960, and again he offered data, but was more expansive in his positive report. He chose first to describe the situation in the Oklahoma City School District, that it had one high school, one junior high school, and several elementary schools in that part of the city where only Blacks reside and that the district sufficiently met legal and educational purposes. Continuing, he wrote that there were eight communities where the town, school board, teachers, and students were all Black. In summation of integration, he wrote: "We have treated it as a strictly local problem and we let the local boards of education decide when their people are ready to move into this program." In explaining his statistics, he failed to explicate the twenty remaining districts' refusals to integrate their high schools. Generally, all of the state's "remarkable progress" was achieved "without any unpleasantness at all."[71]

Oklahoma's minimalistic approach to compliance with the Supreme Court's decision was not surprising given its constitutional underpinning in 1907. "Because the State Board of Education had stopped short of denying all state aid to segregated local districts, a large number of school systems, particularly in the southeastern corner of the state, continued to maintain separate facilities. Moreover, even those districts that had abolished de jure segregation usually, continued to assign children to schools on a geographic basis."[72] What the court did not address sufficiently were districts with multiple elementary schools at all levels, usually city school districts but sometimes smaller cities with only one high school and several elementary schools. These districts were less affected by the judicial mandate than the smaller rural areas.

Neither the Board nor Hodge offered sympathy for the Black teachers who suffered job losses because of integration. White teachers could retain their jobs regardless of competence while Black teachers often lost theirs just because they were not white. The Department knew about these teachers because its personnel section kept all of the records on teacher certification. Most likely, the same was true with Black principals. Fewer positions were open to them than to teachers. What happened was that Black schools were closed, the students were transferred to the predominantly white schools, and the principals and teachers lost their jobs. In the five-year period of the Superintendent's surveys (Septembers of 1956-1960), the state added 1,300 teachers, but 379 Black teachers lost their jobs. In the same period, the number of districts decreased by 369 (table 12.2). No leadership or support was forthcoming from the Department to assist these educators. Nowhere in his annual reports did Hodge include anything about the Department's efforts to address these conditions. Desegregation focused on students, not the welfare of Black teachers and administrators, and the Board did not show much interest in going beyond its basic mandate. For Hodge and the Board desegregation compliance was a local district issue that did not need Departmental assistance or interference. Hiring and terminating teachers was beyond the purview of the Department; furthermore, it would not have been prudent for the agency to meddle in local affairs, especially when the issue was purely racial.

There is no indication that the Department marshaled any resources to provide districts with funds to prepare the white teachers for the infusion of Black students. Since integration was the domain of the district, it was at that level that the adjustments, if any, were made. Whatever resentment or dissatisfaction arose, the responsibility for addressing it was local. Whatever overt and covert opposition developed, the district was the locus of control. Hodge's biennial reports presented a Superintendent, Board, and agency hewing to a consistent approach: little of substance was mentioned regarding desegregation. For example, in 1956: "During the past biennium the separate school program in Oklahoma has been abandoned because of the Supreme Court decision abolishing legal segregation. Integration of the races in our schools is not complete but it is proceeding in a satisfactory manner and without unpleasant community incidents."[73] Hodge's recommendations for legislative changes omit any addressing desegregation. Two years later the report vaguely refers to "periods of considerable confusion and opposition to recognized objectives and educational processes."[74] Again, no recommendations relating to integration, and the pattern continued in 1960.[75]

Maintaining the Progress: the Second Five Years

Annual surveys discontinued after 1960, suggesting that it was no longer imperative that critical information be collected to provide guidance to an interpretation of the success or lack thereof of the state's integration efforts. Given the significance of the desegregation movement impelled by the Supreme Court's two decisions, and the weight attached to the Superintendent's biennial reports, Hodge's omissions of either statistical examples of progress made or recommendations for improvements are surprising. In those reports, the recommendations were directed toward legislative changes, but Hodge could have included a separate section devoted to a description of the extent of desegregation efforts and progress. While he was required to report on specific topics, provide statistical data, and proffer recommendations, he was not restricted to those basic components.

A window through which to ascertain Hodge's thinking after five years of desegregation is a letter to a Georgia state senator in which he wrote that no state laws were changed relative to segregation. That was a true, but incomplete, statement, for the citizens voted for the Better Schools Amendment in 1955 and the Legislature re-wrote the laws financing the public schools, in essence ending the dual system of Black schools and white schools. It was accurate in that the constitutional and statutory provisions mandating separate schools had not been removed. Regarding that, he said that we "consider that all of our laws pertaining thereto are unconstitutional." Hodge also wrote that, from the beginning, the state determined that desegregation was a local issue: "When the local communities are ready, we have found that they move into this program."[76]

One consequence of the desegregation movement, the elimination of the dual system and its need for an accurate accounting of the Black and white students for school financing purposes, was the decision of the Department to cease collecting such data. By the early 1960's the Department had no subgroup data on the number of Black students as it had for Native American students, a federal requirement. No data resulted in an incomplete picture of the extent to which districts were integrating, an omission matched only by Missouri and West Virginia. Ironically, in Oklahoma the health department compiled racial data in school districts, but the two state agencies did not share their records.[77]

A Decade Later and Beyond: Progressed Stalled

Ten years after *Brown v Board of Education* II, Hodge reported that fifty-seven of the state's 1,100 school districts still had not "submitted statements of compliance or plans for compliance with Federal [sic] school integration requirements."[78] It seems that "all deliberate speed" in Oklahoma was interpreted by some districts to be a snail's pace. If compliance was not accomplished in a decade, what confidence was there that it would ever occur? Lack of compliance after a decade allowed to reach the goal was evidence of the insufficiency of the permissive approach of the government officials. Hodge would have had more compelling data had he continued the survey after the initial five years. Another issue was the districts' ability to continue to operate if they received less money from the state. Possibly they had sufficient local taxes to operate their schools or they squeezed every penny they could and operated on the edge of financial bankruptcy. Regardless, the state's laissez-faire approach to integration, moderately success in the early period, was no longer working and needed a more aggressive stance by the executive and legislative branches. The ultimate pressure to achieve compliance could have been applied through the federal court system, but there was little desire to pursue that avenue.

An Oklahoma Human Rights Commission was complimentary of the early efforts of Governor Gary and his administration in the middle 1950s, but chagrined and disheartened by the slow progress by the mid to late 1960s:

> The State of Oklahoma at the end of 1968 is in the midst of an education crisis that has not yet fully surfaced or abrasively manifested itself. Unless measures are soon taken to resolve the situation, irreparable harm can be done to the state's image; her schools; domestic tranquility; and most important of all, many, many school children…A large part of the opposition by white school patrons to integration centers around the contention that the entry of Negroes into previously all-white schools lowers the general academic tone and penalizes white students. This contention can well be interpreted as a tacit admission for the first time, that in many areas Negro children have previously been condemned to an inferior education.[79]

Hodge was pleased, for the most part, with the state's and school districts' efforts to achieve compliance with the court's decisions directing them to desegregate in good faith and with all deliberate speed. Most of the districts had reached a minimal level, and many of the remaining ones were submitting plans or committing to do so, even if only reluctantly. The two inner city districts deemed they met the court's mandate and explained that whatever segregation existed was because of housing patterns, something beyond their ability to modify. Under the leadership of the Board and the Superintendent, the Department directed most of its resources to the smaller and rural districts. Desegregation of the inner-city school districts was yet to come, an evolution that further exacerbated the problem of mixing the races.

A Career's Legacy

Hodge, who was the only Superintendent to have no children and to die in office and thus be granted no post-Superintendency time to appreciate his legacy, left one that deserves some emphases. He was a formidable politician who was reelected five times and only ever once faced an opponent. Patronage, as he pursued it, was acceptable at that time in history, and thus he avoided any opprobrium. For example, he used the resources available to him to strengthen and ensure his position, all the while couching his activities as providing political information to him and to the educators across the state. The longer he was in office, the more the Department became fixed in the minds of people as the creation of Oliver Hodge. Within six years of his death a building was constructed to house the many offices and personnel of the Department and in honor of his service it was named after Hodge and dedicated through the unveiling of a bronze bust. Hodge's wife Faye honored him by establishing the Oliver Hodge Memorial Scholarship Fund as yet another part of the effort to remember his contribution to education in Oklahoma. His influence was widely felt and not shortly forgotten.[80]

Not long into his tenure he had earned significant stature with the Governor and the legislators that he could be influential in the legislative process. Term limits applied only to governors; consequently, he was able to acquire a lengthy institutional history that he could use strategically when imploring the legislators to improve the education system. It was fortuitous for Hodge that the Legislature at the onset of his tenure passed a comprehensive statewide school district consolidation law and soon thereafter a revised school code with significant additional money. By the mid-1950s the Better Schools Amendment altered the state's school finance scheme, but inadequate and inconsistent funding plagued the common schools. Two profound and permanent external forces during his tenure affected the state and the Department, and he played a key role in the way those pressures evolved. His particularly close relationship with Governor Gary served the state well through the precarious first few days and years after the *Brown v Topeka Board of Education* decisions. It was also during the 1950s that the federal government expanded its influence through an infusion of funds but with strings attached. The state's desperation for a steady source of money was sufficient to overcome resistance to federal intrusions in the state's affairs. Hodge played a key role in communicating how the Department and the Board could accept and use the funds to the betterment of the education system without compromising state and local control.

It would be fair to assess Hodge's leadership of the Department's response to the *Brown* decisions, and it is obvious that the citizens were satisfied with his performance. With his position being elective he was not going to initiate bold steps that might anger the voters nor was he going to create problems for the Governor. Hodge could have provided greater leadership to improve the educational opportunities of the African American students and the employment of African American teachers and administrators through directing the Department to collect and analyze in-depth data to describe the status of curricular offerings for white and Black students. Most likely he would have engendered the opposition of the Board members and stirred enmity within the schools and the general population. This is but one example of how the dynamics of an elective office without term limits mitigate bold leadership initiatives. On the other hand, continuity in office can encourage consistency in positive directions if the incumbent is able to overcome the inertia that is endemic.

During his tenure the US government initiated steps to provide financial assistance to schools, not a popular idea for many people fearful of the encroachment of federal regulation. Aid for vocational education, in effect for decades and continued during his tenure, the school lunch program, and the Elementary and Secondary Education Act of 1965 are examples. The Civil Rights Act of 1964 was viewed as another external effort to constrict the prerogatives of state officials. And, of course, insufficient funding was a perennial issue with concomitant challenges of too few qualified teachers, partially caused by inadequate compensation, and the inability to plan budgets over extended periods of time.

Accolades were frequent both during his life and for years afterward. Over 1,000 attended a celebration fest for him about ten years into his tenure. Even the Governor attended and offered his enthusiastic support.[81] Within a month of this event the Board commended Hodge, "It is gratifying to have a noble leader like you to guide us in the solution of our many problems in this complex age. Your life has been uplifting and inspiring at all times. No problem that affects the education of the children of Oklahoma has been too small to receive your attention."[82] Frosty Troy, a frequent critic of politicians and their antics, as a young reporter for the *Tulsa Tribune* in the early 1960s, was chided by Hodge for never attending Board meetings. Eventually Troy did, and then he started traveling the state to visit schools, becoming an outspoken advocate for public education and critic of the appalling conditions in which many students were expected to learn.[83] Troy learned what Hodge experienced early on. Both relished the opportunities to traverse the state to communicate their passion for education and to represent the needs to the decision makers and the masses.

The staunchly Republican *Oklahoman*, eulogized him: "Holding a political job, Dr. Hodge was less politician on the surface than almost any other elected official during his career…Under his leadership school financing was done with closer accountability… There was improvement in the selection of state teacher college presidents over the former patronage system."[84] The paper emphasized the political nature of the position at the pinnacle of the state's education system. The longer Hodge was in his position, the less he needed to worry about his job security, a status that allowed for expansive educational leadership and reduced political contrivances. It gave him political capital if he had wanted to offer bold initiatives.

Chapter 13
Creech and Tuxhorn: Stepping In to Fill the Vacancy
(1968-1971)

Hodge's untimely death, after two years of suffering heart ailments, handed Governor Dewey Bartlett a conundrum. For more than two decades voters had placed their trust in a Democrat, even continuing him in office twice when a Republican governor was elected. But Bartlett was not about to name a Democrat who would then have three years to establish his reputation to use in his platform for an elected four-year term. The Governor was complimentary of Hodge's effectiveness and success—describing him as a friend, someone willing to tackle tough problems, and leader in education—but political considerations trumped any thought of naming a Democrat. Republicans held so few state executive level positions in Oklahoma history that a vacancy was certainly not going to a Democrat. Rep. Pauline Tabor, a Durant Democrat, preemptively attempted to stymie Bartlett's prerogative to appoint a replacement by suggesting an amendment to the law that would require the Governor to call a special election to fill a vacancy created by retirement, resignation, or death. Emotions were running high because of several controversial issues confronting the Superintendent, the Board, and the Legislature: a consolidation plan to eliminate 300 small schools, 27,000 teachers threatening to strike for higher pay, and Bartlett's effort to create a new governing board for vocational education. Bartlett appointed the Agency's deputy superintendent, sixty-one year old Edgar Haskell (E. H.) McDonald, as Interim until he could name a willing and acceptable replacement. The Governor had a person in mind and hoped to name him, Pryor's superintendent D. D. Creech, but the latter refused to accept the job unless the salary was increased. Bartlett decided that he would try to convince the Legislature to raise the salary, a constitutional move dubious at best. One important and advantageous factor for the Governor was the smooth functioning of a stable Board membership over the past few years that would remain so until the end of his term.[1]

The Interim: January 14–April 14, 1968

E. H. McDonald had held administrative positions in multiple small school districts in southwestern Oklahoma and had served in the army before being hired in the Department May 1, 1947, to be the teacher certification director. Advancement to top-level administrative positions over the next two decades qualified him to be the logical choice for this temporary position, but his political affiliation mitigated any appointment to complete Hodge's term. Dutifully, he guided the Department for three months through the period of mourning of the popular Superintendent and the preparation for his replacement. McDonald then returned to his previous duties until his retirement in 1976, ending a twenty-nine-year employment in the Department where he served four Superintendents. He was able to enjoy his retirement until August 1984 when he succumbed to injuries suffered in an automobile accident one month earlier.[2]

The Reluctant Transient: April 15, 1968-December 31, 1969

Eligibility criteria for Bartlett was that the designee should be someone with district superintendent experience, a Republican holding a doctorate, and willing to work for the relative low pay approved by the Legislature. Hodge had held an earned doctorate and had been highly respected as an educator, convincing the Governor that his Republican replacement should be equally qualified and would be competitive in the 1970 election. McDonald's resumé satisfied the first of these, and he was respected in his narrow sphere of influence and would probably have served for the salary of $300 less than his current one. Leading contenders were Danten Dayle (D. D.) Creech and Scott Tuxhorn. While Creech's acceptance was contingent upon the Legislature approving a higher salary, pay was not a stumbling block for Tuxhorn who commanded a salary of only $9,000 (set to be raised to $11,000) for the 1968-69 school year as the Jet-Nash School District superintendent. Creech was Bartlett's preferred choice, but the Governor knew he had to sweeten the salary to entice him. Even success at that effort eventually would prove insufficient to keep Creech until the expiration of the term in January 1971. The Pryor superintendent had his eyes focused on a college presidency and used the twenty-one months in Oklahoma City as a springboard to his ultimate goal. Creech's political instincts were keen enough to surmise that no Republican in 1970 would win the Governorship or the Superintendency.[3]

From his childhood days, Creech was immersed in the ethos of public education resulting from both parents whose careers were in teaching and administration. He earned bachelor's and master's degrees at Southwestern Oklahoma State University and OSU respectively and capped his career preparation by earning a doctorate at OU in 1965. Creech gained teaching and administrative experience in rural school districts in northwestern Oklahoma (teacher at Royal and Mutual, principal at Sharon High School and superintendent at Fargo, Arnett, and Velma-Alma school districts) before he moved 250 miles east to Pryor School District, an attractive and highly prized superintendency because of a tax base enlarged by the development of an industrial park. The Governor was able to convince the reluctant Creech to leave Pryor only after persuading the Legislature to expeditiously increase the salary to a level attractive to him, from $16,500 to $19,000 or about $2,000 more than he was to be paid the next year at Pryor. He transitioned to Oklahoma City at the persistent request of the Governor, but then stayed only a short time. His "assets" to be considered for the statewide position included experience as a teacher and administrator, high esteem by educators and school board members alike, and, not least, registered as a Republican.[4]

D. D. Creech

2012.201.B0148.0147, The Oklahoman, Oklahoma Publishing Company Photography Collection, Oklahoma Historical Society

Patience on Creech's part and a successful election in 1970 would have resulted in a salary of $25,000 beginning in January 1971 (see appendix I). April 15 Creech was beginning a job with little preparation or experience for the duties. Previously he had attended only one meeting of the Board, but now he was the chair of the Board. To his advantage, most of the Department's supervision and oversight was focused on small and rural schools. But, as with several of his predecessors, he had no experience with the Legislature, not a primary focus of his assignment, or with the Commissioners of the Land Office, the state textbook process, and the teacher education institutions.[5]

The Board, under McDonald's direction, met four times in the first three months of 1968, twice in regular session and twice in special meeting, with all six members present, all appointed by Republican governors. Creech attended the late March special meeting to observe the process and to understand the topics under discussion and potential action. Not surprisingly and not for the first time, school consolidation was the focus. Hodge and an earlier Board attempted to accomplish desegregation through a financing scheme that eliminated some districts. Now, the Board voted to tackle the problem straightforward through a unanimous resolution to support SB 462, designed to replace the seventy-seven county superintendents with not more than fifteen coordinators to be named by the Board. This action would result in consolidation and purportedly more efficient governance, but conversely, it would shift considerable power to the State. No such consolidation ensued.[6]

In twenty-one months in office, Creech presided at all twenty-three regular and special sessions of the Board. Many mundane topics were discussed and actions taken to move the educational process forward. Exceptional, however, was a move to reconfigure the Department to achieve more efficiency, an attempt not surprising now that Republicans held key positions for the first time since statehood. Creech's analysis produced recommendations consistent with those of Bartlett's management study conducted two years previously: combining the duties of the field men in the auditing division, creating a research division, and enlarging the data processing division. Without a thrust of research and a database, Department administrators were unable to accomplish informed decisions.[7]

Board approval of Creech's plan in late July 1969 allowed the Superintendent to align the Department with the evolving needs anticipating it to be fully operational by the beginning of the 1970-71 school year. Fundamentally, the plan did not alter the overall organization, for the four major departments (administration, finance, state and federal programs, and instruction) and the number of top management positions remained the same; only relatively minor adjustments resulted in some shifting of divisions within the departments. Enlarging capacity for research and data processing became feasible through the efficiency of combining auditing duties.[8]

Three critical curriculum controversies captured Creech's attention. First was the need for pre-school education to be offered, not an inexpensive proposition and not acceptable to everyone. Years later such a suggestion would be criticized as government intrusion in parental child rearing. While superintendent at Pryor, Creech was convinced of the efficacy of an early childhood program, and the district had funds to offer kindergarten classes at no expense to the parents. Now he was in a position where he could lead an effort to implement this thrust statewide. Second, the House passed a bill prohibiting sex education in the schools as a result of pressure from some constituents who had identified themselves as members of Sanity on Sex. Creech was summoned to the Governor's press conference to offer his opinion on the bill and, with the Board's support, criticized any attempt by the Legislature to mandate how local boards and citizens approached this subject. They believed components of the science and home economics curricula were sufficient to educate the students in this critical area. Third, and most controversial by far, was the implementation of minimum enrollment standards for both elementary and high schools. For the latter, those numbers were fifty-five, sixty-five, and seventy-five for the current and the next two years, respectively. The decision to set these requirements had occurred the previous summer, long enough time for legal action to be threatened.[9]

Creech argued, from experience and intuition, that extremely small schools could not offer the course diversity and sequence requisite for a basic and enriched curriculum. Student performance on the ACT was reflective of the school enrollment with the average scores in small high schools lower than in large high schools. The opposite was true in student average GPA: the smaller the school, the higher the GPA. Achieving consolidation by various methods seemed feasible and desirable. First during the late 1960s was the Board's plan to set minimum enrollments. Strong opposition forced the Board to compromise its criteria. Next, cooperation between the Governor and the Board produced a large financial assistance plan, but only for school districts with high schools.

All 226 dependent districts would be eliminated, but the schools would not necessarily be forced to close for they could be merged administratively with adjacent independent districts. Closure of some of the schools would allow the students to augment the small enrollments of nearby elementary schools in independent districts. Not then, nor for the next forty-five years, were these districts forced to close because the rural interests in the Legislature coalesced in opposition and outweighed political party affiliations.[10]

Creech did not have to contend with desegregation as did his predecessor. Not all school districts met the federal courts' standards with a few rural districts dilatory in implementing their plans. Desegregation thinking was evolving and, while districts met the letter of the law, some were still deficient in meeting the spirit of the law. No coordinated complaints against the Board for total inattention to the issue arose and the Board was not focused on raising the topic. Although facilities were deplorable in some rural districts where Blacks were dominant, that problem was a local and county issue rather than a Board concern. The two large urban districts, Oklahoma City and Tulsa, were still free to operate some segregated schools, but the era of busing was just over the horizon.[11]

Educators' perspectives about the dearth of funding for the public schools persisted throughout the state's history, but for the concern to be escalated by the first Republican Superintendent during the term of a Republican governor was unique. Creech was vocal in stating the Department's need for greater funds and a different funding scheme, calling the program for financing public school education "absolutely obsolete." Heretical to his party and the Governor, he informed the legislators and Bartlett that $44,000,000 were needed to reach the regional per pupil and teacher salary averages: "It is discouraging to hear comments by Governor Bartlett that there is no crisis in Oklahoma's public schools." In a farewell at his final Board meeting, he solicited the members' support for increased funding.[12]

The Legislature separated the Division of Vocational Education from the Department to form the State Department of Vocational and Technical Education, effective July 1, 1968, and created the Board of Vocational and Technical Education with the Superintendent *ex-officio* chair to govern that agency. That first Vo-Tech Board hired Francis Tuttle to lead the vocational system, a wise choice of the one who crafted the nationally regarded education program.[13] Creech had attended only a few meetings of the Board before the split, but he was at the helm of the Vo-Tech Board when it made the critical decision to hire Tuttle, who would oversee the development of the finest career technical system in the United States. Because Creech's knowledge of the vocational-technical programs was limited, the creation of the separate department and the choice of Tuttle to lead it narrowed his realm of responsibility for this component of the overall curriculum. At the governance level, the division between common schools and vo-tech benefitted both entities, yet the statutory advantage given the latter through State Question 434 providing a generous funding scheme became the envy of the common schools as the two education divisions competed for scarce local and state tax dollars.

Bartlett hoped Creech's performance and reputation would get him elected to the position in the fall of 1970. However, after only a few months in office, Creech pursued the Cameron University presidency, unsuccessfully, but it was obvious that he aspired to be a college president and continued to focus on that effort. Creech resigned in fall 1969 to move to Miami, Oklahoma, to become president of Northeastern Oklahoma A&M College, a position that compensated financially more than either the Pryor schools or the Superintendency. His transition from the Superintendency to the NEO presidency was not entirely smooth, caused partially by the Governor's attempts to persuade him to remain as head of the education system. The Board of Regents for OSU and A&M Colleges (NEO's governance board) met in November intending to hire Creech for the NEO position, but he mysteriously failed to attend. Later he admitted Bartlett had tried to discourage his resignation, but all he would say was "I can't talk about it anymore."[14] After all, Bartlett expended some political capital to get the Legislature to raise the salary, and the Governor knew finding a suitable replacement (the fourth person to fill the position in three years) to serve for just one year while competitively campaigning for the office would be a challenge.

Twelve and one-half years later, and at age 65, Creech retired, ending a 40-year career in education, interrupted only by a four-year stint in the US Army during WWII. Creech was rural and small town to the core, and lived his entire life in that environment with the exception of the hiatus in the Superintendency. He was born August 1, 1917, married to Dorothy Buss, June 5, 1947, and they had three children. Civic affairs participation and active involvement in various Methodist churches were his foci outside of his professional responsibilities. He died at age 82 August 2, 1999, in Miami, Oklahoma.[15]

A Sacrificial Lamb: January 1, 1970-January 10, 1971

In December 1969 Governor Bartlett again searched for someone with the qualifications he stated almost two years earlier, knowing that finding such a person would be a challenge. A mere twelve months remained on the term, so the expectations of this substitute were minimal. Scott Tuxhorn, EdD, superintendent at Jet-Nash School District, received a phone call from the Governor offering the opportunity to serve. "The governor was looking for a Republican who held a doctorate and had experience in the public schools. I met all three criteria."[16] Bartlett was desperate and down to his third choice. He preferred William Anderson, EdD, assistant superintendent in the Midwest City School District, but he declined the Governor's offer because only one year remained. Whoever accepted the chief executive's offer, if he wished to continue in office, he would have to fulfill the duties and campaign for the office simultaneously. A second person, Tom Smith, EdD, in a similar position in the Oklahoma City School District, was then approached. His credentials included helping that district navigate its early path toward desegregation. Smith declined the offer for the obvious reasons and was eventually promoted to that district's top position.[17]

When Tuxhorn accepted the offer and assumed the duties in January 1970, he was fully aware of the time constraints to influence the direction of the Department and to mount a campaign should he decide to compete for the office as the incumbent. No neophyte to the political process, he had been elected to one term as a state representative previously. Tuxhorn's career trajectory, begun in 1951, included teaching and administrative stops in small towns in southwestern Kansas and northwestern Oklahoma. As principal at the Helena Training School for Boys only slightly more than a decade earlier he had gained notoriety when he administered three swats with a paddle to twenty-nine boys during an investigation into a coach's missing wristwatch. An attorney general's favorable opinion permitted him to avoid a charge of criminal liability with the decision contingent on the fact the incident occurred during the school day and at the school.[18]

Scott Tuxhorn
2012.201.B1301.0709, The Oklahoman, Oklahoma Publishing Company Photography Collection, Oklahoma Historical Society

School employment permitted him to be bi-vocational, so he engaged in farming and, in his "spare" time, participated actively in Republican politics, eventually running for a House seat in Alfalfa County in 1962. He beat his primary opponent 840 to 719 and won the general election 2,271 to 1,384, but in a reelection attempt two years later, he was bested by a Democrat. With the legislative session lasting only a few months and in odd numbered years only, in 1963 now-Representative Tuxhorn contemplated a teaching position, but first he needed to request Attorney General Charles Nesbitt's opinion whether one could be a legislator and a teacher simultaneously. The inquiry surprised Governor Bellmon whose lawyer was also working on a similar request, one the Governor considered highly explosive. Bellmon objected to legislator-educators being able to vote on their own raises and was no doubt miffed that a freshman legislator initiated a request that did not address all of the nuances, desired by the Governor, to be weighed. Several decades earlier the attorney general had ruled that teachers serving in the Legislature could continue receiving their pay as long as the funds were local and not state aid. Replying to Tuxhorn's request, Nesbitt determined that local funds and state aid were co-mingled, prohibiting payment for teachers serving in the Legislature. In a slight twist of the decision, if a school district received no state aid, its teachers could receive their pay while serving as lawmakers.[19]

Legislator Tuxhorn's earlier educational experience was auspicious when a controversy emerged in 1963 regarding the authority of the North Central Association of Secondary Schools and Colleges to sanction schools where students exceeded the maximum number of absent days allowed for participation in extracurricular activities. The Association threatened to withdraw accreditation if schools failed to comply. Given the priorities particularly of rural schools, it is little wonder that such a threat reached the politicians. Representative Tuxhorn reminded the participants at a hearing that membership in the Association was voluntary and that they could withdraw if they wished, but if they withdrew, adverse consequences would ensue. Oliver Hodge was on the periphery of this issue and stated the Board's preference for the locus of control of activities to lie with an independent state association.[20]

After completing his duties in the sole legislative session in which he served, Tuxhorn went to work for a year for the Division of Vocational Education in Stillwater as the coordinator for the industrial cooperative program. From there he served as superintendent at Jet School District for one year. Oklahoma's vocation-technical program was expanding, but its organizational framework was yet to be solidified and implemented. Tuxhorn added to the discussion of the optimal organization through his doctoral dissertation in 1967 when he studied the attitudes and opinions of various stakeholders. An advocate of vocational programs, he focused his energies during his Superintendency toward greater funding of vocational education, winning support from educators across the spectrum.[21]

Farmer, state representative, schoolteacher, district superintendent, and vo-tech employee Tuxhorn added to his repertoire of experiences when Bartlett named him chairman of the State Board of Affairs, just seven months prior to his appointment as Superintendent. He resigned his position as superintendent of the recently consolidated Jet-Nash School District immediately and moved to Oklahoma City for a salary of $15,000, a propitious move when the Governor came calling a second time. Events moved quickly, and on his first day as Superintendent, he led the Board to develop its legislative goals based on Creech's planning for this agenda. The first recommendation, the elimination of dependent districts so that all districts would offer K-12 instruction, was followed by a statement that the present school finance law was obsolete and needed to be rewritten. Other highlights were: a $5.25 million increase in special education, an increase in textbook funding of $7.00 per student, a transportation funding increase of $3 million, an allocation of $15.5 million for reduction in class size, and a request for counselors, nurses, teacher aides, and library/media center personnel. Ambitious requests to say the least, the Republican-dominated Board exerted its best effort to convey to the Governor and Democrat-majority Legislature requisites to achieve a quality education. The Board's request for additional funds for special education, reducing class size, and hiring personnel to support teachers and students was offset partially by the estimate of a cost reduction from the elimination of all dependent districts.[22] However, rural Oklahoma would oppose consolidation regardless of what incentives might be offered, and the Democrats in the Legislature had other priorities.

What option did Tuxhorn have but to support the Board's agenda even if he might have disagreed with parts of it? New on the job but with an eye toward campaigning for the office seven months in the future, he was supportive. The agenda, after all, was a compromise of money-saving school district consolidation, expansion of services, reduction in class sizes, and an urgent call for modernizing the finance law. Having lived and worked in conservative, Republican, northwestern Oklahoma, he was aware of the trend in the loss of population since statehood in that quadrant of the state and saw firsthand as the superintendent at Jet-Nash the resulting constriction of school districts. Fewer dependent districts (grades 1-8) remained in the western half of the state, so he could support consolidation of those schools without excessive political damage. Consolidation of independent districts (1-12) for lack of students would continue apace despite citizen desire otherwise.

The sex education or, as Tuxhorn framed it, family life education, controversy of the previous spring reached a resolution of sorts when the Board at its January 23rd meeting unanimously adopted a policy to guide school districts in curriculum planning. Tuxhorn, chairing only his second Board meeting and new to the discussion, was following Creech's leadership; and as the Board's and Department's communicator, he pronounced, "I firmly believe that all the curriculum should be decided on by the local school boards because they know the needs of their local school districts."[23] Assigning this issue to the local level allowed the Board to deflect criticism and to shift responsibility for implementing this contentious component of the curriculum.

Tuxhorn's experience as a teacher and legislator a decade earlier served as a backdrop to his perspective and informed his approach to pushing for greater financial advantages for educators. His election year Superintendency gave him a sense of political urgency to do his utmost to benefit educators and to establish his credentials statewide. To him, it seemed the right time to announce his support of legislative efforts to enhance teacher retirement benefits. In March Tuxhorn announced at a news conference a "new" way to reconfigure the system, only to be knocked down within minutes by a Democratic senator who proudly proclaimed that such a proposal had already been offered by a Democratic state representative.[24] Apparently Tuxhorn's idea was better than his timing. No way was an elected member of the Democratic Party going to allow a short-term Republican appointee to capture the attention of the news media.

Lack of sufficient teacher compensation and demands for improvements falling on legislators' deaf ears were providing fertile grounds for stronger collective action of Oklahoma's teachers who were becoming more aware of the unionization wave sweeping across the country. In fact, Oklahoma's pro management history and culture mitigated efforts of employees to join together to demand greater financial benefits and due process rights. Increased compensation was an attractive political plank that might ameliorate the discontent among teachers, but the Republicans opposed higher taxes and public employee unionization. Hard into the campaign season Tuxhorn proposed to the Board the selection of a lay citizen advisory committee to develop legislative recommendations for an improved teacher salary structure.[25]

In campaign literature and through speaking engagements Tuxhorn highlighted his ideas to address the numerous pressing needs of the common schools. Elimination of the elementary school districts would allow the re-allocation of money to improve the ratio of students to teachers. Consistent with his predecessor's efforts, he proposed expansion of early childhood education programs. Tuxhorn pushed for funds for classes for the gifted and a high school curriculum that included an awareness of ecological problems and significance of natural resource conservation. At the annual OEA conference in October candidates Tuxhorn and Les Fisher pitched their ideas for the next four years. Fisher wanted the calculation for state aid to school districts to be average daily membership rather than average daily attendance because ADM was a more beneficial determinant where costs were the same regardless of which measure was used. To Tuxhorn, students must be convinced to invest themselves in the future, something that could only be achieved by improved instruction. Fisher received a rousing round of applause for advocating more money for salaries and Tuxhorn a polite one for suggesting teachers improve their performance, a harbinger of what occurred shortly thereafter.[26]

Oklahoma's eight-year experience with the Republican Party leading the state came to an end in 1970 when the Democrats swept all of the executive level offices. Tuxhorn captured only 38 percent in a typical campaign where many voters chose to be efficient by selecting the straight party option.[27] Tuxhorn was thrust into a difficult position, a sacrificial lamb, when he responded affirmatively to Bartlett's invitation to finish Hodge's term. Cast into an elective office with little time to develop a history of success and to campaign for election, and representing the minority party, created a formidable mountain to climb. Leveling the field somewhat, neither candidate in the general election was an accomplished and polished speaker.

Tuxhorn went down in history as the shortest-tenured, non-acting Superintendent and also as the only one of five Superintendents from 1968 to 1986 who finished his last term. Multiple positions marked his career, most of which he sought and was successful getting; however, the Superintendency came his way and he could not refuse the Governor's request to serve. Out of office in January 1971, Tuxhorn went to work for the first of three federal agencies beginning with the Regional Office of the US Department of Health, Education, and Welfare in Dallas. With a Republican in the White House, this was viewed as a patronage payoff compliments of then Senator Bellmon. Ten years later he moved on to a three-year stint in the Secretary of Education Regional Office also in Dallas before finishing his career with a nine-year stint at the Ft. Worth office of the US Department of Transportation. Tuxhorn died September 26, 2015, in Highland Village, Texas, at the age of 87. He had three children and was active in the Masonic Lodge and the Christian Church. His wife Dolores Marie preceded him in death in 1976.[28]

Chapter 14
Fisher: Directing Rapid Department Growth and Expansion of Services
(1971-1984)

Leslie Robert Fisher (Les) built a resumé through teaching and administrative employments at small school districts in near proximity to Ardmore in the south-central region of the state and then at Moore in the Oklahoma City area. He was born January 17, 1922, grew up in Madill, and earned a bachelor's degree at Southeastern State College in Durant. Pursuit of his degree was interrupted with three years of military service during WWII. Following three years of teaching at Springer and an equal time as principal at Lone Grove, he was superintendent of the Mountain Home School District near Ringling and at Elmore City for three and four years, respectively. In 1961 he moved to Moore where he served as superintendent for nearly a decade leading the district through a 500 percent growth, a harbinger of the Department's expansion in his fourteen years as the Superintendent. Early in his Moore tenure he studied at OU and wrote his dissertation on the patterns of liability decisions in public schools. Obligatory (for a school administrator) civic duties included membership in a local Lions Club and on the board of directors of the Moore Chamber of Commerce.[1]

Competing Against a Professional Friend…and Eliminating Any Competition

Nineteen seventy's election cycle was unique in that the three candidates had school district superintendent experience, almost exclusively in small districts, and it involved two rarities. In the Democratic primary, two current district superintendents, Fisher and Charles Holleyman contested for the right to enter the general election and in that election a sitting Superintendent fought a district superintendent. Although Fisher and Holleyman competed against each other their collegial relationship was sufficiently strong that Fisher hired Holleyman in the Department soon after the election. Significant for this election cycle was that it proved to be the last one in which district level superintendent experience played a large part. Incumbent and Republican Scott Tuxhorn ran as a substantial underdog. But before Fisher could contend with Tuxhorn, he needed to dispatch with Holleyman, superintendent of Mustang Public Schools, and with whom he shared the commonalities of serving as superintendents in districts on the fringes of Oklahoma City and previously in small rural school districts in southern and southwestern Oklahoma and as officers in the Oklahoma Association of School Administrators.

Among educators, at least, both of the primary contenders had gained some statewide recognition through their involvement in professional associations. In 1965 Fisher assumed the presidency of the Oklahoma Association of School Administrators while Holleyman became its vice-president. A year earlier Holleyman provided leadership to the OEA as a member of a general committee for Oklahomans For Better Education, an endeavor to steer the OEA's efforts to secure passage of four constitutional amendments. Three failed to gain a majority and the fourth one passed, but then failed to overcome the constitutional hurdle of receiving a majority of the total votes cast in that election. By 1968 Holleyman raised his political fortunes to capture the presidency of the OEA. However, it was an extremely contentious period for the state's largest educational advocacy group, partly because the school administrators held most of the leadership positions yet the teacher numbers far exceeded those of the administrators. Nationwide, teachers were demanding collective bargaining rights, placing their professional organizations at odds with the administrators.[2]

After graduating from Chilocco Indian School, Holleyman, a Creek-Cherokee, matriculated to Bacone College, near his home, where he earned an associate degree, before transferring to East Central State College to complete his undergraduate education. Later he was awarded a master's degree at OU. Near the end of his career, he obtained an honorary doctorate from a small private college in West Virginia. He taught at Velma-Alma Public Schools from 1951 to 1955 followed by two years as high school principal at Comanche and then eight years as superintendent in that district of thirty-six teachers. In the six years he led the Mustang district the number of teachers doubled from thirty-nine to seventy-seven. Although he hailed from northeastern Oklahoma, all of his experience was gained in southwestern Oklahoma. At forty-one years of age, Holleyman focused his energy on winning the primary election, "I am running as a professional educator for an office that needs to be filled by an educator, not a politician."[3] Fisher had already announced his intentions, so now the Democrats were offered a choice.

Although both were novice politicians, Fisher's campaigning success and larger war chest bested Holleyman in the August 25, 1970 primary election 59.8 percent to 40.1 percent, capturing 194,612 votes to 130,672 and boding well for the general election. Buoyed by the compelling results and calculating that his toughest competition was behind him, Fisher prepared for the general election and his Republican opponent. The results were similar to those of the primary election, even capturing a slightly larger 62 percent of the votes. Holleyman's campaign expenditures were $15,309 while Fisher's amounted to $52,140 for the entire election season. For the general election Tuxhorn amassed nearly $20,000 but more than 60 percent of that was his own money. Running political campaigns was not an inexpensive endeavor and forced aspirants into speaking engagements and dipping into their personal assets. Because neither man was known well across the state, and many voters typically chose the party ticket, an obvious disadvantage accrued to the Republican candidate.[4]

Holleyman's post-election career trajectory followed twists and turns when he was initially hired by Fisher as the director of federal programs in the Department. Then he became a Bacone College administrator from 1972 to 1974, before returning to the Department as the assistant administrator of school plant services. He left for a short stint as superintendent at the forty-teacher Little Axe School District in 1980 before rejoining the Department in its auditing unit. A brief hiatus as superintendent in the

Oaks Mission district concluded his peripatetic career. Throughout the '70s and early '80s Fisher graciously treated his opponent through hiring him for various positions. Holleyman died April 26, 2005.[5]

Fisher's retention of the position for fourteen years, required little effort beyond that initial campaign. With the 1970 election as recent history, Fisher settled into a comfortable political environment for more than a decade. Although he drew no opponent in 1974, the Board wished to communicate its satisfaction of his performance through a resolution to "express appreciation and commendation to Leslie Fisher for the outstanding job being done as state superintendent of public instruction."[6] No opponent surfaced in the 1978 election, possible because he "has strong support throughout the state and has well-oiled campaign machinery,"[7] and only nominal force in 1982, when Charles Sandmann filed on the Republican ticket. Immediately upon filing, Sandmann was contacted by the state Republican Party with offers of financial assistance. Part of his decision to run emanated from his intuition that he was passed over for promotions in the Department because of his political affiliation. Sensing political alignments that were pitting employees in the Department against one another, he quickly resigned and invested no time or money in the election. The working environment was dominated by a "good ole boy network under Fisher" and he, Sandmann, was not going to be promoted to assistant or deputy superintendent.[8]

Sandmann had been employed at the Department for sixteen years when he decided to test the political waters. He had prepared himself for a range of opportunities in the early years of this tenure by earning a doctorate at OU. Initially assigned as the administrator of human relations and finally as director of federal financial assistance programs, with three other duties interspersed, he gained knowledge of the inner workings of the Department. But he was a member of the minority political party and unknown beyond the confines of the Department; thus, his political assets were minimal and mitigated any effective run for a statewide office. Given the political tenor at the time, and Fisher's popularity, Sandmann would have wasted his resources had he decided to compete for the position. Eight years later and ensconced in the oil business, he showed his bipartisanship by offering space to Sandy Garrett for her election campaign headquarters.[9]

Halfway through his fourth term, comfortable with the extent of the preparation of his protégé, and looking for a greater political challenge, Fisher resigned from office in late 1983, effective at the end of June 1984, to lay the groundwork for a run for the governorship two years later. If he thought his fourteen years as Superintendent gave him the name recognition and garnered him political capital sufficient to sustain an expensive campaign, he grossly miscalculated, for, in a crowded field of six candidates in the Democratic primary, he came in a very distant third with only 6.5 percent of the vote. His education and political careers were over.[10]

Expanding the Department's Staff, Programs, and Expenditures

Fisher, who in early 1971 had concluded a decade of leading a relatively small school district through rapid growth, was confident in his ability to lead a state agency. He was given the support of voters statewide to guide and coordinate the state's education system. Voters were not well informed of the Department and its functions, but the local media would keep a watchful eye on its operations. Fisher would not hesitate to expand services where he determined the need to do so, and the federal and state governments would provide him the rationale and funding to grow the agency. Uncertainty and job security faced the Department's employees in January 1971 when they were to have their fourth Superintendent since 1968. Rapid turnover of the Department's chief administrator produced anxiety as, no doubt, did Fisher's request to the Legislature to enact statutory provisions removing dozens of top administrative and supervisory positions from merit system protections. Employees with access to due process obtained less positional status and reputation but appreciated the trade-offs. Legislatures generally preferred state professional employees to be at-will and subject to the expectations of the administrator in charge. Thus, Fisher's appeal found receptivity among a cooperative group of solons and the Governor who enacted the necessary statute.[11]

Fisher then set out to re-organize the administrative units and generate a new organizational chart to clarify lines of authority. A new policy handbook, when presented to the Board for approval, received unanimous support. Three services were to be rendered by the Department: instructional, administrative, and operational. "To administer with justice the policies contained herein, the State Superintendent of Public Instruction may modify or delete any part at his discretion," communicated to him that he could assume sole prerogative to change Department policy.[12]

Early in his tenure he had the unique opportunity to be integrally involved with the design, construction, lease, move to, and occupation of the new headquarters of the Department. An agreement was formed in 1971 between the Board and the Oklahoma Capitol Improvement Authority to have a building erected by the latter and leased to the former for the housing of the Department. Culmination of the planning efforts was

Oliver Hodge Memorial Education Building,
photo by Lois E. Brandt

December 8, 1974, when the Oliver Hodge Memorial Education Building was dedicated. Fisher coordinated the move of the agency's offices and personnel to the first three floors and those of the Oklahoma Teachers Retirement System and Oklahoma State Regents for Higher Education to the fourth and fifth floors, respectively. Offices scattered in several locations, inhibiting effective communication, were now placed in close proximity, increasing the efficiency and effectiveness of the agency.[13]

Elimination of the merit system protections did not result in the discontinuance of the "good ole boy" composition of the Department, but one noteworthy exception that showed Fisher's willingness to support and advance a person whom he deemed highly competent and destined for greater things was John Folks. Folks did not fit the stereotypical mold in that he was young and lacked school district administrative experience yet in about a decade he was promoted often and to advanced levels sufficient for Fisher to recommend him to Governor Nigh to replace him in 1984. Folks's ascension to more expansive influence and responsibility was a measure of the confidence and trust that Fisher placed in males capable of performing at a high level. He became a key linchpin in the overall governance of the Department and one to whom Fisher looked when he needed the exuberance of youth and the maturity of experience. Fisher's relationship to Folks communicated to the other top executives a standard they might wish to emulate.[14]

Les Fisher
Courtesy of Oklahoma Education Association

Events and actions nationally affected what was happening within Oklahoma and local school districts. Supreme Court decisions in the mid-1950s forced state legislative bodies, school districts, and state education agencies to confront segregation and to change the way the education system operated. Affected the greatest for the first two decades after *Brown v Board of Education, Topeka,* were the rural schools, forcing the Department to accept the mantle of leadership in complying with the court's decision. By the early 1970s, urban districts were scrutinized by the Supreme Court and given mandates of busing to comply with desegregation orders. Oklahoma City was no exception and was placed under a federal court order and Tulsa also had to develop its plan. Different from its earlier supervision of rural school desegregation, now the Department became more an observer of the court's actions and the districts' plans.

Essentially freed from direct involvement in urban desegregation, the Department could direct its energies to complying with federal and state legislation. Extension and clarification of civil rights in a variety of areas and expansion of President Johnson's Great Society promises through legislation and federal money for education necessitated changes in the Department. The Elementary and Secondary Education Act of 1965 pumped massive sums of money into states for distribution to schools. Expansion of the vocational/career programs was given impetus through funding increases in the late 1960s resulting in creating the Vocational-Technical Department for supervising that segment of education in Oklahoma. By Fisher's first day on the job in 1971 these programs were becoming mature in their implementation.[15]

State legislation in 1971, HB 1325, dramatically changed the dynamics between teachers and administrators in the local schools and to a lesser extent in the Department. Legislators across the country and the general public were becoming more receptive to granting public employees rights to collective bargaining. Oklahoma teachers were given more power, ameliorated somewhat because the state has always been management oriented, to negotiate their compensation and working conditions resulting in a more severe line of demarcation between management and workers. Simultaneous to this evolving change in the employment interactions in schools was the separation of administrators from teachers' organizations and the founding of joint administrator associations. The expansion of the Department and the state's education system along with the concomitant growth and maturation of the teacher and administrator subgroups forged the anvil upon which reforms were designed and implemented.[16]

The Legislature and the various components of the education system expanded the rights and opportunities of students with learning disabilities as early as the late 1960s. In the 1969-70 school year special education programs across the state enrolled 33,753 students and engaged 718 teachers. A short five years later in the Prescriptive Teaching Act of 1974, the Legislature created Regional Education Service Centers as an intermediate level between the Department and the local school districts and under the supervision of the Department. Twenty RESCs, designed strategically and situated geographically to provide testing, diagnostic, and instructional services, were staffed with administrators, psychologists, psychometrists, and secretaries, eventually adding 180 positions to the Department's expanding staff. The PTA of 1974 was designed to assist the Department with the crucial responsibility for implementing the Education for All Handicapped Children Act. This legislation enlarged the federal government's involvement in the public schools and infused tens of millions of dollars, expanded the rights of an estimated 10 to 15 percent of the students, and resulted in Fisher's Department adding programs and mid-level administrators and supervisory personnel to achieve compliance with the law. Districts geared up for the programs and colleges/universities expanded to prepare the teachers and other critical specialized personnel.[17]

Growth of the Agency during Fisher's term was nothing short of phenomenal. Physically located in the State Capitol and other auxiliary facilities until 1974, the Department expansion would have been difficult without the move to the Hodge Building. A staff of 273 members in 1971-72 more than doubled under Fisher's tenure to 587 in 1983-84 (see table 14.1). A 700 percent growth in state appropriations and a six-fold increase in the Department's total budget over fourteen years seem incomprehensible, even accounting for inflation, and especially when the state's pupil enrollment dropped by 26,957 or 4.18 percent. Growing concern over the enlargement of the Department would manifest itself within a few years.

The decline in enrollment numbers, the skyrocketing Departmental expenditures as displayed in table 14.1, and the growing number of teachers would eventually attract scrutiny but any serious assessment of the situation by the Board was not a priority. During Fisher's tenure school districts hired 28 percent more teachers. For legislators and *The Oklahoman* pursuing more efficiency and effectiveness, their voices for consolidation were dismissed as the number of districts declined by a mere 4.5 percent and those

Table 14.1 School district and Department data 1971-1984

Year	Enrollment	Teach./admin.	Staff*	Number of districts			Department expenditures		
				K-8	K-12	Tot.	State	Federal	Total
71/72	644,841	31,231	273	187	457	644	2,276,256	1,324,256	3,600,512
72/73	636,820	31,186	263	181	456	637	2,335,671	1,775,377	4,111,048
73/74	630,437	32,191	287	178	456	634	2,469,671	1,773,053	4,667,651[†]
74/75	625,800	32,861	311	173	455	628	3,276,900	2,553,149	5,830,049
75/76	625,568	33,738	301	168	456	624	3,269,350	2,222,657	5,492,007
76/77	628,230	34,577	311	166	457	623	3,642,866	2,922,644	6,565,510
77/78	626,519	35,510	359	165	457	622	4,148,576	3,211,383	7,359,958
78/79	620,167	36,551	386	163	457	620	5,110,982	3,419,372	8,530,355
79/80	616,951	37,751	433	162	457	619	5,974,660	4,597,063	10,571,723
80/81	611,246	38,464	492	161	457	618	9,684,253	4,760,517	14,444,770
81/82	620,781	38,894	578	159	457	616	13,898,863	4,320,577	18,219,440
82/83	622,630	39,901	565	159	457	616	15,961,763	4,012,006	19,973,768
83/84	617,884	39,950	587	158	457	615	16,326,681	3,642,089	19,968,769

Sources: Enrollment numbers are from the *Annual Report 1987-88*, Vol. 2, SDE, 84. Teacher and administrator numbers are from the *Annual Report 1984-85*, Vol. 2, SDE, 97. Department staff numbers, number of districts, and department expenditures are found in these *Annual Reports*: 71/72, 5; 72/73, 2; 73/74, 2; 74/75, 2; 75/76, 2; 76/77, 2; 77/78, 3; 78/79, 1; 79/80, 2; 80/81, 2; 81/82, 2; 82/83, 2; 83/84, Vol. 1, 23.

Notes: The dip in the number of staff in 82/83 reflects the statewide hiring freeze.

*Department employees.

† Reason for the discrepancy of $424,927 in the total for state and federal amounts is unknown.

were only K-8 districts with a negligible total enrollment. Fisher's rural background and political base mitigated any possibility for formulating consolidation overtures. Most Board members represented interests in maintaining the status quo, especially given the mandated implementation of a barrage of state and federal legislation and an absence of any incentive or force to combine districts. Key to the teacher growth figures was the employment at the district level of large numbers of teachers to implement the provisions of the law mandating services to students with disabilities. The 215 percent increase in Department staff and an astonishing 717 percent rise in state-sourced expenditures did not go unnoticed. Somewhere over the horizon there would be a time of reckoning but it was not imminent in 1984.

An undercurrent to the growth of federal influence and money and calls for the expansion of teachers' rights began to coalesce in the late 1960s. More funding for the schools and growing collective teacher power, a second consecutive Republican governor in office to urge changes, the formation of the State Department of Vo-Tech Education as a totally separate and stand-alone agency, and rumblings of higher expectations of teacher and student performance in schools, formed the basis for the Legislature in 1969 to create the Oklahoma Commission on Education. Annually for six years the Commission, divided into the subcommittees of Education and Finance, issued a report culminating in a final one in 1976. It was in the third report of 1971 that the topic of accountability was broached. Eight legislators, joining twenty-three others spread across the medical, business and legal sectors and within which there were eight women, averred: "A topic of increasing concern in public education is that of accountability. Educators, administrators, members of the Legislature, and the public in general are with the passage of time becoming more and more insistent that the educational needs of all students are more effectively met at the lowest possible costs to the taxpayers." Without representation on the Commission educators and administrators were listed first as being insistent on greater efficiency and producing better results with the least possible financial effect on taxpayers. As a starting point it posited that a "good system of accountability should include a joint venture between local communities and the State Department of Education."[18] There was a key role for the Superintendent and the Department to provide leadership and to assist local school districts to establish measurable goals and methods and instruments to evaluate the progress. The Commission offered a draft bill for the Legislature to consider that was modeled after one recently passed in Colorado.[19]

Accountability proved to be an attractive concept, particularly to the politicians. In 1973 the Legislature injected itself into an arena with a concept that would prove to have lasting consequences. Joining thirty-two states, it passed a resolution that required the Department to develop a systems analysis, widely used in business and industry, to be applied to education.[20] An accountability approach, with little attention given to the significant differences in purpose and operation between for-profit companies and nonprofit service agencies, to solving the perceived inefficiencies and ineffectiveness of schools and improve their efficacy was deemed the preferred and best avenue to pursue.

Teacher and school district accountability and school choice were complementary ideas that needed time to ferment. Initially, little heed was given to the choice issue partly because Oklahoma historically enrolled a high percentage of eligible students in public schools, indicative of parental satisfaction with the schools, and a large majority of the population was Protestant. Only 5 percent of school age students attended Catholic schools and few other students attended Protestant/private schools. Citizen satisfaction with the schools held steady with few demands for greater options.[21] Also important to remember is that after a 1940s Oklahoma Supreme Court decision placed responsibility on the schools for proving inadequate quality of homeschooling efforts, public school districts with limited resources almost never pursued parents who were suspected of abdicating their responsibilities.

In June 1980 the Legislature determined that it was necessary to change how teachers were prepared by higher education and how their knowledge of curriculum in their field and practices should be assessed; how new teachers were oriented and integrated into school districts; and how they should continue their professional learning. House Bill 1706 was the embodiment of the Legislature's intent to improve instruction in the classroom. Most responsibility for implementation of the law was assigned to the Department: develop curriculum exams, design the Entry Year Assistance Program, and create procedures and guidelines for staff development programs. Fisher's Department geared up for this major overhaul of the instruction occurring in the classroom.[22]

Oklahoma's economy, as with all energy producing states' economies, was booming at the beginning of the 1980s, but within two years, its sizeable dependence on the energy sector suffered a severe blow. The pendulum swung quickly in the opposite direction, passing from a boom to one of its periodic "busts," exacerbated by the fall of Penn Square Bank and the consequent shock that reverberated through the economy. Although state appropriations were quickly curbed, the Department was expected to implement 1706's provisions, but with fewer resources. Once again, Oklahoma's education system was reminded of the extent to which the vicissitudes of the oil and gas industry determined its destiny. Those who believed the education funding was more than adequate felt no compulsion to seek additional resources to maintain the status quo.

Prior to the blow to the energy industry the Board, chaired by Fisher, decided in the fall of 1980 to pressure the Legislature to increase his salary immediately to a respectable level. Constitutionally, increasing a salary during a current term was impermissible. But the Board seized most importantly upon the notion that since HB 1706 was a significant reform with many attendant duties and responsibilities for the Department and oversight from the Superintendent, a salary raise was justifiable. Adding to the Board's thinking was the perceived inequity between Fisher's salary and school district superintendents' salaries. Fisher was viewed as a quality Superintendent, so the Legislature complied with the request through enactment of SB 401. To justify the increased compensation five additional "duties" were enumerated, the fulfillment of which qualified him for an increase of $10,000 to accompany his rather meager $35,000 salary. Among those specified duties were implementation of HB 1706 guidelines and regulations, improvement of automated reporting by school districts, developing educational leaders, and assisting school districts with asbestos removal and abatement. Not everyone was pleased for, within nine months, the Attorney General nullified the extra compensation as unconstitutional under article 23, section 10 prohibiting raising the pay during a term of office.[23]

Increating the compensation of the Superintendent in 1980 was not the first instance adequate remuneration for the office was considered. The Board's seven members were *ex officio* members of the thirteen-member State Board of Vocational-Technical Education that typically convened in the afternoon of the day each month when the Board met in the morning. Chaired also by the Superintendent, the Vo-Tech Board's foremost responsibility was to employ and set the compensation for the director of that agency. Because it was under no statutory or constitutional restraint when determining the director's pay, pressure was there to set the director's salary more competitive with the vocational-technical district superintendents' salaries, resulting in more attention on the Superintendent's inadequate compensation. To address the considerable discrepancy the State Vo-Tech Board adopted a resolution in February 1977 urging the Legislature to increase the salary of the Superintendent from its current $30,000 to $42,000 for the next term beginning in January 1979. Then at the next month's Board meeting member Harry Shackelford presented the same resolution for approval, which was granted unanimously. The Legislature granted the request for an increase, but, in true form, raised the amount only to $35,000. No doubt the solons felt constrained to augment the salary anymore by the structure used to set the salaries of all of the elected executive officers.[24]

Fisher served in a period of rapid expansion of the federal government into what historically had been the prerogative of the states as established by the Tenth Amendment to the Constitution and of influences swiftly crossing the county expanding the rights of teachers. Large amounts of federal funds flowed to the states to continue and expand the provisions of the various civil rights laws. The US Supreme Court rendered opinions clarifying student rights relative to access to education and disciplinary procedures. Simultaneously, Oklahoma's Legislature expanded the rights of teachers through collective bargaining, and women's access and advancement to administrative positions began to take root. Fisher's reign for the most part exhibited the characteristics of the positive nature of growth without the necessity of contraction. Only near the end of his tenure did the state's energy sector "bust" and the economy collapse causing a squeeze on the funds available. By then it was time for Fisher to transition into another chapter of his life and to pass the challenges to his handpicked successor.

Before Fisher left, and as the economy was teetering on the brink of disaster, the Legislature commissioned a survey by Peter Hart Research Associates to ascertain public opinion regarding the status of education. Among the findings were that the public desired higher standards for a high school diploma and they would be willing to pay higher property taxes to support education. Two-thirds said the state should spend more money on education and that teachers deserved more pay. Fisher directed one of his deputies John Folks to summarize these findings and to present them to the Board in its October 1983 monthly meeting.[25] The survey findings carried substantial weight subsequently in Folks's development of his reform agenda when he assumed the Superintendency eight months later. He had credible evidence to gauge the public's support for his ideas.

To allow a smooth transition resulting from his resignation mid-term, Fisher announced to the Board at its December 14, 1983, meeting: "DR. JOHN M. FOLKS, Associate Deputy State Superintendent, has been designated by Governor George Nigh to be State Superintendent of Public Instruction to finish out his term."[26] Six days earlier Fisher's retirement was announced to be effective June 30, 1984. Fisher had groomed

Folks for the position and then recommended him to the Governor. Not coincidentally, Fisher had invited the Governor as a special guest to the previous month's special Board meeting where Folks led a discussion of "current education issues." Nigh wanted to see firsthand what kind of person he would soon appoint to complete Fisher's term.[27]

Federal and state constitutional and statutory laws, court decisions, and regulations undergirding and guiding the various agencies and branches of government as well as school districts became more complex, eventually causing Fisher to recommend to the Board the hiring of legal counsel. At his final meeting with the Board, and acting on his recommendation, the Board hired a fulltime attorney to assist the agency to ensure compliance with the myriad laws under which it operated and to represent the Board and the Department in lawsuits against them. Until that time Associate Superintendent Tom Campbell addressed queries from school district administrators about legal issues within their districts and lawyers were hired as needed to represent the Department in court.[28]

Fisher served through the terms of three governors, David Hall, David Boren, and George Nigh, all Democrats. By all appearances Fisher, as an elected officer also, enjoyed generally positive, professional relationships with them, with the exception of disagreements at times with Boren. This trio of governors was supportive of education and the efforts of the Department to provide the prerequisite leadership for the schools. Fisher's personality and commitment to be part of a team to carry out the government's mandate to provide educational opportunities to the students earned him high regards.[29]

No allegations of misfeasance or malfeasance surfaced during his tenure and only one minor issue arose when Fisher transferred 103 employees from the protection of the merit system. That act along with his generosity regarding employee absenteeism and pay formed the bulk of a legislative audit team's accusation of low efficiency. In a rousing defense of his leadership, he stated that the auditors did not perform satisfactorily and that he was ashamed that he could not pay his key employees better salaries.[30] What was not addressed was whether or not the efficiency was low. Instead, he averred the audit was deficient and, furthermore, what can you expect when employees are insufficiently compensated?

Not surprising was the Legislature's complicity in the controversy over the merit system actions by Fisher when it was that very body that provided the mechanism for his decision. His request to the Legislature in May 1971, after four months on the job, to enact a law to remove all supervisory personnel in the Department from the merit system was granted to him. His wish was to expand his prerogative, but not totally, to hire and remove personnel.[31] This development harkened back to Crable's administration in the early 1940s when he lost his patronage authority in a gasp of legislative acrimony.

The anticipated and earned congenial and professional relationship between Fisher and the Board was exemplified in the Board's conveyance through several resolutions at the beginning, during, and end of his tenure of recognition of excellent performance. The initial resolution was adopted at the Board's regular February meeting when it "unanimously approved that a vote of confidence be given Dr. Fisher and…that the Board is looking to him for this leadership." The reference to leadership followed Fisher's stated intent to "provide efficient leadership…which should result in a progressive program."[32]

A second indication of support came after the filing period closed in June 1974 and was based on Fisher's drawing no opponent as an indication of the quality of his performance. Also, the Board had heard no meaningful criticism of his administration and leadership. The third and final commendation and appreciation of his service was through a unanimous resolution at its May 24, 1984, meeting. In part it read, "Whereas, no matter what position he held, or what recognitions he received, his first concern was always for the school children of Oklahoma."[33]

"Show and Tell," second grade classroom, 1986, Stillwater, Oklahoma

Fisher was no innovator of major thrusts or encourager of bold ideas and new directions. Moving the status quo forward incrementally and responding to external forces expediently marked his administration. First and foremost, he was a rural educator who viewed the Department's primary role as serving the interests and needs of rural schools. New federal and state legislation impelled the shifting focus of the Department. Fisher's success emanated from his personality and leadership perspective as exhibited through his gregariousness. He liked people and would listen to any argument or persuasive attempts without showing agreement or disagreement. "This is going to be the best school year in the state's history" is how he described the 1973-74 year.[34] His political instinct was convincing, until his run for governor when his ideas did not resonate with the public. Not autocratic, he displayed an eye for good talent and then supported excellent leadership within the agency.

Custodian of the School Lands

Some controversy, not unusual, surrounded the Commissioners of the Land Office during Fisher's first term on the Board. Corruption and politics have plagued this Commission from its founding given its oversight of assets, financial duties, and susceptibility to influence. The elected officials who serve *ex officio*, with the Governor the *ex officio* chair, are accountable to the voters and not to the Governor. Selection and employment of the secretary, the critical administrator of the Commission, is a process oftentimes fraught with intrigue and maneuvering. In early 1972 Governor David Hall wished to name a new secretary, so the incumbent was demoted and the assistant secretary was promoted to the top position. Controversy erupted six months later over the propriety of a school land auction, and, after another six months, the secretary resigned. Fisher, not hesitant to oppose the Governor, and one of two Commission members to dissent against the Governor's nominee, did so because that person was the subject of an investigation.[35]

From January of 1971 to June 1975 the Commission had five secretaries with one serving only eight days. Both Hall and his successor David Boren encountered opposition from the other Commission members, especially in the naming of the secretary. Political machinations were causing frequent turnover in this key position and instability in the Commission. This government agency supervised considerable assets that were to benefit public education, yet frequently through multiple incidents and decisions did not represent the best interest of students. Fisher, adamant about protecting the asset and opposing the sale of any school land, looked askance at any potentially politically motivated transactions. More than a decade of service to the Commission gave him an in-depth understanding of its purpose and operation, and the significance of the financial support to the state's schools.[36]

Influencing the Selection of College Presidents

His tenure on the Board of Regents of Oklahoma Colleges, as a member only, informed him of the operation of those higher education institutions primarily responsible for preparing the teachers and principals for the schools. That venue allowed him to explicate the close connection particularly between the secondary schools and colleges relative to the curriculum demands of the former and the preparation of teachers by the latter. When HB 1706 passed requiring the joint efforts of many of the state's higher education institutions, the Department, and the common schools, Fisher assigned his assistant-in-waiting, Folks, to lead the Department's efforts. Fisher, as a regent *ex officio*, participated in the selection of two of his fellow superintendents in 1975 for university presidencies (Leonard Campbell, SWOSU and Bill Lillard, UCO).

Participating in the Creation of the Moore-Norman Vo-Tech District

By January 1971 the separation of the governance of vocational and technical education from the Board and the Department, and the development of a free-standing agency and department in Stillwater, were two and one-half years under way. The eight area vo-tech schools either in operation or approved for opening in 1968, by 1975, had grown to nineteen plus two nearly completed. Rapid growth of area school districts and in the personnel to operate them caused the Vo-Tech Department to enlarge its staff to offer assistance and guidance to them. Fisher chaired the board *ex-officio* in these early heady days of expansion and enjoyed particular delight in overseeing the creation of the Moore-Norman district and facility, an area with which he was thoroughly familiar. He offered a district superintendent perspective to the discourse when contemplating the interfacing of the K-12 and vocational-technical districts.[37]

Unfortunately Only a Short Retirement

About a year prior to going public with his decision to retire Fisher suffered cardiovascular disease leading to surgery. His retirement announcement omitted any reference to his health status, but his physical fitness was raised by the media when, in late June 1986, he suddenly, and belatedly, inserted himself into the already crowded field of five for the Democratic primary for Governor. Four successful statewide elections gave him the confidence to decide to proclaim his intention to compete again, and he judged his ailment not to mitigate his chances for success. Fisher attempted to succeed at what only one of his predecessors tried—use the Superintendency as a springboard to the governor's chair—and failed. As with R. H. Wilson in 1922, he could not parlay his experience and name recognition into higher office. Different from Wilson who nearly won the Democratic primary, Fisher's attempt on August 26 was an abysmal failure when he placed a distant third with only 6.5 percent of the vote. Rather incongruously, one of his platform planks was that state government needed shrinking and that, if elected, he pledged to eliminate many high-level jobs.[38]

Longevity of life was not to be his fate for he died of heart failure January 2, 1988, at age sixty-five. Surviving him were his wife Ernestine to whom he had been married for forty-six years, one son, and two daughters. At Fisher's death Governor Nigh eulogized his leadership in guiding the Department through growth and expansion: "He deserves a lot of the credit for the great progress we have made during these past years in strengthening the quality of the state's public schools."[39]

Chapter 15
Folks: Pursuing an Ambitious Reform Agenda
(1984-1988)

For the fifth time in history (1927, 1936, 1968, and 1970) a governor was faced with choosing someone to finish an unexpired term, and, as on all previous occasions, a male was selected. Named was a current Department employee, a first, but he held not the highest position in the administrative hierarchy; rather, he was one of three associate deputy superintendents. Governor Nigh was given plenty of advance notice of the vacancy when Fisher informed him of his resignation more than six months prior to the effective date. Nigh wasted little time in selecting John Folks to assume the reins upon Fisher's departure, midway through the four-year term.

John Max Folks began life March 17, 1948, in Sayre, Oklahoma, when he was born into a family where both parents were educators who provided a home environment where the importance of earning a quality education was instilled in him. Conservative in religion, Democratic in politics, and living in Republican western Oklahoma, the Folkses were deeply rooted in Oklahoma values: honesty, integrity, diligent work, and high expectations. By his teen years, his family had moved to the Oklahoma City area where he graduated from Moore High School in 1966. He matriculated at Oklahoma Christian University where he played on the basketball team his freshman year before transferring to OU and earning a mathematics degree in 1970. Folks aspired to be an FBI agent, but learned he was ineligible because he was not yet twenty-three.[1]

Stifled by the age restriction he opted to pursue another avenue at least for a year, after which he would decide his career's direction. With a math degree it was not difficult to secure a teaching position and he accepted an offer to teach mathematics at Thomas Jefferson High School in the Port Arthur, Texas, Independent School District. John and his wife were ecstatic when the district offered her an elementary teaching position sight unseen. They were off to Texas where they stayed for two years after which he accepted a secondary teaching and coaching position in the Western Heights School District near Oklahoma City. Close proximity to Norman, fond memories of his student days at OU, and the realization that he needed a master's degree if he wished to advance his career drew Folks to pursue a secondary education degree. Sometime during his third year in the district Folks's superintendent Leonard Campbell was asked by his friend and professional colleague Les Fisher if he knew of a young talent who might want to work at the Department. Folks was encouraged to apply, was hired, and assigned. Less than a decade after high school graduation, Folks, on a fast track, was employed in the Department by Fisher, his superintendent while a high school student.[2]

Aggressive Pursuit of Opportunities to Reach the Apex

Preceding Folks to the Department was his father, Cecil, who was first hired in 1965 by Hodge. Cecil held several administrative positions in the Department during his ten-year tenure prior to reaching the agency's mandatory retirement age of sixty-five: two years each as assistant director of School Plant Services and director in the State Aid Section, and three years each in the Finance Division and as assistant state superintendent and director of Finance. Coincidentally, the day after Cecil retired, John began his ascent to the Superintendency somewhat knowledgeable of the inner workings of the Department from his father's perspective. Cecil's professional competence and warm relationship with Fisher, along with high praise from Campbell at Western Heights, convinced Fisher of the high probability of John's success.[3]

They had different personalities: Cecil was quiet, reserved, and meticulous with an accountant-like personality while John was loquacious, ebullient, and extroverted. The elder served well in a supportive role as did the younger; but the latter exhibited high expectations that evolved into aspiring to the top and projecting the image of the Department. At twenty-seven, Folks was younger than most new employees at the Department, particularly for persons in administrative positions. Nevertheless, he was hired as assistant controller to aid the controller to prepare budget requests for the Governor and Legislature and to administer expenditures for Departmental supplies and employee salaries. One year later he was promoted to controller where he had the additional tasks of developing a computerized accounting system and an internal data processing system for the Department.[4]

John Folks
Courtesy of the Oklahoma State Department of Education

Folks's assignment shifted significantly in 1978 with his new title of director of Secondary Education. Now he was ensconced in responsibilities coordinating secondary curriculum at the Department and throughout Oklahoma. Through the Department curriculum coordinators, he shared in the planning, development, and implementation of innovative projects across the state. Although his emphasis centered on curriculum, he was never far from the political arena. Only thirty, Fisher named him legislative liaison for the Department for all matters relating to education.[5] Not a few within the Department noticed the increasing responsibilities assigned to this youthful protégé, and no doubt wondered about what the future held for him.

Such perspectives gained further credence when Folks was named associate deputy state superintendent of public instruction in 1981 with primary responsibility to supervise all of the programs in the instruction division of the Department and the 200-person cadre administering those programs. Satisfactory performance as the legislative liaison earned him continuation of that assignment, but now the stakes were higher, for the Legislature provided the framework for improving the quality of teacher preparation, implementing an orientation/transitional period for new teachers, and establishing professional development for all teachers.[6]

House Bill 1706, proclaimed a major step forward for Oklahoma's educational system, included funds for the Department to create a teacher testing system, for higher education faculty assistance in first year teaching assessment, and to compensate experienced teachers for their role in guiding neophyte teachers to navigate their first year of teaching. The law provided a means for easing the transition from college student to teacher, but, typical of many legislative enactments to improve education, the bill lacked any research underpinning. Pragmatically, principals and professors were unhappy because they received no extra compensation as did the "consulting teachers," and the professors perceived their assignment as another onerous, time-consuming duty. Folks was not deterred by what he considered unnecessary distractions, but then he lacked any experience as a principal, consulting teacher, or professor.

Folks's formal educational preparation continued during these years in the Department as he worked toward his Doctorate in Education at OU in 1982. Apropos to his career was the focus of his dissertation: "An Analysis of Opinions of H.B. 1706 as Perceived by Certain Selected School-Related Groups." Administrators, teachers, board members, and professors of education were asked their thoughts regarding the various components of this cutting-edge legislation. With this knowledge and analysis, Folks not only satisfied the degree requirements, he also gained a sense of the education establishment and where challenges to the bill's successful implementation might arise in the next several years. The Department's role in directing the teacher-testing component, for example, was unique because this was the first instance in more than half a century that teachers were tested by the Department to qualify for certification. Tied to the testing qualification was the Entry Year Program where school principals, experienced teachers, and professors of education were being asked to assume additional responsibilities for the joint supervision of beginning teachers. House Bill 1706 identified teachers as the only group to receive compensation for their increased duties. Folks gained the perspectives of these various groups, but he rarely, if ever, expressed any concern over the expansion of duties sans extra pay. His perspective was that principals were given more license to assist and evaluate their neophyte teachers and professors would not be overly burdened with the duty. Furthermore, professors could gain valuable knowledge about the strengths and weaknesses of the undergraduate programs, and mitigating their resentment over the arrangement was just not an important concern for Folks.[7]

Folks relished the opportunity and visibility to represent the Department as liaison to the Legislature and advocate for its efforts. Communicating to the policymakers the needs of the ever-expanding Department gave him the platform from which to launch his political career. Quick to grasp the inner workings of the Department through holding several positions, and being assigned more substantial responsibilities within a short time period, gained him political capital internally and steered his career toward the Superintendency. His rapid ascension within the Department administrative hierarchy was not unnoticed and conveyed to the Agency's employees the vital role he played and the advantages he enjoyed because of his close relationship with Fisher. Occasionally Fisher would hint that he might not finish his term, "I might retire one of these days and you might be interested."[8] He was not in robust health, with heart problems that seemed intractable. His popularity was not in doubt, and he most likely would have won reelection in 1986. When Fisher announced his resignation in December 1983 to be effective June 30 of the next year, Governor Nigh wasted no time naming Folks to complete the term, a decision that surprised few people and culminated nearly a decade of effort to serve the Department.[9] He achieved the position he believed potentially most influential to improving education in Oklahoma. Not one to shy away from a challenge, he grabbed the reins and spurred everyone to continue efforts to reform the schools and education.

The "Reformation" of 1984-1988

Folks's brief teaching stint in Port Arthur gave him insight into a Texas education system built on the needs of education rather than settling for what was possible with limited funds. It was not hindered by the same constraints present in Oklahoma, for example, where the Legislature had a history of bleeding education, having almost never funded it adequately, and was subject to the vicissitudes of the boom-and-bust energy industry. He appreciated a well-funded system and then returned to Oklahoma when the state and the country were dealing with energy and political crises. Folks now had some out-of-state experience and context in which to construct his ideas of possibilities in Oklahoma. The danger lay in trying to replicate the well-funded Texas model in Oklahoma where there existed a different mindset and decades of talking about the good education system while rarely funding it beyond a minimal level. Oklahoma politicians often prated about offering a quality system, but displayed a history of mediocre funding built on a primacy of low taxes. To some extent Folks's notion of possibilities was based on what Texas was accomplishing. Though a neophyte teacher, he observed and learned about the secondary school math curriculum, standards, and expectations. His appreciation of the generous funding of Texas's schools grew to frustration as he subsequently experienced the relative low level of support in Oklahoma. In the Department he believed that eventually he might be able to positively influence the state's financial commitment and expectations. After all, the public seemed to be responsive to efforts to reform schools and improve students' academic performance.[10]

Folks assumed the Superintendency informed of the expectations of the position and the political context in which it functioned equal to, if not better than, any of his predecessors. No predecessor spent as much time and in various positions in the Department prior to his Superintendency as he did. Legislators knew him, Department employees knew him, the Board was familiar with his work there, and many school superintendents had interactions with him. If knowledge of the Agency, the schools, the political environment, and the teacher education segment of higher education were critical to his success, he was prepared. The naysayers within the Department and the rural schools who were critical because of his lack of district superintendent experience and perspective, and thus unqualified for the job, were about to be proven wrong as Folks set out to show them the error of their judgment.[11]

As Folks was set to undertake the Department's leadership, he and Fisher were challenged by *The Oklahoman* to defend the rapid expansion in staff and the budget. Essentially, they, primarily Fisher, explained that growth was a necessary and expected result of new education laws and mandates. In January 1984 the situation was precarious with the state's economy in the doldrums and education funding was being curtailed, causing a reduction of one million dollars in the Agency's budget. Folks determined that was not going to hinder initiation of his ambitious reforms. Using his swearing-in ceremony at the Capitol as the venue, he outlined his reform ideas that would be included in a package for the Legislature by late fall. Assessment of student progress and teacher preparation for the classroom; improvement of instruction in mathematics, science, foreign languages, and computers; and a career ladder for teachers would constitute the emphasis of a reform initiative.[12]

Folks desired to increase the amount of time students spent in school by adding a year at the beginning of elementary school and more closely regulating high school attendance. He believed that if Oklahomans thought kindergarten accessibility were important, they would support mandatory attendance and the lowering of the required age to attend from six to five. At the secondary level he supported a more restrictive, Board-approved, regulation setting the maximum number of student absences permitted for participation in extracurricular activities. As might be expected, and similar to the outcry in 1962, the most vociferous parent and educator opposition voiced at a hearing in September originated with the rural schools, and especially from the agriculture advocates who saw the restrictions infringing upon local district prerogative. The Board held firm on a 4-2 vote, supported by the director of the Vo-Tech system, Francis Tuttle. Folks was highly committed to upgrading the expectation of increased student classroom attendance, believing one's presence was imperative for maximum learning.[13]

Completing the reform package was a proposed statewide testing program. Never before had the state attempted to test all students at certain grade levels; rather, it was deemed local prerogative and paid from the district's budget. Under the Department proposal all students in grades three, seven, and eleven would be examined using a criterion-referenced test followed by a randomly-selected group of 2,000 students at each of the three grade levels completing a norm-referenced test so the results could be compared with other states.[14] Not known then, but evident later, this experiment with testing would explode into testing schemes costing tens of millions of dollars annually. In spite of the comprehensive testing regime over the next thirty years, Oklahoma's norm-referenced test results have not reflected improvement relative to the national average.

By mid-July 1985 unsolicited laudatory comments coming his way and the results of his efforts boosted his confidence: "Educational leadership in Oklahoma rests with the state superintendent. This office has to be the focal point of leadership and the public schools should look to our office for direction."[15] Simultaneously he had weathered blistering comments and opposition for his support of the Board's upgrade of the classroom attendance regulations. Also, he led the effort to create learner outcomes for grades one to eight and the beginning of an evolution that would lead to a parental revolution in less than a decade. Folks's optimism after his first year in office was aided significantly by the Legislature's increased appropriations for schools. Overcoming a history of inconsistent and somewhat paltry financial support with a relatively generous infusion of funds sparked enthusiasm.

Consolidation of school districts, highly unpopular with rural schools, was never a priority with Folks who focused his attention on curriculum, testing, instruction, teacher compensation, and the high school to college transition. His support from the rural schools was tentative at best, and he did not hesitate to propose reforms that he surmised would alienate them further. He knew the topic of consolidation was a political minefield, but he advocated for an open transfer policy that would potentially achieve a similar result. Regardless, the number of school districts operating was less concerning to him than was the quality of the curriculum offered to students and the level of achievement gained.[16]

Table 15.1 provides a statistical portrait of the status of education during Folks's tenure when almost no change occurred in the number of school districts and only a slight reduction of Department employees was evident. Teacher numbers initially increased but then declined overall by slightly more than 600, the same pattern as student numbers that ultimately dropped approximately 6,500. There were fewer teachers, students, and a minimal decrease in Department employees, yet the budget's growth of 10 percent continued the direction existing under his predecessor. A cursory glance at these data

Table 15.1 School district and Department data 1984-1988

Year	ADM	T/Ad*	DE†	No. of districts††			Department expenditures†		
				K-8	K-12	Tot.	State	Federal	Total
84-85	614,082	39,903	564	156	457	613	15,853,794	4,389,017	20,242,811
85-86	617,931	40,889	560	156	457	613	17,614,347	4,707,534	22,321,881
86-87	612,723	39,653	547	156	456	612	15,427,450	4,413,034	20,858,856‡
87-88	607,738	39,281	552	155	455	610	17,068,074	4,711,657	22,374,904‡

Sources: Annual Reports 1984-85 through 1987-88, Box 16, Oklahoma Documents Collection, OSA, ODL, OKC.
Note: ADM—average daily membership, T/Ad—teachers and administrators, DE—Department employees.

* *Annual Report 1987-88*, vol. 2, 83, 84.

† *Annual Reports: 84/85*, vol. 1, 59; *85/86*, vol. 1, 48; *86/87*, vol. 1, 52; *87/88*, vol. 1, 356.

†† *Annual Reports: 84/85*, vol. 3, 2; *85/86*, vol. 1, 114; *86/87*, vol. 2, 89; *87/88*, vol. 2, 89.

‡ Includes state revolving and state dedicated funds: 86/87, $637,123 and $381,249; 87/88, $590,607 and $4,566.

could arouse suspicion about why a significant increase in expenditures, a trend that laid the groundwork for some of the problems encountered by Folks's successor, occurred when there was a corresponding decrease in the numbers of students and teachers.

Folks was more concerned with substantive reforms than with attempting to explain the growing discrepancy between increasing expenditures and fewer students and teachers. He relied on his ability to explain the symbiotic relationship between legislative mandates and Department services and based his success on his tenacity to get things accomplished by refusing to show any temerity in dealing with the Legislature or rural schools. Folks proved to be a bridge that spanned his predecessor's success based on the political support of the rural constituency to that of the next elected successor's support generated from the urban areas and business sectors. Fisher's and Sandy Garrett's backgrounds were essentially rural, but neither was quite as dismissive of the rural schools as Folks. Garrett shared Folks's priority of what was desired. Different from Fisher and then Hoeltzel, with their rural power bases, Folks appealed to the city and larger school districts and sought support from the urban areas and business sectors. Not inconsequential, both Folks and Garrett had no prior school district administrative experience and both had several years within the Department to develop their understanding of the agency.

As Henry Bellmon was gearing up for his second gubernatorial term late in 1986 after a twenty-year hiatus, he set in motion Oklahoma's recently created cabinet system by naming Smith Holt, Arts and Sciences Dean at OSU, to be the Secretary of Education and directing him to coordinate the three branches of the state's education system. Holt excelled in this bully pulpit in part because it allowed him to espouse his highly critical opinion and assessment of the preparation of teachers. He served at the pleasure of the Governor who gave him wide latitude regarding what he could do and say. Aggressive pursuit of his agenda achieved mixed results because of the constitutional and statutory structures of the education branches. It was difficult to force cooperation and achieve effective compliance, and Holt was only the first to experience frustration with such a herculean task as subsequent Secretaries have discovered.[17]

Folks's leadership at the Department began nearly the same time as the US Department of Education released *A Nation at Risk*. Viewed by many primarily as a political document, but highly touted as an accurate description of the nation's schools and a blueprint for the future, the report generated a massive amount of discussion regarding how the public schools were failing and what action should be taken. The report's release resulted in states examining their schools and creating various approaches to improvement. For Folks, it confirmed his convictions and affirmed his call for reform, necessary prerequisites for success in implementing change. Viewing his election success as a mandate for continuation of his energetic push for improving the schools, he was explicit in his recommendations. Below par performance on middle school tests was proof that standards should be increased. Many students who wrestled with below level reading competence should be required to take reading courses. If more students were competent in reading, they would score higher on achievement tests.[18]

Oklahoma in 1982 was the first state to require curriculum examinations for prospective teachers, but other states soon followed. Five years later scrutiny of that hurdle to the profession portrayed a not-so-pleasing picture of its status, and Oklahoma was a prime example of the dismal situation. Wide variations in pass rates among various subject areas were evidence of inconsistency in difficulty of items. Questioned was how the exams were graded and scored, including the essay portions. Folks was a strong advocate of the exams as a filter to bar incompetent persons from entering the profession and believed, in spite of the analysis and critique, that that assessment measure's overall effect was worthwhile.[19]

What proved to be Folk's last salvo for significant reform was carefully packaged into "Our Children's Future: Programs for Progress" and presented to the Governor and Legislature in late December 1987. He never entertained the idea that his plan was a chimera. He had not lost his enthusiasm for quantifying educational achievement and holding schools accountable regardless of the socioeconomic status of their students and communities. Pressing his point, he said the minimum number of units should be raised from twenty to twenty-two with thirteen core and nine elective, one semester of reading instruction in the seventh and eighth grades would be mandatory, student transfers between districts would need the approval only of the receiving districts, and capping the reforms would be a statewide assessment and comparison of all school districts: graduation and dropout rates, test results, and student socioeconomic backgrounds. He frequently expressed the adage that "what gets measured gets done."[20] Folks's educational philosophy and quantitative mindset meshed easily with that of the national administration of the 1980s where the most important educational endeavors were those that could be measured. By thus narrowing the curriculum, it was only logical that curriculum would be aligned with the tests. Testable standards needed to be designed. Overlaying a for-profit, business model on the nonprofit, services model was selected to be the prod for greater results. Competition would spur teachers, administrators, and boards to improve schools; thus, tests were necessary, so schools could be compared and graded.

Not to be deterred, and not concerned with school official or parental reactions, Folks pressed on. By the time the Legislature convened he urged lengthening the school year by ten days and initiating a three-tiered diploma plan. Secretary Holt, nearing the end of his brief time in that role, chimed in to say that schools must do more to serve students on both ends of the learning continuum. With great passion, lots of energy, consistent vision, political acumen, and dogged persistence, Folks pursued his reform agenda. In the end, legislator opposition and inertia, inconsistent and inadequate state revenue, and focused hostility to reform proved too successful and kept him from considering other options within his role. Consequently, June 15, 1988, he sent his resignation letter to Governor Bellmon expressing his pleasure at being able to serve the state and announcing his employment as superintendent in the Mid-Del schools "in order to place me closer to the classroom."[21]

Folks's indefatigable pursuit of his reform agenda did not go unnoticed by the *Tulsa Tribune*: "Folks has not always succeeded in his efforts for school reform and better school financing. But his straightforward presentation of school needs has been refreshing." Continuing, "He has set a pattern for real leadership in the state superintendent's office…For all our sakes, Gov. Bellmon must find someone other than a chair-warmer to hold that position until the 1990 election."[22] The nature of the position and the political ramifications precluded the Governor from succeeding in his quest in spite of the *Tribune's* prescience.

From his tenure in the Department prior to being appointed Superintendent Folks was fully informed of Fisher's intent to advance women to upper management positions to achieve some parity within the agency. An intent clearly stated, unfortunately, did not materialize into significant results under Fisher. When handed the reins, Folks assigned strategic priority to hiring women. In his short tenure, he compensated for the historical negligence by identifying key women and intentionally promoting them to positions to match their potential and competence. Folks engaged in incremental promotions by assigning women to human relations and curriculum positions, typically viewed as appropriate for women, but not to deputy superintendent or administrator of finance or law, domains favorable to men (see chapter 6).

With his resignation public and before his final day in the office, Folks lamented the state of the economy and the failure to fund schools sufficiently. What was imperative was a sound, sustainable tax structure that would provide funds to schools to accomplish their mission. Also, public attitudes, while they could be forward-looking, were none-the-less colored by their fear of the unknown, particularly in small rural districts. About 500 districts fit this category, neither an insignificant number nor a minimal political force. These districts feared an open transfer policy, and Folks was convinced of the prudence of offering options to force some competition.[23]

Regardless of the mixed success of his reform agenda, and the rigor of campaigning for the office, his tenure as the top public servant in the education sector was the most satisfying and fulfilling of the various employments of his career. It was exhilarating to be at the pinnacle of the profession and to move resources toward improving the educational environment for the students and the teachers. Conversely, it was detrimental to his ability to be a father to his sons at a critical age of their maturation and development. To resign mid-term and thus disappoint those who campaigned for him and those who placed their faith in him was excruciatingly difficult, the most difficult decision of his career.[24]

Ex-officio Contributions

In his role as an *ex-officio* member of the Commissioners of the Land Office in the mid-80s the most challenging issue was whether or not to sell the state-owned land and mineral rights. The precipitous drop in energy prices devalued the royalties and the amount of money available to the education fund, and pressure mounted on the Commissioners to liquidate some of the assets. Folks objected to any quick fix in favor of a longer perspective. Historically, the energy industry experienced booms and busts so, as far as Folks was concerned, selling assets during a bust was not prudent. Instead, the Legislature needed to develop a taxation scheme that would provide, to the extent possible, a consistent stream of revenue.[25]

While serving *ex-officio* on the Board of Regents for Oklahoma Colleges, presidencies opened at three universities and focused Folks's time in the filling of those vacancies. Adjusting budgets and operating with fewer resources consumed most of the regents' time, but this experience provided insight into the curricula of the teacher preparation programs at the several universities and helped prepare him for a brief tenure several years later as Dean of the School of Education at Southwestern Oklahoma State University. In general, he believed that these institutions should be preparing higher qualified teachers and that improvement would result from mandating certification exams and publicizing the scores by institution.[26] By the mid-1980s other curricular departments on the campuses (e.g., engineering and business) were increasing their strategies to recruit bright female students with the tantalizing potential to earn greater compensation in employment, thus resulting in teacher education programs being challenged more-so in the recruitment competition.

As *ex-officio* chair of the Career Technology Board Folks was able to learn and view all of K-12 and career technology in one unified form. Fifteen years as a separate agency was more than enough time to develop into a well-established branch of the total education system. No doubt the most important action the Career Tech Board took during Folks's leadership was to hire Roy Peters to replace the retiring Dr. Francis Tuttle, the "father" of the career tech system. Peters, an associate director in the Vocational Education Division with responsibility for the Area Vocational-Technical Schools and Training Services unit was the logical choice of the Career Tech Board. For Folks it was extremely satisfying to be part of the acknowledged best career education system in the United States and to provide leadership in that branch of education. Especially rewarding was leading that board when it chose Tuttle's successor.[27]

A Need to Campaign to Keep the Office

Hotly contested elections for the top education official were anomalous for the forty-year period from 1946 to 1986. Multiple contenders vied for the position in the mid-1940s and then, for the next four decades, with the exception of 1970, oftentimes no Republican filed for the office or filed and then opted not to campaign actively. Folks's tenure at the Department included the 1978 and 1982 elections where he observed that having no opposition or no credible opposition allowed Fisher to breeze through the election period with little interruption to his regular duties. With Fisher's resignation, a smooth transition to his assumption of the office, and two years to push for his reforms, Folks hoped that he would be able to avoid any competition in 1986 that might slow or de-rail his efforts to implement his agenda.

No one gave any early indications of contesting for the office. As late as the first day of the filing period there was no announcement. By mid-day of the third and final day July 9 Folks was thrilled and filled with anticipation of not having to contend for the position that he believed was rightfully his. After all, he had espoused multiple reform ideas in the previous five years and believed he was politically astute enough to bring those ideas to fruition. Late that Wednesday afternoon Folks was prepared to celebrate his good fortune in not having drawn any opposition and not having to mount a campaign when, much to his disquietude and surprise, he learned that a Republican filed for the office. That someone had the audacity to contest the office when he was performing so admirably created a palpable frustration and anger. Quite possibly a sense of entitlement had crept into his thinking and clouded his judgment.[28]

Unknown and new to the political arena, David Evans, high school principal at Billings, Bellmon's hometown, filed. Earlier that afternoon Evans received a phone call from the state Republican headquarters requesting him to file for the office and offering to pay the filing fee. That party in those days was struggling for relevance but still wanted candidates to contest all positions. With little thought and no planning, he consented, drove to Oklahoma City and completed the application, and then almost immediately rued his decision. He would need to run a campaign for which he had no forethought, preparation, experience, or fortitude.[29] Evans was not going to win the election, and he became a sacrificial lamb for a weak party whose primary objective was winning the Governorship but wanting candidates to compete in the other executive offices. With Bellmon running Republicans were hopeful he would win and have coattails long enough to carry other offices.

Folks quickly organized his campaign and raised in excess of $80,000 over the next several months to support the printing of stationery and flyers, to buy billboard space, and to purchase television ads.[30] His campaigning was slightly different from previous Superintendents, in part, because he had never been a district superintendent and he did not have the kindred spirit. He believed he would win the election, but he wanted to ensure that he would be the victor. To win, it would be crucial to broaden his political message to appeal to voters beyond the public education arena. Advancing media opportunities, quite expensive, became more critical to communicating with the public. With cash flowing in, he was able to diversify his communication strategies. Studying history, he could have assumed some confidence in the fact that no one other than a Democrat had previously been elected to the position. Voter registration was approximately two to one in favor of the Democrats and the Superintendency was considered a down ticket position. However, Bellmon, who won with 55 percent of the gubernatorial vote in 1962, was, after a hiatus of twenty-four years, eight of which he represented Oklahoma as a Senator in Washington, DC, running for the top position once again.[31]

Evans was critical of Folks and accused him of improperly involving school superintendents in his campaign by having them work on his political behalf. Folks had sent a letter in early August asking superintendents for support. In defending his action, Folks said he sent the letter to his county campaign chairmen, most of whom just happened to be superintendents, proving yet again the advantage of the incumbent over the challenger in that murky area of acceptable ethical behavior while electioneering. School superintendents typically supported the candidate they estimated most likely to win and, in 1986, they did not deviate from that vantage point.[32]

Bellmon's campaign gave hope to the Republicans that they might be able to capture other positions. Disappointment was their misfortune for he won narrowly and all of the other executive offices went to Democrats. Folks garnered 61 percent of the 864,120 votes cast after a robust campaign while Evans received 39 percent sans campaigning, proving once again that for a perceived secondary, relatively-unknown position, voters hued to the party ticket. Folks would have won had he spent no money and not even campaigned. However, by aggressively seeking to remain in the position, he had a platform from which to defend his reform efforts and to convince the public and Legislature that he was moving the education establishment in the best direction. Affirmed by the public's support, and that of *The Daily Oklahoman*, he continued his reform efforts relentlessly. He had been distracted by an onerous, four-month political campaign, and now he had four years to etch his mark permanently on Oklahoma's education system. Evans, on the other hand, eventually served as principal in two other districts before departing the state permanently. He soured over the election process, was threatened with professional blackmail through middle-of-the-night harassing phone calls in violation of federal election statutes, and believed that the Democrats had railroaded him, with some good reason.[33]

A year after Folks was appointed to the Superintendency and the same length of time before running for the office, he expressed his opinion that the office should be elective rather than appointive to make that person accountable to the public. Hindsight, gained from his appointment and election in Oklahoma, and superintendent employment in Texas where the commissioner was a gubernatorial appointee, refocused his perspective considerably to where he now believed the Superintendent should be appointed by the Board regardless of whether the Board is elected by the people or appointed by the governor.[34] Folks's vacillation on the method by which the Superintendent should be chosen was no different from others whose perspectives have changed subject to the specific conditions at the time.

A Circuitous Path to District Superintendent

"I want to be closer to seeing actual progress in the classroom, closer to the teaching and learning process," quipped Folks, announcing his resignation June 14, 1988, to become superintendent of the Mid-Del School District.[35] Intriguing is this statement particularly since he was a math teacher prior to going to work in the Department and had the opportunity to do just that. No doubt at least two other factors entered into the consideration: an increase in salary from $55,000 to $76,000 and never having to campaign in a reelection bid. Rare was it for someone in the 1980s to be hired for a district's highest position with no building or upper-level district administrative experience.

After six years at the Mid-Del district, he shifted direction and broadened his resume as Dean of the School of Education for three years at SWOSU before leaving Oklahoma for Texas. With his career moves and experience, the presidency of one of Oklahoma's regional universities would have been an attractive draw, but by then, the pattern in Oklahoma was changing. District superintendents were no longer competitive for presidencies, although he offered a variation of that with his deanship. An opportunity for him to return to a superintendency came from the Spring Independent School District near Houston. Folks continued his career as the superintendent there for five years and then topped off his career with a decade-long stint at the rapidly growing Northside Independent School District near San Antonio. In retirement he lives in the San Antonio area with his wife Wyvonna, a high school classmate he married June 27, 1969. Their two sons and families reside in Oklahoma.[36]

Chapter 16
Hoeltzel: Grappling with Excess in the Department
(1988-1991)

Folks's rather abrupt resignation forced Governor Bellmon into searching for a replacement within a short timeframe, a situation reminiscent of twenty years earlier in 1968 when another Republican governor needed to appoint someone to complete the unexpired term of Oliver Hodge. Then Governor Bartlett sought a Republican, rural school superintendent who would eventually decide to seek a full term. Complicating Bellmon's predicament in 1988 was that not only did he need a Superintendent, but it was also imperative that he named a Secretary. Secretary of Education was a critical office and, because his first appointee Smith Holt, who had never been confirmed by the Senate, just resigned after serving for a year, Bellmon was faced with two appointments. He interviewed Sandy Garrett for the Superintendency; but then, with additional thought and pushback from Republicans who did not wish to have a Democrat appointed to an elective position, he named her to be Secretary, leaving him with the challenge of finding a Superintendent.[1] For the sixth time since 1927, a governor needed to name a Superintendent to complete an unexpired term.

Bellmon reportedly considered several people for the position as *The Oklahoman* speculated about who might be named. Current and former politicians, county and district school superintendents, and his former Secretary Holt were possibilities, as were employees of the Department. The legislators hailed from northwestern Oklahoma while the superintendents were from across the state. Smith Holt, a Republican, pursued the opportunity briefly but had to reconsider after he discovered he was ineligible because he did not meet the ten-year residency stipulation. Clarence J. Oliver Jr., PhD, a long-time Broken Arrow superintendent, was currently serving his second term as a member of the State Board of Vocational-Technical Education. He first was appointed to that Board by Governor George Nigh, a Democrat, and then re-appointed by Bellmon. Oliver's notable professional stature earned him the attention of governors so it was not unusual for him to receive a phone call requesting him to consider assuming the vacant post. He was a conservative, registered Democrat, and the Governor showed his commitment to find the best person regardless of political affiliation. Bellmon needed a savvy Superintendent who was well known among district administrators, school business officials, and school board members across the state and at the national level.[2]

Oliver met with Bellmon to discuss the possible appointment and the educational objectives that Oliver had been seeking through legislative initiatives and that he most likely would pursue if chosen Superintendent. He was a proponent of a year-round school plan, or at minimum increasing the school year to 200 days, with twenty additional days for professional development, increasing the length of the school day to seven periods, and requiring all extracurricular activities and athletic practices to be held before and after school hours. Oliver had already led the Broken Arrow district to shift to an outside-of-school-day schedule for all extracurricular activities and practices and to require all students to enroll in six class periods, but his preferences for these arrangements were not shared by rural school district superintendents and rural citizens. While Oklahoma's school year was one of the shortest of the fifty states and the in-school extracurricular activities scheme was practically unique in the country, they were acceptable outside of the urban areas. Bellmon, an extremely adept politician, was keenly aware of the rural perspective.[3]

Having briefly offered his educational objectives and aspirations for the schools and the students, Oliver then opined that the Superintendency should be appointive rather than elective so that the person could focus on educational issues rather than spending time and energy on raising money to get reelected. He indicated his willingness to complete the unexpired term if the Governor would seek a constitutional amendment to make the position appointive and legislative change to require the Superintendent to also serve as the Secretary. When Bellmon replied that he did not believe he could accomplish these changes in the executive office, Oliver thanked him for consideration. Oliver rejected the offer more because the office was elective, not appointive, and less because of the expectation that he would run for the office in 1990.[4] Oliver's ingrained philosophy of designing the state's education system to benefit students provided the foundation for a great distaste of the politicization of education.

Bellmon's pursuit of Oliver informed him of the urban perspective, but failure to gain Oliver's acceptance forced Bellmon to widen the talent pool for his recruitment to leaders of small school districts. He settled on a little-known superintendent in a nondescript town in conservative, northwestern Oklahoma, Gerald Hoeltzel of Watonga. If anyone represented rural education in Oklahoma, it was Hoeltzel who when he received the call from Bellmon was preparing for the opening of another school year in a district with declining enrollments and about seventy teachers. Hoeltzel and Bellmon had never met previously although they had commonalities: both were farmers from rural areas of northwestern Oklahoma and members of the Republican Party. Hoeltzel gained visibility among school administrators in his quadrant of the state through his leadership in the mid-1980s to protect the gross production tax from redistribution to the metropolitan areas. The oil boom of the late '70s and early '80s left school districts in that part of the state flush with money, and they did not view favorably the efforts of the Oklahoma City legislators to shift some in their direction. Hoeltzel led the Northwest Oklahoma School Officials Association to organize a protest at the Capitol and, by doing so, advanced his reputation as a leader among his peers.[5]

When the Governor summoned Hoeltzel to Oklahoma City to talk, not only did he desire someone to fill the unexpired term, but he also needed someone who could and would oppose legislators' efforts to get "pork." Bellmon, in his folksy approach, stated that he loathed lawmakers who tried surreptitiously or blatantly, for whatever reason, to secure money outside of the administrative process. Though not discussed, Hoeltzel thought Bellmon desired someone to continue the reform commitment of Folks. By accepting the invitation, he would have two years, until the mid-1990 primary election, to focus on the progress underway and exhibit the ability to reshape the Department to serve the schools more effectively. After two or three days of considering the Governor's offer, he resigned the Watonga superintendency to lead the Department for the next two and a half years at a salary of $9,000 over his current $46,000. He assumed the reins August 2, 1988, for the term ending January 8, 1991. By becoming the Superintendent, he was forced to share access to the news media with the Secretary who was to be paid $60,000 to assess an education system that included Hoeltzel's domain and to inform the Governor of ways to improve it. If there ever were a formidable challenge, Hoeltzel just agreed to try to succeed.[6]

Gerald Earl Hoeltzel's biography began with his birth December 17, 1934, at Carrier, Oklahoma, and continued with his playing basketball and earning a Bachelor's Degree in Geology in 1957 at Phillips University. While teaching he earned a Master's Degree in Education Administration at Northwestern Oklahoma State University in 1968. Teaching and administrative positions in the four small, rural school districts of Freedom, Tyrone, Covington and Watonga in northwestern Oklahoma comprised his resumé from 1958 to 1988. Now Hoeltzel, with assets in descending priority being political party affiliation, experience, and availability, was suddenly named to lead the largest of the three education agencies. He was perceived as a neophyte politician competing with a newly appointed Secretary who answered only to the Governor.[7]

In the end, Bellmon chose a person who was the epitome of those he would be leading, someone who could speak their language and understand their constituents, but the timing was inauspicious.[8] Citizens and teachers were clamoring for accountability and increased compensation, respectively, but Hoeltzel was optimistic he would be able to conquer the headwinds and deliver on a few significant reforms. Bellmon was not pleased with his selection options initially and his reservations about Hoeltzel were confirmed the longer the Superintendent was in office, but those perspectives were offset to some extent by the performance of Secretary Garrett.

An Almost Accidental Superintendent Struggles to Find Direction

Five hundred employees in the Department worked in various divisions administered by a deputy superintendent, three associate and five assistant superintendents. Under Hoeltzel's direction, the department was reorganized in 1989 with only minor modification at the administrative level: one additional associate and one less assistant superintendent. Subsequently, an external review recommended a major overhaul to lessen duplication and waste. That assessment by Gerald Bass, PhD, formerly a superintendent of small, rural school districts in North Dakota and Minnesota and now a professor at OSU, determined that a major change was imperative in the leadership structure and that the 527 employees (see table 16.1 for some slight discrepancy with official reporting of number of employees) could be reduced by at least 175. One deputy superintendent would be sufficient to direct the Department's overall operation while the Superintendent should work with the Board, Governor, and Legislature to represent the interests of all of the public education system. Hoeltzel resisted the recommendations of the external study that came in the middle of the 1990 election campaign and chose not to implement them. The consequence proved to be a significant nail in the coffin for Hoeltzel as he approached the November election.[9]

Twenty years of school district superintendent duties provided frequent interactions with Department personnel, thus Hoeltzel was not uninformed or naïve of the various functions and political environment in which the Department operated. Leading a Department whose employees were hired by his Democratic predecessors caused him little concern because he believed these educators to be dedicated regardless of political affiliation. Eventually when Hoeltzel discovered that the director of the north central accreditation unit eyed his position, he began to realize that he had both internal and external opposition and criticism.[10] As a lifelong Republican, he was cognizant of the difficulty he would encounter were he to run for the office in two years. More time to assess the political winds and to design at least a small reduction in the Department employee ranks could potentially have produced more positive results. To be a stalwart within his own party and be in good stead with the faithful, he needed to show strong leadership and courage, but exigencies prohibited a robust effort. Often, timing is critical for success and, in Hoeltzel's case, more so. A substitute, overshadowed by a Secretary flexing her muscle, and expectations of significant change blended for a perfect storm.

Gerald Hoeltzel
2012.201.B0553.0723, The Oklahoman, Oklahoma Publishing Company Photography Collection, Oklahoma Historical Society

Hoeltzel outlined his general direction in an interview with the editor of the *Oklahoma Educator* shortly after taking office. He would continue his predecessor's direction because he believed many innovative ideas germinated in the 1980s both at the Department and in the local schools should be permitted time to come to fruition. He said he would advocate for increased funding for the schools, some of which would be used to increase teacher compensation. Secretary Garrett, a couple of months later, laid out her ideas to *The Oklahoman.* There must be a decrease in the school dropout rate, a lengthening of the school year, more recruiting of minority teachers, a lowering of student-teacher ratios, and increased parent involvement in the schools. She advocated greater teacher involvement in the management of schools and tougher high school graduation requirements. All of these merited a refocused attention on K-12 schools, but not all were consistent with Hoeltzel's priorities, especially teacher involvement in the school's management. It was easy for the Secretary to articulate and advocate when not responsible for their implementation.[11]

Shortly after he took office, Hoeltzel's "pork" conversation with the Governor assumed real life when he received a "napkin list" request from a southern Oklahoma legislator. The Department had discretionary grant money available to school districts that completed the application process, and this legislator wanted to circumvent the process and be given priority. After Hoeltzel's denial of the request and subsequent nasty name calling, the Governor, privy to the events, called him to reaffirm his support.[12]

Outlined in Hoeltzel's first budget request in October were more money and higher salaries for teachers, a Technical Assistance Program to Support Effective Teaching that was targeted for grades one to three, phased in over three years, and specifically focused on low performing schools. By late November he announced the formation of a thirty-seven-member Teacher Advisory Council, a counterpart to the existing Superintendent Advisory Council. A little more than a month later he advocated creating a district report card. He was anxious to establish a pattern of pursuing innovations that would increase student performance and accountability that would communicate to parents his intent on raising test scores but not run afoul of teacher and administrator interests.[13]

The 1989 Legislature complied with his request by enacting the Oklahoma Educational Indicators Program to measure the performance of public schools and districts. Hoeltzel's enthusiasm for this "accomplishment" was dampened when Garrett succinctly assessed the Legislature's action, "Unfortunately, not much action has taken place." With little to hinder her commentary and much expectation that she would offer her thoughts, she launched into the necessity and value of district report cards so that the public could compare academic performance.[14] It was then only natural that the next reasonable step was to permit and encourage parental choice. For Hoeltzel's kindred spirits among the small, rural superintendents and public schools, these recommendations were anathemas that threatened their existence. For educators whose knowledge of the complexities of the learning process and the challenges facing schools enrolling students with various learning abilities and representing families from diverse ethnic, racial, and economic backgrounds, any accountability schemes that centered on one report card, were to be viewed with skepticism and alarm. Keen observers of the machinations of politics and government were given advance notice of the beliefs and persuasions of the person who was to become the next Superintendent.

Test results' significance in the summer of 1989 led Hoeltzel to announce that the Department would identify "lighthouse" districts and those that were "academically at risk." The former would be identified as models and studied to determine how they were achieving great success, some in spite of all odds, while the latter would likewise be studied to determine how extra guidance and counseling might help. In the "lighthouse" districts, teacher governance, administrative leadership styles, and parental input would be assessed to detect their influence.[15] Extensive and intensive examinations of school districts in subsequent decades show the quaintness of these rather superficial criteria, but the attention was misplaced without sharp focus on the quality of the instruction.

Hoeltzel had the unenviable duty to oversee a large bureaucratic department that provided services to school districts while nudging compliance with education standards, and accomplishing this in a political environment with the Secretary looking over his shoulder. A Secretary with no school district superintendency experience was now announcing to the media her notions of improving education across the entire spectrum of K-12, career tech education, and higher education. One commanded a bureaucracy and the other a microphone having an open-ended agenda. Partially because of, or in spite of, the efforts and actions of Hoeltzel, Garrett and others, a significant milestone was accomplished when the Legislature, in one of its finest moments, passed HB 1017 in 1990. Governor Bellmon defied his party when he pushed for a bill that raised taxes and infused a large amount of money into the schools to reduce class sizes and increase teacher salaries. The act afforded Hoeltzel the opportunity to reconfigure the Department for ease of implementation of the act's provisions, but the political campaign was foremost in his mind, and his experience and capability prohibited him from comprehending how to change. Rather, he incurred the wrath of politicians by stating that he would need sixty-seven additional employees to implement the bill.[16]

In recalling his greatest achievements three decades later, Hoeltzel described his efforts to expand early childhood options, increase opportunities for at-risk students, and allocate more funds to small, rural school districts. Hoeltzel's lengthy experience afforded him a comprehension and appreciation of the critical necessity of the services provided by the Department to districts with low net assessed valuations and lacking economies of scale. While there was plenty of money for most districts in his area of the state because of the tax revenues from the energy industry, they were a small segment of the state's rural schools. Under his administration, Department services to small schools became a priority, for the larger schools could more easily fend for themselves. As Superintendent he attended as many legislative committee meetings as possible to convey the Department's priorities and needs. By comparison, Hoeltzel said Fisher sent Folks as his spokesman rather than going himself.[17]

Table 16.1 provides a three-year portrait key to an understanding of Hoeltzel's administration. Statewide student enrollment increased 1 percent as the number of teachers grew by 5 percent. Passage of HB 1017 providing for smaller class sizes resulted in the need for additional teachers, the beginning of a trend of expanding costs across the state. Department personnel declined by 10 percent, about a third of what Bass recommended, while the number of districts was reduced by thirty-one, a 5 percent decline. For his brief time in office, district consolidation occurred at a rate faster than for his predecessors and successors, but that happened primarily without the Superintendent's affirmative support.

Table 16.1 School district and Department data 1988-1991

Year	Student enrollment	Ave. daily attendance	District personnel	Department employees	Number of districts		
					K-8	K-12	Total
1988-89	605,771	542,693	40,052	553	154	455	609
1989-90	604,276	543,170	40,659	535	152	452	604
1990-91	611,534	548,387	42,034	500	136	442	578

Sources: *Annual Report 1988-89: Statistics on Oklahoma School Districts*, vol.1, 351, vol. 2, 83-84, 89; *Annual Report 1989-90: Statistics on Oklahoma School Districts*, vol. 1, 341, vol. 2, 89; *Annual Report 1990-91: Statistics on Oklahoma School Districts*, vol. 2, 89, vol. 3, 15.

Notes: The State Department of Education had approximately 500 employees by June 30, 1991, but most of the reduction occurred under the new Superintendent during the first half of 1991. The *1990-91 Report*, generated by Sandy Garrett, discusses a restructuring where sixty-four positions were eliminated, twenty-two employees were transferred to another state agency, and an unspecified number of positions were created.

State funding for Department operations dropped slightly from the 1988-89 school year to the following school year, but was more than offset by an increase of one million dollars from federal sources and a substantial increase in the state revolving fund. Not displayed in table 16.2 are the respective sources for the third year of Hoeltzel's tenure, but it is safe to say that state funding increased considerably in 1990-91 from the mandates of HB 1017. In a caretaker status it would have been challenging for Hoeltzel to try to cause radical change, especially not knowing if he would be in office beyond the current term. He experienced precisely the reasons Oliver raised when he declined the offer from Bellmon.

Table 16.2 Sources and amounts of Department expenditures 1988-1991

Year	State	Federal	State revolving	Total
1988-89	18,485,326	5,549,613	542,828	24,577,767
1989-90	18,420,930	6,577,824	971,522	25,970,275
1990-91	n/d	n/d	n/d	29,107,027

Sources: *Annual Report 1988-89: Statistics on Oklahoma School Districts*, vol. 1, 351; *Annual Report 1989-90: Statistics on Oklahoma School Districts*, vol. 1, 341.

Notes: Department Annual Reports beginning with FY 91 discontinued including the *Department Agency and Support Expenditures*. Thus the total for this year was determined by summing the various categories as displayed in the *Governor's Executive Budget Historical Data* for 1991.

Hoeltzel's brief time in this high office gave him some limited insight into the Commissioners of the Land Office where he served *ex officio*. The oil boom had "busted," but a lot of money flowed into the Commission from royalties and the sale of mineral rights. Although he intuitively sensed that an insufficient amount of that money was going to the schools, he did not take the time to investigate. Lack of knowledge of the operation of the Land Commission and its vast assets hindered him from asking probing questions and providing any meaningful input into its operation. He trusted the secretary to the Commissioners to administer the agency within the legal parameters of the Constitution and statutes and free from political interference and favoritism.[18]

A Murky Crystal Ball

Indecision described Hoeltzel's political ambitions, and timing determined some of his public announcements regarding his plans. The amount of time between his appointment and the next election cycle equaled that of the average of the five previous Superintendents who were initially appointed so in that regard he was not placed in a unique situation. But the timing, the presence of a Secretary speaking freely, and the political pressure for downsizing the Department formed some headwinds. To his benefit the Superintendency invitation, and subsequent incumbency, caused a redirection in the trajectory of his career and opened doors previously unimagined. Bellmon wanted to appoint someone who would be interested in vying for the full term in 1991, an interest Hoeltzel no doubt shared with the Governor and expressed formally when interviewed for his appointment. By late November 1989 Hoeltzel decided his future was not to compete in the 1990 election for the Superintendency: "I don't feel I have the time or the inclination to run a statewide political race. It would be hard to win as a Republican. I am a realist."[19] Rather, he was considering an overture to run for the state senate or to continue pursuing the Elk City School District superintendency. Regardless of the direction, he still had more than thirteen months remaining in his current obligation.

Seven months passed before Hoeltzel declared his intentions. Neither the state senate nor the Elk City opportunity materialized, and his thinking on a run for his position evolved. What caused him to reconsider is at least partially known. According to Hoeltzel, it was because of the passage of the massive reform bill and the excitement of being able to lead the implementation of the reforms. However, winning a statewide race as a Republican would be no easier in November 1990 than he calculated in late 1989. Regardless, he would campaign from May to November while assuming his responsibilities as Superintendent.[20]

He understood the significance of *The Oklahoman* in shaping the thinking of its readers and believed its support was requisite to winning a statewide race. Early in the campaign he approached the editor to solicit the paper's assistance only to be rebuffed for a decision of several months earlier when a tie vote by the Board required Hoeltzel to declare his position. By casting the deciding vote to oppose consolidation and represent the interests of the rural schools and communities, it cost him the support of the state's most influential newspaper.[21] *The Oklahoman*'s position on consolidation to save money was well known then and has not changed since.

His renewed interest and announcement surprised at least one person, David Fisher, son of Les Fisher and a former employee of the Department who was fired by Hoeltzel for his public statements assessing the advantages and disadvantages of HB 1017. He was terminated also for allegedly campaigning for the office during the workday, giving credence to Clarence Oliver's prescience when he expressed the potential for such shenanigans and voiced his loathe of the political machinations. As in the several previous instances when Department employees left their positions to run against their former bosses, Fisher would be unsuccessful.[22]

While Hoeltzel was assessing the political landscape, Garrett was likewise for, in May, she announced she would not run only to change her mind five days later. Her reason for the decision reversal was that "she spent most of the weekend 'doing nothing but answering the phone' from supporters urging her to reconsider her decision. 'I was flabbergasted, to tell you the truth.'"[23] Hoeltzel delayed his filing as long as possible, providing further evidence of his ambivalence and waiting until the last day to announce his interest to run. Even then it was a question of which office would he seek. Immediately afterward he saw Garrett who said, "I'm glad you filed. You did file for the senate seat?" He stated he filed for the Superintendency.[24] Much to her chagrin, she would now have to wage both a primary and a general campaign. She hoped to have a relatively easy primary race and avoid any further campaigning, well aware that history was not favorable to the Republican Party's efforts to capture the office.

In the 1990 primary race Hoeltzel, age fifty-five, was an observer to the contest between Democrats Fisher, thirty-eight, and Garrett, forty-seven, both former Department employees: he as director of accreditation and she as director of rural programs, both mid-management positions. Fisher's campaign spent almost $68,000 in a losing effort where he captured only 36 percent of the vote. His primary mode of campaigning was placing ads on billboards. Garrett won two to one, primarily by buying advertising time on radio and television (see appendix J for campaign expenditures). The primary election over, she quickly focused on beating the incumbent in the general election.[25]

Hoeltzel ran a lackluster campaign that exhibited less than an enthusiastic interest. He detested having to ask people for money to support his campaign, so he refused to participate in fundraisers and spent only $14,818. He seemed to think the outcome was a fait accompli. Defeating Fisher in a general election was conceivable, but, when Garrett entered the race, he perceived her visibility as Secretary for two and a half years to be insurmountable. Also, by the election Hoeltzel had been chastised several times by *The Oklahoman* as anti-reform while she was praised for her calls for reform and expressed the goal of streamlining the Department to increase efficiency. Garrett's war chest allowed her to spend three times the combined amount of the Fisher and Hoeltzel campaigns. Also, in her favor was the fact that the majority of voters were registered Democrats and that party's candidates won the statewide offices in 1990. After Garrett garnered 72 percent of the votes, *The Oklahoman* offered this postscript for the outgoing Superintendent, suggesting that newly elected Governor David Walters not "Give a job to anti-reform Republican educator Gerald Hoeltzel."[26]

After the Limelight

Vacating his office did not mean Hoeltzel would have no good career options in his future. The Oklahoma City School District wanted to place him somewhere in their yet undecided administrative reorganization. Although he stated he had superintendent opportunities beyond the boundaries of Oklahoma, he chose instead to become the interim executive director of the Cooperative Council of Oklahoma School Administrators, an organization comprised largely of rural school administrators. Shortly thereafter, the Waukomis School District hired him to be its superintendent from 1991 to 1994, and then Barlow and Associates, Inc., a consulting firm assisting school districts in employee relations, contract negotiations, fiscal management, and other administrative duties, employed him until his retirement. This last stint found him working in school related services, primarily to small rural districts. With his career ended, he devoted his energy to enjoying time with his wife Mary Ann (Broome) whom he married before a justice of the peace in Medford in 1957, to running his farm near Carrier, and being the family patriarch.[27]

Chapter 17
Quintessential Politician Garrett: Maneuvering Through Two Decades
(1991-2011)

Stilwell, the county seat of Adair County located near the Arkansas border in northeastern Oklahoma, has been the home of famous outlaws and high-profile politicians. Of the former there were the James brothers and "Pretty Boy" Floyd, and of the latter long-tenured state representatives, W. H. Langley Sr. and Larry Adair who served as Speaker from 2001 to 2004, and the first female elected Superintendent, Sandy Garrett. The small town of approximately 4,000, five times its population in 1900, was once served by the Southern Belle (Kansas City Southern) passenger rail line, but now the major access is via U. S. 59 and Oklahoma 51 highways. Several industries and a major retail store provide commercial opportunities along with the signature strawberry production leading to the moniker Strawberry Capital of the World. On health, general welfare, and economic standards Stilwell compared poorly nationally and to similar towns in Oklahoma. In 2015 it had the poorest economy in the state and there were only 79.6 males for every 100 females age eighteen and older.[1] It was this geographical and cultural environment that formed the early impressions on Sandy Garrett.

From Small Town to the Big Time

Sandy's father W. H. Langley Sr. was born in Wauhillau, Indian Territory, about six miles northwest of Stilwell in 1900, graduated from high school in neighboring Westville, and decided to be a professional gambler in Fayetteville, Arkansas. He was athletic and competitive, wild in his young life, liked to box and fought to see who was toughest. After three years of living this lifestyle, he was urged by his father W. F. Langley to earn a living at a respectable occupation. When W. H. "reformed" (He could still be "mean as a snake.") and became a politician, he overcame quite a legacy. Government service seemed an attractive option seeing that the elder Langley was an alternate delegate to the Constitutional Convention and then was Adair County's first court clerk. W. H. sought, and was elected to, the office of county assessor where he served for six years before becoming the county treasurer for the following eight years. In the latter office he began to analyze financial concepts that formed the basis for his greatest achievement (see below) as a state representative from 1940 to 1960 with the exception of 1942-1944.[2]

Approaching age forty, W. H., a staunch Democrat, entered into marital bliss with Katy Lee Garrison, a bride of only sixteen and a die-hard Republican. She was a housewife with a high school education who taught Sunday School classes, and together they instilled respect in their children by example and expectation through the precepts of the

Ten Commandments, the Lord's Prayer, and the Golden Rule. Never to imbibe alcohol, she was the life of every party. This happy couple raised two daughters who became lifelong educators, the elder one Superintendent and the younger one an English teacher, and between them a son who was a businessman.[3]

Sandra Lee (Sandy) arrived February 8, 1943, in Muskogee, Oklahoma, just as her dad's state political career was budding. She attended Stilwell Elementary School except in the winter/spring of the odd numbered years when the Legislature was in session in Oklahoma City. Then, her father would pack up the whole family and move them to the capital city where the children were enrolled in the Oklahoma City Public Schools. Politics was an integral part of Sandy's growing up years for she traveled with her gregarious, suave, and debonair father to campaign speeches and rallies across the county. Sandy distributed flyers and bumper stickers along with other campaign materials. When they were homeward bound, what she had just experienced was a frequent topic of discussion. Her father was the most influential person in her life, and he imbued within her the strong conviction that one can be fiercely partisan while running for office but must be willing to reach across the aisle to succeed in political office. When Secretary she once told a reporter, "A lot of them don't know whether I am a Republican or Democrat."[4]

Significant to W. H.'s legacy, and that of Stilwell, Adair County, and northeastern Oklahoma, was a Cherokee heritage. He, and his father, were proud members of the Cherokee Tribe and eligible for all of the benefits afforded to tribal members. Sandy inherited that legacy and carried a tribal card showing her blood quantum at 1/64. Pride in her heritage as a Cherokee was rooted in part in the extent to which her ancestors overcame the forced liquidation of their assets in Georgia because having Indian blood precluded land ownership. The more recent ancestors survived the arduous journey to Oklahoma, initially by rail, and then by horseback from Van Buren, Arkansas. Pride of original success in Georgia and prevailing over obstacles while migrating to start a new home in Indian Territory mixed to form a respectful attitude and stance. Those who have succeeded in Oklahoma appreciate the struggles and feel a sense of obligation to help their tribal brothers and sisters to achieve likewise.[5]

Sandy was involved as a typical teenage girl, in the late 1950s/early 1960s, high school milieu, and then college. As a senior at Stilwell High School she was band and basketball queen attendant, majorette, member of student council, president of the Future Homemakers of America, and editor of the Big Chief Newsletter. Succinctly put, she wanted to be the "queen bee" in her world with an ambition to major in home economics in college. Leaving the protected world of small town Stilwell upon high school graduation in 1961, Sandy enrolled at OU to join her boyfriend, John C. Garrett, who had matriculated a year earlier. Marriage and the birth of their son interrupted her studies briefly.[6]

After a hiatus of about three years, Sandy pursued her Bachelor's degree in Elementary Education and then a Master's degree in Counseling and Guidance at NSU, earning the degrees in 1968 and 1980, respectively. In this twelve-year span she taught at Hilldale Public Schools before beginning a two-year stint in 1980 as that district's gifted programs administrator. Prior to the latter assignment, she honed her political skills as the teachers' negotiator at the contract bargaining table. Her son's graduation from high school gave her the freedom and flexibility to accept a position in the Department that entailed some travel across the state so she moved to Oklahoma City and assumed the responsibility of assisting with the coordination of the Department's gifted and talented programs. Hired initially by Les Fisher, Sandy devoted her full energy toward strengthening the Department's oversight of the growing programs for the state's gifted and talented students. From her childhood days she knew what it was like to attend schools where instruction was to the whole class without extra resources for the most capable students. Her experience at Hilldale involved students who were of above average intelligence and capable of benefitting from a richer learning environment than was typically available. Part of her role in the Department was giving technical assistance and in-service programming to local school districts to expand and enrich educational opportunities for qualified students.[7]

When Folks became Superintendent in mid-1984, he committed to hiring women in administrative positions within the Department. So, when the director of rural education position opened late that year, Garrett was deemed most capable to lead this section that was growing in importance because of the desire of the Legislature to enhance the curriculum and educational opportunities for students in small, rural schools. Exciting and innovative technologies such as satellite delivered instruction were becoming accessible to schools with limited enrollments and resources. The director would be on the cusp of a new era with promising opportunities, and it did not hurt that the Legislature appropriated one million dollars for small school cooperative grants. Garrett's enthusiasm and competence convinced Folks that she was the best director he could find, and for two years she led this program.[8]

A re-organization of the Department in 1987 created a subdivision of Educational Services led by an executive director. Several of the programs previously under Garrett's authority were grouped into this enlarged unit along with media and library resources. Her title and salary were upgraded commensurate with the more expansive authority. She was not long in this position before Governor Bellmon came looking for replacements for Folks as Superintendent and Smith Holt as Secretary. The Governor considered Garrett for the Superintendency, but eventually selected her as Secretary and Hoeltzel as Superintendent.[9]

Honing Political Skills as Secretary of Education

Garrett was tabbed from a lower echelon of relatively unknown administrators in the Department than what the Governor would have had to choose, but his preference was Garrett and she was named. Plucked from a seemingly obscure position, she was announced as the Secretary to exercise oversight of the three major segments of education in Oklahoma: common schools, career-technical education, and higher education. Bellmon advocated for rural schools and needed someone with a similar conviction to expand curriculum options to these schools. He was aware of her work and deemed her savvy and most proficient to facilitate his efforts to improve education.[10]

Bellmon invited Garrett to his office to discuss the Superintendent vacancy and, during the "interview," she informed or reminded him that she was a registered Democrat. The experienced politician that he was, he assured her he was aware of her political affiliation and said she could have a little time to consider the offer. Whether they discussed the twenty-first legislative session in 1947 when he and Sandy's father served together in the House is unknown, but not long after she returned to her office, he called again, this time asking her to serve as Secretary instead.[11]

Not only was she not well known, but she was also succeeding Smith Holt, a Republican who was a dean on-leave from OSU and was a highly visible and vocal critic of public schools and teacher education programs in the universities. At the same time, he advocated satellite-delivered instruction especially to rural high schools, no doubt in part because his College of Arts and Sciences offered that format at OSU. The Governor gave Garrett the flexibility and support to tackle some of the more intransient challenges facing the educational establishment knowing that the three major segments functioned mostly independent of each other. With the Superintendent elected and the chancellor of higher education appointed by the State Board of Regents, the Secretary lacked any real authority. In the background, fellow resident of Stilwell, a House member, and eventual speaker of that body, Larry Adair, was quietly admiring Garrett's star rising.

With no prior experiential oversight or involvement in career-technical education or the higher education institutions in Oklahoma, she was now to be the "voice" of education and the Governor's advisor on all educational things. Marching orders were prepared for the Cabinet Council on Education with the overarching priority to "make Oklahoma's educational program…focused on excellence in all areas." Secretary Garrett was appointed chair of the council and announced that all meetings would be open to

Sandy Garrett
Courtesy of the Oklahoma State Department of Education

the public The educational resources were to be coordinated to develop a better delivery system for its citizens after "the curriculum needs, requirements and standards in all areas of education" were assessed. Her thoughts were that school buildings should be used longer than eight hours daily, preferably for adult programs in the evenings and after-school; expanded student enrichment activities; higher college tuition rates; and expanded high school senior concurrent enrollments. Vocational-technical schools and programs were not mentioned in this initial expression of her observations and analysis.[12]

Four months after her appointment, but still prior to her Senate confirmation, Garrett had time to assess the education landscape and better organize her ideas and priorities for new programs and upgraded practices from pre-school to the universities: early childhood programs for four-year-olds and full day kindergarten, increased college entrance requirements, expanded school management to include teacher voices, increased graduation requirements, and academic competition to parallel athletics. Preliminary estimates were favorable for an increase in funding at all levels, so it was apropos that she highlighted those aims and other possibilities: lengthening the school year, recruiting more minority teachers, improving teacher-student ratios and increased appropriations for OSU and OU.

Nowhere in her comments did she reference vocational-technical education and its relationship to common schools and the universities. It is understandable that she did not urge additional funding for Vo-Tech, for it had a solid tax base, but failure to connect it to the other two is mystifying. Five months later when queried by a reporter she stated, "Vo-Tech officials seem to be doing all the right things. We can be proud of that system."[13] It was exciting and exhilarating to capture the attention of a reporter for the state's major news organization and to delve into pressing needs of the education system without any budgetary or political constraints. She had a platform to shed light on the status of the state's education with no governing board or political constituency to mollify. It was an opportunity to test her ideas with the taxpayers and gauge their reactions in a climate favorable to improving education, albeit with accountability in expenditures.[14]

Her public pronouncements aligned well with the minority Republican agenda of nonpublic options with public money and the Democrats with more accountability from local school districts. For example, one idea for improving school districts was to create competition through a report card generated from a compilation of several assessments. Those districts deemed deficient would be given a warning and placed on probation with a subsequent "emergency plan of improvement." Open transfer options offered to students would force districts, especially small ones, to improve their curriculum and instruction.[15] Choice, as a concept within public schools, was evolving and had not yet achieved a frequent voice, but an expansion of that concept to include public funding of non-public schools was appearing on the horizon.

Garrett also spoke publicly about Oklahoma's higher education system that prioritized access over quality. Many factors have been integral to the evolution of that system, most crucially politics and the populism thread woven into the culture. Greater investment was essential in the two comprehensive universities if esteemed professors were to be valued and retained.[16] It seemed a mark of pride that tuition was lower than that in almost every other state so that admission was available to any student academically qualified. Neither OSU nor OU had yet begun to increase their minimum standards to levels comparable to similar universities in neighboring states. Possession of only a superficial comprehension of the administration of colleges and universities or the operation of the post-secondary system discouraged any more substantive commentary on its operation.

When the Legislature acted late in the session in 1989 to require high school seniors to pass competency tests in five areas beginning in 1992, Garrett deemed the decision a responsible one because it was one of her goals and because employers would know what competencies students possessed. Failure to achieve a passing score would result in the student receiving a certificate of attendance rather than a diploma. Superintendent Hoeltzel anticipated a major change in the way schools operated, but was supportive if more accountability would be accompanied by more funding.[17]

As 1989 slipped into 1990, several individuals were weighing the political landscape to decide whether or not to compete for the Superintendency. With the appointed incumbent suffering the indignation of severe criticism from *The Oklahoman* and announcing he would not be a candidate, the climate seemed favorable for a run by a moderate Democrat. Garrett initially declared she had no interest in mounting a campaign, only to reverse her decision after her supporters convinced her otherwise. Quite possibly she recalled memories of campaigning with her father, meeting his constituents, and sharing the thrill of winning, and she experienced firsthand the challenges of schools in impoverished rural communities. She was not the only one to have a change of heart, for Hoeltzel reconsidered likewise.[18]

Garrett's performance as Secretary convinced Governor-elect David Walters to reappoint her for his administration. While this may have made economic sense, it communicated a lot about how the Secretary's role was defined. If, previously, the Secretary and the Superintendent were two bona-fide positions, how could one person complete both roles' responsibilities? For *The Oklahoman* it was a positive move to save approximately $200,000 of taxpayers' money. Conversely, it acknowledged that HB 1017 omitted provisions for public money to support parental choice in non-public education and for the consolidation of school districts, closing a window of opportunity for the moment and minimizing the need for a Secretary's megaphone to advance the conservative newspaper's agenda. With minimal expectations for the Secretariat, Garrett focused on reducing the size of the Department while assisting school districts with implementing the reform act.[19]

With Democrat Governor Walters not seeking reelection in 1994, the door opened for the charismatic Republican Frank Keating to lead the state. The combined responsibilities of Secretary and Superintendent had evolved into a pattern unacceptable to the new Governor who preferred ruffling the feathers of the education establishment. Keating first chose Linda Murphy, but she failed to earn Senate approval. Next, he named Floyd Coppedge, a Democrat, who espoused public money for private schools and more accountability for secondary schools to reduce the demand for zero credit courses in higher education. Coppedge enunciated the specifics and Keating maximized the bully pulpit opportunity to criticize the common schools and the higher education community by condemning them for their mediocre efforts and results. Audacious to think he should have been permitted to sit at the table when the Board convened their regular meetings, the Secretary chaffed when not invited to do so.[20] Garrett was neither intimidated nor forced into indefensible positions, choosing instead to exercise her political acumen to diffuse situations and to maintain her acceptance level with educators.

Keating was oppositional, impatient, and offensive to the education establishment in his elitist efforts to attain his goals of obtaining public money for private schools, parental choice, and implementation of an academic curriculum that required all students to be college ready. Coppedge was to represent those efforts with intentional effect on the Department and the Superintendent's ability to do her statutorily-required duties. After two terms of the Keating administration Garrett was freed from the barrage of negativity and criticism, as well as any expectation to serve in a Secretary capacity, when Brad Henry was elected governor and chose not to name a Secretary. For the last eight years of her tenure, she was able to work with a moderate Democrat who was non-confrontational and who supported her actions and appreciated her efforts.

Two Decades of Political Engagement, a Pragmatic Democrat

When Garrett initially vacillated, but eventually decided she aspired to the position and was willing to expend her energies to achieve it, she calculated that Hoeltzel would be an unpopular candidate who represented the minority party and was viewed as ineffective. Bellmon was term limited. Likely, the Democratic candidate for governor would be successful, benefitting those Democrats down the ticket. An additional arrow in her expanding political quiver was having served as campaign manager for her boss, Folks, four years earlier and learned the "tricks of the trade."[21]

Year of the Novices: Election 1990

Three novices in directing their own election campaigns competed for the Superintendency in 1990: two in the Democratic primary and one on the Republican ticket in the general election. Candidate Garrett had a slight advantage gained in 1986. All three had the singular commonality of Department experience; Hoeltzel and David Fisher were currently employed and Garrett was from 1982-1988. Hoeltzel had his thirty-month record to defend while Garrett could continue to emphasize the positions she had staked out during the same time period. Fisher lacked a statewide reputation beyond the education community and faced an uphill battle to succeed in competing with the Secretary who had ready access to the media.

Fisher, hired in July 1985 as administrator in the North Central Accreditation office and son of former Superintendent Les Fisher, calculated the benefits he could accrue from name recognition in his quest for the office. Prior superintendent employment in the Paoli and Calumet school districts, and teaching and administrative experience at Elk City schools, burnished his credentials with the state's rural community. Five years supervising the accreditation of schools under two Superintendents gave him insight into the operation of the Department, and degrees in business education and school administration prepared him for work in schools as well as the ownership of a tree nursery.[22]

Garrett set out to change history and attain a level no other women had achieved, and only three attempted: election to the state's highest education office. Two women in 1926 and one in 1934 ran unsuccessfully on Republican tickets, but she was a Democrat, which increased her odds of success. From her vantage point as Secretary working for a respected and bipartisan Republican governor, she was able to gain name recognition and stake out her political position, most importantly offering more options to parents and students within the public schools. She was free to oppose the incumbent and emphasize his lack of leadership. Assisting as a campaign manager was a young, energetic, recent graduate of OU, Lealon Taylor, who would subsequently serve a key role in her administration.[23]

Hoeltzel also communicated ambivalence about his intentions, first running, then not, and running again. Did he really want the position and could he get the support of the Governor and the media? *The Oklahoman*'s critical commentary of his mediocre performance, even though he was a Republican and typically would have received a sympathetic ear, damaged his odds of success. He, like Garrett, was trying to make history, albeit by becoming the first Republican elected to the Superintendency.[24]

Critical to the politics was HB 1017, passed in the 1990 legislative session, a comprehensive law that was full of "reforms" in education. Governor Bellmon expended an immense amount of political capital to ensure its passage and funding, and he desired a highly competent person to lead the implementation of the bill's programs. Although Hoeltzel was a fellow Republican, the Governor was not confident of his ability to head the Department for a full four-year term. Conversely, Garrett performed admirably in her forward-looking role and deserved Bellmon's endorsement.

For the first time in twenty years, and only the second time since 1946, there was a Democratic primary election. Garrett had no difficulty dispatching Fisher who was fired by Hoeltzel after he received a letter from the Governor asking him to investigate reports that employees were allegedly campaigning on the job and opposing some provisions of HB 1017. Most people were somewhat familiar with the planks in her platform, and she had been honing her political and oratorical skills for three years. Fisher espoused a trite description of the status of education: "I feel we're at a critical crossword of education here in Oklahoma. Through the legislature, the people of our state are demanding a complete evaluation and required revamping of our entire educational system." Six months before the primary, he said he planned to continue his job in the Department and would campaign on weekends. When Hoeltzel announced he would not be a candidate, Fisher opted to throw his hat into the ring, knowing that his candidacy would not be oppositional to his boss.[25]

Fisher's termination from the Department freed him to campaign however he deemed best which meant that he could travel the state and appeal to the rural interests. He tapped into a reservoir of opposition to the reform bill that eventually would lead to an unsuccessful effort to overturn it in October 1991. Expenditures for Fisher's status quo campaign were considerable, amounting to $67,816. The strong rural support he gained proved insufficient to mount any serious opposition to Garrett who enthusiastically endorsed the comprehensive reform legislation and whose victory margin of twenty-eight percentage points buoyed her spirits for the upcoming general election. Advantageous to her was editorial support of the *Tulsa World*, "She has been a staunch proponent of education reform and has been in the forefront of efforts to improve the public education system."[26]

In late summer and early fall Garrett campaigned across the state, with nothing to defend and only to propose what she believed important. Hoeltzel, on the other hand, had to explain why the Department had so many employees, why its budget was excessive, and why he had no innovative ideas for school improvements. Somewhat incredulously, he said he would spend time in the schools helping them to administer services. He represented everything that many citizens in larger towns and cities wanted changed. She was forward looking and he was defending the status quo. She adopted the catchy slogan, "First by the Twenty-First," to encapsulate her goal of making Oklahoma the premier state in public education.[27] Anyone with even a cursory knowledge of Oklahoma's history, its populist tendencies, and the influence of the energy industry knew that her ambitious goal stretched credulity, but it was an appealing message.

Voters chose Garrett over Hoeltzel by a wide margin—71.5 percent to 28.5 percent. He raised a paltry $14,678 while her coffers overflowed with a remarkable $155,891 for the entire election season. Educators seeking financial support for campaign expenses face a daunting task because their strongest supporters typically do not have deep pockets. Sandy was no exception, but she had the support and commitment of many people including her savvy brother to scour the land for contributions. Success was achieved on the election night and she had a proven record of soliciting funds for her reelection campaign four years hence.[28]

Garrett ran a shrewd campaign and earned editorial support of the state's two largest newspapers; Hoeltzel had their derision, especially *The Oklahoman*'s. He suffered the ignominious fate of receiving the second lowest percentage of the vote as a Republican in a general election in the state's history. The election's three contestants were a harbinger of the next two decades when Garrett would attract at least one or more opponents in all of her efforts for reelection. A relatively easy competition the first go-round proved far different from what would materialize in the next election season.

Controversy Matters: 1994 Election

Four years later it was Garrett's turn to defend her record and convince the public that they had chosen well in 1990 by placing their confidence in her capability to change the Department and to improve the state's schools. When Governor Walters chose not to seek reelection because of pleading guilty to an election violation, she did not receive the advantage accruing from having a successful incumbent at the top of the ticket. Garrett also was subjected to a barrage of criticism from *The Oklahoman* because she was a Democrat and her teaching experience was in "government-funded schools," connoting inferiority and hostility to private schools.[29]

When Earl Garrison, formerly a professor at Rose State College and regional accreditation officer in the Department with solid credentials among the rural superintendents, and current superintendent of the Ft. Gibson school district, declared in March 1994 for the Democratic primary, he epitomized the waning influence of the good 'ole boy network with strong ties to rural schools where few women held superintendent positions. Pronouncements from Garrett's office celebrating the success of HB 1017 were met with skepticism, Garrison said, because insufficient time had passed to allow such unqualified positive assessments. Also, he believed the greatest parental concern was school violence, a topic he would address if he were elected. Garrett garnered the support of the *Tulsa World* for her reduction of the Department's budget and implementation of the reform package. Garrison's fund-raising efforts generated the inconsequential amount of $9,000 compared to the tens of thousands Garrett raised to supplement the $25,000 raised from her election four years previous and in the interim since then. She moved on to the general election, besting him by a 3-2 margin.[30]

Garrett was in for the political fight of her life that fall. Controversy swirled over the issue of outcomes-based education, and her Republican opponent, Linda Murphy, was waging a fierce battle. Still simmering among many citizens who resented the intrusion of the state into what was deemed local prerogative were the issues over HB 1017 and its attempted overturn, even though some of the legislative provisions were to improve schools through smaller class sizes and greater accountability. Murphy, a daughter of a Baptist preacher, earned a bachelor's degree in education from Southwestern Oklahoma State University. For several years she operated a private clinic specializing in aiding children with visually related learning challenges. A dark horse with only three years of public school teaching experience and no prior political engagement, Murphy chose a propitious moment to challenge Garrett in the general election. Believing that curriculum decisions should reflect a back-to-the-basics emphasis, she was opposed to "total inclusion" because it hindered other students' learning, a lesson learned as a special education teacher. But the catchall, defining term was "outcomes-based education" or OBE, and she was totally opposed to any radical education initiatives. Also, any talk of directing public money to nonpublic schools was irresponsible and against the US Constitution, a plank not favorable to the Republicans hoping to expand their influence.[31]

Republicans Frank Keating and Mary Fallin were running for Governor and Lieutenant Governor, both winning by pluralities. Of the other five executive positions, Democrats won three and Republicans two, some with narrow margins. A harrowing election all around, of the 978,115 votes cast, Garrett won by a mere 9,259. To keep her office and to fend off all opposition she spent about $180,000 while Murphy spent only about a third of that amount, $63,500, for the general election.

What was paramount in this Superintendency election was OBE. In the summer and fall of 1994 opposition to OBE was heated nationally with conservative Christian groups and organizations expressing alarm at the perceived loss of the pro-Christian philosophy they believed the Founding Fathers intended the nation to embody. Permeating the opponents' positions were misunderstandings of the concept, authenticity of outcomes and their measurement, and the roles of the federal and state governments in conjunction with local district prerogatives. Garrett staked her campaign largely on the benefits of Priority Academic Student Skills (PASS) and the necessity of implementing the program in the schools. Rather incredulously, she disavowed any connection to OBE, never having met or heard its creator; was critical of its alleged liberal slant, and contraindicated its use. Her first *Annual Report of May 1992* was a sufficient refutation of her subsequent denial. As she judged the changing political environment, she waffled and sought a compromise position, believing it necessary to be successful in the election. She was repudiated for her initial position when the Legislature rejected the standards. Post-election she announced unequivocally that OBE had "become an albatross around Oklahoma's neck." She had learned a critical lesson that would make her wary of supporting any future revolutionary ideas or schemes.[32]

Not long after the election, the Senate Education Committee in a controversial hearing rebuked Keating for nominating Murphy to be his Secretary when, by a vote of twelve to five, they rejected her. Not to be outwitted, he named her his education advisor. How the Governor believed Murphy could have been a successful Secretary with oversight of the Superintendent and Department is mystifying at best, but it did represent his antipathy toward public education. Furthermore, Keating, unlike Bellmon, would never have named Garrett to be his Secretary for any reason; such was the depth of his criticism for the work of tens of thousands of educators. All was not lost for Murphy, and her star continued rising, albeit slowly, when Keating appointed her over the next four years to several commissions. Then, in January 1998 Labor Commissioner Brenda Reneau appointed her deputy commissioner, but she resigned five months later to campaign anew for the Superintendency.[33]

Déjà vu: Election 1998

Early in 1998 *The Oklahoman* fired a tentative salvo in responding to Garrett's plucking the positive segments of a national report, praising her for the progress evident in the schools, but emphasizing the overwhelming evidence that the state was failing to get its money's worth. As usual, this was the pretext for its larger preference of parental school choice, inferring that public money would accompany such choice. Clarification of the contestants for the Superintendency occurred in the July filing period. Two Republican challengers would compete in the primary, but Garrett would benefit by not having to campaign until nearer the general election. No intrepid Democrat ventured to take her on in the primary. Directing her political effort and becoming chief of staff in the Department was the now thirty-one-year-old, Lealon Taylor.[34]

Linda Murphy's appeal had waned by 1998, drawing an opponent, but essentially an inconsequential one, when Tod Williams, a thirty-six-year-old superintendent of the tiny elementary school district of Garrett filed for the Republican primary. Only five teachers were employed in that isolated, rural district in Beaver County in the Panhandle, thus Williams's name recognition statewide even among Republicans was negligible. The results were a bit surprising when he spent little time and money campaigning yet he received 35 percent of the votes. His antipathy toward Murphy and her platform was so strong that, post-primary, he pledged his support to Garrett.[35]

Murphy was confident of the election outcome, only uncertain over how large the margin might be, claiming strong grassroots support across the state. She was excitedly awaiting the general election because she did not intend to lose again. Near success four years earlier and Keating's effort to get her into several positions and advance her career buoyed her hopes. By mid-September the challenger and incumbent were trying to distinguish their differences and the efficacy of their positions. On some issues they agreed: phonics being the preferred approach to teaching reading; desirability of charter schools; school choice, but opposition to vouchers; opposition to state-forced consolidation; more money for education with concomitant accountability; and support of student prayers in the public schools, but according to the law. Less earmarking of federal money and more state flexibility through block grants found common ground.[36]

They differed on the importance of the amount of money allocated actually being spent in the classroom (Murphy wanted more). Garrett opposed any scheme to direct public money to parents to choose a nonpublic option, but Murphy supported the concept, saying that tax credits would allow parents to use their own money. Also, Murphy alleged that over the past four years, no improvement was achieved in implementing and evaluating academic standards. Memory of the outcome of the election four years earlier caused anxiety and concern for Garrett. Contributions more than doubled to nearly $410,000 of which she spent about 85 percent compared to her nemesis collecting and spending less than 10 percent of that amount. Campaign rhetoric did not match the heights of the '94 election, for the incumbent was a more experienced if not chastened candidate. With the severest test of her political career in the background, she was a more calculating incumbent and savvier politician.[37]

Garrett appreciated the editorial support of *The Oklahoman* just three days before the election, even though it was qualified: she was moving in the right direction on educational reforms and deregulatory success and, with another term, would continue that commitment. Hardly a ringing endorsement, nonetheless, Garrett appreciated the critique of this influential newspaper, even if it were tempered. Voting results reverted to their historical pattern with the Democrat garnering 60 percent of the 863,561 votes cast and the Republican the balance. The split in the final results also mirrored closely the respective parties' registrations in 1998. Keating's reelection bid was successful, but his influence did not sway many to vote for Murphy whose recent history was littered with his failed attempts to get her a position in government. Garrett's and Keating's victory margins were nearly identical with the Superintendent actually receiving more total votes than the Governor.[38]

Opposition Wanes: Election 2002

The 2002 election, for Garrett, was absent the particular drama of her previous elections for she drew neither a primary opponent nor was challenged by Murphy or any other formidable candidate. Only one person filed on each ticket, leaving campaigning for early fall. Voter registration in the state was not trending in her favor with Democrats losing and both Republicans and Independents gaining. Her challenger dealt with his own issues, the race evolved into a nasty fight with dirty tricks on both sides, a lawsuit was threatened, and Garrett emerged victorious, but not untainted. Sufficient complaints were lodged that the State Ethics Commission sent a letter to all school superintendents advising them of conduct that violated the commission's ethics rules. No legal restrictions would have prohibited the Superintendent from preempting the ethics commission through a directive from her office ahead of the election season cautioning these public officials from temptations to cross any ethical barriers while campaigning for her, even for a minor offense such as affixing political bumper stickers to district owned vehicles.[39]

Challenging Garrett was a former assistant superintendent of the Western Heights

School District and current professor of education at the University of Central Oklahoma. In an early salvo months before the mid-summer filing period Lloyd Roettger, PhD, accused a Department official with illegal campaigning for the Superintendent. As the spring months of 2002 passed, and more campaign mud was flying, Garrett responded with a letter to the editor of *The Oklahoman* defending her tenure and its accomplishments, and denying any use of state funds for political purposes. She defended the use of yellow school buses for her annual fall tours, saying they were donated privately, as if money were the sole issue. Garrett announced her candidacy July 5 with an electioneering release that claimed a cumulative $37.5 million saving in the Department in twelve years. Truancies were reduced, parents had more school choice, class sizes were smaller (a result of HB 1017 which passed before she took office), and accountability was greater. In prior elections she had conquered all opponents and now there was no reason to anticipate different results with Roettger.[40]

Roettger, 55, was born in Evansville, Indiana, earned a doctorate at Iowa State University, and had moved to the Oklahoma City area to work as an administrator at Western Heights School District. With this background and the urging of the Republican Party, he decided to enter the contest for the Superintendency. Politicians' penchants for selectively choosing quantitative data to boost their positions and then castigating their opponents for resorting to the same strategy, surfaced in this race and provided fodder for allegations. Roettger harped at Garrett's inability to raise the state's ACT average, while Garrett stated that Oklahoma had a higher percentage than the national average of its seniors taking the test. Over her tenure the percent of the seniors taking the test increased from 50 to more than 70 and resulted in scores regressing toward the mean. Trenchant in his commentary, Roettger was unable to find a chink in Garrett's armor. Eternal optimism, grandiose delusions, downright political huckstering, or desperation was evident in a claim that he would eliminate politics in the state education system. Because public education is by definition political, only those who commit to following the maxim of doing what is best and proper for students can mitigate the political scheming.[41]

Five days prior to the election Roettger threatened legal action if the Garrett campaign did not cease running a particular set of derogatory advertisements against him that claimed, "he lied about his credentials, that he was forced to resign at a local school district, that he had put pornography on a school computer."[42] He was incensed that his character was being denigrated in a race to be the state's premier education official. Garrett brushed the allegation aside and captured the endorsement of *The Oklahoman*. Garrett, adroit at courting the media, earned that paper's support through her efforts to improve schools over the previous decade by successfully implementing legislatively mandated reforms and standards. The editorial acknowledgement of the difficulty of managing the educational system in a highly charged political environment, and Garrett's success within that milieu, framed the rationale for the support. Prohibiting the state from greater progress was opposition to consolidation of tiny districts, "conflicting legislative directives and a culture of indifference to a first-class education."[43]

The outcome was predictable: Garrett won 60 percent to 40 percent a margin of victory similar to that of the previous election. The result appeared to have been achieved by some of the ever-growing number of Independent voters marking her box as the number of Democratic registrations was dwindling. Garrett, the consummate politician, was returned to office once again by a considerable majority of the voters who expressed their satisfaction with her performance and faith in the future.

As the incumbent, she possessed all of the benefits of the office, a twelve-year history of mostly favorable commentary from *The Oklahoman*, strong Democratic support, and an ability to achieve her political aspirations. Roettger, on the other hand, faced an uphill battle in this race from the beginning. He was an unknown novice in the political arena with financial support only a small fraction of his opponent's. His war chest of slightly less than $87,000 could not compete with Garrett's funds in excess of five times that amount. Regardless, election outcomes typically more closely paralleled voter registration than amount of money spent.[44]

Political Finale: Election 2006

Sixteen years in office and four previous successful statewide campaigns made Garrett a formidable candidate, eliminating any qualified individuals who were willing to challenge her. The political ship was listing to the right and giving Republicans more hope than ever, but Brad Henry, a popular governor, was seeking a second term. He squashed his opponent two-to-one, and all of the executive offices went to the Democrats by fairly large margins. This outcome was achieved even though the voter registration ratio was five Democrats to four Republicans and one Independent. Garrett, having received the endorsement of *The Oklahoman*, defeated Bill Crozier three to two.[45]

Crozier, an eccentric who had been a frequent candidate for various offices over twenty-five years, was never hesitant to espouse extreme positions. At age 60 he now presented himself as a "serious" candidate to be the Superintendent, but his campaign committee name was Crozier for Superman 2006. Many people scoffed at some of his ideas, not the least of which was that students could use obsolete textbooks to shield themselves from shooters' bullets. Consistent with the tenets of his church, Assembly of God, he supported teaching the narrative of intelligent design as the explanation of the beginning of humans versus Darwinism. More conventionally, he advocated strengthening the teacher retirement system and increasing teacher salaries to a level comparable to Texas and then adding 7 percent to compensate for the then Oklahoma income tax rate. Suggestions such as these were an anathema to his party. Disciplinary options for students' unacceptable behavior should include more liberal use of corporal punishment. In spite of such questionable tactics and ideas, excepting the strengthening of the teacher retirement system, Crozier got 344,000 voters to support him, affirming a function of Oklahoma's practice of allowing the option of straight party voting.[46]

Donations in this campaign were so lopsided in favor of Garrett that it seems incredulous. Garrett, the doyen of Superintendents in campaigning, received $310,000 while Crozier collected no funds. During the entire election period, the latter spent only $600. As the incumbent her funds were so plentiful that she transferred $38,670 to the Friends of Sandy Garrett 2010 at the end of 2006. Excess funds and uncertainty of her ultimate plans caused her to enter a deposit for four years hence should she decide to run again in 2010.[47]

No More Campaigns

The 2006 election proved to be Garrett's finale as she chose to retire at the end of her term in January 2011. Midway through the term she began to lose the fire and inspiration that previously burned within; age was a factor with her reaching retirement eligibility; her long-term partner and best friend was experiencing major health challenges; and the Republican party was gaining steam.

She drew one or more opponents in each of the five election cycles of her tenure, and dispatched of them readily with the one exception of the 1994 general election. Only then did she not gain the endorsement of *The Oklahoman* when it opted to remain neutral. In 2006, when the Republican candidate was totally unqualified, the paper tepidly commented: "Garrett, a Democrat with a bipartisan bent, has earned a fifth term." Her performance gained the attention of the *Tulsa World* over the several elections to the extent that the paper offered its readers its support. Garrett was a successful and efficient administrator of the Department, an innovator and advocate of technology, and an implementer of HB 1017. In the lead-up to the 2010 election when she could enjoy the status of an observer and supporter, her choice for her replacement was Senator Susan Paddack of Ada. Paddack had extensive teaching experience in three states and served for nine years as the director of Local Education Foundation Outreach for the Oklahoma Foundation for Excellence.[48]

Garrett was the only Superintendent ever to have to contend with a governor of the opposing party for eight years. Governor Keating's education agenda, advocated aggressively by his Secretary Lloyd Coppedge who was expected to imprint it on the education system, contained elements too controversial for the education establishment and the voting public. Keating's curriculum standard of four-by-four was rejected as was his call for merit pay. The Governor fervently believed in the value of competition from offering extra pay to excellent teachers to designing vouchers for nonpublic school students. Garrett countered eventually with a four-by-three curricular standard and the national board certification plan for teachers.

Politics as Usual: Ethical and Legal Concerns

Typically, because incumbents benefit from the perquisites of the office and the visibility inherent to the position, regardless of what the office holder does or says, it is intended or interpreted to have political overtones. Garrett understood well how her decisions affected her political status and frequently reminded Department employees against overtly blending work responsibilities and campaign activities. She weighed every decision for political significance, how it would affect her next reelection effort. Provision of educational services is a governmental responsibility and everything in the delivery of that mandate is political—the mantra of Garrett's modus operandi—with a savvy politician figuring out how to accomplish a responsibility and simultaneously campaign for reelection.[49]

Excursions to schools across the state allowed for contact with local VIPs. Garrett desired to communicate with the common folk through the local newspaper editors and radio stations, by speaking at civic clubs, and highlighting meetings with superintendents. In many small towns across Oklahoma, the Superintendent was the face of executive government. On occasion she traveled around the state in a yellow school bus, not the most comfortable mode of transportation, to visit school districts and to talk to district personnel. Critics accused her of syphoning state money for her political gain, but she responded emphatically with denials and informed that the bus company provided the vehicle at no cost to the state. Given no legitimacy was the fact that the bus company's business with the school districts could give an air of conflict of interest. Explanations for the purpose of such activity could get murky, given the ethical angles and the public's perception.[50]

More discrete, apparently legal, but questionable ethically, was the understanding whereby school superintendents who wanted to be members of Garrett's "advisory team" were expected to donate private funds to her reelection campaigns. Advisory team members were invited to monthly meetings at the Department where she would give them, for example, early notice of upcoming modifications in regulations or the amount of their districts' share of funding for projects. Also, these meetings were opportunities for the Superintendent to hear from all parts of the state, thus keeping her ear to the ground. Obviously, those superintendents who chose not to donate put their districts at a disadvantage while several superintendents attending these meetings traveled there in district provided vehicles and with publicly funded per diem accounts.[51]

Allegations of misconduct surfaced early in the 2002 campaign season when Roettger accused Garrett's chief of staff for using his position to solicit funds for her reelection. Roettger stated that several superintendents who wished to remain anonymous lest their districts' funding would be reduced reported that they were called during business hours and asked for contributions. Garrett's response: "Absolutely no campaign activities are conducted at the State Department of Education, and no complaints have been received by us from school administrators regarding the professor's baseless allegation."[52] A stretched credulity would be imperative to believe that superintendents, in a highly charged political environment, would complain publicly about such chicanery.

Certainly, more questionable ethically and legally was the practice of creating "restroom breaks" in management level meetings for a top administrator to discuss with the Department's administrators how they were expected to participate in campaign efforts. A fifteen-minute break in the middle of a two-hour meeting would be devoted to the various campaign efforts and how those present would participate (e.g., highest level administrators would host fund-raising receptions and lower-level ones would donate designated amounts of money). As with her long-tenured predecessor of fifty years earlier Oliver Hodge, Garrett's attitude toward employees contributing to election campaigns was benign and gratuitous. After all, if a staff member wished to support the boss, that was a sign of loyalty (and a hope for job stability).[53]

When Garrett filed for reelection June 5, 2006, she led a group of public elementary school students wearing T-shirts supporting her candidacy from her Oliver Hodge Building office to the Capitol filing office. Possibly only a few might view this as unacceptable, and while it is but a minor instance, it represents the incumbent's advantage and lack of a transparent attempt at unquestionable ethical behavior.[54] Oklahoma's political climate for more than 100 years has been receptive to standards lower than those considered by persons desiring ethical and legal government operations. When the original drafters of the Constitution preferred elective selection of the Superintendent with no term limits, they opened the door for potential unethical/illegal practices of incumbents to use the advantages of the office. Garrett was not hesitant to employ acceptable as well as questionable benefits to their maximum effect.

Managing the Department and Supervising the Education System

Chaos, then Relative Calm

Garrett's tenure as Secretary, when she explicitly stated what reforms were necessary, combined propitiously with the passage of HB 1017 to give her a broad base of appeal as she assumed the mantle of Superintendent. The bloated Department needed restructuring, consolidation of positions, and refocusing of purpose. Simply, she was given the mandate to create a more nimble Department to lead the implementation of the reforms. If a shakeup of the Department would initially generate internal resistance, the consequence was acceptable for she had promised the citizenry better custodianship of its tax dollars. As opposition arose and coalesced around a state question to overturn HB 1017 with its reform provisions, Garrett was chagrined to learn the extent of the resistance to the bill. With considerable tireless effort progressive supporters across the state guaranteed failure of the opponents to stymie progress and gave her the green light to continue executing the various thrusts of the bill.[55]

Her childhood habituated her for her eventual career in politics. She lived in an environment where politics was an important topic of discussion her entire life before leaving home to attend college and she resided in a small town in an economically poor county and area. Stability at home and at school provided her a consistent and positive outlook on life. Not everyone in her social sphere enjoyed such advantages. Seeing classmates and other students confronted with greater challenges instilled in her the desire to do whatever she could do to improve the chances of success for the less fortunate, especially for those who shared a Cherokee heritage. Now she was center stage and in position to tackle the necessary issues.

Garrett's assignments in the early days of her Department employment broadened her insight into how the state's resources could be used to further the educational opportunities of students, particularly in rural areas. As time passed and she became more informed and aware of the intransient problems of the inner cities, she pondered how she and the Department might be able to improve learning environments regardless of the size and location of the schools. By becoming the Superintendent, she could influence the discussion about curriculum content, quality of instruction originating within the classroom or beyond, direction of resources, district consolidation, length of school day and school year, and other topics.

Her maneuverability in the political environment of the Capitol allowed her to succeed whether she was forced to react to legislative mandates or to propose changes. The Superintendency was a political position first and foremost, but she needed to have sufficient skills to manage a large bureaucracy and to supervise the state's effort to provide every child a basic education. By experience and intuition Garrett comprehended the extent of inertia, particularly among the small school districts and those on the brink of consolidation resulting from dwindling enrollment. She also sensed that talk of consolidation was political suicide and thus couched any language on the subject in terms of local control. A firm believer in local control but, at the same time, frustrated with the difficulty of creating and maintaining high quality schools, she was acutely aware of the number of districts where the extreme emphasis on athletics worked to the detriment of the academic program. When she created a task force to study consolidation, she gave it the mandate to generate cost estimates of several scenarios without expressing a preference for any specific one.[56]

"It will take a strong-willed individual to implement reforms in HB 1017—and to assure Oklahomans that the new tax revenues will be put to good use." This challenge was not formidable, for she was someone who could "tell you how the cow ate the cabbage."[57] With that description, Garrett set the standard against which she would be measured. Never did she then imagine that the citizens would give her two decades to implement the reforms, defend them, and ultimately fight to keep forward momentum.

Simultaneous to Garrett's assumption of the office was the growth of a new financial mechanism for cash management in government entities including school districts. Stifel, Nicolaus & Co., the program's underwriter, defended the arrangement while conceding that some districts were abusing it. Garrett was no expert in this arena and expected the state's Attorney General to investigate. She solicited the support of Clifton Scott, State Auditor and Inspector, and House Speaker Glenn Johnson to join her in requesting a formal opinion from Robert Henry, Attorney General. At least for this early public relations challenge she was able to hand it off to someone more knowledgeable. How ironic that her father, W. H. Langley Sr., was known for his efforts in the Legislature in the 1940s to get state bond reform and now she was confronted with a bond fund and cash management issue.[58]

Garrett set about reorganizing the Department through eliminating administrative and curricular positions and transferring others to the Health Department, slashing its budgetary needs, and creating positions necessary for HB 1017 compliance. *The Oklahoman* was complimentary of her decisions all the while suggesting that future efforts of the Department and the Legislature should include adoption of open transfer and parental choice.[59] Feigning support by using that avenue to push their agenda was typical for that newspaper. Meanwhile, it was remarkable that, external to the Department and in two months' time, she was able to study the agency sufficiently to determine the people and positions to be eliminated and design the new structure and focus.

The Superintendent was proud of her success at streamlining the Department, both in the first year and in the years thereafter. Efficiency of the bureaucracy was quantifiable and evidence that her management skills were superior to her predecessor and proof to the taxpaying public that the confidence they expressed in her election in 1990 was justified. In the first month sixty-four positions were eliminated (but several new positions were created) and another twenty-two were transferred to the health department enlarging its FTE. Through a six-fiscal-year-period beginning in 1991 she was able to display a $21.6 million total saving to the Department. Table 17.1 reflects a leveling of the decreases after FY 94, and it does not account for inflation.[60]

Table 17.1 Department budget FY 91-FY 96

FY	Amount (dollars)	Percent decrease FY 91	Dollar change from previous FY	Cumulative savings	FTE
91	22,020,448	n/a	n/a	n/a	513
92	18,907,788	14.14	-3,112,660	3,112,660	486
93	18,354,462	16.65	-553,326	6,778,646	496
94	17,083,505	22.42	-1,270,957	11,715,589	482
95	17,167,554	22.04	+84,049	16,568,483	482
96	17,001,228	22.79	-166,326	21,587,703	471

Sources: *1994-95 Annual Report: Statistical Report on Oklahoma Schools and the State Department of Education* (OKC: SDE, 1996), 93; FTE for FYs 91 and 92, *FY-94 Executive Budget*, 173, Oklahoma Publication Clearing House (750.6) ODL, OKC; FTE for FYs 93 and 94, *FY-96 Executive Budget and Historical Data*, 171; FTE for FYS 95 and 96, *FY-98 Executive Budget and Historical Data*, 171.

Note: Garrett's FTE numbers as discussed in the above narrative are discrepant with the Governor's annual *Executive Budget and Historical Data*.

Total Department FTE reached the zenith of 587 in 1983-84 and retracted slowly until Garrett's assumption of the Superintendency in 1991 when it dropped by twenty-seven as shown in table 17.1. Incremental change up and down describes the next eleven years until 2003-04 when a major decrease of 124 FTE resulted from the closure of the regional education service centers. Numbers fluctuated for the remainder of her tenure, dropping to 329 at its end for a cumulative reduction of 36 percent (see table 17.2 for data for five-year intervals and appendix M for all of the years 1970-2014).

Without much fanfare from the Department and the media, school district numbers declined slowly over Garrett's tenure while ADA and the number of certified staff increased. Consolidations averaged 2.6 per year, certainly a minimal effort at right-sizing school districts. Meanwhile, the ADA edged upward at approximately 3,420 annually. Certified staff numbers followed an upward trajectory, hitting almost 59,600 in 2006-07, before precipitously declining by 2010-11. The 11.1 percent ADA growth for the two decades was two-thirds of the 18.2 percent rate increase in the certified staff numbers. Table 17.2 certified staff numbers reflect the infusion of funds through HB 1017's implementation in the early 1990s and then the economic pressure in the latter half of the 2000s.[61]

Table 17.2 School district data and Department FTE 1991-2011

School year	School districts	ADA	Certified staff	Dept. FTE
1990-1991	578	548,387	42,034	513
1995-1996	549	574,440	46,558	471
2000-2001	544	580,744	49,920	476
2005-2006	540	591,486	58,310	357
2010-2011	524	616,775	51,388	329

Source: *2013-2014 Annual Report: Statistical Report on Oklahoma Schools and the State Department of Education* (OKC: SDE, 2015), 4-7.

Changing student demographics challenged the resources available both to the Department and the school districts, and those responsible for the management of those entities. Rapidly increasing numbers of Hispanic students needing English as a Second Language programs stretched the capability of local districts to serve these students. Displayed in table 17.3 is a snapshot of the statewide enrollment by race/ethnicity showing the numbers of non-white students approaching 50 percent with Hispanics comprising nearly 15 percent. White students' parents increasingly were opting for home schooling or private and parochial schools while pressure increased to improve the high school graduation rate. Less political support for traditional public education and increasing clamor for public financing of nonpublic options, more challenging students to teach, and a collapsing national economy evident in its effect on Oklahoma's economy, created a maelstrom, ideal for a dramatic change in political direction.[62]

Table 17.3 Enrollment by race/ethnicity 2012-13

Race	Indian	Black	White	Hispanic	Asian	Two+*	Total
Number	105,995	63,381	354,323	95,014	12,439	42,331	673,483
Percent	15.74	9.41	52.61	14.11	1.85	6.28	100.0

Source: "Public Education in Oklahoma," https://ballotpedia.org/Public_education_in_Oklahoma, 5/20.
*Two or more races/ethnicities.

Structural and Curricular Thrusts

Garrett pushed for a longer school day and school year, and for the reduction and elimination of disruptions during the school day. Metropolitan area school superintendents supported moving athletics outside of the school day, but there was sufficient rural opposition to stifle any efforts to do so, even though Oklahoma was the only state still allowing athletics within school hours. Because Oklahoma had one of the shortest school years, she pushed for additional days to give students more classroom learning time. The OEA supported this effort as long as teachers received the per day rate for currently taught days and an increase in their salaries. Regardless of her efforts, these ideas gained no traction during her tenure.[63]

An idea that germinated and gained appeal was the opening of the school districts to various forms of choice. Garrett was an early advocate of open transfers between school districts for students, primarily in the rural areas. Districts underperforming or not offering subjects or extracurricular activities preferred by the parents and students or both, and home district schools further distant geographically than neighboring district schools were arguments in favor of more openness. Enlarging choice within the public schools was desirable for the needs of students, and was thought strategically important to dampen the clamor for public funding of nonpublic schools.

That each of the state's two metropolitan areas had one large urban district and several suburban districts in close proximity allowed parents with financial means to change their residency to districts of their preference. Many families in the two inner city districts, however, were unable to move elsewhere. Garrett desired these parents to have options, believed charter schools to be the preferred model, and pushed for legislation and creation of such schools in Tulsa and Oklahoma City. As a staunch proponent of public schools, deeply aware of the extreme challenges facing the inner city schools, and perceptive of the rising tide in conservative circles for publicly supported nonpublic options, she advocated greater flexibility within the public school districts.

A rewrite of the Elementary and Secondary Education Act of 1964 and its subsequent amendments and iterations occurred in 2001 through the No Child Left Behind Act that set the standards by which schools receiving federal funds would be measured. Accountability became the watchword for teachers, students, and schools. Annual standardized tests and school report cards would determine adequate yearly progress. Garrett's announced hopes as Secretary twelve years earlier were given the necessary impetus to achieve fruition. Receipt of federal dollars, critical resources for Oklahoma's financially starved schools, would now be contingent upon setting standards and designing the curriculum and testing schemes to assess performance. With enthusiasm, the Superintendent led the statewide effort to achieve compliance by adjusting current practices, anticipating resistance from teachers who balked at the idea of narrowing the curriculum to achieve expected test results. Eventually, the federal plan encountered major challenges and failed to achieve its initial intentions.[64]

High School Graduation 1994, Brandt Family Private Collection

Strong academic standards and expanded curriculum offerings were frequent emphases of the Superintendent. Small districts did not have sufficient enrollments or resources to justify an expansive curriculum. Two methods to solve this deficiency were satellite delivery systems initially and later the internet and, beginning in the late 1980s when she was Secretary, the Oklahoma School for Science and Mathematics. Technology-delivered instruction expanded educational opportunities to all students across the state while the high-quality program of the elite OSSM catered to the academically gifted students in science and math. But what was not equally valued and created was a similarly purposed school for students gifted in the arts and music. Without a school to serve the rural interests, student talent in the performing arts was perpetually underdeveloped, and there was little hope of the establishment of such an opportunity.

Possibly her signature effort was her interest in and strong support of early childhood education through half day programs for four-year-olds and all-day kindergarten for five-year-olds. She was a staunch proponent of an appropriate learning environment for these children, encouraged by her assistant state superintendent Ramona Paul, PHD. Unfortunately, for many urban students benefiting from these early experiences, the elementary schools they subsequently attended were understaffed or staffed by novice teachers, underfunded, and thus unable to build sufficiently on the students' early growth.

Improving the quality and the image of teachers was approached through several ways. Garrett advocated higher standards and expectations, but was frustrated at being unable to create a plan and convince the Legislature to provide a sustainable funding mechanism. For the most part, the legislators talked a lot about the priority of education, yet failed to fund all teachers' salaries adequately. Governor Keating wanted a merit pay scheme but it was opposed by the OEA. A compromise of sorts was to reward teachers who met some national standards. When the Legislature created and funded the national teacher certification scheme, it was begun with much fanfare and excitement. The Superintendent was delighted to take some credit for the program's initiation in Oklahoma. Resources were generated to assist teachers to achieve the designation of National Board Certification, and the Legislature in 1997 appropriated $5,000 per year (one of the most generous rewards nationally for earning the certification) for ten years for each teacher completing the program. Unwilling to appropriate enough money to reward all teachers better, the Legislature funded a few very well and then the state received national attention for the number of such persons and the amount of compensation they received. True to form, with the passage of time, legislative commitment faltered to near elimination of the funding of the program.[65]

Lost in all of this attention was whether the program actually resulted in better instruction over time and what was the instructional effect on students during the qualifying year for the teacher. For example, it was not unusual for an elementary school teacher who was pursuing board certification to be assigned a select class of students given that instruction scenes were videotaped for evidence of quality teaching. Non-random selection benefited one teacher for the year but adversely affected the teachers of the other classes of the same grade level. Regardless, many excellent and highly devoted teachers pursued the certification primarily to hone their instructional skills to benefit their students, and the extra stipend was recognition of that motive and energy.

Adequate teacher supply continued to plague the state as fewer college graduates in select areas (e.g., math, science, and special education) were entering the profession. Females graduating from high school were aggressively recruited by universities to their math and science degree programs, and subsequently by employers seeking to diversify their gender ratios. Not only were teacher salaries substantially below those offered by companies, they were thousands of dollars less than those offered by surrounding states.[66] Even more challenging than the gender supply was the minority shortage. University teacher preparation programs graduated few minority students, leaving school districts the near impossibility of hiring minority teachers in any curricular area.

Throughout the state's history, when a shortage of qualified and certified teachers occurred, the response was to lower the standards and accept subpar individuals rather than provide the additional funds to maintain the preferred level. This consistent legislative response communicated no sense of substantial urgency and debased the relative importance attached to the teaching profession. Oklahoma is a typical southern state where a large majority of the teachers are female and, with the exception of Texas, perceives no need to compensate them well. Additionally, in rural areas where teacher pay is comparable to, and oftentimes better than, wages earned by others, little impetus exists to raise taxes to improve their salaries.

Consistent with her philosophy of choices and a pragmatic approach to the teacher shortage, Garrett pushed for alternative certification to open the door wider to potential entrants to the profession, particularly in the critically-short STEM areas (science, technology, engineering, and math). In the latter half of her tenure, this approach fit well with the legislators' attitudes toward teaching: solve the teacher shortage by opening the door wider rather than by increasing compensation and properly funding education. Troops to Teachers, a thrust where former military personnel with college degrees could become certified to teach with the acquisition of several hours of coursework, became one of the options. Unfortunately, no funds were appropriated to determine the success of this program. Did these teachers find this opportunity attractive over time? How difficult was the transition from the culture of the military to that of a public school classroom?

A point of pride for the Superintendent was the Teacher of the Year program. Annually, local district winners across Oklahoma were winnowed to a list of a dozen teachers who were invited to the State Fair for the highly publicized announcement and recognition of the winner. No doubt excellent teachers were recognized, but the immediate effect was the removal of the winner from the classroom for a year of touting the state's education accomplishments. After returning to their teaching positions, oftentimes it was not long before these winners soon left their classrooms for advancement in other venues. But the practice was good politically for the Fair and every fourth year the annual celebration occurred at the height of the quadrennial campaign season.

Formal preparation standards and requirements for school building and district administrative positions also came under review with the same attitude as with teachers. However, one distinct difference existed between teachers and administrators—there was no shortage of the latter. Regardless, Garrett worked with the Board to lower the requirements. For athletic coaches desiring to transition to administrative positions and maintain their high salaries, it would require less coursework, time, and effort. Alternative pathways would allow non-traditional (i.e., having no teaching preparation and/or school administrative experience) seekers to pursue district leadership, and reduced coursework would allow persons a shorter path to certification eligibility. Leadership in the business world was sufficient evidence of the requisite skills to lead a district or building, but the inverse was rarely assumed. No special knowledge was necessary to head a public education entity. Few instances offered much confidence of great success by business leaders who were hired to lead large urban school systems in Oklahoma and across the country.

Near the end of Garrett's tenure, the Legislature passed the Lindsey Nicole Henry Scholarship for Students with Disabilities Act and secured the Governor's signature by naming the scholarship after one of his daughters. Its purpose was to channel state funds to students with disabilities in private schools, and it opened the door to an avalanche of tax money schemes to finance virtual and traditional nonpublic schools.[67]

Department Chief

Garrett's longevity in the Department facilitated an environment that fostered the maturation of innovative programs and thrusts and, at the same time, allowed her to know everything about the organization. Department administrators were allowed time to coordinate with school districts to initiate and conduct innovative curricular projects without constant interruptions. Frustration was frequently a threat caused by recurring limited and diminishing resources, recalcitrant problems of the multitude and variations of districts, and frequent meddling of legislators for special consideration of grants for their districts. Garrett had the fortitude to continue "slogging" onward, to provide students in every district the best education possible. She valued the informed opinions of everyone from a secretary to the top-level administrator and allowed employees flexibility in performing their duties, but she was very much hands-on and nothing escaped her approval. Regular communication with the administrators occurred in Tuesday morning meetings formalized by an agenda. Wanting to understand everything, she was a voracious reader, from Department-prepared reports to proposed standards, bills, laws, etc. Consequently, a tendency to micromanage occasionally resulted in bogged down processes.[68]

Garrett assumed Board members wished to be supportive and, thus, needed to be informed. Agendas for meetings were sent to these members and then either she or the chief of staff initiated a phone call to discuss the items, the background information, and reason for placement on the agenda. This forum allowed members to ask questions for clarification and implication and subsequently to be knowledgeable when casting their votes in the official meetings. Always attentive to her public persona, Garrett wished not to be embarrassed by appearing to be uninformed or ill prepared, and she desired the Board to be a joint effort in leading the education system.[69]

She was highly adept at anticipating sources of support and opposition with the exception of the blip in 1993-94 over OBE, a lesson she learned well. Overall, she had a vision of what she wished to accomplish and then proceeded toward the goal. Three endemic challenges to achieving her goals were the Department bureaucracy, the perceptions of the legislators, and the low pay for the agency's top administrative positions. Because the Board, including Garrett, was loath to pay Department employees' salaries exceeding the Superintendent's compensation, it was difficult to attract the desired quality and experience needed and preferred.[70]

Investigative Reports

Garrett's tenure was tainted by the findings of three investigative reports (two described here) completed in 2012 by the State Auditor and Inspector's Office (SAIO). In the first instance, the Oklahoma Curriculum Improvement Commission, the nonprofit organization operating under the auspices of the Department and funded from school district memberships, offered workshops and seminars to school personnel. Governed by a board of educators that met two or three times each year, it had a long history within the Department. The OCIC board members were aware that Department officials were managing one operating account, but were uninformed that those officials had opened and were operating two separate accounts under the commission. Solicited donations from companies contracting for services with the Department were being funneled through these two secret accounts and used to purchase alcohol, beer, and choice food for attendees at conferences. High-level Department administrators were involved in the transfers of funds between accounts to keep the actions hidden from public view. According to the SAIO, "The accounts we identified appear to have been operated as slush fund accounts allowing OSDE officials to issue payments shielded from governmental oversight as well as public scrutiny. Over a period of 10 years, in excess of $2.3 million has been expended from these accounts."[71]

A second investigation was triggered by Garrett's successor over the private, non-profit organization, Oklahoma Foundation for Innovation in Education, created to organize and offer the Innovation 2011 summer conference. Barresi was early in her tenure and chaos reigned in the Department, in part from the conflict between long time employees and new hires, some being paid through private funds and hired sans Board action. The SAIO determined that Department personnel were mixing state and private funds: "OSDE officials exercised substantial 'operational control' over both the fund raising and disbursement activities of the Foundation." One example was when SDE used state funds to pay $16,429.50 for an overdue bill (related to the 2011 conference) that appeared to be a foundation obligation and not a debt to the state.[72]

Repercussions from the investigative reports did not include any court actions or persons being held accountable for questionable practices. In spite of Department personnel recalcitrance to heed requests to be interviewed by the SAIO, no negative consequences ensued either to these employees or to the Department overall for engaging in a quasi-legal activity. Quite possibly it was because the third and final report included a statement that it was considering surveying other departments and agencies to determine the prevalence of similar activities.[73] Discovery of such widespread practices might mitigate charges against any specific agency.

Never Far from Politics

Garrett retired from the Superintendency in January 2011, but not from involvement in education. Though she and Janet Barresi had a professional and personal relationship, she did not encourage Barresi to run for the office, and Garrett was sought after by both successors Barresi and Joy Hofmeister for her assistance in helping them to navigate the complexities of the office. She continued her involvement in the Democratic Party by speaking frequently at various Party related functions. Significant to her acclaim was to have been the first woman in seventy-five years to be elected to a statewide office and her Cherokee heritage and tribal membership. After more than thirty years living in Oklahoma City, she moved to Tulsa to be nearer her son Chuck, an executive of Cherokee Nation Businesses, and his wife. After her twelve year marriage to John Garrett ended in 1974, she never remarried. Her long time "beloved partner in life," Jerry Hefner, died September 21, 2017. He and Garrett met in 1989 when he was a state representative from Muskogee and Wagoner counties and she was Secretary of Education. After he left the Legislature in 2004, he was elected as a Wagoner County commissioner and served until 2008.[74]

Chapter 18
Barresi: Faltering in the Changing of the Guard
(2011-2015)

Garrett's decision to retire in 2010 opened the door for a newcomer in a political environment where the Democrats were fading and the Republicans were flexing their muscle. Years earlier rural educators had seen their political strength ebb under Garrett who struck a middle ground to achieve success in her education agenda. She cultivated the urban, business community to garner support for tax increases and reforms, but understood intuitively that she was dependent upon the rural schools for support. Age and political reality dictated it was time for her reign to end and to pass the torch to someone else. All signs pointed to a resounding takeover of government executive positions by the long-suffering Republican Party. It was now their turn to impose their will on the citizens and to show their ability to govern. Having chaffed for so many decades, they were given the opportunity to lead, and their education leader was going to be Janet Marion (Costello) Barresi, a retired dentist.

A Charter School Disciple

Barresi was not the typical candidate when she announced her intent to run for the position. Most of her career was spent in operating a small business and she was bringing that expertise to the Superintendency and the Department. She espoused the basic tenants of the Republican Party, competition was the bedrock of free enterprise, private entities should be permitted to compete with public schools, and public funds should be allocated to these non-public options. Barresi was convinced that the only way the public schools would improve would be through competition with private options. If direct support were not deemed constitutionally sound, then a compromise option of charter schools was the next best goal. She seemed also to harbor a lack of confidence in local school district administration and governance by suggesting that the Department, with Board approval, should be able to intervene in local affairs either by hiring a private company to operate the district or by the Department assuming the prerogative itself.

Barresi earned a Bachelor's degree in Speech and Hearing at OU prior to working toward her Master's degree in Speech Pathology. As an undergraduate she was a member of several organizations including Young Democrats. After graduation Barresi was employed as a speech pathologist for several years in the Harrah and Norman school districts when she decided to pursue the doctorate in dentistry at OU, graduating in 1984. With degree in hand she began private practice.[1]

When her sons entered Quail Creek Elementary School in Oklahoma City, Barresi became a very involved parent. By the time the boys were in the fourth grade, she, along with several other parents, grew concerned over where their children would attend middle school within the Oklahoma City Public Schools. Hoover Middle School received students from Quail Creek, but the concerned parents claimed Hoover was crowded and inadequate to serve northwest Oklahoma City. From what they knew, they did not see any viable options on the horizon, so they decided to raise the issue of creating an alternative. They presented their concerns to the school board and the superintendent and couched in part that many students leave the city district following elementary school to go to suburban districts or to private schools.[2]

The Oklahoma Legislature had not yet provided the legal means for establishing charter schools or other options from the traditional public school, trailing a nationwide movement to address some of the inner city school problems. Administrators in the Oklahoma City district were sympathetic to the concerns of the parents, sufficiently for them to press the board with a plan that would have the district contract with the parents to operate an alternative school. Under the state's deregulation statutes, administrators believed they had the flexibility to create "enterprise schools," a limited form of charter schools with a moniker borrowed, in part, from the economic term "free enterprise." This initial contract, extensive and addressing every aspect of the school, the teachers, and the curriculum, was finalized by the school board in its March 1998 meeting.[3]

The concerned parents became organized and informed of events in other states so that they could present a coordinated effort to achieve the goal of having options. Barresi, one of the leaders, opined what an ideal middle school for her sons and the other students would be like: a cozy public school with no more than 225 students, mandatory uniforms, and tough disciplinary requirements. Parents would be required to sign a contract promising to volunteer at the school three hours each week. All students would have computers with which to do schoolwork and to e-mail their teachers in the evening. So successful were the parents that by spring 1998 there were advertisements for slots at a new north Oklahoma City middle school. Barresi was now the leader and spokesperson for the energized group. Publicity emphasized the features: student uniforms, mandatory parental involvement at school, and a core curriculum presented via team teaching. Fifth grade students in the six elementary feeder schools, and sixth and seventh grade students in other middle schools were eligible to attend.[4]

The Oklahoman frequently ran articles highlighting Barresi's efforts and activities in the Oklahoma City School District to challenge the status quo with her cause célèbre playing perfectly into the paper's agenda. Beyond the district little interest was generated in her efforts and successes, but time would tell that she was tapping into a concept that would roil the education establishment and lead to her capturing the state's top education position. She was elated over the results of her efforts to establish Independence Enterprise Middle School viewed by many as getting the proverbial camel's nose under the tent. "We're establishing competition in this school district," she was quoted. "With competition, you increase quality, decrease costs and increase the number of customers that come to your business."[5] Supplanting the education model with a business model, for this practicing dentist, was a panacea for the problems facing inner city schools.

Janet Barresi
Courtesy of the Oklahoma State Department of Education

Barresi continued her crusade to expand the options to the traditional school model through a Point of View article in *The Oklahoman*. Here she distilled the arguments for and against a law for charter schools by describing the essence as people, power and politics. Couched in the lexicon typical of a businessperson, the argument was that charter schools could practice entrepreneurism and innovation within the free market economy to provide a superior education for students. Interestingly enough, her excitement and activities, and that of like-minded parents, centered on beginning a school where their children would attend, rather than on the most problematic schools in the district.[6]

Propelled by the success of IEMS while her sons were enrolled there, and that they were now finishing middle school and needing an acceptable option for high school, Barresi in 2002 authored a proposal to expand Independence to include a college preparatory high school. Her proposal became stymied when she also entered the discussion over the location of a new John Marshall High School. The district was willing to go only so far in ceding authority for charter school oversight. School board president Cliff Hudson shared her enthusiasm, but was hesitant to go too far. Yet, he lauded her success, "The school district has got to create schools that's [sic] as good as what Janet builds."[7] Barresi's commitment to creating a high school to serve students in the middle academically continued unabated into the spring of 2003. Her group had not yet succeeded in finding a location and facility, but diligent efforts were being expended to do so. The school board had granted a charter, but location was a stumbling block. Its academic program was to be a college-preparatory curriculum requiring all students to complete four years of English, science, math, and social studies. Specifically identified for recruitment were children of the families where parents and other family members had not attended college. Students would be required to wear uniforms, provide their own transportation, and complete fifty hours of volunteer service.[8]

Her influence waxing ever greater, she took to criticizing the Oklahoma City school board over a decision to limit charter schools. By now an active participant in the MAPS project, a recognizable person in the Oklahoma City area, she was the face of the charter school movement, gaining the respect and support of the power brokers. Simultaneously, her efforts were drawing louder opposition from the education establishment and some of the state's politicians. Barresi was a constant and consistent critic of the status quo and missed no opportunity to accuse educators and school boards of recalcitrance in their approach. She believed she had proven the efficacy of charter schools and wished to compare their students' performances against those of students in the traditional schools.[9]

An issue she did not confront in the establishment of IEMS, offering a comprehensive extracurricular program, proved to be an insurmountable challenge for her personally when her sons reached high school level. Since charter secondary schools tend to tout their expertise to offer a quality academic curriculum, they are not prepared or equipped to offer a comprehensive curriculum, co-curricular activities, and athletics. Not successful in convincing the Oklahoma City school board to build or offer the kind of high school she desired for her sons, when they were high school age, her personal and private interest in charter schools shifted and she transferred them from the Oklahoma City Public Schools to a high school in Edmond where they excelled in football.[10] Edmond North offered a comprehensive academic curriculum and athletics so she no longer needed to pursue charter school options for her sons. Her ardor for school options, however, became a driving force in her decision to run for the Superintendency, and she had the support of Cliff Hudson who was influential in the Oklahoma City area.

Barresi's "education" in the lead up to her decision to run for the Superintendency included increased opportunities to participate in the debate over the design of education and the value of charter schools. In 2007 she was a member of the ACE (Achieving Classroom Excellence) Task Force that participated in the effort to get statutory provision for end-of-instruction exams. "The economic future of this state and our viability as a national and global competitor depends on our ability to provide highly educated workers to our present and future state corporations."[11] Accolades received by Harding Charter Preparatory High School were highlighted by Barresi in 2009 when she proudly announced that graduates were admitted to prestigious universities in spite of the fact that fifty-four percent of the students qualified for reduced lunches. She was immensely pleased of the success of the school guided by the board that she chaired.[12]

Arguably, Barresi's political skills were honed over the decade leading up to the 2010 election. Sustained, active leadership in establishing two charter secondary schools during the infancy of the charter school movement exhibited her ability to accomplish the exceptional. Granted, some of her success was due to timing. The foresight and excitement of the MAPS project lent an air of creative experimentation. Initially, she found a receptive school administration willing to work with her to attempt a new venture. She was motivated personally as a concerned parent to have her sons enrolled in a positive, challenging, and enriched environment. And, nationally the movement toward school options was gathering speed. Regardless, she worked tirelessly for a decade, all the while attracting the attention of the Oklahoma City business community. Although she did not possess a typical resumé, she refused to allow that potential disadvantage to discourage her ambitions; rather, she viewed it as an asset to be non-traditional. The Constitution's short list of eligibility criteria for the Superintendency allowed a career dentist to qualify to lead the Department of several hundred employees and the vast common school system with its multi-billion dollar slice of the state budget.

Flexing an Expansive Personal Financial Muscle

The 2010 election season got kicked off October 6, 2009, when Barresi chose to begin her quest to capture the Superintendency. Announcing a run for the position, she said that the educational bureaucracy had failed the children through maintenance of the status quo and that the solution was school choice because it promoted competition. As the election season warmed up, all of the candidates were addressing the dire shortage of funds in the state's coffers. Solutions posited were higher taxes to generate more money, improved administrative and paperwork efficiency, volunteerism, and innovation. Timing proved to be consequential. Since the election of 1922, no incumbent either elected or appointed was running for the office. Twenty ten produced a wide-open race with no candidates needing to defend a record. In part because of the effects of term limits on the Legislature, and because of a wave of Republican successes across the country, conditions were ripe for a sweep of the election. The 2010 election was the first since 1934 that involved both a Democratic and Republican primary and, coincidentally, in both years at least one woman was competing in the Republican primary. Both primaries were split between one man and one woman and, in both instances, the women were victorious as shown in table 18.1. In the Republican primary, Barresi defeated Brian Kelly by a near two-to-one vote while in the Democratic race Susan Paddack won with a three-to-one margin. Kelly was a retired teacher and coach and Jerry Combrink a long-tenured superintendent at Blue and Boswell school districts in southeastern Oklahoma.[13]

Paddack was hoping her education and political background would be sufficient to carry her to the Superintendent position. She earned a Bachelor's Degree in Education in 1974 at the University of Colorado and later a Master's Degree in Secondary Education at East Central University. Several years she taught science in public schools in Colorado, Oklahoma, and Texas. After teaching she was hired by The Foundation for Excellence

Table 18.1 2010 Primary election results

Republican			Democratic		
Candidate	Votes	Percent	Candidate	Votes	Percent
Janet Barresi	145,433	62.7	Susan Paddack	183,550	73.3
Brian Kelly	86,430	37.3	Jerry Combrink	66,697	26.7
Total	231,863	100.0	Total	250,247	100.0

Source: www.ok.gov/elections.

as the first director of local education foundation outreach. Her star was rising so she ran for the state senate from Ada and was first elected in 2004. As a senator she was appointed to serve on three education organizations: Achieving Classroom Excellence Task Force, Southern Regional Education Board, and Education Commission of the States.[14]

With the men dispatched rather easily, Barresi and Paddack moved on to the general election where they were joined by a third contestant, Richard Cooper, an Independent with a long career teaching social studies and English that was followed by serving as the education director at Sylvan Learning Center in Oklahoma City. The two main candidates went on the speaking and fundraising circuit and were joined by Cooper in the speaking forums only because he expressly refused to accept donations, undercutting his ability to run a successful campaign.

Barresi campaigned on improving standards, reforming testing, and developing teacher effectiveness; Paddack espoused fiscal responsibility and focused on creating and implementing a vision for education; and Cooper pushed for evaluating the curriculum and testing, and implementing quality physical education. Adding intrigue and interest to the election was State Question 744 with wording that would require the state to increase education funding to the regional per student average. Cooper and Paddack expressed strong support while Barresi opposed because it was an ill-conceived policy. She believed that Oklahoma should determine its tax needs and structure without needlessly tying its level with those of surrounding states. Historically, raising taxes to support education was extremely difficult, so binding the state to the regional average would give leverage to education supporters. Opponents of the tax increase were given a strong reason to vote both against the state question and for Barresi.[15]

For the first time since statehood a Republican captured the Superintendency when Barresi won with almost 56 percent of the vote after spending nearly 1.25 million dollars as shown in table 18.2. Financial support for her election differed vastly from previous candidates' as reported by the Oklahoma State Ethics Commission. Whereas former candidates garnered most of their support from educators and friends of public education, Barresi received large donations (legal maximum amount allowable was $5,000) from family members, individuals and groups external to the state, energy companies, private foundations, and owners of some of the largest non-energy companies headquartered in Oklahoma. Personally, she donated to, or loaned, her campaign in excess of $700,000,

Table 18.2 2010 General election results and total campaign expenditures

Candidate	Party	Votes	Percent	Expenditures
Janet Barresi	Republican	573,716	55.9	1,223,232.80
Susan Paddack	Democratic	387,007	37.7	852,661.00
Richard Cooper	Independent	65,243	06.4	3,249.02
Total	n/a	1,025,966	100.0	2,079,142.82

Source: www.ok.gov/elections; see C1-R Campaign Contributions and Expenditures Report for each candidate at https:pay.apps.ok.gov/ethics/crs/c1r/view_c1r.php?reg_id=110093&action=public& report_num=73083 (Barresi); id=110166, num=68516 (Paddack); id=110472, num=65324 (Cooper).

Note: Expenditure totals are for both the primary and general elections, but they exclude the combined amount of $13,312.67 for Brian Kelly and Jerry Combrink in the primary election.

more than she received from all other sources combined. Big money was now flowing into the campaign for Superintendent with more than $2,000,000 spent. Even the amount Paddack spent was more than twice any candidate in any previous election.[16]

Republicans for the first time swept the major executive offices as well as the House and Senate and the voters expressed a strong distaste for a tax increase requested through State Question 744. By 81 percent to 19 percent they overwhelming defeated the proposed amendment. The reason for the question was a dire shortage of funds, a shortage that developed in part through the Legislature's multiple reductions of the top level of the state's income tax scheme. Voters were in no mood for Democratic policies or higher taxes.[17]

Political dynamics for the 2014 election cycle still had the Republicans in charge, but the incumbent Superintendent was facing an uphill battle that began early in December 2012 when the superintendent of the tiny Bennington School District in Bryan County announced her candidacy. Although she never followed through with her announced intent, it alerted Barresi to the forthcoming battle to be waged, one that she did not hesitate to inflame. Two months prior to this announcement, Barresi lashed out at Board member Joy Hofmeister who had been a member only since January. Shortly after the public confrontation, *The Oklahoman* offered some perspective on the political fallout from such obstreperous behavior in a description of what happened to her counterpart in Indiana who also tried to implement an aggressive education reform agenda. He and Barresi had similar approaches that had them forge ahead with little thought to consider those who were closest to the students, the teachers. "At times her words and actions have lacked grace and diplomacy, which has served as a distraction and eroded relationships with many of the state's educators."[18] If she so adamantly wished to see the fulfillment of her reform agenda, building a consensus was imperative. The skirmish caused an unbridgeable rift that led to Hofmeister's resignation in April 2013 and shortly thereafter plans to contend for the Superintendency.

Regardless of the chiding by the newspaper, Barresi's modus operandi and personality, if they changed at all, were imperceptible. Her narrowing political base was staunchly supportive of her, hopeful that she could be more than a one-term Superintendent. But, in the year leading up to the 2014 election quite a bit of energy was spent vilifying her primary opponent. Fewer and fewer donations to her campaign caused her to dip heavily into her personal finances to support her reelection efforts. By June 30, 2013, Hofmeister had raised $166,056 to Barresi's $1,100, forcing the latter to loan her campaign $100,000. In the next quarter Hofmeister received $91,853 to Barresi's $48,850. More than a year in advance of the primary election *The Oklahoman* was reporting on the sizes of the war chests, indicative of the negative side of an elective Superintendency. Barresi, in 2013, "loaned" her campaign $350,000 which was almost half of the $731,345 she "loaned" her 2010 campaign. Officially the money was loaned, but then she repaid herself in her first campaign only $60,000. Of course, this opened her up to allegations by Hofmeister that she was buying the job. Hofmeister's total contributions for 2013 were $321,663, and election year had not yet arrived.[19]

Campaign rhetoric, mudslinging, and political chicanery grew during spring and early summer 2014. Hofmeister's volunteer involvement with Jenks Public Schools and close connections to that district's administrators along with other Tulsa area districts' administrators were used to acquire information that became the basis for allegations of law breaking. Through an open records request Barresi's campaign asked for all communication records between Hofmeister and Jenks School District's employees dating to 2007. A bit presumptive, but with barely a veneer of sincerity, that early date was so the campaign could detect where Hofmeister stood on a range of education issues. Dating only to 2011, the emails initially numbered 3,661, but eventually involved more than 7,000. Legally required to do so, the campaign paid the Jenks district for the time and costs involved with complying with the request.[20] It was not long before the political machinations expanded and Barresi's campaign sent a barrage of requests to other districts in Tulsa County "for any communication—written or electronic—that contains the name 'Joy Hofmeister.'"[21] Not surprisingly, allegations of illegal use of school computers followed solely with the Jenks district since that is where she lived and had interactions with school officials. Fortunately for Hofmeister, who had solicited Superintendent Kirby Lehman's support in May 2013, he politely refused, saying he could not use school resources to comply with her request.[22]

The June 2014 primary drew multiple candidates in both parties with Republicans Barresi and Hofmeister joined by the 2010 primary entrant Brian Kelly. The incumbent's modus operandi and agenda were repudiated when Hofmeister won by capturing more than 50 percent. Only tepid support from *The Oklahoman*, highlighting Barresi's attempts at reform while recognizing the mistakes, proved insufficient to carry Barresi to victory. When the results were tallied, Barresi achieved a unique distinction for the Superintendency by finishing third in a primary field of three, losing even to her 2010 primary opponent whom she had bested two to one. The loss came with a high price tag since she was committed to winning regardless of the financial cost. Barresi seemed to have an ample reservoir of financial resources, personally and through family members, as evidenced through her giving to several politicians and political campaigns both in Oklahoma and beyond its borders. Eventually, she would donate in excess of three million dollars with the bulk of that going to her own campaigns. Of the $1,470,231 she raised in the 2010 campaign, $1,010,345 was her own money. Self-reelection efforts and support for others four years later totaled $2,027,367.[23] A low voting outcome and a high expenditure, as shown in table 18.3, compute to a cost of $28/vote.

Table 18.3 2014 Republican primary election and campaign expenditures

Candidate	Votes	Percent	Campaign expenditures
Janet Barresi	55,048	21.0	1,544,746
Joy Hofmeister	151,122	57.6	…
Brian Kelly	56,060	21.4	…
Total	262,232	100.0	…

Source: www.ok.gov/elections.

Notes: Hofmeister's campaign expenditures for the 2014 election cycle are aggregated in table 19.1. Kelly filed no report. Candidates who compete in both the primary and general elections do not report expenditures separately for each election making it difficult to compute the cost per vote.

Unpopular and Contentious Leads to a Short Political Career

Barresi's solutions to the problems she identified as facing public schools should have been of no surprise to Oklahomans when she moved into the Superintendent's office on January 10, 2011. She was absolutely convinced of the necessity of applying business assumptions and practices to the composition, operation, management, and evaluation of public education. She was not reticent to transfer her acclaimed success with the charter schools of Oklahoma City to the state writ large. What was good for the state's inner-city schools would be good for all students and schools. Higher standards (e.g., accountability of students through third grade reading threshold retention, end-of-year testing in high school, and a point system for teachers emphasizing student performance) were requisite and urgent, and school choices needed to be expanded. Students and parents became "customers" and competition would drive the schools to success or to close.

Prior to becoming Superintendent, Barresi had established ties with the national movement for school choice, in particular with Florida Governor Jeb Bush who had pushed through reform-centered provisions in that state. Early in her administration she joined a group of like-minded chief state school officers, Chiefs for Change, who provided a national platform for discussion of reforms and methods to implement them. Importantly, her counterpart in Indiana provided external support for her efforts to improve Oklahoma's schools.[24]

Foundation for Excellence in Education, Bush's creation for serving as a resource for school options, proved to be a key participant in Oklahoma's move toward options and public financing of nonpublic schools. Barresi's close connections allowed ideas for state-customized policies to be drafted by personnel at the FEE. At FEE's annual summits, its employees facilitated conversations between education officials from multiple states and its corporate donors and also arranged private meetings between decision makers and company executives. Key financial contributors to FEE were the Walmart Foundation, Bill and Melinda Gates Foundation, the Dick and Betsy DeVos Foundation, book publishing companies, technology companies, and others advocating a marriage of education and corporate America to shape education while providing public monies for all options. "Choice" became the mantra of this network of foundations, corporations, and chief executive officers.[25]

Barresi's naivete about how to lead a large agency of state government, her cavalier move to replace longtime employees within the Department, and chairing the Board whose members were all named by the previous Democratic governor did not stand her in good stead. Immediately following the election and two months prior to assuming the office, she hired several of her campaign staff for influential positions in the Department. To preempt the law, these people were paid with private funds until after she assumed office when they could be placed on the state's payroll and paid with taxpayers' funds.[26]

At her first Board meeting in January 2011, she announced these hires to the dismay of the members, some who reacted angrily and with charges of violating the law. The battle was on, and the media descended on the events. Barresi could not comprehend that she could not proceed so freely, and some Board members were adamant that they would not approve the hires. Marching into this politically charged environment, newly elected Governor Mary Fallin, in a show of solidarity, held a news conference, with Barresi standing nearby, condemning the actions of the Board and pleading for all participants to act civilly toward each other. Defiantly, Barresi announced that the three hires would continue working for her and be paid with private funds. Senate Democratic minority leader Andrew Rice sought an attorney general's opinion to determine the legality of her action. Four months later she received word that her employment actions contravened state law by her acting without Board approval.[27]

So angered were the Republicans in the Legislature over the Board's tiff with Barresi that they acted posthaste through HB 2139 to enlarge the Superintendent's prerogative in hiring personnel in the Department and expanding her influence over the agency itself. Abruptly, the dynamics changed, certainly not a precedent, and she was not going to permit a "minor glitch" to disrupt her plans. Barresi could claim one early victory when she won the exclusive right to hire her own personnel independent of the Board's desires. She was warned that this opportunity carried greater accountability and subjected her to the sword of Damocles, where she would have more authority but would hold it tenuously. Typically, new Superintendents replaced several members of the administrative staff who, by virtue of their positions, were excluded from the merit system. Those members were all the more vulnerable when the Superintendent retired or chose not to run for another term and the incoming one represented the other party. Rancor was particularly evident when Barresi exercised her prerogative to replace several of these individuals.[28]

Four months into her term drastic change was evident. A whole new Board was appointed by the Governor and the Superintendent replaced long tenured, knowledgeable personnel with some of her most active political operatives who had no insight into the workings of the agency. Intentionally, much institutional history was lost but, at the same time, leading a large agency with hundreds of employees responsible to the public and over 500 school districts serving 700,000 students demanded leadership skills and political acumen. Time would determine whether Barresi possessed such capability, and the public would be the judge.

The Legislature's enactment of the law to shift authority for personnel decisions away from the Board and to the Superintendent only became effective ninety days following the adjournment of the legislative session. Unable to muster the sufficient vote for the emergency clause in the House, the law's implementation would have been delayed except that Barresi requested the Board at the May 9 meeting to have the authority immediately. A unanimous decision by the all-new Board gave Barresi permission to terminate employees the next day and some were dismissed with no advance notice.[29]

Barresi's successful initiation into the Superintendency was hindered also by her outspoken criticism of State Question 744 which would have raised more money for education. Its failure and continuing insufficient money to fund the full amount of the bonuses for National Board Certified teachers exacerbated the ill feeling between the teachers and Superintendent. Unfortunately, they were harbingers of things to come and would bedevil Barresi throughout her term.[30] The Legislature and Governor were not making life any easier for the Superintendent for they were pushing cuts in the state's income tax while assuring citizens that tax revenue in the future would actually increase with the subsequent expanded productivity. New laws were enacted siphoning off public money for nonpublic school vouchers and virtual schools. Meanwhile, the state's public schools were forced to downsize when the highly acclaimed revenue increases failed to materialize.

Reform ideas and processes were advocated seemingly with suggestions generated out-of-state. Two months into her term Barresi laid out her reform agenda: improve literacy, prepare students for college and workforce, and improve curriculum and instruction in STEM (science, technology, engineering, and math). Her ideas were not nearly as controversial as were her methods to achieve them. What testing process would be best and how to interpret the results captured headlines. By May the Governor signed into law mandatory retention of third grade students who failed the qualifying test and a report card system for grading schools, both strongly opposed by educators.[31]

Barresi was on a mission and she was not going to be stymied by any opposition, for she believed she had been given a mandate to introduce chaos into the status quo and she had four years to implement her experiment. Counting on a governor and legislature sympathetic to her efforts and education philosophy led her to believe she could parlay her successes leading charter schools into effective leadership of the schools statewide.

Intimate connections and frequent contacts with Jeb Bush's FEE provided fuel to the heated controversies surrounding her espousal of ideas held contemptible by educators and especially in light of the Legislature's enthrallment with reducing the income tax rate and overall taxes. Should reforms be implemented and competition lauded, the anticipated result would be schools operating more efficiently. School district consolidation, an oft-discussed solution, was encouraged by conservative groups and *The Oklahoman*. However, rural influence on the Legislature was a tour de force, and consolidation was not accomplished during Barresi's term, even though this was one of her highest priorities.[32]

In her first year Barresi tackled key issues and problems by requesting from the federal government waivers to the requirements of the No Child Left Behind Act of 2001 and by restructuring the Department's technology infrastructure with its concomitant implementation of the WAVE, a website to collect student demographic and test data. Errors in the statewide testing plan produced additional cacophony in the system. Any one of these was sufficient to cause significant dissonance, but organizing chaos, though not unexpected by Barresi, nevertheless proved nigh impossible.[33]

Late in the fall of 2011 one of the Board members unexpectedly resigned forcing Governor Fallin to name another member. She chose Joy Hofmeister, someone Barresi anticipated would be sympathetic to and supportive of her goal to transform the state's public education system. Only eight months had passed since the appointment of all new members, so Hofmeister joined a Board still attempting to form a cohesive dynamic team to oversee an increasingly discordant Department. In mid-January 2012 Barresi convened the Board in a two-day planning session in Lawton to allow the members to get to know each other and to lay out her plans for the next year.[34]

With a year of experience to determine the Board's perspectives and expectations and to gauge the support of the Legislature, Barresi offered her preferences for legislation to implement changes: ending third grade social promotion via a reading test, a new teacher evaluation system, and letter grades for schools. Additionally, she stated it was imperative to install a system to allow collection and analysis of more data. To prepare for this increase in accountability a technology and digital learning summit was held. Semantics are important in analyzing one's position, and for Barresi this was critically important. Terminology from the FEE was integral in the Superintendent's description of what she was trying to accomplish: end of social promotion, teacher accountability, letter grades for schools, digital learning, and a summit for dissemination of ideas. Her learning about, and comprehension of, these ideas was gained in part from attending summits, some organized by FEE, where educators hobnobbed with people in business and industry who measured success quantitatively.[35]

About the same time, school districts began to learn that the waiver requesting release from No Child Left Behind included a provision to permit the Department to hire a private company to take over and manage failing schools as soon as the 2012-2013 school year. Not surprisingly, reaction was swift both from educators and some legislators. Barresi attempted to soften and deflect the criticism by emphasizing that these would be partnerships and that these "private education management companies" would be required to hire Oklahoma certified teachers. Such public assurance was not comforting to the state's public educators.[36]

By fall 2012 the A-F school grading system became a flashpoint in the continuing saga of Department and Barresi versus public schools with the former averring that input was sought and the latter deriding the process. Governor Fallin had named a Board sympathetic to Barresi's philosophy, and the latter's hires, unencumbered by backgrounds in education, provided a united front to the common schools establishment. Barresi labeled school administrators as obstreperous and administrators described the Superintendent as having a deaf ear to any concerns. Anyone who critiqued the Superintendent's decisions was immediately labeled as an obstructionist. Several researchers and statisticians at OSU and OU jointly analyzed the state's test results and grading formula and determined problems inherent in the formula. Barresi sought to discredit this examination of one of her most important goals even to the point of stating publicly not only that the researchers had recanted their analysis and renounced their conclusions, but that their results were politically motivated. Unable to defend her position, she resorted to casting aspersions on these apolitical researchers who were seeking to analyze facts to develop an appropriate system to meet the needs of diverse students.[37]

Questions of her ability to lead the education system mounted throughout 2013 when, in April, computer servers crashed during the state's testing process, interrupting testing across the state and naturally causing consternation for the students, parents, and educators. Later, in July, Barresi announced that the state would create its own tests for the new Common Core curriculum standards rather than use those developed by a consortium of more than twenty states, resulting in the necessity for greater expenditure of public funds and in an apparent duplication. Compounding the problem was the controversy over using Common Core standards. The whole realm of student testing, standards, and curriculum was enmeshed in political controversy that increasingly included more of the state's politicians.[38]

A statistical summary of personnel and budgets during Barresi's term, as shown in table 18.4, depicts the Department in a downsizing trend beginning with a 13.7 percent decrease in the number of Department staff and a corresponding 10.9 percent drop in total Departmental expenditures during her first year in office. She was obviously committed to reducing personnel, enjoying her expanded patronage authority and purging the agency of unwanted employees, and money. Over the next two years small numbers of additional staff were hired, but the Department's expenditures continued to be significantly less than in 2010-11. By 2014-15 only 275 employees worked in the Department, a number reduced to 267 (a decrease of almost 20 percent during her term) in 2015-16, her successor's first year in office and before she had an opportunity to determine her staffing needs.[39]

Table 18.4 Department personnel and budget 2010-11 to 2013-14

Year	DE staff	% +/-	Department expenditures					
			State	% +/-	Federal	% +/-	Total	% +/-
2010-11	329	n/a	23,198,326	n/a	52,768,074	n/a	75,966,400	n/a
2011-12	284	-13.7	21,471,858	-7.4	46,179,697	-12.5	67,651,555	-10.9
2012-13	289	-12.2	24,363,867	+5.0	34,815,888	-33.0	59,179,755	-22.1
2013-14	297	-10.0	27,826,521	+20.0	38,158,619	-27.3	65,985,140	-13.1

Sources: *Executive Budget Historical Document of the Governor,* vol. 2 for the number of employees. Department expenditures data were received by the author, October 9, 2019, through an Open Records Request.

Notes: Change columns represent the amount of difference from the baseline 2010-11 data. State expenditures (including revolving funds) and federal program amounts were summed for total Department expenditures for employee compensation, travel, supplies, equipment, and contractual expenses.

Barresi believed her performance to be satisfactory in the face of much ingrained opposition, and that this record and financial and political support from her staunchest supporters in Oklahoma City would be enough to carry her to reelection. Alas, to her disappointment she was unable to make it through her party's primary in June 2014. Undaunted and somewhat flagrantly as a lame duck, in September, Barresi created a new assistant state superintendent of accreditation and compliance position and hired the husband of her general counsel to fill it. His background was in law enforcement although he held a Doctorate in Educational Leadership from the University of Texas at San Antonio. *The Oklahoman's* prescience in April 2011 warned that the Superintendent's newly acquired authority to hire could be used inappropriately.[40]

In the lengthy interregnum between the primary and inauguration day, Barresi resorted to her authority, not given to any previous superintendents, to hire and fire personnel. Beyond the instance cited above, she promoted two employees and gave them $5,000 raises each and, in her final week in office, hired five new ones at a cost of $290,500. Between the beginning of November and early January there were thirteen new hires in the Department.[41] She had no ethical reservations about saddling her successor with patronage appointments and spending taxpayer funds to apply salve to her hurt feelings and injured ego. Her behavior strengthened the position that Board oversight of personnel decisions was necessary to ensure defensible expenditures of public funds.

The four years of her term were a period of relative stability in the local school districts with student enrollments growing by slightly more than 1 percent, about the same rate of growth as reflected in the attendance rate and number of district personnel. Table 18.5 reflects a 5 percent drop in the number of PK-8 districts and a decrease of just two PK-12 districts, reducing the overall number of districts statewide by seven, a negligible amount. Barresi initially supported consolidation but her priorities lay with alternatives to the traditional public school; consequently, statewide the system accommodated itself to her personal quirks, opinions, and obstructions. Not accounted for in the Department's records was the number of students statewide who left the public schools for nonpublic or home school options. Oklahoma law does not permit the Department to gather any data on the number of students taught at home or in nonpublic schools or the curriculum followed.

Table 18.5 School district data 2010-2014

Year	Enrollment	Attendance	District personnel	Number of school districts		
				PK-8	PK-12	Total
2010-11	652,958	616,775	51,388	103	421	524
2011-12	659,537	624,410	51,719	102	420	522
2012-13	667,983	630,766	52,380	101	419	520
2013-14	675,534	639,376	52,395	98	419	517

Sources: *Annual Report of the State Department of Education: 2010-11*, 7, 12, 93; *Annual Report of the State Department of Education, 2011-12*, 3, 7, 12; *Annual Report of the State Department of Education, 2012-13*, 3, 7, 12; *Annual Report of the State Department of Education, 2013-14*, 3, 7, 12.

Note: Because the Department discontinued reporting data in the typical format in 2013-2014, it is difficult to compare data for the subsequent years. The National Center for Education Statistics reported slightly different enrollment/membership data for the years displayed in this table. For example, NCES reported the enrollment/membership for 2013-14 was 681,578. See http://nces.ed.gov/.

Her staunchest advocate, *The Oklahoman*, gave Barresi one last opportunity to assess her term and the extent to which she was able to achieve her goals. As to be expected, she blamed opposition on the recalcitrance of educators and politicians who benefitted from continuation of the status quo. She "laughed off claims that she's cold and indifferent, that she doesn't listen to schools and superintendents and doesn't care about teachers, calling such claims 'ridiculous.'" Continuing, "I am a gal that is very plain-spoken. I will tell people when I see a problem."[42] Barresi seemed to conflate educators' resistance to her modus operandi and educational philosophy as simply their reaction to her form of communication rather than to sincerely held beliefs about how the state should be implementing its constitutional mandate to provide educational opportunities for the students.

Within Oklahoma's education governance schematic of the Superintendent presiding over both the Board and also *ex-officio* over the State Board of Career and Technology Education, Barresi influenced the hiring of the director of Career Technology in April 2013. Her contacts with school option advocates and devotees around the country familiarized her with Robert Sommers, CEO and managing director of Carpe Diem Learning Systems, a for-profit charter school management organization operating on-line charter schools. Governor Fallin three months later named him Secretary of Education and Workforce Management. The seventh Career Tech director, but the first one chosen from out-of-state, commuted from Ohio the entire fourteen months he served. Similar to Barresi, he was a destabilizing force as he brought new, and sometimes unpopular ideas to Oklahoma's highly reputable career technical system. However, because the position is appointive the Board had the flexibility to choose an outsider, something impossible under the elective arrangement for Superintendent.[43]

Barresi was in a hurry to change the education system, and many of her ideas came from external connections. The influence of the FEE and subsequently Chiefs for Change was instrumental in aiding her to formulate her notions of what to do and how to do it. How much of her success or failure resulted from her personality and approach and how much from the concepts, ideas, and implementation efforts are subject to one's interpretation. One thing is relatively certain: her performance was not conducive to great success in administering the agency receiving more than half of the state's allocation of public funds and a sizeable portion of federal funds also.

Her aspiration from the beginning was to disrupt the status quo through stimulating competition and diverting public money for private options. She desired to test the strength of the state's constitution prohibiting the funneling of public funds for private and church-related schools and their students. Viewed through the prism of an ineffective public school system needing a firm corrective stimulus, her approach was to siphon money from a historically, financially-starved, and constitutionally-required government function and channel it through alternatives that might compete and force improvement. In part, she achieved her goal. Millions of dollars were redirected into non-brick and mortar schools while the Legislature became adept at bleeding the traditional schools financially.

Barresi was unable to expand her influence through reelection and another four years from a combination of her abrasive personality and animosity toward the public school community. Had she proven to be a listener and worked to build support for her ideas she might have been able to generate more support to initiate her desired reforms. Barresi vacated the office January 12, 2015, and re-entered the world of private citizen, preferring obscurity and avoiding the controversies that hung over her term like a thick fog.[44]

Her biography states that while studying for her graduate degree she married John R. Barresi who played football for the Sooners and was focusing on petroleum land management. August 9, 1975, was their wedding date, and they were married until his death in March 2009 at the early age of 59. Twin sons were born in 1987 and eventually followed their father's footsteps by playing football in college. It was her strong parental interest and efforts to secure a quality education for her sons in the urban Oklahoma City School District that led her to the path to seek the Superintendency. Her initial campaign for the office occurred in the immediate aftermath of her husband's untimely death.[45] She joined the first elected Superintendent E. D. Cameron in the dubious distinction of serving only one term and then losing in the primary election for a second term.

Chapter 19
Hofmeister: Campaigning on Limited Qualifications
(2014 and the Quasquicentennial Anniversary)

Joy Hofmeister's rapid rise to the Superintendency was aided immensely by Barresi's inability to form a cohesive Board. Unknown in the public school arena beyond the Jenks School District prior to her appointment to the Board by Governor Mary Fallin in January 2012, Hofmeister came from relative obscurity to run for the office of Superintendent. A member of the Board when chaos reigned at the Department, she served for fifteen months trying to work with the Superintendent, but became exasperated and resigned. Certainly, she thought, someone else needs to be in charge to end the strife within the Board and the Department.[1]

Born in St. Louis, Missouri, September 7, 1964, she spent her formative years in Tulsa where she graduated from a church-sponsored high school, entered college at Southwest Baptist University in Bolivar, Missouri, and eventually earned a Bachelor's Degree in Education from Texas Christian University. Her undergraduate studies qualified her for teaching certificates in English and elementary education, the latter she used to obtain a lower elementary grade teaching position in Ft. Worth. After a brief stint of no more than one year of teaching, she and her family moved to Jenks where she settled into a career of operating for-profit Kumon Math and Reading Centers in the Tulsa area, serving on the board of directors for the Jenks Public Schools Foundation, providing lay perspective on the Select Committee for the Study of School Finance in Jenks, and participating in multiple civic and professional endeavors.[2]

Board Member Insight

Tumult encompassed the Board in early 2011 when Governor Henry's appointees refused to support personnel changes sought by Barresi. When the First Congressional District representative (a Board member is selected from each Congressional District) from Tulsa, Tim Gilpin, left his position on the Board in March, Phil Lakin was appointed to complete the term. Six months later, in October, when the Legislature's newly enacted SB 435 giving the Governor power to name a new Board became effective, Lakin was reappointed only to resign within two months because of his election to the Tulsa City Council. The vacancy guaranteed that a third person would fill this position within a span of nine months,[3]

Preston Doerflinger, Oklahoma's secretary of finance and revenue, recommended his friend and fellow Jenks resident, Hofmeister, to Governor Fallin for appointment to complete the unexpired term. The Governor appreciated the advice and named Hofmeister who joined the Board with enthusiasm, trepidation, and commitment to civic duty knowing that she was about to embark on a potentially perilous journey. Major issues attracting media coverage were confronting the Board, thus she anticipated their continuation during her term. She fully committed to completing her term, but served only from January 2012 to April 2013 when she resigned following a confrontation with Barresi who was not known for smoothing ruffled feathers. Hofmeister was chagrined to say the least over the episode. Barresi relentlessly pushed her especially controversial A-F grading scheme for schools and districts and the expanding options for public school students. Adding to the challenge was that the Governor fired three of the Board members in September 2011, another resigned, and now most of the members had not worked together previously. Consequently, Board members were attempting to learn their positions, functioning in a new dynamic atmosphere with a Superintendent committed to non-conformity, and trying to implement a challenging reform agenda that included accountability through student testing, reading benchmarks for promotion to third grade, assignment of grades (A-F) to schools and districts, and greater involvement of private companies in the management and operation of schools.[4]

Hofmeister, who learned how to operate a company through ownership of a private tutoring service and how some students struggled and needed extra assistance to learn math and to read well in school, proved her mettle in advocating for the students. She attended every one of the twenty-one Board meetings during her tenure, abstaining only once in a vote. As a new member, she listened, learned, and only after six months, did

Joy Hofmeister
Courtesy of the Oklahoma State Department of Education

she offer a motion for consideration. Of the approximately 214 votes taken during her tenure she initiated motions only nine times and seconded motions thirty-three times.[5] She staked out her position rather early and held consistent throughout her brief tenure. Where there was apparent school district negligence in the implementation of state law and Board regulations, resulting in perceived harm to students in their academic pursuit, Hofmeister advocated for the students and chided the district administration for incompetence. The cavalier approach to solutions exhibited through the impatience of Barresi, who disdained anyone seemingly opposed to her competitive agenda, placed Hofmeister as a neophyte Board member in the Superintendent's crosshairs. Exacerbating the situation were the complexity of the reform efforts and the tensions among educators statewide over the diversion of limited resources to nonpublic options and virtual schools.

Tulsa area school officials found a sympathetic ear in their representative, and they kept her informed of the inconsistencies and inequities resulting from Department and Board decisions. She focused on student testing, district and school letter grades, and what she deemed best for students. While Barresi saw her as an obstructionist and the pawn of the Tulsa educators, Hofmeister viewed Barresi as obstreperous. Hofmeister rarely voted against the majority but was not hesitant to ask pointed questions about purpose and clarity. Insufficient and ineffective Department communication with educators, especially refusal to hear input, and the agency's overall attitude that the educators were united in their efforts to stifle implementation of reforms, caused her to resign from the Board and to run for the Superintendency.[6]

Distilling the toxic brew of Barresi, the Board, the Department, the education system, and Republican politics to ascertain the most significant ingredients and what was politically feasible was a challenge to the Republican establishment. Barresi had a diminishing cadre of staunch supporters while the majority of Republicans yearned for a more viable candidate. She was determined to win at any financial cost and was not hindered by any ethical restraints as shown by her willingness to harass the Jenks School District with a request for all electronic communications involving her opponent. Thus, Barresi's tactics to smear Hofmeister caused consternation and substantial extra work as the district responded to the demand.

Growing the Brief Republican Legacy

Republicans were determined to employ the successes of the 2010 election as a springboard for candidates in the 2014 election, and they had no intent on ceding to the Democrats any gains in statewide power. But, in the Superintendent, they had a highly contentious and fractious person who had alienated many voters and most of the educators. Also at hand was the internal struggle raging in the Republican Party caused in part by groups external to Oklahoma attempting to control events within the state. Stepping into the fray to present an alternative was the short tenured, little-known, previous Board member. Hofmeister, with no experience at state level governance, but with perceived political capital, began to capture the attention of political kingmakers. She could be a strong candidate to compete against Barresi in the 2014 election. She had an inside look at the incumbent, knew her strengths and weaknesses, and, anticipating the support of the education constituency as well as much of the Republican establishment, she threw her hat into the ring. Those who were familiar with her knew her to be passionate about students and frustrated with the incumbent.

Hofmeister began her journey for the Superintendency early in 2014 by hiring a campaign manager to operate out of a small office in the rear of her company's headquarters in Tulsa. Initially, resources were limited as she was preparing for a political fight against an incumbent of her own party. Once before, in 1946, another Tulsan, Oliver Hodge, challenged the incumbent of his own Democratic Party, and now Hofmeister was trying to accomplish the same as a Republican but without the visibility benefiting Hodge. She traversed the state speaking to many Republican women's clubs, precinct committee meetings, and school district administrator and teacher meetings, receiving friendlier receptions by the former two and penetrating questions by the latter. Sometimes condescendingly and other times disbelieving, the educators communicated their apprehensions regarding her minimal qualifications.[7]

As with any newcomer to the political arena, and specifically one with such a paucity of public school experience, her positions evolved and matured over time. Suspicion swirled about the extent, if any, of her teaching experience. The media reported that she had teaching experience, per her campaign website and printed literature, but Hofmeister never sought to clarify the issue or provide evidence. Generalized positions slowly became more focused through the crucible of the campaign as she was compelled to elucidate her goals: "advocate for standardized testing reform and accountability system updates…current A-F school grading system is broken and must be fixed…like to see some legislation to 'decrease costly bureaucracy' to ensure more education funding gets to classrooms."[8] She struggled to flesh out her thoughts with exiguous personal experience in public education.

Preparing for the June 23 primary, she solicited and obtained the endorsement of forty-five state senate and house members or almost one-third of the membership of the two chambers, a phenomenal achievement by any measure. Of course, the Legislature was by now majority Republican by a large margin. Continuing to advise her were the executive director of the Cooperative Council of School Administrators, Ryan Owens, the Secretary, Phyllis Hudecki, and the Tulsa Public Schools superintendent, Keith Ballard. A "viable" candidate meant one minimally qualified and registered Republican, for the political environment strongly favored the party with the elephant symbol. Counterbalancing was her status as an outsider competing against the incumbent. As events unfolded, three contestants entered the fray, expanding the options and further complicating Hofmeister's efforts to win. Simmering general dissatisfaction with the incumbent engendered through some high-profile controversies played satisfactorily into Hofmeister's campaign. After crushing her opposition without a runoff, capturing 57.6 percent of the votes, she was set to challenge the eventual Democratic candidate who had a runoff election himself (see table 19.1).[9]

The Democratic primary attracted four candidates with none garnering more than 41 percent. Winnowed to two, John Cox and Freda Deskin competed in the August 26 runoff with the former capturing almost 63 percent of the vote. Cox, with no prior statewide campaign experience, minimal interest and support from the Democratic Party, and needing to overcome his opponent's support from former Democratic governors, represented the rural interests. Democrats' support for Deskin materialized because she was viewed as a stronger choice against the incumbent. Like Barresi, Deskin was from the Oklahoma City area and was intimately involved in founding a charter school, not a plank friendly to a Democrat's platform but apropos to a line adapted from Shakespeare's The Tempest, "Politics make strange bedfellows." Both parties' candidates were now set for the November general election.[10]

Cox, superintendent of the Peggs Elementary School District in Cherokee County, sought and received the support of the rural educators, particularly the school administrators, through his leadership in the Organization of Rural Oklahoma Schools. He campaigned on a platform of experience of twenty-eight years in public schools with twenty of those years as superintendent, a Doctorate in School Administration, and leadership in statewide organizations. Working against him were his image-suffering, high compensation for the superintendency of a small, rural, elementary school district; representation of the minority party; opposition to district consolidation; lack of charisma compared to Hofmeister; and inability to convince the voter of his capability to move the state forward. Also, his fundraising for the primary, runoff, and general elections amounted to less than half that of Hofmeister. Proof of the extent to which the state had swung Republican and conservative, she garnered more votes than Cox in every one of the seventy-seven counties.[11]

Table 19.1 2014 Election results and campaign expenditures

Candidate	Party	Election	Votes	Percent	Expenditures
John Cox	Dem	Primary	68,889	41.0	...
Freda Deskin	Dem	Primary	64,135	38.2	...
Jack Herron	Dem	Primary	22,335	13.3	24,225.21
Ivan Holmes	Dem	Primary	12,504	7.5	13,696.22
John Cox	Dem	Runoff	60,370	62.9	...
Freda Deskin	Dem	Runoff	35,621	37.1	295,547.07
Brian Kelly	Rep	Primary	56,060	21.4	n/d
Janet Barresi	Rep	Primary	55,048	21.0	1,544,746.00
Joy Hofmeister	Rep	Primary	151,122	57.6	...
John Cox	Dem	General	361,878	44.2	460,159.62
Joy Hofmeister	Rep	General	457,053	55.8	818,932.06

Sources: www.ok.gov/elections; C1-R Campaign Contributions and Expenditures Report for each candidate at https: pay.apps.ok.gov/ethics/crs/c1r/view.

Notes: Expenditures are cumulative for each candidate and are listed for the final election in which the candidates participated. Brian Kelly failed to report.

Costs escalated rapidly in the elections where Republicans dominated the outcomes, but the amounts reported were skewed by the deep pockets of Barresi. Regardless, expenditures for the 2010 election exceeded two million dollars with Republicans accounting for 60 percent of the total. Four years later, the sum increased more than 50 percent to $3,157,306 with the Democrats' share only 33.6 percent of the overall amount. While Hofmeister's campaign invested more than did the Democrats' combined efforts, her expenses were still only slightly more than half of Barresi's.[12]

Sworn into office January 12, 2015, as the eleventh elected, fourteenth overall, and the third consecutive female Superintendent, Hofmeister assumed the duties and began working with the Board that had four members with whom she had worked while a member. Although distinguished by being the first Superintendent to have previously been a Board member, she faced the immediate necessity of compressing a lot of learning about leading the Department and a chronically underfunded common school system. Graduating from a Baptist high school and TCU shielded her from the environment of public education until her brief teaching stint introduced her to the challenges facing teachers even in the reasonably well-funded schools of Texas. Operating a local franchise of a for-profit tutoring company, JLH Resources, gave her insight into the business world and the opportunities for profit-based companies to benefit from those parents who had the financial capacity to acquire supplementary education for their children. With this background she was selected to serve on the Board responsible for oversight of almost 700,000 students who were majority minority and two-thirds of them qualified for free/reduced lunches. Service on the Board occurred when Department personnel were demoralized and the entire state public school system was chaotic resulting from a Superintendent whose personality and modus operandi failed to measure up against all that was requisite for the effective operation of the Board and Department.

Tulsa Public School classroom 2021, photo by Lois E. Brandt

Hofmeister accepted appreciably the editorial support and positive coverage of her campaign from her hometown newspaper, the *Tulsa World*, while *The Oklahoman* aggressively pushed the candidacy of Barresi. She was a relative newcomer and novice politician, but she presented herself as a viable alternative to the feisty and combative incumbent. She also earned the endorsement of the OEA and the Cooperative Council of Oklahoma School Administration. Her perspectives were couched in the language of the business world, placing her in good stead with the business community. In an acknowledgement of her limited credentials, less than a week following the 2014 election Hofmeister formed a nine-member team to assist her with the transition to the office. School district superintendents, former Superintendent Garrett, a Republican Party official, a Board member, and the owner of a company were named to the committee. The overture to the school administrators was Hofmeister's initial attempt to reach out to an important segment of the education community that supported her and seemed to be held in disdain by her predecessor.[13]

Hofmeister's term began with little fanfare, many challenges, and an immediate commitment to lower the level of chaos in the Department. The Republican dominated Legislature, executive offices, and various agencies were beginning to feel the pressure of accumulating losses of revenue from reductions in the state income tax rate and the downturn in the energy sector with all of the related effects on companies directly tied to gas and oil exploration, drilling, and production. Reduced revenue was not novel to Oklahoma, but that part of history was no consolation to a new Superintendent who was to represent the interests of the state's ethnically-diverse public school students. One thing is certain, she benefitted from the minimal requirements to be Oklahoma's Superintendent. Compared to all of her elected and appointed predecessors, she offered the least qualifications to lead Oklahoma's public school system: the first Superintendent since Crable (1936-1947) to have earned no degree above a bachelor's degree, only one year of teaching experience, no formal educational preparation for an administrator's certificate, and no public school administration experience.[14] She was conservative politically and in her religious affiliation, married to a municipal judge, lived in an upper middle class, predominantly white suburb, and enjoyed the benefits of a family of four children. She was now handed the responsibility to provide leadership and direction to the Board, a Department of hundreds of employees, and more than 500 school districts, and to oversee the expenditure of funds exceeding $2,000,000,000.

A description and critique of Hofmeister's performance and tenure would have continued the theme of this historical analysis and added substance to the overall depiction of the Superintendency in Oklahoma. Because the design from the beginning was to set the parameters to be from the establishment of the Superintendency in December 1890, early in the Territorial period, through the quasquicentennial anniversary, this book now ends.

Epilogue

My goal over several decades of research was to investigate and analyze in-depth the nature and dynamics of the Superintendency as it evolved from the meager beginnings of the territorial period to the oversight of the Department of hundreds of employees, a statewide system of more than 500 school districts with more than 55,000 teachers, and an annual budget of 2-3 billion dollars. What was expected of the Superintendent as the administrator of the statewide system and the gatekeeper to fulfilling the constitutional mandate of providing a free public education to the students of the state? Superintendents had to confront the challenges of a perennially underfunded system, a structure of systemic racism, major blows from the Great Depression, two world wars, the Dust Bowl, the vicissitudes of the energy industry, and the more recent move to public funding of non-public school options. The cornerstone theme, which is indirectly related to the job responsibilities of the Superintendent, is the nature of the position and the decision-making attendant to competing for, and retaining, the office. The elective Superintendency places it squarely in the midst of political forces both in the effort to gain and keep the office. The strength of a democracy is determined in part by the quality of people aspiring to positions and the rigor of the process to select the best candidate.

Most Oklahomans are not informed well of the Superintendency and the limitations, intentional and otherwise, constraining the selection and operation of those who hold the office. Citizens cling tightly to their prerogative to engage in the selection of the Superintendents rather than to delegate that authority to others. Highly qualified education administrators weigh whether or not they wish to subject themselves to the politics of the election process. Many such persons decide not to engage in what they consider anathema to their life's mission to provide a non-politicized, excellent educational environment for learning. Self-selection required of the elective option leaves the citizens to the whims and motives of the few who contend.

Several governors from the 1920s to the 1980s commissioned studies to examine how to improve the efficiency and effectiveness of state government. Some of these leaders' motivation stemmed from a desire to increase their authority and prerogative over the operation of the education system through being able to appoint the Superintendent, but to date, those attempts have proven futile. What was lacking was a thorough examination of the consequences of the elective option and the subsequent development of a sufficient argument for having the top education official appointed either by the Governor, the Board, or some other method. Citizens generally support change when there is an emergency or when they are convinced of the value of doing so. For example, Republicans wanted a two-term limit because they could not get one of their own elected, and in the 2010 election when the state swung solidly to the right politically, the voters approved a constitutional amendment to accomplish that. Now that the Republicans dominate the political structure in Oklahoma they have the responsibility to provide the best leadership. The reality is that oftentimes the forces for change arise from the opposing party but when that party is so weak, it is nigh impossible to generate sufficient thrust for meaningful improvement.

Should time and an educational effort to convince the voters to shift to the appointive method through a constitutional amendment be unsuccessful, two other aspects need further explication—the constraints of the ten-year durational residency rule (average length for the thirteen states that still elect their Superintendents is four years) and the low salary relative to what the local school superintendents are paid.[1] Both of these would appea to be easier, but not necessarily easy, hurdles to cross than the selection provision. Almost never is the residency rule's purpose evaluated or debated and it is referenced only when someone's eligibility comes into question. The efficacy of the criterion needs to be examined in an environment free of any specific person's qualification. Regarding the relative paltry salary, the Legislature is loath to approve a salary scheme in which any elected official is paid more than the Governor. Additionally, district superintendent salaries are the highest in the urban areas, and the Legislature is dominated by rural interests mitigating sufficient resolve to increase the Superintendent's compensation. If leadership of a medium or large district is a preferred criterion for leading the Department and the statewide public education system, a higher salary must be offered to entice these superintendents.

What is desperately needed in the Superintendency is creative leadership, a willingness to take more risks to effect significant change, and a profound desire to elevate the role and respect of the teachers through encouraging politicians to act through positive commentary and provision of reasonable financial compensation.

An enlarged perspective of the possibilities for a public education system might come from the selection of a person who has developed experience in another state. Oklahoma's constitutional provisions effectively narrow unnecessarily those eligible for the Superintendency, but one must assume that as long as the citizens are satisfied with the status quo it will be difficult to accomplish a significant change. After conducting this lengthy study, I believe that if the politicians, influential citizens, and the media better comprehended how the elective method constrains the quality of the individuals available for the Superintendency and the political calculations of those who serve, they might muster the courage and resources to mount an effort to overcome a somewhat provincial attitude and lack of knowledge present in a large swath of the citizenry. Year after year of being in the bottom fifth of the states in educational outcomes, but with a great resource for a century being extracted from deep in the earth seems inconsistent.

Abbreviations in the Notes and Appendices

ARS—Annual Report

ARSSPI—Annual Report of the State Superintendent of Public Instruction

AROSDE—Annual Report of the Oklahoma State Department of Education

ARSROSSDE—Annual Report: Statistical Report on Oklahoma Schools and the State Department of Education

BR—Biennial Report

BRDPIO—Biennial Report of the Department of Public Instruction of Oklahoma

BRSDEO—Biennial Report of the State Department of Education of Oklahoma

BRSSPI—Biennial Report of the State Superintendent of Public Instruction

BRTSPI—Biennial Report of the Territorial Superintendent of Public Instruction

CCER—Campaign Contributions and Expenditures Report

DE—Department of Education

EBCFCE—Election Board Candidate Filings and Campaign Expenses

EOHC—Encyclopedia of Oklahoma History and Culture

GPO—Government Printing Office

IT—Indian Territory

JCP of the …—Journal of Council Proceedings…

OA—Oklahoma Almanac

ODE—Oklahoma Directory of Education

OEA—Oklahoma Education Association

ODL—Oklahoma Department of Libraries

OED—Oklahoma Educational Directory

OHC—Oklahoma History Center

OHSRC—Oklahoma Historical Society and Research Center

OK—Oklahoma

OKC—Oklahoma City

OSA—Oklahoma State Archives

OSU—Oklahoma State University

OT—Oklahoma Territory

OU—The University of Oklahoma

RSBE—Report of the State Board of Education

SBE—State Board of Education
SBEMM—State Board of Education Meeting Minutes
SCC—Superintendents Correspondence Collection
SDE—(Oklahoma) State Department of Education
SEB—(Oklahoma) State Election Board
SEC—(Oklahoma) State Ethics Commission
TBEMM—Territorial Board of Education Meeting Minutes
TW—Tulsa World
TT—Tulsa Tribune
TO—The Daily Oklahoman/The Oklahoman

Endnotes

Introduction

1. Angie Debo. *Oklahoma Foot-loose and Fancy-free* (Norman: University of Oklahoma Press, 1949), 9.
2. *Third Biennial Report of the Department of Public Instruction State of Oklahoma* (Guthrie: Leader Print, 1910), 18.
3. R. H. Wilson, *A Brief Statement of the Growth of the Schools of Oklahoma for the Past Four Years 1912-1915* (Oklahoma City: 1915), 4.
4. The slogan was an integral component of her campaign literature as well as included on the front covers of the annual *Educational Directory* and the annual reports.

Chapter 1

1. *Journal of the First Session of the Legislative Assembly of Oklahoma Territory, Beginning August 17, 1890* (Guthrie, 1890*)*, 37; *JCP of the Third Legislative Assembly of the Territory of Oklahoma, Beginning January 8, 1895 and ending March 8, 1895* (Guthrie, 1895), 334.
2. Statutes of Oklahoma 1890 § 6369 (Guthrie, 1891*)*; *Report of the Governor of Oklahoma to the Secretary of the Interior 1895* (Washington, DC, 1895), 15-16; Statutes of Oklahoma 1890 §§ 409, 3718; Territory of Oklahoma S.L. 1897, ch. 16, § 1, ch. 1, § 1 (Guthrie, 1897).
3. Statutes of Oklahoma 1890 §§ 6440, 6176; Territory of Oklahoma S.L. 1895, ch. 43, § 1-2 (Pub. NA, 1895*)*; *Report of the Governor of Oklahoma to the Secretary of the Interior for the Fiscal Year Ended June 30, 1898* (Washington, DC, 1898), 70*;* Territory of Oklahoma S.L. 1895, ch. 35, § 47*;* Statutes of Oklahoma 1893 § 152 (Guthrie, 1893).
4. Statutes of Oklahoma 1890 §§ 6384, 6385.
5. *Norman Transcript,* August 19, 1892, 1; Department of Commerce, *US Census of Population: 1900,* Kingfisher County, O. T. (Washington, DC, 1900); D. W. Wilder, *The Annals of Kansas, New Edition 1541-1885* (Topeka, 1886), 709-10, 924, and 1042.
6. Wilder, *The Annals of Kansas,* 1068-71, 1095; Kirche Mecham, ed., *The Annals of Kansas 1886-1925* (Topeka: Kansas State Historical Society, 1956), 11, 71; https://www.kshs.org/p/kansas-superintendents-of-public-instruction/1100#lawhead; G. W. Martin, ed., *Transactions of the Kansas Historical Society, 1903-1904, together with Addresses at Annual Meetings, Miscellaneous Papers, and a Roster of Kansas for Fifty Years,* 8 (Topeka: Geo. A. Clark, 1904), 511, 521.
7. (Guthrie, O. T.) *Oklahoma State Capital,* August 29, 1892, 1; *Journal of the First Legislative Assembly,* 765-66; *Weekly Oklahoma State Capital,* December 27, 1890, 7; January 14, 1891, 2.
8. *TBEMM,* January 14, 1891, RG 18-1, DE, OSA, ODL, OKC.
9. *TBEMM,* February 6, 1891; February 19, 1891; April 9, 1891.
10. *TBEMM,* January 20, 1892; May 25, 1892.
11. *Norman Transcript,* August 19, 1892, 1; A. Kenneth Stern and Janelle L. Wagner, "The First Decade of Educational Governance in Kansas, 1855-1865," *Kansas History,* Spring 2001, 36-53; Thomas Arthur Hazell, Leroy H. Fischer, ed., *Oklahoma's Governors, 1890-1907: Territorial Years* (OKC: OHSRC, 1975), 10, 21-22.
12. George M. Platt, "Possess Thou the West and the South: The Frontiers of Reverend Joseph Homer Parker: A Son of the Eastern Townships," *Journal of Eastern Township Studies,* 22 (Spring 2003): 53-73.
13. Ibid.; J. H. N. Tindall, *Makers of Oklahoma* (Guthrie: State Capital, 1905), 53; *Portrait and Biographical Record of Oklahoma* (Chicago: Chapman, 1901), 193-94. *US Census of Population: 1890,* Kingfisher County, O. T. (Washington, DC, 1890) shows that Parker was forty-seven years old, and thus would have been born in 1843. However, his tombstone in Kingfisher Cemetery states his birth as February 20, 1848. Platt, "Possess Thou the West," 58; *US Census of Population: 1900,* Kingfisher County; *Portrait and Biographical Record,* 193-94.
14. *Weekly Oklahoma State Capital,* January 3, 1891, 7; September 9, 1893, 2; *JCP of the Second Legislative Assembly of the Territory of Oklahoma, Beginning January 10, 1893* (Guthrie, 1893), 100.
15. *TBEMM,* November 2, 1892; Statutes of Oklahoma 1893 § 5876; *TBEMM,* April 5, 1893.
16. *TBEMM,* May 4, 1893*;* July 15, 1893; October 26, 1893.
17. *Weekly Oklahoma State Capital,* June 10, 1893, 1; June 17, 1893, 1.
18. *Weekly Oklahoma State Capital,* September 9, 1893, 2; *Cameron, Superintendent of Public Instruction v. Parker,* 38 P. 16 (Okla. 1894).
19. *Portrait and Biographical Record,* 194; *Kingfisher (O. T.) Free Press,* July 9, 1915, 3.
20. *Cameron v Parker*; R. L. Williams, "Rev. Evan Dhu Cameron," *Chronicles of Oklahoma,* 11 (March, 1933); 740-43.

21. Williams, "Rev. Evan Dhu Cameron;" *Minutes of the Annual Conference of the Methodist Episcopal Church, South for the Year 1889* (Nashville: Publishing House of the Methodist Episcopal Church, South, 1890), 105, 111.
22. *TBEMM,* March 21, 1894; May 3, 1894-January 11, 1896. *TBEMM* are not extant from January 12, 1896 to January 18, 1904.
23. *Second BRTSPI in the Governor's Message to the Third Legislative Assembly of the Territory of Oklahoma* (Guthrie, 1895), 10.
24. "Cameron to Resign," *Guthrie Daily Journal*, November 16, 1896, 1; *JCP of the Third Legislative Assembly*, 481; *Third BRTSPI of Oklahoma, July 1, 1894-June 30, 1896* (Guthrie, 1896), 3; Williams, "Rev. Evan Dhu Cameron," 743.
25. *Second BR of the Territorial Auditor* (Guthrie, 1895), 20; *JCP of the Fourth Legislative Assembly of the Territory of Oklahoma, Beginning January 12, 1897, Ending March 12, 1897* (Guthrie, 1897), 1139.
26. *Joplin* (Missouri) *Globe,* July 14, 1954, 11; Robert Cutting (A. O. Nichols's grandson), phone interview with the author, April 21, 1997; *Oklahoma Daily Press Gazette,* March 14, 1894; *JCP of the Fifth Legislative Assembly of the Territory of Oklahoma, Beginning January 10, 1899, Ending March 10, 1899* (Guthrie, 1899). The *Territorial Auditor's Report* was included in its entirety in this volume on pages 78-95.
27. *Manual for Lincoln County Teachers*, 2 (Chandler, O. T.: Chandler News, 1896).
28. *El Reno* (*O. T.*) *News,* April 30, 1897, 1.
29. *El Reno News*, July 2, 1897; September 3, 1897, 1; *JCP of the Fifth Legislative Assembly*, 78-95; Cutting, interview; *Joplin Globe*, July 13, 1954, 11.
30. *Guthrie* (*O. T.*) *Daily Leader*, September 26, 1897, 4.
31. *Portrait and Biographical Record*, 21-22.
32. *Ibid.; Oklahoma School Herald*, December 1895, 15; November 1897, 10; Joe Hubbell, "The Oklahoma Education Association, 1884-1974," 9 (unpublished manuscript, OEA, OKC).
33. *Norman Transcript*, June 1, 1894, 1; *TBEMM*, June 5, 1894; *JCP of the Fifth Legislative Assembly*, 1100; *JCP of the Sixth Legislative Assembly of the Territory of Oklahoma, Beginning January 8, 1901, Ending March 8, 1901* (Guthrie: State Capital, 1901), 335-36.
34. *TO*, February 18, 1899, 3; *El Reno News*, February 24, 1899, 1. Habeas corpus is a writ requiring a person under arrest to be brought before a judge especially to secure the person's release unless lawful grounds are shown for that person's detention. *El Reno News*, April 7, 1899, 2.
35. *Oklahoma School Herald*, March 1899, 3; February 1899, 2.
36. Fifth BRTSPI, July 1, 1898-June 30, 1900 (Guthrie: State Capital, 1900), 10-11, 6.
37. *Southwest World*, March 16, 1901, 4; *El Reno Democrat*, March 21, 1901, 7; *The Normal School for Oklahoma 1900-1901*, Edmond, Oklahoma, 9. In the next year the name was changed to *Annual Catalogue of the Officers and Students of the Territorial Normal School. Oklahoma City School Board Meeting Minutes* for these dates: June 11, 1909, March 7, 1910, September 25, 1911, April 5, 1912, April 7, 1913, May 21, 1914, August 28, 1915, June 19, 1916, May 26, 1919, May 13, 1920, and October 20, 1921, OKC School District Office.
38. *TO*, November 9, 1934, 16; Francis Coram Oakes, *A Story of Central State College of Edmond, Oklahoma*, (Edmond, OK: 1953) 48-49, Library Archives, UCO, Edmond; *Portrait and Biographical Record*, 22.
39. *Oklahoma School Herald*, April 1901, 2; *Edmond* (*O. T.*) *Sun*, December 20, 1906, 4; *US Census of Population: 1900*, Oklahoma County; *Edmond Sun*, November 30, 1900, 1; December 21, 1900, 1.
40. "Annual Meetings and Presidents of the State Teachers Organization in Oklahoma," OEA, OKC; *Guthrie Daily Leader*, December 30, 1896, 4; January 10, 1897, 1; July 25, 1897, 3; October 7, 1897, 4; (Guthrie, O. T.) *Southwest World*, April 6, 1901, 1.
41. Oakes, *Story of Central State College*, 28; *The Normal School for Oklahoma, 1897-98. Catalogue and Report of the President and Faculty*, 7.
42. Oakes, *Story of Central State College*, 48-49.
43. *JCP of the Seventh Legislative Assembly of the Territory of Oklahoma, Beginning January 13, 1903, and ending March 13. 1903* (Guthrie: State Capital, 1903), 297; *JCP of the Eighth Legislative Assembly of the Territory of Oklahoma, Beginning January 10, 1905, and ending March 17, 1905* (Guthrie: State Capital, 1905), 240.
44. *Sixth BRTSPI of the Territory of Oklahoma for the Two Years Beginning July 1, 1900 and ending June 30, 1902* (Guthrie: State Capital, 1902), 8-12.
45. Ibid., 11-12.
46. *Seventh BR of the Territorial Auditor of Oklahoma, November 30, 1902 to November 30, 1904* (Guthrie: State Capital Printing Company, 1904), 6-7.

47. *Edmond Sun*, December 20, 1906, 4.
48. *Ibid.*; *TT*, March 7, 1935, 9.
49. *Lawton (O. T.) Constitution*, December 19, 1906, 2; Alumni Records, Archives Office, University of Kansas, Topeka; (Wellington, KS) *Monitor*, September 1, 1892, 1; *Horton, Kansas, Alumni Directory, 1991*. This Directory lists all of the superintendents in the history of the Horton School District. *TO*, December 27, 1926, 1-2; Charles Black, *The Lawton Directory, 1902* (Lawton, O. T.: George W. McCoy, 1902), 17; *TO*, December 27, 1926, 1-2.
50. *TBEMM*, January 10-October 19, 1907; *Guthrie Daily Leader*, October 18, 1907, 1.
51. *Oklahoma Elections: Statehood to Present*, vol. 1 (OKC: SEB, 1994), C-1; *TO*, December 27, 1926, 1-2; *US Census of Population: 1910*, Grady County, OK (Washington, DC, 1910); *TO*, December 27, 1926, 1-2.
52. Statutes of Oklahoma 1893 § 268-69; Territory of Oklahoma S.L. 1895, chapt. 4, § 2-3; Territory of Oklahoma S.L. 1899, chapt. 3, art. 2, § 4 (Guthrie, 1899); Territory of Oklahoma S.L. 1905, ch. 4, § 6 (State Capital 1905).
53. United States Office of Indian Affairs, *Annual Report of the Commissioner of Indian Affairs for the Year 1896* (Washington, DC: GPO, 1896), 245, images.library.wisc.edu/History/EFacs/CommRep/AnnRep96/reference/history.annrep96.i0019.pdf; George Posey Wild, "History of Education of the Plains Indians of Southwestern Oklahoma Since the Civil War," (EdD diss., OU, 1941), 269-74; Sells to West, 24 December 1913 (Cheyenne and Arapaho Files, Cantonment, Indian Archives), OHSRC; Clyde Ellis, "American Indians and Education," *EOHC*, vol 1 (OHSRC, OKC, 2009), 42.
54. A. Kenneth Stern and Dan D. Chavez, "From Clerk to Professional: New Mexico's Superintendency and the Superintendents of Public Instruction, 1891-1916," *New Mexico Historical Review* (Spring, 2005): 192-95.

Chapter 2

1. Dawes Act (1887), https://www.ourdocuments.gov/print-friendly.php?flash=false&page=&doc=50&title=Dawes+Act+%281887%29; *Report of the Commissioner to the Five Civilized Tribes*, November 20, 1894, Senate Misc. Doc. 24, 53rd Cong., 3rd sess., 1894-95, vol. 1 (Washington, DC, 1894), 17.
2. An Act for the Protection of the People of the Indian Territory, and for Other Purposes, 55th Cong., 2d sess., 30 Stat. 95, chapt. 517 (1898). The principal author was Charles Curtis, Senator from Kansas who was mixed-blood Kansa, Osage, Potawatomi, French, and British.
3. Angie Debo. *The Road to Disappearance, A History of the Creek Indians* (Norman: OU Press, 1941), 352; John D. Benedict, *Report of Superintendent of Schools for Indian Territory, August 19, 1899*, 3, Grant Foreman Collection, Box 3, F 13, OHSRC.
4. *Report of the Commissioner to the Five Civilized Tribes*, 1-12; *Official Register of the United States, Department of the Interior*, 1 (Washington, DC, 1899), 960.
5. www.doi.gov/whoweare/past_secretaries#bliss; Earl S. Pomeroy, *The Territories and the United States, 1861-1890* (Philadelphia: University of Pennsylvania Press, 1947), 6, 7, 15; Autobiography of John Downing Benedict (undated), Grant Foreman Collection, Box 3, F 11, OHSRC.
6. Autobiography of John Downing Benedict, 1-3. John Benedict was born May 27, 1854.
7. Ibid., 5-6.
8. Undated biography of John Benedict, 1, John D. Benedict Collection, Box 1, FF 1, 2, OHSRC.
9. Ibid., 3; Pomeroy, *The Territories and the United States, 1861-1890*, 78-79.
10. Undated biography of John Benedict, 4-5; An Act for the Protection of the People of Indian Territory, chapt. 517, § 19.
11. *Official Register of the United States*, 960-61; S. N. Hopkins. *Sixth BR of the Territorial Auditor of Oklahoma for the Two Years Beginning December 1, 1898 and Ending November 30, 1900* (Guthrie: State Capitol, 1900), 39-51. The report shows monthly payments of $150.00 for the Superintendent. *www.doi.Gov/whoweare/past_secretaries#bliss*; Undated biography of John Benedict, 5.
12. Muriel H. Wright, "John D. Benedict: First United States Superintendent of Schools in the Indian Territory," *Chronicles of Oklahoma* 33, no. 4 (1955): 473.
13. Angie Debo. *And Still the Waters Run* (Princeton, NJ: Princeton University Press, 1940), 66-69.
14. John D. Benedict, *Report of Superintendent of Schools for Indian Territory, August 19, 1899*, 19.
15. Ibid.; United States Indian Inspector for Indian Territory, *Report to the Secretary of the Interior 1899*, (Washington, DC: GPO, 1899), 19; Angie Debo, "History of the Choctaw Nation From the End of the Civil War to the Close of the Tribal Period," (PhD diss., OU, 1933), 406.
16. United States Indian Inspector for Indian Territory, 19; See Benedict's ARs 1899-1907; John D. Benedict, *Report of the Superintendent of Schools for Indian Territory, August 19, 1899*, 19.
17. Green McCurtain to E. A. Hitchcock, 27 October 1899, Superintendent for Five Civilized Tribes, vol. 2, 309-12, Grant Foreman Collection, OHSRC.

18. Hitchcock to Green McCurtain, 15 November 1899, Superintendent for Five Civilized Tribes, vol. 2, 327-32, Grant Foreman Collection, OHSRC.
19. John D. Benedict, *Report of the Superintendent of Schools for Indian Territory for 1900*, July 25, 1900, 4, Grant Foreman Collection, Box 3, F 13, OHSRC.
20. *Report of the Superintendent of Schools for Indian Territory*: (1899, 7; 1900, 6; 1901, 10; 1902, 9-10; 1903, 7-8; 1904, 7-8; 1905, 8-9; 1906, 9-10; 1907, 7), Grant Foreman Collection, Box 3, F 13, OHSRC.
21. *Report of the Superintendent, 1900*, 7-8.
22. *Report of the Superintendent, 1901*, 10.
23. Ibid., 10-11.
24. *Report of the Superintendent, 1903*, 7-8.
25. *Report of the Superintendent, 1906*, 10; Debo, *And Still the Waters Run*, 68.
26. *Report of the Superintendent, 1899*, 8-9.
27. *Report of the Superintendent, 1901*, 20-21; *Report of the Superintendent, 1904*, 5-6.
28. *TBEMM*, May 28, 1904, RG 18-1, DE, OSA, ODL, OKC.
29. *TBEMM*, June 12, 1904; September 13, 1904, RG 18-1, DE, OSA, ODL, OKC.
30. *Oklahoma School Herald*, June, 1905, 2.
31. *Report of the Superintendent, 1899*, 12-13.
32. Ibid.; *Report of the Superintendent, 1903*, 11; Benedict's ARs 1899-1907; *Report of the Superintendent, 1903*, 11; *Report of the Superintendent, 1905*, 7.
33. Debo, *And Still the Waters Run*, 70; Edward E. Dale and Morris L. Wardell, *History of Oklahoma* (Englewood Cliffs, NJ: Prentice-Hall, Inc., 1948), 478.
34. *School Herald*, January 1906, 31; "That the tribal existence and present tribal governments of the Choctaw, Chickasaw, Cherokee, Creek and Seminole tribes or Nations of Indians in the Indian Territory are hereby continued in full force and effect for all purposes under existing laws until all property of such tribes, or the proceeds thereof, shall be distributed among the individual members of the said tribes unless hereafter otherwise provided by law." As one section of the more comprehensive law that was first introduced in early March, debated and exchanged several times between the House and Senate, it was finalized into law April 26. "That the Secretary of the Interior is hereby authorized and directed to assume control and direction of the schools of the Choctaw, Chickasaw, Cherokee, Creek, and Seminole tribes, with the lands and all school property pertaining thereto, March fifth, nineteen hundred and six, and to conduct such schools under rules and regulations to be prescribed by him, retaining tribal educational officers…until such time as a public school system shall have been established under Territorial or State government, and proper provision made thereunder for the education of the Indian children of said tribes…." Concurrent to the consideration of this law was that of the framework for the admission of the combined Indian and Oklahoma Territories to form the state of Oklahoma. An Act to Provide for the Final Disposition of the Affairs of the Five Civilized Tribes in the Indian Territory, 59th Cong. rec. sess. I, vol. 40, chapt. 1876, secs. 10-11, 140-41 (1906); Grant Foreman, "John D. Benedict, Pioneer Educator in Oklahoma," *Oklahoma Teacher*, May 1946, 18; Joe Jackson, "The History of Education in Eastern Oklahoma from 1898 to 1915" (EdD diss., OU, 1950), 394.
35. Debo, *And Still the Waters Run*, 66-70.
36. Daniel F. Littlefield Jr., *Alex Posey: Creek Poet, Journalist, and Humorist* (Lincoln: University of Nebraska Press, 1992), 78, 81, 82, 101, 104.
37. Ibid. 82, *Constitution of the Proposed State of Sequoyah 1905,* babel.hathitrust-org/cgi/pt?id=mdp.35112105063251&view=1up&seq=42.
38. Littlefield, *Alex Posey, 97*; Jonita Mullins, "Muskogee County," *EOHC*, vol. 2 (OKC: OHSRC, 2009), 998; Charles Ballard, "Posey, Alexander (1873-1908)," *Encyclopedia of the Great Plains* (Lincoln: University of Nebraska—Lincoln Press, 2011), http://plainshumanities.unl.edu/encyclopedia/doc/egp.it.061.
39. Jackson, "The History of Education," 133.
40. Ibid., 396, 424; *Second BR, Department of Public Instruction, State of Oklahoma, 1908,* (Guthrie, State of Oklahoma, 1908), 107; Benedict to D. Frank Redd, 18 January 1908, Dawes Commission Records: Letters Sent and Received and Other Documents, 1907-08, 49, OHSRC.
41. The initial amount of $300,000 was continued to the county schools as general aid annually until 1915 as shown in these reports: *Report of the Commissioner to the Five Civilized Tribes to the Secretary of the Interior* (Washington: GPO, 1908), 49; 1909, 77; 1910, 65; 1911, 85; 1913, 58; 1914, 57; *AR of the Department of the Interior 1912* (Washington: GPO, 1912), 513; Jackson, "The History of Education," 402.
42. Jackson, "The History of Education."
43. Joseph B. Thoburn and Muriel H. Wright, *Oklahoma, A History of the State and its People* (New York: Lewis Historical, 1929), 644; "Superintendent Cameron Invokes Support of Chickasaw Executive," *Guthrie*

Leader, January 10, 1908, 6; "Would Imprison Benedict," Ibid., January 13, 1908, 6; *Report of the Commissioner to the Five Civilized Tribes, 1908, 51.*

44. *Oklahoma Red Book*, vol. 2 (Tulsa: Press of Tulsa Daily Democrat, 1912), 141, 145; *Third BRSSPI 1908-1910* (Guthrie: State Capital, 1910), 14; Autobiography of John Downing Benedict (Undated), Box 3, 41, Grant Foreman Collection, OHSRC; Ballenger to Benedict, 10 February 1910, John D. Benedict Collection, Box 1, F 4, OHSRC.
45. Wright, "John D. Benedict: First United States Superintendent of Schools in Indian Territory," 473; Undated biography of John Benedict, Box 1, F 1, OHSRC
46. Undated biography of John Benedict, 17.
47. Ballenger to Benedict, 19 June 1909, John D. Benedict Collection, Box 1, F 3, OHSRC; Autobiography of John Downing Benedict, 18; *Oklahoma School Herald*, April 1908, 3.
48. The letter of 6 January 1910 is referenced in Benedict to Ballenger, 22 January 1910, John D. Benedict Collection, Box 1, F 4, OHSRC; *Oklahoma Red Book*, 145.
49. Benedict to Ballenger, 22 January 1910 and Benedict to Ballenger, 26 January 1910, John D. Benedict Collection, Box 1, F 5, OHSRC; Benedict to Ballenger, 10 February 1910, Box 1, F 6, OHSRC; Ballenger to Benedict, 19 February 1910, John D. Benedict Collection, Box 1, F 6, OHSRC.
50. Benedict to Ballenger, 21 February 1910, John D. Benedict Collection, Box 1, F 6, OHSRC.
51. "Benedict Opens Fight Against Rep. Creager," *TO*, January 15, 1910, 14; James T. Brady, ed., *The State of Oklahoma, Its Men and Its Institutions* (OKC: Oklahoman, 1908), 94.
52. Wright, John D. Benedict, 473; Foreman, "John D. Benedict, Pioneer Educator in Oklahoma," 18.
53. Foreman, "John D. Benedict;" *Muskogee Daily Phoenix*, January 29, 1946, 3; John D. Benedict, *Muskogee and Northeastern Oklahoma*, vol. 1 (Chicago: S. J. Clarke, 1922). Speeches by honored and revered Indian authorities are included in their entirety.

Chapter 3

1. State Question No. 436 adopted May 3, 1966.
2. *Journal of the First Session of the Legislative Assembly of Oklahoma Territory, Beginning August 17, 1890* (Guthrie, 1890), 697. S. N. Hopkins was arrested and charged with refusal to produce records and vouchers to an investigating committee. Eventually, the charges were dropped with many believing the whole affair was a political maneuver.
3. Statutes of Oklahoma 1890, art. 5, §§ 4-10 (Guthrie, 1891); *Governor's Message to the 2nd Legislature of Territory of Oklahoma, January 19, 1893*, 66-012, File 12, Special Collections and University Archives, Edmon Low Library, OSU.
4. William H. Murray, *Memoirs of Governor Murray and True History of Oklahoma*, vol. 2 (Boston: Meador, 1945), 37; Okla. Const. of 1907, art. XIII, § 7.
5. Statutes of Oklahoma 1893, chapt. 73, art. 11, §§ 5-10 (State Capital, 1893); O.S. 1908, chapt. 54, art. 8, §§ 4399-405 (State Capital, 1908).
6. O.S. 1908, chapt. 2, art. 6, § 300; Okla. Const., of 1907, art. VIII, § 7.
7. O.S. 1931 §§ 6748-6755, 6759 (Harlow 1931).
8. 70 O.S. 1941 §§ 915.2-915.5 (West 1941); Hodge got patronage via 70 O.S. 1951 § 2A-4 (West 1951).
9. 70 O.S. 1971 §§ 3-104-107 (West 1971); 70 O.S. 1981 § 3-108 (West 1981); A.G. Op. 80-173 (1980).
10. www.law.justia.com/codes/Oklahoma/2014/title-70/section-70-3-107.1/.
11. *2013-2014 AR: Statistical Report on Oklahoma Schools and the SDE* 13, https://sde.ok.gov; *Twenty-Fourth BRSDEO 1952* (OKC: SBE, 1952), 11, 19-22.
12. *Fifth BRSSPI together with the Second Report of the SBE, OK, 1914*, (OKC: Warden, 1914) 14; *Rural School Consolidation, A Bulleting of Information Issued by the SBE*, 3-4.
13. Kenneth McKinley, e-mail correspondence with author, March 18, 2021.
14. Leroy Fischer, ed., *Oklahoma's Governors 1890-1907: Territorial Years* (OKC: OHSRC, 1982), 85-86.
15. Murray. *Memoirs of Governor Murray*, 45-46.
16. Ibid.
17. *Public Education in Oklahoma: A Report of a Survey of Public Education in the State of Oklahoma, made at the Request of the Oklahoma State Educational Survey Commission, Under the Direction of the United States Commissioner of Education*, (Washington, DC: Department of the Interior, Bureau of Education, 1922), report pages are unnumbered.
18. Ibid.; The county superintendent position was eliminated by the Legislature effective July 1, 1993, 70 O.S. Supp. 1993 § 4-101 (West 1993), and all dependent school districts were required to hire persons holding the appropriate superintendent certificate.

19. *Public Education in Oklahoma*, page unnumbered.
20. The Institute for Government Research of the Brookings Institution, *Report on a Survey of Organization and Administration of Oklahoma* (OKC: Harlow, 1935), 14, 390; H. V. Thornton, Corbitt Rushing, and John Wood, *Problems in Oklahoma State Government* (Norman: Bureau of Government Research, 1957), 25-28.
21. Thornton, Rushing, and Wood, 227-28.
22. *Oklahoma Public Schools: A Survey Report to the Oklahoma Governor's Advisory Committee on Common School Education* (Nashville: Division of Surveys and Field Services, George Peabody College for Teachers, 1964), 20-21.
23. "Sweeping Changes Urged in State Government," *TO*, October 26, 1967, 1-2; 70 O.S. 1993 § 4-101 (West 1993); A Preliminary Report on a Statewide Assessment of Elementary and Secondary Education in Oklahoma Under Title III ESEA, 1969, "Optimizing Educational Opportunity for the Children of Oklahoma," (SCREL of Little Rock, 1969), page unnumbered.
24. Commission on Reform of State Government, *Oklahoma, Report and Recommendations* (OKC, 1984), 1.
25. 74 O.S. 1991 §§ 10.1-10.3 (West 1991); Oklahoma Reorganization Council, *Comprehensive Plan for Executive Branch Reorganization* (OKC: 1987), 1, 25.
26. David Morgan, Robert England, and George Humphreys, *Oklahoma Politics and Policies: Governing the Sooner State* (Lincoln: University of Nebraska Press, 1991), 111-12.
27. *The State of Oklahoma Governor's Performance Team: Final Issue Papers,* presented to The Governor's Commission on Government Performance, October 17, 1995; ED-19; *TO*, October 26, 1967, 1-2.
28. *Fourteenth BRSSPI and the Eleventh BRSDE, OK* (OKC: SDE 1932), 8.
29. "Proposal to Let Governor Name State Superintendent," *TO*, December 10, 2003, 6A; "50 State Comparison: K-12 Governance Structures," http://www.ecs.org/k-12-governance-structures/.
30. Robert Darcy, "Woman Suffrage in Oklahoma," in Bob Darcy and Jennifer Paustenbaugh, *The Oklahoma Women's Almanac* (Stillwater, OK: OPSA, 2005), 16-17.
31. 70 O.S. Supp. 1965 § 1-6 (West 1965); A. G. Op. 81-43. It was rumored that a politician lacking the statutory requirements desired to run for the office and needed clarification from the attorney general. No such person ran for the office in 1982.; O.S.L. 1990, chapt. 29, § 6 (West, 1990).
32. Superintendents' salaries before statehood are shown in the Territorial Auditors' BRs and since statehood are listed in OK's Session Laws. The federal government's territorial governors' salaries are listed in the *Official Register of the United States* for the years 1899 and following.
33. In 1994 the Legislature enacted a law that equated the Superintendent's compensation to that of a district judge effective in 1995. Three years later [O.S.L. 1997, chapt. 384, §§ 1,3,7 (West 1997)] the Governor's salary was to be equal to that of the Supreme Court Chief Justice beginning in 1999. The seven member Board of Judicial Compensation (two members appointed by the Senate pro tempore representing labor and civic organizations, two members appointed by the Speaker of the House representing communications media and retail business, two members appointed by the Governor selected from manufacturing and professional fields not otherwise mentioned, and one member appointed by the Supreme Court Chief Justice representing agriculture; no more than four members from any party) determined judicial and legislative salaries and, by operation, executive office salaries [74 O.S. Supp. 2011 § 250.4 (West 2011)]. Through SB 549 on May 18, 2015, the Legislature set the executive officers' salaries for the next four years. The Governor expressed her displeasure with the bill by vetoing it only to have her veto overridden by the Legislature.
34. "School Chief Pay Hike Bill Vote Delayed," *TO*, January 31, 1968, 3; "Bartlett Given Boast in Filling School Post," *TO*, March 14, 1968, 10; 70 O.S. 1981 § 3-108 (West 1981). Through SB 401 in 1980 the Legislature enumerated five additional responsibilities for the Superintendent for which his pay would be increased by $10,000. A. G. Op. 80-173 (1981) examined the constitutional provisions relating to executive officer pay during the term of office and concluded that SB 401 was unconstitutional.); www.oklegal.onenet/oklegal_cgi/isearch.
35. Executive officers' salaries are usually included in the Session Laws every four years in Title 74.
36. http://www.sde.ok.gov.
37. *Twenty-Third BRSDEO* (OKC: SBE, 1950), 288, 293-94.
38. *OED and Requirements for State Certificates 1909-1910* (Guthrie: SDE, 1909), 81-93; *OED 1919-1920* (OKC: SDE, 1919), 10-29.
39. "Hodge to Seek Former Power Held by Crable," *TO*, December 21, 1946, 29.
40. Steve Housel, "Oklahoma's Adoption of the Merit System: J. Howard Edmondson and Cooperative Federalism, *Oklahoma Politics*, 23 (2013): 69-70, ojs.library.okstate/osu/index.php/OKPolitics/article/view/2342/2043.
41. "Changes Proposed in Merit System," *TO*, May 18, 1971, 12; "Merit System Change Wins OK in House," *TO*, June 3, 1971, 32.

42. "Education Board Spars with New Schools Chief," *TO*, January 28, 2011, 1A; "Barresi's Hires' Salaries Studied," *TO,* February 17, 2011, 9 West; "Schools Superintendent is Lightning Rod for Opinions," *TO*, August 18, 2013, 12A; O.S.L. 2011, chapt. 31, § 1-7 and chapt. 316, § 1 (West 2011) show the modifications with the amended version at 70 O.S. 2011 §§ 1-105, 3-104, 3-107, 3-101 (West 2011); 70 O.S. 2001 §§ 1-105, 3-101, 3-104 to 3-107.1; "Education Politics Continue," *TW*, March 24, 2011, A 17.

Chapter 4

1. *Oklahoma Elections: Statehood to Present, vol.1 (OKC: SEB, 1994)*, C13-C-23; "Election Laws in Bad Way in State," *TO*, August 28, 1910, 32, http://archive.newsok.com/Olive/APA/Oklahoman/Print.Article.
2. *Oklahoma Red Book*, vol. 2 (Tulsa: Press of the Tulsa Daily Democrat, 1912), 355-58; *Oklahoma Elections*, C1-C2. "At the primary election held in August, 1914, any party which has a national recognition as a party shall be recognized as a political party in Oklahoma," O.S.L. 1913, ch. 157, § 9 (Cooperative 1913).
3. "Rev. E. D. Cameron Presents His Views on School Questions," *Sulphur Democrat*, March 28, 1907, 2; "Robert L. Knie, Political Advertisement," *TO*, June 5, 1907, 3; "Returns Come Slowly: Results Not Certain," *TO*, June 9, 1907, 1; *Cordell Weekly Beacon*, June 20, 1907, 1; *TO*, June 19, 1907, 1, 6.
4. "Frantz Victory Gives Him Full Control in His Party," *TO*, August 3, 1907, 1-2.
5. www.ok.gov/elections/documents/1907-1912_RESULTS.pdf.
6. *Oklahoma Elections*, C-322, C-329, and C-334.
7. Ibid., C1-C639; www.ok.gov.
8. *Oklahoma Elections*, all pages.
9. Included in the fifteen is E. H. McDonald, deputy state superintendent, who served for three months in 1968 as acting Superintendent during the interim between Oliver Hodge's death and D. D. Creech's assumption of the position.
10. *OA 2015-2016* (OKC: ODL, 2015), 606-8; www.ok.gov/ethics/Commission.
11. www.ok.gov.
12. Statewide voter registration records have been compiled only since 1960. Currently, only three political parties are recognized: Democratic, Republican, and Libertarian. Independents are registered voters not affiliated with a recognized political party.
13. Political candidates were required to file expenditures only for primary campaigns prior to 1974, and those records are housed in the OSA, ODL, OKC. 26 O.S. Supp. 1968 §§ 423.2-423.3 (West 1968). Since then, reports must be completed for all elections and by candidates who receive contributions of $500 or more, and they are held in the SEC Office. 74 O.S. Supp. 2014, ch. 62: Rule 257:10-1-13 specifies great detail for reporting according to the Revised Constitutional Ethics Rules.
14. [15] A Democratic, but no Republican, primary election occurred in 1907. The Legislature that year wrote the statute governing the financial reporting for future primary elections, and it was printed in O.S. 1908 § 2764. "Candidates before any primary election, for all offices for which the voters of more than a county have the right to vote, shall file with the secretary of the State Election Board...." The original law was expanded in 26 O.S. Supp. 1968 § 3. "Every candidate for state office who receives a contribution of the value of Five Hundred Dollars ($500.00) or more shall file a written report thereof as hereinafter provided." www.ok.gov/ethics/Commission/Commission_History/.
15. CCER for the 2010 and 2014 election cycles for Janet Barresi filed with the SEC and accessed at https://pay.apps.ok.gov/ethics/crs.
16. EBCFCEs for E. D. Cameron and R. H. Wilson, Democratic Primary 1910, Box 1-15, RG 24-4-1, EBCFCE, OSA, ODL, OKC; *Oklahoma Elections*, C-14; Republican Primary 1910, Box 1-15, RG 24-4-1, EBCFCE, OSA, ODL, OKC. The 1908 statute mandating the filing of campaign expenditures did not stipulate the exact form, format, and ethical principles attached to the reporting process. Thus, in the 1910 primary election, G. D. Moss, superintendent of Cheyenne Public Schools and Republican candidate, filed his report on the District's official stationery. Candidates John Evans, E. D. Cameron, and R. H. Wilson listed their expenses on standard legal size paper.
17. R. H. Wilson's EBCFCE, Primary Election 1914, Box 3-19, RG 24-4-1, OSA, ODL, OKC (all of these EBCFCE documents are housed at the OSA.); EBCFCE, Primary Election 1918, Box 9-23, RG 24-4-1, EBCFCE; Democratic Primary Election 1922, Box 12-9, RG 24-4-1, EBCFCE; Primary Election 1926, Box 15-16, RG 24-4-1, EBCFCE. Fourteen years after the original statute required reporting a president of one of the state colleges used official stationery to file his report. Apparently, the political environment tolerated such activity.
18. Primary Election 1930, Box 18-23, RG 24-4-1, EBCFCE; Primary and Run Off Elections 1934, Box 23-16, RG 24-4-1; Primary Election 1938, Box 28-15, RG 24-4-1; Primary Election 1942, Box 33-7, RG 24-4-1; Primary and Run Off Elections 1946, Box 36-24, RG 24-4-1.

19. The US Bureau of Labor Statistics' Consumer Price Index shows that $1.00 in 1910 was worth $24.92 in 2014. Thus, Wilson's campaign cost of $1,454.34 in 1910 would have exceeded $35,000 in 2014.
20. The CCERs for all three candidates for the 1970 election cycle are filed with the SEB in OKC.
21. Access the 2014 candidates' CCERs, Form C1-R, at http://pay.apps.ok.gov/ethics/crs/c1r/view.
22. "No Apologies Needed, Says Oliver Hodge," *TO*, May 27, 1950, 5, www.archive.newsok.com.
23. John Bennett, interview by the author, November 20, 2001. Bennett was Director of School Personnel Records and Manager of the Criminal History Program at the Department from 1994-2006.
24. "R. H. Wilson, Candidate for State Superintendent of Public Instruction," *TO*, June 23, 1918, 18; Chickasha *Daily Express*, June 24, 1910, 1; *Oklahoma School Herald*, September, 1910, 14-15; "State Superintendent Who Has Made Good," *Harlow's Weekly*, April 25, 1914, 47; "Four Years of Educational Progress," *Harlow's Weekly*, July 31, 1915, 80-1. Box 1, F 1-1, RG 18-3-3, Superintendent of Public Instruction 1914-1922 (correspondence by subject), OSA, ODL, OKC. Examples are: R. H. Wilson to Almeda Pickens, 19 December 1921; R. H. Wilson to Orval Pfifer, 22 February 1922; R. H. Wilson to Dan Perry, 22 April 1922; Mack Phillips to R. H. Wilson, 17 January 1922;
25. The John Dunning Political Collection, Democratic Party Materials 1940s, Box 26, FF 3, OHSRC, has various artifacts including these referenced in the text. The Women's Democratic Council of Oklahoma booklet lists the members for 1945, and the 1940 Speakers' Manual, issued by the Democratic State Central Committee of Oklahoma, includes the statement by A. L. Crable. Campaign advertisements were in: *A Digest of Oklahoma Democracy* (OKC: B+W Publishing, 1940), pages unnumbered and *The Voice of the Democratic Women of Oklahoma*, July 1942, 13.
26. https://pay.apps.ok.gov/ethics/crs/c1r/schedule_a/view_sched_a.php; https://pay.apps.ok.gov/ethics/crs/c1r/schedule_e/view_sched_e.php.
27. "Superintendents Get Ethics Warning," *TO*, March 24, 2003, A1.

Chapter 5

1. Richard L. Fox and Jennifer L. Lawless, "Gaining and Losing Interest in Running for Public Office: The Concept of Dynamic Political Ambition," *The Journal of Politics*, 72, no. 2 (2011), 444, https://www.jstor.org/stable/10.1017/s0022381611000120; Matt A. Barreto and Matthew J. Streb, "Barn Burners and Burn Out: The Effects of Competitive Elections on Efficacy and Trust," paper presented at the annual meeting of the Midwest Political Science Association, Chicago, IL, April 12, 2007.
2. C. S. Lewis. *Collected Letters Volume One: Family Letters 1905-1931* (Glasgow, UK: HarperCollins, 2009), 67.
3. Seth Motel, "Who Runs for Office? A Profile of the 2%," https://www.pewresearch.org/fact-tank/2014/09/03/who-runs-for-office-a-profile-of-the-2/.
4. "Summary for the United States, by Divisions and States," 28, www2.census.gov/prod2/decennial/documents/06229686v32-37ch5.pdf; "QuickFacts Oklahoma," www.census.gov/quickfacts/fact/table/OK/RH1825219.
5. Eugene D. Mazo, "Residency and Democracy: Durational Residency Requirements From the Framers to the Present," *Florida State University Law Review*, 43, no. 2 (Winter, 2016): 651, ir.law.fsu.edu/cgi/viewcontent.cgi?article=2546&context+ir. Six states have no durational residency requirements and the average length of the other forty-four states is five years.
6. W. H. Langley, Jr., interview by the author, January 9, 2020.
7. Marriage and Divorce Statistics 1990-2015, Oklahoma State Department of Health, www.ok.gov/health/Data_and_Statistics/Center_For_Health_Statistics/Health_Care_Information/Vital_Statistics/Vital_Statistics_Data_and_Reports/Index.html.
8. John Folks, interview by the author, February 15, 2018.
9. "Religious Landscape Study, 2014," Pew Research Center, https://www.Pewforum.org/religious-landscape-study/state/oklahoma.
10. "Summary for the United States, by Divisions and States," 28; "QuickFacts Oklahoma."
11. Because this book covers the timeframe of December 1890 through January 2015 no information and demographics of Joy Hofmeister's first term in office are included.

Chapter 6

1. Statutes of Oklahoma 1890, art. 8, § 1 (Guthrie 1891).
2. "Women May Sit on School Board," *DO*, May 29, 1908, 7.
3. By initiative petition, State Question No. 8 in 1910 asked voters to authorize women to vote. www.ok.gov/elections. The question was voted down 128,928 to 88,808.

4. www.ok.gov/elections. Eight years later State Question No. 97 asked voters again to institute universal suffrage and it passed 106,909 to 81,481.
5. *EOHC*, vol. 1 (OKC: OHSRC, 2009), 100. There was one exception to the exclusion of females from executive office—the office of Commissioner of Charities and Corrections. Kate Bernard was elected in 1907 and reelected in 1910. Legislators became upset with her unionizing efforts and criticism of the state's handling of prisoners, orphans, and Native American children so they defunded her position, forcing her from office. Additionally, the constitutional requirement of a majority of all voters voting in an election needing to pass individual amendments was changed by State Question 496, Legislative Referendum No. 199, adopted at the primary election held August 27, 1974. *Oklahoma Elections*, C-531. By a count of 354,644 to 341,341 voters amended the constitution to require only a majority vote for amending the constitution.
6. *OA 2015-2016* (OKC: ODL, 2015), 785, 824, 826; Christine Pappas, "Lamar Looney," *EOHC*, vol. 1 (OKC: OHSRC, 2009), 865; Christine Pappas, "Amelia Elizabeth Simison McColgin," *EOHC*, vol. 2 (OKC: OHSRC, 2009), 914. Representative Bessie McColgin was a Republican from Roger Mills County, and Senator Lamar Looney, a Democrat from District 4 (Harmon and Greer counties). McColgin served one term only while Looney was reelected three times. (Looney v Leeper, 292 P. 365, 145 Okl. 202). Advantageous to Mrs. Looney, the Oklahoma Supreme Court supported her and ordered Leeper to submit the proposed amendment for a vote at the next general election. The court ruled that the constitutional provision requiring a two-thirds majority meant two-thirds of the total membership of the Senate and House, respectively. Thus sixty-five votes were needed in the House and only sixty-three were obtained. Okla. Const., art. XXIV, § 1. Amendments could be proposed in either branch of the Legislature but approval for submission to the people for a vote required a majority of those elected to each house of the Legislature; the vote of the people was to be at the next regular general election "except when the legislature [*sic*], by a two-thirds vote of each house, shall order a special election for that purpose;" and, "If a majority of all the electors voting at such election shall vote in favor of any amendment thereto, it shall thereby become a part of this Constitution." Suzanne H. Schrems, "Women's Legislative Council," *EOHC*, vol. 2 (OKC: OHSRC, 2009), 1641-42. Women's clubs and organizations (e.g., YWCA, Woman's Christian Temperance Union, and Daughters of the American Revolution) in the early to mid 1920s worked through the WLC to initiate state legislation "for the betterment of humanity in general, women and children especially." In this politically active time for women and their interests, leadership and governance in education were natural ingredients in the general mix of politics.
7. The *OED* for the years 1925-26 through 1934-35 list her as the Woodward County superintendent. Oklahoma Elections 1934-1938, www.ok.gov/elections/documents/1934-1938_RESULTS. pdf, C-9.
8. I Timothy 2:12 states "I permit no woman to teach or to have authority over men." Revised Standard Version.
9. Chapter 79, art. 6, § 3 (6397) of the Statutes of Oklahoma 1890 provided that anyone age twenty-four or older who held a diploma from a state normal school or a territorial certificate or a first grade county certificate was eligible to be a county superintendent. *Fifth BRTSPI 1898-1900* (Guthrie, O. T.: State Capital, 1890), 141. *OED 1919-1920* (OKC: SDE, 1919), 10-30; *OED 1929-1930* (OKC: SDE, 1929), 34-35; *OED 1990-1991* (OKC: SDE, 1990), 10-115. The county superintendent position was abolished in 1992.
10. *OED*, 2009-2010, 1-134.
11. "State Board of Education, A Brief History," (Unpublished manuscript, SDE, 1986); *OED 1926-1927* (OKC: SDE, 1926), 4-5. *OED* published annually by the Department and *Biennial/Annual Reports of the State Superintendents* include a listing of the Board members. *SBEMM* for the meetings of February 5, 1935 to August 19, 1936 list the members present. Kate Galt Zaneis, Jane Cole Clark, and Grace Norris Davis served during this time, but never were more than two of them on the Board.
12. *SBEMM*, July 6, 1935.
13. *SBEMM*, June 2, 1936.
14. See *OED*s referenced in note 8.
15. Begun as normal schools in Oklahoma Territory and later in Indian Territory, these institutions were upgraded legislatively to teachers colleges in 1917 and eventually to universities. Around 1940 a second name change eliminated the word "teachers" and, in 1974, a final renaming resulted in the six institutions being designated as universities. "Zaneis, Kate Galt," *EOHC*, vol. 2 (OKC: OHSRC, 2009), 1667.
16. "Oral History Interview with Joe Anna Hibler," July 20, 2007, Inductees of the Oklahoma Women's Hall of Fame Oral History Project, Special Collections and University Archives, Edmon Low Library, OSU.
17. *OED, 1914-1915* (OKC: SDE, 1914), 3; *OED*, 1919-1920, 29; *OED*, 1926-27, 3.
18. *Seventh BRSSPI together with the Fourth Report of the SBE, OK, 1918* (OKC: Allied Printing, 1918), 3; "Vocational Education," *Oklahoma Home and School Herald*, March, 1918, 107; "Directory," *Oklahoma Teacher*, December, 1919, 2; *Fourth Annual Report to Congress of the Federal Board for Vocational Education*, 162.

19. Annual editions of the *OED*, *1971-72* through *1983-84*; "Educator's Background Leads to New Position," *TO,* March 17, 1972, 7.
20. *OED*, 1969-70, 36.
21. "Women's Rights Backers Praise Official's Candor," *TO*, February 20, 1981, 94; Annual editions of the *OED*, *1984-85* through *1987-88*.
22. *SBEMM*, July 29, 1982, 92.
23. Velta (Reed) Johnston, interview by the author, March 15, 2021; *SBEMM*, July 26, 1979, 66; June 26, 1980, 49. Yarbrough was to be paid $20,000 for the 1980-81 school year. He previously served school superintendencies at Snyder and Port Neches, Texas, and held various positions in the education section of the federal department of Health, Education, and Welfare (became the Department of Education in 1979). To compare, Fisher's salary for that year was $35,000 (see appendix I).
24. Clarence G. Oliver Jr., interview by the author, March 2, 2021. Women were not deemed qualified for principal and superintendent positions until the late 1970s. As late as the 1950s and early 1960s some of the administrators (all male) would meet periodically for fraternal purposes to discuss issues they confronted in their positions. One component of this good ole boys club, The Secret Order of the Red, Red Rose was an initiation to the Order which could sometimes become vulgar and ribald. Clarence's Angels was a variant of the title of the TV show Charlie's Angels that ran from 1976 to 1981 and featured three attractive police detectives. "Department of Education, State of Oklahoma, Resolution," *SBEMM*, January 22, 1981, 29.
25. Acknowledgement is given to these superintendents as representative of those who intentionally advanced women: Clarence G. Oliver Jr., Broken Arrow Public Schools; George Rowley, Edmond Public Schools; and Kara Gae (Wilson) Neal, Glenpool Public Schools.
26. "State Council of Administrative and Executive Women in Education," *Minutes of the Conference on Teacher Training*, November 29, 1917, OEA Collection, OEA Proceedings 1917.
27. Johnston interview; Custer County Schoolmasters, a typical association of the school district administrators within many counties, met monthly during the school year to share a dinner and discuss current issues and problems. Because of Southwestern Oklahoma State University's proximity and with a primary goal to prepare teachers and administrators for the school districts, the Dean and male professors in the School of Education were invited to these meetings. However, not until the early 1980s were the districts' female administrators and female professors at SWOSU invited to participate. Prior to that time the only exception to the norm occurred when the host institution, either a school district or Southwestern (annually), invited its female administrator(s) or School of Education female faculty. The exclusion at the district level was particularly poignant because only one of the seven districts hired a female principal and she was invited only when that district hosted the meeting. The Dean's tacit approval was no doubt based on the perceived need to maintain good relations with the districts' administrators and the university's administration. Irony was obvious ten years later when the university hired a female president. The author was an Assistant Professor of School Administration in the School of Education at SWOSU from 1976-1980. The Dean and, by extension, the male faculty were invited to attend and participate in the monthly meetings. After two years of participating and feeling uncomfortable over the exclusion of his female colleagues and the one female school principal, the author declined to attend future meetings until the women were also invited. Women were still being excluded when he left the University.
28. Superintendents seated around the table from left to right: Lucy Smith, McAlester; JoAnn (Bates) Thompson, Harshorne; Virginia Webb, Caney Valley; Phyllis (Rottmann) Murphy, Ralston; Kara Gae (Wilson) Neal, Tulsa County; Velta (Reed) Johnston, Western Oklahoma Area Vo-Tech; Sandy Garrett, Secretary: Pat Sholar, Tupelo; Lynn Kinnamon, Jet-Nash; Kathy Roberts, Healdton; unknown; Edna Manning, Shawnee; Dee Dee Graham, Snyder; and June Knight, Hobart.
29. Johnston interview; *OED* for the years 1980-81 to 1990-91 list the persons, positions, and employers of the educators.
30. *ODE 2001-2002* (OKC: SDE, 2001), 151, 155-59; *ODE 2005-2006* (OKC: SDE, 2005), 141-42, 163-64.

Chapter 7

1. O.S.L. 1907-1908, chapt. 5, art. 21, § 2 (Oklahoma, 1908).
2. The Constitution of Oklahoma, art. XVII, § 8, assigned the county names and boundaries and § 2 included the county superintendent in the offices of county government.
3. For additional biographical information, see chapter 1, subsection E. D. Cameron, Minister and Democrat. *Oklahoma School Herald*, 2, no. 6, April 1894, 2; R. L. Williams, Necrology, "Rev. Evan Dhu Cameron," *Chronicles of Oklahoma*, 11, no. 1 (1933): 740-43; "Rev. E. D. Cameron Presents His Views on School Questions," *Sulphur Democrat*, March 28, 1907, 2. As the first pastor of the First Methodist Episcopal Church of Norman, Cameron was chosen to turn the first spade of dirt in the foundation of the initial building of OU.

4. Williams, Necrology, 743; Sidney Henry Babcock and John Y. Bryce, *History of Methodism in Oklahoma*, vol. 1 (OKC: Times Journal, 1935), 257-63, 287; *Minutes of the Annual Conferences of the Methodist Episcopal Church, South for the Year 1898* (Nashville: Publishing House of the Methodist Episcopal Church, South, 1898), 83-84, 86 (see also the *Minutes* for the years 1899 [92 and 94] and 1900 [82-83[); Babcock and Bryce, *History of Methodism*, 289. Williams, Necrology, 287; *Proceedings of the Baptist General Convention of Indian Territory, November 7-12, 1906* and *Proceedings of the Baptist General Convention of Oklahoma, October 31-November 4, 1907*, Oklahoma Baptist Archives, Shawnee, OK.
5. *Closing Exercises of the Normal School for Oklahoma, Edmond, OK, 1897*, Special Collections & University Archives, Edmon Low Library, OSU; James T. Grady, *The State of Oklahoma, Its Men and Institutions* (OKC: Oklahoman, 1908), 19.
6. "Rev. E. D. Cameron Presents His Views;" https://worldpopulationview.com/states/Oklahoma-population/; *Proceedings of the Baptist General Convention of Indian Territory* and *Proceedings of the Baptist General Convention of Oklahoma.*
7. "One Man Right," *Oklahoma Farm Journal*, January 15, 1907, 7; "The New President," *School Herald*, February 1906, 5; Joe C. Jackson, "The History of Education in Eastern Oklahoma From 1898 to 1915," (EdD diss., OU, 1950), 142, 278.
8. "Some of the Things, Briefly Stated, Advocated by Robert L.Knie, Candidate for State Superintendent of Public Instruction," *Oklahoma Farm Journal*, June 1, 1907, 14.
9. Ibid.; "Robert L. Knie, Candidate for State Superintendent of Public Instruction Will Win in the Race for That Important Office," *TO*, June 5, 1907, 3; "Washita County," *School Herald*, April 1906, 24; "Rev. E. D. Cameron Presents His Views;" (political advertisement) "Professor E. D. Cameron," *TO*, June 7, 1907, 2. S. M. Barrett was Lawton schools superintendent in 1907, author and professor of psychology and teaching at OU in 1911, and later commandant of the Oklahoma Military Academy. He authored several books on Native Americans. *OA 2015-2016* OKC: ODL, 2015), 824; *Harper's Weekly*, January 6, 1923, 4; *Harper's Weekly*, January 20, 1923, 4, 15. Knie was an ambitious county superintendent on a career trajectory that would place him in political offices within a decade. A sizeable landowner in his hometown and well known in the community, he parlayed his superintendency into a sixth district Senate seat in 1918 and 1920, and then was named Secretary to the School Land Commission by Governor Walton in 1923, a highly controversial action since Knie had an outstanding loan of $10,000 with the Commission. *The Official Gazette of the United States Patent Office*, 492, no. 1 (Washington, DC: GPO, 1938), 560. Knie was multi-talented as a farmer, educator, politician, and inventor who in 1938 was awarded a patent for a ventilated toilet seat.
10. "Rev. E. D. Cameron presents his views."
11. Ibid.: *Second BRTSPI, Governor's Message to the Third Legislative Assembly of the Territory of Oklahoma, January 8, 1895 (Guthrie, 1895)*, 9-10.
12. *Sulphur Democrat*, March 28, 1907; *Official Register of the United States, US Department of the Interior, 1903*, vol. 1 (Washington, DC: GPO, 1903), 987. Beginning in 1899 Benedict's salary was set at $3,500. O.S.L. 1907-1908, chapt. 5, art. 6, § 1 (Oklahoma, 1908); *Oklahoma Elections: Statehood to Present*, vol. 1 (OKC: SEB, 1994), C-2.
13. *First Report of the Superintendent of Public Instruction of the State of Oklahoma 1908* (Guthrie: State of OK, 1907), 2.
14. Ibid., 47-50; *Second BRDPIO 1908* (Guthrie: State of Oklahoma, 1908), 99, 132-33.
15. *Second BRDPIO*, 73, 109.
16. Ibid., 75.
17. Joseph B. Thoburn and Muriel H. Wright, *Oklahoma, A History of The State and Its People*, vol. 2 (New York: Lewis Historical, 1929), 644.
18. *First Report of the Superintendent*, 19, 36-37, 45-46, 50-52; Second BRDPIO, 52-56, 59, 64, 181-82. William Murray, president of the Constitutional Convention, did not want to determine locations of institutions during the Convention because of the intense politics involved. Those feelings had not abated by the first two legislative sessions.
19. Compiled Laws of Oklahoma 1908 § 300 (Pipes Reed, 1908); Compiled Laws of Oklahoma 1909 § 7115 (Pipes Reed, 1909).
20. *Second BRDPIO*, 132-33; Compiled Laws of Oklahoma 1908 § 6620. The law of 1908 was carried forward verbatim from the Statutes of Oklahoma 1893 § 5888.
21. *Second BRDPIO*, 133-34.
22. J. M. Davis to Haskell, 18 August 1909 and George Bruce to Haskell, 19 November 1909, Box 2, F 7, RG 8-A-4, Governor Charles Haskell, Application and Appointment Files, SBE 1909, OSA, ODL, OKC; *Second BRDPIO*, 52-56, 59, and 64.
23. Joe Hubbell, *The Oklahoma Education Association, 1884-1974* (undated), 37-38.

24. Ibid.
25. Francis Coram Oakes, "A Story of Central State College of Edmond, Oklahoma," (Edmond: Unpublished Manuscript, 1953), 116-18.
26. Hubbell, *The Oklahoma Education Association*, 37-38.
27. *First Report of the Superintendent*, 50; *Second BRDPIO*, 181; W. C. Rogers to Hon. C. N. Haskell, 4 January 1908, *Journal of the House of Representatives of the Regular Session of the First Legislature of Oklahoma* (Guthrie: Leader, 1908), 112-13; Compiled Laws of Oklahoma 1909 §§ 8326, 8329, 8323.
28. Edmond Normal School was established by the Statutes of Oklahoma 1890 § 3716 (Guthrie: State Capital, 1891). Northwestern Normal School in 1897 (Compiled Laws of Oklahoma 1908 § 6536) and Southwestern Normal School in 1901 (Compiled Laws of Oklahoma 1908 § 6538) were formed after Cameron resigned from office. W. B. Richards, *The Oklahoma Red Book*, vol. 2 (Tulsa: Tulsa Daily Democrat, 1912), 141, 146. In 1907 Cameron was elected by the Normal School Board as its president and held that position during his term as Superintendent.
29. *Oklahoma School Herald*, February 1909, 21-22; www.americanhumane.org/about-us/history/.
30. *Alva Pioneer*, July 8, 1910, 6; "Cameron Delivers Address," *Chickasha Daily Express*, July 7, 1910, 1.
31. *Alva Pioneer*, July 8, 1910, 6.
32. "Cameron Hit by Circular of Opponents," *OKC Times*, July 17, 1910, 2; "Anarchy, Yells Cameron at his Mad Enemies," *OKC Times*, July 20, 1910, 6; "Cameron Criticized," *Chickasha Daily Express*, July 13, 1910, 3.
33. "More About Politics in the Schools," *Chickasha Daily Express*, July 20, 1910, 2.
34. "Cameron Will Move Office to Oklahoma City," *OKC Times*, July 25, 1910, 5; Compiled Laws of Oklahoma 1909 §§ 8335, 8408, 7955; Richards, *The Oklahoma Red Book*, 144-47.
35. *Oklahoma Elections*, C-14; *Third BRSSPI 1908-1910* (Guthrie: State Capital, 1910), 8-10, 30.
36. *Third BRSSPI*, 427-29; O.S.L. 1910-1911, chapt. 131, §§ 1,3 (Co-operative, 1911).
37. Second BRDPIO, 5-6.
38. *Third BRSSPI*, 315, 18.
39. *Arrow-Democrat*, June 1, 1922, 4; *Oklahoma Elections*, C-120; *Sulfur Democrat*, March 28, 1909, 4; Williams, Necrology, 743. Cameron served the Baptist denomination from 1910 throughout the remainder of his life and held pastorates in Guthrie, Claremore, Checotah, Okmulgee, Henryetta, and Ardmore. He was active both in the Anti Saloon and Anti Divorce leagues and in the founding of the National Anti Divorce League. "Rev. E. D. Cameron Dies Suddenly," *Arrow-Democrat*, August 2, 1923; www.findagrave.com/memorial/159943469/evan-dhu-cameron; www.findagrave.com/memorial/159943553/clara-w-cameron. Cameron's political career ended in 1910, allowing him to devote all of his energies to his ministry for the next thirteen years, and until his death. The father of six children, five sons (one predeceased at a young age), several who became lawyers, and a daughter, Cameron died suddenly in Tahlequah July 29, 1923 at age sixty-one. He was buried in Okmulgee where his wife Clara, born five years after him, was buried alongside him when she died in 1959. Other higher education entities besides Cameron University named after distinguished Oklahomans are Rogers State University (named after Rogers County which was named for Clement Vann Rogers, I. T. judge and Cherokee Senator) and Rose State College (named after Oscar Rose, Mid-Del School District Superintendent].

Chapter 8

1. *Second BRDPIO 1908* (Guthrie: OK, 1908), 4.
2. Ibid., 24.
3. Joseph B. Thoburn, *A Standard History of Oklahoma*, vol. 3 (Chicago: The American Historical Society, 1916), 1106-10.
4. "Robert H. Wilson, 1873-1937," *Chronicles of Oklahoma*, 15, no. 4 (1937): 498; Thoburn, *A Standard History*, 1106; "Chickasha Citizens Denounce Libel," *TO*, July 28, 1910, 16.
5. "Working for County High School," *Chickasha Journal*, November 22, 1907, 1; "Chickasha Citizens Denounce Libel."
6. "Pres. Wilson's Address," *Oklahoma School Herald*, February 1909, 19; "The Grady County Plan," *Oklahoma School Herald*, June 1908, 6.
7. Thoburn, *A Standard History*, 1107; "Grady County News," *Oklahoma School Herald*, December 1908, 8.
8. "Pres. Wilson's Address."
9. Ibid., 20.
10. *Second BRDPIO 1908*, 134.
11. Testimony by R. H. Wilson to the Committee Investigating the Board of Education, August 26, 1911, Box

30, F 6, RG 8-B-2, Governor Cruce Collection, OSA, ODL, OKC; See *Annual* and *Biennial Reports* for 1907-1910.

12. *Second BRDPIO 1908*, 134. Placing educators (school men) in state education leadership positions was a hot topic in 1910 and 1911. Francis Coram Oakes, "A Story of Central State College of Edmond," (Edmond: unpublished manuscript, 1953), 118. *Cordell Weekly Beacon*, June 20, 1907, 4; *Oklahoma Elections: Statehood to Present*, vol. 1 (OKC: SEB, 1994), C-14; Democratic Primary 1910, Box 1-15, RG 24-4-1, EBCFCE, OSA, ODL, OKC.

13. *Oklahoma Elections*, C-18; *Oklahoma School Herald*, September 1910, 17; EBCFCE, Republican Primary 1910, Box 1-15, RG 24-4-1, EBCFCE, OSA, ODL, OKC.

14. *Oklahoma Elections*, C-26; (Political announcement), *Oklahoma School Herald*, September 1910, 17; Jim Bissett, *Agrarian Socialism in America: Marx, Jefferson, and Jesus in the Oklahoma Countryside, 1904-1920* (Norman: OU Press/Red River Press, 2002), 10.

15. *Marshall Tribune*, April 24, 1914, 1. Several references were made to his campaigning in the May and June issues of the *Tribune*, but no references were found in other publications. Thoburn, *A Standard History*, 1107; Democratic Primary 1914, Box 3-19, RG 24-4-1, EBCFCE, OSA, ODL, OKC; *Oklahoma Elections*. C-46; "Republican State Preferential Convention," *Perry Republican*, April 16, 1914; Republican Primary 1914 and General Election 1918, EBCFCE, OSA, ODL, OKC. The expenses of $2,011.80 were primarily for the general election when only primary expense reporting was mandatory.

16. Thoburn. *A Standard History*, 1107; "C. G. Vannest Speaks at Enid," *Perry Republican*, October 1, 1914.

17. *Oklahoma Elections*, C-64; "Progressive Candidate for State Superintendent," *TO*, November 1, 1914, B2; "Socialism a Menace to Present Political Order," *Harlow's Weekly*, September 25, 1915, 10; J. O. Welday, "The Socialist Pary in Oklahoma," *Oklahoma Graphic*, February 1915, 11-12, www.marxisthistory.org/history/usa/parties/spusa/1915/0200-welday-oklahomasp.pdf.

18. *Advance-Democrat* (Stillwater), June 27, 1918, 4; *Bulletin of the Oklahoma Agricultural and Mechanical College, Twenty-Seventh Annual Catalog 1917-1918* (April-June, 1918), V-VI; (political ad) "Chas. W. Briles, Candidate for State Superintendent of Public Instruction," *TO*, June 30, 1918, B6; "An Inspiring Story," *Advance-Democrat*, July 4, 1918, 1. A political ad paid by Rev. Wilmoore Kendall and typical for that era. Joe Hubbell, *The Oklahoma Education Association, 1884-1974*, 19-20, 35-40, 50; *Fourth Annual Report to Congress of the Federal Board for Vocational Education, 1920* (Washington, DC: GPO, 1920), 162; (political ad) "George Wilson, Candidate for State Superintendent of Public Instruction," *TO*, July 7, 1918, B16; https://go.okstate.edu/about-osu/past-osu-presidents.html. Five years later Gov. Walton ordered the National Guard to remove A&M President James Eskridge from campus so he could "install his political favorite George Wilson." After thousands marched Wilson, who did not hold a college degree was forced to resign.

19. "Several Faculty Members Leave," *Orange and Black*, January 12, 1918, 1; "Prof. Briles Returns From Extended Trip," *Orange and Black*, April 6, 1918, 1; "Prof C. W. Briles Makes Tour of State," *Orange and Black*, July 20, 1918, 1; "Briles Quits Race for Superintendent," *TO*, July 26, 1918, 1; *Oklahoma Elections*, C-88; Democratic Primary 1918, Box 9-23, RG 24-4-1, EBCFCE; "To the Democratic Voters of Oklahoma," *Advance-Democrat*, August 1, 1918, 5; *Oklahoma Elections*, C-88; General Election 1918, Box 9-23, RG 24-4-1, EBCFCE. Report of the Resolution Committee of the OEA included this resolution: "As our worthy State Superintendent of Public Instruction, Hon. R. H. Wilson, has received the hearty indursement (sic) of the citizens of Oklahoma with his re-election to the high and responsible office which he holds, we hereby renew our allegiance to him and pledge our undivided support in his efforts to upbuild the schools of Oklahoma to a state of efficiency and power commensurate with our duty in the great work of reconstruction." Meeting held Nov. 29-Dec. 1., 1918.

20. *Fourth BRSSPI together with the FRSBE, OK, 1912* (Guthrie: State of OK, 1912), 76-78, 231, 54, 56, 62-70, 13; *Third BRSSPI 1908-1910* (Guthrie: State Capital, 1910), 14; *Journal of the Proceedings of the Senate of the Regular Session of the Third Legislature of the State of Oklahoma, 1911* (OKC: Warden, 1911), 112-13.

21. *Fourth BRSSPI*, 13-15.

22. Testimony by R. H. Wilson to the Committee Investigating the Board of Education, August 26, 1911, Box 30, FF 8, 7, RG 8-B-2, Governor Cruce Collection, OSA, ODL, OKC; *Journal of Proceedings of the Senate of the Regular Session of the Third Legislature*, 115.

23. Testimony, Box 30, F 8, RG 8-B-2, Governor Cruce Collection; Testimony by Robert Dunlop to the Committee Investigating the Board of Education, August 31, 1911, Box 30, F 8, RG 8-B-2, Governor Cruce Collection; O.S.L. 1910-1911, ch. 47, §§ 1-3 (Co-operative, 1911).

24. "Educational Reform, Oklahoma in Forefront," *Oklahoma School Herald*, March 1911, 9.

25. Boxes 7, 12, 13, FF 1-4, RG 8-B-2, Governor Cruce Collection; Cruce to T. D. Duncan, 6 April 1911, Box 12, F 6, RG 8-B-2, Governor Cruce Collection; "New State Board of Education Named Saturday by Governor Cruce," *TO*, April 9, 1911, 26; "Personnel of the State Board of Education," *Oklahoma School Herald*,

May 1911, 7; Wilson to Cruce, 15 July 1912, Box 10, F11, RG 8-B-2, Governor Cruce Collection; Testimony by R. H. Wilson, 11.

26. Wilson to Cruce, 15 July 1912,
27. Testimony by R. H. Wilson, 11. 14, 17; SBEMM April-June, 1911, RG 18-1, DE, Box 1, File 3, OSA, ODL, OKC.
28. Governor to J. M. Brody, 9 May 1911, Box 12, F 3, RG 8-B-2, Governor Cruce Collection; Grant Evans to Cruce, 30 June 1911 and Evans to Cruce, 11 July 1911, Box 30, F 1, RG 8-B-2, Governor Cruce Collection. Both of these documents are embedded within the oral testimony given during the investigation of the Board of August 1911 and included in the written record.
29. J. E. Dyche to Cruce, 30 July 1911, Box 30, F 5, RG 8-B-2, Governor Cruce Collection. See note 25. Many letters, telegrams, and affidavits were sent supporting the Board members: Box 7, FF 79-80, RG 8-B-2 Governor Cruce Collection.
30. Executive Order of Governor Cruce, July 29,1912, Box 30, F 11, RG 8-B-2, Governor Cruce Collection.
31. Wilson to Cruce, 15 July 1912.
32. "Both Factions of Board Turned Down by the Senate," *TO*, December 8, 1912, 1; "With Hands Full Senate Wants to Adjourn Tuesday," *TO*, December 10, 1912, 1; "Four Members of Board are Named," *TO*, January 31, 1913, 1; "Four Members of Board Confirmed," *TO*, February 2, 1913, 4.
33. O.S.L. 1910-1911, chapt. 131, §§ 1-3; *Fifth BRSSPI together with the Second RSBE, OK, 1914* (OKC: Warden, 1914), 14, 142; *Rural School Consolidation, A Bulletin of Information Issued by the OK SBE*, 3-4; O.S.L. 1913, chapt. 239, § 1.
34. *Journal of the Senate of the Fourth Legislature of the State of Oklahoma 1913*, (OKC: Warden, 1913), 82-83; *Fourth BRSSPI*, 18-19.
35. *Fourth BRSSPI*, 16-19; Fifth BRSSPI, 137.
36. *Fifth BRSSPI*, 9, 13-15.
37. Ibid., 13-14; *Eighth BRSSPI together with the Fifth RSBE, OK, 1920* (Oklahoma City: Allied, 1920), 42; Wilson to Cruce, 15 July 1912.
38. *Eighth BRSSPI*, 41.
39. *Fifth BRSSPI*, 14.
40. Hubbell, *The Oklahoma Education Association*, 44; O.S.L. 1913, chapt. 219, art. 1-17 (Cooperative 1913).
41. *The OEA*, 48.
42. *Fifth BRSSPI*, 27-28.
43. Hubbell, *The OEA*, 49; *Fourth BRSSPI*, 6-8.
44. *Sixth BRSSPI together with the Third RSBE, 1916* (OKC: Warden, 1916), 7, 71-72.
45. *Fourth BRSSPI*, 16; O.S.L. 1913, chapt. 219, art 6; *Sixth BRSSPI*, 9-10.
46. R. H. Wilson, *A Brief Statement of the Growth of the Schools of Oklahoma for the Past Four Years 1912-1915* (Oklahoma City: 1915), 5; *Sixth BRSSPI*, 7.
47. *Sixth BRSSPI*, 12.
48. O.S.L. 1919, chapt. 274, § 1 (Harlow 1919); *Eighth BRSSPI*, 42. The General Education Fund, a philanthropic thrust initiated by John D. Rockefeller, provided money to help rural white and Black schools in the South from 1902 to circa 1950.
49. *Sixth BRSSPI*, 17-18.
50. Smith-Hughes Act of 1917, Pub. L. No. 64-347, 39 Stat. 929 (1917); O.S.L. 1917, chapt. 155, §§ 1-6 (Cooperative 1917).
51. *Seventh BRSSPI together with the Fourth Report of the SBE, OK, 1918* (OKC: Allied, 1918), 3; "Vocational Education," *Oklahoma Home and School Herald*, March, 1918, 107; "Directory," *Oklahoma Teacher*, December, 1919, 2; *Fourth Annual Report to Congress of the Federal Board for Vocational Education*, 162.
52. O.S. 1921 §§ 10246-10247 (Bunn 1922).
53. Ibid., §§ 10855-10863, 10803-10820, 10766-10779, 10848-10854, 10699-10703, 10717-10744, 10821-10837; *Eighth BRSSPI*, 80.
54. O.S. 1921 §§ 10306-10310, 10674-10688, 10666-10673; Hubbell, *The Oklahoma Education Association*, 64.
55. *Journal of the Senate of the Seventh Legislature of the State of Oklahoma Regular Session January 7 to March 29, 1919*, 295; Leroy Fischer, ed., *Oklahoma's Governors, 1907-1929: Turbulent Politics* (OKC: OHSRC, 1981), 98-99.
56. *Harlow's Weekly*, XVI, no.3, January 15, 1919, 8, https://gateway.okhistory.org/ark:/67531/metadc1601375/m1/8/.
57. *Ninth BRSSPI together with the Sixth RSBE, OK, 1922* (OKC: Warden, 1922), 66; *Eighth BRSSPI*, 72.
58. *Oklahoma Elections*, C-118; Hubbell, *The OEA*, 66-67; *Eighth BRSSPI*, 10.
59. O.S. 1921 §§ 10888-10891; *Public Education in Oklahoma, A Report of a Survey of Public Education in the*

State of Oklahoma (Washington, DC: Department of the Interior, Bureau of Education, December 11, 1922), vii, https://babel.hathitrust.org/cgi/pt?id=loc.ark:/13960/t7pn9qq8v&view=1up&seq=40. The Commission was to be comprised of the state superintendent of public instruction as *ex-officio* chair, Martin Brumbaugh of Philadelphia, Pennsylvania, and three others from the National Bureau of Education. All educators were to assist them to have access to information, records, and data. The legislature appropriated $20,000 for travel, lodging, honoraria, and printing costs.

60. *Public Education in Oklahoma, viii.*
61. *Public Education in Oklahoma*, 363-89.
62. *Ninth BRSSPI*, 2.
63. *Fourth BRSSPI*, 4; *Ninth BRSSPI*, 3-11.
64. O.S.L. 1917, 536-37; O.S.L. 1919, 501-02; O.S.L. 1921, 293-95; "Directory," *Oklahoma Teacher*, December 1919, 2.
65. Stanley Frost, "Night-Riding Reformers: The Regeneration of Oklahoma," *Outlook*, November 14, 1923, 40, 438.
66. "Both Owen and Wilson Have Lead Over Radical League Candidate," *TO*, July 30, 1922, 1; "Catholic Vote Defeats Ku Klux Klan," *TO*, August 4, 1922, 1; Carter Blue Clark, "A History of the Ku Klux Klan in Oklahoma," (PhD diss., OU, 1976), 175; *Oklahoma Elections*, C-120.
67. *Oklahoma Elections*, C-203; "Wilson's Body to Lie in State," *Oklahoma City Times*, October 5, 1937, 10; "Heart Stroke Proves Fatal to R. H. Wilson," *TO*, October 5, 1937, 1.

Chapter 9

1. *Oklahoman*, September 10, 1922, 9C; Lyle H. Boren and Dale Boren, *Who is Who in Oklahoma* (Guthrie: Cooperative, 1935), 372; *Handbook of Texas Online*," Robert Wooster, "Tryon, TX (Hardin County)," http://www.tshaonline.org/handbook/online/articles/hyt64; Francis Coram Oakes, "A Story of Central State College of Edmond, Oklahoma" (unpublished manuscript, 1953), 86; "Longtime Educator Dies Here," *Edmond Evening Sun*, May 12, 1981, 2A; "Nash Resigns as School Head," *Blackwell Sunday Tribune*, April 10, 1927, 1; *Oklahoma County Marriage Records, 1889-1951*, Book 26, 224, OHSRC. For additional demographic information, see appendix A.
2. *Oklahoma High School Manual 1919*, SDE, 1; O.S. 1921 §§ 10306-10310 (Bunn 1922).
3. Joe Hubbell, "The Oklahoma Education Association, 1884-1974" (unpublished manuscript, 1974), 66, 84; Boren and Boren, *Who is Who in Oklahoma*, 372.
4. *Oklahoma Elections: Statehood to Present*, vol. 1 (OKC: SEB, 1994), C-123, C-127, C-135; Democratic and Republican Primaries 1922, Box 12-9, RG 24-4-1, EBCFCE, OSA, ODL, OKC.
5. *Oklahoma Elections*, C-121; Democratic and Republican Primaries 1922, EBCFCE; (political ad with testimonials by four Alva ministers), *TO*, July 24, 1922, 5; "The League's Selections," *TO*, July 30, 1922, 5; bls.gov/data/inflation_calculator.htm; "Guilt Denied by Dodson in License Deal," *TO*, July 9, 1922, 8.
6. Democratic and Republican Primaries, EBCFCE; *Oklahoma Elections*, C-135; *TO*, July 30, 1922, 6.
7. "Where Age and Youth Work Together," *TO*, September 10, 1922, 9 C; *Oklahoma Elections*, C-135.
8. "Only Twelve in List Know School Chief," *TO*, June 19, 1926, 5.
9. *Oklahoma Elections*, C-160; Republican Primary 1926, Box 15-16, RG 24-4-1, EBCFCE; *Oklahoma Elections*, C-168.
10. *Chickasha Express*, April 12, 1927; Rex F. Harlow, *George W. Austin, His Life and Work* (OKC, 1927), 135.
11. "Nash Gives up State Post to Head College," *TO*, April 10, 1927, 5.
12. "He Wants One Third of Gross Production Tax in School Fund," *TO*, January 23, 1923, 5.
13. *Eleventh BRSSPI together with the Eighth RSBE, OK, 1926* (OKC: SDE, 1926), 67; O.S.L. 1923, chapt. 174, §§ 1-21 (Harlow 1923). Nash summarized the appropriations for 1923 and 1924 in this *Eleventh BRSSPI of 1926*, something he did not include in the *Tenth BRSSPI of 1924*. By the time of his *1924 Report* he would have known the figures.
14. "The Textbook Controversy," *TO*, September 14, 1921, 6; *Eleventh BRSSPI*, 7-8.
15. O.S.L. 1925, chapt. 16, § 1 and chapt. 10, §§ 1-5 (Harlow 1925); *Oklahoma Elections*, C-171.
16. "Farmers Open Fight for Vote," *TO*, April 19, 1925, 77; "Nash Assailed on Book Order by Farm Union," *TO*, April 30, 1925, 13; "Darwin Theory Repealed, Too?" *TO*, June 18, 1925, 10; "State to Vote on Evolution," *TO*, June 21, 1925, 8.
17. *Eleventh BRSSPI*, 67.
18. *Tenth BRSSPI together with the Seventh RSBE, 1924* (OKC: SDE, 1924), 9; *Eleventh BRSSPI*, 31-34, 6-8; Edgar W. Knight, *Education in the United States* (New York: Ginn, 1929), 555. John Fox Slater, New England manufacturer, created a one million dollar endowment in 1882 to aid Blacks to get an education with a

Christian influence. Funds were used for salaries, buildings, and operating expenses principally in normal and industrial training.
19. Tenth BRSSP, 10-12; *Public Education in Oklahoma, A Report of a Survey of Public Education in the State of Oklahoma* (Washington, DC: Department of the Interior, Bureau of Education, December 11, 1922), 319-20.
20. Tenth BRSSPI, 11.
21. *Public Education in Oklahoma*, 315.
22. Tenth BRSSPI, 6-7.
23. Ibid., 10-12.
24. E. E. Brown, *A Statistical Survey by Counties of Education in Oklahoma 1925* (OKC: SDE, 1925), 3, 55-61; *Eleventh BRSSPI*, 6-8.
25. *Eleventh BRSSPI*, 25.
26. Ibid., 52-53.
27. Ibid., 5; *SBEMM*, March 21, 1927, RG 18-1, SDE, OSA, ODL, OKC.
28. *OED 1926-1927*, 31-32.
29. Ibid., 4; O.S.L. 1927, chapt. 90, § 1 (Harlow 1927). Chapter 90 reported the institutional appropriations for fiscal year 1928-1929. Enrollment figures for the same year ranked the Oklahoma College for Women fifth in a group that included the six teachers colleges. *Twelfth BRSSPI together with the Ninth RSBE, OK, 1928* (OKC: SDE, 1928), 144-48.
30. *Edmond Evening Sun*, May 12, 1981, 1.
31. "Resolution," Oklahoma State Regents for Higher Education, May 27, 1981; State Superintendent's Letter, *Oklahoma Teacher*, September 1923, 8.
32. Editorial. *TO*, April 11, 1927, 8; "Nash Resigns as State Superintendent," *Oklahoma Teacher*, May 1927, 8.

Chapter 10

1. "Nash Gives up State Post to Head College," *TO*, April 10, 1927, 5; Lyle H. Boren and Dale Boren, *Who is Who in Oklahoma* (Guthrie: Cooperative, 1935) 508; *Handbook of Texas Online*, Stephen L. Hardin, "Thompsonville, Texas," http://tshaonline.org/handbook/online/articles/hnt19; "John Vaughan is Dead at 65," *TO*, January 22, 1951, 1; *Third BRSSPI 1908-1910* (OKC: Warden, 1910), 402; *Fifth BRSSPI together with the Second RSBE, OK, 1914* (OKC: Warden, 1914), 185; *OED 1917-1918* (OKC: SDE, 1917), 13.
2. *OA 2015-2016* (OKC: ODL, 2015), 825; *Kingston Messenger*, July 21, 1916, 10; *Kingston Messenger*, August 4, 1916, 8. The primary vote was current state representative from Marshall County, J. J. Clark with 1,025 and Vaughan with 1767. Clark received twenty-one more votes in Johnston County while Vaughan garnered a net 763 in Marshall County. *Kingston Messenger*, August 14, 1916, November 10, 1916, 4.
3. *Journal of the Senate of the Regular Session, Sixth Legislature* (OKC: Warden, 1917), 2016; O.S.L. 1917, chapt. 155, § 3 (Warden 1917).
4. *Journal of the Senate of the Seventh Legislature of the State of Oklahoma* (OKC: Warden, 1919), 2408; O.S. 1921 §§ 10601, 10666-10673, 10397-10403, 10385-10390 (Bunn 1922).
5. *Journal of the Senate of the Seventh Legislature*, 2116, 2120.
6. "The Holisso," Southeastern Oklahoma State University's yearbook for the years 1920-1924, https://www.se.edu/library/serials-department/electronic-resources/southeastern-annuals/; *Public Education in Oklahoma, A Report of A Survey of Public Education in the State of Oklahoma* (Washington, DC: Department of the Interior, Bureau of Education, 1922), vii-viii, https://babel.hathitrust.org/cgi/pt?id=loc.ark:/13960/t7pn9qq8v&view=1up&seq=40.
7. "John Vaughan is Dead at 65," *TO*, January 22, 1951, 1; *SBEMM*, July 21, 1925; December 21, 1925, RG 18-1, DE, OSA, ODL, OKC.
8. Joe Hubbell. *The Oklahoma Education Association 1884-1974* (unpublished manuscript, 1974), 70-73; Oscar W. Davison, "Early History of the Oklahoma Education Association," *Chronicles of Oklahoma*, XXIX, no. 1, (1951): 57-59; *Oklahoma Elections: Statehood to Present*, vol. 1 (OKC: SEB, 1994), C-172. Vaughan served as a vice president of the National Education Association 1927-28, his first year as Superintendent. *Public Education in Oklahoma, A Report of a Survey*, 32-33.
9. Hubbell, *The OEA*, 74.
10. *Blackwell Morning Tribune*, April 12, 1927, 7; *SBEMM*, March 21, 1927; April 4, 1927; April 22, 1927, RG 18-1, DE; "State Board of Education From 1911-Present," (unpublished manuscript, n.d.), SBE, 1986.
11. *Model and Accredited Elementary School Bulletin No. 118, May 21, 1928* (OKC: DE, 1928), 7-19; *Model and Accredited Elementary School Bulletin No. 118-H, July 1936* (OKC: DE, 1936), 5-14.
12. *Model and Accredited Elementary School Bulletin No. 118-G, July 1935* (OKC: DE, 1935), 5; *Model and Accredited Elementary School Bulletin No. 118*, 51-58; *Model and Accredited Elementary School Bulletin No. 118-H*, 14.

13. *Twelfth BRSSPI together with the Ninth RSBE, OK, 1928* (OKC: SDE, 1928), 4-7.
14. LeRoy Fisher, ed., *Oklahoma's Governors, 1907-1929: Turbulent Politics* (OKC: OHSRC, 1981), 189-91; Hubbell, *The OEA*, 74.
15. Hubbell, *The OEA*, 76.
16. O.S. 1931 §§ 6694-6695, 7189, 6756 (Harlow 1935).
17. O.S. 1931 § 7007; *Thirteenth BRSSPI and the Tenth BRSBE* (OKC, SDE, 1930), 125.
18. *Thirteenth BRSSPI*, 1-6.
19. *Fifteenth BRSSPI and the Twelfth BRSBE*, Oklahoma (OKC: SDE, 1934), 96, 101.
20. Ibid., 2-11; *SBEMM*, December 3, 1934.
21. "Vaughan Sees Peril for Schools in Tax Measures," *TO*, November 16, 1931, 1,16.
22. "Vaughan Explains Bills at School," *TO*, December 11, 1931, 9.
23. "Murray Plea on Tax Held to be False," *TO*, November 3, 1932, 1-2.
24. "Valuation Cut to Trim State School Terms," *TO*, April 9, 1933, 12; "Vaughan Points Out Weak Spots in School's Support," *TO*, August 4, 1933, 4.
25. "Early Relief Action is Due," *TO*, February 20, 1934, 1; "John Vaughan, The New Deal for Education," *Oklahoma Teacher*, March, 1934, 9; William H. Murray, *Wm. H. Murray Educational Foundation* (Tishomingo, OK: William H. Murray, 1949), 5-6. In the heart of the depression, in April 1934, Governor Murray, with the help of friends, established the Wm. H. Murray Educational Foundation to assist deserving college students (excluding communists, Zionists, atheists, and persons of any race with less morality than the American Nordic Whites or different from Anglo-Saxon Germanic race, and Aryan American Indian of bad character) by loaning them money to pay for their college expenses. Henry Bennett was one of the founders ($100 minimum) and a trustee. This Foundation was part of the textbook litigation of a decade later and involved royalties from textbooks written by Bennett, president of Oklahoma A&M. "State Board to Meet for Action on Aid," *TO*, May 11, 1935, 2.
26. *Sixteenth BRSSPI and the Thirteenth BRSBE, OK* (OKC: SBE, 1936), 128; *SBEMM*, February 5, 1935; *SBEMM*, May 11, 1935; *SBEMM*, August 19, 1935. *OED* for 1947 to 1953. Kate Zaneis was hired by Oliver Hodge to work in the school lunch division of the Department.
27. "More College Heads to Lose Out in Change," *TO*, May 12, 1935, 24.
28. Compiled Laws of Oklahoma 1921 §§ 10246-10281 (Bunn 1922); O.S.L. 1929, chapt. 260, §§ 1-2 (Harlow 1929); Okla. Const. art. XIII, § 6; O.S. 1931 (Harlow 1931); "Price Cuts on Texts Deep, is Board Report," *TO*, July 26, 1929, 11; "Rebound Text Sales Not Common, Claim," *TO*, September 4, 1929, 5.
29. "Comment on Unsupported Alibi," *TO*, December 17, 1931, 8.
30. Ibid.
31. "Vaughan Questions Appointment Order," *TO*, May 10, 1933, 2.
32. "Vaughan Raps Governor for Book Threat," *TO*, May 21, 1933, 21; "Text Bidding Still Veiled in Secrecy," *TO*, June 22, 1933, 16.
33. "Ruling Shears Text Adoption by 40 Percent," *TO*, July 15, 1933, 1.
34. "Murray Balks at Text Hike," *TO*, September 26, 1933, 14; "Schools Shun New Text Use," *TO*, October 19, 1933, 2.
35. "Murray Book Order Flayed, *TO*, October 9, 1934, 4; "Vaughan Reiterates Texts Never to Be Used," *TO*, January 3, 1935, 2.
36. "Vaughan Asks Quality Study," *TO*, June 15, 1935, 5; "Texts Change is Blocked by State Board," *TO*, July 20, 1935, 1; "U.S. Court Gets State Book Fight," *TO*, July 23, 1935, 1; "Text Changes Avoided Here," *TO*, September 13, 1935, 1.
37. "Evans is Offered Westminster Job," *TO*, August 5, 1930, 19; Primary Election 1930, Box 18-23, RG 24-4-1, EBCFCE, OSA, ODL, OKC; "Charles Evans, Democrat for State Superintendent of Public Instruction," *TO*, July 26, 1930, 23; "Citizens! Taxpayers! Hear These Candidates Speak!" *TO*, July 21, 1930, 5. These two advertisements were typical forms of politicking in that era. *Oklahoma Elections*, C-182, C-194.
38. *Oklahoma Elections*, C-220 and C-226.
39. "Kerr, Candidate to Resign State Post," *TO*, March 28, 1934, 3. Kerr was re-hired in the Department in 1941 as one of six school examiners, was promoted to division level director in 1947, and served as such for three different divisions until his retirement in 1962.
40. "Woman, Seven Men Seeking House Posts as Democrats," *TO*, June 10, 1934, 14A; *Oklahoma Teacher*, May 1924, 44; "Vote on Faculties Sought by Vaughan," *TO*, June 16, 1934, 9; "Teacher Vote Fight Carried into Schools," *TO*, June 27, 1934, 5.
41. Editorial. *"Texted and True,"* *TO*, July 16, 1934, 8; "Who Killed Cock Robin?" *TO*, July 22, 1934, 44.
42. *Oklahoma Elections*, C-220, C-226, C-229, and C-235.
43. A. L. Beckett, *Report of the Secretary to the Commissioners of the Land Office to the Honorable Wm. H.*

Murray, Governor and to the Fourteenth Legislature, (n.d.), 1-4, Box 1, F 1, RG 8-1-2, Governor William Murray Papers, OSA, ODL, OKC. Secretary Beckett reported to the Chair who was the governor, resulting in confusion as to when Murray was functioning as governor and when as chair of the Commission.

44. Ibid., 4; Examples: Murray to Judge A. L. Beckett, 10 February 1931 (R. A. Hopper for a clerical position) and Murray to Judge A. L. Beckett, 23 January 1931 (Joe Neeley for appraiser); Murray to Mr. Meigs Murray, 18 May 1931, Box 1, F 1, RG 8-1-2, Governor William Murray's Papers, OSA, ODL, OKC. Meigs Murray was unrelated to Governor Murray as deduced from the written notes of an interview of him by Lula Austin October 19, 1934, as part of the Works Progress Administration's Indian-Pioneer History Project for Oklahoma. https://digital.libraries.ou.edu/cdm/singleitem /collection/indianpp/id/855/rec/6.
45. Beckett, "Report of the Secretary"; Earl R. Willson to Murray, 10 February 1932, Box 1, F 1, RG 8-1-2, Governor Murray's Papers; Governor's Executive Order, October 26, 1932, Governor Murray's Papers; E. R. Willson to Murray, 10 March 1933, Governor Murray's Papers.
46. *State of Oklahoma, ex rel, Commissioners of the Land Office v Sam A. Pollard and American Surety Co.*, a Corporation, Box 1, F 2, RG 8-1-2, Governor Murray's Papers; bls.gov/data/inflation_calculator.htm. The equivalent amount was calculated from June 1928 to June 2014.
47. A. L. Beckett to Murray, 20 April 1933, Box 1, F 1, RG 8-1-2, Governor Murray's Papers; HB 187 passed in the Extraordinary Session of the Fourteenth Legislature and was signed by Governor Murray July 18, 1933. With no emergency clause, the law became effective ninety days after the Legislature's adjournment, October 14. Military Executive Order, May 16, 1933, Box 1, F 1, RG 8-1-2, Governor Murray's Papers.
48. *Past Transactions of the School Land Commission Composed of the Governor, State Auditor, State Superintendent, President of the State Board of Agriculture and Secretary of State; Report of the Committee on School Lands Designated As a Special Committee for the Purpose of Investigating the School Land Department*, (n.d.), Box 1, F 2, RG 8-1-2, Governor Murray's Papers.
49. *Commissioners of the Land Office Meeting Minutes*, October 17, 1933, Box 1, F 1, RG 8-1-2, Governor Murray's Papers.
50. Ibid.
51. Ibid.
52. Ibid.
53. Glenn Young to Murray, 27 October 1933; Murray to Homer Boughman, 5 June 1934: Box 1, F 1, RG 8-1-2, Governor Murray's Papers. Murray succeeded in persuading the legislature to grant him the authority to appoint the Commission secretary.
54. "Evidence taken in the Special School Land Investigation 1935," 814, Box 2, F 1, RG 8-J-4, Governor Marland's Papers, OSA, ODL, OKC.
55. Ibid., 43, 590, 592; bls.gov/data/inflation_calculator.htm. See note 46.
56. Ibid., 685, 743.
57. *Commissioners of the Land Office Meeting Minutes*, October 17, 1933.
58. "Evidence taken in the Special School Land Investigation," 571.
59. Ibid., 814-16.
60. Ibid., 817; *OA 2016-2016* (OKC: ODL, 2015), 271. The Commission's membership changed through State Question 514 that was approved July 22, 1975 and effective January 8, 1979.
61. *OA*, 271; *Commissioners of the Land Office 2019 Annual Report*, http://clo.ok.gov/wp-content /uploads/2020 /01/2019-Final-Annual-Report-1.pdf.
62. *SBEMM*, August 19, 1936, RG 18-1, DE, OSA, ODL, OKC; *Sixteenth BRSSPI*, 128.
63. "John Vaughan is Dead at 65," *TO*, January 22, 1951, 1.
64. "His Work Will Live," *TO, January 23, 1951, 8.*

Chapter 11

1. "It's Busy Day, From Teacher to Statehouse," *TO*, August 20, 1936, 5; *SBEMM*, August 19, 1936, RG 18-1, DE, OSA, ODL, OKC.
2. Rex Harlow and Victor E. Harlow, *Makers of Government in Oklahoma* (OKC: Harlow, 1930), 661-62; "It's Busy Day, From Teacher to Statehouse;" Lyle H. Boren and Dale Boren, *Who is Who in Oklahoma* (Guthrie: Co-operative, 1935), 113; Alvin L. Crable Jr., interview by the author, April 6, 1998; *Marietta Monitor*, September 9, 1921, 1; Robert C. Fite, *A History of Oklahoma State University Extension and Outreach* (Stillwater: OSU, 1988), 19.
3. Boren and Boren, *Who is Who in Oklahoma.*
4. *Eleventh BRSSPI Together with the Eighth RSBE 1926* (OKC: DE, 1926), 42; O.S.L. 1925, chapt. 66, § 1 (Harlow 1925); "Report of High School Inspectors," *Twelfth BRSSPI Together with the Ninth RSBE, OK,*

1928 (OKC: DE, 1928), 72. The report states that the Superintendent was to be the head of the Department of High School Inspectors and he was to appoint three inspectors at an annual salary of $2,400. For that term of office the Superintendent's salary was $2,500. O.S.L. 1919, chapt. 80, § 1 (Harlow 1919); Crable Jr., interview.
5. Fite, *A History of Oklahoma State University*, 19-20.
6. "It's Busy Day, From Teacher to Statehouse;" *SBEMM*, August 19, 1936; *Twelfth BRSSPI*, 3; Sixteenth BRSSPI and the Thirteenth RSBE, OK (OKC: SBE, 1936), iv-v.
7. "Crable, Scott to Draw Fire in Two Races," *TO*, June 6, 1937, 28; James C. Milligan, "Zaneis, Kate Galt," *EOHC* (OKC: OHSRC, 2009), 1667.
8. "Crable Place Eyed by City School Chief," *TO*, February 8, 1938, 20; "McCool Enters State School Job Contest," *TO*, April 20, 1938, 5.
9. "McCool Enters State School Job Contest;" *Oklahoma Elections: Statehood to Present*, vol. 1 (OKC: SEB, 1994), C-264; Primary Election 1938, Box 28-15, RG 24-4-1, EBCFCE, OSA, ODL, OKC.
10. *Oklahoma Elections*, C-274; "For State Superintendent of Public Instruction," *TO*, November 6, 1938, 18A.
11. "For State Superintendent;" "Measure Appropriating $1,000,000 for Relief of Schools is Passed by House," *TO*, March 2, 1935, 4.
12. "Crable Favored Over Fisher in School Contest," *TO*, July 4, 1942, 20; *The Voice of the Democratic Women of Oklahoma*, July 1942, 13, John Dunning Political Collection, Democratic Party Materials 1940s, Box 26, FF 3, OHSRC; *Oklahoma Elections*, C-298; Primary Election 1942, Box 33-7, RG 24-4-1, EBCFCE.
13. "Crable Favored Over Fisher in School Contest;" *Oklahoma Elections*, C-297-8, 305.
14. See election results for the several elections in *Oklahoma Elections*.
15. "Text Scandals Might Cause Crable Defeat," *TO*, May 20, 1946, 5; *Oklahoma Elections*, C-322; Primary Election 1946, Box 36-24, RG 24-4-1, EBCFCE.
16. "Crable Raps Gilmer Charge," *TO*, July 14, 1946, 17A; Political ad. "A. L. Crable," *TO*, July 16, 1946, 10.
17. Political ad. "To the School Patrons of Oklahoma," *TO*, July 14, 1946, 17; Political ad. "Oliver Hodge Democrat for State Superintendent of Public Instruction," *TO*, July 22, 1946, 22.
18. *Oklahoma Elections*, C-329, 334; Primary Runoff Election 1946, Box 36-24, RG 24-4-1, EBCFCE; "Crable Raps Gilmer Charge;" *TO*, July 21, 1946, 11A; "Bassett, Doyle Also Defeated, Arnold Wins," *TO*, July 24, 1946, 2.
19. *Sixteenth BRSSPI*, 1-2.
20. *Seventeenth BRSSPI and the Fourteenth RSBE, OK* (OKC: DE, 1938), 30-31, 267-68.
21. *Sixteenth BRSSPI*, 3-4.
22. Ibid., 5; *Eighteenth BRSSPI and the Fifteenth RSBE* (OKC: DE, 1940), 86.
23. *Nineteenth BRSDEO and the Sixteenth RSBE* (Guthrie: Co-operative, 1942), 4. While James Staten, Board secretary, prepared both the Department and the Board sections, the report was submitted to the governor under Crable's name.
24. See the Superintendent's "Summary and Recommendations" sections of the *Sixteenth* through *Eighteenth BRSSPIs* and the *Nineteenth BRSDEO*, and the "Schools for Negroes" sections of the *Twentieth* and *Twenty-First BRs. Twenty-First BRSDEO* (Guthrie: Co-operative, 1946), 29. The *Twentieth* and *Twenty-First BRS-DEOs* were printed under Crable's name, but were prepared under the aegis of the Board by its secretary W. T. Doyel. The change occurred when Crable was stripped of his supervision and patronage in 1942 and did not revert to the previous format when Hodge was given control of the SDE in early 1947.
25. *Seventeenth BRSSPI*, IV-V, 7-10; *Sixteenth BRSSPI*, IV-V. In 1936 Vocational Rehabilitation, with its primary office in the State Capitol, was listed under the Vocational Education Division which had offices at OSU in Stillwater. By 1938, it was listed as a separate division in the SDE.
26. *Sixteenth BRSSPI*, 13.
27. *Eighteenth BRSSPI*, 15-18.
28. *Oklahoma Elections*, C-293.
29. *Nineteenth BRSDEO*, 13-18.
30. "School Group Urges Teacher Retirement Act," *TO*, October 6, 1938, 9; "Pension Urged for Teachers," *TO*, October 14, 1938, 7; "Silent Vote Likely to Defeat Six Referendums," *TO*, October 16, 1938, 6A.
31. "Approval Seen at Polls for Teachers' Plan," *TO*, July 12, 1942, 9; *Oklahoma Elections*, C-303; 70 O.S. Supp. §§ 964.1-964.9 (West 1943); *Twentieth BRSDEO and the Seventeenth RSBE* (Guthrie: Co-operative, 1944), 231.
32. *Nineteenth BRSDEO*, 2-3; "State is 1,000 Teachers Shy, Survey Shows," *TO*, October 7, 1942, 1.
33. "New Teacher Sources Urged to Meet Crisis," *TO*, April 8, 1943, 7.
34. "State Relaxes Teaching Rules," *TO*, April 9, 1943, 14.
35. *Twenty-First BRSDEO*, 140-46; *Nineteenth BRSDEO*, 62.

36. 70 O.S.L. 1947, chapt. 21, art. 2, § 1 (Cooperative 1947); David Baird, in discussion with the author, December 20, 1984.
37. "Two Put Off State Board by Governor," *TO*, August 2, 1936, 1; "Three Named Aids on State School Board," *TO*, August 4, 1936, 1; Editorial. *TO*, August 5, 1936, 8.
38. "Marland Plan for Balanced Budget Aired," *TO*, December 20, 1936, 1; "Two Put Off State Board by Governor;" *Thirty-First BRSDEO* (OKC: DE, 1966), 271-72.
39. No speaker of the House served more than one term from statehood to the mid 1950s. LeRoy H. Fischer, ed., *Oklahoma's Governors, 1929-1955: Depression to Prosperity* (OKC: OHSRC, 1983), 104-5; *Seventeenth BRSSPI*, 113.
40. "Phillips Relies on Board Votes to Curb Crable," *TO*, October 29, 1939, 1.
41. Ibid., 2.
42. Editorial, *TO*, January 1, 1941, 20.
43. "Budget Trims State Requests by 7 Millions," *TO*, January 10, 1941, 1-2.
44. "Phillips Asks Curbs on School Buses," *TO*, January 25, 1941, 1; "Crable Calls School Bus Costs 'Fair;'" *TO*, January 28, 1941, 12.
45. *Eighteenth BRSSPI,* 107-19; *OA 2015-2016* (OKC: ODL, 2015), 792-95, 825-29.
46. *Sixteenth BRSSPI*, IV-V; *Eighteenth BRSSPI*, IV-V.
47. "Crable Calls School Bust Costs 'Fair;'" *OA*, 731; O.S.L. 1939, Appropriations, 591 (Cooperative 1939); O.S.L. 1941, Appropriations, 499 (Guthrie: Cooperative, 1941).
48. "Bill Would Slash 14 Off Education Office Pay Roll," *TO*, January 31, 1941, 2; *OA*, 792.
49. "School Battle to Flare Again," *TO*, February 3, 1941, 9; "Phillips to Let Crable Do All Tulsa Talking," *TO*, February 4, 1941, 2.
50. "Crable Demands All Revenues Go to General Fund," TO, February 8, 1941, 4.
51. "Phillips Levels Against Crable, To Press Reorganization Bills," *TO*, February 13, 1941, 1.
52. "Crable to Seek Votes Against 2 Amendments," *TO*, February 23, 1941, 1; "Governor to Talk to State Teachers,"*TO*, February 25, 1941, 13.
53. "Pay Raises Promised Teachers By Governor If Act Passes," *TO*, March 7, 1941, 2; "Crable Mails 15,000 Attacks on Amendment," *TO,* March 2, 1941, 1, 8A. Crable had 50,000 copies printed initially and was prepared to print that many more.
54. Editorial. "We Write a Constitution," *TO*, March 5, 1941, 8.
55. Governor Leon Phillips's radio address, March 3, 1941, Box 1, F 13, RG 8-K-2, Governor Phillips Collection, OSA, ODL, OKC.
56. "Phillips Takes to Radio to Ask Support in Special Election," *TO*, March 4, 1941, 18; "Phillips Plans Special Message on State Budget," *TO*, March 9, 1941, 19A; "All Amendments Get Big Majorities; Pension Vote is Overwhelming," *TO*, March 12, 1941, 1; *Oklahoma Elections*, C-293-94.
57. "State Senate Will Present 'Crable's Last Stand' Today," *TO*, April 9, 1941, 12.
58. "Phillips Names Four New Men to School Board," *TO*, April 16, 1941,1; 70 O.S. 1941 §§ 915.4-915.5 (West 1942); "Crable Clipping Bills Advanced in House Test," *TO*, March 26, 1941, 6; 70 O.S. 1941 §§ 915.1-915.5 (West 1942). All of the state's executive officers' salaries were set every four years and remained the same throughout the term. Crable's salary was $4,800 as stated in O.S.L. 1937, chapt. 20, art 9, § 1 (Harlow 1937).
59. "Bill Would Slash 14 Off Education Office Pay Roll," *TO*, January 31, 1941, 2; "Phillips Levels Against Crable, To Press Reorganization Bills;" "Phillips Forces Push Through Tax Freezing," *TO*, March 21, 1941, 7; HB 168, *Journal of the House of Representatives, Eighteenth Legislature, 1941*, 1552-55.
60. "Divided State School Board Fires Three Crable Appointees," *TO,* June 27, 1941, 1; "Board Fires Crable Appointees," *TO*, September 16, 1941, 9.
61. Joseph B. Thoburn, *A Standard History of Oklahoma*, vol. 3 (Chicago: The American Historical Society, 1916), 1193. See Staff pages for DE personnel in the Superintendents' biennial reports from 1914 to 1942. "Board Rejects One Selection Made by Hodge," *TO*, January 9, 1947, 16.
62. SBEMM, August 1936-December 1946, RG 18-1, DE, OSA, ODL, OKC.
63. O.S.L. 1943, 70, chapt. 26, §§ 1-2 (Cooperative 1943); "Men to Direct State's Schools Picked by Kerr," *TO*, February 5, 1943,1; *Oklahoma Teacher*, March 1943, 15.
64. SBEMM, January 8-9, 1947, RG 18-1, DE.
65. HB 168, *Journal of the House, 1941*, 1552-55; HB 120, *Journal of the House of Representatives, Twenty-Second Legislature, 1949*, 1375-76; 70 O.S. 1951 §§ 2A-1 to 2A-10, 2B-3 (West 1951).
66. 70 O.S. 1941 § 971 (West 1942).
67. "Use of Relief Money to Buy Books Proper," *TO*, July 20, 1937, 5.
68. "Textbook Firms Ask Injunction Against Crable," *TO*, January 5, 1941, 29; "Textbook Firms Ask Dismissal of Suit," *TO*, July 22, 1941, 7.

69. "Leaders Eye Phillips' Speeches; Textbook Issue Holds Spotlight," *TO*, October 24, 1942, 30.
70. "Bennett, Scott, 19 Publishing Firms Accused," *TO*, January 1, 1943, 1-2. Including Crable in the creation of the William H. Murray Education Foundation is fascinating because he was not Superintendent then. On the other hand, he was extension director at OSU, a good friend of Bennett, and a former employee in the Department.; bls.gov/data/inflation_calculator.htm. The inflation amount was calculated from December 1942 to December 2014.
71. "Crable Suggests Book Comparison," *TO*, January 5, 1943, 1; "Speeches Hit Whitford On Inquiry Bill," *TO*, February 4, 1943, 10.
72. "Federal Attorney Called for Textbook Testimony," *TO*, February 25, 1943, 20; "Dierker Denies Others Linked in Text Payoff," *TO*, February 26, 1943, 1; "Kerr Signs Bill to Continue Joint Inquiry," *TO*, April 4, 1943, 16A; bls.gov/data/inflation_calculator.htm. The inflation amount was calculated from December 1942 to December 2014.
73. "Crable Heard By Tulsa Jury," *TO*, November 14, 1943, 20; bls.gov/data/inflation_calculator.htm. The inflation amount was calculated from December 1940 to December 2014. "School Chiefs Charged with Major Frauds," *TO*, December 12, 1943, 9.
74. "Crable, Daniel Freed on Bonds After Arrest in Tulsa Inquiry," *TO*, December 14, 1943, 1; "Crable Defends Record, Will Retain Office," *TO*, April 23, 1944, 24; "Gilmer Seeks Perjury Charge Against Crable," *TO*, April 21, 1944, 2.
75. "Crable Defends Record, Will Retain Office;" "Spotlight Now on Hill, Who Said He'd Quit," *TO*, February 16, 1945, 1, 11; "House Fails to Impeach Crable; Hill Quits Post," *TO*, February 18, 1945, 17.
76. George Lynn Cross, *The University of Oklahoma and World War II: A Personal Account, 1941-1946* (Norman: OU Press, 1980), 148-50, 156.
77. Ibid., 151.
78. Ibid., 149.
79. State Question No. 318 (Initiative Petition No. 228), approved November 5, 1946, by a vote of 261,807 to 167,563 amended Okla. Const. art. XIII, § 6. Enabling legislation, HB 399, effective July 1, 1948, specified the composition of the textbook committee.
80. "Crable's Back on Pay Roll," *TO*, February 3, 1948, 19; "Crable's Post Due for Study," *TO*, February 8, 1948, 6; "State Can't Fire Crable, He's on VA Pay Roll," *TO*, February 10, 1948, 1; "Crable Riddle Gets Deeper with Denials," *TO*, February 11, 1948, 2.
81. "Crable Slated to Quit Soon," *TO*, February 20, 1948, 46; *Oklahoma City Times*, August 11, 1976, 22. The *Times* was an evening supplement to *TO* until 1984. http://gateway.okhistory.org/explore/collections/OKCT/.
82. *Oklahoma City Times*, August 11, 1976; "Crable Heads Trustees of Baptist University," *TO*, November 29, 1939, 17; "Lee, Crable Assail Move for Repeal," *TO*, November 16, 1939, 6. Crable and his wife Claudia, whom he married May 8, 1918, had three children. For additional biographical information, see appendix A.

Chapter 12

1. *Sign-Post*, August 1952, 2. The *Sign-Post* was a publication of the Oklahoma Rehabilitation Service. *The Trail: 1917 Collinsville High School Yearbook*, Newspaper Museum, Collinsville, courtesy, Ted Wright, January 4, 2020; *OED* for 1925-26 and 1926-27 show Hodge as high school principal at a salary of $1,500 and $1,575, respectively.
2. *Sign-Post*, August 1952; "Tulsans Have Rosy Outlook on 1931 Court," *TO*, December 15, 1930, 12; "St. John, Warwick Win Golf Doubles," *TO*, December 17, 1933, 27.
3. "2 Candidates Mentioned for State Regents Post," *TO*, June 25, 1941, 20.
4. "John Dillinger Gunned Down," *TW*, July 23, 1997, www.tulsaworld.com/archive; Lola Covington, a woman, was eligible to run for a county office, but not for a statewide office. *TT*, July 5, 1934, 10; *TT*, July 2, 1934, 2; *TT*, July 25, 1934, 1.
5. See *Tulsa Tribune* for these dates for election results: July 9, 1936, 1; November 4, 1936, 1; July 10, 1938, 14; November 9, 1938, 1; July 10, 1940, 1; July 11, 1942, 9; July 12, 1944, 6; November 9, 1944, 11.
6. Tulsa County data were found in the *OED* for the years 1937-1947. Districts were included in the *OED* only if they employed four or more teachers. Tulsa County was one of the seventy counties with at least one dependent school district. 70 O.S. 1941 § 24 (West 1942). Regardless of the number of dependent school districts, every county had a county superintendent even later on when the county had independent districts only.
7. Oliver Hodge, "The Administration and Development of the Oklahoma School Land Department," (EdD diss., OU, 1937), ProQuest (DP10436).
8. *Oklahoma Elections: Statehood to Present*, vol. 1 (OKC: SEB, 1994), C-322, 329, 334. In the 1946 elec-

tion cycle, the statewide offices drew many candidates: nine for governor, eight for lieutenant governor, and eleven for secretary of state. "Hodge, Nelson Seek Crable's Present Post," *TO*, November 3, 1946, 26A.

9. "Eight Key Jobs are Contested on State Ballot," *TO*, November 2, 1958, 20A; *Oklahoma Elections*, C-419, A-6.
10. "Hodge to Seek Former Power Held by Crable," *TO*, December 21, 1946, 29.
11. 70 O.S. 1941 §§ 915.1-915.5 (West 1942); 70 O.S. 1951 §§ 2A-1 to 2B-4 (West 1951); "Truth Will Out! 'Goats' Reveal 25 Percent Tap Was for Hodge," *TO*, May 26, 1950, 1.
12. "Truth Will Out 'Goats'", 2; "No Apologies Needed, Says Oliver Hodge," *TO*, May 27, 1950, 5.
13. "State School Chief Seeks Re-election," *TO*, December 5, 1953, 7.
14. "House Probers to Quiz Hodge," *TO*, January 28, 1955, 12; "Witness Keeps $1,500 Secret," *TO*, February 16, 1955, 1; "Jurors Work Fast on Higgins Probe," *TO*, June 8, 1955, 1; "Eddie Higgins Charged With Taking a Bribe," *TO*, July 9, 1955, 29.
15. "1000 Turn Out to Honor Hodge," *TO*, November 4, 1957, 28; "Hodge in Race for 4th Term," *TO*, January 28, 1958, 9.
16. "Top Educator Backs Gary As Governor," *TO*, May 5, 1962, 29; "Friend of Nance Fired; Gary Feud Gets Blame," *TO*, July 9, 1953, 2. Article VI, § 4 of the Constitution provided, "Governor, Secretary of State, State Auditor, and State Treasurer shall not be eligible immediately to succeed themselves."
17. "Foes Pull Out, Give Boecher, Hodge No Race," *TO*, March 10, 1966, 3.
18. *AROSDE 1981-82* (OKC: Henry McGraw, 1982), 89-90.
19. *Twenty-First BRSDEO* (Guthrie: Co-operative, 1946), 30.
20. *Twenty-Fourth BRSDEO* (OKC: SBE, 1952), 8-9. Article XIII, § 4 of the 1907 Constitution (never amended) requires students to attend school between ages eight and sixteen for at least three months of the year. The Legislature could extend these limits when offering a free public education.
21. *AROSDE 1981-82*, 89-90; *Thirty-Second BRSDEO* (OKC: SBE, 1968), 71-78. Staff numbers were gleaned from the *OED 1962-63*, 4-7 and *OED 1967-68*, 4-8.
22. "Hodge to Seek Former Power Held by Crable;" "Board Rejects One Selection Made by Hodge," *TO*, January 9, 1947, 16.
23. LeRoy H. Fisher, ed., *Oklahoma's Governors 1929-1955: Depression to Prosperity* (OKC: OHSRC, 1983), 133; "Hodge to Seek Former Power by Crable.;" "Hodge Denies Per Capita Plan," *TO*, July 19, 1946, 6.
24. "Turner Names Trio to State School Board," *TO*, May 29, 1947.
25. "Board of Education Calls Meeting After New Law is Upheld," *TO*, July 9, 1947, 38; *Twenty-Second BRSDEO* (Guthrie: Co-Operative, 1948), 98; "Shortage of 500 State Teachers Seen This Year," *TO*, August 26, 1947, 1.
26. "County District School System Urged for State," *TO*, September 17, 1948, 1. *OED* for the school years 1936-37 to 1946-47. While Hodge was Tulsa County superintendent, no consolidation occurred. There were ten independent districts and eight or nine dependent districts (with four or more teachers) in the county with the latter districts enrolling a range from 2,011 to 2,589 students during his tenure.
27. "County District School System Urged for State."
28. *Twenty-Third BRSDEO* (OKC: SBE, 1950), 248; "Debate on Aid to Education Brings Charges," *TO*, July 26, 1956, 10; Guy Lambert and Guy Lankin, "Oklahoma," in Jim B. Pearson and Edgar Fuller, eds., *Education in the States: Historical Development and Outlook* (Washington, DC: National Education Association, 1969), 983.
29. James Scales and Danney Goble, *Oklahoma Politics: A History* (Norman: OU Press, 1982), 9-10; *Twenty-Second BRSDEO*, 154-55; *Twenty-Third BRSDEO*, 245-47. George Lynn Cross, *The University of Oklahoma and World War II: A Personal Account, 1941-1946* (Norman: OU Press, 1980), 148-57. Governor Kerr asked George Cross, president of OU, to chair the State Textbook Committee in 1945 to clean up the corruption in the textbook selections. Reluctantly, Cross agreed to. In 1948 Governor Turner asked him to chair the reconstituted Textbook Committee, and he consented.
30. *Twenty-Second BRSDEO*, 159-60.
31. Ibid., 161-66.
32. Ibid., 19-22; 70 O.S. 1941 § 1063. Beginning in 1941 the Board of Education became also the Board of Vocational Education and both were chaired *ex officio* by the Superintendent. The vocational division for the most part was located in Stillwater and led by the director. Simultaneous to the creation of the State Board of Vocational Education was the voter-approved amendment creating The Oklahoma State System of Higher Education and its governing board (State Question 300, adopted March 11, 1941).
33. "County District School System Urged for State," *TO*, September 17, 1948, 1; "Modern School Code is Sought," *TO*, September 23, 1948, 2; "Study of School Code is Started by Legislature," *TO*, September 28, 1948, 6; "School Code Hits a Bump," *TO*, February 19, 1949, 1-2; "Who Has the Answer?" *TO*, May 3,

1949, 16; "School Reform Whacked Anew in Senate Test," *TO*, May 5, 1949, 1; "School Code Fight Breaks Out Again, May Stall Windup," *TO*, May 25, 1949, 1; "Legislators OK School Bill, Vote to Quit Friday," *TO*, May 26, 1949, 1-2; "Turner Blasts Schools Chief in Aid Bill Row," *TO*, May 4, 1949, 5; www.osrhe.edu. Former state representative and president of SEOSU E. T. Dunlap became the chancellor of higher education July 1, 1961.

34. *Twenty-Third BRSDEO*, 13-14.
35. Ibid., 15-16.
36. Ibid., 287-88, 291-94; *Twenty-Fourth BRSDEO*, 344-45.
37. "Driving Count Names State School Chief," *TO*, May 14, 1950, 1.
38. "Senators Block Probe of Hodge," *TO*, March 30, 1951, 24.
39. "Friend of Nance Fired, 2.
40. "School Official Defends Action," *TO*, February 9, 1955, 4. The annual *OED* from 1949-50 to 1964-65 lists Bugg's employment positions.
41. "School Official Plugs for Firm," *TO*, March 23, 1955, 3. The annual *OED* from 1937-38 to 1962-63 lists Emans's employment positions.
42. "Of General Application," *TO*, April 16, 1955, 6.
43. "Figures that Wobble," *TO*, October 29, 1955, 6; "Skirting the Problem," *TO*, October 30, 1955, A22; "School Chief Given Report by OU Dean," *TO*, November 15, 1955, 18; T. B. Ferguson to D. T. Flynn, 24 January 1903, Ferguson Collection, Western History Collections, OU Library. Partial content of the letter as summarized: Jerry Gill, "Thompson Benton Ferguson, Governor of Oklahoma Territory, 1901-1906," *Chronicles of Oklahoma* (Spring, 1975): 118.
44. "Were We Mistaken?" *TO*, October 31, 1955, 16.
45. "End of Teacher Pensions Seen," *TO*, June 8, 1955, 1; *Twenty-Sixth BRSDEO*, 11.
46. *Twenty-Sixth BRSDEO* (OKC: SBE, 1956), 10; *Twenty-Eighth BRSDEO* (OKC: SDE, 1960), 46, 18. Hodge's biennial reports of 1958, 1960, and 1962 included recommendations for the Legislature to enact the OEA's "program."
47. *Thirty-Second BRSDEO*, 20-24. In four consecutive biennial reports (1960-1968), Hodge recommended to the Legislature that it not siphon off money belonging to education. As the federal government increased financial support, the Legislature acted to shortchange the schools.
48. *Twenty-Seventh BRSDEO* (OKC: SBE, 1958), 9-10; *Twenty-Eighth BRSDEO*, 10; *Twenty-Ninth BRSDE* (OKC: SBE, 1962), 12; *Thirtieth BRSDEO* (OKC: SBE, 1964), 16; *Thirty-First BRSDEO* (OKC: SBE, 1966), 18. These reports also have recommendations regarding adequate funding, per pupil expenditure, and teacher salaries.
49. "Major Milestones of Career & Technology Education in Oklahoma," (Stillwater, OK: Oklahoma Department of Career and Technology Education, 2006), 6, 8-10, www.okcareertech.org/educators/cimc/resources/downloads-1/learning-to-earn/history_of_careertech_lo_res.pdf/view; *Oklahoma Elections: Statehood to Present*, vol.1 (OKC: SEB, 1988), D-474.
50. "Athletic Group to Act on Plan," *TO*, September 30, 1962, 131.
51. Henry Bellmon, *The Life and Times of Henry Bellmon* (Tulsa: Council Oak, 1992), 199-201.
52. 70 O.S. 1971 § 1-105 (West 1971).
53. The lone dissenting associate justice in *Plessy v Ferguson* in 1896 was John Marshall Harlan. In the 1955 follow up decision of the Supreme Court in *Brown v Board of Education of Topeka*, associate justice John Marshall Harlan II, grandson of the former Harlan and recently appointed to the court, concurred with the other eight justices in mandating schools to integrate "with all deliberate speed."
54. O.S. 1921 §§ 10567-10578 (Bunn 1922).
55. Outside resources for example were Jeanes teachers and General Education Board funds.
56. "The Law is the Law," *TO*, May 19, 1954, 18.
57. Hodge to County and District Superintendents, 27 May 1954, Box 1, FF 1-8, RG 18-3-3, Superintendent's Correspondence Collection, OSA, ODL, OKC. In this folder also is a copy of the proposal from the Oklahoma Cooperative Program in Educational Administration to help school districts to transition to a desegregated plan. "Schools to Stand Pat for Present on Segregation," *TO*, May 28, 1954, 1.
58. "Gary Plans to Handle School Segregation Problem as Financial Issue," *TO*, December 26, 1954, 1; Scales and Goble, *Oklahoma Politics: A History*, 298; James C. Milligan and L. David Norris, *The Man On The Second Floor, Raymond D. Gary* (Muskogee, OK: Western Heritage Books, 1988), 86-89; *Oklahoma Elections*, C-397. Amendments in 1966 (SQ 428) and 1978 (SQ 526) removed separate school provisions.
59. "There's Malingering Already," *TO*, April 15, 1955, 12.
60. *Twenty-Second BRSDEO*, 67.
61. "School Chief Favors Leaving Integration up to Local Districts," *TO*, June 8, 1955, 1-2.

62. "Policy Drafted on Integration For Next Year," *TO*, June 18, 1955, 1.
63. "Integration Not Necessary For State Aid," *TO*, July 7, 1955, 19.
64. "Schools Rolling on Integration," *TO*, August 23, 1955, 4; Hodge to Superintendents, 6 September 1955, Box 1, FF 1-11, RG 18-3-3, SSC, OSA, ODL, OKC; *SBEMM*, June 17, 1955, RG 18-1, DE, OSA, ODL, OKC.
65. *SBEMM*, January 13, 1956.
66. "State Draws up Policy on Color Ban in School," *TO*, January 13, 1956, 1; Monroe Billington, "Public School Integration in Oklahoma, 1954-1963," *The Historian*, 26 (1964): 530.
67. See Hodge to Superintendents of Districts operating a Negro high school, 22 March 1956 and the Integration Report of April 4, 1956, Box 1, FF 1-11, RG 18-3-3, SCC, OSA, ODL, OKC.
68. Hodge to Superintendents, 18 September 1956, Box 1, FF 1-13, RG 18-3-3, SCC; Hodge to Superintendents, 6 September 1957, Box 2, F 2-2, SCC; Hodge to Superintendents, 23 September 1959, Box 2, F 2-51, SCC; Hodge to Superintendents, 27 September 1959, Box 3, F 3-15, RG 18-3-3, SSC.
69. Hodge to John Rogers, 12 December 1958, Box 2, F 2-2, RG 18-3-3, SCC.
70. Ibid.
71. See Paul H. Douglas to Hodge, 5 May 1959 and Hodge to Douglas, 12 May 1959, Box 2, F 2-31, RG 18-3-3, SCC; Hodge to Robert S. Kerr, 1 April 1960, Box 2, FF 2-51, RG 18-3-3, SCC.
72. Scales and Goble, *Oklahoma Politics: A History*, 299.
73. *Twenty-Sixth BRSDEO*, 10-11.
74. *Twenty-Seventh BRSDEO* (OKC: SBE, 1958), 8-10.
75. *Twenty-Eighth BRSDEO* (OKC: SBE, 1960), 8-10.
76. Hodge to Wm. Ingram, 26 January 1961, Box 3, F 3-14, RG 18-3-3, SCC.
77. "School Records By Race Debated," *TO*, February 14, 1962, 8.
78. "State Integration Near 100 Percent," *TO*, April 20, 1965, 13.
79. Oklahoma Human Rights Commission, "Problems in Oklahoma Education," www.digitalprairie.ok.gov/cdm/compoundobject/collection/okresources/id/30650/rec/11.
80. "New Education Building Formally Dedicated," *TO*, December 3, 1974, 53; "Oliver Hodge Memorial Scholarship Fund is Established by Wife of Late State Educator," *Oklahoma Signpost*, February, 1968, 1.
81. "1000 Turn Out to Honor Hodge."
82. *SBEMM*, December 18, 1957, RG 18-1, DE.
83. Frosty Troy, "The Crisis in Public Education." Address of the annual meeting of Americans United for Separation of Church and State, Washington, DC, November 12, 1994, http://lighthousecommunities.org/publiceducation.htm.
84. "Oklahoma Loses One of its Brightest Stars," *Oklahoma Teacher*, March 1968, 18-20.

Chapter 13

1. "Dr. Hodge, Head of Schools, Dies," *TT*, January 15, 1968, 4, 17; "Bartlett Leans to Republican," *TO*, January 20, 1968, 3; "Hodge Death Gives School Post to GOP," *TT*, January 15, 1968, 4, 17; "Bartlett Given Boost in Filling School Post," *TO*, March 14, 1968, 10; "School Chief Pay Hike Bill Vote Delayed," *TO*, January 31, 1968, 3. Governor Bellmon replaced four Board members during his term and Bartlett replaced one in his first year. Charles Mason, appointed by Governor Howard Edmondson, served on the Board from 1962 to 1973. From 1967 to 1971 only one position changed: Lester Reed replaced Don Garrison who died in December 1969.
2. Oliver Hodge, "Education Department," *Oklahoma Teacher*, September 1947, 32; Kathryn McDonald, phone discussion with the author, May 27, 1985; Work experience documents, Box 14, F 14-3, RG 18-3-3, SCC, OSA, ODL, OKC; "Funeral Set for Veteran Educator," *TO*, August 24, 1984, 21.
3. "No Candidate Leads Pack for State School Chief Job," *TO*, January 18, 1968, 13; "School Chief Pay Increase Gets Go Ahead," *TO*, February 6, 1968, 6; "School Chief's Pay is Factor," *TO*, January 28, 1968, 21; "Creech Seeks College Post?" *TO*, October 29, 1969, 54.
4. D. D. Creech, interview by the author, April 7, 1998; "New School Chief Highly Qualified," *TT*, March 29, 1968, 37; Danten Creech, "The Development and Application of an Evaluative Check-list [*sic*] for Professional Associations of School Administrators," (EdD diss., OU, 1965), 1; "Bartlett Given Boost in Filling School Post;" Governor Bartlett's Order of Appointment, Box 14, F 1, RG 18-3-3, SCC, OSA, ODL, OKC.
5. "New School Chief Highly Qualified," 37, 43.
6. *SBEMM*, January 19, 1968; February 6, 1968; March 8, 1968; March 25, 1968, RG 18-1, DE, OSA, ODL, OKC.

7. "School Plans Get Go Ahead by State Board," *TO*, July 26, 1969, 32; "Board Backs Creech Plan to Overhaul Department," *TO*, July 26, 1969, 35.
8. See the *OED* for these years: 1968-69, 1969-70, and 1970-71.
9. "Teachers Hear Early Childhood Plan by Creech," *TO*, August 18, 1968, 26; Rosemary Hardy, "Oklahoma's State Superintendent of Public Instruction," *Oklahoma Teacher*, May 1968, 16; "Due Clearing Up," *TO*, March 21, 1969, 4; "State Board of Education Backs Creech," *TO*, March 22, 1969, 19; "Compromise in Mill to Save State's Small Schools," *TO*, February 7, 1969, 67.
10. "Small Schools' Graduates Stumble in College Tests," *TO*, September 21, 1968, 37; "Plan to Scrap 226 Districts Gets Backing," *TO*, January 3, 1970, 46.
11. "School Integration Case Testimony Ends," *TO*, July 26, 1969, 33; Oklahoma Human Rights Commission, "Problems in Oklahoma Education," 1-2, www.digitalprairie.ok.gov/cdm/compoundobject/collection/okresources/id/30650/rec/11.
12. "OEA, Creech Rap Bartlett," *TO*, November 12, 1969, 25; "Creech Urges Hugh Increase in School Cash," *TO*, December 20, 1969, 1.
13. Carl Tyson, *The History of Vocational and Technical Education in Oklahoma* (Stillwater, OK: Department of Vocational and Technical Education, n.d.), 7, 53-54.
14. "Creech Seeks College Post?" *TO*, October 28, 1969, 1; "Creech Stays Home, Regents Puzzled," *TO*, November 8, 1969, 2; "Bartlett Lauds School Chief," *TO*, December 5, 1969, 12; Creech, interview.
15. Creech, interview; Hardy, "Oklahoma's State Superintendent,"16; www.findagrave.com.
16. Scott Tuxhorn, interview by the author, December 18, 1998; Personal Data Sheet of Dr. Scott Tuxhorn (n.d.), Box 14, F 2, RG 18-3-3, SCC, OSA, ODL, OKC.
17. "Governor Picks School Job Man," *TO*, December 4, 1969, 1; "Tuxhorn Gets School Post," *TO*, December 18, 1969, 1-2; "School Board to Ask Delay," *TO*, December 19, 1969, 2.
18. Personal Data Sheet of Dr. Scott Tuxhorn; "Helena School Paddling Quiz is Completed," *TO*, January 23, 1958, 35; "Helena School Paddling Held Legal by State," *TO*, February 25, 1958, 7.
19. "Incumbents for State House Posts Trail in 5 Counties," *TO*, May 2, 1962, 45; "Oklahoma Voters Decide 48 Races in Legislature," *TO*, November 7, 1962, 7; *OA 2015-2016* (OKC: ODL, 2015), 799, 801; "Ruling Sought on Teachers," *TO*, July 16, 1963, 33; "Teacher-Legislators to Fight Nesbitt Opinion, Hamilton Says," *TO*, October 25, 1963, 3.
20. "Legislators Hit School Rules on Activities," *TO*, March 29, 1963, 40.
21. "Personal Data Sheet of Dr. Scott Tuxhorn;" Scott Tuxhorn, "The Educational Unit for Administration, Organization, and Supervision of Area Vocational-Technical Schools in Oklahoma," (EdD diss., OSU, 1967), 136-38; Tuxhorn, interview.
22. "Tuxhorn Named to Affairs Board," *TO*, May 30, 1969, 19; Tuxhorn, interview; *Oklahoma Teacher*, February 1970, 19-22; *SBEMM*, January 2, 1970, RG 18-1, DE; "Plan to Scrap 226 Districts Gets Backing," 46.
23. *SBEMM*, January 23, 1970, RG 18-1, DE; "Sex Education Policy Decided," *TO*, January 26, 1970, 11.
24. "Schools Chief Offers Plan for Retirement," *TO*, March 19, 1970, 22.
25. *SBEMM*, September 25, 1970, RG 18-1, DE.
26. Harriett Tuxhorn Collection, Campaign Materials, Box 1, FF 21, OHSRC; "1500 Teachers Hear Fisher, Tuxhorn," *TO*, October 22, 1970, 25.
27. *Oklahoma Elections: Statehood to Present*, vol. 1 (OKC: SEB, 1994), C-507.
28. Tuxhorn, interview; "Many May Feel Ruling's Impact," *TO*, January 16, 1972, 22; Scott Tuxhorn Obituary, http://legacy.newsok.com/obituaries/oklahoman/obituary.aspx?pid=…; "Educator's Wife Dies," *TO*, January 19, 1976, 7.

Chapter 14

1. Public school employment record, Box 14, F 5, RG 18-3-3, SCC, OSA, ODL, OKC; "State Association Picks Moore Man," *TO*, July 6, 1965, 33. Brief biography of Leslie R. Fisher, SDE, circa 1981. *OED* (OKC: SDE, annual editions for the years 1961-62 to 1970-71); Leslie Fisher, "An Analysis of Patterns of Liability Decisions in the Public Schools of Selected States of the United States," (EdD diss., OU, 1963).
2. "State Association Picks Moore Man;" *OEA Board of Directors Meeting Minutes*, March 27, 1964; *OEA Executive Committee Meeting Minutes*, April 17, 1964. Minutes are located at the OEA headquarters in OKC. *Oklahoma Elections: Statehood to Present*, vol. 1 (OKC: SEB, 1994), C-459, C-460. Until the voters approved State Question 495, August 27, 1974, passage of constitutional amendments required the support of not just a simple majority on the question, but a majority of the votes cast in that election. "Key Opponents Heal Perilous Breach in OEA," *TO*, August 13, 1968, 6.
3. "Bacone College President Named," *TO*, March 31, 1974, 5A; "State Association Picks Moore Man;" *OED*

(OKC: SDE, annual editions for the years 1958-59 to 1970-71); "Hat Thrown by Holleyman," *TO*, June 12, 1970, 10.
4. *Oklahoma Elections*, C-501, C-507; Primary and General Elections 1970, Box 54, RG 24-4-1, *EBCFCE*, OSA, ODL, OKC.
5. *OED* (OKC: SDE, annual editions for the years 1971-72 to 1991-1992); www.legacy.newsok.com /obituaries/Oklahoman/obituary.aspx?n=charles-douglas-holleyman&pid=3477235.
6. *SBEMM*, July 11, 1974, RG 18-1, DE, OSA, ODL, OKC.
7. *SBEMM*, March 25, 1982.
8. "State Superintendent Seeking Re-Election," *TO*, January 22, 1978, 11; Charles Sandmann, interview by the author, November 27, 2001; Charles Sandmann, *"CCER C-1,"* December 3, 1982 (final report for the 1982 election campaign), SEB, OKC.
9. Charles Sandmann, "An Evaluation of the General Aptitude Test Battery in Predicting Success in Area Vocational-Technical Centers," (EdD diss., OU, 1969), 1; *OED* (OKC: SDE, annual editions for the years 1966-67 to 1981-82); Lealon Taylor, interview by the author, January 26, 2020.
10. "State School Superintendent Resigns," *TO*, December 9, 1983, 1; *Oklahoma Elections,* C-603.
11. "Changes Proposed in Merit System," *TO*, May 18, 1971, 12; "Merit System Change Wins OK in House," *TO*, June 3, 1971, 32.
12. *SBEMM*, September 16, 1971, RG 18-1, DE.
13. *SBEMM*, November 19, 1971, RG 18-1, DE; "Education Building Dedication Set," *TO*, December 3, 1974, 39.
14. Clarence G. Oliver Jr., interview by the author, January 30, 2018.
15. Elementary and Secondary Education Act of 1965, Pub. L. No. 89-10, 79 Stat. 27 (1965).
16. 70 O.S.1971 §§ 509.1-509.8 (West 1971).
17. *AROSDE 1969-70* (OKC: SDE, 1970), 200; 70 O.S. Supp. 1974 §§ 1210.271-1210-281 (West 1974); Education for All Handicapped Children Act of 1975, Pub. L. No. 94-142, 89 Stat. 773 (1975).
18. *Third Annual Report of the Oklahoma Commission on Education* (for the Year Ended December 1971), (State Capitol, Oklahoma City, 1971), 11.
19. Ibid., 12-19.
20. "'Accountability' Roots Planted," *TO*, September 9, 1973, A23.
21. *OED 1974-75*, 41-43. During the 1974-75 school year, twenty-four Catholic, five Protestant, and one private elementary schools operated in the state. Four Catholic, eight Protestant, and one private secondary school enrolled students.
22. "Attitudes of Oklahoma Teachers Toward House Bill 1706," *Journal of Teacher Education*, March 1, 1983, http://journals.sagepub.com/doi/pdf/10.1177/002248718303400206. O.S.L. 1980, chapt, 318, § 1 (West 1980); A. G. Op. 80-173 (1981), www.oklegal.onenet.net/oklegal-cgi/isearch.
23. *SBEMM*, March 24, 1977, 29-30, RG 18-1, DE.
24. *SBEMM*, October 27, 1983, 93, RG 18-1, DE.
25. *SBEMM*, December 14, 1983, RG 18-1, DE.
26. *SBEMM*, November 2, 1983, RG 18-1, DE.
27. *SBEMM*, June 28, 1984, RG 18-1, DE.
28. "State School Superintendent Seeking Re-Election."
29. "Audit Allegations Denied," *TO*, February 13, 1976, 27.
30. "Changes Proposed in Merit System," *TO*, May 18, 1971, 12.
31. *SBEMM,* February 26, 1971, RG 18-1, DE.
32. *SBEMM*, July 11, 1974; *SBEMM*, May 24, 1984, 29.
33. Oliver, interview; "Best School Year in History, State Superintendent Predicts," *TO*, August 26, 1973, 4.
34. "School Land Commission Parley Asked," *TO*, November 24, 1971, 1-2; "New Secretary Named," *TO*, June 28, 1972, 62; "School Land Secretary Defends Contract," *TO*, July 28, 1972, 12; "Land Commission has Long Stormy History," *TO*, November 30, 1972, 41; "School Land Commission Schedules Meeting Today," *TO*, December 15, 1972, 4; "School Land Commission Position Filled," *TO*, December 19, 1972, 1.
35. "School Land Commission Gets Secretary," *TO*, June 5, 1972, 23; "Land is Forever," *TO*, May 7, 2002, 6-A.
36. Carl Tyson, *The History of Vocational and Technical Education in Oklahoma* (Stillwater, OK: State Department of Vocational and Technical Education, n.d.), 54.
37. "Former Superintendent to Run for Governor," *TW*, June 25, 1986; "Candidate Fisher Seeks Return to Leadership Days of Old," *TW*, August 20, 1986, 8; *Oklahoma Elections*, C-603; "Fisher Would Eliminate Jobs at Top as Governor," *TO*, June 30, 1984, 4.
38. "Former State School Chief Dead at 65," *TO*, January 3, 1988, 1-2.

Chapter 15

1. John Folks, interview by the author, February 15, 2018.
2. Ibid.; John Folks, Resumé, April 16, 1998.
3. *OED* (OKC: SDE) for the years 1965-66 to 1974-75; Folks, interview.
4. Clarence G. Oliver Jr., interview by the author, January 30, 2018; Folks, Resumé.
5. Folks, Resumé; Folks, interview.
6. Folks, interview; 70 O.S. 1981 §§ 6-150-165 (West 1981).
7. John Folks, "An Analysis of Opinions of H.B. 1706 as Perceived by Certain Selected School-Related Groups," (EdD diss., OU, 1982), ProQuest (8224195).
8. Folks, interview.
9. "State School Superintendent Resigns," *TO*, December 9, 1983, 1; *SBEMM*, December 14, 1983, RG 18-1, DE, OSA, ODL, OKC.
10. Folks, interview.
11. Ibid.
12. "Agency Budget Soared in '70s," *TO*, January 14, 1984, 57; Folks, interview; "New School Head Plans to Propose Reform Package," *TO*, July 3, 1984, 35.
13. "State Educators Eye Mandatory Kindergarten," *TO*, November 16, 1984, 119; "Class Absence Limits Draw Heavy Objection," *TO*, September 28, 1984, 103.
14. "Educators Propose Statewide Testing Program," *TO*, December 14, 1984, 130.
15. "School Superintendent Unflinching Over Past Year," *TO*, July 15, 1985, 3.
16. "Folks Calls Funding the Key," *TW*, June 21, 1988, B1.
17. "Education Official Plans to Coordinate System," *TO*, December 28, 1986, 15.
18. "School Official Urges Tougher Middle Grades," *TO*, May 29, 1987, 6.
19. "Teacher Exams Still Backed by State," *TO*, August 30, 1987, 7; Folks, interview.
20. "Education Reforms Outlined," *TO*, December 18, 1987, 97; Folks, interview.
21. "Folks Lobbies for Plan To Extend School Year," *TO*, January 20, 1988, 3; John Folks to Henry Bellmon, 15 June 1988, Box 14, F 7, RG 18-3-3, SCC, OSA, ODL, OKC.
22. Editorial, "Room at the Top," *TT*, June 14, 1988.
23. "Folks Says Better Funding is Key to Better Schools," *TT*, June 21, 1988.
24. Folks, interview.
25. Ibid.
26. Ibid.
27. Ibid.; *Major Milestones of Career Technology Education in Oklahoma, A Discussion Guide* (Stillwater: Oklahoma Department of Career and Technology Education, 2006), 17; *OED* (OKC: SDE, 1985-86), 21,
28. "672 Hopefuls File for State Offices; 13 Pursue Top Job," *TO*, July 10, 1986, 1-2; Files, SEB. Evans was number 667 of the 673 who filed.
29. David Evans, conversation with the author, July 14, 1986; Charles Sandmann, interview by the author, November 27, 2001. Political shenanigans after his filing threatened Evans's professional future. For example, over the weekend following the filing period, Evans twice received phone calls at 3 a.m. where the caller, a superintendent of one of Oklahoma's largest school districts, warned that if he, Evans, actively campaigned for the office, he would be blackballed from any other school administrator position in Oklahoma. Evans, shakened, phoned the Republican candidate in 1982, Charles Sandmann, to report the incidents and to seek his advice. Sandmann then called that superintendent to inform him that any further threats on his part would result in him, Sandmann, reporting his actions to the federal authorities for his tampering with election laws, a federal crime.
30. John Folks, internet correspondence exchange with the author, November 17, 2020. Multiple requests to the SEC from 2017-2020 to obtain the donations and expenditures reports of the 1986 Superintendent election were unsuccessful. Folks provided an estimate according to his recollection.
31. Statewide Registration by Party 1960-1995, SEB, https://www.ok.gov/elections/Voter_Info/Voter_Registration_Statistics/index.html; *Oklahoma Elections: Statehood to Present*, vol.1 (OKC: SEB, 1994), C-445, C-495, C-537.
32. "Opponent Gives Superintendent 'F' as Leader," *TO*, October 29, 1986, 100.
33. *Oklahoma Elections*, C-610; "Folk Deserves Retention," *TO*, October 19, 1986, 20. Also, see note 29 above.
34. Folks, interview.
35. "Education Reformer Quits to Head Mid-Del Schools," *TO*, June 14, 1988, 1.
36. Folks, interview.

Chapter 16

1. "2 Named to Education Posts," *TO*, July 20, 1988, 1; "Holt to Return as OSU Dean of Arts and Science," *TO*, January 15, 1988, 11.
2. "State School Superintendent Candidate List Packed," *TO*, June 18, 1988, 16; "Front-Runner for State Education Post Withdraws," *TO*, June 24, 1988, 9; Clarence G. Oliver Jr., summary to the author, September 29, 2020.
3. [3] Oliver, summary.
4. [4] Ibid.
5. Gerald Hoeltzel, interview by the author, March 1, 2018.
6. Ibid.; Clarence G. Oliver Jr., interview by the author, January 30, 2018; "2 Named to Education Posts."
7. "Phillips Topples Central, 72-65," *TO*, February 26, 1956, 71; Gerald Hoeltzel, Resumé, April 23, 1998; *OED* for the years from 1985-86 to 1990-91 (OKC: SDE).
8. "State School Superintendent Candidate List Packed."
9. Organizational Charts of the SDE, December 1988 and 1989; Jerry Bass, "The Oklahoma State Department of Education: Mission, Organizational Structure, Administration, and Staffing," A Report Submitted to Gerald Hoeltzel, State Superintendent of Public Instruction, and to the SBE, July 26, 1990; "Education Office Under Fire," *TO*, August 22, 1990, 1.
10. Hoeltzel, interview.
11. *Oklahoma Educator*, September 1988, 1; "Education Secretary Outlines School Plans," *TO*, December 8, 1988, 12.
12. Hoeltzel, interview.
13. *Oklahoma Educator*, November-December 1988, 2; January 1989, 2-3.
14. *Oklahoma Educator*, January 1990, 2-3; "Sandy Garrett: School Districts Ought to Be Graded," *TO*, May 15, 1989, 9.
15. "Test Results to Play Role in State School Policies," *TO*, June 11, 1989, 1.
16. "Legislators Rip School Chief's Proposal," *TO*, May 4, 1990, 84.
17. Hoeltzel, interview.
18. Ibid.
19. "2 Named to Education Posts," 2; "Hoeltzel Says He Won't Seek State School Superintendent Post," *TO*, November 29, 1989, 8.
20. "Superintendent Changes Mind, Seeks Re-election," *TO*, July 12, 1990, 10.
21. Hoeltzel, interview.
22. Ibid.; "Learning the Hard Way," *TO*, February 13, 1990, 8.
23. "Education Secretary Won't Run," *TO*, May 16, 1990, 10; "Ex-candidate Rethinking Plans," *TO*, May 22, 1990, 5.
24. Hoeltzel, interview.
25. *OED* (OKC: State Board of Affairs, 1986), 9-10; *Oklahoma Elections: Statehood to Present*, vol. 1 (OKC: SEB, 1994), C-631, C-639; "State Superintendent Race Grew Heated Early On," *TO*, August 26, 1990, 20.
26. Hoeltzel, interview; "Profiles in Cowardice," *TO*, July 13, 1990, 8; *Oklahoma Elections*, C-639; "Memo to: David Walters," *TO*, December 29, 1990, 12.
27. "City Schools Trying to Hire Hoeltzel," *TO*, January 3, 1991, 1; Hoeltzel, Resumé; Hoeltzel, interview.

Chapter 17

1. Rachel Whitaker, "Adair County," *EOHC*, vol. 1 (OKC: OHSEC, 2009), 5; http://www.census.gov/prod/www/decennial.html; "The Poorest Town in Each State," https://247wallst.com/special-report/2015/06/05/the-poorest-town-in-each-state/; Bureau of the Census, "American FactFinder Results," https://factfinder.census.gov/faces/tableservices/jsf/pages/productview.xhtml?src=bkmk.
2. *US Census 1940*; www.findagrave.com; *OA 2015-2016* (OKC: ODL, 2016), 792-98; W. H. Langley, Jr., interview by the author, January 9, 2020; W. H. Langley, Jr., email correspondence with the author, January 29, 2020. W. H.'s grandfather gained notoriety as a gunslinger. Four times he found himself in Hanging Judge Parker's court in Ft. Smith for killing a man in a gunfight and four times he was exonerated. In the 1942 re-election attempt W. H. Langley Sr. agreed with his Republican opponent C. W. Waters to "allow" him to win with the understanding that he would serve in only one legislative session and never run again. Waters said he wanted to be able to say that he was once a state representative.
3. Langley, Jr., interview.
4. Ibid.; "Sandy Garrett: Bellmon's Pupil," *TO*, October 17, 1999, 10; "Graduation Coaches Wise Investment," *TO*, November 23, 2007, 15A; Charles Garrett, interview by the author, November 22, 2019; Sandy Langley

Garrett Resumé, SDE, November 5, 1998; "Garrett, Teaching and Learning," *TO*, October 20, 1999, 8.

5. www.okhistory.org/research/dawesresults (William F. Langley's roll number was 22529 and blood quantum 1/16 and William H. Langley Sr.'s numbers were 27079 and 1/32.); Langley, Jr., interview; Langley, Jr., email correspondence.
6. Adair High School Yearbook, *The Warrior 1961*, 12; Langley, Jr., interview; Garrett, Resumé; "'Educator First,' Garrett Downplays Political Ambitions," *TW*, September 9, 1991, A1; Garrett, interview.
7. Garrett, Resumé; "'Educator First;'" Lealon Taylor, interview by the author, January 26, 2020; *AROSDE 1983-84* (OKC: SDE, 1984), 22; *SBEMM*, July 29, 1982, RG 18-1, DE, OSA, ODL, OKC.
8. *SBEMM*, January 24, 1985, RG 18-1, DE; *AROSDE 1985-86* (OKC: SDE, 1984), 11.
9. Garrett, Resumé; "2 Named to Education Posts," *TO*, July 20, 1988, 1; "Educator First."
10. "Educator First."
11. Taylor, interview.
12. "2 Named to Education Posts," 14; "Education Cabinet Formed by Bellmon," *Journal Record*, August 10, 1988; "Democrats, Women May Get Chance at Job," *TO*, June 15, 1988, 6.
13. "Education Secretary Outlines School Plans," *TO*, December 8, 1988, 12; "Sandy Garrett: School Districts Ought to Be Graded," *TO*, May 15, 1989, 9.
14. "Attitude Key to Better Schools," *TO*, December 12, 1988, 7.
15. "Sandy Garrett: School Districts;" "Education Secretary Pushes 'Report Cards' for Schools in State," *TW*, March 30, 1989, 1A.
16. "Sandy Garrett: School Districts." The Legislature created a professorship endowment scheme matching state funds with private donations but then failed to match the success of the universities to generate private funds.
17. "State to Require High-School Competency Tests by 1992," *TW*, June 3, 1989, 8A.
18. "Education Secretary Won't Run, *TO*, May 16, 1990, 10; "Ex-candidate Rethinking Plans," *TO*, May 22, 1990, 5.
19. "…And There's More Good News," *TO*, January 6, 1991, 77.
20. "Coppedge—Consolation Choice," *TO*, June 1995, 8: Taylor, interview.
21. Governors were limited to one term until State Question 436 passed in May 1966 allowing two terms. Bellmon's first term was 1963-1967 and his second term 1987-1991. Taylor, interview.
22. *SBEMM*, July 25, 1985. See the *OED* for the years 1985-86 to 1990-91.
23. "Garrett Back in Superintendent Race," *TW*, May 27, 1990, A2; Taylor, interview.
24. "Education Office Under Fire," *TO*, August 22, 1990, 1-2.
25. "Ex-teacher Begins Campaign for State's Education Office," *TO*, January 25, 1990, 44; "Fired Official Still Campaigning," *TO*, February 12, 1990, 18; "Learning the Hard Way," *TO*, February 13, 1990, 8.
26. www.ok.gov/elections. On October 15, 1991 State Question No. 639 (initiative petition No. 347) asked voters to replace HB 1017 with the laws existing before the bill was enacted. The repeal measure was rejected by a 360,318 to 428,680 vote. David Fisher, *CCER C-1*, December 6, 1990 (final report for the 1990 primary election), SEB, OKC; *Oklahoma Elections: Statehood to Present,* vol. 1 (OKC: SEB, 1994), C-631; "For Sandy Garrett," *TW*, August 8, 1990, 10A.
27. "Pair Urges Education Changes—Candidates Differ on State's Role," *TW*, October 22, 1990, 3A; *AROSDE 1990-91* (OKC: Office of Public Affairs, 1992), 5.
28. *Oklahoma Elections*, C-639; Gerald Hoeltzel, *CCER, C-1*, May 16, 1991 (final report for the 1990 election campaign), SEB, OKC; Langley, Jr., interview.
29. "Sandy Garrett Hits Linda Murphy's Credentials," *TO*, November 1, 1994, 8.
30. "Two Plan Bids for State Education Post—Fort Gibson Pair Will Challenge Garrett," *TW*, March 15, 1994, N9; Earl Garrison, *CCER C-1R*, December 9, 1994 (final report for the 1994 Democratic primary), SEC; Sandy Garrett, *CCER C-1R*, July 15, 1996 (final report for the 1994 election campaign), SEC; www.ok.gov/elections. Some years later Garrison served as superintendent of Indian Capital Technology Center and in 2004 he was elected state senator from Muskogee by capturing 65 percent of the vote, eventually serving for three terms until he was term limited.
31. "Keep Focus on Education, Murphy Says," *TO*, September 25, 1998, 4; "State Education Chief Draws 2 Challengers," *TO*, August 14, 1994, 116; "Two Plan Bids for State Education Post;" "For Scott, Garrett," *TW*, August 18, 1994, N16.
32. For an excellent description of OBE and an analysis of the reasons for opposition, see William G. Spady, *Outcome-Based Education: Critical Issues and Answers* (Washington, DC: American Association of School Administrators, 1994), files.eric.ed.gov/fulltext/ED380910.pdf. General Election Results for 1994, https://www.ok.gov/elections/Election_Info/Election_Results/1994-Election_Results.html; Garrett, *CCER C-1R*, July 15, 1996; Linda Murphy, *CCER C-1R*, January 15, 1998 (final report for the 1994 election campaign),

SEC; AROSDE 1990-91, 32; "Linda Murphy vs. Sandy Garrett," *TO*, October 30, 1994, 16; "Opponent Cites Negative Ads in Garrett's Victory," *TO*, November 4, 1998, 15; "Changing Course—Outcome-Based Education Declared Dead," *TW*, December 9, 1994, N1.
33. "About Linda Murphy," https://lindamurphyoklahomaeducator.wordpress.com/about/.
34. "Spin and Sandy (II)," *TO*, January 16, 1998, 6; Sharon Lease, interview by the author, December 3, 2019. Lease was a top-level administrator in the SDE during Garrett's tenure.
35. "Fewer Candidates File on Second Day," *TO*, July 8, 1998, 8; *1997 OED* (Stillwater: State Department of Vo-Tech, 1998), 5; *OA 2015-2016 (OKC: ODL, 2015)*, 595; "Defeated Republican Endorses Democratic Party Nominee," *TO*, August 26, 1998, 98.
36. "Murphy Ahead for Superintendent," *TO*, August 26, 1998, 106; "Candidates Support Phonics in Schools," *TO*, September 18, 1998, 6; "Murphy, Garrett Face Key Issue: School Standards," *TO*, October 29, 1998, 1,9; "Keep Focus on Education."
37. "Murphy, Garrett Face Key Issue;" Sandy Garrett, *CCER C-1R*, August 1, 2001 (final report of the 1998 election campaign), SEC; Linda Murphy, *CCER C-1R*, (final report of the 1998 election campaign), SEC.
38. "For Sandy Garrett," *TO*, October 31, 1998, 4; *OA*, 595.
39. "Superintendents Get Ethics Warning," *TO*, March 24, 2003, A1.
40. "Garrett Foe Charges Wrongdoing," *TO*, February 26, 2002, 5-A; "Education Claims Baseless," *TO*, June 16, 2002, 6-A; Press Release, "State Superintendent Sandy Garrett Announces Candidacy," July 5, 2002. The total expenditures for the Department for 1990-91 were $29,107,027 and increased every year except 1997-98 through 2001-02 when the amount was $54,262,000. If Garrett's reference were to reduction in staff and thus reduction in total staff compensation, those FTE numbers were 513 in 1990-91 and 476 in 2001-02.
41. "Teachers' Salaries a Top Concern for Superintendent Candidates," *TO*, August 18, 2002, 66-D; Lloyd Roettger, interview by the author, December 3, 2002; Roettger and his wife Caroline had five children. "Schools Chief Race Focuses on ACT Scores," *TO*, August 23, 2002, 8-A; "Candidate Vows to Eliminate Politics in State Education System," *TO,* September 4, 2002, 4-A.
42. Candidate Demands Retraction," *TO*, November 1, 2002, 3-A.
43. "Roettger, interview; "For Sandy Garrett, Voters Should Keep Her Superintendent," *TO*, October 31, 2002, 6-A.
44. *OA,* 600; Lloyd Roettger, *CCER C-1R*, January 31, 2003, (final report of the 2002 election campaign), SEC; Sandy Garrett, *CCER C-1R*, July 30, 2003, (final report of the 2002 election campaign), SEC.
45. "Our Choices, Five Incumbents Deserve New Terms," *TO*, October 22, 2006, 16A.
46. "Book Armor Idea Put to Target Test on Shooting Range," *TO*, November 1, 2006, 1East; "Superintendent of Public Instruction," *TO*, July 16, 2006, 10V; "Schools' Race Pits Challenger, 4-Term Incumbent," *TO*, October 21, 2006, 14A; *OA*, 603.
47. Sandy Garrett, *CCER C1-R*, April 10, 2007, (final report of the 2006 election campaign), SEC; Bill Crozier, *CCER C1-R*, January 29, 2007, (final report of the 2006 election campaign), SEC; Friends of Sandy Garrett, "Schedule G. Written Monetary Transfers," December 30, 2006, SEC.
48. Taylor, interview; "For Sandy Garrett," *TO*, October 31, 1998, 4; "For Sandy Garrett;" "Our Choices, Five Incumbents;" "For Sandy Garrett," *TW*, August 8, 1990, 10A; "For Scott, Garrett," *TW*, August 18, 1994, N16; "For Sandy Garrett," *TW*, October 6, 1994, N12; Taylor, interview; *OA*, 118-19.
49. Taylor, interview.
50. Ibid.; "Garrett, Teaching and Learning;" "Superintendent Candidates Find Agreement Only on Few Issues," *TO*, October 26, 2002, 8-A.
51. Clark Ogilvie, interview by the author, October 1, 2018.
52. "Garrett Foe Charges Wrongdoing," *TO*, February 26, 2002, 5-A.
53. John Bennett, interview by the author, June 10, 2019. Bennett was administrator in the Department in charge of criminal issues with teacher certificate applications. Taylor, interview.
54. "Official Hears Footsteps on Way to File for Re-Election," *TO*, June 6, 2006, 7A.
55. *Oklahoma Elections*, C-645.
56. "Task Force to Unveil Consolidation Scenarios," *TO*, January 24, 2003, 3-A.
57. "New Superintendent of Schools Says Voters Endorsed HB 1017," *TO*, November 8, 1990, 21; Langley, Jr., interview.
58. "Caution Urged on Cash Plan," *TO*, March 10, 1991, 1, 17A: "Schools Chief to Seek Bond Fund Opinion," *TO*, February 5, 1991, 1, 9: "Langley 'Sells' Plan to Save Bond Interest," *TT*, December 22, 1949, 8.
59. "A Good Start," *TO*, February 3, 1991, 12.
60. Ibid.; AROSDE 1990-91, 10; ARSROSSDE 1994-95 (OKC: SDE, 1996), 93; ARSROSSDE 2007-08 (OKC: SDE, 2009), 8. Garrett discontinued the practice of her predecessors of including Department expenditures and FTE in her ARs. Thus, the data for her tenure were taken from the Governor's Annual *Executive Budget*

Historical Data and from data provided by the Department through an Open Records Request, October 9, 2019. Neither FTE data nor expenditures match.
61. ARSROSSDE 2013-14 (OKC: SDE, 2015), 4-7, https://sde.ok.gov.
62. "Public education in Oklahoma," https://ballotpedia.org/Public_education_in_Oklahoma; Because Oklahoma laws do not allow for any data collection relating to home schools, only anecdotal information is available regarding such school participation.
63. "Calendar Outdated," *TO*, August 5, 2007, 21A; "A Matter of Time, Disruptions Hamper Student Learning," *TO*, July 13, 2008, 16A.
64. Pub. L. 89-10, 79 Stat. 27; Pub. L. 107-110, 115 Stat. 750.
65. "Certification to Pay Off for Teachers," *TO*, November 20, 1998, 57. This additional stipend was not included in the formula for determining retirement compensation.
66. "Digest of Education Statistics," National Center for Education Statistics, Table 211.60, Estimated average annual salary of teachers in public elementary and secondary schools, by state: Selected years, 1969-70 through 2015-16, https://nces.ed.gov/programs/digest/d16/tables/dt16_211.60 .asp; "Public education in Oklahoma." By the 2012-13 school year Oklahoma had the highest student to teacher ratio also.
67. 70 O.S. 2011 § 13-101.1-101.2 (2011 West) with recent amendment O.S.L. 2017, chapt. 249, § 1 (West 2017).
68. Lease, interview; Taylor, interview.
69. Taylor, interview.
70. Ibid.
71. "Supplemental Investigative Report, Oklahoma State Department of Education," Oklahoma State Auditor and Inspector, March 7, 2012, ii, iii.
72. "Special Investigative Report, Oklahoma State Department of Education, Innovation 2011 Conference," (January 10, 2011-June 30, 2012), Oklahoma State Auditor and Inspector, October 29, 2012, i-ii.
73. Ibid., iii.
74. "Keeping it Real," *Tulsa People*, www.tulsapeople.com/Tulsa-People/November2017/Keeping it Real; "Jerry Wayne Hefner," *TW*, September 29, 2017; Garrett Resumé; "Educator First."

Chapter 18

1. "Five Couples' Engagements Announced," *TO*, February 23, 1975, 66; "Janet Barresi," https://votesmart.org/candidate/biograph/biography/124960/janet-barresi#.WJ8jchA2jRO; "Retired Dentist to Seek Superintendent Job," *TO*, October 7, 2009, 20 West; "Candidates' Views Vary on Issues," *TO*, September 12, 2010, 8A.
2. "Middle Schools Due Study by City District," *TO*, June 7, 1996, 70.
3. "'Enterprise Schools' Proposed for City," *TO*, May 6, 1997, 1; "Enterprise School Pact Approved," *TO*, March 30, 1998, 34.
4. "New Middle Schools Needed, Group Says," *TO*, September 28, 1997, 1; "Enterprise School Seeking Students," *TO*, February 4, 1998, 62.
5. "School Boasts 'Parent Power,'" *TO*, June 29, 1998, 37.
6. "It's Time to Pass a Charter School Law," *TO*, January 30, 1999, 4.
7. "Charter Idea Complicates School Plans," *TO*, October 10, 2002, 1A.
8. "Charter School Confronts Hurdles," *TO*, May 10, 2003, G4.
9. "Charter Schools Boost Education," *TO*, June 7, 2004, 11A.
10. "Band of Brothers," *TO*, August 21, 2004, 2C.
11. "Diluting ACE Law a Mistake," *TO*, May 2, 2007, 9a.
12. "Blueprint for All Schools," *TO*, June 26, 2009, 11A.
13. "Retired Superintendent to Seek Superintendent Job," *TO*, October 7, 2009, 20 West; *OA 2015-2016* (OKC: ODL, 2015), 605; "Candidates Call for Education Reform," *TO*, June 17, 2010, 2A; "State Superintendent Race Focuses on Funds," *TO*, July 22, 2010, 2A.
14. "Candidates' Views;" *OA*, 119.
15. "Paddack, Barresi Capture Parties' Spots in School Races," *TO*, July 28, 2010, 2A; "Candidates' Views;" "Philosophies Differ Among Candidates," *TO*, October 17, 2010, 6A.
16. Oklahoma SEB Election Results for November 2, 2010, www.ok.gov/elections; C-1R and C-4R campaign finance reports for the 2010 election, respectively: https://pay.apps.ok.gov/ethics/crs /c1r/view; https://pay.apps.ok.gov/ethics/crs/c1r/schedule.
17. Oklahoma SEB Election Results for November 2, 2010.
18. "Barresi Draws Opponent for 2014," *TO*, December 23, 2012, 16A; "Barresi Lashes Out at Board Member," *TO*, October 9, 2012, 3A; "Working to Build Consensus Could Aid Barresi in the Long Run," *TO*, November 15, 2012, 8A.

19. "Superintendent's Challenger Outraising State Incumbent," *TO*, August 2, 2013, 16A; "GOP Challenger Outraises Barresi," *TO*, November 2, 2013, 1A. See SEC website for the quarterly C1-R CCERs for the several candidates. "Barresi's Loans to Campaign Draw Opponent's Criticism," *TO*, February 4, 2014, 9A.
20. "Barresi Campaign Requests All Records Related to Jenks Schools, Challenger," *TO*, March 17, 2014, 4A.
21. "Barresi's Campaign Seeks Records from Five Districts," *TO*, May 16, 2014, 14A.
22. "Barresi's Manager Accuses Hofmeister of Breaking Law," *TO*, June 19, 2014, 3A.
23. *OA*, 608; "Reform-Minded Barresi Merits GOP Voters' Nod," *TO*, June 15, 2014; Once, in the 1910 Democratic primary, incumbent Cameron lost to the challenger, Wilson, and in the crowded 1946 Democratic primary of six candidates, incumbent Crable forced a two-way runoff before losing to Hodge. https://www.followthemoney.org/entity-details?eid=8737700&default=candidate; https://www. followthe money.org/tools/election-overview/?s=OK&y=2010; https://ballotpedia.org/Janet_Barresi; https://www.followthemoney.org/tools/election-overview/?s=OK&y=2014.
24. "Working to Build Consensus."
25. "Chiefs for Change Education Advocacy Group is Headed for More Change," *Washington Post*, March 10, 2015, https:www.washingtonpost.com/local/education/chiefs-for-changeeducati…0/2e98a510-c73f-11e4-a1996cb5e63819d2_story.html?utm_term=.1b1bd44e61dd; ExcelinEd, https://www.excelined.org/about/approach/; "Our Donors," ExcelinEd, https://www.excelined.org/about/meet-our-donors/.
26. "Education Board Spars with New Schools Chief," *TO*, January 28, 2011, 1A.
27. Ibid.; "Barresi's Hires' Salaries Studied," *TO*, February 17, 2011, 9 West; "Schools Superintendent is Lightning Rod for Opinions," *TO*, August 18, 2013, 12A; A. G. Op. 2011-6, http://www.oscn.net/applications/oscn/DeliverDocument.asp?CiteID=462382.
28. 70 O.S. 2011 § 3-107.1 (West 2011); 70 O.S. 2001 §§ 1-105, 3-101, 3-104-107.1 (West 2001); "Education Politics Continue," *TW*, March 24, 2011, A 17; "Stakes Higher Than Ever for Schools Superintendent," *TO*, April 18, 2011, 8A; "Ex-state Workers Speak Out," *TO*, May 13, 2011, 11A.
29. *SBEMM*, May 9, 2011, SBE Office, Oliver Hodge Building.
30. "Education Board Spars with New Schools Chief."
31. "Schools Chief Unveils Her Agenda for Reform," *TO*, March 16, 2011, 1A.
32. "Professor Makes the Case for Consolidation," *TO*, December 28, 2015, 8A.
33. "State Will Apply for Federal Education Law Exemption," *TO*, September 29, 2011, 2A; "Test Score Blunder Causes Headaches for Districts, Kids," *TO*, August 24, 2011, 1A; "Barresi Tackles Technology Barriers," *TO*, August 29, 2011, 8A.
34. *SBEMM*, January 15-16, 2012, SBE Office, Oliver Hodge Building.
35. "How Do Politics Help a Child Learn How to Read," *TO*, January 15, 2012, 19A; "Foundation Influences State School Policies, Laws," *TW*, February 10, 2013, http://infoweb.newsbank.com/resources/doc/print?p=NewsBank&docrefs=news/1446462AEB8A6C60.
36. "Barresi Tries to Quell Fears of State Takeover," *TO*, February 12, 2012, 10A.
37. "Barresi Defends Staff, Grading Despite Criticism from Schools," *TO*, October 6, 2012, 14A; "Authors Dispute Claim by Barresi," *TW*, February 14, 2013, http://infoweb.newsbank.com/resources/doc/print?p=NewsBank& docrefs=news/144796AAF86B2938.
38. "Schools Superintendent is Lightning Rod."
39. *State of Oklahoma Fiscal Year 2016 Executive Budget*, Office of Management and Enterprise Services, February 2, 2015, 58, www.omes.ok.gov/sites/g/files/gmc316/f/bud16.pdf; *State of Oklahoma Fiscal Year 2017 Executive Budget*, Office of Management and Enterprise Services, February 1, 2016, 78, www.omes.ok.gov/sites/g/files/gmc316/f/bud17.pdf.
40. "Barresi's Move to Create New Position is Questioned," *TO*, September 25, 2014, 3A.
41. "Barresi Goes on 11th Hour Hiring Spree," *TW*, January 10, 2015; http://infoweb.newsbank.com /resources/doc/print?p=NewsBank&docrefs=news/152EF4EC1569E730; "Barresi Defends Hiring, Raises," *TW*, January 17, 2015, http://infoweb.newsbank.com/resources/doc/print?p= NewsBank$docrefs=news/152EF4EC1569E730.
42. "It's Time for the State to Continue to Move Forward," *TO*, December 28, 2014, 15A.
43. "Dr. Robert Sommers," http://www.okcareertech.org/digital-learning-forum/speakers/dr.-robert-sommers; "Robert Sommers, Oklahoma Secretary of Education, Resigns," *TW*, July 16, 2014, http:// www.tulsaworld.com/news/education/robert-sommers-oklahoma-secretary-of-education-resigns /article_a1a36e23-f811-500d-97fl-c0db02920bac.html.
44. A written request August 2016 for an interview received no reply.
45. "Services for OU Lineman," *TO*, March 20, 2009, 2C; "Band of Brothers."

Chapter 19

1. "Tulsa Woman Named to Education Board," *TO*, January 14, 2012, 16A; "State School Board Member Resigns," *TO*, April 25, 2013, 10 South.
2. Author sent written request for information, December 27, 2017, but received no reply. "Hofmeister Prepares for Her New Job," *TO*, November 11, 2014, 14A; "Hofmeister Wins by a Comfortable Margin," *Edmond Sun*, November 4, 2014, in.com/news/local_news/hofmeister-wins-by-a-comfortable-margin/article_a53fe65e-64a9-11e4-8cae-7714dd46cdaa.html; "Tulsa Woman Named to Education Board."
3. "Education Board May Have More Turnover," *TO*, September 27, 2011, 13 West; "Tulsan Appointed to State Board," *TO*, April 2, 2011, 17 Norman; "Can New Education Board Keep Fireworks in Check?" *TO*, October 2, 2011, 20A; "Letter Campaign Opposes Tulsa Postal Center Closing," *TO*, December 13, 2011, 15A.
4. Ellen Dollarhide McCoy, interview by the author, February 4, 2019; McCoy was Hofmeister's campaign manager from January to the June primary. "Education Board May Have More Turnover."
5. See *SBEMM*, January 2012-March 2013, SBE Office, Oliver Hodge Building.
6. McCoy, interview; Clark Ogilvie, interview by the author, October 1, 2018.
7. McCoy, interview.
8. "Schools Chief Candidates Set Policy Goals," *TO*, June 15, 2014, 5A.
9. "Joy Hofmeister Biography," www.JoyforOklahoma.com; McCoy, interview; *OA 2015-2016* (OKC: ODL, 2015), 608.
10. *OA 2015-2016*, 607; John Cox, interview by the author, January 29, 2019.
11. www.ballotpedia.org/John_Cox_(Oklahoma); www.ballotpedia.org/Joy_Hofmeister.
12. Financial data on the C1-R CCERs for the 2010 and 2014 election cycles accessed at www.ok.gov/ethics.
13. "State Superintendent-elect Hofmeister Forms Transition Team," *TO*, November 7, 2014, 12A.
14. "Oklahoma State Schools Superintendent Joy Hofmeister Charged with Campaign Violations, Conspiracy," *TO*, November 3, 2016, www.newsok.com/article/5525407. Months after the election Hofmeister and several others were charged with violation of the state's campaign and election laws governing fundraising and with conspiracy. She was arrested, booked, photographed, and fingerprinted, before posting bail. Allegations of political chicanery surfaced because the Oklahoma County district attorney was a Democrat. Almost a year later suddenly and mysteriously the charges were dropped. Obviously a major relief to her, she maintained all along that she was innocent. What the circumstances revealed were some questionable actions on the part of the state school boards association funneling money into a campaign account. Several hundred thousand dollars were donated via a "dark money" account by a highly reputable Oklahoma City insurance company that coveted anonymity. The company's donation was legal, but how it was handled caught the interest of the SEC. "Joy Hofmeister Leaves Jail after Posting Bond," *TO*, November 4, 2016, www.newsok.com/article/5525512; John Cox, interview; "Hofmeister Wins by a Comfortable Margin."

Epilogue

1. "Superintendent of Schools (state executive office)," https://ballotpedia.org/Superintendent_of_Schools_(state_executive_office); Eugene Mazo, "Residency and Democracy: Durational Residency Requirements From the Framers to the Present," *Florida State University Law Review*, 43, no. 2, (2016), 651.

Appendix A
Superintendent Demographics 1907-2015

Superintendent	Birthdate	Birth state	Children*	Married	Age**
E. D. Cameron	Feb. 26, 1862	North Carolina	1d, 5s	1890	44
R. H. Wilson	July 25, 1873	Kentucky	1d, 1s	1899	37
M. A. Nash	July 20, 1890	Texas	1d, 3s	1916	32
John Vaughan	Oct. 29, 1885	Tennessee	1d	1914	41
A. L. Crable	Nov. 27, 1889	Texas	1d, 2s	1918	47
Oliver Hodge	Sept. 24, 1901	Missouri	0	1924	45
E. H. McDonald†	Sept. 18, 1907	Oklahoma	1d, 1s	1944	60
D. D. Creech††	Aug. 1, 1917	Oklahoma	1d, 2s	1947	50
Scott Tuxhorn††	Mar. 4, 1928	Oklahoma	1d, 2s	1952	41
Leslie Fisher	Jan. 17, 1922	Oklahoma	2d, 1s	1941	48
John M. Folks	Mar. 17, 1948	Oklahoma	2s	1969	36
Gerald Hoeltzel††	Dec. 17, 1934	Oklahoma	1d, 2s	1959	53
Sandy Garrett	Feb. 8, 1943	Oklahoma	1s	1962‡	47
Janet Barresi	Mar. 6, 1952	Oklahoma	2s	1975‡‡	59
Joy Hofmeister	Sept. 7, 1964	Missouri	2d, 2s	1984	50

* d=daughter, s=son

** Age when first appointed or elected

† Acting for three months only

†† Appointed but never elected

‡ Divorced in 1974

‡‡ Widowed prior to term

Superintendent Demographics 1907-2015 Cont.

Superintendent	Death date	Death place	Age	Denomination
E. D. Cameron	July 29, 1923	Tahlequah, OK	61	Methodist/Baptist*
R. H. Wilson	Oct. 4, 1937	Oklahoma City, OK	64	Baptist
M. A. Nash	May 10, 1981	Edmond, OK	90	Baptist
John Vaughan	Jan. 21, 1951	Tahlequah, OK	65	Baptist
A. L. Crable	Aug. 10, 1976	Oklahoma City, OK	86	Baptist
Oliver Hodge	Jan. 14, 1968	Oklahoma City, OK	66	Christian
E. H. McDonald	Aug. 22, 1984	Oklahoma City, OK	76	Baptist
D. D. Creech	Aug. 2, 1999	Miami, OK	82	Methodist
Scott Tuxhorn	Sept. 26, 2015	Texas	89	Christian
Les Fisher	Jan. 2, 1988	Moore, OK	65	Baptist
John Folks	n/a	n/a	n/a	Church of Christ
Gerald Hoeltzel	n/a	n/a	n/a	Lutheran
Sandy Garrett	n/a	n/a	n/a	Methodist
Janet Barresi	n/a	n/a	n/a	Catholic
Joy Hofmeister	n/a	n/a	n/a	Baptist

* Initially a Methodist minister and later became a Baptist minister

Appendix B

Alphabeticized List of Candidates, Year, Election, and Party Affiliation 1907-2014

Candidate	Year	Election	Party
Allen, Clinton	1914	Primary	Democratic
Ballard, Calvin	1907	General	Republican
Barresi, Janet	2010	Primary	Republican
		General	
	2014	Primary	
Battenberg, J. P.	1922	Primary	Democratic
Briggs, Thomas Jefferson	1934	Primary	Republican
Briles, Charles	1914	Primary	Democratic
Brock, Andrew Jackson	1946	Primary	Democratic
Burns, John C.	1934	Primary	Republican
		General	
Butterfield, Ralph	1942	General	Prohibition
Cameron, E. D.	1907	General	Democratic
	1910	Primary	
Cannon, Jack	1934	Primary	Democratic
Choate, Issac	1926	Primary	Republican
Combrink, Jerry	2010	Primary	Democratic
Cooper, Richard	2010	General	Independent
Cox, John	2014	Primary	Democratic
		Runoff	
		General	
Crable, A. L.	1938	Primary	Democratic
		General	
	1942	Primary	
		General	
	1946	Primary	
		Runoff	
Creekmore, H. G.	1946	Primary	Democratic
Crockett, David	1946	Primary	Democratic
Crozier, Bill	2006	General	Republican
Deskin, Freda	2014	Primary	Democratic
		Runoff	
Dowell, Horace	1922	Primary	Republican
Dyche, J. E.	1910	Primary	Republican
Evans, Charles	1930	Primary	Democratic
Evans, David	1986	General	Republican

Name	Year	Election	Party
Evans, John P.	1910	Primary	Republican
		General	
Fisher, David	1990	Primary	Democratic
Fisher, Earl	1942	Primary	Democratic
Fisher, Leslie	1970	Primary	Democratic
		General	
	1974	General	
	1978	General	
	1982	General	
Floyd, M. R.	1942	General	Republican
Folks, John	1986	General	Democratic
Garrett, Sandy	1990	Primary	Democratic
		General	
	1994	Primary	
		General	
	1998	General	
	2002	General	
	2006	General	
Garrison, Earl	1994	Primary	Democratic
Gilmour, Geen	1938	General	Republican
Grow, Russell	1946	Primary	Democratic
Hamilton, J. N.	1918	General	Republican
Hanna, Joseph	1907	General	Socialist
Herron, Jack	2014	Primary	Democratic
Hodge, Oliver	1946	Primary	Democratic
		Runoff	
		General	
	1950	General	
	1954	General	
	1958	General	
	1962	General	
	1966	General	
Hoeltzel, Gerald	1990	General	Republican
Hofmeister, Joy	2014	Primary	Republican
		General	
Holleyman, Charles	1970	Primary	Democratic
Holmes, Ivan	2014	Primary	Democratic
Ingle, William	1926	Primary	Republican
Jones, Jenella	1934	Primary	Republican
Kelly, Brian	2010	Primary	Republican
	2014	Primary	
Kerr, Clay W.	1934	Primary	Democratic
Knie, Robert L.	1907	Primary	Democratic
McCool, R. M.	1938	Primary	Democratic

Name	Year	Election	Party
McCord, Otis L.	1922	Primary	Republican
Moss, G. D.	1907	Primary	Republican
	1910	Primary	
	1922	Primary	
		General	
Munson, Mary Abrams	1926	Primary	Republican
Murphy, Linda	1994	General	Republican
	1998	Primary	
		General	
Murray, John	1934	Primary	Democratic
		Runoff	
Nash, M. A.	1922	Primary	Democratic
		General	
	1926	Primary	
		General	
Nelson, Martin B.	1946	General	Republican
Nelson, Merrill A.	1934	General	Progressive
	1938	General	Prohibition
Nelson, Tivis	1934	Primary	Democratic
Paddack, Susan	2010	Primary	Democratic
		General	
Parrick, Cyris	1914	General	Progressive
Peak, C. N.	1922	Primary	Republican
Price, Edson	1930	General	Republican
Record, Ralph	1922	Primary	Republican
Roettger, Lloyd	2002	General	Republican
Sandmann, Charles	1982	General	Republican
Smallwood, Clyde G.	1958	General	Republican
Smith, S. S.	1910	General	Socialist
Tuxhorn, Scott	1970	General	Republican
Vannest, C. G.	1914	General	Republican
Vaughan, John	1930	Primary	Democratic
		General	
	1934	Primary	
		Runoff	
		General	
Welday, J. O.	1914	General	Socialist
Welton, W. Roy	1934	Primary	Democratic
White, J. C.	1938	Primary	Democratic
Williams, Tod	1998	Primary	Republican
Willis, Anna	1926	Primary	Republican
		General	
Wilson, George	1918	Primary	Democratic

Wilson, R. H.	1910	Primary	Democratic
		General	
	1914	Primary	
		General	
	1918	Primary	
		General	

Appendix C

Number of Candidates for the Superintendency 1907-2014

Election	Year	No. Dem	No. Rep	No. Other	Total
Primary	1907	2	2	0	4
General	1907	1	1	1	3
Primary	1910	2	3	0	5
General	1910	1	1	1	3
Primary	1914	2	1	2	5
General	1914	1	1	2	4
Primary	1918	3	1	0	4
General	1918	1	1	0	2
Primary	1922	2	5	0	7
General	1922	1	1	0	2
Primary	1926	1	4	0	5
General	1926	1	1	0	2
Primary	1930	2	1	0	3
General	1930	1	1	0	2
Primary	1934	6	3	0	9
Dem. runoff	1934	2	NA	0	2
General	1934	1	1	1	3
Primary	1938	3	1	0	4
General	1938	1	1	1	3
Primary	1942	2	1	0	3
General	1942	1	1	1	3
Primary	1946	6	1	0	7
Dem. runoff	1946	2	NA	0	2
General	1946	1	1	0	2
General	1950	1	0	0	1
General	1954	1	0	0	1
General	1958	1	1	0	2
General	1962	1	0	0	1
General	1966	1	0	0	1
Primary	1970	2	1	0	3
General	1970	1	1	0	2
General	1974	1	0	0	1
General	1978	1	0	0	1
General	1982	1	1	0	2
General	1986	1	1	0	2
Primary	1990	2	1	0	3
General	1990	1	1	0	2
Primary	1994	2	1	0	3

General	1994	1	1	0	2
Primary	1998	1	2	0	3
General	1998	1	1	0	2
General	2002	1	1	0	2
General	2006	1	1	0	2
Primary	2010	2	2	0	4
General	2010	1	1	1	3
Primary	2014	4	3	0	7
Dem. runoff	2014	2	NA	0	2
General	2014	1	1	0	2

Sources: *Oklahoma Elections: Statehood to Present,* vol.1, *1994* (OKC: SEB, 1994); Election Results 1996-2014 in *OA 2015-2016* (OKC: ODL, 2015), 593-608.

Appendix D
Candidates' Ages at Filing Time 1907-2014

Election	Candidate	Age	Election	Candidate	Age
1907	E. D. Cameron	45		William A. Ingle	35
	Calvin Ballard	54		Mary Abrams Munson	46
	Joseph Hanna	35			
	Robert Knie	35	1930	Charles Evans	60
	G. D. Moss*	40		John Vaughan	43
				Edson Price	53
1910	E. D. Cameron	48			
	R. H. Wilson	36	1934	W. Roy Welton	37
	J. E. Dyche	44		Jack Cannon	36
	John Paul Evans**	31		Clay W. Kerr	44
	G. D. Moss*	43		Tivis Nelson	45
	S. S. Smith**	31		John Murray	43
				John Vaughan	48
1914	Clinton Allen	35		John C. Burns	40
	R. H. Wilson	40		Jenella D. Jones	45
	G. G. Vannest	35		Thomas J. Briggs	41
				Merrill A. Nelson*	37
	J. O. Welday†				
	Cyrus H. Parrick	41	1938	Merrill A. Nelson*	41
				A. L. Crable	48
				R. M. McCool	52
1918	George Wilson	47		J. C. White	33
	R. H. Wilson	44		Geen Gilmour	37
	Charles Briles	45			
	J. N. Hamilton	37	1942	Earl Fisher	45
				M. R. Floyd	65
1922	M. A. Nash	32		Ralph E. Butterfield	52
				A. L. Crable	52
	J. P. Battenberg	33			
	G. D. Moss*	55	1946	Oliver Hodge	44
	Horace F. Dowell	37		A. L. Crable	56
	Otis L. McCord	38		H. G. Creekmore	50
	Ralph Record	32		David Crockett	40
	C. N. Peak	55		Andrew J. Brock	52
				Martin B. Nelson†	
1926	M. A. Nash	36		Russell Grow	44
	Isaac Choate	50			
	Anna Willis	44	1950	Oliver Hodge	48

Election	Candidate	Age	Election	Candidate	Age
1954	Oliver Hodge	52	1994	Linda Murphy*	43
				Earl Garrison	49
1958	Oliver Hodge	56		Sandy Garrett	51
	Clyde G. Smallwood	40			
			1998	Linda Murphy*	47
1962	Oliver Hodge	60		Tod Williams	36
				Sandy Garrett	55
1966	Oliver Hodge	64			
			2002	Lloyd Roettger	55
1970	Charles D. Holleyman	41		Sandy Garrett	59
	Scott E. Tuxhorn	42			
	Leslie R. Fisher	48	2006	Sandy Garrett	63
				Bill Crozier	60
1974	Leslie R. Fisher	52			
			2010	Janet Barresi	58
1978	Leslie R. Fisher	56		Susan Paddack	57
				Jerry Combrink	69
1982	Charles W. Sandmann	54		Richard Cooper†	
	Leslie R. Fisher	60		Brian Kelly*	46
1986	David Evans	34	2014	Janet Barresi	62
	M. Folks	38		Joy Hofmeister	49
				John Cox	50
1990	Gerald E. Hoeltzel	55		Brian Kelly*	50
	David L. Fisher	38		Jack Herron	68
	Sandy Garrett	47		Freda Deskin	65
				Ivan Holmes††	77

Sources: For the early elections filing applications can be viewed at the OSA, ODL, OKC and, for more recent elections, at the Oklahoma State Election Board Office. There were sixty-seven males and nine females for a total of seventy-six. Only one (interim) Superintendent, D. D. Creech did not seek the office through an election.

*Candidates who ran multiple times and never won.

**Youngest candidates.

†Unable to determine age at filing time.

††Oldest candidate at first election participation.

Appendix E

Superintendency Candidates' Other Political Activities 1907-2014

Name	Election	Party	Other political activity
E. D. Cameron*	**1907**	Democratic	**Ran in 1910 for Superintendent and lost the primary**; ran for lieutenant governor in 1922 and lost the primary
Robert Knie	1907	Democratic	Elected in 1917 and 1919 to the state senate; appointed secretary of the Commissioner of the Land Office in 1923
Calvin Ballard	1907	Republican	None
G. D. Moss	1907	Republican	Lost the 1910 Republican primary; won the 1922 Republican primary and lost the general election
Joseph Hanna	1907	Socialist	None
E. D. Cameron	**1910**	Democratic	See above
James E. Dyche	1910	Republican	Former Territorial Superintendent in 1907; ran for state auditor in 1907 and lost
John P. Evans	1910	Republican	Was elected in 1907 to represent the flotorial district of Alfalfa and Grant counties in the House of Representatives
G. D. Moss	1910	Republican	See above
R. H. Wilson	**1910**	Democratic	**Won 1914 and 1918 elections for Superintendent;** ran for governor in 1922 and lost in the Democratic primary; ran for U.S. Congress, Fifth District in 1932 and lost the Democratic primary
S. S. Smith	1910	Socialist	None
R. H. Wilson	**1914**	Democratic	See above
Clinton Allen	1914	Democratic	None
C. G. Vannest	1914	Republican	None
J. O. Welday	1914	Socialist	None
Cyris H. Parrick	1914	Progressive	None
R. H. Wilson	**1918**	Democratic	See above
George Wilson	1918	Democratic	Ran for U.S. Senator in 1924 on the Farm-Labor Party; lost
Charles W. Briles	1918	Democratic	None
J. N. Hamilton	1918	Republican	None
J. P. Battenberg	1922	Democratic	Ran for the U.S. Congress in 1928 from District 8 and won the primary; won the runoff and lost the general election.

Name	Year	Party	Notes
M. A. Nash	1922	Democratic	Won general election for Superintendent in 1926
Horace F. Dowell	1922	Republican	None
Otis L. McCord	1922	Republican	Ran for Congress-at-large in 1938 as a Democrat and lost the primary
G. D. Moss	1922	Republican	See above
Ralph H. Record	1922	Republican	None
C. N. Peak	1922	Republican	None
M. A. Nash	1926	Democratic	See above
Issac Choate	1926	Republican	None
Anna Willis	1926	Republican	None
Mary Abrams Munson	1926	Republican	None
William A. Ingle	1926	Republican	None
Charles Evans	1930	Democratic	None
John Vaughan	1930	Democratic	Won general election for Superintendent in 1934
Edson Price	1930	Republican	None
John Vaughan	1934	Democratic	See above
W. Roy Welton	1934	Democratic	None
Jack Cannon	1934	Democratic	None
Clay W. Kerr	1934	Democratic	None
Tivis Nelson	1934	Democratic	Ran for governor in 1954 Democratic primary and lost
John Murray	1934	Democratic	Ran for clerk of the Supreme Court in 1934 and 1958 and lost both times
Jenella Jones	1934	Republican	None
Thomas Jefferson Briggs	1934	Republican	None
John C. Burns**	1934	Republican	Ran for state auditor in 1926 and lost the primary; ran for secretary of state in 1930 and won the primary and the runoff but lost the general election; ran for Congress-at-large in 1936; won the primary and the runoff, but lost the general election; ran as a Democrat for Congress-at-large in 1938 and lost the primary; ran for the corporation commission as a Democrat in 1940 and lost the primary; ran for the corporation commission as a Republican in 1944 and lost the primary; ran for the commission of insurance in 1946 as a Republican and lost the general election; ran for the corporation commission in 1948 and 1952 as a Republican, losing the general election and the primary, respectively
Merrill A. Nelson	1934	Progressive	Ran for the Superintendency in 1938 on the Prohibition ticket and lost the general election

Name	Year	Party	Notes
A. L. Crable*	1938	Democratic	**Ran for the Superintendency in 1942 and won the general election; ran for the same position in 1946 and lost the runoff.**
R. M. McCool	1938	Democratic	Ran for president of the state board of agriculture in 1930 and 1942 and lost in the primary; ran for U.S. Senate in 1932 and lost in the primary; ran for corporation commission in 1936 and lost in the primary; ran for governor in 1946 and lost in the primary
J. C. White	1938	Democratic	Ran for corporation commission in 1936 and lost in the primary
Geen Gilmour	1938	Republican	None
A. L. Crable	**1942**	Democratic	See above
Earl Fisher	1942	Democratic	None
M. R. Floyd	1942	Republican	None
Ralph E. Butterfield	1942	Prohibition	Ran for U.S. Congress, District 8, on the Prohibition ticket in 1940 and won the primary; lost in the general election
A. L. Crable	**1946**	Democratic	See above
Russell Grow	1946	Democratic	None
Oliver Hodge	**1946**	Democratic	**Won the general election for Superintendent in 1950, 1954, 1958, 1962, and 1966**
H. G. Creekmore	1946	Democratic	None
David Crockett	1946	Democratic	None
Andrew Jackson Brock	1946	Democratic	None
Martin B. Nelson	1946	Republican	None
Oliver Hodge	**1950**	Democratic	See above
Oliver Hodge	**1954**	Democratic	See above
Oliver Hodge	**1958**	Democratic	See above
Clyde Smallwood	1958	Republican	None
Oliver Hodge	**1962**	Democratic	See above
Oliver Hodge	**1966**	Democratic	See above
Leslie R. Fisher	**1970**	Democratic	**Won the general election for Superintendent in 1974, 1978, and 1982; ran for governor in 1988 and lost in the Democratic primary**
Charles D. Holleyman	1970	Democratic	None
Scott E. Tuxhorn	1970	Republican	State representative from Alfalfa County 1962-1964
Leslie R. Fisher	**1974**	Democratic	See above
Leslie R. Fisher	**1978**	Democratic	See above
Leslie R. Fisher	**1982**	Democratic	See above
Charles W. Sandmann	1982	Republican	None
John M. Folks†	**1986**	Democratic	None
David Evans	1986	Republican	None

David L. Fisher	1990	Democratic	None
Sandy Garrett	**1990**	**Democratic**	**Won the general election for the Superintendent in 1994, 1998, 2002, and 2006**
Gerald E. Hoeltzel	1990	Republican	None
Sandy Garrett	**1994**	**Democratic**	See above
Linda Murphy	1994	Republican	Ran for Superintendent in the general election in 1998 and lost
Earl Garrison[††]	1994	Democratic	Won Senate District 9 in 2004, 2008, and 2012
Sandy Garrett	**1998**	**Democratic**	See above
Linda Murphy	1998	Republican	See above
Tod Williams	1998	Republican	None
Sandy Garrett	**2002**	**Democratic**	See above
Lloyd Roettger	2002	Republican	None
Sandy Garrett	**2006**	**Democratic**	See above
Bill Crozier[‡]	2006	Republican	Ran for Fourth Congressional District in 1972 and lost; ran for the U.S. Senate in 1984, won the primary, and lost general election; ran for governor in 1986 and lost primary; ran for lieutenant governor in 2010 and lost the primary
Susan Paddack[‡‡]	2010	Democratic	Was elected to State Senate District 13 in 2004, 2008, and 2012
Jerry Combrink	2010	Democratic	None
Janet Barresi*	**2010**	**Republican**	**Lost the 2014 Republican primary for Superintendent**
Brian Kelly	2010	Republican	Lost in the 2014 Republican primary for Superintendent
Richard Cooper	2010	Independent	None
John Cox	2014	Democratic	None
Freda Deskin	2014	Democratic	None
Jack Herron	2014	Democratic	None
Ivan Holmes	2014	Democratic	None
Brian Kelly	2014	Republican	See above
Joy Hofmeister	**2014**	**Republican**	**NA**
Janet Barresi	**2014**	**Republican**	**See above**

Note: Excludes the county superintendency. Bold print identifies the Superintendents and their involvement in elections for the Superintendency. Nineteen candidates ran a total of forty times for positions other than Superintendent. Sixty-five candidates ran unsuccessfully for the Superintendency.

* Lost a reelection bid in the primary or runoff election.

** In the 1930s and 1940s he ran nine times for various offices as a Republican or Democrat, but was always unsuccessful.

† Only elected Superintendent who was involved in only one election

†† Only candidate for Superintendent who then ran successfully for the state senate, serving twelve years

‡ Used several variations of his name over the decades of campaigning

‡‡ Member of the state senate when she ran for the Superintendency

Appendix F
Superintendency Election Results 1907-2014

Election Candidates	Year	Votes	Percent
	1907		
Democratic Primary—June 8		...	...
E. D. Cameron			
Robert L. Knie			
Republican Primary—August 2		...	...
Calvin Ballard			
G. D. Moss			
General election—September 17			
E. D. Cameron, Democrat		132,962	54.8
Calvin Ballard, Republican		99,912	41.1
Joseph Hanna, Socialist		9,678	3.9
Total		242,552	99.9
	1910		
Democratic primary—August 2			
E. D. Cameron		47,433	43.2
R. H. Wilson		62,337	56.7
Total		109,770	99.9
Republican primary—August 2			
James E. Dyche		22,035	31.9
John P. Evans		25,706	37.2
G. D. Moss		21,269	30.8
Total		69,010	99.9
Socialist primary—August 2			
S. S. Smith		13,015	100.0
General election—November 8			
R. H. Wilson, Democrat		118,628	50.3
John P. Evans, Republican		93,549	39.6
S. S. Smith, Socialist		23,642	10.0
Total		235,819	99.9
	1914		
Democratic primary—August 4			
Clinton M. Allen		37,084	36.3
R. H. Wilson		64,807	63.6
Total		101,891	99.9
Republican primary—August 4			
C. G. Vannest		26,581	100.0

Socialist primary — August 4		
J. O. Welday	15,700	100.0
Progressive primary — August 4		
Cyris H. Parrick	2,103	100.0
General election — November 3		
R. H. Wilson, Democrat	107,686	44.7
C. G. Vannest, Republican	75,705	31.4
J. O. Welday, Socialist	52,658	21.8
Cyris H. Parrick, Progressive	4,584	1.9
Total	240,633	99.8

1918

Democratic primary — August 6		
George Wilson	32,872	35.9
Charles W. Briles	10,445	11.4
R. H. Wilson	48,101	52.6
Total	91,418	99.7
Republican primary — August 6		
J. N. Hamilton	40,054	100.0
General election — November 5		
R. H. Wilson, Democrat	101,775	56.4
J. N. Hamilton, Republican	78,818	43.6
Total	180,593	100.0

1922

Democratic primary — August 1		
M. A. Nash	132,337	61.9
J. P. Battenberg	81,240	38.0
Total	213,557	99.9
Republican primary — August 1		
G. D. Moss	17,688	24.8
Horace F. Dowell	13,101	18.4
Otis L. McCord	12,885	18.1
Ralph H. Record	14, 610	20.5
C. N. Peak	12,892	18.1
Total	71,176	99.9
General election — November 7		
M. A. Nash	289,417	63.5
G. D. Moss	165,892	36.4
Total	455,309	99.9

1926

Democratic primary — August 3		
M. A. Nash	149,998	100.0

Republican primary — August 3

Isaac Choate	7,565	14.3
Anna Willis	18,234	34.6
William Ingle	14,946	28.4
Mary Abrams Munson	11,876	22.5
Total	52,621	99.8

General election — November 2

M. A. Nash, Democrat	203,005	57.7
Anna Willis, Republican	148,558	42.2
Total	351,563	99.9

1930

Democratic primary — July 29

Charles Evans	97,414	39.9
John Vaughan	146,527	60.0
Total	243,941	99.9

Republican primary — July 29

Edson Price	57,378	100.0

General election — November 4

John Vaughan, Democrat	285,719	64.7
Edson Price, Republican	155,365	35.2
Total	441,084	99.9

1934

Democratic primary — July 3

W. Roy Welton	29,269	7.4
Jack Cannon	53,970	13.8
Clay W. Kerr	63,012	16.1
Tivis Nelson	12,449	3.1
John Murray	91,377	23.4
John Vaughan	140,401	35.9
Total	390,478	99.7

Republican primary — July 3

John C. Burns	33,226	61.9
Jenella D. Jones	11,877	22.1
Thomas Jefferson Briggs	8,568	15.9
Total	53,671	99.9

Democratic runoff primary — July 24

John Murray	140,914	37.3
John Vaughan	236,493	62.6
Total	377,407	99.9

General election — November 6

John Vaughan, Democrat	353,345	66.7
John C. Burns, Republican	174,312	32.9

Merrill A. Nelson, Progressive	1,515	0.2
Total	529,172	99.8

1938

Democratic primary — July 12		
A. L. Crable	239,196	52.2
R. M. McCool	150,509	32.8
J. C. White	68,115	14.8
Total	457,820	99.8
General election — November 8		
A. L. Crable, Democrat	305,439	68.9
Geen Gilmour, Republican	135,032	30.4
Merrill A. Nelson, Prohibition	2,633	0.5
Total	443,104	99.8

1942

Democratic primary — July 14		
A. L. Crable	158,820	54.9
Earl Fisher	130,329	45.0
Total	289,149	99.9
General election — November 3		
A. L. Crable, Democrat	184,539	54.8
M. R. Floyd, Republican	149,671	44.5
Ralph E. Butterfield, Prohibition	2,419	0.1
Total	336,629	99.4

1946

Democratic primary — July 2		
Russell Grow	25,076	8.5
Oliver Hodge	98,497	33.5
A. L. Crable	82,635	28.1
H. G. Creekmore	30,658	10.4
David Crockett	40,901	13.9
Andrew Jackson Brock	15,994	5.4
Total	293,761	99.8
Runoff Democratic primary — July 23		
Oliver Hodge	216,713	69.3
A. L. Crable	95,854	30.6
Total	312,567	99.9
General election — November 5		
Oliver Hodge, Democrat	263,751	58.6
Martin B. Nelson, Republican	186,185	41.3
Total	449,936	99.9

1950
General election — November 7
    Oliver Hodge, Democrat   352,180   100.0

1954
General election — November 2
    Oliver Hodge, Democrat   347,026   100.0

1958
General election — November 4
    Oliver Hodge, Democrat   350,472   74.7
    Clyde Smallwood, Republican   118,373   25.2
    Total   468,845   99.9

1962
General election — November 6
    Oliver Hodge, Democrat   548,500   100.0

1966
General election — November 8
    Oliver Hodge, Democrat   695,518   100.0

1970
Democratic primary — August 25
    Leslie R. Fisher   194,612   59.8
    Charles D. Holleyman   130,672   40.1
    Total   325,284   99.9
General election — November 3
    Leslie R. Fisher, Democrat   384,397   62.1
    Scott E. Tuxhorn, Republican   234,357   37.8
    Total   618,754   99.9

1974
General election — November 5
    Leslie R. Fisher, Democrat   822,026   100.0

1978
General election — November 7
    Leslie R. Fisher, Democrat   (unopposed)

1982
General election — November 2
    Leslie R. Fisher, Democrat   511,176   64.2
    Charles W. Sandmann, Republican   284,443   35.7
    Total   795,619   99.9

1986

General election—November 4
 John M. Folks, Democrat   527,477   61.0
 David Evans, Republican   336,643   38.9
 Total   864,120   99.9

1990

Democratic primary election—August 28
 David L. Fisher   180,636   35.8
 Sandy Garrett   323,790   64.2
 Total   504,427   100.0

General election—November 6
 Sandy Garrett, Democrat   618,008   71.5
 Gerald E. Hoeltzel, Republican   246,435   28.5
 Total   864,443   100.0

1994

Democratic primary—August 23
 Sandy Garrett   255,827   59.7
 Earl Garrison   172,479   40.3
 Total   428,306   100.0

General election—November 8
 Sandy Garrett, Democrat   493,687   50.5
 Linda Murphy, Republican   484,428   49.5
 Total   978,115   100.0

1998

Republican primary—August 25
 Linda Murphy   75,310   64.9
 Tod Williams   40,633   35.1
 Total   115,943   100.0

General election—November 3
 Sandy Garrett, Democrat   520,270   60.2
 Linda Murphy, Republican   343,291   39.8
 Total   863,561   100.0

2002

General election—November 5
 Sandy Garrett, Democrat   609,851   59.7
 Lloyd Roettger, Republican   411,814   40.3
 Total   1,021,615   100.0

2006

General election—November 7
 Sandy Garrett, Democrat   576,304   62.6

Bill Crozier, Republican	343,900	37.4
Total	920,204	100.0

2010

Democratic primary — July 27		
Susan Paddack	183,550	73.3
Jerry Combrink	66,697	26.7
Total	250,247	100.0
Republican primary — July 27		
Janet Barresi	145,433	62.7
Brian Kelly	86,430	37.3
Total	231,863	100.0
General election — November 2		
Janet Barresi, Republican	573,716	55.9
Susan Paddack, Democrat	387,007	37.7
Richard Cooper, Independent	65,243	6.4
Total	1,025,966	100.0

2014

Republican primary election — June 24		
Janet Barresi	55,048	21.0
Joy Hofmeister	151,124	57.6
Brian Kelly	56,060	21.4
Total	262,232	100.0
Democratic primary election — June 24		
John Cox	68,889	41.0
Jack Herron	22,335	13.3
Freda Deskin	64,135	38.2
Ivan Holmes	12,504	7.5
Total	167,863	100.0
Democratic runoff election — August 26		
John Cox	60,370	62.9
Freda Deskin	35,621	37.1
Total	95,991	100.0
General election — November 4		
Joy Hofmeister, Republican	457,053	55.8
John Cox, Democrat	361,878	44.2
Total	818,931	100.0

Sources: Oklahoma Elections: Statehood to Present, vol. 1 (OKC: SEB, 1994), C-1 to C-639; *OA 2009-2010* (OKC: ODL, 2009), 597-99; *OA 2015-2016* (OKC: ODL, 2015), 595, 600, 603, 605-08.

Notes: The 1907 Democratic primary final results are not extant, but, with two counties' results not yet reported, E. D. Cameron was leading by 15,000 votes out of 150,000 tallied. The Republicans chose Calvin Ballard over G. D. Moss by a narrow margin at their convention.

For an unopposed candidate, the State Election Board recorded either the total votes cast in that election, the total votes actually cast for that candidate, or just listed the candidate as unopposed.

Appendix G

Superintendency Vote as a Ratio of the Governor Vote 1907-2014

Election	Votes for superintendent	Votes for governor	Supt. vote ratio of governor vote	Ranking
1907	242,552	250,409	.969	7
1910	235,819	247,666	.953	8
1914	240,633	253,687	.949	10T
1918	180,593	194,435	.929	12
1922	455,309	515,616	.885	17T
1926	351,563	387,308	.908	14
1930	441,084	511,320	.863	21
1934	529,172	628,331	.843	22
1938	443,104	507,956	.873	19
1942	336,629	378,871	.889	16
1946	449,936	494,599	.910	13
1950	n/a	644,276	n/a	n/a
1954	n/a	609,194	n/a	n/a
1958	468,845	538,839	.871	20
1962	n/a	709,763	n/a	n/a
1966	n/a	677,258	n/a	n/a
1970	618,754	698,790	.885	17T
1974	n/a	804,848	n/a	n/a
1978	n/a	777,414	n/a	n/a
1982	795,619	883,130	.901	15
1986	864,120	909,925	.950	9
1990	864,443	911,314	.949	10T
1994	978,115	995,012	.983	6
1998	863,561	873,585	.989	4
2002	1,021,665	1,035,620	.987	5
2006	920,204	926,462	.993	1T
2010	1,025,966	1,034,767	.992	3
2014	818,931	824,831	.993	1T

Sources: *Oklahoma Elections: Statehood to Present 1994*, vol. 1 (OKC: SEB, 1994); www.ok.gov/elections.

Note: Incumbent drew no opponent in 1950, 1954, 1962, 1966, 1974, and 1978.

Appendix H

Oklahoma Voter Registration 1960-2017

Year	Democrat Number	Democrat Percent	Republican Number	Republican Percent	Independent Number	Independent Percent	Total
1960	863,529	82.0	179,645	17.6	3,585	0.4	1,019,759
1970	922,158	76.7	267,284	22.2	6,622	0.6	1,201,666*
1980	874,895	75.8	263,008	22.8	15,830	1.4	1,153,733
1990	1,239,275	64.9	624,801	32.7	46,567	2.4	1,910,643
2000**	1,189,332	56.7	734,382	35.0	174,649	8.3	2,098,750†
2010**	999,855	49.0	813,158	39.9	225,607	11.1	2,038,620
2017**	852,447	39.4	989,358	45.8	316,109	14.8	2,161,881††

Source: Voter Registration Statistics, State Election Board, oklahoma.gov/elections/voter-registration/voter-registration-statistics.

*Includes 5,602 registered as American Party.

**As of January 15; numbered registered increases by November 1.

†Includes 267 registered as Libertarian Party and 120 Reform Party.

††Includes 3,967 registered as Libertarian Party.

Appendix I

Ratio of Superintendent's Salary to Governor's Salary 1890-2015

Year	Superintendent	Governor	Ratio
1891-92	1,800	2,600	.69
1893-94	2,000	2,600	.77
1895-96	2,000	2,600	.77
1897-98	1,800	2,600	.69
1899-00	1,800	2,600	.69
1901-02	1,800	2,600	.69
1903-04	1,800	3,000	.60
1905-06	1,800	3,000	.60
1907-10*	2,500	4,500	.55
1911-14	2,500	4,500	.55
1915-18	2,500	4,500	.55
1919-22	2,500	4,500	.55
1923-26	2,500	4,500	.55
1927-30**	2,500	4,500	.55
1931-32	6,000	7,500	.80
1933-34***	4,000	6,000	.67
1935-38	4,000	6,500	.62
1939-42	4,800	6,500	.74
1943-46	4,800	6,500	.74
1947-50†	4,800	6,500	.74
1951-54	12,000	15,000	.80
1955-58	12,000	15,000	.80
1959-62	12,000	15,000	.80
1963-66	15,000	25,000	.60
1967-70††	16,500	27,500†††	.60
1971-74	25,000	35,000	.71
1975-78	30,000	42,500	.71
1979-82	35,000	48,000	.71
1983-86	55,000	70,000	.79
1987-90	55,000	70,000	.79
1991-94	55,000	70,000	.79
1995-98‡	55,000	70,000	.79
1999-02‡‡	88,511	101,140	.875
2003-06‡‡‡	95,898	110,299	.869
2007-10#	102,529	117,571	.872
2011-14	102,529	117,571	.872
2015-18##	102,529	117,571	.872

Note: The territorial legislature met biennially and set the salaries for the biennial periods. Beginning at statehood and continuing to 1967, the Legislature met in the odd numbered years, but the salaries of executive officers were set for four years (the terms of the offices). A constitutional amendment (State Question 435) in May 1966 provided for the Legislature to begin meeting annually, but the salaries still were set for the four-year terms.

* Oklahoma Constitution 1907, Art. XIII, § 10: "…in no case shall the salary or emoluments of any public official be changed after his election or appointment, or during her term of office, unless by operation of law enacted prior to such election or appointment…." Legislative Referendum 169 to eliminate this provision was offered to the voters as State Question 456 August 27, 1968, but it failed to pass. Thus, the wording in the original 1907 constitution is operative today. State officers' salaries are found in 74 O.S. § 250.4, not every four years, but only when the Legislature specifies a different salary for the next term.

** The 1929 Legislature in SB 36 set the salaries at $6,000 and $7,500 for the Superintendent and the governor, respectively, and they were paid those amounts for 1931 and 1932.

*** The 1933 Legislature appropriated only $4,000 and $6,000, respectively, for 1933 and 1934. During this period the salaries were reduced because the state's revenues declined dramatically.

† Although the Legislature set the salaries for 1949 and 1950 at $7,200 and $15,000, it appropriated only $4,800 and $6,500. The constitution prohibited the Legislature from increasing the salary during a four-year term, but it did not prohibit the Legislature from appropriating less than the statutory amount approved.

†† An exception concerned the Superintendent's salary in 1968. Oliver Hodge died in mid-term and Governor Bartlett wanted to name D. D. Creech to the position. Creech, as superintendent at Pryor, was receiving a larger salary than that of the Superintendent. *Oklahoman*, February 6, 1968, 6. Bartlett lobbied the Legislature to raise the salary from $16,500 to $19,500.

††† The governor's salary is included in the list of state officers' salaries in 1961 for the period 1963-1967 (74 O.S. 1961, § 250.4), but not in 1965 for the 1967-71 term (O.S.L. 1965, chapt. 502, § 2. The governor's salary is then included in 1970 for 1971-1974 (O.S.L. 1970, chapt. 85, § 1). If, from 1963-66 to 1967-70, the Superintendent's salary increased 10 percent, one could extrapolate the governor's salary to have been $27,500.

‡ Legislated in 1994 and beginning in 1995, the Superintendent's salary was tied to that of a district judge (O.S.L. 1994, chapt. 239, § 3. Judicial salaries were set by the Board of Judicial Compensation.

‡‡ Enacted in 1997, effective in 1999, the governor's salary was equal to that of the chief justice of the state supreme court (O.S.L. 1997, chapt. 384, §§ 1, 3, 7).

‡‡‡ O.S.L. 2000, chapt. 37, §§ 2, 6.

O.S.L. 2004, chapt. 499, §§ 1, 8.

Through O.S.L. 2015, chapt. 338, § 1 (amending 74 O.S. 2011, § 250.4), the Legislature decoupled the executive office and judicial salaries commencing with the terms beginning in 2019. SB 549 set the salary for any term beginning after 2016. For the 2019-2023 term the salary will be $124,373.

Appendix J

Candidates' Campaign Expenditures 1910-2014

Primary and runoff elections 1910-1966

Year	Candidate	Expenses	Year	Candidate	Expenses
1910	E. D. Cameron (D)	1,428.79	1934	John Vaughan (D)	1,015.82
	R. H. Wilson (D)	1,454.34*†		John Murray (D)	1,110.00
	J. E. Dyche (R)	82.85		Tivis Nelson (D)	212.08
	John Paul Evans (R)	421.33*		Clay Kerr (D)	1,332.00
	G. D. Moss (R)	225.81		Jack Cannon (D)	854.00
	S. R. Smith (S)	n/a		Roy Welton (D)	746.81
	Total	**3,613.07**		Jenella Jones (R)	F/R
				Thomas J. Briggs (R)	F/R
1914	Clinton Allen (D)	793.32		John C. Burns (R)**	5.00*
	R. H. Wilson (D)	1,460.92*†		**Subtotal**	**5,340.71**
	G. G. Vannest (R)	1,790.00			
	J. O. Welday (S)	n/a	1934	Democratic runoff	
	C. H. Parrick (P)	n/a		John Vaughan	199.11*†
	Total	**4,044.24**		John Murray	255.00
				Subtotal	**454.11**
1918	George Wilson (D)	1,480.10		**Total**	**5,794.82**
	Charles Briles (D)	Withdrew			
	R. H. Wilson (D)	1,481.50*†	1938	A. L. Crable (D)††	1,478.19*†
	J. N. Hamilton (R)	n/a		R. M. McCool (D)	725.00
	Total	**2,961.60**		J. C. White (D)	.53
				Geen Gilmour (R)	.60
1922	M. A. Nash (D)	1,243.90*†		M. A. Nelson (P)	2.50
	J. P. Battenburg (D)	1,168.58		**Total**	**2,206.82**
	G. D. Moss (R)	12.00*			
	Horace F. Dowell (R)	276.75	1942	Earl Fisher (D)	1,143.21
	Otis McCord (R)	102.95		A. L. Crable (D)	1,494.53*†
	Ralph Records (R)	367.50		M. R. Floyd (R)	…
	C. N. Peak (R)	115.10		**Total**	**2,637.74**
	Total	**3,286.78**			
			1946	Andrew Brock (D)	F/R
1926	Isaac Choate (R)	.59		H. G. Creekmore (D)	F/R
	Anna Willis (R)	.95*		David Crockett (D)	911.70
	William Ingle (R)	10.00		Russell Grow (D)	803.00
	Mary Munson (R)	<25.00		Oliver Hodge (D)	1,079.00
	M. A. Nash (D)	196.85†		A. L. Crable (D)	1,423.64
	Total	**233.39**		Martin B. Nelson (R)	…
				Subtotal	**4,216.63**
1930	Charles Evans (D)	1,200.00	1946	Democratic runoff	
	John Vaughan (D)	1,094.51*†		Oliver Hodge	837.70*†
	Edson Price (R)	1.02		A. L Crable	1,486.40
	Total	**2,295.53**		**Subtotal**	**2,324.10**
				Total	**6,540.73**

Oklahoma's Chief of Public Instruction / 401

Year	Candidate		Year	Candidate	
1950	Oliver Hodge	Unopposed	1962	Oliver Hodge	Unopposed
1954	Oliver Hodge	Unopposed	1966	Oliver Hodge	Unopposed
1958	Oliver Hodge	No primary			

All elections 1970-2014

Year	Candidate	Expenses	Year	Candidate	Expenses
1970	Leslie Fisher (D)	52,140.16*†	2002	Sandy Garrett (D)	458,746.98†
	Charles Holleyman (D)	15,308.96		Lloyd Roettger (R)	86,881.32
	Scott Tuxhorn (R)	19,709.39		**Total**	**545,628.30**
	Total	**87,158.51**			
			2006	Sandy Garrett (D)	375,617.44†
1974	Leslie Fisher (D)	Unopposed		Bill Crozier (R)	600.00
				Total	**376,217.44**
1978	Leslie Fisher (D)	Unopposed			
			2010	Janet Barresi (R)	1,223,232.80*†
1982	Leslie Fisher (D)	n/a		Brian Kelly (R)	8,349.99
	Charles Sandmann (R)	-0-		Susan Paddack (D)	852,661.00*
	Total	**n/a**		Jerry Combrink (D)	4,962.68
				Richard Cooper (I)	3,249.02
1986	John Folks (D)	80,000.00		**Total**	**2,092,455.49**
	David Evans (R)	n/a			
	Total	**80,000.00**	2014[17]	John Cox (D)	460,159.62
				Freda Deskin (D)	95,547.07
1990	Sandy Garrett (D)	247,626.27*†		Jack Herron (D)	24,225.21
	David Fisher (D)	67,815.99		Ivan Holmes (D)	13,696.22
	Gerald Hoeltzel (R)	14,817.90		Janet Barresi (R)	1,544,745.58
	Total	**330,260.16**		Joy Hofmeister (R)‡	818,932.06*†
				Brian Kelly (R)	F/R
1994	Sandy Garrett (D)	202,883.28*†		**Total**	**3,157,305.76**
	Earl Garrison (D)	8,930.05			
	Linda Murphy (R)	63,491.97	2014	Democratic runoff	
	Total	**275,305.30**		John Cox*	
				Freda Deskin	
1998	Sandy Garrett (D)	421,834.63†			
	Linda Murphy (R)	30,132.52*			
	Tod Williams (R)	1,040.79			
	Total	**453,007.94**			

Sources:

1910 Primary election report, Box 1, F 15, 24-4-1, Election Board Filings and Campaign Expenses, OSA, ODL, OK
1914 Primary election report, Box 3, F 19
1918 Primary election report, Box 9, F 23
1922 Primary election report, Box 12, F 9
1926 Primary election report, Box 15, F 16
1930 Primary election report, Box 18, F 23
1934 Primary and Democratic runoff election reports, Box 23, F 16

1938 Primary election report, Box 28, F 15

1942 Primary election report, Box 33, F 7

1946 Primary and Democratic runoff election reports, Box 36, F 24

1950-1966 no primary or runoff elections

1970-1990 Primary and general election results are available in the OSA, ODL and the State Election Board at the State Capitol.

1994-2014 Primary, runoff, and general election results are held by the State Ethics Commission at the State Capitol with the records from 2008 to 2014 accessible at www.ok.gov/elections

Notes:

In 1907 the Democrats chose between E. D. Cameron and Robert Knie in a primary election while the Republicans chose between Calvin Ballard and G. D. Moss at their convention. Neither primary nor general election candidates were required to file expenditure reports. From 1910 to 1966 expenditure reports were required only for primary and runoff elections, but some candidates filed reports when unnecessary (Vannest in 1914, Nash in 1922, Price in 1930, and Gilmour in 1938). Two Republican in 1934, two Democrats in 1946, and one Democrat in 2014 failed to report their expenditures. All candidates from 1970 to 2014 were required to file expenditure reports for all elections.

From 1908 to 1930 elections were determined by pluralities rather than by majorities. In several election cycles the "winner" received fewer than half of the votes (as low as 24.8 percent in the Republican primary of 1922).

The totals for the elections of 1970, 1990, 1994, 2010, and 2014 include Democratic primaries, and totals in 1998, 2010, and 2014 include Republican primaries. A Democratic run off occurred in 2014.

Neither the State Election Board nor the State Ethics Commission can locate the donation and expenditure reports for the 1982 and 1986 election cycles. It is assumed these records are not extant. Most probably Fisher spent only a small amount given Sandmann did not campaign at all. The same can be said for Evans who quickly announced after filing that he would not campaign for the office. Folks, on the other hand spent in excess of an estimated $80,000.

Expenditures of all candidates:
    1910-1968 primary and runoff election $33,614.72
    1970-2014 all elections $7,297,328.90
    Total $7,330,943.62

* Primary/runoff winner

** Won the primary with 62% of the vote

† General election winner

†† Won the primary with 52% of the vote

‡ Won the primary with 57.6% of the vote

Appendix K

School Age Population, Enrollment, Number of Teachers, State Population, and Number of School Districts for Select Years 1891-2014

Year	School age population	Enrollment	No. of teachers	Total state population	No. of school districts
1891	21,335	9,395	438	61,832	n/a
1901	145,843	116,971	2,503	297,075	n/a
1908	497,211	297,075	8,736	1,414,177	5,656
1914	557,004	496,908	12,390	1,657,155	5,880
2014	...	675,534	52,395	3,878,000	517

Sources: *Fourth Biennial Report of the State Department of Education 1912* (Guthrie: State of Oklahoma, 1912), 226; *Eighth Biennial Report of the State Superintendent of Public Instruction 1920* (OKC: Allied, 1920), 5.; *Twenty-Second Biennial Report of the State Department of Education of Oklahoma* (Guthrie: Co-operative, 1948), 1; Census data for 1910, www2.census.gov/prod2/decennial/documents/06229686v32-37ch5.pdf; *2013-2014 Annual Report: Statistical Report on Oklahoma Schools and the State Department of Education* (OKC: SDE, 2104), 3, 5, https://sde.ok.gov; www.google.com/search (the Population of Oklahoma 2014).

Notes: The number of districts for 1891 and 1901 and the school age population for 2014 were unlisted.

Appendix L

Number of Districts and Teachers 1907-2014

Year	Districts	Teachers	Year	Districts	Teachers	Year	Districts	Teachers
1907-08	5,656*	6,386**	1943-44	4,448	17,272	1979-80	619	37,751
1908-09	n/a	8,736†	1944-45	n/a	16,931	1980-81	618	38,464
1909-10	5,725	8,315	1945-46	4,416††	17,863	1981-82	616	38,894
1910-11	5,820	9,215	1946-47	4,450	18,312	1982-83	616	39,901
1911-12	n/a	10,282	1947-48	2,664‡	18,097	1983-84	615	39,950
1912-13	5,861	10,779	1948-49	2,338	18,447	1984-85	615	39,903
1913-14	5,880	11,876	1949-50	2,332	18,885	1985-86	613	40,889
1914-15	5,845‡‡	12,390	1950-51	2,177	19,244	1986-87	613	39,653
1915-16	5,843	12,721	1951-52	2,100	19,477	1987-88	611	39,281
1916-17	5,838	13,565	1952-53	1,989	19,411	1988-89	609	40,052
1917-18	5,752	14,204	1953-54	1,888	19,695	1989-90	604	40,649
1918-19	5,716	14,727	1954-55	1,802	20,075	1990-91	578	42,034
1919-20	n/a	15,711	1955-56	1,738	20,512	1991-92	569	44,164
1920-21	5,414	16,611	1956-57	1,643	20,683	1992-93	554	45,123
1921-22	n/a	17,274	1957-58	1,468	20,698	1993-94	551	45,949
1922-23	5,190	17,988	1958-59	1,372	20,858	1994-95	550	46,630
1923-24	5,159	18,404	1959-60	1,322	21,530	1995-96	549	46,558
1924-25	5,142	18,390	1960-61	1,274	21,983	1996-97	549	46,882
1925-26	5,103	18,393	1961-62	1,232	22,466	1997-98	547	47,655
1926-27	5,078	18,813	1962-63	1,180	23,026	1998-99	547	48,659
1927-28	5,024	19,130	1963-64	1,160	23,687	1999-00	544	49,607
1928-29	4,978	19,565	1964-65	1,118	24,377	2000-01	544	49,920
1929-30	4,933	20,146	1965-66	1,049	25,380	2001-02	543	50,536
1930-31	4,869	19,978	1966-67	998	27,062	2002-03	541	49,346
1931-32	4,836	19,842	1967-68	940	27,979	2003-04	541	48,042
1932-33	4,825	19,510	1968-69	705	28,567	2004-05	540	56,536
1933-34	4,816	19,300	1969-70	664	29,355	2005-06	540	58,310
1934-35	4,791	19,617	1970-71	646	30,272	2006-07	540	59,592
1935-36	4,760	19,858	1971-72	644	31,231	2007-08	539	52,008
1936-37	4,738	20,459	1972-73	637	31,186	2008-09	533	52,167
1937-38	4,697	20,874	1973-74	634	32,191	2009-10	527	52,901
1938-39	4,646	20,938	1974-75	628	32,861	2010-11	524	51,388
1939-40	4,644	20,980	1975-76	624	33,738	2011-12	522	51,719
1940-41	n/a	20,276	1976-77	623	34,577	2012-13	520	52,380
1941-42	4,518	19,391	1977-78	622	35,510	2013-14	517	52,395
1942-43	n/a	18,084	1978-79	620	36,551			

Sources: For the years 1907-08 to 1959-60 see *The Twenty-Eighth Biennial Report of the State Department of Education of Oklahoma* (OKC: SBE, 1960), 370-72. For the years 1962-2014, see the biennial reports of 1962, 1964, 1966, and 1968 and annual reports thereafter. Data are unavailable for the years showing no data.

* *The Twenty-Second Biennial Report of the State Department of Education of Oklahoma* (Guthrie: Co-operative, 1948), 1. This *Report* states: "In 1908 when the work of setting up school districts in the new state was complete, we found ourselves with 5656 school districts." Creating school districts was apparently not complete until 1913-14 when the largest number is recorded.

** *Second Biennial Report, Department of Public Instruction* (Guthrie: NA, 1908), 132-33. Includes actual number of teachers in twenty-six counties of the former O. T. and an estimate of the number in the former I. T. *Twenty-Second Biennial Report of the State Department of Education,* 370 does not include any data for 1907-08 and 1908-09.

†The *Twenty-Second Biennial Report* also states the number of teachers in 1908 to be 8,091. Given the rapid expansion of the state's responsibilities in the former I. T., it is not surprising to find discrepancies in statistics.

†† *The Twenty-First Biennial Report of the State Department of Education of Oklahoma* (Guthrie: Co-operative Publishing Co., 1946), 242. The total is stated as the number of districts reporting scholastic enumeration September 1, 1946.

‡ Of the 1,786 eliminated, 1,105 had no enrolled students. Another 438 were annexed by the county superintendents under the provision of SB 5 of the 1943 Legislature, leaving only 243 to be consolidated or annexed by the districts' patrons.

‡‡ *The Sixth Biennial Report of the State Superintendent of Public Instruction together with the Third Report of the State Board of Education* (OKC: SBE, 1916), 20.

Appendix M

ADA, Number of Teachers, Department FTE, Number of Districts, and Department Expenditures 1970-2014

School Year	ADA	Teachers/ admin.	FTE	No. of dist. K-8	K-12	Total	Expenditures* State	Federal	Total
71/72	566,857	31,231	273	187	457	644	2,276,256	1,324,256	3,600,512
72/73	558,034	31,186	263	181	456	637	2,335,671	1,775,377	4,111,048
73/74	549,061	32,191	287	178	456	634	2,469,671	1,773,053	4,667,651
74/75	548,337	32,861	311	173	455	628	3,276,900	2,553,149	5,830,049
75/76	548,538	33,738	301	168	456	624	3,269,350	2,222,657	5,492,007
76/77	547,990	34,577	311	166	457	623	3,642,866	2,922,644	6,565,510
77/78	544,539	35,510	359	165	457	622	4,148,576	3,211,383	7,359,958
78/79	540,288	36,551	386	163	457	620	5,110,982	3,419,372	8,530,355
79/80	538,454	37,751	433	162	457	619	5,974,660	4,597,063	10,571,723
80/81	542,701	38,464	492	161	457	618	9,684,253	4,760,517	14,444,770
81/82	547,385	38,894	578	159	457	616	13,898,863	4,320,577	18,219,440
82/83	556,115	39,901	565	159	457	616	15,961,763	4,012,006	19,973,768**
83/84	553,237	39,950	587	158	457	615	16,326,681	3,642,089	19,968,769
84/85	552,857	39,903	564	156	457	613	15,853,794	4,389,017	20,242,811
85/86	553,365	40,889	560	156	457	613	17,614,347	4,707,534	22,321,881
86/87	550,949	39,653	547	156	456	612	15,427,450	4,413,034	20,858,856***
87/88	547,149	39,281	552	155	455	610	17,068,074	4,711,657	22,374,904
88/89	542,693	40,052	553	154	455	609	18,485,326	5,549,614	24,577,767
89/90	543,170	40,659	535	152	452	604	18,420,930	6,577,824	25,970,275
90/91	548,387	42,034	513	136	442	578	n/a†	n/a†	29,107,027
91/92	556,609	44,164	486	131	438	569	n/a	n/a	30,711,925
92/93	560,744	45,123	496	120	434	554	n/a	n/a	32,214,732
93/94	565,489	45,949	482	118	433	551	n/a	n/a	33,648,444
94/95	570,358	46,630	482	117	433	550	n/a	n/a	34,303,287
95/96	574,440	46,558	471	116	433	549	n/a	n/a	35,984,173
96/97	580,572	46,882	471	116	433	549	n/a	n/a	40,962,910
97/98	582,459	47,655	475	116	431	547	n/a	n/a	40,853,902
98/99	586,310	48,659	486	116	431	547	n/a	n/a	43,610,624
99/00	586,266	49,607	474	114	430	544	n/a	n/a	45,506,000
00/01	580,744	49,920	476	113	431	544	n/a	n/a	46,135,000
01/02	580,796	50,536	476	112	431	543	n/a	n/a	54,262,000
02/03	581,767	49,346	462	111	430	541	n/a	n/a	56,629,000
03/04	583,933	48,042	338	111	430	541	n/a	n/a	63,329,000
04/05	599,297	56,536	341	111	429	540	n/a	n/a	59,577,000
05/06	591,486	58,310	357††	111	429	540	n/a	n/a	60,580,000

School Year	ADA	Teachers/ admin.	FTE	No. of dist. K-8	K-12	Total	Expenditures* State	Federal	Total
06/07	596,172	59,592	370	111	429	540	18,571,330	33,432,689	52,004,019†††
07/08	596,450	52,008	375	112	427	539	19,220,300	39,401,375	58,621,675
08/09	603,410	52,167	370	107	426	533	26,586,961	37,544,601	64,131,562
09/10	610,019	52,901	368	103	424	527	23,834,793	44,472,570	68,307,364
10/11	616,775	51,388	329	103	421	524	23,198,326	52,768,074	75,966,400
11/12	624,410	51,719	284	102	420	522	21,471,858	46,179,697	67,651,555
12/13	630,766	52,380	289	101	419	520	24,363,867	34,815,888	59,179,755
13/14	639,376	52,396	297	98	419	517	27,826,521	38,158,619	65,985,140

Sources: ADA and teachers/administrators were from the *2013-2014 Annual Report: Statistical Report on Oklahoma Schools and the State Department of Education*, accessed at https://sde.ok.gov. FTE were from the annual reports from the Department for the years 1971-72 to 1989-90 and *Executive Budget Historical Document* (vol. 2) of the governors for fiscal years ending June 30, 1990 to June 30, 2015. The number of districts for 1971-72 to 2007-08 are reported in the *Annual Report: Statistical Report on Oklahoma Schools and the State Department of Education*, Box 16, Oklahoma Documents Collection, OSA, ODL, OKC and for 2009 to 2014 in the *Annual Report: Statistical Reports on Oklahoma Schools and the State Department of Education*. https://sde.ok.gov.

*From 1971-72 to 1982-83 the annual reports were one volume only and included the two primary sources of Department monies: state appropriations and federal sources.

**Beginning in FY 83 and continuing to FY 90 the Department published its Agency and Support Expenditures in its annual report, volume 1 of three volumes, and added a third category, state revolving (not included here). For example, FY 89 the state revolving funds were $542,828 and, if added to the other two categories, results in the total of $24,577,767. FY 90 total includes state revolving funds also.

***The numbers reported by the Department and the *Governor's Executive Budget* for 86-87 to 89-90 are discrepant with the Department typically reporting approximately $1,000,000 less than the Governor's Executive Budget.

†Department Annual Reports beginning with FY 91 discontinued including the Department's Agency and Support Expenditures, thus the numbers for FY 91 to FY 06 were determined by summing the various categories as displayed in the *Governors' Executive Budgets Historical Data* for those years. The *Executive Budget* books were accessed at the Oklahoma Publication Clearing House (750.6), ODL OKC, for FY 91 to FY 06. Only the total expenditures are reported here.

††This number is extrapolated from using the numbers from the five years before and after and matching with the positions listed in the *Oklahoma Directory of Education*. The FTE for fiscal year 06 is not reported in the FY-2008 *Executive Budget Historical Data* document as would be expected, and the *FY-2009 Executive Budget Historical Data* document was missing from the State Documents Collection.

†††State appropriations (including revolving funds) amount and federal programs amount were summed for a total Department expenditure for employee compensation, travel, supplies, equipment, and contractual expenses. The Department provided this data to this author through an Open Records Request, October 9, 2019.

Appendix N

Superintendent Participation on Agencies, Boards, Commissions, and Committees 1890-2015

The Superintendent (or his/her designee) serves by constitutional and statutory authority on numerous agencies, boards, commissions, and committees, and thus is able to affect their direction and influence. Most are listed below alphabetically from the territorial period to 2014. Abbreviations and uppercase lettering used in this listing of those entities (except where there is a direct quotation) are:

Board—State Board of Education and Territorial Board of Education

Government Printing Office—GPO

Superintendent—superintendent of public instruction during the territorial period and statehood

OSU—Oklahoma State University (initially Oklahoma A&M College)

OU—University of Oklahoma

AD VALOREM TASK FORCE, 68 O.S. 2946.1

The Ad Valorem Task Force, created in 1989 (S.L. 1989, chapt. 321, § 23), was to be terminated as of July 1, 1939. Membership included: state auditor and inspector, director of the Ad Valorem Division of the Oklahoma Tax Commission, director of the OSU Center for Local Government Technology, Superintendent, president of the County Assessor's Association of Oklahoma, and six other members.

The Ad Valorem Task Force was abolished in 1993 and the Ad Valorem Transition Oversight Committee was created with the same membership as before. It was to be terminated as of January 1, 1995.

Participation: 1989-1995

ADVISORY BOARD TO THE COMMISSIONERS OF NARCOTICS AND DANGEROUS DRUGS CONTROL/ ADVISORY COUNCIL ON ALCOHOL AND DRUG ABUSE/OKLAHOMA DRUG AND ALCOHOL ABUSE ADVISORY BOARD, 63 O.S. 1971, § 2-104; S.L. 1983, c. 145, § 4; S.L. 1989, c. 116, §§ 1-5; 74 O.S. 1991, §§ 30-3,4

The Advisory Board to the Commissioners of Narcotics and Dangerous Drugs Control was established by S.L. 1971, chapt. 119, § 2-104 to assist and advise the Commissioner in carrying out the duties of his office. Ten members or designees including the Superintendent were named. These provisions were repealed in 1983 (S.L. 1983, chapt. 145, § 4) and replaced by a law requiring seven members (no *ex-officio* members) appointed by the governor.

Session Laws 1991, chapt. 121, § 3, amended S.L. 1989, chapt. 116, §§ 1-5 to provide for a board to be comprised of the governor and his/her designee, attorney general, director of the Oklahoma State Bureau of Investigation, commissioner of public safety, commissioner of the Department of Mental Health and Substance Abuse Services, commissioner of health, Superintendent, and eight others.

The Advisory Board is to meet at least quarterly and has these duties: encourage establishment of a mechanism for the exchange of information and ideas among the missions and efforts to fight drug and alcohol abuse, encourage public and private institutions to create uniform drug policies, create a structure to fight drug and alcohol abuse, etc.

Participation: 1971 to 1983 present, either the Superintendent or his designee was a member; 1983 to present, member

AGRICULTURAL AND INDUSTRIAL EDUCATION (COMMISSION OF), Chapt. 2, Art. VI, O.S. 1908, §§ 298-310, effective May 20, 1908

Membership: Superintendent, chair; president of the State Board of Agriculture; president of A&M College

The commission was to carry out the requirements of the state constitution relating to the teaching of the elements of agriculture, horticulture, stock feeding, and domestic science in the common schools. The commission was to report to the governor at least thirty days prior to the regular sessions of the legislature including the work done and a complete account of all funds and their disbursement. It was to cooperate with all normal schools, the agricultural and mechanical colleges, and the state board of agriculture. The duties of the Superintendent: investigate and determine the character, extent and costs of courses of instruction in the branches provided for in this act; through bulletins and public addresses give information to school boards and communities as to the courses and character of instruction which have proved most satisfactory and best adapted to various schools; to give information where the best trained teachers may be found; formulate and recommend plans for the organization of training and normal schools for the preparation of teachers of said subjects; seek to awaken an active interest among teachers in the subjects and public sentiment to the importance of the teaching of said subjects; and develop the examinations and the grading of the exams for students who wanted to enter the A&M College. (S.L. 1919, chapt. 8, § 10) He was to have the A&M College publish a textbook on agriculture and allied subjects, have a publishing company print it, make it available to the state, and at no cost to the state.

Participation: 1908-1922, chair

APPORTIONMENT COMMISSION, Oklahoma Constitution, Art. V:IIA

If the legislature fails to reapportion following a Federal decennial census or fails to do it according to the time frame or proper process, then such apportionment is to be accomplished by an apportionment commission composed of the attorney general, Superintendent, and the state treasurer. This constitutional amendment was adopted November 2, 1976, through Legislative Referendum 218, State Question 523.

Participation: 1976 to present, member

BANKING BOARD (TERRITORIAL), S.L. 1897, chapt. 4, §§ 1, 47

"The Governor, Secretary, Treasurer, Auditor, and Attorney General of this Territory shall be, and they are, hereby made a Board which shall be designated and known as the Territorial Banking Board of which the Governor shall be president, the Auditor shall be Vice-president...."

"The Territorial Banking Board shall have power to make such rules, and establish such regulations for the government of the banks of this Territory, as in their judgment seem wise and expedient...."

Participation: 1897-1907, member (Territorial Superintendent was *ex officio* territorial auditor and thus served on this board.)

BOARD FOR LEASING SCHOOL LAND (See COMMISSIONERS OF THE LAND OFFICE)

BOARD OF CONTROL FOR MILITARY TRAINING SCHOOLS

The Superintendent was one of five members with duties to arrange contests in military drill and athletics among the high schools that provided military and athletic training. These contests were to be maintained by fees collected from the schools (S.L. 1917, chapt. 246, p. 454, § 3). (*Directory of Oklahoma, 1921*, 44) The law was repealed by 70 O.S. 1949, p. 607, article 20, § 9.

Participation: gubernatorial appointee 1917 and afterward

BOARD OF EDUCATION OF NORMAL SCHOOL FOR THE TERRITORY OF OKLAHOMA

The board to control the Normal School at Edmond and any subsequent normal schools was established through O.S. 1890, chapt. 57, §§ 3718, 3726.

§ 3718 "Said Board of Education shall consist of five members, three of whom shall be appointed by the Governor and by and with the consent of the Legislative Council if in session, one of whom shall hold his office for six years, another for four years, and another for two years…The Treasurer and Superintendent of Instruction shall by virtue of their offices be members of said Board...."

§ 3726 "The Board of Education shall hold four regular meetings in each year."

Participation: 1890-1907, member of the Board and could have been elected president

BOARD OF EDUCATION OF NORMAL SCHOOLS/TEACHERS COLLEGES

The statutes for the Territorial Board of Education of Normal School were carried forward into statehood and are found verbatim in Art. III, chapt. 74 of the Oklahoma Statutes of 1908 (§§ 6532, 6544). This Board functioned until 1911 when it was folded into the Board.

S.L. 1911, chapt. 47, § 2, p. 121. The Board was reconstituted to include many of the previous institutional boards including the "Board of Education now in control of the State Normal Schools…"

S.L. 1939, chapt. 34, §§ 1,3, p. 201. A separate board was created to consist of seven members appointed by the Governor. The Superintendent was not one of the seven. This Board of Regents of Oklahoma Colleges was to succeed the Board in the management and control of the normal schools and the Colored A&M University.

S.L. 1943, Title 70, chapt. 26a, p. 211. The Board of Regents of Oklahoma Colleges was abolished and the supervision management, and control were vested in the Board.

Oklahoma Constitution, Art. XIII-B (State Question 328, adopted at primary election, July 6, 1948.) and S.L. 1949, §§ 2, 4, pp. 799-800. This act vitalized the provisions of the constitutional amendment, "The Board of Regents of Oklahoma Colleges shall succeed the State Board of Education in the management and control…" These provisions remain in effect today relative to the participation of the Superintendent.

Participation:

1907-1911	member of the Board of Education of Normal Schools (could have been elected president)
1911-1939	president of the Board with responsibility for Normal Schools/Teachers Colleges
1939-1943	Board of Regents of Oklahoma Colleges (Superintendent was not a member)
1943-1949	president of the Board (Board of Regents was abolished and control shifted to the Board)
1949-Present	member of the Board of Regents of Oklahoma Colleges (has nine members including the Superintendent who can be elected president)

Changed to **REGIONAL UNIVERSITY SYSTEM OF OKLAHOMA (RUSO)** July 1, 2006

BOARD OF EDUCATION (STATE), Constitution of Oklahoma, 1907, Art. XIII, Section 6

"The supervision of instruction in the public schools shall be vested in a Board of Education, whose powers and duties shall be prescribed by law. The Superintendent of Public Instruction shall be President of the Board. Until otherwise provided by law, the Governor, Secretary of State, and the Attorney General shall be ex-officio members, and with the Superintendent, compose said Board of Education."

"The State Board of Education shall consist of seven members, including the State Superintendent of Public Instruction, who shall be the president, and six members appointed by the Governor by and with the advice and consent of the Senate for a period of six years, except as hereinafter provided…." Two of the six had to be practical schoolmen who shall have had at least four years' experience in actual school work with two of the years in Oklahoma. (O.S. 1911, chapt. 47, § 1)

Over the years other modifications have been made to include representation from Congressional districts. In 2011 the legislature revised the law to require Board members to resign when there is a change in governors so that the new governor can appoint a new Board.

Participation: 1907-present, member and president/chairperson

BOARD OF EDUCATION (TERRITORIAL), Statutes of Oklahoma, 1890, Art. 3, § 6369

"The Territorial Superintendent and the county superintendents of the Territory comprised the Territorial Board. Board members' terms were two years." The first meeting was held January 14, 1891 with the territorial Superintendent and superintendents from six counties. Obviously, as counties formed quickly, Board membership grew to be problematic. The legislature changed membership composition to include the Superintendent; president, Territorial School at Edmond; president, OU; and one district and one county superintendent appointed by the governor. (Statutes of Oklahoma 1893, chapt. 73, Art. 10, § 1)

Participation: 1890-1907, member and secretary most of the time

BOARD OF EQUALIZATION, Oklahoma Constitution, Art. X, Section 21, 68 O.S. 2864

The Board of Equalization was created by legislation (Statutes of Oklahoma, 1890, chapt. 79, § 1) in 1890 and the membership included the Auditor/Superintendent. Membership did not change until statehood when the auditor/superintendent position was split into two positions and the Superintendent was dropped from the board (Oklahoma Constitution, Art. X, Section 21). Thus, the Board of Equalization was comprised of the governor, auditor, state secretary, state treasurer, attorney general, state inspector and examiner, and president of the State Board of Agriculture. In 1975 the constitution was amended (State Question 508 effective January 8, 1979) and the legislature added statutory language (S.L., 1979, chapt. 30, § 162) to make the Superintendent a member of the Board.

Participation: 1890-1907, member; 1979-present, member

BOARD OF HEALTH (TERRITORIAL), Oklahoma Statutes 1890, chapt. 9, §§ 1,3, 4.

The Territorial Board of Health was to be the president, vice-president, and superintendent of public health. "The Superintendent of Public Instruction of said Territory shall be *ex-officio* president of said board." This board was to meet as often as once every six months, and there were nine enumerated duties.

S.L. 1903, chapt. V, § 1, 88. The above law was repealed and a new board of three physicians was created.

Participation: 1890-1903, president of the board

BOARD OF PARDONS (STATE)

In his Thirty-Third Special Message to the Legislature (Guthrie, March 30, 1908), Governor Haskell urged the legislature to create a board of pardons to relieve the Governor's Office of the detail consideration of petitions for pardon and parole. The legislature responded (O.S. 1908, c.hapt 18, Art. 14, § 2283): "…said Board consists of the State Superintendent, President of the State Board of Agriculture, and the State Auditor, and shall meet at the office of Secretary of State on the second Monday in each month…The Superintendent of Public Instruction shall be President…."

S.L. 1913, chapt. 217, § 2. The Board of Prison Control was created and was to have three members appointed by the Governor, excluding the Superintendent.

Participation: 1908-1913, president

BOARD OF PRIVATE SCHOOLS (Oklahoma), 70 O.S. 21-102, S.L. 1970, chapt. 65, § 2 (effective 7-1-70)

The Board of Private Schools was created and was to have nine members of whom three are to be the *ex-officio* voting members of the Oklahoma State Accrediting Agency or their designated representatives (Chancellor of Higher Education, Superintendent, and State Director of Career Technical Education). The Board is to issue licenses to private schools that are defined as a privately owned business school, flight school, trade or other school offering resident or correspondence courses in Oklahoma that gives training for a consideration or remuneration. The name was changed to the Oklahoma Board of Private Vocation Schools (S.L. 1986, c.hapt 258, §§ 11-12) and the wording altered to read, "…9 members of whom three shall be the Director of the State Department of Vocational and Technical Education, the Chancellor of the Regents for Higher Education, and the State Superintendent of Public Instruction or their designated representatives."

Participation: 1970- present, member

BOARD OF RAILROAD ASSESSORS (Territorial), S.L. of Oklahoma 1895, chapt. 43, § 2.

The territorial auditor/superintendent was a member of this board that had the responsibility for overseeing the assessment of the railroads of the Territory. At statehood the state auditor continued on the board (Oklahoma Statutes 1908, chapt. 72, Art. IV, § 6111).

Participation: 1895-1907, member as *ex officio* auditor

BOARD OF REGENTS OF COLORED AGRICULTURAL AND NORMAL UNIVERSITY/LANGSTON UNIVERSITY, S.L. 1897, p. 37

"Said Board shall consist of the State (sic) Superintendent of Public Instruction, Treasurer, and three other…

Members shall elect the president and secretary." A minor modification was added in the appointment process and the duties were specified in 1907 (Oklahoma Statutes 1907, c. 74, Art. V, §§ 6381-6383). The board was to consist of the Superintendent, state treasurer and three others to be appointed by the governor by and with the advice of the Senate. Duties included appointing a president of the institution and assistants to take charge and fix the salaries of each. They were to "...prescribe the various books and make and prescribe such laws as may be necessary for the good government and management of the same." Rules and regulations for the admission of students were to be ordained. At least four meetings were to be held each year and the president of the board had to submit a full and complete report of the results of the school. Begun during the Territorial period, this board continued until it was subsumed under the Board in 1911 (S.L. 1911, chapt. 47, § 2). Eight years later (S.L. 1919, chapt. 303, §§ 1-2) the legislature reconstituted the Board of Regents: five members with four appointed by the governor and the fifth to be the Superintendent who was to be the chair of the board. For twenty years this arrangement existed and, in 1939, the Board of Regents of the Colored Agricultural and Normal University ceased to exist. Legislation effective April 27, 1938 (S.L., 1939, chapt. 34, Art. 19) assigned supervision of this institution to the newly reorganized Board of Regents of Oklahoma Colleges. This new board did not include the Superintendent. In 1943 Langston was moved under the State Board of Agriculture when the Board of Regents of Oklahoma Colleges was abolished and the supervision of the state colleges was placed under the Board.

Participation: 1897-1911, member and president of the Board; 1919-1939, member and chair of the board

BOARD OF REGENTS OF THE STATE UNIVERSITY (University of Oklahoma)

Established by the legislature (Oklahoma Statutes 1893, § 6145), the board was ten members including the governor. In 1911 the Board of Regents of the State University was subsumed under the Board (S.L. 1911, chapt. 47, § 2, p. 121); thus, the Superintendent presided over the Board responsible for the supervision of OU until 1919 when a new board of regents was formed consisting of seven members appointed by the governor. (S.L. 1919, chapt. 293, p. 423)

Participation: 1911-1919, member and president of the Board

BOARD OF VOCATIONAL EDUCATION (State), 70 O.S. §§ 14-101-103

The State Board of Vocational Education was created in 1917 (S.L. 1917, chapt. 155, p. 245-46) and consisted of these five members: chairman of the Board (Superintendent), the president of the Board of Agriculture, the president of the State University, the president of the Agricultural and Mechanical College, and one member to be appointed by the governor. This board was established as a response to an Act of Congress (P.L. No. 347, 64th Congress), "An Act to provide for the promotion of vocational education; to provide for co-operation with the states in the promotion of such education in agriculture and the trades and industries; to provide for co-operation within the states in the preparation of teachers of vocational subjects; and to appropriate money and regulate its expenditures." The board's duty was to "...cooperate...with the Federal Board for Vocational Education in the administration of the provisions of said act and to do all things necessary to entitle the state to receive the benefits thereof."

Twelve years later (S.L. 1929, chapt. 267, § 1, p. 391) the statute was changed to "The State Board of Education shall include in its functions and duties all the duties now pertaining to the State Board of Vocational Education which functions shall be transferred to and directed and controlled by the State Board of Education, and the State Superintendent is hereby designated as the director of Vocational Education. It shall be the duty of said Board, and it is hereby empowered to cooperate, as provided in and required by the aforesaid Act of Congress, with the Federal Board for Vocational Education in the administration of the provisions of said Act and to do all things necessary to entitle the State to receive the benefits thereof."

After another twelve years (S.L. 1941, Title 70, p. 415), the statute was amended to read, "The State Board of Education is hereby designated as the State Board of Vocational Education. It shall be the duty of said Board '...to designate and fix the salary of a director of Vocational Education, such director to be under the control and authority of said Board.'"

The legislature in 1949 (S.L. 1949, Title 70, Art. 2, 9, p. 523) required the Board to constitute the State Board of Vocational Education and to perform all powers and duties prescribed by law. It had the power and duty to exercise jurisdiction and supervision over vocational education.

Twenty years later the legislature created the State Department of Vocational and Technical Education to be under the control of the State Board of Vocational and Technical Education (S.L. 1969, chapt. 237, § 1, p. 300). The State Board of Vocational Education became an entity of its own the previous year (S.L. 1968, chapt. 183, § 1, p. 280) when legislation was written providing for a separate board. The new board was to succeed to all of the powers and duties invested in the State Board for Vocational Education. Membership on this new board included the Superintendent and the six appointed members of the Board as *ex officio* members plus six members appointed by the governor. The chair of the board was to be the Superintendent while the director of Vocational Education was to serve as an *ex officio* nonvoting member and the Executive Officer of the Board.

The director of the Division of Vocational Education was changed to the director of the Department of Vocational and Technical Education (S.L. 1971, chapt. 281, Art. 14, § 101, p. 692) and the name of the department was changed from the State Department of Vocational and Technical Education to the Oklahoma Department of Vocational and Technical Education (S.L. 1995, chapt. 144, § 1). In 2000 another name change resulted in the Oklahoma Department of Career and Technology Education (2000 O.S.L. sec. 209; 70 O.S. 2001, § 14-101) with nine members to include the Superintendent, two members of the Board *ex officio*, one member of each Congressional district (5) and one member at large.

Participation: 1917-1929, member and chair of the State Board of Vocational Education; 1929-1941, member and chair of the Board; 1941-1968, member and chair of the Board which was also designated as the State Board of Vocational Education; 1968-present, member and chair of the Board and *ex officio* member and chair of the State Board of Career and Technology Education

CHILD GUIDANCE BOARD (Oklahoma), S.L. 1959, Title 11, chapt. 3, p. 34. (effective 7-17-59)

The *ex-officio* board was the Superintendent (chair), dean of the OU College of Medicine, director of Mental Health, director of Public Welfare, and the state Commissioner of Health. The board was to adopt rules for its governance, establish standards for county child guidance clinics, establish standards for employees in these clinics, and determine if need existed to create a county clinic. This statute was repealed (S.L. 1984, chapt. 158, § 2, p. 571). The *Directory of Oklahoma* for the years 1971-1983 stated, "The Board has been inactive since its inception."

Participation: 1959-1984, member and chair

COMMISSION FOR TEACHER PREPARATION (Oklahoma), 70 O.S. 6-178: consolidated with the Office of Educational Quality and Accountability through SB 1797, effective July 1, 2014

The Oklahoma Commission for Teacher Preparation began June 1, 1992, and had twenty-eight members including the Superintendent and the chancellor of the Oklahoma State Regents for Higher Education as *ex officio* members (S.L. 1992, chapt. 308, § 8). The major responsibility was to develop the new teacher preparation system. By 1995 the membership decreased to twenty, and there were four *ex officio* members: Superintendent, chancellor, director of State Department of Vocational-Technical Education, and the Secretary of Education or their designees. The Commission's charge in 1995 was to create a competency-based teacher preparation system.

Pursuant to SB 1797, passed in 2012 and effective July 1, 2014, the Oklahoma Commission for Teacher Preparation was consolidated with the Office of Educational Quality and Accountability. The OCTP serves as Oklahoma's independent standards board for teacher education. The agency assumes three primary responsibilities: the accreditation of teacher education programs, the assessment of teacher candidates, and the ongoing growth and development of classroom teachers.

Participation: 1992 to 2012, member

COMMISSION OF EDUCATIONAL SURVEY (The)

The 1921 legislature authorized this commission and imposed upon it "…the duty of making a comprehensive survey of the public educational system of Oklahoma including all schools and educational institutions supported in whole or in part from public funds to determine the efficiency of same and to report its findings to the Governor before the 1st of September 1922" (*Directory, State of Oklahoma 1921*, 43). The Superintendent, R. H. Wilson, chaired the commission with four other members.

Participation: 1921-1922, member and chair

COMMISSION ON CHILDREN AND YOUTH (OKLAHOMA), 10 O. S. 601.1

The commission was formed as a result of legislation in 1982 (S.L. 1982, chapt. 312, § 1). There were fifteen members initially (now sixteen) including the director of the Department of Human Services, state Commissioner of Health, commissioner of the Department of Mental Health and Substance Abuse Services, Superintendent, and the Chair of SJR 13 Oversight Committee or their designees. The Commission is to hold at least four regular quarterly meetings annually. Duties are to establish and maintain the Office of Planning and Coordination for Services to Children and Youth, establish and maintain the Office of Juvenile System Oversight, receive reports from the Child Death Review Board, designate district and regional planning and coordination areas and district and service coordination among public and private agencies that provide services to youth, prepare and publish reports, etc. Its current mission is to improve services to children by facilitating joint planning and coordination among public and private agencies and to provide independent monitoring of the children and youth service system.

Participation: 1982-present, member *ex officio* or designee

COMMISSION ON SCHOOL AND COUNTY FUNDS MANAGEMENT (OKLAHOMA), 60 O.S. 2016, § 177.2

Membership on this commission (S.L. 1985, chapt. 322, § 44) is the Superintendent, the director of the Oklahoma Department of Career Technology, and the state Bond Advisor. Its duties are to receive requests of school districts and counties for authorization to participate in a short term cash management program where the proceeds will be used to facilitate cash-flow management: process requests and respond accordingly; establish reasonable limits for fees, commissions and other compensation paid to persons or firms involved with the proposed short term cash management program; submit to the house speaker, senate pro tem, and governor by October 15 a report detailing the participation of each school district and county for the prior fiscal year in the short term cash management programs; etc.

Participation: 1985-present, member

COMMISSIONERS OF THE LAND OFFICE, Oklahoma Constitution, Art. VI, § 32

In March 1891, Congress authorized the governor to lease the school lands for a term not to exceed three years.

Report of the Governor of Oklahoma to the Secretary of the Interior, 1896 (Washington: GPO, 1896), 20.

"By an act of Congress approved May 4, 1894, the board for leasing school land, composed of the governor, secretary, and superintendent of public instruction, was created and authorized to proceed with the leasing of these lands under rules and regulations heretofore prescribed by the Secretary of the Interior until such time as the legislative assembly should provide rules and regulations."

Report of the Governor of Oklahoma to the Secretary of the Interior, 1895 (Washington: GPO, 1895), 15.

The School Land Board adopted new rules and regulations governing the leasing of lands May 3, 1899.
Report of the Governor of Oklahoma to the Secretary of the Interior, 1900 (Washington: GPO, 1899), 23.

When the Oklahoma Constitution was written in 1907, article 6, section 32 provided: "The Governor, Secretary of State, State Auditor, Superintendent of Public Instruction, and the President of the State Board of Agriculture shall constitute the Commissioners of the Land Office, who shall have charge of the sale, rental, disposal and managing of the school lands and other public lands of the state, and of the funds and proceeds derived therefrom, under rules and regulations prescribed by the legislature." A constitutional amendment (S.Q. 514, July 22, 1975, effective January 8, 1979) replaced the secretary of state with the lieutenant governor.

Participation: 1894-present, member

COUNCIL OF CHIEF STATE SCHOOL OFFICERS

The CCSSO is a "nonpartisan, nationwide, nonprofit organization of public officials who head departments of elementary and secondary education…it provides leadership, advocacy, and technical assistance on major educational issues. It seeks member consensus on major educational issues…" www.CCSSO.org/who_we_are .html

Participation: The Superintendent has been a member for many years.

CRIPPLED CHILDREN'S COMMISSION, (10 O.S. 1941, § 171.9)

The legislature created this commission (S.L. 1935, chapt. 14, art. 2, § 9, p. 14) with three members: dean of the OU School of Medicine, Oklahoma Commissioner of Health, and the Superintendent. The commission's purpose was to conduct a program of medical care for children who were crippled or who were suffering from conditions leading to crippling. It was to appoint a director who was to be the *ex officio* secretary of the commission and to be the administrator of the department. Through S.L. 1959, Title 10, chapt. 8 all of the Crippled Children's Commission was transferred to the Oklahoma Public Welfare Commission effective July 1, 1959, and the membership was to be all medical personnel.

Participation: 1935-1959, member

DORMITORY BONDS FUNDING COMMISSION, 70 O.S. 1951, § 1946.2 (S.L. 1945, p. 303, § 2)

The commission's membership consisted of five *ex officio* members: governor, attorney general, Superintendent, president of the State Board of Agriculture, and the chancellor of higher education. Its purpose was to issue dormitory funding bonds to take up and replace outstanding bonds against any of the state schools of higher education, subject to restrictions set forth in the law. This commission was dissolved in 1965 (S.L. 1965, chapt. 396, §§ 1309, 741.)

Participation: 1945-1965, member

EDUCATION COMMISSION OF THE STATES, 70 O.S. 2014, § 70-506.1

Within the Compact for Education is the Educational Commission of the States. With S.L. 1967, chapt. 123, § 1, Oklahoma joined the Commission as a party state. Its seven members are the governor, chancellor of the State Regents for Higher Education, the Superintendent, two members of the state legislature, and two members appointed by the governor. The commission has authority to "…collect, correlate, analyze and interpret information and data concerning educational needs and resources; encourage and foster research in all aspects of education, but with special reference to the desirable scope of instruction, organization, administration, and instructional methods and standards employed or suitable for employment in public educational systems; develop proposals for adequate financing of education as a whole and at each of its many levels, etc.

Participation: 1967-present, *ex officio* member

EDUCATION COUNCIL (OKLAHOMA)

The Oklahoma Education Council was formed as part of the legislation establishing Oklahoma's participation in the Compact for Education (1967). The members of the Educational Commission of the States and ten others appointed by the governor made up the council. In 1979 the council was abolished.

Participation: 1967-1979, *ex officio* member

GOVERNOR'S COMMITTEE ON EMPLOYMENT OF THE HANDICAPPED, (74 O.S. 1991, § 9.31)

Founded in 1957 (S.L.1957, § 1, 522) the committee was not to have more than seventy-five members from state leaders of industry, business, agriculture, labor, veterans, women, religious, educational, civic, fraternal, welfare, scientific, medical, and other professions. The committee, which elects its officers, is to assist in the employment of the physically, mentally, emotionally and otherwise handicapped citizens of Oklahoma. In 1980 it was renamed Governor's Advisory Committee on Employment of the Handicapped (S.L. 1980, chapt. 135, §§ 10,

16) and in 1996 renamed once more to Governor's Advisory Committee on Employment of People with Disabilities (S.L. 1996, chapt. 132, § 8).

The Superintendent has never been an *ex officio* member of this board. In 1965 Oliver Hodge was a technical advisor (*Directory of Oklahoma, 1965,* 42) and from 1974 to 1981 Leslie Fisher was a member (*Directory of Oklahoma,* 1973, 1975, 1977, 1979, and 1981).

INDUSTRIAL INSTITUTE AND COLLEGE BOARD OF REGENTS/OKLAHOMA COLLEGE FOR WOMEN

The Institute, known as the Oklahoma Industrial Institute and College for Girls, was to be governed by a Board of Regents consisting of the Superintendent, who was to be the *ex-officio* president of the board. The president of the Board of Agriculture and three others were to be appointed and confirmed by the Senate, two of whom were to be women (Oklahoma Statutes, 1907, chapt. 70, Art. I). The board functioned until March 1911 when it was subsumed under the Board (S.L. 1910-11, chapt. 47). In 1916 the name of the institution became the Oklahoma College for Women (S.L. 1916, 32). After operating under the supervision of the Board for eight years, the legislature created a separate Board of Regents (S.L. 1919, chapt. 295, § 1) consisting of five members with one member being the Superintendent who was to be the chairman, an arrangement that continued until 1965 when the Superintendent was dropped from the board (S.L. 1965, chapt. 510, § 602).

Participation: 1907-1911, member and president of the Board of Regents; 1911-1919, member and president of the Board; 1919-1965, member and president of the Board of Regents of the Oklahoma College for Women

INSTITUTION FOR THE FEEBLE-MINDED (OKLAHOMA)

When it was founded, this Institution had a Board of Managers of five persons including the governor as *ex-officio* chairman (Oklahoma Statutes, 1909, p. 534). In 1911 this board and the institution were subsumed under the reconstituted Board (S.L. 1911, chapt. 47, § 2, p. 121). Eight years later the legislature moved the supervision of the institution under the State Board of Public Affairs (S.L. 1919, chapt. 57, § 1, p. 91).

Participation: 1911-1919, member and president of the Board

INTERDISCIPLINARY COUNCIL ON THE PREVENTION OF JUVENILE SEX OFFENSES, S.L. 1990, p. 1911

The Interdisciplinary Council was created to oversee implementation of a comprehensive approach to prevent sex offenses by juveniles; develop a uniform coding system for juvenile sex offenders; implement a training program for mental health professionals in the assessment and treatment of juvenile sex offenders; oversee the establishment of a continuum of treatment services; support programs for victims of juvenile sex offenses; and to make recommendations to the legislature for funding for statewide needs assessments. Membership is seventeen including the Superintendent or designee.

Participation: 1990-present, member of designee

LIBRARY COMMISSION (OKLAHOMA), S.L. 1919, chapt. 32, pp. 51-53

The Oklahoma Library Commission was established in 1919 to "…give advice to all schools, free, and other public libraries, and to all committees which may propose to establish them, as to the best means of establishing and maintaining such libraries, the selection of books, cataloguing and other details of library management…." The commission was to have five members: the Superintendent and four members appointed by the governor. The duty of the commission "…was to work with and under the supervision of the president of each normal school for lectures on book selection, use and care of books, cataloging and library administration. Rules and regulations for librarians throughout the state were to be promulgated by the State Superintendent…." The commission was to report annually to the legislature.

The legislature in 1953 (S.L. 1953, Title 65, chapt. 2) transferred, "The powers, rights, privileges, duties, responsibilities and authority heretofore exercised by the Oklahoma Library Commission…" to the state librarian. The four appointive members and the Superintendent were to serve as an advisory board to the State Librarian on library extension matters. This arrangement ended in 1965 when the legislature repealed the law providing for the advisory board (S.L. 1965, chapt. 129, p. 151).

Participation: 1919-1953, *ex-officio* member; 1953-1965, *ex-officio* member and chair

LITERACY INITIATIVE COMMISSION, S.L. 1989, chapt. 210, § 2

This commission was created to encourage and assist coordinated efforts by the public agencies, by volunteers, and by the enterprises of the private sector for the improvement of the level of literacy in all parts of the state. Every five years it must be recreated to continue. There are thirty eight members and the secretary of education is the chair.

Participation: 1991-1994 chair while serving as both Superintendent and secretary of education

MINORITY TEACHER RECRUITMENT ADVISORY COMMITTEE, 70 O.S. 6-129.1

Created in 1992 (S.L. 1992, chapt. 324, § 9) and amended in 1995, 1998, and 2004 (S.L. 2004, chapt. 24, § 1) this committee has a membership of nineteen including the Superintendent or a designee. Its purpose is "to work with the Oklahoma State Regents for Higher Education in the interests of recruiting, retaining and placing minority teachers in the public schools of the State of Oklahoma."

Participation: 1992-present, member or designee

OKLAHOMA EDUCATIONAL TELEVISION AUTHORITY, S.L. 1953, p. 552

The OETA was created in 1953 and became an entity May 18. Originally it was to consist of thirteen members: president of OU, Superintendent, chancellor of the Oklahoma State Regents for Higher Education, president of one of the state supported four-year colleges, president of one of the state supported junior colleges, and seven members appointed by the governor by and with the consent of the Senate to serve seven year terms. Now the board of directors numbers twelve. Among the powers of the Authority are to accept, assume and control the television channels assigned by the FCC to Oklahoma for educational purposes and to construct, maintain, repair, and operate TV facilities which with their access connections are designed ultimately to extend and include all sections and areas of Oklahoma.

Participation: 1953-present, member

OKLAHOMA LITERATURE COMMISSION, 21 O.S. 1957, § 1040

This commission was created effective June 6, 1957, and was to include the commissioner of Charities and Corrections (as secretary), the attorney general or his designee, and the Superintendent or his designee. Its duty "…shall make such investigations as may be necessary into sales of literature which it has reason to suspect is detrimental to the morals of the citizens of this State. The Commission shall submit an annual report of its activities to the Governor and to the State Legislative Council." The Commission was to hold hearings and make findings on literature it found to be obscene. Eleven years later the act creating the Commission was repealed by 21 O.S. 1968, § 1040.26.

Participation: June 6, 1957-April 4, 1968

OKLAHOMA PARTNERSHIP FOR SCHOOL READINESS FOUNDATION, 10 O.S, 2003, § 640.1A

The OPSRF is a non-profit 501(3)(c) organization established in 2003 to support Smart Start Oklahoma through the use of private funds. It works in partnership with fifteen state agencies, private citizens, etc. to ensure children are healthy and ready for school. The mission is to lead Oklahoma in coordinating an early childhood system focused on strengthening families and school readiness. The OPSR is Oklahoma's early childhood advisory council. In 2015 the OPSR board adopted a new, innovative structure: using affinity groups to address legislative changes—people representing perspective of state agencies responsible for administering state and federally funded early childhood programs/services. www.smartstartok.org; www.opsrfoundation.org.

Participation: The Superintendent became a member of one of the "affinity groups" in May 2015.

PROFESSIONAL STANDARDS BOARD, S.L. 1971, chapt. 281, § 6-123

The Professional Standards Board (PSB) was created "to provide leadership for the improvement of teacher education and standards for the certification of teachers and other educational personnel in Oklahoma and shall serve in an advisory capacity to the State Board of Education in all matters of professional standards and certification.…" The original board had twenty-six members including the Superintendent, the chancellor of higher education, executive secretary of the Oklahoma Education Association, the director of teacher education and certification in the State Department and other members. The educator members were to be appointed by the Board from a list of nominees from the teaching profession while the non-educator members were to be appointed by the Board.

In 1991 the PSB was renamed the Educational Professional Standards Board and the Superintendent or designee was to be one of the nineteen members (S.L. 1991, chapt. 67, § 7). The legislature changed its mind in 1992 and repealed the above law (S.L. 1992, chapt. 308, § 15) effective July 1, 1995.

Participation: 1971-1991, member; 1991-1995, member or designee

REGENTS *EX-OFFICIO* OF THE OKLAHOMA SCHOOL FOR THE BLIND

Oklahoma Statutes, 1908, chapt. 67, § 5801 provided an appropriation for the temporary school for the blind that had been established during territorial days. At statehood, supervision was vested in the Board comprised of the governor, secretary of state, attorney general, and Superintendent (*Oklahoma Educational Directory 1909-1910* shows that the governing board, Regents *Ex-officio*, was the Board.). Supervision was placed under the Board in 1911 when it was reconstituted (S.L. 1911, chapt. 47, p. 121). From 1911-1965 the School for the Blind was under the control of the Board. In 1965 jurisdiction was transferred to the Oklahoma Public Welfare Commission (S.L. 1965, chapt. 193, p. 339).

Participation: 1907-1911, member of the Board; 1911-1965, member and president of the Board

REGENTS FOR THE OKLAHOMA SCHOOL FOR THE DEAF

Chapter 70, Art. II, of the Oklahoma Statutes 1907 provided: "The government and management of the Oklahoma School for Deaf shall be vested in a board of control, to consist of the State Superintendent of Public Instruction, and three trustees to be appointed by the Governor and confirmed by the Senate...." This board was to select its president and to hold quarterly or oftener if necessary meetings at the school. In 1911 it was subsumed under the reconstituted Board (S.L. 1911, chapt. 47, § 2). The governance status did not change until 1965 (S.L. 1965, chapt. 193, p. 339) when jurisdiction was transferred to the Oklahoma Public Welfare Commission.

Participation: 1907-1911, member of the board of trustees; 1911-1965, member and president of the Board

SCHOOL LAND COMMISSION (See Commissioners of the Land Office)

SCHOOL OF MINES (MIAMI), governing board, S.L. 1919, chapt. 75, p. 117

When the Miami School of Mines was created, effective March 17, 1919, management was vested in the Board. Eighteen days later (S.L. 1919, chapt. 302, p. 439) the legislature changed the earlier decision and vested governance of the institution in a board of regents consisting of five members, four to be appointed by the governor and one to be the Superintendent who was to be chairman of the Board of Regents. Control shifted to the Board of Regents of Oklahoma Colleges in 1939 (S.L. 1939, chapt. 34, Art. 20, 202).

Participation: 1919-1939, member and chair of the board of regents

SCHOOL OF MINES (WILBURTON), governing board, O.S. 1910, §§ 8044, 8049

The Wilburton School of Mines, established in 1910, was to be under the supervision of a three-member board of regents to be selected by the governor from the Board of Regents of the State Agricultural and Mechanical College. Supervision shifted to the Board in 1911 (S.L. 1911, chapt. 47, § 2, p. 121). Eight years later a separate board was created for the school consisting of the governor, three members appointed by the governor, and the Superintendent (S.L. 1919, chapt. 178, p. 252). After twenty years with a separate board, the legislature transferred jurisdiction to the State Board of Agriculture (S.L. 1939, chapt. 34, Art. 18, p. 200).

Participation: 1911-1919, member and president of the Board; 1919-1939, member of the Board of Regents of the School of Mines (name was changed to Eastern Oklahoma College of Agriculture)

SCHOOL OF SCIENCE AND MATHEMATICS (OKLAHOMA), 70 O. S. 2011, § 1210.401B

The Oklahoma School of Science and Mathematics, a two-year public, residential high school, located in Oklahoma City, was established in 1983 (S.L. 1983, chapt. 331, § 1) with a board of trustees of twenty-five members. Six are *ex-officio* nonvoting members: chair of the Oklahoma State Regents for Higher Education or designee, chancellor of OSRHE or designee, Superintendent or designee, and the deans of Arts and Sciences at OSU, OU, and the University of Tulsa. This board of trustees is to prepare a budget request and submit it to the legislature and governor by October 1 of each year. Additionally, it has the authority to promulgate rules and regulations.

Participation: 1983-present, *ex-officio* member

SECRETARY OF EDUCATION, S.L. 1989, chapt. 27, § 2

Governor Henry Bellmon persuaded the legislature to create a cabinet system to improve the efficiency of state government. Oklahoma's three major segments of education (common schools, vocational-technical, and higher education) were all grouped under the auspices of the secretary of education. The secretary is responsible for reviewing and making public comment on progress and effectiveness of all of education. Sandy Garrett served as secretary of education (appointed by Gov. Henry Bellmon July 19, 1988) and then both as Superintendent and secretary of education (appointed by Gov. David Walters December 27, 1990) from 1991 to 1995. During the Frank Keating administration (1995-2003) Floyd Coppedge served while Governor Brad Henry chose not to appoint a secretary (2003-2011). Two secretaries, Phyllis Hudecki and Robert Sommers, served during Governor Mary Fallon's first term (2011-2015).

Participation: 1991-2015, secretary

SOUTHERN REGIONAL EDUCATION COMPACT/SOUTHERN REGIONAL EDUCATION BOARD, 70 O. S. 2011, § 2127

Through legislative enactment (HJR No. 10, S.L. 1949, p. 790), Oklahoma joined the Compact one year after it was founded when the governor signed the resolution April 26, 1949. Membership involved the governor and three citizens from each state appointed by the governor with at least one being from the field of education. In 1969 Oklahoma withdrew its membership from the Compact (S.L. 1969, c. 47, § 1), the only state to ever do so. Sixteen years later when Oklahoma rejoined the Compact (S.L. 1985, c. 198, § 1), it was allowed four members: the governor and three members appointed by the governor, one of whom must represent education. Meetings are annually and the Board has the power to enter into agreements with any of the states and with education institutions or agencies to provide adequate services and facilities for graduate, professional, and technical education for the benefit of the citizens of the states within the region. The Superintendent is a member only if appointed by the governor.

Participation: Oklahoma participated from 1949-1969 (The Superintendent was not a member.), withdrew from 1969 to 1985, and has been a member since 1985 (The Superintendent has been a member some of the years since 1985.)

STATE ACCREDITING AGENCY, 72 O.S. 2015, § 341; 74 O.S. § 3908

Public Law 346 was passed by the US Congress in 1944 and amended by P.L. 610 in 1950 establishing a procedure for federal funding of the retraining of veterans. Subsequent legislation, the Veterans' Readjustment Assistance Act of 1952, provided for each state to have a "State approving agency." The State Accrediting Agency (*Oklahoma Almanac 2015-2016*, p. 230) "was established in 1949 and is responsible for the approval and the monitoring of education and training programs for veterans, their dependents, active-duty military, and reservists in Oklahoma. The agency's membership was the Superintendent, the director of Vocational Education, the chancellor of the Oklahoma State Regents for Higher Education, and two honorably discharged war veterans appointed by the governor. These five members selected their officers. The three *ex-officio* offices may be held by their designees (S.L. 1983, chapt. 176, p. 534).

Participation: 1952-1983, member; 1983-present, member or designee (usually designee)

STATEWIDE VIRTUAL CHARTER SCHOOL BOARD, S.L. 2012, chapt. 367, § 3

The Statewide Virtual Charter School Board was established in 2012 and the provisions were modified through S.L. 2013, chapt. 212, § 4, effective September 1, 2013. The board has the sole authority to authorize and sponsor statewide virtual charter schools. It is composed of five voting members, one each from the five Congressional districts, and two *ex-officio* nonvoting members, the Superintendent or designee and the secretary of education or designee.

Participation: 2012-present, *ex-officio* nonvoting member or designee

TASK FORCE 2000, HJR 1033, 70 O.S. § 1210.801-803

Task Force 2000: creating Twenty-first Century Schools was formed to develop strategic educational policies that recognize the interrelated nature of the problems which impact society's ability to provide educational opportunity for the youth, to eliminate literacy, etc. It was created in 1989 (S.L. 1989, HJR No. 1033, p. 1662) to "establish a set of goals to determine the steps to be taken annually so that Oklahoma will reach or exceed regional averages in salaries and funding per student and in all other aspects of education by the year 1995 and national averages by 2000; to make annual recommendations to the governor and legislature regarding amounts and sources of new funds necessary for meeting next year's steps...." The membership is thirty-one including the Superintendent as an *ex-officio* nonvoting member. Meetings were held at the call of the chair.

Participation: 1989-2000, *ex-officio* nonvoting member

TEACHER RETIREMENT SYSTEM (OKLAHOMA), 70 O.S. 2016, § 17-106 (2a)

S.L. 1919, chapt. 79, p. 123 created the Oklahoma State Teachers' Retirement and Disability Fund to be used to pay annuities to persons engaged in teaching. Governance of the fund was entrusted to a board of trustees of five members: Superintendent, state treasurer, and three persons appointed by the governor. State Question 306, adopted July 14, 1942, became article 5., section 62 of the Oklahoma Constitution. It read, "The legislature may enact laws to provide for the retirement for meritorious service of teachers and other employees in the public schools, colleges, universities in this State...." Membership on the Board of Trustees was changed through S.L. of 1943 (Title 70, chapt. 27) to: the Superintendent *ex-officio* or designee, member of the State Tax Commission *ex-officio*, state treasurer and state insurance commissioner *ex-officio*, and other members. The Board is responsible for the general administration and proper operation of the retirement system and for making effective the provisions of the Act. Members select their chair.

Participation: 1919-present, member

TEXTBOOK COMMISSION (TERRITORIAL PERIOD), Oklahoma Statutes 1890, § 2., Art. 3, chapt. 79

The legislature established a free textbook law providing for the Territorial Board to "...adopt a uniform series of textbooks, to be purchased and distributed by said Board of Education." Three years later county adoption of textbooks was permitted with expected uniformity for a period of five years (Sec. 2, Art. 12, chapt. 73, Statutes of Oklahoma 1893). More legislation occurred in 1897 (Art. 9, chapt. 34, § 2) to require the territorial Superintendent to determine what textbooks were used in the territory and to contract with the publishers for a period of five years so there would not be any changes in textbooks or prices.

Participation: 1890-1907, member

TEXTBOOK COMMISSION/COMMITTEE (STATE)

At statehood the legislature created a textbook commission consisting of the governor and six other persons who were residents of the state, were of recognized ability and a majority of whom were experienced educators (Oklahoma Statutes 1907, chapt. 77, Art. 8). These six were appointed by the governor and approved by the Senate to serve for a five-year term. (Note: There is an inconsistency here in the number of appointed members and the length of their terms.) When the Board was reconstituted in 1911, this textbook commission was dissolved and the duties were transferred to the Board (S.L. 1911, chapt. 47, p. 12). After eight years with this arrangement, the legislature created the seven-member Textbook Commission consisting of the governor who was to be the *ex-officio* chairman, the Superintendent who was to be the *ex-officio* secretary, and five other persons appointed by the governor to serve until the adoption was made for the books (S.L. 1919, chapt. 12, § 1, p. 11). The commission was to adjourn sine die when the adoption was finished. Modifications both in membership and duties were legislated in 1929 (S.L. 1929, chapt. 260, § 1, p. 370) when membership did not include the governor and increased to six the number appointed by the governor. No *ex-officio* officer positions continued since the commission selected its own officers. Deposited in the Superintendent's Office were to be a record of the proceedings, votes, and actions of the commission. In 1949 the name was changed to the State Textbook Committee and the membership increased to eight not including the Superintendent (S.L. 1949, p. 524). The Superintendent was to serve as the secretary and was to vote only where there was a tie. Almost twenty years later the Superintendent was given the latitude to name a designee to the committee to serve as secretary and to vote only where there was a tie (S.L. 1968, chapt. 408, § 1, p. 360). The Superintendent calls the committee together to elect its chair and vice chair.

Participation: 1911-1919, member and president of the Board; 1919-1929, member and *ex-officio* secretary of the Textbook Commission; 1929-1947, member and office holder only if elected; 1947-1968, secretary and voting in case of tie only; 1968-present, secretary and voting in case of tie only or naming a designee to serve as secretary and voting in case of tie only (70 O.S. 2016, § 16-101)

UNIVERSITY PREPARATORY SCHOOL AT TONKAWA (NORTHERN OKLAHOMA COLLEGE)

The University Preparatory School at Tonkawa, from its founding in 1901 until 1911 had its own board. When the board was reconstituted in 1911, the Prep School Board was dissolved and its duties transferred to the Board (S.L. 1911, chapt. 47, p. 121) which had supervisory responsibilities for the next eight years. In 1919 the school was given its own board again (S.L. 1919, chapt. 118, p. 173).

Participation: 1911-1919, member and president of the Board

Index

Page numbers in italics refer to figures and tables. References to the appendix are noted as page number followed by the appendix number only for appendix N (e.g., 423apN). The sixty-two Superintendency candidates, who did not serve as Superintendents, are included in the data in appendixes B, D, E, F, and J, and are shown as apsB,D,E,F,J. Biographical data for the fourteen Superintendents are found in appendix A. Page numbers for appendixes A, C, G, H, I, K, L, and M are omitted here.

accountability
  campaign expenditures, of, 134
  Department, participation in, 260, 324
  education
    financing and expenditures, 242, 293-94
    permeated HB 1017, 298
    schools and districts, 62, 260, 293-94, 300
    student performance 283, 309, 323, 332
    system of, 334
    teacher, 260, 281, 309, 323, 326
    zero credit courses, 294
  entered lexicon, 112
  profit v non-profit assumptions of, 260
  technology, facilitated by, 326
  tribal governments, of, 25
  tribal schools, 27, 41
Achieving Classroom Excellence Task Force (ACE), 318, 320
Act Creating a Comm. of Educ. Survey, An, 170
Act for the Protection of the People of the Indian Territory, An, 25, 28-29
Act to Provide for the Final Disposition of the Five Civilized Tribes in the Indian Territory, An, 35, 346n34
Adair, Larry, 289
Ad Valorem Task Force, 409apN
African American
  educational opportunities, 232, 241
  state racial composition, 87-88, 90
  student enrollment, 308
  teachers and administrators, 241
Agent for Negro Education, 223
Agricultural and Industrial Education, Commission of, 126, 409-10apN
Allen, Clinton M., apsB,D,E,F,J
American Book Company, 8, 13, 149, 211-12
Anna T. Jeanes Fund, 161, 198
Apportionment Commission, 410apN
Atoka agreement, 37
auditor, territorial
  burden on Supt. *ex officio*, 1, 3-4, 12, 18, 21
  criminal charges, 9, 15
  member of boards, 4, 410apN, 412apN
  salary of, 348n32
Austin, George, 158

Bacone College, 35, 254
Baird, David, 362n36
Ballard, Calvin, 34, 65, 117, apsB,D,E,F,J
Ballard, Keith, 334
Ballenger, Richard, as Interior, Secretary of, 38
Barlow and Associates, Inc., 288
Barnard, Kate, 351n5
Barnes, C. M., 13
Barresi, Janet
  ACE Task Force, 318, 320
  biography, *56, 87, 92*, 315, 329
  Board controversy, 321, 323-24
  as chair, Bd of Career and Technology Educ., 328
  business perspective, 315-17, 323
  charter school, 91, 316-18
  Department
    chaotic four-year term, 326-27
    curriculum and instruction, 323, 325-26
    district takeover, 315, 326
    employees/patronage, 62, 323-24, 327
    personnel and budget, 327, *327*
  district data, *328*
  election, 2010, 67, *69*, 75, 319-21, *319*, apsA,B,D,E,F,J
  election, 2014
    campaigning and candidates, 67, *69*, 76, 321-22, apsA,B,D,E
    expenditures and results, 321, *322, 335*, apsF,J
  external influences, 317-18, 323, 325, 329
  grading schools, 325, 326
  MAPS participation, 318
  national board certification, 324
  non-public school funding, 323
  Oklahoman, The, support of, 316, 322, 328
  patronage, 62, 323-24, 327
  personality
    business oriented, 315, 323, 325-26
    confrontational, 111, 321, 329
  politics, 315, 321
  tenure, *86*, 112
Barrett, S. M., 117, *138*, 353n9
Bartlett, Dewey
  appointments of
    Creech, 59, 66, 243, 247
    McDonald, *86n*, 243
    Tuxhorn, 67, 248, 250

Governor's Management Study Committee, 53
Superintendency eligibility criteria, 244
Superintendent salary, 243, ap1*n*
Bass, Gerald, 281, 284, 370n9
Battenberg, J. P., 76, 157, apsB,D,E,F,J
Baxter, L. W.
  biography, *6*, 16, 19, 21
  as Superintendent, 16-18, 34
Beckett, A. L., 180-81, 183
  See also Commissioners of the Land Office; Murray, Alfalfa Bill
Bellmon, Henry
  appointments, 86*n*, 96, 366n1
  cabinet system implemented, 54, 420apN
  HB 1017, passage of, 75, 284
  Hodge, relationship with, 231
  Oklahoma Ethics Commission, advocate of, 75
  Oklahoma Public Schools: A Survey Report to the Oklahoma Governor's Advisory Committee on Common School Education, 53
  women's advocate, xiv, *108*
Bellmon, Shirley, xiv, *108*
Benedict, John
  biography, 2, 27-28, 39-40, 41
  federal government hierarchy, 27, 29
  federal supervisor, Indian Territory
    administrator development, 34
    appointment, 28, 117
    build public school system, 35
    funding oversight, 37, 113
    meshing territorial education systems, 34-38, 113, 120 (*see also* Cameron)
    reports to Secretary of the Interior, 25, 29-32
    teacher preparation, 32-33
  government intervention, 25, 28, 31
  salary, *58*, 353n12
  Textbook Committee appointment, 38
Bennett, Henry G.
  amendments, supporter of, 207
  Crable, relationship to, 195, 213, 217, 363n70
  member, Murray Educational Foundation, 359n25
  political kingpin, 191-92
  as president, Oklahoma A&M College, 189-91
  president, SESTC, 169
  textbook corruption, 195, 210-12
Bennett, John, 372n53
Bennett, Truman, 219
Benson, Ann, 109
Better Schools Amendment Act, 1920, 149
Better Schools Amendment Act, 1923, 170
Better Schools Amendment Act, 1955, 234
  See also desegregation; Gary; Hodge
Bizzell, W. B., 207
Black schools. *See under* separate schools
Bliss, Cornelius, 27-28, 31
Board for Leasing School Land. *See* Commissioners of the Land Office

Board of Career and Technology Education. *See* vocational education
Board of Control for Military Training Schools, 410apN
Board of Education, New Mexico Territory, 23
Board of Education, Normal School
  statehood
    Cameron, as president, 354n28
    functioned 1907-1911, 410-11apN
    hiring teachers, 125
    membership, 410-11apN
    merged into Board, 411apN
  territorial period
    Board of Educ., Territorial, separate from, 8
    established, 17, 410apN
    institutions, governance over, 3, 354n28
    membership, 3, 8, 410apN
    replacing presidents, 17
    territorial statutes in statehood, 410-11apN
Board of Education, State
  augmenting Superintendent's salary, 226.
  as Board for voc. educ. (*See* vocational educ.)
  controversies, 100-1, 112, 177, 323
  Department, authority over, *150*
  desegregation, implementation of. *See* desegregation; Hodge
  duties and powers
    actions, 100, 137
    addressing student absenteeism, 271-72
    authority, 138-39, 147-48, 151, 206, 219
    biennial reports of, 221
    certification (*see* certificates)
    college presidents' employment, 192
    curriculum, 89, 246, 251
    Department growth facilitated, 260
    eleemosynary institutions, oversight of (*see* eleemosynary institutions)
    failure to perform, 133, 140
    interference with, 141
    intervention in local districts' affairs, 315
    legal counsel hired, 263
    patronage (*see under* Barresi; Crable; Fisher, Leslie R.; Garrett, Sandy; Hodge; merit system)
    personnel decisions, 48, 61-62, 208, 227
    policy handbook approved, 256
    proposal to specify duties, 225
    salary setting, 59, 60, 226, 231, 312
    secretary to, in charge, 196, 200, 205, 207
    significance of, 139
    statutory, 47, 137
    Superintendent qualifications, 232
    teachers colleges oversight (*see under* teachers colleges)
    textbook rules and regulations, 224
  establishment of
    constitution, by, 47, 99
    free of politics, to be, 139

political maneuvering acute, 138-39
  separate board requested, 137-38, 141
  statute, by, 99, 112, 137 (see also under Cruce;
    Wilson, R. H.)
headquarters, 137, 240, 257
history of, 411apN
investigation of, by Cruce, 140
meetings
  first, 139
  minutes, xii, 122, 136, 341
  rancorous, 312, 323-24
  secretary, chair of, 208-9
  Supt., as presiding officer, 47, 50, 122, 410
  Vaughan, hired as pres. of NESTC, *186*, 191
membership
  cohesion, lack of, 331
  changes in number, 207, 209
  educators, preferred for, 129-30, 133, 137, 139
  ex officio, 47, 113, 122, 127, 141
  first appointed Board, 136, 139
  gubernatorial appointees
    changes to, recommended, 142
    congressional district representation, 331
    controversy over, 139, 140-41, 176, 202
    general, 55, 61-62, 99, 100, 223
    Hofmeister, as member, 100-1, 171, 325,
      331-33
    inexperience of, 202, 326, 332
    resignations expected, 209, 324
  terms, 62
  women as (see under women)
Supt., relationship with, 208-9, 219, 223, 241
as used in text, ix
Board of Education, Territorial
  advice to Superintendent, 113
  history of, 17, 411apN
  meetings
    frequency, topics, 5-6, 11, 15, 18-19, 136
    minutes, not extant 1896-1904, xii
  membership, 14, 16-17, 411apN
    Superintendent, *ex officio* member, 3, 7
Board for Leasing School Land. See Commissioners of
  the Land Office
Board of Equalization, 4, 412apN
Board of Health, Territorial, 412apN
Board of Pardons, 412apN
Board of Private Schools, 412apN
Board of Railroad Assessors, Terr., 4, 412apN
Board of Regents of Okla. Coll., 102, 265, 410-11apN
Board of Regents of the State University. See
  University of Oklahoma
Board of Regents of the University of Oklahoma. See
  University of Oklahoma
Boren, David, 265
Brandenburg, W. A., 139
Brandt, Joseph, 200
Brickell, Ben, 220
Briggs, Thomas Jefferson, apsB,D,E,F,J

Briles, Charles, 135-36, apsB,D,E,F,J
Brock, Andrew J., 194, apsB,D,E,F,J
Brown, E. E. 163
Brown v Board of Education, Topeka. See under
  desegregation; segregation
Bugg, Ira, 227, 365n40
Burford, John H., 15
Burns, John C., 68, 180, apsB,D,E,F,J
Bush, Jeb, 322-23
Butterfield, Ralph, 193, apsB,D,E,F,J

Cabinet Council on Education, 292
Cameron, E. D.
  biography
    early years in North Carolina, 10, 114, 127
    experience in educ., 2, 10, 20, 57, 91, *92*, 98
    general, 6, *21*, 87, 352n3, 354n39, apA
    ministerial work, 10, 13, 21, 93, 114-15, 352n3
    qualifications, *56*, 114-15
  bi-vocational thrust, 11, 114-16, 125, 134
  Department, 122, 126, 133
  election, 1907, 64-65, *73*, 116-18, 134, apsB,D
  election, 1910
    campaign, 76, 125, 133-34, apsB,D,J
    results, 67, 76, 91, 126, 134, 329, apF
  Normal schools/teachers colleges, 124
  OBU, founding member of, 115
  OTA presidency, 123
  salary, *58*, 61, apI
  as Superintendent, State
    audacious claim, xi, 120, 127
    Benedict, relationship with, 37-38, 120
    biennial report, 118, 120-22, 126
    Board of Education of Normal Schools, 124,
      129-30, 410-11apN
    Board relations, 122-23, 129, 133, 136
    boards and commissions, member of, 122, 126
    district creation in Indian Territory, 126-27
    duties, 121, 123
    equilibrium, struggling for, 85
    legislation recommended, 121, 124, 126
    patronage, 134
    politics, 111, 114, 123-25, 127, 129, 133
    segregation, 11, 115, 117-18, *119*, 127
    setting precedent, 84, 118
    tenure, *86*, 90, 112
    women on boards, 96
  as Superintendent, Territorial, 6, 9-11
Cameron State School of Agriculture, 128
*Cameron, Superintendent of Public Instruction v
  Parker*, 343n18
Campbell, Leonard, 265, 267-68
Campbell, Tom, 263
Cannon, Jack, 179-80, apsB,D,E,F,J
Cardiff, Ethel, 100, 171
Carpenter, J. L., Commissioners of the Land Office,
  secretary to, 181-82
Carpenter v Carter, 183

Carroll, Hugh, 209
Carter, Frank, auditor and *ex officio* member, Commissioners of the Land Office, 180-82, 183
Casteel, John H., 183
Castle, A. D., 221
Cates, L. H., 216-17
Catholic, 23, *87*, 261, 368n21, apA
Catholicism, 90
Caucasian, 88
Central State Teachers College, x
certificates
   administrator, 57, 232, 311, 337, 347n18
   alternative, 311
   applicant screening, 49, 111, 372n53
   Board supervision, 8, 18
   conductors and instructors, 8, 22
   county superintendent eligibility, 351n9
   Department role
      coordination, 151, 163, 171
      sole responsibility, 162, 172-73, 238, 243
      supervision, 18, 49, 122, *143*, 164, 217
   issuance/testing
      county superintendents
         problems with, 137, 142-43, 162-63, 171
         responsibility for, 27, 98, 122, 200
      Department
         number of, 122, 142
         problems with, 157
         responsibility for, 19, 111, 137, 142-43, *143*
         testing, 19, 173, 269, 276
            general, 11, 21, 32
            Indian Territory, 32
   levels, 6, 18, 122, 142-43, 200
   professional development, 114, 280
   revocation, 47, 49
   standards
      national, 303, 310, 324
      Professional Standards Board, 418-19apN
      relaxed, 200
      state, 57, 137, 142, 149, *150*, 172, 209
      territorial, 18, 22, 32
   teachers, 11, 19, 22
   wage determination, 6
Chambers, Leslie, 192
charter schools, 300, 316-18
Cherokee heritage. *See* Garrett, Sandy
Cherokee Nation schools, 30, 32, 124
Cheyenne and Arapaho Files, 345n53
Chickasaw Nation, summer normal schools, 32, 37
Chiefs for Change, 323, 329
Child Guidance Board, Oklahoma, 414apN
Choate, Issac, apsB,D,E,F,J
Choctaw Nation, 31-32, 34, 117
Choctaw people, 31, 117
Christian
   denomination, *87*, *375*
   loss of influence of, 298

religious practices in schools, 89
citizenship
   criteria for the Superintendency (*see under* Superintendency, state)
   position or status of being a citizen, xii, 36, 149
Civil Rights Act, 1964, 230
Clark, Jane Cole, 351n11
Cleveland, Grover, 8, 51
collective bargaining, 231, 254, 258, 262
Colored Agricultural and Normal University, ix, 137, 146-47, 412-13apN
Combrink, Jerry, 319, *319*, *320n*, apsB,D,E,F,J
Commission of Educational Survey, 52, 149-50, *150*, 171, 356-57n59
Commissioner of Indian Affairs, Report of, 1896, 22, 345n53
Commission on Children and Youth, Oklahoma, 415apN
Commission on Reform of State Government, 53-54, 348n24
Commission on School and County Funds Management, Oklahoma, 415apN
Commissioners of the Land Office
   Board for Leasing School Land, established as, 415apN
   corruption, 181-84
   expansion of statutes governing, 181-82, 184
   Governor to the Secretary of the Interior, Reports of the, 343c1n2
   membership, 3, 50, 181, 183
   Murray, as chair, 180-83, 185, 360n43
   secretary controversy 1971-75, 264-65
   State of Oklahoma, ex rel, Commissioners of the Land Office v Sam A. Pollard and the American Surety Co., 360n46
Commissioners of Narcotics and Dangerous Drugs Control, Advisory Board to, 409apN
Commissioners of the School Land. *See* Commissioners of the Land Office
Common Core curriculum standards, 326
common education
   administration dominated by men, 102
   coordinated by Secretary, 54
   Department administration of, *103*, *103n*,
   Department leadership program of, 106
   efforts to improve, 152
   school code codification, 225
common schools
   Board, oversight of, 139, 153
   campaign planks about, 117, 251
   cooperation with higher education, 265
   criticism of, 294
   curriculum for, 15, 18, 49, *143*, 225
   financing of, 196, 199-200, 241
   instruction in, improving, 165
   major education branch, xi
   perspectives of, 8
   Secretary, oversight of, 291, 293

separation from vo-tech education, consequences of, 225, 247
status of, 137, *199*, 173, *174*
Superintendent at the apex, 114, 158
Comprehensive Plan for Executive Branch Reorganization, 54
compulsory attendance
   constitutional provisions, 120, 364n20
   enforcement, 122, 163, 221
   segregation mandated, 120
   strengthening, 124, 126, 161-63, 172
Con Con. *See* Constitutional Convention
consolidation, school district
   achieved through
      enrollment standard, 51, 53, 221, 224, 243
      financial inducement, 146, 225
      population loss, 224, 251, 285
      statute, 201, 224, 241
   desegregation effect
      ambivalence, 236
      elimination of schools, *236*
      funding mechanism, 235, 245
   efficiency of, 91, 127, 152, 245, 251, 306
   election platform, 117
   failure to achieve, 143, 171, 221, 247, 294
   need for, ameliorated through
      rural supervisor, 146
      technology, 50, 291-92, 309
      transportation, 202
   opposition to
      as campaign plank, 286, 300-301, 335
      closure of dependent districts, 246-47, 250
      enrollment standards, 246
      general, 259, 272
   politics of
      campaign literature, 125
      political minefield, 260, 272, 306
      small district inertia, 305
   priority, 325, 328
   urged by, 50, 141-42, *143*, 224, 286
Constitution, Oklahoma
   agricultural and domestic science, 123
   amending standard, 351n5
   Commission of the Land Office, 3, 50, 181, 183
   compulsory attendance, 120, 364n20
   education provisions, found in, 36
   executive office eligibility criteria, 45, 53, 56,
   free public education, xiv
   Posey, Alexander Lawrence, contributions to, 36
   sectarian control, prohibited, xiv
   suffrage to women, 96
Constitutional Convention
   Con Con, informal name of, 45, 47, 51, 55, 121
   delegates, 55, 96-97
   education committee's draft, 47
   Executive Branch Committee, 51
   excitement surrounding, 116
   "federal interference," distaste for, 121

Murray, as president of, 51, 353n18
politicization of appointments, 113
Cooper, Richard, 320, *320*, apsB,D,E,F,J
Cooperative Council of Oklahoma School Administration, 288, 334, 337
Coppedge, Floyd, 294-95, 420apN
Cordell, Harry, 180
Council of Administrative and Executive Women in Education, State, 107
Council of Chief State School Officers, 415-16apN
Council of Presidents of the Teachers Colleges, 100
county superintendency. *See* superintendency, county
county supt. *See* superintendent, county
Covington, Lola, 216, 363n4
Cox, John, 334-35, apsA,B,D,E,F,J
Crable, A. L.
   appointment, 90, 189, 191
   biography
      career, 84, *92*, 98, 189-91, 202, 214, 337
      post-Superintendency, 93, 213-14
      pre-career, *87*, 189, apA
      Superintendency, *56*, 207, 223
   as Board president
      approbation of, 209
      chair, 185, 192, 202
      hired Vaughan to presidency, 202
      leading the Department, 207
      meetings, attendance at, 208-9
      membership turnover, 202, 209
      reorganized, 207, 209
   budget amendment, opposition to, 86, 206-7
   Commissioners of the Land Office, member of, 191, 217
   Department
      county superintendent, 196, 202
      county supervision unwieldy, 196
      curriculum deficiencies, 195
      data to Governor, refusal to provide, 203
      dependent district teacher preparation, 196
      district consolidation, 201
      expanded services, employees, 197, *198*, 204
      external donations to schools, 198, *198*
      as high school inspector, 164, 190-91
      instruction quality subpar, 195
      junior colleges excess, 196
      Legislature's involvement in, 203, 205, 207-8
      national calamities, effect on, 189, 199n, 205
      school construction, 201
      student transportation, 202, 204, 207
      taxation and funding, 197-99, 199*n*
      teacher salaries inadequate, 195
      teacher shortage, WWII, 200
      vocational units, 197, 198*n*
   election, 1938, *73*, 191-92, apsB,D,E,F,J
   election, 1942, *73*, 193, apsB,D,E,F,J
   election, 1946, *73*, 77, 193-94, 217, apsB,D,E,F,J
   equilibrium, struggle with, 85
   governor relations

Marland, 193, 202
Phillips
    feuding with, 193-94, 204-7, 217
    independence from, 111, 203
    political maneuvering, 203-4, 209
    transportation issues, 204
higher education amendment opposed, 204, 206-7
Hodge, familiar with, 217
Oklahoma A&M, 189
patronage
    hiring political hacks, charged with, 204
    stripped from, 206-9
    summary of issues, 361n24
politics, 82, 111, 191
separate/Black schools, 196-99, 361nn23,24
teacher retirement system, 199-200
teacher shortage, 200-201
tenure, *86*, 112, 217
textbook issues
    controversies, 209-10, 214
    General Welfare Board purchases, 210
    scandals, 194-95, 210-12, 359n25, 363n70
    State Textbook Committee, 209, 212-13, 364n29
women, 100-101, 192, 200
Creager, Charles, 40
Creech, D. D.
    biography, *56, 87, 92*, 98, 244, apsA,B,D,E,F,J
    Board meetings, 245-46
    college presidencies, 93, 244, 247-48
    curriculum controversies, 246
    Department reorganized, 246
    district consolidation, advocated, 246-47
    funding increase requested, 247
    Superintendency
        appointment, 66, 111, 243, 245
        never a candidate, 57, *70n*, apD*n*
        resignation from, 70, 90, 93
        salary insufficiency, 59, 90, 243-45, apI*n*
        tenure, *86*, 112
    Voc. and Technical Education, Board, chair of, 247
Creekmore, H. G., 194, apsB,D,E,F,J
Creek Nation, 32, 117,
Crippled Childrens Commission, 416apN
Crockett, David, 194, apsB,D,E,F,J
Cross, George, 212, 364n29
Crozier, Bill, 68, *79*, 302
Cruce, Lee,
    Board
        attempt to manipulate, 152
        charge to, 139
        communication with Wilson, 141
        creation of, 137, 138*n*
        investigation of, 140
        letters of concern, 140, 356n29
        members, 138-42
        Normal schools, abolition, 142
        textbook adoption, 140

Curtis Act. *See* Act for the Protection of the People of the Indian Territory, An
Curtis, Charles, 345n2
Custer County Schoolmasters, 352n27
Cutting, Robert, interviewee, 344n26

Daniel, T. J., 210
Davis, Grace Norris, 351n11
Davis, Mary, 107
Dawes Act/General Allotment Act of 1887, 25
Debo, Angie, xi, 25, 29-30, 33, 35
decision making, kinds of, xi
Democratic Committee, 76
Democratic Party, 67, *68*, 349n12, apsB,E,F
Democratic State Central Committee Speakers' Manual, 82, 350n25
Denoyer-Gebbert Co., 227
Department of Career-Tech. Education. *See under* vocational education
Department of Education, State
    ability to perform duties, 164
    certificates (*see under* certificate, Department)
    data, statistical comparison, *259*
    divisions
        Administration, 164, 246
        Annexation and Consolidation, 60
        Auditing, 18, 246, 254
        Educational Services, 291
        Elementary Education, 229
        Finance, Admin. of, 60, 102, 105, 227, 268
        Head Examiner, 61
        High School Inspection, 141, 148, 156, 164, 360-61n4
        Instruction, 103, 105, 246
        Negro Education, 223
        Personnel/Professional Services, 105
        Reports and Statistics, 164
        Research and Service, 174, 246
        Rural and Elementary Education, 60, 164, 227
        Rural School Supervisor, 102, 164
        Schoolhouse Planning, 174, 201
        School Improvement, 105
        School Lunch, 224, 359n26
        School Plant, 254, 268
        Secondary Education, 60, 229, 269
        Special Education, 105, 225
        State Aid, 257, 268
        State and Federal Programs, 103, 246
        Television Instruction, 229
        Transportation and Safety Education, 61
desegregation
    Better Schools Amendment Act, 1955, 234
    Board
        approach minimalistic, 235-38, 247
        disagreement with, 235
        funding disincentives for segregated districts, 235-36
        local district control, 89, 235, 237, 239

Oklahoma Cooperative Program in Educational Administration, 234, 365n57
  policies adopted, 235
Brown v Board of Education, Topeka, Kansas
  effect on rural schools, 258
  Harlan, John Marshall, II, 365n53
  Oklahoma's response, 234-35, 237-41
  "with all deliberate speed," 232
  Department
    Black educators, lack of support of, 238
    data collecting, discontinuation of, 237, 239
  legal prohibitions (*see under* segregation)
Deskin, Freda, *68*, 334, *335*, apsB,D,E,F,J
Dierker, Charles, 211
disabilities, children with
  Division of Special Education, 105, 225
  Educ. for All Handicapped Children Act, 49, 258
  Henry, Lindsey Nicole, Scholarship, 312
  initial program, 225
  institutions for, 139, 146, 152
  Prescriptive Teaching Act (PTA), 258
  regional educ. service centers (RESC), 258, 306
Doerflinger, Preston, 331
Dormitory Bond Fund, 50
Dormitory Bonds Funding Commission, 416apN
Douglas, Paul, 237
Dowell, Horace, 157, apsB,D,E,F,J
Doyel, W. T., 361n24
Drake, Howard, textbook corruption, 211
Duke, E. A., Department employee, 208
Dunlap, E. T., as state representative, 225
Dunlop, Robert
  as Board member, 140-42, 355n23
  co-drafter of bill to create Board, 138
  as state treasurer, 139
Dust Bowl
  Comm. of the Land Office, challenges to, 181
  Department upheaval, 189
  massive emigration, 179
  state budget, effect on, 174, 205
  state's national image, xii
Dyche, J. E.
  biography, *6*, 19, *21*
  post-Superintendency, 20, 134, 140, apsB,D,E,F,J
  as Territorial Superintendent, 19-20, 118

Edmond Normal School, 8, 16-17, 34, 122, 354n28
Edmondson, Howard, 61
Education, Secretary of
  Education and Workforce Management, 329
  member, Statewide Virtual Charter School Board, 420apN
  position, 54, 292, 329, 420apN
  relationship to governor, xi, 54, 279, 281
  as Superintendent, 280, 294
  title used as, in book, ix
  See also Garrett, Sandy
Education, State Board of. *See* Board of Educ., State

Educational Survey Commission (ESC). *See* Commission of Educational Survey
Education and Workforce Management, Secretary of. *See* Education, Secretary of
Education Commission of the States, 416apN
Education for All Handicapped Children Act (EAHCA), 49, 258
education opportunities for children, admin. of eleemosynary institutions, 123, 136-37, 147-48, 419apN
Indian Territory
  Blacks, separate schools for, 32, 34
  freedmen and whites, schools
    Atoka agreement, constraints of, 34, 37
    kinds and numbers, 1, 30, 32, 34-35
  Indians
    critique of schools, 25, 29, 31, 33, 35
    curriculum focus, 33
    as students, 30-31, 33
    tribal school governance, 25, 30-31, 33-34
Oklahoma Territory
  Blacks
    equal quality urged for, 117-18
    Plessy v Ferguson, effect on (*see under* segregation, *Plessy v Ferguson*)
    separate schools, 115
  Indians, public schools, 22-23
  whites, thousands of districts created, 1
physically and mentally challenged. *See under* eleemosynary institutions
pre-school, 246, 293
pre-territorial Indian boarding/day schools, 22
statehood, during
  available to all, 36
  Brown v Board of Education, 234-40, 258
  definition of "Black" and "white," 120, 232
  Native Americans. *See* Native Americans
  Plessy v Ferguson, 115, 118, *119*, 199, 232
  public schools, 11, 34 (*see also* segregation, separate schools)
"education" v "instruction," xi
election tampering, 369n29
elections. *See* Superintendency, state
eleemosynary institutions, 123, 136-37, 147-48, 419apN
Elementary and Secondary Education Act (ESEA). *See under* federal involvement
Emans, Roy, Department employee, 227, 365n41
Enabling Act 1906, silent on education, 45
enterprise schools, 91, 316, 318,
Entry Year Assistance Program. *See* HB 1706
Evans, Charles, 178, apsB,D,E,F,J
Evans, David, 276-78, 369nn28,29, apsB,D,E,F,Jn
Evans, Grant, 140
Evans, John P., 67, 134, 349n16, apsB,D,E,F,J
Executive Branch Committee. *See under* Constitutional Convention

Fallin, Mary, 101, 298, 324, 331
Falwell, Walter, 40
Farmers Union, 51, 160,
federal involvement
  appropriations, 121
  legislation
    Civil Rights Act, 1964, 230
    Elementary and Secondary Education Act, 230, 241, 258, 309
    Indian education, supervision of, 1956, 229
    National Defense Education Act, Title V-A, 229
    National School Lunch Program, 224
    See also vocational education
  supervision, 1, 19, 113, 117, 121
Ferguson, Leslie Guy, 217
Ferguson, Thomas, 17, 228
"First by the 21st," xii, 297
Fisher, David L., 79, 286, 295-96, apsB,D,E,F,J
Fisher, Earl, 193, apsB,D,E,F,J
Fisher, Leslie R.
  "accountability," 260
  biography
    career pre-Superintendency, 84, 91-92, 98, 253
    post-Superintendency, 93, 264, 266
    pre-career, *87*, 253, 266, apA
    president, OASA, 254
    qualifications of Superintendency, *56*
  collective bargaining, effect of, 258, 262
  Department
    federal funds, growth in, 253, 258, 262, 271
    "good ole boy network," 255, 257
    growth of, 256, 259, *259*, 271
    HB 1706, implementation of, 261
    Holleyman, employed in, 253-55
    legal counsel position, 263
    legislative audit of, finding of, 263
    merit system reduction, 61, 256, 263
    policy handbook, rewritten, 256
    regional educ. service centers, created, 258
    re-organization of, 256
    systems analysis, 260
    women's advancement, 103-5
  dissertation author, 255, 367n1
  election, 1970, *73*, 77-79, 252-54, apsB,D,E,F,J
  election, 1982, *73*, 255, apsD,E,F,J
  elections, general
    challenger free, 67, 276
    comfortable political environment, 255
    gubernatorial candidate, 68, 93
    rural power base, 273
  Penn Square Bank failure, 261
  Peter Hart Research Associates, findings of, 262
  salary enhancement, 261-62
  as Superintendent
    Board commendations, 255, 263-64
    chair, Board of Vo-Tech Education, 265-66
    gender issues, 103-6, 108, 275
    harmonious relationships with governors, 263
    leadership program initiated, 106
    member, Board of Regents of Okla. Coll., 265
    member, Comm. of the Land Office, 265
    moved offices, 257
    recommended Folks to finished unexpired term, 257, 262-63, 270
    resignation, 88, 255, 262, 267, 270
    tenure, *86*, *112*, 263
Five Civilized Tribes. *See* tribes
Floyd, M. R., 193, apsB,D,E,F,J
Folks, Cecil, 268
Folks, John
  appointment, 89, *92*, 262-63, 267, 270
  biography, *56*, 57, 84, *87*, 267-71, apA
  chair, Board of Career and Tech. Educ., 276
  Department
    expenditures, *272*
    familiarity with, 57, 271
    Fisher, relationship with, 257
    FTE, *272*
    generally, 265, 269
    growth and expansion, 271
    HB 1706 implementation, 269, 273-74
    Legislature, liaison to, 269-70, 284
  dissertation, 269
  election, 1986
    alleged tampering, 278, 369n29
    campaigning and platform, 67, 277
    candidates, 276, apsB,D,E
    expenditures and results, *73*, 78n, 277, 369n30, apsF,Jn
    Garrett, campaign manager, 295
  member, Board of Regents of Okla. Coll., 275-76
  member, Commissioners of the Land Office, 275
  persona, 257, 268, 272
  political acumen, 271
  reforms, 262, 267, 271-74
  resignation, 86, 93, 274-75, 278
  rural schools, relationship with, 273, 275
  tenure, *86*, 112
  women, advancement of, *105*, 108, 275, 291
Follett Publishing Co., 212
Fordyce, Susan, 107
Foundation for Excellence in Education (FEE), 323, 325, 329
Fourteenth Amendment, 231
Frantz, Frank, 18-19

Garfield, James, 27, 37-38
Garrett, Sandy
  biography
    career pre-Supt., 91, *92*, 99, 105, 273, 290
    Cherokee tribal member, 88, 90, 305
    politician's daughter, 209, 294, 306
    post-Superintendency, 66, 69, 93, 313-14, 337
    pre-career, *56*, *87*, 89, 273, 289-90, apA
  Board, relationship with, 312

Department
  acad. standards and curricular offerings, 309
  advancing women, *105*
  downsizing, 62, 294, *307*, 312, 372n40
  early childhood education, proponent of, 310
  election fundraising schemes, 80-81, 304
  employment in, *92*, 291, 295, 305
  HB 1017, 294, 298, 303, 305-6
  investigative reports, 313
  Priority Academic Student Skills (PASS), 298
  reorganization, 285n, 306
election, 1990, *73*, *79*, 84, 287, 294-97, 305, apsB,D,E,F,J
election, 1994, 72, *73*, *79*, 297-98, apsB,D,E,F,J
election, 1998, *73*, *79*, 299-300, apsB,D,E,F,J
election, 2002, *73*, *79*, 300-302, apsB,D,E,F,J
election, 2006, *73*, *79*, 302, apsB,D,E,F,J
elections, general
  fundraising, 80-81
  gender transition, 68, 70, 87, 99, 109
  races contested, 66
  support base enlargement, 75, 315
political machinations, 289, 301, 303-5
salary, 60
Secretary of Education
  Cabinet Council on Education, chair of, 292
  governor-appointed, 96, 107, 279, 291, 294
  honed political skills, 75, 283, 296, 305
  performance, 281, 296
  platform, 91, 283, 293-94
  satellite-delivered instruction, 292
as Superintendent
administrative skills, 306
advocated
  accountability measures, 309
  administrator certification requirements, reduction in, 311
  "advisory team," 304
  early childhood programs, 310
  longer school day, 308
  Outcome Based Education, 72, 298, 312
  school choice options, 308-9
  teacher certification, pathways to, 311
  teacher recognition, 303, 310-11
  cash management system, 306
  governors, relationship with, 294-95, 299
  inertia, challenges of, 312
  leadership style, 312
  pinnacle of educ. governance, 108-9, 295-96
tenure, *86*, 112
women's advocate, 107-8
Garrett, John C., 290
Garrison, Don, 366n1
Garrison, Earl, 68, *79*, 297-98, 371n30, apsB,D,E,F,J
Gary, Raymond, 234
General Education Board (GEB)
  charitable foundation, 143, 174
  Department positions funded, 143, 146, 174
  General Education Fund, amount of, *198*,
  separate schools, funding for, 161, 167
  southern rural schools, support for, 356n48
General Educ. Fund, *See* General Education Board
Gill, Jerry, 365n43
Gilmer, Dixie, 194, 212
Gilmour, Geen, 192, apsB,D,E,F,J
Gilpin, Tim, 331
Glenn, Scott, 138-40
Government Allotment Act of 1887, 25
Governor's Commission on Government Performance, 54, 348n27
Governor's Committee on Employment of the Handicapped, 416apN
Governor's Management Study Committee, 53
Graham, Dee Dee, 352n28
Great Depression, effects of
  Department personnel, increases in, 47, 205
  Dust Bowl, combined with, 174, 179, 181, 189
Great War
  effects of, 151-52
  navigating years of, 145-47
Grimes, William, 17
Grow, Russell, 194, apsB,D,E,F,J
Gruber, June, 103

Hall, David, 263, 265
Hamilton, J. N., apsB,D,E,F,J
Hanna, Joseph, 118, apsB,D,E,F,J
Harding Charter Preparatory High School, 318
Harlan, John Marshal, 365n53
Harlan, John Marshal, II, 365n53
Haskell, Charles
  Benedict, friends with, 40
  Board member, 129
  Cameron's report, 121
  Garfield, Secretary, agreements with, 37-38
  public buildings of the Five Civilized Tribes, 124
Hayes, O. F. (Frank), as Board member, 139-40
HB 1017
  Department responsibilities, 306-7
  effort to overturn, 305, 371n26
  factor in election, 296
  provisions, 284-85, 294
HB 1706, 261, 269
Henry, Brad, 295, 302
Henry, Lindsey Nicole, Scholarship, 312
Henry, Robert, 306
Herron, Jack, *335*, apsB,D,E,F,J
Hibler, Joe Anna, 102
Higgins, Eddie, 220, 227
High School Inspection, Department of, 141, 148, 156, 164, 360-61n4
Hitchcock, Ethan, Interior, Secretary of, 27-28, 31
Hodge, Oliver
  accolades, 241-43
  athletics sanctioning, 231, 250
  Better Schools Amendment Act of 1955, 234, 241

Oklahoma's Chief of Public Instruction / 431

biography
    career pre-Superintendency, *56*, *92*, 98, 215-16, 218, 363n1
    death, 59, 66, 88, 93
    pre-career, *56*, *87*, 89, 215, 240, apA
Board
    duties expanded, enumerated, 219
    membership reconfigured, 219, 223
    textbooks, promulgate rules for, 224
    women members, 100
compulsory attendance, 221
district consolidation, 221, 224-25, 241. *See also* consolidation, school district
Department
    curriculum inadequacy, 221, 228
    data collection, 226, 236-37, 239
    desegregation (*see* desegregation)
    federal funds
        administration of, 224, 229
        infusion of, 226, 230
        loss of control of, 224, 230, 241
        supplanting of, Legislature by, 230, 365n47
    legislative recommendations, 221, 226, 230
    program growth, 229
    role re-alignment, 221
    scandals, 80, 219-20, 227-28
    stability and continuity, 215
    students with disabilities, program for, 225
    textbook program, administration of, 224
    used for political purposes, 220
dissertation topic, 363n7
election, 1946, *73*, 194, 217-18, 223, 334, apsB,D,E,F,J
election, 1958, *73*, 218, 220, 258, apsB,D,E,F,J
elections challenger free, 66-67, *73*, 221
political calculation, 215
school code codified, 225
Superintendency
    common school system growth, 221, *222*
    financial aid, distribution of, 223, 225
    leadership in, 223
    patronage, 219, 223, 240, 347n8, 361n24
    position status, 218, 232, 244
as Superintendent
    Comm. of the Land Office, member, 217
    desegregation
        advised continuation of status quo, 235
        advocacy of, 241
        attitude toward, 233, 237-38
        out-of-state tuition, funds for, 234
        progress toward, assessment of, 237-40
    governors' relationships, 85, 220, 231-32, 241
    responsible for ethos, 228
    salary, 226
    teacher retirement system, 225, 228, 421apN
    teachers, salary insufficient, 230
    welcomed federal funds, 224
tenure, *86*, 89, *112*, 279, 304

textbook law enacted, 224
Tulsa County superintendency
    administration, 196, 217, 224, 364n26
    elections, 84, 90, 216-17
vocational education, 230-31
women, 100
Hodge, Oliver, Memorial Educ. Building, 240, 257
Hodge, Oliver, Memorial Scholarship Fund, 240
Hoeltzel, Gerald
    achievements, 284
    appointment, 280-81
    biography
        post-Superintendency, 93, 280
        pre-career, *87*, 281, apsA,D,E
        pre-Superintendency career, 91-92, 98, 280-81
        qualifications, *56*
    Department
        agency and district data, *285*
        downsizing difficulty, 281-82
        expenditures, *285*
        external study, recommendations of, 282
        HB 1017, implementation of, 284
        Okla. Educational Indicators Program, 283
        services to rural schools, 284
    election, 1990, *73*,*79*, 282, 286-87, apsB,F,J
    rural power base, 273, 280, 286
    as Superintendent
        advisory councils appointed, 283
        competing with Secretary, 281, 284
        leadership directionless, 85, 279
        legislative contacts, 283-84
        "lighthouse" and "at risk" districts, 284
        as member, Board of Regents, 102
        member, Comm. of the Land Office, 285-86
    tenure, *86*, 112, 281
Hofmeister, Joy
    advisors to, 313, 337
    biography
        career pre-Supt., 84, 91, *92*, 331, 334, apsD,E
        JLH Resources, owner, 336
        pre-career, *87*, 88, apA
        private schooling only, 92
    as Board member
        appointment, 101, 325, 331-32
        confrontation with Barresi, 321, 333
        priorities, 333
        resignation, 101
        voting record, 333
    election, 2014
        campaign violations charged, 373n14
        campaigning and platform, 321-22, 334, 337
        candidates, 321-22, 335, *335*, apB
        expenditures and results, 109, 321, *322*, apsF,J
    tenure, *86*, *87*, 112, 336
Holleyman, Charles
    biography, 253-55
    election, 1970, 77, 79, 253-54, apsB,D,E,F,J

Holloway, William J.
   co-founder, Murray, William H., Education Foundation, 211
   education advocate, 172-73
   Textbook Commission member, 176-77, 220
   Vaughan, directive to, 172-73
Holmes, Ivan, *335*, apsB,D,E,F,J
Holt, Smith, 273-74, 279, 292
home schooling, 261, 308, 328, 373n62
Hopkins, S. N.
   biography, 13-14, 16, *21*
   Board investigation testimony, 140
   Edmond Normal School, 16-17
   tenure, *6*
   as Territorial Auditor, 15, 344n34
   as Territorial Board member, 14, 21
   as Territorial Superintendent, 13-15
   as Territorial Teachers Association president, 14
horse feed, 63, 74, 76
House Bill, 1017. *See* HB 1017
House Bill, 1706. *See* HB 1706
House Special School Land Investigation Committee, 183-84
Hudecki, Phyllis, 334
Hudson, Cliff, 317-18

Independence Enterprise Middle School, 91, 316
Independent Party, 67, *68*, 68n, *74*, apsB,E,F
Indian Trust Periods, 162
Industrial Institute and College for Girls, 126
Industrial Institute and College for Girls, Board of Regents, 417apN
Ingle, William, apsB,D,E,F,J
Institute for Government Research of the Brookings Institution, 22, 348n20
Institution for the Feeble-Minded, 417apN
instruction v education, xi
Instructional Report/Score Card, 171-72
Interdisciplinary Council on the Prevention of Juvenile Sex Offenses, 417apN
Interior, Department of
   Cameron, conflict with, 38, 120
   Commission of Educational Survey, 52, 150n
   federal supervisors, appointed by, 31
   supervision of education system necessary, 25
Interior, Secretary of, 27-28, 31, 37-38

Jasper Sipes Book Depository, 211-12
Jenkins, William, 17
John F. Slater, 357n18
John F. Slater Fund, 161, *198*
Johnson, Glen, 206
Johnson's, Lyndon, Great Society, 258
Johnston, Douglas H., 37
Johnston, Henry, 17, 167, 171-72
Johnston, Velta (Reed), 107, 352n28
Jones, Jenella, 68, *69*, 97, 99, 179, *180*, apsB,D,E,F,J
Judicial Compensation, Board of, 59, 348n33, apIn

Julius Rosenwald Fund, 161, *198*

Keating, Frank
   critical of public schools, 295, 299, 303
   elections, 294, 298, 300
   Governor's Performance Team, 54, 348n27
   merit pay for teachers, advocated, 309
   Secretary appointees, 294, 299
Kelly, Brian, 319, 320n, *322*, *335*, apsB,D,E,F,J
Kerr, Clay W., 179, *180*, apsB,D,E,F,J
Kerr, Robert
   appointees, 209, 212-13, 364n29
   Board re-organization, 209
   as senator, 237
   textbook corruption investigation, 211
Kinnamon, Lynn, 352n28
Knie, Robert L., 65, 68, 117, 353n9, apsB,D,E,F,J,Jn
Knight, June, 352n28
Ku Klux Klan, 152, 166, 173

Labor Union, 51
Laidlaw Brothers, 212
Lakin, Phil, 101, 331
Langley, W. F., 289, 370n17-2
Langley, W. H., Jr., 370n17-2
Langley, W. H., Sr., 289-90, 306, 370n17-2
Langston University. *See* Colored Agricultural and Normal University
Latino, 88, 90
Lawhead, D. B., 11
Lawhead, J. H., 4-6, *6*, *21*
Leach, Judy, 105
Lease, Sharon, 105n, 107, 372n34
Leeper, Graves, 97, 351n6
Lehman, Kirby, 322
Libertarian Party. *See under* political party
lighthouse districts. *See under* Hoeltzel
Lillard, Bill, 265
Linscheid, A., 210
Literacy Initiative Commission, 417-18apN
Looney, Mrs. Lamar, 97, 351n6
Looney v Leeper, 351n6
Lyles, Victoria, rural school supervisor, first, 102
Manning, Edna, 352n28
MAPS, 318
Marland, E. L.
   appointments of
      Board members, 101, 202
      college presidents, influence on, 101, 176
      Superintendent, 185, 189
   as Governor, 178, 193, 195, 202, 211
   member, Commissioners of the Land Office, 185
Mason, Charles, 366n1
Massey, Guy, 211
McClintock, Otis, 213
McColgin, Bessie, 351n6
McCool, R. M., apsB,D,E,F,J
McCord, Otis L., 157, apsB,D,E,F,J

McCoy, Ellen Dollarhide, 375n4
McCurtain, Green, 31
McDonald, E. H., 86n, 243-44, 349n9
McKinley, William, 16, 27
Mercantile Building, Oklahoma City, 137
merit system
    advantage of, 324
    "at will" status, 61
    Department employees fired under, 62, 324
    established, 61, 263
    positions removed from, 256, 263
    See also patronage
Minority Teacher Recruitment Advisory Committee, 418apN
Model School, 144-45, 164, 171-72
Mooneyham, Bob, 106
Moonlight Schools, 144-45
Moore, E. H., 211
Moore-Norman Vo-Tech School, 265-66
Morrill Act, 151
Morrison, Ed, 211
Moss, G. D., 349n16, apsB,D,E,F,J
Munson, Mary Abrams, 97, 158, apsB,D,E,F,J
Murphy, Linda, 69, 72, *79*, 294, 298-300, apsB,D,E,F,J
Murphy, Phyllis (Rottmann), 352n28
Murray, Alfalfa Bill
    governor
        appointed Beckett, 180-81
        candidate for, 123
        chair, Commissioners of the Land Office, 181-85, 360n43
        School Land Department, 181
        Vaughan, controversial reform proposals, 175
    as House Speaker, denounced Benedict's interference, 37
    as president, Con Con, 51, 113, 353n18
    textbook issues, 177-78, 210, 359n25
Murray, John, 179, *180*, apsB,D,E,F,J
Murray, Johnston, 227, 233
Murray, Meigs, 181, 360n44
Murray State School for Agriculture, 192
Murray, William H., Educ. Found., 211, 359n25
Musselman, Ruth, 101

Nash, M. A.
    biography, 85, 155-56, 165, apA
    as chancellor, OSRHE, 93, 142, 165
    Department
        employee compensation, 164
        female employees, 164
        high school inspector, employed as, 84, 156
        insufficient resources, 162-63
        Model School, priority of, 163
        organization and growth, 164
        rural schools, emphasis on, 164
        teacher certificates, issuance of, 161-62
        textbooks, 16, 160
    election, 1922, *73*, 76, 155-58, apsB,D,E,F,J
    election, 1926, *73*, 76, *92*, 98, 156-61, apsB,D,E,F,J
    experience, *92*, 98, 156
    funding scheme
        Educational Survey, proposed by, 159
        Indian Trust Periods, effect of, 162
        inequities, 163
        state's financial capacity, 163
        statewide tax levy, 162
    Indian students, 162-63
    Ku Klux Klan involvement, 157
    leader, 165
    legislation recommended, 159, 161-63
    Oklahoma College for Women, 93, 107, 158-61
    qualifications, *56*, 57, 158
    resigned, 93, 159
    as secretary, OEA, 76, 84, 149, 156, 158, 165
    separate schools, 161
    State Textbook Comm., as *ex officio* chair, 160
    tenure, 85, *86*, *87*, 112
national board certification, 303, 324
National Defense Education Act, Title V-A, 229
National School Lunch Program, 224
Nation at Risk, A, 273
Native American students
    Barnard, Kate, supportive of, 351n5
    Cameron's perspective on, 152
    data categorized by Department, 239
    educators' attitudes toward, 165
    identified as, in Oklahoma constitution, 233
    needs highlighted in, 163
Neal, Kara Gae (Wilson), 106, 108, 352nn25,28
Nelson, Martin B., 194, 217, apsB,D,E,F,J
Nelson, Merrill A., 192, apsB,D,E,F,J
Nelson, Tivis, *180*, apsB,D,E,F,J
Nichols, A. O., 2, 6, 11-13, *21*
Nigh, George, 257, 262-63, 266-67
No Child Left Behind, 309
Normal institutes, 15-16, 18, 34
Normal schools
    Board of Education, governed by, 8, 410-11apN
    growth in number, 17, 22
    Indian Territory, 22, 32
    locations, ix, 22, 351n15, 353-54nn18,28
    mission expanded, 168, *169*
    teacher preparation, 22
North Central accreditation, 282, 295
North Central Association, 149
North Central Association of Colleges and Secondary Schools, 231, 250.
Northeastern Oklahoma A&M College, 93, 193, 248
Northeastern State Normal School, ix, 124
Northeastern State Teachers College (NESTC)
    enrollment and degrees, *187*
    ethics in hiring, *186*, 189, 202
    name changes, ix
    presidents, 93, 185-87, 200
Northern Oklahoma College. *See* University Preparatory School at Tonkawa

Northwestern Normal School (NWSTC), x, 76, 125, 134, 157, 354n28

Oakes, Francis Coram, 344n38, 355n12
OASA, 106, 253-54
OBU, 115, 187, 214
OCW. *See* Oklahoma College for Women
OEA. *See* Oklahoma Education Association
Oklahoma A&M College
   board, 139
   correspondence studies, 189
   established, ix
   member of education system, 137
   offices for vocation department employees, 207
   president of, 355n18
   professors, 135, 210
   See also Bennett, Henry; Crable
Oklahoma Association of School Administrators, 106, 253-54
Oklahoma Association for Teacher Retirement. *See* teachers, retirement
Oklahoma Baptist University, 115, 187, 214
Oklahoma Capitol Improvement Authority, 256
Oklahoma City School District
   administrator as Superintendency candidate, 139, 192, 248
   desegregation, 237
   general, 61, 139, 287
   superintendent, 106, 123
Oklahoma College for Women (OCW)
   Board of Regents
      history of, 417apN
      Superintendent chair, 189, 417apN
   compared to teachers colleges, 165
   enrollment in 1928-29, 358n29
   history of, 417apN
   presidents, 158, 165
   status when Nash hired, 165
Okla. Comm. for Future Educ. Leadership, 106
Okla. Comm. for Teacher Preparation, 414apN
Oklahoma Commission on Education, 260
Oklahoma Constitution. *See* Constitution, Okla.
Oklahoma Cooperative Program in Education Administration, 234, 365n27
Oklahoma Curriculum Improvement Commission (OCIC), 106, 313
Oklahoma Education Association
   executive secretary member of Professional Standards Board, 418-19apN
   elections, involvement in, 151, 173, 252
   free textbooks advocated, 160
   general, 107
   history of, 357n3
   legislation supported, 151, 170, 173, 205, 230
   teacher welfare endorsed, 308, 310
   Superintendency candidate connections to, 178, 193, 218, 254, 337
   women, as majority membership, 107

Oklahoma Education Council, 416apN
Oklahoma Educational Indicators Program, 283
Oklahoma Educ. Television Authority, 418apN
Oklahoma Foundation for Excellence, 303,
Oklahoma Found. for Innovation in Education, 313
Oklahoma High School Athletic Association, 231
Oklahoma Human Rights Commission, 240
Oklahoma Institution for Feeble-Minded, 417apN
Oklahoma Library Commission, 417apN
Oklahoma Literature Commission, 418apN
Oklahoma Partnership for School Readiness Foundation, 418apN
Oklahoma Public Expenditures Council, 224
Oklahoma Public Schools: A Survey Report to the Oklahoma Governor's Advisory Committee on Common School Education, 53
Oklahoma Reorganization Council
   created cabinet organization, 54, 348n24
   Commission on Reform of State Government, established by, 53-54
Oklahoma School for the Blind, Regents for, *ex officio*, 419apN
Oklahoma School for the Deaf, Regents for, 419apN
Oklahoma School of Science and Mathematics, xii, 108, 309, 419apN
Oklahoma School Herald, 12n, 15, 117, 132, 137
Oklahoma School Officers Association, 131-33
Oklahoma Secondary Schools Athletic Assn., 231
Oklahoma State Board of Education. *See* Board of Education, State
Oklahoma State Ethics Commission. *See* State Ethics Commission
Oklahoma State Regents for Higher Education (OSRHE), 142, 165, 257, 292
Oklahoma State University
   abbreviation, ix
   author employed by, xiv
   professors, test data analyzed by, 326
   See also Oklahoma A&M College
Oklahoma Teacher Retirement System. *See* teacher retirement/pension
Oklahoma University. *See* University of Oklahoma
Oklahoma Women in Education Administration (OWEA), 107-8
Oklahomans for Better Education, 254
Oliver, Clarence, J., Jr., 106-7, 279, 352n24
Organic Act 1890, 45, 98
Organization of Rural Okla. Schools (OROS), 335
Outcomes-Based Education (OBE), 72, 86, 298-99, 312, 371n32
out-of-state tuition fund, 234
Owens, Ryan, 334
Ozmun, Charles, 205-7

Paddack, Susan, 303, 319-20, apsB,D,E,F,J
Parent-Teacher Association (PTA), 200
Parker, I. H.
   biography, 6-7, 9, 20, 21, 343n13

forced resignation/legal action, 8-9
Territorial Board of Education, 7-8, 21
Territorial Superintendency, 6, 8, 46
Parrick, Cyrus, 135, apsB,D,E,F,J
patronage
   duties affected, 48
   endemic in political office, 61
   "good ole boy network," 61, 255, 257
   limited in early period, 47
   re-instated/revoked, 48, 209 (*see also under* Barresi; Crable; Hodge, superintendency)
   tribal boarding schools, 25
   unlimited and problematic, 62, 323-24, 327
Paul, Haskell, 184
Paul, Ramona, 107, 310
Payzant, Tom, 106
Peak, C. N., 157, apsB,D,E,F,J
Penn Square Bank, 261
Perkey, J. B., 231, 255
Peter Hart Research Associates, 262
Peters, Roy, 276
Phillips, Leon, 202-3, 211
Phillips, Mack, 81
Plains Indians, 22
Plessy v Ferguson. *See under* segregation
political party
   candidates of
      Democratic, 67, *68*, *74*, 349n12
      Independent, 67-68, 68*n*, *74*, 349n12
      Libertarian, 349n12
      Progressive, 67, 68*n*, 180*n*, apsB,E,F
      Prohibition, 67, 68*n*, 180*n*, 193, apsB,E,F
      Republican, 67, *68*, *74*, 349n12, apsB,E,F
      Socialist, 67, 68*n*, *118*, 134, 144, apsB,E,F
   voter registrations, 64, 74, *74*, 85, apH
   weak party, consequences of, xiii, 83, 97
Pollard, Sam, embezzlement, 181
Posey, Alexander Lawrence, 36, 346nn37,38
Potter, Mabel, 102
Preliminary Report on a Statistical Assessment of Elementary and Secondary Education in Oklahoma Under Title III, ESEA, A, 53, 348n23
pre-school education, 246, 293
Prescriptive Teaching Act, 1974, 254
Price, Edson, 178, apsB,D,E,F,J
Priority Academic Student Skills (PASS), 298
private schools. *See under* school options
Private Schools, Oklahoma Board of, 412aN
Professional Standards Board, 418-19apN
Progressive Party, 67, 68*n*, 180*n*, apsB,D,E
Prohibition Party, 67, 68*n*, 180*n*, 193, apsB,D,E
Protestant, 89-90, 160, 261, 368n21
Public Education in Oklahoma: A Report of a Survey of Public Education in the State of Oklahoma. *See* Commission of Educational Survey

racism, 22, 199, 339
Record, Ralph, H., 157, apsB,D,E,F,J

Reed, Lester, 366n1
Reed, Velta. *See* Johnston, Velta
regional educ. service centers (RESC), 258, 306
religion
   affiliation, 89-90, 111, 127, 211, 298
   Christianity, 89-90, 261, 368n21
   Supts., as ministers, 6-7, 9, 10-11, 114-15
religious denomination
   Baptist
      general, 115, 298, 336
      Supts., as members, *87*, 156, 187, 214, apA
   Catholic, 23, *87*, 261, 368n21, apA
   Christian, *87*, 252
   Church of Christ, *87*, apA
   Congregational, 6-7, 9
   general, 298, 336
   Lutheran, *87*, apA
   Methodist
      Episcopal Ch., South, 10, *21*, *87*, 114-15, 352n3
      United, *87*, 248, apA
   Presbyterian, 16, *21*
Renfrow, William, 8-9, 11, 14
Report of the Commissioner of Indian Affairs, 1896. *See Comm. of Indian Affairs, Report of, 1896*
Report on a Survey of Organization and Administration in Oklahoma, 22, 348n20
Report of a Survey of Public Education in the State of Oklahoma, A, 52, 150, *150*, 170-71
Reports of the Commissioner to the Five Civilized Tribes to the Secretary of the Interior, 346n41
Reports of the Governor of Oklahoma to the Secretary of the Interior, 343c1n2, 415apN
Republican Party, 67, *74*, 349n12, apsB,E,F
Rice, Andrew, 324
Roberts, Kathy, 352n28
Robertson, J. B. A., 148-49
Roettger, Lloyd, 301-2, 304, 372n41, apsB,D,E,F,J
Rogers, John, 237
Rogers, W. C., 124
Roosevelt's New Deal, 176
Rowley, George, 352n25
Rowsey, W. E., 139, 141

Sandmann, Charles, 255, 368n9, 369n29, apsB,D,E,F,J
Sanity on Sex, 246
school district
   administrator of, 57, 61, 81, 152
   authority of, 135, 175
   building construction, 201
   consolidation of (*see under* consolidation, school district)
   county, *169*
   curriculum, 251
   Department assistance to, 260
   dependent
      consolidation, 49, 99, 221, 247, 250
      governance, 150, 164, 171, 347n18, 363n6
      Tulsa County, 217, 364n26

desegregation of (see under desegregation)
elementary, 49, 251, 299, 335
evaluation of, 62, 195
financing of
    assistance plan for consolidation, 246-47
    by ADA or ADM, 252
    corruption losses, 184
    disbursement of funds, 223, 225
    legislator-teacher permitted, 249
    Phillips's opposition, 193, 203-4
    rural schools, 158
general, 22-23, 37, 126, 174
governance of, 152, 175
independent, 147, 168, 267, 278
number in
    Indian Territory, xii, 37, 126, 129
    Kansas, 4, 19
    New Mexico Territory, 23
    Oklahoma Territory, xii, 1, 22, 37, 118
Oklahoma City School District, 61, 139, 287
reports submitted by, 163, 168
rural
    desegregation, effect on, 240, 247
    number of, 49, 98, 146, 167, 174
    resources insufficient, 111, 130, 155, 157, 170
    Supts. employed in, 91, 243-44, 253, 288
separate, 22-23, 197
    See also separate schools
size, by enrollment
    declining, 151, 221, *222*
    greater than 5,600, 49-50, 59, 129
    lesser than 5,600, 37, 127, 136, 174
textbook ownership, 160, 177-78, 225
township, 49
union graded, 168
urban area districts, 92-93, 103, 248
vocational-technical, 230
weak, 175, 194, 223
school district consolidation. See consolidation, school district
School for the Blind, 121, 126, 419apN
School for the Deaf, 121, 419apN
School Land Commission. See Commissioners of the Land Office
School of Mines, Miami, 147, 151, 419apN
School of Mines, Wilburton, 419apN
School of Mines and Metallurgy, 147, 151
school options
    homeschool, 261, 308, 328, 373n62
    non-public
        funding for, 93, 294-95, 312
        parochial, 75, 308, 368n21
        private, 10, 75, 92, 261, 297, 308, 316
        vouchers, 15, 300, 303, 325
    non-traditional, 75, 328
    public
        charter, 300, 316-18, 420apN
        traditional. See under compulsory attendance

Scopes Trial, 160
Scott, A. C., 139, 141
Scott, Joe, 191, 210
Seay, Abraham, 6, 8
Secret Order of the Red, Red Rose, The, 353n24
Secretary of Education. See Education, Secretary of
segregation
    Harlan, John Marshall, 365n53
    out-of-state tuition fund, 234
    "separate but equal"
        Oklahoma Constitution and statutes
            provisions, 36, 120, 137, 232-33
            stricken from, 234, 239, 365n58
        Plessy v Ferguson
            anemic response to slavery vestiges, 199
            competition for limited resources, 155
            legal foundation for, 22, 118, *119*, 120, 232
    separate schools, rapid establishment of, 11
Sequoyah Constitution, proposed in, 36
separate schools
    charitable support of, 161, 233
    compared to southern states, 196
    definition and kind, 120, 232
    ended by, 233
    funding for counties, 161, 233
    governance, 127, 137, 161, 233, 196
    inferior to white schools, 144, 149, 161, 196, 233
    majority Black, 22, 144, 196
    state support, 161, 167, 238
    Supts.' concerns, 22, 144, 149, 152, 165, 196
Senate Special Investigating Committee, 181-82
Shackelford, Harry, 262
Shaw, C. C., 167
Sholar, Patricia, *108n*, 352n28
Sipuel (Fisher), Ada Lois, 233
Sipuel v Board of Regents of the University of Oklahoma, 233
Smallwood, Clyde G., 218, apsB,D,E,F,J
Smith, Lucy, 352n28
Smith-Hughes Act, 103*n*, 147
Smith, S. S., 134, apsB,D,E,F,J
Smith, Tom, 248
Smith, Willis, 211
Sneed, R. A., 181
Socialist Party, 67, 68*n*, 118, 134, 144, apsB,E,F
Sommers, Robert, 328-29
Southern Regional Education Compact, 420apN
Southwestern Normal School, x, 354n28
State Accrediting Agency, 420apN
State Board of Educ. See Board of Education, State
State Council of Administrative and Executive Women in Education, 107
State Ethics Commission, Oklahoma
    campaign finance reporting, 79*n*320,
    created by State Question 627, 75, 80
    funded insufficiently, 75
    repository of records, apJ*n*
    warnings by, 81, 300

State of Oklahoma, ex rel, Commissioners of the Land Office v Sam A. Pollard and American Surety Co., 181, 360n46
State of Oklahoma Governor's Performance Team: Final Issue Papers, 54, 348n27
State Superintendent of Public Instruction. *See* Superintendent of Public Instruction, State
State Textbook Commission. *See* Textbook Commission, State
State University, The. *See* University of Oklahoma
Staten, James, 196, 207, 361n23
State Welfare Board, 210
Statewide Virtual Charter School Board, 420apN
Steele, George W., 3-7, 21, 51
Stern, A. Kenneth
    as women's advocate, 352n27
    author of book, xiii-xiv
Steward, W. P., *138*
Strachan-Forsythe, Grace, 107
straight party voting option, 64, 71, 252, 302
student attendance. *See* compulsory attendance
student transportation, 203-4
superintendency, county
    candidates excluded from, apE
    counties with no dependent schools, 363n6
    duties
        annexation approval, apL*n*
        approve transfers, 235
        assistance and supervision, 22, 98, 196
        filing reports, 15, 196, 225
        hiring teachers, 217
        issuing certificates, 22, 98, 131, 142, 162-63, 200
        Model School established, 144
        reports to the Superintendent, 217
        testing teacher candidates, 98, 131, 142, 163, 200
    elective, 5, 23, 37, 143, 164, 225
    eligibility for, 98, 196, 351n9
    evaluated by, 172
    office of
        obsolete, 49, 98, 245
        eliminated, 49, 53, 84, 91, 347n18, 351n9
        evolution of, 49, 130, 221, 352n2
    political dynamics, 52, 91, 164
    prerogative, limited by desegregation, 235
    reports due to, 15, 124
    reputation, 99, 133, 221
    resources, lack of, 202, 233-34
    salary, 132, 168, *169*
    separate schools, supervision of, 196-97, 233-34
    stepping-stone to Superintendency, 98
    women pursued, 98-99
Superintendency, state
    administration of
        common school system, 84-85, 223, 305, 339
        Department of Education, 48-50
    appointees to, 66-67
    board and commission memberships
        Board, president, 50, 411apN
        Board of Career-Technical Education, State, president, 50, 413apN
        Commissioners of the Land Office, member, 50
        general (*see* appendix N)
        Oklahoma Teacher Retirement System, 421apN
        State Textbook Commission, 421apN
    compensation
        amount, 58, 65, 340
        Board determination, 261-62
        method for determining, 58-59, 348n33
        relative to, 59-61, 62, apI
    duties
        biennial/annual reports, 51
        constitutional, 46-47, 50, 411apN
        evolution of, 231
        expansion of, 84, 133, 261
        extra pay for, 59, 261
        public uninformed of, 158
        reports to governor, 47
        school laws, 47, 144
        statutory, 45, 47-49, 58, 121, 219, 411apN
    elections
        campaign methods, 80-82
        candidates
            age, apD
            alphabetized list of, apB
            female, party, and election, *69*
            number of, 65-66, *66*, 179, apC
            other political activities, 67-68, apE
            political parties, 65, 67, 349n12
            profiles, 68-71, *68*, *69*, *70*
        ethical issues
            campaigning, 80-82, 303-4, 333
            elective method creating, 304-5
            employee involvement, 80-81, 304
            official stationery and postage, use of, 220, 277, 349nn16,17
            reporting, 134
            warnings of, 81, 300
        expenditure records, reports, 349nn13,14,16
        expenditures, 74-80, *78*, *79*, 399-401, apJ
        plurality standard, 64
        results, 72, *73*, 158, 218, apF
        statutory qualifications, 232
        vote ratio to governor vote, 72, apI
    examination and analysis of, 43
    executive office
        constitutional origin of, 45, 208
        elective, xii
        eligibility qualifications
            absence of career experience, 91
            age and citizenship, 53, 56
            gender, 56, 97-98, 351n6
            minimal, 319
            residency duration, 43, 56, 88, 340
            statutory, 57

leadership needed in, 340
patronage, 61-62, 223
political dynamics, 52, 305, 339
selection method, 51-54, 278, 280, 339-40
stability of, 45
stepping-stone to higher office, not a, 43, 266
term limits, 45
as used in the book, ix
Superintendency, territorial
   appointed by, 1-4, 22, 23
   as auditor *ex officio* (see auditor, territorial)
   biennial reports, 11, 18
   Board membership, 411apN
   boards and commissions, 3-4
   compensation, *58*
   duties, 46
   position created, 3, 337
   term, 4, 20-21
Superintendent Advisory Council, 283
superintendent of schools, county
   statehood,
      authority of, 11
      as book salesman, 227
      competency of, 142, 146, 164, 196, 218
      coordinate with Department, 221
      desegregation progress, 235, 237
      duties, 22, 27, 37, 98, 144-45
      prerogative, 122-23, 163, 175, 196, 235
      relationship with, 52, 131, 217
      Report Card completion, 171-72
      reports to Superintendent, 18, 163, 224
      State School Officers Association, 132, 142
      Supt., with experience as, 130-33, 216-17
      women as, 44, 95, 98-99
   territorial
      member of Board, 5, 8-9, 122
      Superintendent previously, 6-7, 9-10, 411apN
Superintendent of Public Instruction, State
   career experience, 91-92, *92*
   credentials of, 55, 57, 84
   demographic data, 86-89, *87*, apA
   duties
      combined with campaigning, xiv, 63, 67, 125, 191, 248
      familiarity with, 84, 245
      time for, 89, 115, 125-26, 133, 248
   exit from office, reason for, 93, 189
   factors to consider, 83
   initially appointed, 89-90
   managing the Department, 111
   political experience, 90-91
   post-Superintendency experience, 88, 93
   qualifications, *56*
   reports to governor, 47
   representative of dominant group, 86
   resigned to assume college presidency, 159, 165, 185-86
   tenures, 85-86, *86*, 112

   as used in the text, ix
   women as, xiii, 86-87, 108-9
Superintendent of Public Instruction, Territorial
   biennial reports submitted, 12, 15, 18, 21
   credentials, 13, 21, *21*
   demographic data, 6, *21*
   duties and expectations, 8, 12, 18, 47, 113-14
   legislative recommendations, 15, 18
   oversight of separate schools, 22
   political dynamics, 8-10, 16, 22-23

Tabor, Pauline, 243
Taft, William, 39
Task Force 2000, 420-21apN
Taylor, J. B., 123
Taylor, Lealon, vii, 81, 296, 299
teacher
   associations
      Oklahoma State Teachers Association, 132
      Oklahoma Teachers Assn., 117, 123, 125-26
      Territorial Teachers Association, 13-14, 16, 22
      See also Oklahoma Education Association
   certification (see *under* certificate)
   collective bargaining, 231, 254, 258, 262
   needs, 32, 269
   preparation
      normal training institutes, 15-16, 18, 34
      Okla. Comm. for Teacher Preparation, 414apN
   recognition
      incentive pay scheme, 310
      national board certification, 303, 324
      Teacher of the Year Program, 311
   shortages of, solved by, 200-201
   testing (see certificates, Department; HB 1706)
Teacher Advisory Council, 283
teacher retirement/pension
   amendments for, 200
   benefits, 225, 251, 302
   board, 419apN
   created, 148
   funding and solvency of, 225, 228
   Oklahoma Assn. for Teacher Retirement, 200
   support, 148, 172, 200, 302
   system, 225, 228, 421apN
teachers colleges
   accreditation standards, 172
   as Council of Presidents of, 100
   enrollments, 185, *187*
   evolved from Normal schools, 351n15
   influenced by, 101, 171, 206
   presidencies, 176, 202
   presidents of, 101-2
territorial auditor. *See* auditor, territorial
Terrrritorial Board of Education. *See* Board of Education, Territorial
Territorial Superintendent of Public Instruction. *See* Supt. of Public Instruction, Territorial
Territorial Teachers Association, 13-14, 16, 22

Textbook Commission (Committee), State
    actions recorded, 211
    authority, 121, 151, 160, 172
    chair, 212-13, 364n29
    established, 121, 138-39, 147, 168, *169*
    history of, xiv, 213, 217, 421apN
    membership, 142, 173, 176-77, 209, 213
    members testifying, 211
    office space for, 224
Textbook Commission, Territorial, 421apN
textbooks
    adoption controversies, 194-95, 209-10, 233
    adoptions, 5-6, 178
    authors, 177, 210
    Board meeting topics, 11, 224
    as campaign plank, 117-18, 135, 157, 178
    content, 160
    contractual obligation of, 13
    corruption, 224 (*see also under* Crable, textbook)
    costs of, 177, 211
    Department service bureau, 161
    funding
        district, 177
        insufficient, 159-60, 230
        parental, 122, 124, 161, 209
        state
            opposition to, 160, 161
            responsible for, 213, 250
            State Welfare Board, 210, 212
            Supts. advocated for, 122, 146, 193, 203
    ownership of, 160, 177
    quality of, 117, 160, 213, 302
    royalties, 359n25
    selection of, 38, 151, 160, 210, 213
    Supt. recommendations, 124, 161, 174-75, 221
Thompson, JoAnn (Bates), 352n28
Thornton, Rushing, and Wood, 52, 53
Trapp, Martin, 97
tribal role numbers and quantum, 371n5
tribal schools. *See under* education opportunities for children, administration of
tribes
    Arapaho, 22-23
    Cheyenne, 22-23
    Comanche, 23
    Five Civilized Tribes, 25, 41, 124
    Kiowa, 22-23
Troops to Teachers, 311
Troy, Frosty, 241-42
Truitt, Bertha, 100, 171
Tuttle, Francis
    Administrator Development Program, 106
    career tech system, "father of," 276
    coordinator of area schools, 230
    student absences, 271
    Vo-Tech director, 231, 247
    See also vocational education

Tuxhorn, Scott
    appointment, 66, 244, 248, 250
    biography, *87*, 93, 248, 252, apA
    curriculum issues, 89, 251
    dependent school districts, elimination of, 250
    dissertation topic, 367n21
    election, 1970, 67, 77-79, 90, 251-52, apsD,F,J
    Helena Training School for Boys, 248
    North Central Assn of Sec. Schools and Coll., 250
    qualifications, 56, 91, *92*, 98
    State Board of Affairs, 250
    state representative, 67, 91, 249, apE
    teacher retirement benefits, 251
    tenure, 66, 85, *86*, 90, 112
University of Central Oklahoma, x
University of Oklahoma (OU)
    abbreviation, ix, 341
    admission to, 234
    Board of Regents, 139, 147, 413apN
    founding, 22
    minimum standards, 294
    part of education system, 137
    as president of,
        chaired commissions, 200, 212
        dismissed by Board, 140
        freshmen unprepared, 228
        member, Territorial Board, 8, 122
        reported to Board, 139
        supported amendments, 207
    professors, test data analyzed by, 326
    reputation, xii
    students assisting Superintendent, 172
    Superintendents with degrees from
        bachelors, 156, 169, 267, 315
        masters, 169, 191, 215, 267, 315
        doctoral, 215, 244, 253, 269, 315
University Preparatory School at Tonkawa, 142, 147, 422apN
Umholtz, Frederick Howard, 17
US Constitution
    citizenship, 56
    commerce with Indian tribes, 31
    suffrage, 96
    Tenth Amendment, 45, 262

Vannest, C. G., 134-35, apsB,D,E,F,J
Vaughan, John,
    appointment, 17, 89, 167, 171
    biography
        common schools, *92*, 98, 167, 169, 172
        general, *56*
        higher education, 84, 168-69
        post-Superintendency, 93, 187
        pre-career, *87*, 167, apA
    as Board president
        college presidency appointments
            NESTC, 185, *186*
            SESTC, 101-2, 176

vacancies in 1935, 176
vocational administration, 173
college administrator, 93, 168-69, 185, *187*
Commission of Educational Survey, executive
  secretary of, 52
constitutional amendment, selection method, 55
Department
  Black high school accreditation, 175
  certification, consolidated under, 173
  common school system 174, *174*
  Division of Research and Service created, 174
  external funding, 174
  funding request to federal government, 176
  Legislature involvement in, 175
  positions, 175
election, 1930, *73*, 178, apsB,D,E,F,J
election, 1934, *73*, *77*, 100, 179, *180*, apsB,D,E,F,J
governor, relationship with
  Holloway, cooperative, 177
  Johnston, appointed by, 171
  Marland, harmonious, 185
  Murray, Alfalfa Bill
    Board appointments, 176
    constraints on authority of, 183
    defiance of, 111
    tax structure overhaul, 175
    as Textbook Commission member, 177-78
instructional leadership, 171-72
legislative recommendations, 172-73, 175
as member, Commissioners of the Land Office
  battling the Governor, 181-85
  chair of, 182
  corruption investigations, 181-84
  ex officio, 180
  guilt by omission, admitted, 184
as president of OCW board, 171
resignation, 185, 191
as senator
  advantage as Supt., 84, 90, 152, 171
  election, 1916, 167
  legislative efforts, 148, 167-68, *169*,
  terms, 178
teacher assn. leadership, 170-71, 173, 358n8
teacher retirement, 225
tenure, 66, *86*, 112
Textbook Commission, *ex officio* secretary, 177
Vaught, Ed, 34
Veterans Administration, 214
Veterans Agricultural Training Program, *103n*
vocational education
  Board of Career and Technology Education, 328,
    413-14apN
  Board of Education
    est., 147, 168, *169*, 225, 364n32, 411-12apN
    chair, Superintendent, 151
  Board of Vocational-Technical Educ., State, 247
  director of, history of, 413-14apN
  gender in employment, 102, *103*, 147

governance of, 173, 230-31, 243
male dominance of leadership, 102
Smith-Hughes Act, 103*n*, 147
supervision of, 112, 197, 198*n*, 225
Vocational and Technical Education, Dept. of, 247
Vocational Rehabilitation
  Division, *103n*, *198n*, 361n25
  employees, increase in, 197
  expansion, *198n*
  funding, 209, 241, 250
vocational-technical district, 262, 266
Voice of the Dem. Women of Okla., The, 350n25
voting patterns
  down ballot effect, 71, 277
  ratio of governor to Superintendent, apJ
  straight party option, 71
voter registrations. *See under* political party
vouchers, 15, 300, 303, 325

Wagner, Janelle L., 343n11
Walters, David, 294
Walton, Jack, 353n9, 355n18
Wardell, Morris L., 35, 346n33
Waters, C. W., 370n17-2
WAVE, 325
weak party consequences, xiii, 83, 97
Webb, Virginia, 352n28
Welday, J. O., 135, apsB,D,E,F,J
Welton, W. Roy, 179, *180*, apsB,D,E,F,J
White, J. C., 192, apsB,D,E,F,J
white and freedmen children, 1, 30-35, 37
Whitford, Charles, impeachment resolution, 211
Wild, George Posey, 345n53
Williams, J. Roy, *138*
Williams, Tod, 299, apsB,D,E,F,J
Williamson, Mac Q., 233-34
Willis, Anna, *69*, 76, 97, 99, 158, apsB,D,E,F,J
Wilson, George, 135-36, 355n18, apsB,D,E,F,J
Wilson, Kara Gae. *See* Neal, Kara Gae
Wilson, R. H.
  association leadership, 131-33, 135, 144-45
  biography
    career pre-Superintendency, *56*, 91, *92*, 133
    Grady County superintendency
      administrative skills, 84, 132
      communication with principals, 142
      competing for, 130
      county schools curriculum, 142
      efficiency in purchasing supplies, 131
      organizing school districts, 131
      political skills, development of, 90
      stepping-stone, 98
    post-Superintendency, 22, 152-53, 157
    pre-career, *87*, 130, 146, apA
  Board
    chaired by, 141
    composition of, 142
    convened first meeting, 139

    educators as members, 141
    governance of boards and commissions consolidated, 139
    oversight of, 142, 147
    review of institutions, 137, 139
    secretary
        appointed, 139
        certificates issued illegally by, 157
    textbook selection, 140-41
Colored Agricultural and Normal University Board, 146
Cruce
    independence from, 111, 129, 141, 152
    relationship with, 138-39
election, 1910, 73, 76, 123-26, 132-34, apsB,D,E,F,J
election, 1914, 73, 134-35, 144, apsB,D,E,F,J
election, 1918, 73, 135-36, apsB,D,E,F,J
Superintendency
    authority increased, 150
    boards and comms., service on, 135, 139, 151
    committed to equal education opportunity, 149, 152
    Department administration
        campaign rallies for better schools, 145
        common school system status, 136
        community centers, advocating for 144-45
        county schools, materials for, 142
        Dept. of High School Inspection, 148-49
        district consolidation, 141-42, 146, 152
        growth, 142, 151
        leadership, 151
        legislation, recommendations for, 143-45
        legislative involvement, 141-42, 146
        Model School establishment, 144
        multi-year contracts for educators, 145
        navigating the war years, 152
        organization, 136-37
        personnel requests, 141, 143
        political acumen, 141, 151-52
        publications, 141, *143*, 144-45
        quality schools (see Model School)
        rural education emphasized, 146-47
        school inspector position, 141,
        separate schools for Blacks, 144, 152
        taxation inequalities, 143-44, 146-49

    teacher certification, 142-43, 157
    teacher retirement system, 148
    teacher termination, reasons for, 145
    tenure a transitional period, 85
    textbook supervision, 146-47
    women in leadership positions, 102, 147
tenure, *86*, 112
Wisley, Sandy, xiv
"with all deliberate speed," 232, 234-35, 239, 240
women
    as Board of Education, State, members, 99-101
    college
        presidencies, 101-2
        presidents (see Hibler; Zaneis)
    competing for the Supt, xiii, 86-87, 108-9
    as county superintendents, 45, 95, 98-99
    as Department employees,102-5, *103*, *104*, *105*
    eligibility for Superintendency, 56, 97-98, 351n6
    as leaders, supporters of
        individuals, 96, 105-8
        Okla. Comm. for Future Educ. Leadership, 106
        Oklahoma Women in Education Admin., 107
        State Council of Administrative and Executive Women in Education, 107
        Women's Christian Temperance Union, 351n6
        Women's Democratic Council of Okla., 350n25
        Women's Legislative Council, 351n6
    limited by cultural and societal norms, 95
    local/county boards of education, eligible to serve on, 96
    as local school district superintendents, 95-96, 99, 101, 107, 109
    positional achievements, 108-9
    suffrage, 96-97, 351n4
    as Supt. (see Barresi; Garrett, Sandy; Hofmeister)
Women's Christian Temperance Union, 351n6
Women's Democratic Council of Oklahoma, 350n25
Women's Legislative Council, 351n6
Works Progress Administration (WPA), 201
Wynne, R. P., *138*

Yarbrough, Cecil, 106, 352n23
Young, Glenn, 183

Zaneis, Kate Galt, 101, 176, 192, 351n11, 359n26

About the Author

A. Kenneth Stern is the author of articles for the historical journals of Kansas, Oklahoma, and New Mexico about the office of superintendent of public instruction during the territorial periods of those states. Born in Roaring Spring, Pennsylvania, he is Associate Professor Emeritus of School Leadership at Oklahoma State University and lives in Tulsa, Oklahoma, with his wife Lois and near his daughter and her family.

www.ingramcontent.com/pod-product-compliance
Lightning Source LLC
Chambersburg PA
CBHW081437070526
44586CB00019B/2159